Roberto de Mattei

The Second Vatican Council

An Unwritten Story

Translated by
Patrick T. Brannan, S.J., Michael J. Miller, and Kenneth D. Whitehead

Edited by Michael J. Miller

Loreto Publications

Cover photos from www.shutterstock.com

First edition: *Il Concilio Vaticano II: Una storia mai scritta,*

Corso Re Umberto 37
10128 Torino, ITALY

Loreto Publications
P. O. Box 603
Fitzwilliam, NH 03447 USA
603.239.6671
www.loretopubs.org

ISBN: 978-1-62292-002-0

The Second Vatican Council

An Unwritten Story

Contents

Introduction

1. Vatican II: a council different from the others

The history of the Catholic Church is at the center of universal history, on account of the primary role that the Church plays in the guidance of souls and the building up of civil society. From this perspective, the importance of the ecumenical councils in universal history is no surprise, since they are one of the highest expressions of the social life of the Church. If the Church has some relationship with the history of humanity, then an ecumenical council will have a relationship with that same history that is similar to the one that it has with the Church.[1]

Councils are called ecumenical (or general) when, under the direction of the pope or of his representatives, they gather bishops from the entire *oikuménē*, which means from the whole inhabited world.[2] In the councils

---

[1] *Cf.* Giuseppe Siri, "Il Concilio ecumenico visto dal piano della teologia della storia," conference held in Genoa on January 25, 1961, published in *La giovinezza della Chiesa: Testimonianze, documenti e studi sul Concilio Vaticano II* (Pisa: Giardini, 1983), 43–50, citation at 43.

[2] Cf. Walter Brandmüller, "Il Concilio e i Concili: Il Vaticano II alla luce della Storia dei Concili," in *Cristianità* 332 (2005): 3–10, citation at 4. On the significance of councils in the history of the Church, see Joseph Hefele, *A History of the Christian Councils from the Original Documents to the Close of the Council of Nicaea*, vol. I (Edinburgh: T. & T. Clark, 1872, 1883[2]), 1–15. See also

the voice of the pope and of the world's bishops united with him speaks up about historic events: this solemn voice makes the history of the Church and, with it, the history of the world.

In the history of the Church twenty-one councils have been held that are recognized by the Church as being ecumenical, or general.[3] The last one was Vatican Council II, opened in Rome in Saint Peter's Basilica by John XXIII on October 11, 1962, and concluded in the same place, after four sessions, by Paul VI on December 8, 1965. From the Council of Nicaea, which after the Council of Jerusalem was the first council written about by historians, to Vatican II, every council has been the subject of an historiographical debate. Every one of these assemblies not only made history, but then had its historians, and each of them brought to his work his own interpretive view.[4]

Unlike the preceding councils, however, Vatican II poses a new problem for historians. Councils exercise, under and with the pope, a solemn magisterium [teaching authority] in matters of faith and morals and set themselves up as supreme judges and legislators, insofar as Church law is concerned. The Second Vatican Council did not issue laws, and it did not even deliberate definitively on questions of faith and morals. The lack of dogmatic definitions inevitably started a discussion about the nature of the documents and about how to apply them in the so-called "post-conciliar period." For this reason the problem of the relation between the council and the "post-conciliar period" is at the heart of the ongoing hermeneutical debate.

---

the "Introduzione" by Pietro Palazzini to the *Dizionario dei Concili* (Rome: Città Nuova, 1963), xi-xxxix; also the articles s.v. "Concile oecuménique" by J. Forget, in DTC, vol. 3 (1908), cols. 636–676 and by Nicolas Juny, in DDC, vol. 1 (1954), cols. 378–381.

[3] There are no official pronouncements by the magisterium concerning the number of ecumenical councils, but the canonical and theological teaching has been firmly established since St. Robert Bellarmine (*De Controversiis christianae fidei*, vol. II, [Venetiae: Apud Societatem Minimam, 1599], Liber I, "De Conciliis et Ecclesia," cap. V, cols. 4–9). In the inaugural address given at the council by John XXII on October 11, 1962, and also in the allocution by Paul VI at the opening of the third session, the two pontiffs refer to the twenty ecumenical councils celebrated previously, considering Vatican I as the last ecumenical council before Vatican II.

[4] See, for example, W. Brandmüller, "Carl Joseph von Hefele: Ein Geschichtsschreiber macht Geschichte," in Pontificio Comitato di Scienze Storiche, *Walter Brandmüller Scripta Manent* (a collection of essays in honor of his 80th birthday), Cosimo Semeraro, ed., (Città del Vaticano: Libreria Editrice Vaticana, 2009), 365–377.

2. The two conciliar hermeneutics

The debate about the Second Vatican Council, even in its complexity and in the articulation of the various positions,[5] can be boiled down essentially to two lines of interpretation: the hermeneutic of "continuity" between the council and the preceding tradition, and the hermeneutic of "discontinuity" or "rupture" with the Church's past. The first line of interpretation has been taken up by the ecclesiastical hierarchy since the pontificate of John Paul II[6] and has been formulated with clarity and conviction by Benedict XVI, especially in his address to the Roman curia on December 22, 2005.[7] This is a theological approach to the Second Vatican Council, which is judged by the sixteen documents of unequal doctrinal value that it produced. As a whole, these documents, according to the supreme authority of the Church, express a non-infallible yet authentic magisterium, which must be read in continuity with the

---

[5] Archbishop Agostino Marchetto presents a survey of contrasting interpretative approaches, while declaring his preference for the hermeneutic of continuity, in *The Second Vatican Ecumenical Council: A Counterpoint for the History of the Council*, translated by Kenneth D. Whitehead (University of Scranton Press, 2010), and in the reviews collected in *Chiesa e Papato nella storia e nel diritto* (Città del Vaticano, Libreria Editrice Vaticana, 2002). See also Claudio Anselmo, "Agostino Marchetto: per una ermeneutica del Concilio Vaticano II," in *Venti secoli di storiografia ecclesiastica: Bilancio e prospettive*, ed. Luis Martínez Ferrer (Rome: EDUSC, 2010), 449–458. For a viewpoint from the perspective of the "School of Bologna," see: Giuseppe Ruggieri, "Recezione e interpretazione del Vaticano II: Le ragioni di un dibattito," in *Cristianesimo nella storia* 28 (2007): 381–406, reprinted in *Chi ha paura del Vaticano II?*, Alberto Melloni and G. Ruggieri, eds. (Rome: Carocci, 2009), 17–44. See also Yves Chiron, "Il y a 40 ans: L'ouverture de Vatican II: Mise en perspective historique," in *Divinitas* 46 (2003): 222–232; David Berger, "Gegen die Tradition oder im Licht der Tradition? Zu neueren Interpretationen des Zweiten Vatikanischen Konzils," in *Divinitas* 40 (2005): 294–316; and, in general, *Vatican II: Did Anything Happen?*, ed. John W. O'Malley (New York-London: Continuum, 2007); Gilles Routhier, *Il Concilio Vaticano II: Recezione ed ermeneutica* (Milan: Vita e Pensiero, 2007); Christoph Theobald, *La réception du Concile Vatican II: I. Accéder à la source* (Paris, Cerf, 2009), esp. 495–654.

[6] On the "normalizing" reading of the Second Vatican Council by John Paul II, see Giovanni Miccoli, *In difesa della fede: La Chiesa di Giovanni Paolo II e Benedetto XVI* (Milan, Rizzoli, 2007), 18–30.

[7] Benedict XVI, "A correct hermeneutic for reading and receiving the council as a great force of Church renewal," Address to the Roman curia, December 22, 2005; Italian original in Benedetto XVI, *Insegnamenti*, 1:1018–1032.

documents that preceded it and that have followed it, in other words "in the light of tradition."

Benedict XVI has returned many times to this topic; in his speech to the participants in the Plenary Meeting of the Congregation for the Clergy on March 16, 2009, for example, he emphasized the need to refer to "uninterrupted ecclesial tradition" and "to encourage in priests, especially in the young generations, a correct reception of the texts of the Second ecumenical Vatican Council, interpreted in the light of the Church's entire fund of doctrine."[8] The one way to make Vatican II credible—Cardinal Ratzinger always maintained and Benedict XVI maintains today—is to present it as a part of the entire, unique tradition of the Church and of her faith.[9]

The second line of interpretation takes a hermeneutical approach that is historical rather than theological. It has its most significant expression in the so-called "School of Bologna" which, under the direction of Professor Giuseppe Alberigo,[10] produced an impressive *History of Vatican II*[11] published in various languages, which, although controversial and

---

[8] "Address to the Members of the Congregation for the Clergy on the Occasion of their Plenary Assembly," www.vatican.va/.../speeches/2009/march/documents/hf_ben-xvi_spe_20090316_plenaria-clero_en.html - 12k - 2009–03–26; *Insegnamenti* 5/1 (2010): 393.

[9] Essays by many scholars follow this line of thinking, such as those collected in Matthew Lamb and Matthew Levering, eds., *Vatican II: Renewal Within Tradition* (Oxford: Oxford University Press, 2008). The 2005 address by Benedict XVI opens the volume, followed by a series of closely argued essays dedicated to the four conciliar constitutions, the nine decrees, and the three declarations of Vatican II. Among the authors are two American Cardinals (Avery Dulles and Francis George) and scholars such as Dominican Father Charles Morerod and the legal philosopher Russell Hittinger. The basic thesis is that Vatican II can be understood only in continuity with the bi-millennial tradition of the Church, according to the formula of Leo XIII, *"vetera novis augere et perficere"* ["to augment and perfect the old things by means of the new"]. Along this same line, see Leo Scheffczyk, *Aspekte der Kirche in der Krise: Um die Entscheidung für das authentische Konzil*, with an introduction by Cardinal J. Ratzinger (F. Schmitt, 1993).

[10] Giuseppe Alberigo (1926–2007), professor of Church History at the University of Bologna, director of the John XXIII Institute for Religious Sciences, and editor of the journal *Cristianesimo nella storia*. On the name and history of the Institute, cf. *L'officina bolognese 1953–2003*, ed. G. Alberigo (Bologna: EDB, 2004). For an analysis of the council from the perspective of this "school," cf. Giuseppe Dossetti, *Il Vaticano II: Frammenti di una riflessione*, ed. Francesco Margiotta Broglio (Bologna: Il Mulino, 1996).

[11] G. Alberigo, *Storia del Concilio Vaticano II*, 5 vols. (Bologna: Peeters/Il Mulino, 1995–2001);

debatable, constitutes an indispensable reference work. For this school, Vatican II, apart from the documents that it produced, was in the first place an historical "event" which, as such, meant an undeniable discontinuity with the past: it raised hopes, started polemics and debates, and in the final analysis inaugurated a new era.[12]

An event is a situation that represents a radical break with the past, "a fact which, once it has happened, changes something in the present and in the future."[13] The Second Vatican Council, according to Alberigo, exhibits very conspicuous characteristics of its own: the way in which it was convoked; the deliberate absence of a specific historical purpose; the almost wholesale rejection of the views and formulations prearranged by the preparatory bodies; the elaboration by the assembly of the general guidelines and of the texts themselves of the decisions; public opinion's perception of the council as a crucial event that was attended and participated in with extraordinary intensity.[14] "For all these reasons," the Bolognese historian writes, "the hermeneutic of Vatican II depends primarily and to a high degree on the event-dimension of the council."[15] The council's identity is defined, from this perspective, not only by the institutional doctrinal documents and the canonical norms followed at the council, but above all by the actual unfolding of the assembly and by the reception of the event by the community of the faithful.[16]

English edition *History of Vatican II*, 5 vols., edited by Joseph A. Komonchak (Maryknoll: Orbis, 1995–2006).

[12] For an overall view of the thesis of the "council-event," besides the volume cited in the previous note, see: *Experience, Organisations and Bodies at Vatican II*, Maria Teresa Fattori and A. Melloni, eds. (Leuven: Bibliotheek van de Faculteit Godgeleerdheid, 1999).

[13] Yves Congar, "Regard sur le Concile Vatican II," in *Le Concile de Vatican II: Son église, peuple de Dieu et corps du Christ* (Paris: Beauschesne, 1984), 53.

[14] G. Alberigo, "Criteri ermeneutici per una storia del Vaticano II," in *Il Vaticano II tra attese e celebrazioni*, ed. G. Alberigo (Bologna: Il Mulino: 1995), 9–26, at 16–17; reprinted in *Transizione epocale: Studi sul Concilio Vaticano II* (Bologna: Il Mulino, 2009), 36–37.

[15] Cf. G. Alberigo, *Transizione epocale*, op. cit., 37.

[16] Besides the study by G. Routhier, *Il Concilio Vaticano II, op. cit.*, see *Réceptions de Vatican II: Le concile au risque de l'histoire et des espaces humains*, ed. G. Routhier (Louvain: Peeters, 2004); *Zweites Vatikanisches Konzil—Ende oder Anfang?* with essays by Wolfgang Seibel, Helmut Krätzl, Herbert Vorgrimler, Karl Lehmann, Salvatore Loiero, ed. Alfred E. Hierold (Münster: Bamberger

The thesis of "discontinuity" is advanced also in the so-called "traditionalist" world, which includes a wide range of dissimilar views. The most important work to have appeared so far is the one by Professor Romano Amerio, *Iota Unum*,[17] which is not situated on the historical level, however, but on the theological and above all philosophical level. Although ignored by the progressive media, it too is an indispensable reference work.

3. The reception and implementation of the council

The hermeneutical conflict over Vatican II is connected also with two different interpretations of the context into which the conciliar gathering thrust itself and of the historical consequences that it had. Cardinal Ratzinger recounts that on the eve of the opening of the proceedings, on October 12, 1962, Cardinal Frings, president of the Conference of German Bishops, invited him to explain to the German-speaking bishops the theological problems that the council fathers would have to confront in the following months. While looking for an introduction that would highlight something relative to the very nature of the council, then-Professor Joseph Ratzinger found a passage by Eusebius of Caesarea, who had participated in the Council of Nicaea in 325, and he summarized in these words his impression of the sessions of his day:

> The most distinguished of God's ministers from all the Churches which abounded in Europe, Libya [Africa], and Asia were here assembled. And a single house of prayer, as though divinely enlarged, sufficed to contain at once Syrians and Cilicians, Phoenicians and Arabians, delegates

Theologisches Forum, 2004); Giacomo Martina, "Una nuova vitalità per la Chiesa: Sulla recezione del Concilio Vaticano II," in *Rivista del Clero Italiano* 86/3 (2005): 170–189.

[17] Romano Amerio (1905–1997), a philosopher and philologist, was an advisor to the bishop of Lugano, Angelo Jelmini, during the work of the Preparatory Commission of the Council. His chief work, *Iota Unum: Studio delle variazioni della Chiesa cattolica nel secolo XX*, edited by Riccardo Ricciardi and published in Milan and Naples in 1985, was translated into English by John P. Parsons from the second Italian edition as *Iota Unum: A study of changes in the Catholic Church in the XXth century* (Kansas City, Missouri: Sarto House, 1996). About that author, see *Romano Amerio: Della Verità e dell'Amore*, ed. Enrico Maria Radaelli, introduction by Antonio Livi (Lungro di Cosenza: Marco Editore, 2005). Other works by Amerio: *Stat Veritas: Seguito a "Iota unum,"* ed. E. M. Radaelli (Turin: Lindau, 2009), and *Zibaldone* (Turin: Lindau, 2010).

> from Palestine, and others from Egypt; Thebans and Libyans, with those who came from the region of Mesopotamia. A Persian bishop too was present at this conference, nor was even a Scythian found wanting to the number. Pontus, Galatia, and Pamphylia, Cappadocia, Asia, and Phrygia, furnished their most distinguished prelates; while those who dwelt in the remotest districts of Thrace and Macedonia, of Achaia and Epirus, were notwithstanding in attendance. Even from Spain itself, one whose fame was widely spread took his seat as an individual in the great assembly.[18]

Behind these enthusiastic words—Father Joseph Ratzinger commented to the German bishops—one recognizes the description of Pentecost given by Luke in the Acts of the Apostles. Eusebius' point was that Nicaea had been a true Pentecost. This was also the point that John XXIII and the council fathers were making about Vatican II: it would be a new Pentecost.[19]

The School of Bologna remained faithful to the Council-Pentecost archetype and sees in John XXIII the unheeded prophet of a new era in the history of the Church. Benedict XVI today, in contrast, is the most renowned representative of those who, in view of the self-destructive reality of the post-conciliar period, changed their judgment on the council over the years, proposing that it be interpreted in the wake of tradition.

After living through the council event and the long years of the post-conciliarpost-conciliar period as a protagonist, Joseph Ratzinger, having ascended to the papal throne with the name of Benedict XVI, applied the image of the Council of Nicaea once again to Vatican II, but in a very different key. In the above-cited address on December 22, 2005, the newly-elected pope confirmed that the reception of the council had undeniably been a difficult process, and then mentioned in this connection the image that St. Basil gives for the Church after the council in 325: he compares it to a naval battle being waged in the dark of night during a raging storm, describing "the cry of the combatants encountering one another in dispute;

---

[18] Eusebius of Caesarea, *Vita Constantini*, III, 7; NPNF 2nd series, 1:521b.

[19] Cf. J. Ratzinger, *Principles of Catholic Theology: Building Stones for a Fundamental Theology* (San Francisco: Ignatius Press, 1987), 367. On the council as a "Pentecost," cf. John XXIII, DMC, October 23, 1958, April 27, 1959 (vol. 1, p. 285), September 12, 1960 (2:496), January 6, April 21, May 8, August 26, September 26, 1962 (4:221, 251, 286, 550, 879). See also Gabriele Cislaghi, *Per una ecclesiologia pneumatologica: Il concilio Vaticano II e una proposta sistematica* (Rome-Milan: Glossa, 2004).

… the inarticulate screams, the unintelligible noises, rising from the ceaseless agitations."[20]

The metaphor that Benedict XVI applies to the post-conciliarpost-conciliar Church, forty years after the conclusion of the council, is therefore that of a naval battle, in the darkness, on a stormy sea. But already twenty years after the close of the conciliar proceedings, in his book-length interview, *The Ratzinger Report,* then-Cardinal Ratzinger considered it "incontestable" that the last twenty years had been "decidedly unfavorable for the Catholic Church."

> Developments since the council seem to be in striking contrast to the expectations of all, beginning with those of John XXIII and Paul VI. Christians are once again a minority, more than they have ever been since the end of antiquity.… What the popes and the council fathers were expecting was a new Catholic unity, and instead one has encountered a dissension which—to use the words of Paul VI—seems to have passed over from self-criticism to self-destruction. There had been the expectation of a new enthusiasm, and instead too often it has ended in boredom and discouragement. There had been the expectation of a step forward, and instead one found oneself facing a progressive process of decadence that to a large measure has been unfolding under the sign of a summons to a presumed 'spirit of the council' and by so doing has actually and increasingly discredited it.… The Church of the post-conciliar period is a huge construction site. But … it is a construction site where the blueprint has been lost and everyone continues to build according to his taste.[21]

The reasons for this profound crisis, according to Cardinal Ratzinger / Benedict XVI, must be sought in a wrong implementation of the council due to an erroneous interpretation of its documents. Therefore it is a question of a hermeneutical conflict.

> The problems in its implementation arose from the fact that two contrary hermeneutics came face to face and quarrelled with each other. One caused confusion, the other, silently but more and more visibly, bore and is bearing fruit.

---

[20] St. Basil, *De Spiritu Sancto,* XXX, 77; PG, vol. 32, col. 213; NPNF 2nd series, 8:48–49.

[21] J. Ratzinger, *The Ratzinger Report: An exclusive interview… with Vittorio Messori* (San Francisco: Ignatius Press, 1985), 29–30.

> On the one hand, there is an interpretation that I would call "a hermeneutic of discontinuity and rupture"; it has frequently availed itself of the sympathies of the mass media, and also one trend of modern theology. On the other, there is the "hermeneutic of reform," of renewal in the continuity of the one subject-Church which the Lord has given to us. She is a subject which increases in time and develops, yet always remaining the same, the one subject of the journeying people of God.[22]

It should be noted that between the crisis situation following the Council of Nicaea and the one in the aftermath of the Second Vatican Council there is a fundamental difference. The crisis after Nicaea was not started as a result of a hermeneutical conflict over the canons of the council in 325, but in an open reaction against those decrees.[23] Faced with this reactionary movement, the Emperor Constantine modified his policy toward Arianism, which led to an expansion of the crisis. The conflict was

---

[22] "The hermeneutic of discontinuity risks ending in a split between the pre-conciliar Church and the post-conciliar Church. It asserts that the texts of the council as such do not yet express the true spirit of the council. It claims that they are the result of compromises in which, to reach unanimity, it was found necessary to keep and reconfirm many old things that are now pointless.... Precisely because the texts would only imperfectly reflect the true spirit of the council and its newness, it would be necessary to go courageously beyond the texts and make room for the newness in which the council's deepest intention would be expressed, even if it were still vague.

"In a word: it would be necessary not to follow the texts of the council but its spirit. In this way, obviously, a vast margin was left open for the question on how this spirit should subsequently be defined and room was consequently made for every whim.

"The nature of a council as such is therefore basically misunderstood. In this way, it is considered as a sort of constituent that eliminates an old constitution and creates a new one. However, the Constituent Assembly needs a mandator and then confirmation by the mandator, in other words, the people the constitution must serve. The fathers had no such mandate and no one had ever given them one; nor could anyone have given them one because the essential constitution of the Church comes from the Lord and was given to us so that we might attain eternal life and, starting from this perspective, be able to illuminate life in time and time itself." (Benedict XVI, "A correct hermeneutic for reading and receiving the council as a great force of Church renewal," pp. 1024–1025; see footnote 7).

[23] Cf. Manlio Simonetti, *La crisi ariana nel IV secolo* (Rome: Institutum Patristicum "Augustinianum," 1975), 99–134 and *passim*. See also the study by Bl. John Henry Newman, *The Arians of the Fourth Century* (1833; London and New York: Longmans, Green, and Co., 1919).

between the supporters of the Council of the Nicaea and its radical and moderate opponents, whereas the meaning of the Nicene Creed was never called into question.

4. A "pastoral" or a "doctrinal" council?

The formula of reading the council in the light of tradition or, if you prefer, the "hermeneutic of continuity," no doubt offers the faithful authoritative direction in clearing up the problem of the right way to take the conciliar documents, but it leaves one fundamental problem open: assuming that the correct interpretation is the one emphasizing continuity, it remains to be seen why after the Second Vatican Council something happened that never happened in the aftermath of any council in history, namely that two (or more) contrary hermeneutics found themselves in conflict and, to use the words of the pope himself, "quarreled" with each other. Then if the post-conciliarpost-conciliar era is to be interpreted in terms of a "crisis," we must ask ourselves whether an erroneous reception of the documents could lead to such a point in historical events and constitute a reason that is sufficient and proportionate to explain the enormity and depth of that same crisis.

The existence of a plurality of heremeneutics, on the other hand, is evidence of a certain ambiguity or ambivalence of the documents. If one must resort to a hermeneutic criterion external to the document in order to interpret the document itself, it is obvious, in fact, that the document is not sufficiently clear in itself: it needs to be interpreted and, inasmuch as it is susceptible to interpretation, can be the object of historical and theological criticism.

The most logical development of this hermeneutic principle is the one proposed by an eminent specialist in ecclesiology, Monsignor Brunero Gherardini.[24] According to the Roman theologian, Vatican II, being a

---

[24] Brunero Gherardini, *Concilio Ecumenico Vaticano II: Un discorso da fare*, Preface by Bishop Mario Olivieri, bishop of Albenga-Imperia, and Introduction by then-archbishop Albert Malcolm Ranjith, secretary of the Congregation for Divine Worship and the Discipline of the Sacraments (Frigento: Casa Mariana, 2009); English translation: *The Ecumenical Vatican Council II: A Much Needed Discussion* (Frigento: Casa Mariana Editrice, 2012). Monsignor Gherardini was born in 1925. After being ordained in 1948 he taught Ecclesiology at the Pontifical Lateran University, where he is now emeritus professor. He succeeded Monsignor Antonio Piolanti as editor of the journal *Divinitas*. For a closely-argued critique of the ambiguity of the conciliar documents, see Atila Sinke

council that described itself as "pastoral," had no "definitional" doctrinal character.[25] The fact that Vatican II cannot claim the status of a dogmatic council, but was characterized by its "pastoral nature," of course does not mean that it was without a doctrine of its own. The Second Vatican Council certainly has its specific teaching, which is not without authority, but, as Gherardini writes, "none of its doctrines, unless ascribable to previous conciliar definitions, are infallible or unchangeable, nor are they even binding: he who denies them cannot, for this reason, be called a formal heretic. He, then, who imposes them as infallible and unchangeable would be going contrary to the council itself."[26] If the Second Vatican Council has an eminently pastoral nature, it is licit to attribute to it a dogmatic character only in places where it reiterates as truths of the faith dogmas that were defined in preceding councils. "The doctrines which are proper to it, on the other hand, absolutely cannot be considered as dogmatic because they are deprived of the requisite form for defining and hence of the related *voluntas definiendi* [intention to define]."[27]

To someone who might object that nothing, in principle, prevents a pastoral council from defining a dogma, one might respond that, apart from the pastoral self-description of the Second Vatican Council, the

---

Guimarães, *In the Murky Waters of Vatican II* (Rockford, Illinois: TAN Books, 1999), 1–296; *idem, Animus Delendi: The Desire to Destroy*, 2 vols. (Los Angeles: Tradition in Action, 2001–2002). The heterogeneous and at times contradictory character of the conciliar documents is admitted also by Antonio Acerbi in *Due ecclesiolgie: Ecclesiologia giuridica ed ecclesiologia di comunione nella "Lumen gentium"* (Bologna: EDB, 1975).

[25] The lack of any intention to define is not contradicted by the adjective "dogmatic" with which the Council describes its two important constitutions: *Lumen gentium* and *Dei Verbum*. In reality they can be considered "dogmatic" only because they accepted and reiterated as truths of faith dogmas that had been defined in preceding Councils. On this point see Arnaldo Xavier Vidigal da Silveira, "Qual è l'autorità dottrinale dei documenti pontifici e conciliari?" in *Cristianità* 9 (1975): 3–7. Apparently less convincing is the thesis of Bernard Lucien, *Les Degrés d'autorité du Magistère: La question de l'infaillibilité: Doctrine catholique, Développements récents, Débats actuels* (Feucherolles: La Nef, 2007), a collection of several articles that had already appeared in the magazine *Sedes Sapientiae*. Contrasting views: Pierre-Marie, O.P., "Le magistère conciliaire est-il infaillible?" and Alvaro Calderon, "Pour une lucidité catholique," in *Le Sel de la Terre* 63 (2007–2008): 37–46 and 47–59.

[26] B. Gherardini, *The Ecumenical Vatican Council II*, op. cit., 60, and, more generally, 55–77.

[27] *Ibid.*, 59

proof that it did not want to define any dogma is supplied also by its acts [*Acta*] and by the tenor of its documents, none of which unequivocally manifests the intention to define.[28] Paul VI himself, in closing the council, declared that in it "the magisterium of the Church ... did not wish to make pronouncements with extraordinary dogmatic judgments"[29] and, on less solemn occasions, reiterated that the council had as one of the points on its agenda "not to issue new solemn dogmatic definitions."[30] If a council has only the authority that the pope wants to attribute to it, the pontifical pronouncements of John XXIII and Paul VI, before and after the promulgation of the conciliar documents, put an end to all doubts that may exist [*sussistere*] in this regard.

The "pastoral" characterization of the Second Vatican Council is underscored also by the School of Bologna,[31] although interpreted from a different perspective. The description of the council as "pastoral" in fact diminishes the importance of its acts and the documents themselves and tends to make the "event" a hermeneutical standard. If one admits the "novelty" of a pastoral council, then it is necessary to acknowledge, with Alberigo, that "the most significant novelty of Vatican II was not its formulations, but rather the very fact of having been convoked and celebrated."[32] The historian Joseph Komonchak emphasizes that the convocation of the council "was a surprise, a break with the normal routine of the Church, in a way that was also independent of what Pope John intended by a council."[33]

The promulgated documents naturally are part of the event, but the "event" is made up of a totality of factors that includes, besides the letter of the texts, also the descriptions transmitted and amplified by the media

---

28 Cf. A. Xavier da Silveira, "Qual è l'autorità dottrinale," *op. cit.*, 7.

29 Address, December 7, 1965, in Paolo VI, *Insegnamenti*, 3:722.

30 Paul VI, Address, March 8, 1967, *ibid.*, 5:704.

31 Alberigo maintains that the adjective *pastoral* appears in texts by Roncalli 689 times in the singular and 168 times in the plural. From his election as pope (October 28, 1958) until his death (1963), the adjective was used 245 times (G. Alberigo, "Criteri ermeneutici," *op. cit.*, 20). See also *idem*, "Le ragioni dell'opzione pastorale del Vaticano II," in *Synaxis* 20 (2002): 489–509.

32 G. Alberigo, *Transizione epocale, op. cit.*, 848.

33 Joseph A. Komonchak, "Riflessioni storiografiche sul Vaticano II come evento," in *L'evento e le decisioni*, 417–439, citation at 419.

that were covering the event. Some sociologists, like Melissa Wilde[34] and Massimo Introvigne,[35] accept the "event" character precisely on account of the depiction of it by the media and because of the "self-image" that many council fathers had of it as it unfolded. Gilles Routhier too emphasized that the hermeneutic of the council cannot ignore the representation of the media and the way in which the council was perceived by the faithful.[36] Catholics, most of whom did not read the conciliar documents, knew the council precisely through the depiction that the media provided for them.

Father John W. O'Malley offers a more in-depth analysis, declaring that the problem concerns not only the way in which the documents were presented, even before the end of the council, but also touches on the very nature of the documents with regard to their form rather than their content.[37] The American Jesuit proposed the figure of Erasmus of Rotterdam as the "key" to interpreting Vatican II,[38] which he describes as

---

[34] Cf. Melissa Wilde, *Vatican II: a Sociological Analysis of Religious Change* (Princeton and Oxford: Princeton University Press, 2007). The volume by Melissa Wilde, a sociologist at the University of Indiana in Bloomington, is particularly innovative. It is based on interviews with the Council fathers compiled by Fr. Rocco Caporale in *Vatican II: The Last of Councils* (Baltimore: Garamond/ Pridemark Press, 1964), drawing from them several important considerations of a sociological character.

[35] Cf. Massimo Introvigne, *Una battaglia nella notte: Plinio Corrêa de Oliveira e la crisi del XX secolo nella Chiesa* (Milan: Sugarco, 2008), 95–101.

[36] Cf. G. Routhier, *Il Concilio Vaticano II, op. cit.*, 118–120.

[37] Cf. John W. O'Malley, S.J., *What Happened at Vatican II?* (Cambridge Mass.: Belknap Press of Harvard University Press, 2008), 45–52 and 290–313. Fr. John O'Malley has presented his thought in relation to rhetorical genres in many volumes, from *Giles of Viterbo on Church and Reform* (1968), and *Praise and Blame in Renaissance Rome* (1979), to *The First Jesuits* (1993) and *Four Cultures of the West* (2004). Less convincing is the proposal by Peter Hünermann to attribute to the conciliar magisterium the status of "constitutional documents," by which he means a new literary genre developed by Vatican II that implies a claim to the "obedience of faith"; see Peter Hünermann, "Der 'Text': Eine Ergänzung zur Hermeneutik des II. Vatikanischen Konzils," in *Cristianesimo nella storia* 28 (2007): 339–358; reprinted in *Chi ha paura del Vaticano II?, op. cit.*, 85–105.

[38] *Cf.* J. W. O'Malley, "Erasmus and Vatican II: Interpreting the Council," in *Cristianesimo nella storia: Saggi in onore di Giuseppe Alberigo*, ed. A. Melloni, D. Menozzi, G. Ruggieri, Massimo Toschi (Bologna: Il Mulino, 1996) 195–197.

an "Erasmian" council.[39] The main parallels [*assonanze*] between Erasmus and Vatican II, in terms of content, have to do with the fundamental theme of "reconciliation," but "the most significant similarity between Erasmus and Vatican II is their language, their vocabulary, their style of discourse."[40]

The "novelty" of the council should be sought, not so much in the contents of the documents, as in their form, according to indications in *Gaudium et spes* and of John XXIII himself in his opening speech: "Provided the meaning and understanding of them is safeguarded..., the deposit and the truths of faith are one thing, the manner of expressing them is quite another."[41] Professions of faith and canons are replaced by a "literary genre" that Father O'Malley calls "epideictic".[42] This mode of expression was, according to the Jesuit historian, "a significant break with past councils."[43] Expressing oneself in terms different from those used in the past means accepting a cultural transformation that is deeper than it may seem. Indeed, the style of a discourse reveals, even more than the ideas, the profound tendencies of the mind of the person who expresses himself. "Style is the ultimate expression of meaning. It does not adorn meaning but is meaning. It is a hermeneutical key *par excellence.*"[44] The pastoral aspect is, normally, accidental and secondary with respect to the doctrinal aspect, but once it becomes an essential and primary dimension, the way in which doctrine is formulated is itself transformed into a doctrine more important than the one that is objectively being conveyed.

The leaders of the council, O'Malley continues, "fully realized that Vatican II as a self-proclaimed pastoral council was for that reason also a teaching council.... Its style of discourse was the medium that conveyed

---

[39] *Cf. idem*, "Egidio da Viterbo and Renaissance Rome," in *Egidio da Viterbo, O.S.A., e il suo tempo: Atti del V Convegno dell'Istituto Storico Agostiniano* (Rome: Studia Agostiniana Historica, 1983), 81.

[40] J. W. O'Malley, "Erasmus and Vatican II," *op. cit.*, 208.

[41] Pastoral constitution *Gaudium et spes*, 62. The same document then refers to the opening speech of John XXIII, in which he had declared, "The substance of the ancient doctrine of the deposit of faith is one thing, and the way in which it is presented is another: and great importance must be attached to the latter, patiently if necessary." (Address on October 11, 1962, in AAS 54 (1964): 792).

[42] J. W. O'Malley, *What Happened at Vatican II?, op. cit.*, 43–52.

[43] *Ibid.*, 44–45.

[44] *Ibid.*, 49.

the message."[45] "This means that Vatican II, the 'pastoral council,' has a teaching, a 'doctrine,' that to a large extent it has been difficult for us to formulate, because in this case doctrine and spirit are two sides of the same coin."[46] The choice of a "style" of language in which to speak to contemporaries reveals a way of being and of thinking, and in this sense it must be admitted that the literary genre and the pastoral style of Vatican II not only express the organic unity of the event, but implicitly convey a coherent doctrine.

In this respect the council undoubtedly signaled a profound change in the life of the Church. Contemporaries would note its epochal character. "There was talk," Komonchak recalls, "about an historical turning point; the end of the counter-reformation or of the Tridentine era, the end of the Middle Ages, the end even of the Constantinian era."[47] "Simply put," Melissa Wilde points out, "Vatican II represents the most significant example of institutionalized religious change since the reformation."[48]

5. The primacy of practice and reform in the Church

Like any "event," Vatican II must be set within the historical context in which it happened: the sixties, which were the years in which so-called "real socialism"—or communism in power—reached the height of its historical trajectory. The intellectual influence of Marxism, as it appeared in those years, was strong in all social circles, including Catholic ones. It is not difficult to understand the "primacy of the pastoral," which was making headway during the years of the council, as the theological transposition of the "primacy of praxis" enunciated by Marx in his *Theses on Feuerbach* in these words: "It is in practice that man must prove the truth, that is, the reality and power, the this-sidedness [this-worldliness]

---

[45] *Ibid.*, 307. See also *idem,* "Vatican II: Historical Perspectives on its Uniqueness and Interpretation," in *Vatican II: The Unfinished Agenda: A Look to the Future*, ed. Lucien Richard, Daniel Harrington, J. W. O'Malley (New York: Paulist Press, 1987), 22–32.

[46] J. W. O'Malley, *Vatican II: Did Anything Happen? op. cit.*, p. 82.

[47] J. A. Komonchak, "Vatican II as an 'event'," in *Vatican II: Did anything happen?*, *op. cit.*, 24–51 at 29.

[48] Wilde, 2.

of his thinking"[49] and "the philosophers have only *interpreted* the world, in various ways; the point, however, is to *change* it."[50] Praxis, which is to say the historical result of political action, is for Marx the supreme criterion of the truth of ideas, because action implicitly contains a doctrine, albeit without articulating it.[51]

Marx's comment on Feuerbach, that philosophers should not know the world but rather transform it, could be paraphrased by a conciliar comment that the task of pastors and theologians is not to understand and transmit the Church's doctrine, but to transform history by means of it.[52] "Ever since the end of the council's first session," Cardinal Agostino Bea writes, "I have repeatedly stated that the fruits of the council were to be sought very largely, before a study of the actual documents could be made, in the experience of those who took part in the council and therefore also of the Christians who were interested in the Conciliar work. This is especially true in the ecumenical field."[53] The theology of liberation carried this principle to its ultimate consequences.[54]

In the post-conciliar period, historical praxis became a *locus theologicus* [theological commonplace],[55] whereby "theology cannot be described as

---

[49] Karl Marx, *Theses on Feuerbach*, in Frederick Engels, *Ludwig Feuerbach and the End of Classical German Philosophy* (Peking: Foreign Languages Press, 1976), 61–65, Thesis II at p. 62.

[50] *Ibid.*, Thesis XI, p. 65.

[51] "Revolution and the meaning of history unite: we have revolution in the meaning of history. History in action becomes the sole judge." Augusto Del Noce, *I caratteri generali del pensiero politico: Lezioni sul marxismo* (Milan: Giuffrè, 1972), 228.

[52] *Cf.* A. Acerbi, "Ortoprassi," in *Nuovo Dizionario di teologia* (Cinisello Balsamo: San Paolo, 1991), 1006–1030; Giovanni Battista Mondin, *Le teologie della prassi* (Brescia: Queriniana, 1973); Walter Kasper, "La prassi scientifica della teologia," in Various Authors, *Corso di teologia fondamentale*, IV, *Trattato di gnoseologia teologica* (Brescia: Queriniana, 1980), 245–281.

[53] Agostino Bea, *The Way to Unity after the Council* (New York: Herder and Herder, 1967), 8.

[54] *Cf.* Carlo Molari, *Introduzione* to the Italian edition of *Mysterium liberationis: I concetti fondamentali della teologia della liberazione*, ed. Ignacio Ellacuria, John Sobrino (Rome: Borla, 1992), 5–31, reference at 12.

[55] See, among other works, *Il Concilio vent'anni dopo: L'ingresso della categoria "storia,"* ed. Enrico Cattaneo (Rome: Ave, 1985); Bruno Forte, "Le prospettive della ricerca teologica," in *Il Concilio Vaticano II: Recezione e attualità alla luce del Giubileo*, ed. Rino Fisichella (Cinisello Balsamo: San Paolo, 2000), 419–429.

a pure science, but rather always as a moment in an historical process."[56] The relation between truth and history was reformulated, emphasizing the historical dimension of theology, which assumed the historical practice,[57] in the form of a "critical theory of Christian and ecclesial praxis."[58] The theology of praxis was postulated as "the consistent application of the theology of the signs of the times (ST) as it was discussed by the council, especially in the Pastoral constitution *Gaudium et spes* (GS)."[59] "Orthopraxis" became the criterion for verifying theology, which was judged in terms of its ability to change the world historically. "The theology that developed in the aftermath of Vatican II is characterized therefore by its peculiar historicity,"[60] writes Monsignor Bruno Forte, echoing the "Manifesto" of Le Saulchoir which stated "The theologian does not and cannot have any hope of encountering his specific datum outside of history...."[61] This is the perspective in which we need to situate the key words of the conciliar period, such as "pastoral," "*aggiornamento,*" and "signs of the times."

The term *aggiornamento* implies that not only do people have to conform to the sacred teachings, but the latter have to be adapted to the people. According to O'Malley this turns on its head the axiom of Cardinal Egidio da Viterbo in his speech at the opening of the Fifth Lateran Council (1512): "*...homines per sacra immutari fas est, non sacra per homines*" ["... it is lawful to change men by means of sacred things, not sacred things by men"].[62] "No previous council ever took the equivalent of *aggiornamento* as a leitmotif, as a broad principle rather

---

56 Giuseppe Ruffini, "Il modello gramsciano della funzione intellettuale ed il suo impiego nella discussione ermeneutico-teologica," in Associazione Teologica Italiana, *Dimensione antropologica della teologia* (Milan: Ancora, 1971), 275–294, ref. at 292.

57 *Cf.* B. Forte, "Le prospettive della ricerca teologica," *op. cit.*, 424.

58 W. Kasper, "La funzione della teologia della Chiesa," in *Avvenire della Chiesa: Il libro del Congresso di Bruxelles* (Brescia: Queriniana, 1970), 72.

59 C. Molari, "Introduzione," *op. cit.*, 12.

60 B. Forte, "Le prospettive della ricerca teologica," in *Il Concilio Vaticano II: Recezione e attualità...*, *op. cit.*, 424.

61 Marie-Dominique Chenu, *Une école de théologie, le Saulchoir* (Kain-lez-Tournai—Etioilles: Le Saulchoir, 1937), 61.

62 Mansi, vol. 32, col. 669.

than as a rare exception, with its implication that the Church should change in certain regards to meet the times rather than the times change to meet the Church."[63]

The pastoral dimension thus becomes a hermeneutical key for recognizing the "historicity of the Church" and for interpreting Christian truth historically. Consistently with this perspective, Giuseppe Alberigo, who wanted to make the School of Bologna the continuation of the School of Le Saulchoir, does not limit himself in his *History of Vatican II* to composing a work of history. He assigns to history the task of the "ecclesiological reform" anticipated by the *"nouvelle théologie"* [new theology] and, even before that, by modernism.[64]

6. "Rewriting" the history of the council

For our part we propose distinguishing carefully between the theological dimension that emerges from the documents and the more properly "factual" dimension that refers to historical events. Distinction, of course, does not mean "separation." Every Church historian carries into his work the baggage of a theological and ecclesiological vision and, even before that, his "theology of history." Furthermore we would say that the historical reconstruction of the conciliar *iter* [journey] is indispensable for understanding the meaning and the significance of those documents of the Church that theologians help us to read in their theological dimension. The theologian reads and discusses the documents in their doctrinal import.[65] The historian reconstructs the events, even though he does not limit himself to the merely factual dimension, but understands occurrences in their cultural and ideological roots and consequences. The historian's task does not consist of deconstructing the past, nor of reconstructing it as a chronicler might, but rather in grasping the

---

63 J. W. O'Malley, *Vatican II: Did Anything Happen?*, *op. cit.*, 64; reprinted as *Theological Studies* 67 (2006): 3–33, citation at 13.

64 Along these lines see G. Alberigo, *La Chiesa nella storia* (Brescia: Paideia, 1988), in which he expresses his conviction that "knowledge of the Christian achievement can lead to critically rigorous results only by retracing its evolution within the history of humanity" (*Ibid.*, 8).

65 *Cf.* for example Karl Rahner, "Interpretazione teologica fondamentale del Concilio Vaticano II," Ital. transl. in *Nuovi Saggi: Sollecitudine per la Chiesa* (Rome: Paoline, 1982), 345–361.

direction of the process and its unifying connection so as to arrive at an "integral" understanding of the events.[66]

The hermeneutic of continuity correctly confirms the primacy of the magisterium but runs the risk of dismissing not only an erroneous theological conception, but also the very fact that is under discussion.[67] The consequence of this operation of dismissing the event is that today there is no serious alternative to the School of Bologna, which has to be credited with offering an initial factual (albeit tendentious) reconstruction of what happened.

For many proponents of the hermeneutic of continuity, the historical dismissal of the conciliar "event" is necessary in order to separate the council from the post-conciliar period and to isolate the latter as a pathology that developed within a healthy body. One might ask, however, whether erasing the council-event leads to an in-depth understanding of what happened in the post-conciliar period. The Second Vatican Council was, indeed, an event that did not conclude with its final solemn session, but was settled with its implementation and historical reception.[68] Something happened after the council as a consequence consistent with it. In this sense one cannot fault Alberigo when he states that the reconstruction of what happened between January 25, 1959, and December 8, 1965, is a necessary premise for serious reflection on Vatican II.[69] The history of the council is therefore to be rewritten, or at least to be completed.

In this spirit I propose a history of the council, "the unwritten story," not so much on account of the novelty of the testimonies and the episodes that emerge from it, as on account of the new reconstruction and interpretation of the facts that is offered. Neither the researcher who "unearths" new documents nor the "chronicler" who piles up the ones that are already known is the real historian, but rather the one who, based on the published or unpublished documentation at his disposal, is

---

66 *Cf.* R. de Mattei, "Per un'assiologia della storia," in *Nova Historica* 1 (2002): 7–16, ref. at 14.

67 "Strangely, some people have the impression," Giuseppe Ruggieri observes, "that *History* is rejected not because it recounts *certain things*, but rather because it *recounts* these things," "Recezione e interpretazione del Vaticano II," *op. cit.*, 391.

68 Cf. Wilde, 28.

69 Cf. G. Alberigo, *Transizione epocale, op. cit.*, 766.

able to order it, understand it, and narrate it, framing the events within a philosophy of history that, for the Catholic historian, is first of all a theology of history.[70]

The following pages are dedicated to the historical reconstruction of the "fact," without claiming to create an artificial dichotomy between the documents and the event, but seeking on the contrary to show the impossibility of separating the doctrine from the facts that generate it. Therefore this is not a work of theological reflection but rather of historical narration, written in the spirit with which Cardinal Sforza Pallavicino confronted the Council of Trent: "The most sublime of all human things is religion," he wrote, "through which we deal with heaven and gain heaven. Therefore these accounts which have religion as their subject matter are as far above the others in their material as the heaven is above the earth."[71]

---

[70] The reference point of these pages is the theology and philosophy of history articulated by the nineteenth and twentieth century papal magisterium and briefly summarized by Plinio Corrêa de Oliveira in *Rivoluzione e Contro-Rivoluzione*, ed. Giovanni Cantoni, 50th anniversary edition (Milan: Sugarco, 2009); English transl. *Revolution and Counter-Revolution* (Fullerton, CA: Educator Publications, 1972).

[71] *Istoria del Concilio di Trento scritta dal padre Sforza Pallavicino della Compagnia de Gesù* (Milan: Tipografia Pirotta, 1843), vol. I, p. xxiv.

Bibliographical Note

The bibliography on the Second Vatican Council is superabundant.[1] As for the sources, the essential point of reference is the edition of the acts and documents, divided into two sections, corresponding to the two phases of the council (preparatory and actual unfolding):[2] the *Acta et documenta Concilio oecumenico Vaticano II apparando* and the *Acta Synodalia Sacrosancti Concilii Oecumenici Vaticani II.*

The phase of the preparation is in turn divided into two parts: the ante-preparatory phase, which runs from the announcement of the council (January 25, 1959) to June 5, 1960; the preparatory phase, which begins on June 5, 1960 with the motu proprio by John XXIII *Superno Dei nutu* and extends to the beginning of the council.

As for the actual unfolding of the council (1962-1965), the *Acta Synodalia* compile the acts of the congregations and of the public sessions, the interventions of the council fathers, both oral and written, the different versions of the schemas, the proposed emendations, and the approbation of the documents.[3] These offer an indispensable help in reconstructing the

---

1 See, just for the three years 2002–2005, Massimo Faggioli, "Concilio Vaticano II: bollettino bibliografico (2002–2005)," in *Cristianesimo nella storia* 28 (2005): 743–768.

2 Cf. Vincenzo Carbone, "Genesi e criteri della pubblicazione degli Atti del Concilio Vaticano II," in *Lateranum* 44 (1978): 579–595; George Lefebvre, "Les Actes du Concile du Vatican II," in *Revue théologique de Louvain* 11 (1980): 186–200.

3 *Acta Synodalia Sacrosancti Concilii Oecumenici Vaticani II* (Città del Vaticano: Typis Polyglottis

conciliar documents, even though the *Acta* lack documentation from the conciliar commissions where the schemas were developed in detail. Finally the texts of the sixteen documents approved by the council fathers have been published in an *editio typica*: *Sacrosanctum Oecumenicum Concilium Vaticanum II: Constitutiones, Decreta, Declarationes* (Città del Vaticano, 1966).

Another very important resource is the Second Vatican Council collection in the Vatican Secret Archives, to which should be added the collections found in several university research centers in Europe and America, in particular the Second Vatican Council archive of the *Istituto per le Scienze religiose* in Bologna, directed by Alberto Melloni, and, in Belgium, the archive of the *Centrum Lumen Gentium* of the *Université Catholique de Louvain-la-Neuve* directed by Claude Soetens, to which we must add the *Centrum voor Conciliestudie Vaticanum II* of the *Katholieke Universiteit Leuven*.

The official documents, although indispensable, are not sufficient to understand what happened in Rome from October 1962 to December 1965. Also important are the documents about everything that happened *a latere* [alongside] the council, influencing it.[4] Many aspects, some of them downright decisive, took place behind the scenes, as Roger Aubert observed. "The official archives are silent about these facts, but references to them, occasionally rather detailed, can be found in the private papers of various protagonists or spectators: letters, diaries, personal notes...."[5] This means that it is necessary to draw on the testimonies of the participants or the spectators at the council, in particular diaries,[6] correspondence, and

---

Vaticanis); vol. 1, *Periodus prima* (1970); vol. 2, *Periodus secunda* (1971); vol. 3, *Periodus tertia* (1973); vol. 4, *Periodus quarta* (1976); vol. 5, *Processus verbales* (1991); vol. 6, *Acta secretariae generalis* (1999).

[4] There is a detailed catalogue of the documentary sources preserved by the protagonists of the Council, in their various localities, thanks to Massimo Faggioli and Giovanni Turbanti. Cf. M. Faggioli and G. Turbanti, Il Concilio inedito: Fonti del Vaticano II (Bologna: Il Mulino, 2001).

[5] Roger Aubert, "Come vedo il Vaticano II," in *Rassegna di teologia* 36 (1995): 134.

[6] A. Melloni, "I diari nella storia dei Concili," in M. D. Chenu, Diari del Vaticano II: Note quotidiane al Concilio 1962–1963, ed. A. Melloni (Bologna: Il Mulino, 1996), 9–53; Joseph Famerée, "Uso comparativo dei diari: Una settimana di lavori conciliari (5–15 novembre 1963)," in L'evento e le decisioni, 321–354; Leo Kenis, "Diaries: Private Sources for a Study of the Second Vatican Council," in The Belgian Contribution to the Second Vatican Council: International

memoirs, as Cardinal Siri already cautioned in 1969: "I still maintain that it will be possible to write an adequate history when the notes or diaries that may have been written by some of the most authoritative members of the council are made public."[7] Since then fundamentally important diaries like the one kept by Siri himself and those of Father Marie-Dominique Chenu, Yves Congar, and Henri de Lubac have appeared in print; likewise the important correspondence of Bishops Giacomo Lercaro and Helder Câmara, to which should be added the still unpublished diaries that we were able to consult, of Monsignor Joseph Clifford Fenton and Doctor Murillo Maranhão Galliez, and the documentation housed in the archives of the Seminary in Ecône and in the *Istituto Plinio Corrêa de Oliveira* in San Paolo (Brazil).[8]

The journalists who followed the council step by step were progressive in their orientation and left tendentious chronicles that are outdated today, such as the ones by Father Antoine Wenger serialized in *La Croix*, by Raniero La Valle in *Avvenire d'Italia*, by Henri Fesquet in *Le Monde*, by Reverend René Laurentin in *Le Figaro*, and by the American Redemptorist Francis X. Murphy under the pseudonym Xavier Rynne in the *New Yorker Magazine*. One exception is the work by the Divine Word Father Ralph M. Wiltgen,[9] director of Divine World News Service and author of an apparently minor body of writings that is actually of first-rate importance, for instance *The Rhine Flows into the Tiber*.

Research Conference at Mechelen, Leuven and Louvain-la-Neuve (12–16 September 2005), ed. Doris Donnelly, J. Famerée, Matthijs Lemberigts, Karim Shelkens (Leuven: Peeters, 2008), 29–53. See also, more generally, A. Melloni, "Tipologia delle fonti per la storia del Vaticano II," in Cristianesimo nella storia 13 (1992): 393–514.

[7] Cf. G. Siri, "Il post-concilium: dal punto di vista storico, dal punto di vista della Providenza," in *La giovinezza della Chiesa, op. cit.*, 177.

[8] For information about the numerous para-conciliar groups, it is indispensable to consult the research of Salvador Gómez y Catalina, *Grupos "extra aulam" en el Concilio Vaticano y su influencia* (three books in nine volumes, for a total of 2,585 pages, an unpublished doctoral thesis in the Biblioteca de la Facultad de Derecho, Universidad de Valladolid).

[9] Ralph Michael Wiltgen (1921–2007), of the Divine Word Congregation, ordained in 1950, completed a doctorate in Missiology at the Pontifical Gregorian University and then published an important study on *The Founding of the Roman Catholic Church in Oceania 1825–1850* (Canberra: Australian National University, 1978). His best-known book however is *The Rhine Flows into the Tiber* (New York: Divine Word Publications, 1967).

Naturally one should not overlook the biographies of the protagonists, recalling that history is not moved only by economic and political interests, but primarily by the ideas and the profound tendencies of the human mind, which inspire ideological systems and the actions that follow from them. In this sense, the council must be considered in the light of the actors and the protagonists who were active in it, such as Cardinals Bea, Döpfner, Felici, Frings, König, Lercaro, Ottaviani, Ruffini, Siri, and Suenens. Recognition must be given to Jan Grootaers for having followed this path.[10]

The history of the Second Vatican Council that we propose is "an unwritten story" because of its new approach to this vast documentation, but it is not yet "the" story of Vatican II, which must wait until all the archives have been explored and all the documents have been brought to light. The surprises that we will be in for then will be much greater than those that this book may hold for many of its readers. But the Church, as Leo XIII confirmed by opening the Secret Vatican Archives to scholars, "must not fear the truth."[11]

---

[10] Cf. Jan Grootaers, *I protagonisti del Concilio Vaticano II* (Cinisello Balsamo: Paoline, 1994); *idem*, ed., *Actes et Acteurs à Vatican II* (Leuven, Leuven University Press, 1988).

[11] Cf. Arnold Esch, "Leone XIII: L'apertura dell'Archivio Segreto Vaticano e la storiografia," in *Leone XIII e gli studi storici*, Atti del Convegno internazionale commemorativo (Città del Vaticano, 30–31 ottobre 2003), ed. C. Semeraro (Città del Vaticano: Libreria Editrice Vaticana, 2004), 20–43, citation at p. 31.

I

The Church in the Age of Pius XII

1. The pontificate of Pius XII: triumph or the start of a crisis?

a) The high point in the Holy Year

The Second World War had caused forty million deaths and covered the world with mourning and with material and moral ruin. While Europe was recovering laboriously from the wreckage of this tremendous conflict, in the Holy Year of 1950 the Catholic Church, governed by Pius XII,[1] arose in the splendor of her liturgy, in the vitality of her doctrine and in her ability to gather crowds from all over the world.

---

[1] Eugenio Pacelli (1876–1958), born into a Roman family, ordained in 1899, undersecretary (1911) and then secretary of the Department of Extraordinary Ecclesiastical Affairs (1914), consecrated bishop and at the same time elevated to the rank of archbishop on May 13, 1917. Nuncio in Bavaria (1917–1929), then created cardinal (1929) and appointed Secretary of State by Pius XI. Elected pope on March 2, 1939 and reigned until October 9, 1958. Despite the abundant literature, relating especially to the conduct of Pius XII with regard to the Jews, there is still no exhaustive monograph on this pope. Meanwhile see the articles by Andrea Riccardi in DSP, 2:1175–1183 and Francesco Traniello in EP, 632–645 with bibliography; Jean Chelini, *L'Église sous Pie XII: 1. La tourmente: 1939–1945; 2. L'après-guerre, 1945–1958* (Paris: Fayard, 1983 and 1989); Philippe Chenaux, *Pie XII: diplomate et pasteur* (Paris: Cerf, 2003); Andrea Tornielli, *Pio XII: Eugenio Pacelli, un uomo sul trono di Pietro* (Milan: Mondadori, 2007).

The culminating moment of the Jubilee Year was the proclamation of the dogma of the Assumption of the Blessed Virgin Mary into heaven, on November 1, 1950, in the presence of more than one and a half million pilgrims. One witness recounts that, from dawn on that day, St. Peter's Square, still immersed in silence, "was transformed into a boundless sea, into which poured streams of humanity, unstoppably and uninterruptedly."[2] All peoples and all nations were represented in this undulating crowd, while hymns and prayers blended harmoniously. Preceded by a procession of bishops vested in white copes and miters, the pope appeared on the *sedia gestatoria*. After imploring the assistance of the Holy Spirit, Pius XII solemnly defined it "to be a divinely revealed dogma: that the Immaculate Mother of God, the ever Virgin Mary, having completed the course of her earthly life, was assumed body and soul into heavenly glory."[3] The whole world, linked by radio to the immense square, rejoiced. "It seemed to be a vision, and yet it was a reality: Pius XII imparted his blessing until nightfall, for the crowd unceasingly clamored for it. After the window had been closed, one stream of people left the square only to be replaced by another. All of them wanted to be blessed once again before the end of that marvelous day."[4]

On October 30, 1950, two days before the definition of the dogma, Pius XII had received the extraordinary grace of seeing, in the Vatican gardens, the same spectacle of the sun dancing in the sky like a ball of fire that had been witnessed by seventy-thousand pilgrims in Fatima, Portugal, more than thirty years before, on October 13, 1917.[5] The "dance of the sun"

---

[2] Pascalina Lehnert, *Ich durfte Ihm Dienen: Erinnerungen an Papst Pius XII* (Würzburg: Naumann, 1986); citations from the Italian translation, *Pio XII: Il privilegio di servirlo* (Milan: Rusconi, 1984), 172.

[3] Pius XII, *Munificentissimus Deus*, in Denzinger-H., no. 3903. See the text in AAS 42 (1950): 767–770.

[4] P. Lehnert, *Pio XII, op. cit.*, 174.

[5] There is a superabundant bibliography on Fatima. The most authoritative sources are the *Documentos de Fátima*, ed. Antonio M. Martins, S.J. (1918–1997) (Porto, 1976), facsimile edition of the handwritten statements of Sister Lucia, with the text in Portuguese and translations in Italian and Spanish. The most in-depth study on the subject is the work of Michel de la Sainte Trinité, *Toute la vérité sur Fatima: Le troisième secret*, 3 vols. (Saint Parres-lès-Vaudes: La Contre-Réforme catholique, 1985); English edition: *The Whole Truth about Fatima*, 3 vols. (Buffalo, NY: Immaculate Heart Publications, 1989). The best compendium is Antonio Augusto Borelli Machado, *Fatima:*

was repeated before the eyes of Pope Pacelli on October 31 and again on November 8. The marvel appeared to the pontiff to be a heavenly seal of approval for the newly-proclaimed dogma and encouragement to develop the great Marian movement which, after the Immaculate Conception and the Assumption, loudly called for the proclamation of Mary as Mediatrix of All Graces and the consecration of Russia to her Immaculate Heart.[6]

Eugenio Pacelli had been consecrated a bishop in Rome on May 13, 1917. On that day began the cycle of Marian apparitions to the three shepherds children of Fatima, Lucia,[7] Jacinta,[8] and Francisco.[9] On October 31, 1942, he had consecrated the Church and the world to the Immaculate Heart of Mary. From then on, the name and message of Fatima had begun to spread throughout the Catholic world. For this reason many considered him to be the "Pope of Fatima" and were convinced that during his pontificate the requests of the Virgin Mary to the three visionaries at the Cova da Iria[10] would be heeded: the spread of the practice of making reparation

---

Message de tragédie ou d'espérance? (French translation, TFP, 2001); after the first edition in Brazil in 1973, the book went through a great number of translations and reprints. See also the story of the apparitions and the contents of the message in *Documents on Fatima and memoirs of Sister Lucia* by Robert J. Fox and Antonio Maria Martins, S.J. (Alexandria, South Dakota: Fatima Family Apostolate, 1992) and Luis Gonzaga Aires da Fonseca, S.J. (1878–1963), *Le meraviglie di Fàtima: Apparizioni, culto, miracoli*, ed., revised and updated by Joaquín María Alonso, C.M.F. (1913–1981), Ital. transl. (Cinisello Balsamo: Edizioni San Paolo, 1997). For an overall interpretation: Stefano M. Manelli, F.I., "Fatima tra passato, presente e futuro," in *Immaculata Mediatrix* 7/3 (2007): 299–431.

[6] Cf. M. de la Sainte Trinité, *The Whole Truth about Fatima, op. cit.*, 3:283–291.

[7] Lúcia de Jesus dos Santos, known as Sister Lucia (1907–2005), after the miraculous apparition, decided to take the habit of the Sisters of Saint Dorothy (1921) and in 1934 she made her solemn vows; in 1948 she entered into the Carmel of Saint Teresa in Coimbra, where she died at the age of ninety-seven.

[8] Jacinta de Jesus Marto (1910–1920), died in the Hospital Doña Estefania in Lisbon, after a long, painful illness, offering all her sufferings for the conversion of sinners, for peace in the world, and for "the Holy Father" who "would have to suffer much."

[9] Francisco Marto (1908–1919) died a holy death on April 4, 1919, in his parents' house.

[10] After the attempt on his life on May 13, 1981, John Paul II made pilgrimages in 1982, 1991, and 2000 to the "Cova di Iria," where the Madonna had appeared to Lucia, Francisco, and Jacinta. On the last-mentioned occasion he declared Francisco and Jacinta Blessed, and announced that their feast day would be celebrated on February 20.

on the first Saturdays of the month and the consecration of Russia to the Immaculate Heart of Mary, solemnly performed by the pope in union with all the bishops of the world.

The historic situation was as favorable as it could be, on account of the unprecedented prestige enjoyed by the Apostolic See. During his speech at the close of the Holy Year on December 23, 1950, Pius XII announced that the excavations undertaken at his request beneath the Confession of St. Peter's Basilica in the Vatican[11] confirmed that the tomb of the Prince of the Apostles had been rediscovered: "The gigantic cupola arches precisely over the tomb of the first bishop of Rome, the first pope, a tomb that was originally quite humble, but over which the veneration of later centuries, in a marvelous succession of projects, erected the massive temple of Christianity."[12]

b) The "theological crisis" of the 1950s

The pontificate of Pius XII was not, however, free of shadows and worrying signs of crisis. The pope himself was aware of this, since in that same year, 1950, he dedicated an important document to the errors creeping into the Church.

In the encylical *Humani generis*, dated August 12, the pontiff denounced the "deadly fruit" produced by "novelties… in almost all branches of theology"[13] and condemned, though without naming them, those who adopted the language and mentality of modern philosophy and who maintained that dogmas could be "expressed also by the concepts of modern philosophy, whether of immanentism or idealism or existentialism or any other system."[14] The principal error condemned by the encylical was relativism, which says that human knowledge never has a real, unchangeable value, but only a relative value. This relativism, which had

---

[11] Cf. Bruno Maria Apolloni Ghetti, Antonio Ferrua, Enrico Josi, Englebert Kirschbaum, *Esplorazioni sotto la confessione di San Pietro in Vaticano eseguite negli anni 1940–1949*, 2 vols. (Città del Vaticano: Tipografia Polyglotta Vaticana, 1951).

[12] Pius XII, "Radiomessaggio natalizio al mondo del 23 dicembre 1950," in DRM 12:377–388 (citation at 380).

[13] Pius XII, encylical *Humani generis* (August 12, 1950), par. 25

[14] Ibid., par. 15.

already characterized the modernism condemned by St. Pius X, was now resurfacing under the guise of "new theology."[15]

Pius XII was well acquainted with the origin and nature of these evils, also because before leaving as nuncio to Bavaria, he had worked closely with Monsignor Umberto Benigni,[16] promoter and organizer of an unceasing battle against modernism under the saintly pontiff Pius X.[17] This was the pontificate to which Pius XII ideally wanted to connect his own, via the beatification of Pope Sarto on June 3, 1951.

Speaking to the pilgrims who had hastened to St. Peter's for the solemn ceremony, Pius XII raised "a hymn of praise and thanksgiving to the Almighty that the Lord allowed to us to raise to the honor of the altars our Blessed Predecessor, Pius X … this pope of the twentieth century, who during the dreadful hurricane caused by the deniers and enemies of Christ, was able to demonstrate from the beginning his consummate experience

---

[15] The label is used by Pius XII in the Allocution *Quamvis inquieti* (September 22, 1946), in AAS 38 (1946): 385.

[16] Umberto Benigni (1862–1934), ordained in 1884, professor of Church History at the "Apollinare," in 1906 called to the Secretariat of State as undersecretary of the Congregation for Extraordinary Ecclesiastical Affairs and was appointed domestic prelate of His Holiness. He remained in that position until March 1911, which he was succeeded by then-Monsignor Eugenio Pacelli. Starting in 1907 he headed the news agency "Corrispondenza romana," then from 1909 to 1912 the *Correspondance de Rome*. In those years, with the encouragement of Pius X, he founded the anti-modernist association Sodalitium Pianum (known also as *La Sapinière*). See the groundbreaking studies by Emile Poulat, *Intégrisme et catholicisme intégral: Un réseau International antimoderniste: La "Sapinière" (1909–1921)* (Paris-Tournai: Casterman, 1969); *idem*, *Catholicisme, démocratie et socialisme: Le mouvement catholique et Mgr. Benigni de la naissance du socialisme à la victoire du fascisme* (Brussels-Paris: Casterman, 1977); see also R. de Mattei, "Modernismo e antimodernismo nell'epoca di Pio X," in Michele Busi, R. de Mattei, Antonio Lanza, Flavio Peloso, *Don Orione negli anni del modernismo*, introduction by Annibale Zambarbieri (Milan: Jaca Book, 2002), 29–86; Jean Madiran, *L'intégrisme: Histoire d'une histoire* (Paris, Nouvelles Éditions Latines, 1964). On Benigni's relations with Monsignor Pacelli, see for example Sergio Pagano, "Documenti sul modernismo romano dal fondo Benigni," in *Ricerche per la storia religiosa di Roma* 8 (1990): 223–300, esp. 259.

[17] Although it never received formal canonical approval, the Sodalitium Pianum, the anti-modernist association founded by Monsignor Benigni in 1909, was encouraged by the Holy See, particularly by the Sacred Consistorial Congregation, with Cardinal Gaetano De Lai (1853–1928) as prefect, and by Pius X himself, who sent three handwritten papal blessings and secured for it an annual subsidy. The sodality was dissolved after the death of Pius X, only to be reactivated in 1915, by an agreement with the Consistorial Congregation; it was definitively dissolved on November 25, 1921.

in handling the rudder of the barque of Peter, but whom God called to himself while the tempest was raging even more violently." To the critics who had spoken out against Pius X on behalf of those who thought that he had been excessive in "repressing" modernism,[18] Pius XII responded: "Now that the most minute examination has thoroughly scrutinized all the acts and events of his pontificate, now that the sequel of those events is known, no hesitation, no reserve is possible any more, and it must be acknowledged that even in the most difficult, roughest times that were most fraught with responsibility, Pius X, assisted by the magnanimity of his most faithful Secretary of State, Cardinal Merry del Val,[19] gave proof of that enlightened prudence which never fails in the saints, even when in its application it finds itself in grievous but inevitable conflict with the misleading claims of human and merely worldly prudence."[20]

Supernatural prudence, so different from human prudence, is the first virtue required of someone who governs, and particularly someone with

---

[18] These critiques continually reemerge. See for example, among recent publications: *La condanna del modernismo: Documenti, interpretazioni, conseguenze*, ed. Claus Arnold, Giovanni Vian (Rome: Viella, 2010); Guido Verucci, *L'eresia del Novecento: La Chiesa e la repressione del modernismo in Italia* (Turin: Einaudi, 2010).

[19] Rafael Merry del Val y Zulueta (1865–1939), born in London to an aristocratic Spanish family, ordained in 1888, titular archbishop of Nicea (1900), appointed Secretary of State by Pius X and created a cardinal in 1903, then secretary of the Congregation of the Holy Office (1914–1930). Cf. Pio Cenci, *Il Cardinale Merry del Val: Segretario di Stato di San Pio X Papa*, (Rome-Turin: L.I.C.E., R. Berruti, 1955) (the work was actually composed by Cardinal Nicola Canali); Girolamo Dal Gal, *Il servo di Dio card. Raffaele Merry del Val* (Rome: Paoline, 1956); José M. Javierre, *Merry del Val* (Barcelona: Juan Flors, 1965).

[20] Pius XII, "Discorso per la Beatificazione di Pio X" (June 3, 1951), in DRM, 13:125–136 (citations at 127, 128, 131). The "minute examination" to which Pius XII refers is that of the *"Disquisitio"* composed by Father, then Cardinal, Ferdinando Antonelli to evaluate the accusations leveled against Pius X that he lacked prudence in repressing modernism. The examination confirmed, in this case as well, the pontiff's heroic virtue (F. Antonelli, *Sacra Rituum Congregatio Sectio Historica, n. 77 Romana Beatificationis et Canonizationis Servi Dei Pii Papae X Disquisitio circa quasdam obiectiones modum agendi Servi Dei respicientes in Modernismi debellatione una cum Summario Additionali ex Officio compilato* (Città del Vaticano: Typis Polyglottis Vaticanis, 1950). There is a good French translation of it edited by Emmanuel du Chalard de Taveau, *Conduite de saint Pie X dans la lutte contre le modernisme: "Disquisitio": Enquête des procès de béatification et de canonisation* (Versailles: Publications du "Courrier de Rome," 1996). The chapter relating to the Sodalitium Pianum was published in Italian by the Centro Librario Sodalitium (Turin: Verrua Savoia, 2005).

the exalted duty of governing the Church. In order to confront current events, it is not enough to be a "good" pope, one must be a "holy" pope, and Pius X proved to be such a pope in his work, which, as Pius XII declared on the day of the canonization, "in circumstances that were sometimes dramatic, had the appearance of a struggle by a giant to defend a priceless treasure, the internal unity of the Church in its deepest foundations: the faith."[21]

The encylical *Humani generis*, in which Pius XII condemned the errors of his own time, did not however have the doctrinal force of *Pascendi*,[22] the document with which Pius X had denounced modernism in 1907. Above all, *Humani generis* was not followed by the repressive acts that had enabled Pope Sarto to crush the new heresy, if only temporarily. Furthermore, among the closest collaborators of Pius XII there were some who sought to diminish the importance of the encylical. A few weeks after the publication of the papal document on September 8, 1950, the French philosopher Jean Guitton[23] met at the Vatican with the *sostituto* of the Secretary of State Giovanni Battista Montini[24] and revealed to him his concern that Rome might look askance at the "progress of thought" in France. Monsignor Montini endeavored to dispel this impression, telling Guitton that *Humani generis* condemned no errors, but only recommended caution about those living and vital cultural trends, which would be able to develop in the Church in an unhurried, prudent manner.

---

[21] Pius XII, "Discorso per la Canonizzazione di Pio X" (May 29, 1954), in DRM, 16:29–37 (citation at 33).

[22] Cf. Pius X, encylical *Pascendi dominici gregis* (September 8, 1907), in ASS 40 (1907): 593–628. The encylical was preceded by the decree *Lamentabili* of the Holy Office (July 3, 1907), in ASS 40 (1907): 470–478, and was followed by the anti-modernist oath *Sacrorum antistitum* dated September 1, 1910 (AAS 2 [1910]: 655–680), which completes it.

[23] Jean Guitton (1901–1999), French writer, member of the Académie Française, was personally invited to attend the Council and sat, during the First Session, in the section for Catholic observers, then among the lay auditors.

[24] Giovanni Battista Montini (1897–1978), member of the clergy of Brescia. Ordained in 1920, deputy to the Secretary of State for Ordinary Affairs (1937–1952); pro-Secretary of State for Ordinary Affairs (1952–1954); archbishop of Milan (1954), Cardinal (1958). Elected supreme pontiff on June 21, 1963, with the name Paul VI. See the article about him by Giovanni Maria Van, in EP, 657–674, with bibliography, and the works cited later in this volume.

> You doubtless yourself noted the shades of meaning written into this papal text. For example, the encyclical never speaks of errors (*errores*). It only speaks of opinions (*opiniones*). This indicates that the Holy See aims to condemn not errors, properly speaking, but modes of thought which could lead to errors, but which in themselves remain respectable.
>
> On the other hand there are three reasons why the encyclical is not distorted. I want to confide to you the first: it is the express will of the Holy Father. The second is the mentality of the French hierarchy, broadminded in their views and open to contemporary currents of thought…
>
> In Rome we have the duty to watch over the doctrinal side as well. We are particularly sensitive to anything that could alter the purity of the doctrine that is truth. The supreme pontiff must guard the deposit, as St. Paul says. And so I arrive at the third reason. It can be summed up in two words: The French are intelligent….
>
> Although the French have often received warnings from the Holy See (and sometimes warnings to the contrary), this is due, I would say, to their qualities of warmth, vitality, creativity, and, I repeat, intelligence. I wish to add something that a philosopher like you will understand very easily. One does not correct what is asleep, what is dead. Or in other words, one corrects only what is alive and, in correcting it, admires it. And I would even go so far as to say that sometimes one envies it. The French are wrong to take as a condemnation the warning, the call to prudence and to the slow ripening [of their ideas].[25]

Monsignor Montini's words offered a glimpse of a substantial sympathy for the doctrinal inclinations that worried Pius XII, as well as the conviction that the era of ideological conflict between modernism and anti-modernism had been definitively surpassed by the "modern times" that were opening up for the Church.

---

[25] Jean Guitton, *The Pope speaks: dialogues of Paul VI with Jean Guitton* (New York: Meredith Press, 1968), 10. [Only the first paragraph of the excerpt appears in the English edition; the rest is translated from the Italian edition, *Dialoghi con Paolo VI* (Milan: Mondadori, 1967), 25–27.] See also *idem*, *Paolo VI segreto,* Ital. transl. (Rome: Edizioni Paoline, 1981), 40–47. See also R. Aubert, *La théologie catholique au milieu du XXe siècle* (Paris: Casterman, 1954), 84–86; G. Martina, "The Historical Context in Which the Idea of a New Ecumenical Council Was Born," in *Vatican II: Assessment and Perspectives: Twenty-five Years After*, ed. René Latourelle, S.J. (New York & Mahwah: Paulist Press, 1988), 30–39.

2. The modernist "reform" of the Church

a) The "historical-critical method"

The term "modernism" was used officially for the first time in the encylical *Pascendi* by St. Pius X as a way to trace back to one movement a complex of errors in all fields of Catholic doctrine (sacred scripture, theology, philosophy, worship).[26] The root causes and reasons for this movement are found in the attempt to establish a "dialogue" between the Church and the process of secularization following the French Revolution.[27]

In the nineteenth century, Pius IX had established a line of defense against this revolutionary process at three solemn events of his pontificate: the definition of the dogma of the Immaculate Conception (1854); the condemnation of modern errors with the encylical *Quanta Cura* and *The Syllabus of Errors* (1864); the proclamation of the dogma of the Roman pontiff's primacy of jurisdiction and infallibility at the First Vatican Council (1870).[28] Each of these acts constituted a theological bastion that made a frontal attack difficult. The "reform" of the Church, which had been the goal of the major heterodox movements of the eighteenth and nineteenth centuries, would have to be accomplished by other means.

In the course of history, "the heretics of the heretics", according to Lucian Canfora, were "the founders of philology,"[29] a science that,

---

[26] The papal document was, according to the modernist Ernesto Buonaiuti, "the only unified definition of the multiple approaches included under the generic name of modernism" ("Modernismo," in *Dizionario delle Opere* [Milano: Bompiani, 1947] 1:158). This movement appeared like "a fluid, incandescent matter" (*idem, Storia del Cristianesimo* [Milan: Dall'Oglio, 1943], 3:622), and its distinctive characteristic "was the very indeterminacy of its program" (*ibid.*, 618).

[27] The bibliography on modernism is by now extensive. For an interpretation in the light of the traditional teaching of the Church, see, in addition to R. de Mattei, "Modernismo e antimodernismo," *op. cit.*, the dense article by C. Fabro, in EC, 8:1190–1191; *idem, Dall'essere all'esistente* (Brescia: Morcelliana, 1957), 71–125; Ramón García de Haro, *Historia teológica del modernismo* (Pamplona: Universidad de Navarra, 1972).

[28] For an analysis of the three pontifical acts, cf. R. de Mattei, *Blessed Pius X*, translated by John Laughland (Gloucester: Gracewing, 2004), 93–102.

[29] Luciano Canfora, *Filologia e libertà: La più eversiva delle discipline, l'indipendenza di pensiero et*

ever since the days of Lorenzo Valla and Erasmus of Rotterdam, was brandished as a tool to subvert natural and divine truth. At the end of the nineteenth century, under the influence of positivism, this philological instrument was applied to sacred scripture by some theologians and exegetes who invoked the autonomy of scientific research from the Church's magisterium and claimed that philologists determine the authentic *interpretatio* of the sacred texts. So it was that, during the pontificate of Leo XIII, the successor of Pius IX, the historical-critical "method" resurfaced, the tool with which Erasmus had paved the way for the protestant revolution three centuries earlier.[30]

Within the *Institut Catholique* founded in Paris in 1875, Monsignor Louis Duchesne[31] began to apply the new method to Church history. Working with him was a young priest, Alfred Loisy,[32] who intended to apply his master's lessons to the field of biblical studies.

---

il diritto alla verità (Milan: Mondadori, 2008), 13. Canfora mentions the name of Spinoza, from which follows, as a logical development, the exegetical work of the Oratorian Richard Simon, which in turn serves as the background for Loisy.

[30] Cf. Henri-Irénée Marrou, "Philologie et histoire dans la période du pontificat de Léon XIII," in *Aspetti della cultura cattolica nell'età di Leone XIII*, ed. Giuseppe Rossini (Rome: Cinque Lune, 1961), 71–106; Hans-Joachim Kraus, *Geschichte der historisch-kritischen Erforschung des Alten Testaments von der Reformation bis zur Gegenwart* (Neukirchen-Vluyn: Neukirchener Verlag, 1969); Joseph G. Prior, "The Historical Critical Method," in *Catholic Exegesis* (Rome: Pontificia Università Gregoriana, 1999); François Laplanche, *La crise de l'origine: La science catholique des Evangiles et l'histoire du XXèmesiècle* (Paris: Albin Michel, 2006). On the subversive character of Erasmus' philological-critical method, see for example R. García de Haro, *op. cit.*, 235–289; R. de Mattei, *A sinistra di Lutero* (Rome: Città Nuova, 2001), 17–20 and *passim.*

[31] Monsignor Duchesne (1843–1922), French priest ordained in 1867, professor at the *Institut Catholique* in Paris (1877–1885), then director of the *École archéologique française* in Rome (1895–1922); see the Acts of the convention organized by the *École française* in Rome, *Monseigneur Louis Duchesne (1843–1922)* (Rome: École française de Rome, 1992); L. Duchesne, *Correspondance avec Madame Bulteau (1902–1922)* (Rome: École française de Rome, 2009).

[32] Alfred Loisy (1857–1940), ordained in 1881, professor of biblical science at the *Institut Catholique* in Paris from 1889 to 1893, excommunicated March 7, 1908, broke off relations with the Church and, unlike his modernist friends, abandoned Christianity. Cf. Friedrich Heiler, *Der Vater des katholischen Modernismus: Alfred Loisy* (1857–1940) (Monaco: Erasmus, 1947); Emile Goichot, *Alfred Loisy et ses amis* (Paris: Cerf, 2002).

In the slim volume *L'Évangile et l'Église*[33] (1902), a response to the interpretation of Christianity of the protestant exegete Adolf von Harnack,[34] Loisy, applying the historical-critical method, denied or nullified the revealed character of the Old and New Testaments, the divinity of Christ, the institution of the Church, the hierarchy, and the sacraments. Looking back on his work, he declared that he had attempted "an essential reform of biblical exegesis, of the whole field of theology, and finally of Catholicism in general."[35] Loisy later recalled: "my reasoning… implied at the same time the abandonment of those absolute theses which are professed by the scholastic theology touching the formal institution of the Church and its sacraments by Christ, the immutability of its dogmas, and the nature of its ecclesiastical authority. Thus I did not confine myself to a criticism of Professor Harnack, but paved the way, discreetly yet definitely, for an essential reform in biblical exegesis, in the whole of theology, and even in Catholicism generally."[36] The horizon that he opened was a plan to transform Christianity into a nebulous "religion of humanity." Some of the great Catholic exegetes, such as the Dominican Father Marie-Joseph Lagrange,[37] refuted Loisy's theological and philosophical theses, but

---

33 The work, published by Picard in 1903, was listed on the Index of Forbidden Books together with four other works by Loisy, who was personally excommunicated on March 7, 1908. Cf. A. Loisy, *My Duel with the Vatican: The Autobiography of a Catholic Modernist*, transl. Richard Wilson Boynton (New York: E. P. Dutton & Co., 1924). On the discussion about the booklet by Loisy, see E. Poulat, *Storia, dogma e critica nella crisi modernista*, Ital. transl. (Brescia: Morcelliana, 1967), 53–68, 85–122 (with all the pertinent biographical notes). Poulat also wrote *Critique et mystique: Autour de Loisy ou la conscience catholique et l'esprit moderne* (Paris: Centurion, 1984).

34 Adolf von Harnack (1851–1930), protestant theologian, professor at the Universities of Leipsiz, Giessen, Marburg, and Berlin. For a summary of the debate, cf. Guglielmo Forni, *L'"essenza del Cristianesimo": Il problema ermeneutico nella discussione protestante e modernista* (1897–1940) (Bologna: Il Mulino, 1992).

35 A. Loisy, *Choses passées* (Paris: Noussy, 1913), 246.

36 Alfred Loisy, *My Duel with the Vatican: The Autobiography of a Catholic Modernist*, transl. Richard Wilson Boynton (New York: E. P. Dutton & Company, 1924), 228. [This English translation of Loisy's autobiography condenses the description of his unorthodox beliefs. The Italian translation reads: "Historically speaking, I did not admit that Christ had founded the Church and the sacraments; I professed that the dogmas had developed gradually and that they were not unchangeable; I said the same thing about ecclesiastical authority, which I made into a ministry of human education…."]

37 Marie-Joseph Lagrange (1855–1938), French Dominican friar, ordained in 1879, founded

accepted his method and were censured by ecclesiastical authority for the errors implicit in their approach to the sacred texts.[38]

Leo XIII, in the encylical *Providentissimus Deus*[39] (1893), upheld the teaching already defined by the Council of Trent and Vatican I, that the magisterium of the Church, the sole repository of the word of God, is the supreme norm for establishing the true meaning of sacred scripture,[40] and on October 30, 1902, he founded, with the apostolic letter *Vigilantiae studique*,[41] the Pontifical Biblical Commission. The document by Leo XIII, after citing the formula of the councils, defined the very reason for the existence of the commission in the principle that, in matters of dogma and morals, "God has not delivered the scriptures to the private judgment of the learned, but has confided the interpretation of them to the teaching authority [magisterium] of the Church."[42]

---

the School of Biblical Studies in Jerusalem, where he lived for forty-five years. *L'École biblique de Jérusalem* and the General Chapter of the Dominican order have introduced the cause for his beatification. See François-Marie Braun, *L'oeuvre du Père Lagrange: Étude et bibliographie* (Fribourg: Éditions Saint Paul, 1943); Bernard Montagnes, *Le Père Lagrange (1855–1938): L'exégèse catholique dans la crise moderniste* (Paris: Cerf, 1995); *idem, Marie-Joseph Lagrange: une biographie critique* (Paris: Cerf, 2004); Jerome Murphy O'Connor, O.P., *The École biblique and the New Testament: a century of scholarship, 1890–1990* (Freiburg, Switzerland: Universitätsverlag; Göttingen: Vandenhoeck & Ruprecht, 1990), 6–28.

[38] Other scholars belonging to the school of Lagrange were the Jesuits Ferdinand Prat (1857–1938), Franz-Xavier Funck (1840–1907), and Franz von Hummelauer (1841–1914), who were refuted by the confreres Santo Schiffini, in the volume *Divinitas scripturarum adversus odierna novitates asserta et vindicata* (1905), and Louis Billot, in *De inspiratione Sacrae Scripturae* (1903). Cf. Giovanni Sale, *"La Civiltà Cattolica" nella crisi modernista* (1900–1907) (Milan: Jaca Book, 2001), 157–160. See also the critique of the "wider school" of Lagrange, in Alphonse J. Delattre, S.J., *Autour de la question biblique: Une nouvelle école d'exégèse et les autorités qu'elle invoque* (Liège: H. Dessain, 1904). It was well known that even the master general of the Dominicans, Bl. Hyacinth M. Cormier (1832–1916), had reservations with regard to Lagrange.

[39] Cf. Leo XIII, encylical *Providentissimus Deus* (November 18, 1893), in ASS 26 (1893/1894): 279–291; Denz.-H., nn. 3280–3294.

[40] Cf. Pius XII, encylical *Divino afflante Spiritu*, in AAS 35 (1943): 338; *idem*, encylical *Humani generis*, AAS 42 (1950): 569.

[41] Leo XIII, apostolic letter, *Vigiliantiae studique* (October 30, 1902), in ASS 35 (1902/1903): 234–238.

[42] *Ibid.*, 236.

b) The principle of immanence

Perhaps the most significant document of modernism is the *Program of the Modernists*, which was published in Rome anonymously in October 1907, but was primarily the work of Don Ernesto Buonaiuti,[43] professor of Church history at the Apollinare Seminary, who was convinced that the historical method was "destined to become the true *locus theologicus* of the Christian revolution."[44] The *Program*[45] affirmed the intrinsic and unlimited evolution of dogmas, the meaning and value of which does not come from their unchangeable content, but from the subjective emotion that it can evoke in human consciousness.

The theological framework of the movement, however, must be credited to the Irish priest George Tyrrell,[46] a convert from Calvinism to Anglicanism, and then to Catholicism (1879), whereupon he entered the

---

[43] Ernesto Buonaiuti (1881–1946), ordained in 1903, was excommunicated in 1925. See the article on him by Fausto Parente in DBI 15 (1972): 112–122 with bibliography, and the one by Annibale Zambarbieri in DSMCI 2:58–66; *idem, Il cattolicesimo tra crisi e rinnovamento: Ernesto Buonaiuti ed Enrico Rosa nella prima fase della polemica modernista* (Brescia: Morcelliana, 1979). His autobiography is still basic reading, *Pellegrino in Roma* (Rome: Darsena, 1945). On modernism in Italy: Maurilio Guasco, *Modernismo: i fatti, le idee, I personaggi* (Cinisello Balsamo: San Paolo, 1995).

[44] E. Buonaiuti, *Pellegrino in Roma, op. cit.*, 139.

[45] *Cf. idem, Il Programma dei modernisti italiani: Risposta all'enciclica di Pio X "Pascendi dominici gregis"* (Rome: Società Internazionale Scientifico-Religiosa, 1907), 100. A decree of the vicariate of Rome (ASS 40 [1907]: 720) excommunicated those who had written, or in any way taken part, in the production of the volume.

[46] George Tyrrell (1861–1909), Irish, converted from Calvinism to Anglicanism and again to Catholicism (1879) and then entered the Society of Jesus (1880). Ordained in 1891, he was excommunicated in 1907. About him see Domenico Grasso, "La conversione e l'apostasia di G. Tyrrell," in *Gregorianum* 38 (1957): 446–480; Daniele Rolando, *Cristianesimo e religione dell'avvenire in George Tyrrell* (Florence: Le Monnier, 1978), and the doctoral thesis in theology by Stefano Visintin, O.S.B., *Rivelazione divina ed esperienza umana: La proposta di George Tyrrell e la risposta di Karl Rahner* (Berna: Peter Lang, 1999). Important documents for understanding his thought are the *Autobiography and Life of George Tyrrell* (London: Edward Arnold, 1912) by Maude Petre (1863–1947), who after meeting the Jesuit at a spiritual retreat, in the religious congregation of which she was the provincial superior, had herself laicized so as to follow him as his disciple and "vestal virgin."

Society of Jesus, from which he was expelled in 1907. In the development of his thought, 1899 stands as an important year with the publication of his article "On the Relation of Theology to Devotion" in the magazine *The Month*; it was then republished in 1907 under the new title "*Lex orandi, lex credendi*" in the anthology *Through Scylla and Charybdis*. Tyrrell identified revelation with religious experience, which is achieved in the conscience of every man; therefore the *lex orandi* is to dictate the norms of the *lex credendi*, and not vice versa. The revelation-experience, indeed, "cannot be put into us from outside; it can be occasioned, but it cannot be caused, by instruction."[47] The "religious experience" of the believer simultaneously replaces reason and faith.

On the pages of the *Annales de philosophie chrétienne* edited by the Oratorian Lucien Laberthonnière,[48] Maurice Blondel, developing the basic theme of his doctoral thesis *L'Action: Essai d'une critique de la vie et d'une science de la pratique* (1893),[49] proposed a new form of apologetic through the "method of immanence" which would make it possible to accept revelation in terms of the needs of the human spirit.[50] In order to avoid "intellectualism," Blondel's apologetic was founded on a "religion of the heart" against a subjectivist and immanentist background.

Buonaiuti mentions the "indelible furrow" cut by Blondel's *Action* in his soul[51] and the "intimate sense of voluptuous satisfaction with

---

[47] G. Tyrrell, *Through Scylla and Charybdis* (London: Green and Co., 1907), 306.

[48] Lucien Labertonnière (1862–1932), Oratorian, ordained in 1886 and editor of the review *Annales de philosophie chrétienne* from 1905 to 1913; an important work by him together with Maurice Blondel is *Correspondance philosophique*, ed. Claude Tresmontant (Paris: Seuil, 1961).

[49] Maurice Blondel, *Action, 1893: essay on a critique of life and a science of practice* (Notre Dame, IN: University of Notre Dame Press, 1984). About Blondel (1861–1949), a professor of philosophy at the University of Aix (1896–1927), see René Virgoulay, *Blondel et le Modernisme: la philosophie de l'action et les sciences religieuses (1896–1913)* (Paris: Cerf, 1980); *Idem, "L'Action" de Maurice Blondel: 1893: Relecture pour un centenaire* (Paris: Beauchesne, 1992). Also important is Blondel's *Correspondance* with Pierre Teilhard de Chardin (Paris: Beauchesne, 1965) and Johannès Wehrlé (Paris: Aubier, 1969) with a commentary by Fr. Henri de Lubac.

[50] Blondel's theses were incisively refuted by Joseph de Tonquédec, S.J. (1869–1962), *Immanence: Essai critique sur la doctrine de Maurice Blondel* (Paris: Beauchesne, 1912). See also the article by Fr. Hervé Gresland, "Maurice Blondel et sa méthode d'immanence: Un grand-père de Vatican II," in *Le Sel de la Terre* 57 (2006): 30–77, which summarizes and reapplies the critique of Fr. de Tonquédec.

[51] Cf. E. Buonaiuti, *Pellegrino in Roma, op. cit.*, 63.

which I spent the first night of the twentieth century reading this work by Blondel."[52] Tyrrell too emphasizes his affinity with the French thinker,[53] although he preferred Laberthonnière and Le Roy "who has the advantage of being clear."[54]

In the encylical *Pascendi* and the decree *Lamentabili,* Pius X condemned the principle of immanence, which was the nucleus of modernism, and along with it the primacy of the believer's "religious experience," from which springs the possibility of the evolution of dogmas and of religious truth. The motu proprio *Sacrorum antistitum*, which rounds out preceding documents, rejects "the heretical invention of the evolution of dogmas, passing from one meaning to another, different from that which the Church first had,"[55] and emphasizes that the faith is not a "blind religious feeling bursting forth from the recesses of the subconscious" but rather "the true assent of the intellect."[56]

c) Between modernism and anti-modernism: the "Third Party"

The term "Third Party" was coined by the French historian Emile Appolis, in several studies on eighteenth-century religious currents.[57] Once it had been condemned by the Church, Jansenism produced, according to Appolis, a "Third Party" composed of ecclesiastics of various ranks who

---

[52] Ibid., 43.

[53] G. Tyrrell, *Autobiography and Life, op. cit.*, 90–91.

[54] *Lettres de Georges Tyrrell à Henri Brémond* (Paris: Aubier-Montaigne, 1971), 271. According to Edouard Le Roy (1870–1954), a disciple and successor of Henri Bergson at the Collège de France, dogmatic truth is only an orienting factor for praxis, and a god who "becomes" contemporaneously with creation cannot be proven, but only translated into ethical action. About him see Rudolf Michael Schmitz, *Dogma und Praxis: Der Dogmenbegriff der Modernisten Edouard Le Roy kritisch dargestellt* (Vatican City: Libreria Editrice Vaticana, 1993).

[55] Denz-H., n. 3541.

[56] Ibid., 3542.

[57] Cf. Emile Appolis, "Entre jansénistes et constitutionnaires: un tiers parti," in *Annales* 2 (1951): 154–171; then *Entre jansénistes et zelanti: Le Tiers Parti catholique au XVIIIème siècle* (Paris: A. & J. Picard, 1962). See also Antonio De Castro Mayer, "Il Giansenismo e la Terza Forza," transl. Ital. in *Cristianità* 1 (1973): 3–4 and 2 (1973): 3–4.

offered to the Jansenists the possibility of prospering within the Church. These ecclesiastics, of course, did not declare themselves Jansenists and even condemned Jansenism, but they did not fight it and maintained that it would quietly disappear if the anti-Jansenists would cease any campaign against it. In the ranks of Catholics, alongside the Jansenists and the followers of the Roman authority, a third party arose which was also opposed to those faithful to Rome, whom it accused of being exaggerated, uncompromising, and enemies of charity. Applying this polarization, other historians have talked about the existence during this period of a "center" movement between the orthodox right of the Jesuits and the Gallican and Jansenist "left."[58] However inappropriate these categories may be, there is no doubt that estrangement from the reference point of integral orthodoxy occurred in variously nuanced ways that allow us to talk about the existence of a "third force" between the fullness of truth and outright error.

At the First Vatican Council as well, a "Third Party" had formed between the "infallibilists" and the "anti-infalliblists," which was composed not so much of "moderate infalliblists" like Archbishop Spalding[59] of Baltimore, as of "anti-infalliblists" like Monseigneur Lavigerie[60] who, realizing that they had met with defeat, sought to the very end to mitigate the terms in which the dogma was formulated for the sake of "political expediency."[61] This same mechanism was repeated with modernism, which also produced a "Third Party" between the positions of the Roman authority and those of heterodoxy. Blondel, who was "not modern enough for some, nor modernist enough for others,"[62] sought to mark out an "intermediate" way between modernism and anti-modernism, and he can be considered, like Father Lagrange, a significant example of that "Third Party" that would dominate

---

[58] Cf. Lucien Ceyssens, "Le jansénisme: Considérations historiques préliminaires à sa notion," in *Nuove ricerche storiche sul giansenismo* (Rome: Gregoriana, 1959), 28–29. See also R. de Mattei, *Idealità e dottrine delle Amicizie* (Rome: Biblioteca Romana, 1981), 15–22.

[59] Martin John Spalding (1810–1872), American, ordained in 1834, was bishop of Louisville 1850) and then archbishop of Baltimore (1864).

[60] Charles-Martial Allemand Lavigerie (1825–1892), French, ordained in 1849, bishop of Nancy (1863), then of Algiers (1867), created cardinal in 1882.

[61] R. Aubert, "Documents concernant le tiers parti au concile du Vatican," in *Abhandlungen über Theologie und Kirche: Festschrift für Karl Adam*, ed. Marcel Reding (Düsseldorf: Patmos-Verlag, 1952), 241–259.

[62] Étienne Fouilloux, *Une Église en quête de liberté* (Paris: Desclée de Brouwer, 2006), 30.

Catholic thought in the following decades.[63] "You were indeed inspired," his friend Ferdinand Mourret wrote to him, "to call your synthetic principle by its traditional name of tradition. If you had had the idea of calling it the collective experience of the Church or the action of the infallible spirit upon the Christian community, or in some other similar way, you would have been severely compromised. If you had had the misfortune to baptize it immanent evolution, you would have been ruined."[64]

After the death of Pius X, in the 1920s, a third force took shape which, while distancing itself from modernism, in fact assured its continuance even after it was condemned.[65] This "Third Party" asserted itself thanks to the support of Cardinal Pietro Gasparri,[66] Secretary of State for Benedict XV and then for Pius XI, until 1930, when he was succeeded by Cardinal Eugenio Pacelli. The disappearance of anti-modernism, which was replaced by the ecclesiastical policy of the "Third Party," fostered in the 1930s the birth of movements and trends that, in one way or another, reaped the legacy of modernism: the "biblical movement," the "liturgical movement," the "philosophical-theological movement," of which the *"nouvelle théologie"* was an expression, as well as the "ecumenical movement" in which all the other movements converged.

3. The biblical movement

In the encylical *Pascendi* and the decree *Lamentabili* (1907), Pius X condemned the distinction between theological-pastoral exegesis and scientific-critical exegesis;[67] reaffirmed the principle that the authentic interpretation of sacred scripture is the duty of the magisterium and

[63] Cf. ibid. For Fouilloux, the "new theology" of the forties and fifties is "the legitimate daughter of the Third Party of the 1900s" (p. 33).

[64] Letter from Mourret to Blondel dated February 20, 1904, in René Marlé, *Au coeur de la crise moderniste: Le dossier inédit d'une controverse* (Paris: Aubier-Montaigne, 1960), 128.

[65] Cf. R. de Mattei, "Modernismo e antimodernismo nell'epoca di Pio X," *op. cit.*, 68–71.

[66] Pietro Gasparri (1852–1934), ordained in 1877, titular archbishop of Caesarea (1898), created cardinal in 1907; in autumn 1914 Pope Benedict XV appointed him Secretary of State, a post that he continued to hold under Pius XI.

[67] Cf. Saint Pius X, encylical *Pascendi dominici gregis*. English edition *On the Doctrine of the Modernists* (Boston: Pauline Books & Media, 1980).

not of the exegetes; set guidelines for an authentic renewal of biblical studies through the creation of the Pontifical Biblical Institute (1909) as a rival project to Fr. Lagrange's School of Jerusalem; and promoted in the seminaries a reform of the curriculum that gave a prominent role to the biblical spirituality of the clergy.[68] Later on, the encylical *Spiritus Paraclitus*[69] by Benedict XV, dated September 15, 1920, and dedicated to St. Jerome as the model of Catholic exegesis, confirmed the divine inspiration of the sacred books and their freedom from all error, and condemned the theory of "historical appearances," which had been debated and defended by Lagrange as well.

The origins of the post-modernist biblical movement go back to the early 1920s, when the new method of *Formgeschichte* ("history of forms") appeared in Germany, thanks especially to the books of Martin Dibelius, *Die Formgeschichte des Evangeliums* (1919), and of Rudolf Bultmann, *Geschichte der Synoptischen Tradition* (1921). This movement, which profoundly influenced exegetical studies in the following years, especially in central Europe, claimed to explain the life of Jesus in a rationalistic way, considering the formulation of the gospel texts as the product, not of particular authors or of definite literary sources, but of a slow anonymous process within the early Christian communities.[70]

In those same years the Pontifical Biblical Institute, founded by St. Pius X, was the center of a gradual surrender of Catholic exegesis to

---

[68] See, besides the cited documents, the motu proprio *Praestantia scripturae sacrae* (ASS 40 [1907]: 723–726), which acknowledged the normative character on the doctrinal level of many decrees and responses of the Pontifical Biblical Commission.

[69] Cf. Benedict XVI, encylical *Spiritus Paraclitus* dated September 15, 1920, in AAS 12 (1920): 385–422. English translation at Vatican website. See also the article by Pietro Nober in EC 11:1162–1163.

[70] On *Formgeschichte* and in particular on Rudolf Bultmann (1884–1976) see B. Gherardini, *La seconda riforma* (Brescia: Morcelliana, 1966), 2:366–496. See also the articles by Francesco Spadafora, "Ermeneutica" and "Generi letterari" in the *Dizionario Biblico* (Rome: Studium, 1963): 209–212 and 263–266; *Idem, Razionalismo, Esegesi cattolica e Magistero* (Rovigo: Istituto Padano di Arti, no date); *Idem, Leone XIII e gli studi biblici* (Rovigo: Istituto Padano di Arti Grafiche, 1976). See also Ermenegildo Florit, *Il metodo della Storia delle Forme e la sua applicazione al racconto della Passione* (Rome: Pontificio Istituto, 1935); Salvatore Garofalo, "Gli studi biblici in Italia da Leone XIII a Pio XII," in *Problemi di storia della Chiesa del Vaticano I al Vaticano II* (Rome: Edizioni Dehoniane, 1988).

the historical method.[71] The ultimate responsibility for this belonged to Father Agostino Bea,[72] who for nineteen years, from 1930 to 1949, held the key position of rector of the Institute, while Father Alberto Vaccari was vice-rector.[73] Bea's position was reinforced by the appointment of two disciples of Fr. Lagrange to the board of the Pontifical Commission in 1938-1939: Cardinal Eugenio Tisserant[74] (president) and the Belgian Dominican Jacques-Marie Vosté[75] (secretary); the latter was a personal friend of Fr. Bea. A historian of exegesis, Mauro Pesce, emphasized "the extraordinary strategy" of Bea, which was of "crucial importance" not only in constructing the crucial alignment of the Pontifical Biblical Institute with the Pontifical Biblical Commission and the papacy in the

---

71 On the foundation and the history of the Biblical Institute, cf. G. Martina, S.J., "A novant'anni dalla fondazione del Pontificio Istituto Biblico," in *Archivium Historiae pontificiae* 37 (1999): 129–160.

72 Augustin Bea (1881–1968), of the Society of Jesus, German, ordained priest in 1912, from 1924 professor of sacred scripture, and from 1930 rector of the Pontifical Biblical Institute. On December 14, 1959, he was created cardinal by John XXIII. About him see Stjepan Schmidt, S.J. *Agostino Bea, Il cardinale dell'unità* (Rome: Città Nuova Editrice, 1987); *Idem, Agostino Bea: Cardinale dell'ecumenismo e del dialogo* (Milan: San Paolo, 1996); Jan Willebrands, "Il cardinale Agostino Bea: il suo contributo al movimento ecumenico, alla libertà religiosa e all'instaurazione di nuove relazioni con il popolo ebraico," in *Atti del Simposio Card. Agostino Bea (Roma, 16–19 dicembre 1981)* (Rome: Pontificia Università Lateranense — Istituto "Ut unum sint," 1983); J. Grootaers, "Agostino Bea," in Grootaers, *I protagonisti*, 67–82. Cf. Stanislas Lyonnet, S.J., "Le cardinal Bea et le développement des études bibliques," in *Rivista Biblica* 4 (1968): 371–392. By Bea, see "La scienza biblica da Leone XIII a Pio XII," in *Divinitas* 4 (1959): 598–634.

73 Alberto Vaccari (1874–1965), of the Society of Jesus, professor at the Pontifical Biblical Institute, of which he was vice-rector from 1924 on, qualificator of the Holy Office (1924), consultor of the Pontifical Biblical Commission (1929). John XXIII appointed him a member of the Preparatory Theological Commission and afterward a conciliar *peritus*. Cf. A. Bea and V. Boccaccio, "In memoriam," in *Biblica* 47 (1966): 158–162.

74 Eugène Tisserant (1884–1972), French, ordained in 1907, created cardinal in 1936, titular bishop of Iconium (1937), secretary of the Congregation for Oriental Churches from 1936 to 1959. Librarian and archivist from 1957 to 1971, dean of the College of Cardinals; he was a member of the Académie Française from 1971 on.

75 Jacques-Marie Vosté (1883–1949), Belgian Dominican, ordained in 1936, student at the École Biblique de Jérusalem, then professor of sacred scripture at the Angelicum. On the relations of Vosté and Bea, cf. Schmidt, *Bea*, 109–110.

1930s and 40s, but also in the 1950s, when he succeeded in creating a close-knit set of alliances among the central administrative bodies of the Church.[76] The historical exegesis of the Biblicum and of the Pontifical Biblical Commission considered only the literal sense of the sacred texts, dissociating the historical, philosophical, and archaeological data from theological and spiritual reflection. The study of sacred scripture would have to limit itself to textual criticism of the biblical texts, through literary analysis and the comparative study of the multifarious ancillary sciences.[77]

The method recommended by the Church, however, was to begin with the literal sense, without being limited to it, as the encylical *Spiritus Paraclitus* by Benedict XV had recalled, pointing out the example of St. Jerome, who counsels us several times "that we must not stop at the simple literal sense: 'Just as we have to search for gold in the earth, for the kernel in the shell, for the chestnut's hidden fruit beneath its hairy coverings, so in holy scripture we have to dig deep for its divine meaning.'"[78] Indeed, Benedict XV emphasizes that the goal of studying the scriptures is to find in them the "Bread that cometh down from heaven," and to nourish our spiritual life by meditation on them, so "that from the bible's pages we learn spiritual perfection."[79]

Bea operated on two fronts. On one hand he championed the historical method against the traditional exegetes who were faithful to St. Jerome's method; on the other he combated the "new theology" of the Blondellian philosophical stamp, which during that same period proposed a spiritual

---

[76] Cf. Mauro Pesce, "Il rinnovamento biblico della prima guerra mondiale alle soglie del Concilio Vaticano II," in *SC I cattolici nel mondo contemporaneo (1922–1958)*, ed. M. Guasco, Elio Guerriero, and Francesco Traniello (Rome: Edizioni Paoline, 1991), 593–605; *Idem,* "Dalla enciclica biblica di Leone XIII *Providentissimus Deus* (1893) a quella di Pio XII *Divino afflante Spiritu* (1943)," in Carlo Maria Martini, Giuseppe Ghiberti, and M. Pesce, *Cento anni di cammino* (Milan: Vita e Pensiero, 1995), 38–100 at 63–64.

[77] Cf. M. Pesce, "Il rinnovamento biblico," *op. cit.*, 575–610; *idem,* "Esegesi storica ed esegesi spirituale nell'ermeneutica biblica cattolica dal pontificato di Leone XIII a quello di Pio XII," in *Annali di Storia dell'Esegesi* 6 (1989): 261–291; *idem,* "Dalla enciclica biblica di Leone XIII," *op. cit.*, 64.

[78] Benedict XV, encylical *Spiritus Paraclitus*, 51, citing St. Jerome, *In Eccles.* 12, 9 ff.

[79] Ibid., 47.

exegesis of the sacred texts unmoored from historic historical-literal sense.[80] Among the representatives of this "pneumatic" exegesis, which looked to Origen as its model, were the theologian Joseph Coppens[81] of Louvain and the Jesuit Fathers Daniélou[82] and de Lubac.[83] The "new theology" was not mistaken in laying claim to the teaching of the Church fathers that had been abandoned by the rationalist exegetes, but it erred profoundly in trying to eliminate the literal sense from the Old Testament and to claim for it only the spiritual and "typical" sense. Equally reductive, however, was the position of those who aligned themselves with the historical-literal sense while suppressing or, worse still, ridiculing the spiritual and allegorical sense, in the name of an alleged historical-scientific "objectivity."

A typical example of this reductive vision was the veritable persecution conducted by the Biblical Institute and the Biblical Commission against Don Dolindo Ruotolo,[84] a pious and learned Neapolitan priest who dared

---

80 Cf. M. Pesce, "Esegesi storica ed esegesi spirituale," *op. cit.*, 286–291; *idem,* "Un 'bruit absurde'? Henri de Lubac di fronte alla distinzione tra esegesi spirituale e esegesi storica," in *Annali di Storia dell'Esegesi* 10 (1993): 301–353; E. Poulat, "Comment lire la Bible: Exégèse critique et sens spirituel de Loisy à Claudel," in *Le retour aux écritures: Fondamentalismes présents et passés*, ed. Evelyne Patlagean and Alain Le Boulleuc (Louvain-Paris: Peeters, 1993), 217–234.

81 Joseph Coppens (1896–1981), Belgian priest, professor of exegesis at the University of Louvain, dean of the Faculty of Theology from 1964 to 1967. By him see *L'histoire critique de l'Ancien testament: Ses origines: Ses orientations nouvelles: Ses perspectives d'avenir* (Tournai-Paris: Casterman, 1939).

82 Cf. Jean Daniélou, S.J., *Origen* (New York: Sheed and Ward, 1955); *idem, Sacramentum futuri: Études sur les origines de la typologie biblique* (Paris: Beauchesne, 1950).

83 Cf. H. de Lubac, S.J., *History and Spirit: the understanding of scripture according to Origen* (San Francisco: Ignatius Press, 2007); *idem, Medieval Exegesis* (Grand Rapids, MI: W. B. Eerdmans, 1998 f.). The original French editions were published in Paris by Aubier in 1950 and 1959–1961 respectively.

84 Dolindo Ruotolo (1882–1970), ordained in 1905, ministered chiefly in Naples at the church of San Giuseppe dei Nudi, of which his brother Elio was pastor and in which he is now buried. His cause for beatification has been introduced. His principal work, published under the pseudonym Dain Cohenel is *La Sacra Scrittura: Psicologia — Commento — Meditazione*, in thirty-three volumes from Genesis to Apocalypse, concluded in 1974, under the auspices of the bishop of Sessa Aurunca, Vittorio M. Costantini (1906–2003). About him see *Fui chiamato Dolindo, che significa dolore: Pagine di autobiografia* (Sessa Aurunca-Naples-Riano: Apostolato Stampa, 1972); Antonio Gallo, *Un prete del Duemila* (Naples: Edizioni Apostolato, 1974).

to challenge the new rationalist orientation by undertaking a commentary on sacred scripture based on the traditional exegetical method of the fathers and doctors of the Church. Don Ruotolo combined the study of sacred scripture with prayer and meditation and set out to heal the rift between science and faith in the field of exegesis. Two prelates, Monsignore Giovanni Maria Sanna,[85] bishop of Gravina and Irsina, and Monsignore Giuseppe Palatucci,[86] bishop of Campagna, intervened in his defense,[87] contrasting Don Ruotolo's exegetic approach to that of the Biblicum, which they interpreted as "an encouragement of certain methods and approaches from a rationalistic and modernistic background."[88] Despite the authoritative and strong support of these and other illustrious Italian prelates, Don Ruotolo was condemned by the Holy Office under pressure from Father Alberto Vaccari.[89] The Neapolitan priest responded with a short work published in May 1941[90] that was presented to the pope by the Cardinal Alessio Ascalesi[91] of Naples, which took aim at historic exegesis,

[85] Giovanni Maria Sanna (1873–1956), of the Friars Minor Conventual, ordained in 1896, bishop of Ampurias and Tempio in Sardinia (1915–1922), then bishop of Gravina and Irsina di Puglia from 1922 to 1953, where he founded the Franciscan Missionary Sisters of Jesus Crucified. Remembered as a holy pastor, many await the cause of his beatification.

[86] Giuseppe Maria Palatucci (18929–1961), of the Friars Minor Conventual, ordained in 1915, was bishop of Campagna from 1937 until his death. On December 12, 2006 he was awarded a Medal of Honor for civil valor for his heroic assistance to the Jews interned in Campagna.

[87] Cf. G. M. Sanna and G. M. Palatucci, *La Sacra Scrittura: Psicologia-Commento-Meditazione del Sac. Dain Cohenel: Difesa dalle incriminazioni dei pretesi errori segnalati dal P. Alberto Vaccari s.j.* (Gravina di Puglia: Apostolato Stampa, 1939); G. M. Sanna, *Risposta al R.P.A. Vaccari s.j. riguardo ai pretesi errori da lui precisati in una lettera al Vescovo stesso sull'Opera La Sacra Scrittura: Psicologia-Commento-Meditazione del Sac. Dain Cohenel* (Gravina di Puglia, Apostolato Stampa, 1939).

[88] Ibid., 36.

[89] AAS 32 (1940): 553. On the incident, cf. M. Pesce, "Il rinnovamento biblico," *op. cit.*, 593–598.

[90] "Un gravissimo pericolo per la Chiesa e per le anime. Il sistema critico-scientifico nello studio e nell'interpretazione della Sacra Scrittura. Le sue deviazioni funeste e le sue aberrazioni" (48–page booklet dated May 24, 1941). ["A very serious danger for the Church and for souls. The critical-scientific system in the study and interpretation of sacred scripture. Its disastrous errors and its aberrations."]

[91] Alessio Ascalesi (1872–1952), ordained in the Congregation of the Most Precious Blood in 1895. Bishop of Muro Lucano (1909–1911) and of Benevento (1911–1916), was created cardinal

seeing in Vaccari's approach the danger of an "intellectual dictatorship in biblical matters." The booklet by Don Ruotolo was censured by the Pontifical Biblical Commission,[92] but the concerns that it expressed were not unfounded. The watchword of the biblical scholars in the 1950s, and of the liturgists as well, seemed to be Erasmus' motto: "Let us return to the sources!"[93] But Erasmus, as his biographer Huizinga emphasizes, "did not realize the extent to which his philological-critical method would shake the structure of the Church to its foundations."[94]

Father Bea, "strategist" of this biblical reductionism, was able to wield considerable influence on the encylical *Divino afflante Spiritu* by Pius XII (1943). The document forcefully restated the principle that the authentic interpretation of sacred scripture rests solely with the Church's magisterium,[95] as opposed to the post-modernist exegetes who in the 1940s sought to limit divine inerrancy to the truths of faith and morality, but identified the chief purpose of exegesis as the determination of the literal sense of the text. This meant the abandonment of patristic, theological, and spiritual exegesis, in the name of an historical-literary exegesis that was purely scientific and rational. The encylical therefore cut the ground from under scriptural exegesis: not only the symbolic hermeneutic of the "*nouvelle théologie*" that was unmoored from the magisterium and scholastic theology, but also the traditional exegesis that had not renounced the symbolic interpretation of the fathers of the Church. The progressives not mistakenly saw a victory in the document of Pius XII which, in order to be correctly understood, must be read in the light of the encyclicals *Spiritus Paraclitus* by Benedict XV and *Humani generis* by Pope Pacelli himself. On the other hand, even the condemnation by *Humani generis* of the errors of the "*nouvelle theologie*" was presented by Cardinal Bea as

in 1916. Archbishop of Naples from 1924 until his death.

92 AAS 23 (1941): 465–472. Cf. Alberto Vaccari, S.J. *Lo studio della S. Scrittura: Lettera della Pontificia Commissione Biblica con introduzione e commenti* (Rome: La Civiltà Cattolica, 1943).

93 "*Ad fontes!* Let us return to the old classical, scriptural, patristic sources! This was the battle cry of the humanists of the Renaissance like Erasmus. It was for the most part the battle cry of the Council, although in its documents it was whispered rather than shouted" (J. W. O'Malley, "Erasmus and Vatican II," *op. cit.*, 200).

94 Johan Huizinga, *Erasmus and the Age of Reformation* (New York: Harper, 1957).

95 encylical *Divino afflante Spiritu, op. cit.* See also Mario Merenda, "Il Magistero della Chiesa: Norma prossima per l'esegeta," in *Palestra del Clero* 49 (1970): 203–220, 396–404, 473–484.

approval of the historical-critical method, which continued to dominate the exegetical field in the fifties and sixties and, as one scholar points out, managed to bring about "profound changes in Catholic theological thought without ever aiming directly at a reform of theology as such."[96] Bea, moreover, would be the confessor of Pius XII from 1945 until the latter's death in 1958. In a conference held on December 8, 1957, at the Pontifical Biblical Institute to commemorate the fiftieth anniversary of the encylical *Pascendi,* the German Jesuit on the one hand pointed out that a significant number of propositions condemned by the encylical *Pascendi* and by the decree *Lamentabili* of Pius X concerned biblical modernism; on the other hand he denied that those errors had spread in Italy, reducing biblical modernism to a mere philosophical tendency personified by the now-forgotten Alfred Loisy.[97]

4. The liturgical movement

Liturgy was, along with exegesis, the other great field in which modernism toiled, claiming that Christian religious experience cannot be expressed adequately in intellectual formulas such as dogmas, but must have its chief expression in the *lex orandi.* Dom Prosper Guéranger,[98] the great nineteenth-century restorer of the Roman liturgy, had intended to renew monastic life by returning to the traditional Roman liturgy, after the devastation wrought by protestantism and, within the Catholic Church, by Gallicanism and Jansenism. The *new* liturgical movement, however, had an essentially anti-Roman inspiration and functioned independently of the directions of the Holy See, and often in overt opposition to it.

---

96 M. Pescse, "Un 'bruit absurde,'" *op. cit.*, 326–327.

97 Cf. A. Bea, S.J., "L'enciclica 'Pascendi' e gli studi biblici," in *Biblica* 39 (1958): 121–138.

98 Dom Prosper Guéranger (1805–1875), ordained in 1827, abbot of the Benedictine Priory of Solesmes and founder of the Congregation of France of the Order of Saint Benedict, was the restorer of monastic life in France. By him see the *Institutions liturgiques*, 4 vols. (Paris: Société Générale de Librairie Catholique, 1878–1885). About him, see Paul Delatte, O.S.B., *Dom Guéranger: Abbé de Solesmes* (Sablé-sur-Sarthe: Abbaye de Solesmes, 1984 [1909]) and Cuthbert Johnson, O.S.B., *Prosper Guéranger (1805–1875): a liturgical theologian* (Rome: Pontificio Ateneo S. Anselmo, 1984). See also the articles by B. Heurtbize, in DCT 6 (1920): 1894–1898 and by Jacques Hourlier, in DSp 6 (1967): 1097–1106.

St. Pius X had outlined a program of authentic liturgical renewal, which followed in the wake of the movement started by Dom Guéranger. Expressions of this renewal were the decrees *Sacra Tridentina*[99] dated December 20, 1905, and *Quam singulari*[100] dated August 8, 1910, which recommended frequent Holy Communion and the Communion for children; the letter to Cardinal Pietro Respighi dated June 14, 1905, in which the pope asked for the completion of a catechism on the liturgical feasts; and the Bull *Divino afflatu*[101] dated November 1, 1911, which promulgated a reform of the Breviary.

The postmodernist liturgical movement[102] had its chief interpreter in Dom Lambert Beauduin,[103] a Belgian Benedictine of Mont-César, whose

---

99 ASS 38 (1905/1906): 401–405.

100 AAS 2 (1910): 894–897.

101 Bull *Divino Afflatu*, in Bellocchi, vol. VII: *Pio X (1903–1914)*, 470–473.

102 On the "liturgical movement," cf. Olivier Rousseau, O.S.B., *The Progress of the Liturgy: an historical sketch from the beginning of the nineteenth century to the pontificate of Pius X*, Engl. transl. (Westminster, MD: Newman Press, 1951); Didier Bonneterre, *Le Mouvement liturgique* (Escurolles: Éditions Fideliter, 1980); Burkhard Neunheuser, "Movimento liturgico," in *Liturgia*, ed. Domenico Sartore, Achille Maria Triacca (Cinisello Balsamo: San Paolo, 2001), 1279–1293; Various Authors, *Liturgia: temi e autori: Saggi di studio sul movimento liturgico*, ed. Franco Brovelli (Rome: Edizioni Liturgiche, 1990); Matias Augé, "Il movimento liturgico: Alla ricerca della fondazione 'spirituale' della liturgia," in *Ecclesia Orans* 24 (2007): 335–350; Alcuin Reid, O.S.B., *The Organic Development of Liturgy: The Principles of Liturgical Reform and their Relation to the Twentieth Century: Liturgical Movement prior to the Second Vatican Council*, with a preface by Cardinal J. Ratzinger (London: St. Michael's Abbey Press, 2004); Bernard Botte, O.S.B., *Le Mouvement Liturgique: Témoignage et souvenirs* (Paris: Desclée, 1973).

103 Lambert Beauduin (1873–1960), Belgian Benedictine, ordained in 1897, monk of the Benedictine Abbey of Mont-César, near Louvain (1907), then founded the monastery of Union in Amay (Liège), which was transferred to Chevetogne, in the province of Namur. He was dismissed from the abbey in 1932 but remained a point of reference for ecumenism. About him see the biography by Raymond Loonbeek and Jacques Mortiau, *Un pionnier: dom Lambert Beauduin (1873–1960): Liturgie et unité des chrétiens* (Louvain-la-Neuve: Chevetogne, 2001), 2 vols. An abridged version was published by Éditions du Cerf in 2005 with the title: *Dom Lambert Beauduin: Visionnaire et précurseur (1873–1960): Un moine au coeur libre.* See also André Haquin, *Dom Lambert Beauduin et le renouveau liturgique* (Gembloux: J. Duculot, S.A., 1970); Louis Bouyer, *Dom Lambert Beauduin (1823–1960): Un homme d'Église* (Paris: Casterman, 1964); Francesco Ricossa, "L'eresia antiliturgica dai Giansenisti a Giovanni XXIII (1668–1960): I tre secoli di gestazione delle riforme conciliari," in *Sodalitium* 11 (1986): 8–16.

speech at the *Congrès National des Oeuvres Catholiques* in Malines on September 23, 1909, is considered the beginning of the new movement.[104] In his talk, the monk from Mont-César maintained that the liturgy is not just the public worship of the Church, but the true prayer of the faithful, through which a powerful bond of union is established.[105] The liturgical assembly, in his opinion, had lost its communal character and had been reduced to the form of a private and interior devotion. During his novitiate, Beauduin had summarized his idea of "liturgical renewal" in the phrase "it is necessary to democratize the liturgy."[106] In order to achieve this he developed the notion of "active participation of the faithful,"[107] a short phrase by Pius X, Gilles Routhier notes, that had passed unnoticed at the end of the third paragraph of his motu proprio *Tra le sollecitudini.*[108] In 1912, when Maurice Festugière,[109] a Benedictine

---

[104] "The Congress of Malines in September 1909 offers the occasion to consolidate our good intentions, to determine a program of action, to coordinate a campaign plan, and also to create a liturgical movement" (L. Beauduin, O.S.B., "Introduction" in *Cours et conférences de la semaine liturgique de Maredsous 19–24 août 1912* [Maredsous: Abbaye de Maredsous, 1913], xiii-xvi at xv).

[105] "La vraie prière de l'Église: Resumé du rapport de dom Lambert Beauduin au Congrès de Malines," in *Questions liturgiques et paroissiales* 40 (1959): 218–221.

[106] L. Beauduin, O.S.B., "Autour du Jubilé du mouvement liturgique 1909–1959," in *Questions liturgiques et paroissiales* 40 (1959): 208, cited in Reiner Kaczynski, "La liturgia come vissuto religioso," in *SC, I cattolici nel mondo contemporaneo, op. cit.*, 400.

[107] J. Lamberts, "L'évolution de la notion de 'participation active' dans le Mouvement liturgique du XXe siècle," in *La Maison-Dieu* 241 (2005): 77–120; *Active Participation Revisited—La participation active: 100 ans après Pie X et 40 ans après Vatican II*, ed. Jozef Lamberts (Louvain: Peeters, 2005).

[108] Cf. G. Routhier, *Il Concilio Vaticano II, op. cit.*, 100–101.

[109] Maurice Festugière (1870–1950) entered the Benedictine monastery of Maredsous in 1895, was ordained in 1900, and professed solemn vows at Sant'Anselmo in Rome, where he completed a doctorate in theology. From 1911 to 1913 he wrote various articles for the *Revue Liturgique et Bénédictine*. His "La Liturgie catholique: Essai de synthèse" appeared in 1913 in the *Revue de philosophie* and was then published as a separate volume (Maredsous, 1913). Subsequently he published articles on philosophy, theology, morality, and spirituality. Cf. Edmond Yawo Amekuse, *Le rôle de la liturgie dans l'économie chrétienne: La contribution de Maurice Festugière au mouvement liturgique* (Rome: Pontificium Athenaeum S. Anselmi, 2008).

of Maredsous,[110] published his work *La liturgie catholique*,[111] in which he launched an all-out attack of Ignatian spirituality, Dom Beauduin described the work as "the beginning of the scientific phase of the liturgical movement"[112] and became an impassioned supporter thereof. Festugière and Beauduin considered the "liturgical action" as a method of asceticsm and spirituality which contrasted with other "schools," such as the Ignatian school which until then had been dominant in the Church. "A profound battle of ideas," wrote Dom Beauduin, "is in the making in the field of piety and ascetism."[113] One year later, Beauduin published the booklet *La piété de l'Église: Principes et faits* [*The Church's piety: principles and facts*], which is considered by many to be the keynote text of the nascent liturgical movement. In that same year 1914, in Italy, Emanuele Caronti,[114] a monk of Praglia, founded the *Rivista liturgica* [*Liturgical Review*] in which, from the very first issues, he adopted the "program" of Dom Beauduin, contrasting the "descending sacramental value" of worship and its "ascending latreutic" value.[115] The Benedictine Salvatore Marsili[116] began his collaboration with the journal in 1934 and

---

[110] The abbot of Maredsous was Dom Columba Marmion (1858–1923), who followed the polemics of those years in a balanced way. Cf. Benjamin Marie Morineau, *Dom Marmion Maître de sagesse* (Paris: DDB, 1944).

[111] Cf. Maurice Festugière, O.S.B., "La liturgie catholique: Essai de synthèse, suivi de quelques développements," in *Revue de philosophie* (1913): 692–886. Cf. Annalisa Girolimetto, "Liturgia e vita spirituale: Il dibattito sorto sugli anni 1913–1914," in *Liturgia: temi e autori, op. cit.*, 211–274.

[112] Cited by M. Augé, "Il movimento liturgico," *op. cit.*, 338.

[113] Letter dated October 12, 1913, in *Lettres de dom Beauduin à dom R. Thibaut, 1909–1955,* cited in E. Y. Amekuse, *op. cit.*

[114] Emanuele Caronti (1882–1966), Benedictine, abbot of the Monastery of San Giovanni di Parma (1919) and then abbot general of the Benedictine Congregation of Subiaco (1937). See his programmatic articles in the first volume of the review: "La liturgia: nozioni e principi," in *Rivista Liturgica* 1 (1914): 7–13, 88–108.

[115] Cf. Salvatore Marsili, O.S.B., "Storia del movimento liturgico italiano dalle origini all'enciclica 'Mediator Dei,'" in O. Rousseau, O.S.B., *Storia del movimento liturgico, op. cit.*, 263–369; Paolo Tomatis, "Lo spirito della liturgia nei primi 50 anni di 'Rivista liturgica' (1914–1964)," in *Rivista Liturgica* 90/2–3 (2003): 341–356; Manlio Sodi, "Tra movimento, riforma e rinnovamento: il servizio di 'Rivista Liturgica,'" in *Rivista Liturgica* 90/6 (2003): 931–964.

[116] Salvatore Marsili (1910–1983), Benedictine, ordained in 1931, cofounder and first president of

edited it from 1939 to 1948. Among the admirers of Dom Beauduin in Italy was the Oratorian from Brescia, Giulio Bevilacqua,[117] to whom the young Giovanni Battista Montini owed his liturgical formation.[118]

In Germany, the point of departure of the "liturgical movement" is considered the celebration of the "Community Mass"[119] that took place on August 6, 1921, in the Crypt of the German Abbey of Maria Laach,[120] in the Rhineland, under the auspices of Abbot Ildefons Herwegen.[121] Certain individuals must be mentioned in connection with the liturgical movement of Maria Laach, such as its own monk Odo Casel,[122] and Father Romano Guardini,[123] whose contacts with the abbey in the initial years of his priestly ministry played a decisive role.[124] In 1918, through

---

the Pontifical Liturgical Institute in Rome, abbot of the Abbey of Santa Maria di Finalpia from 1972 to 1979. Cf. Adele Colombo, "Il teologo Salvatore Marsili, profetico fautore delle scienze umane in liturgia?" in *Rivista Liturgica* 90/5 (2003): 745–764.

[117] Giulio Bevilacqua (1881–1965), priest of the Oratory, ordained in 1908 in Brescia. Was spiritual director in Brescia of Giovanni Battista Montini who, when elected pope, created him cardinal in 1965. About him, cf. Antonio Fappani, *Padre Giulio Bevilacqua, il cardinale-parroco* (Brescia: Queriniana, 1979).

[118] Cf. Godfried Danneels, "Paul VI et la réforme liturgique," in *Istituto Paolo VI* 10 (1985): 55–70 at 56–57.

[119] R. Kaczynski, *op. cit.*, 401.

[120] Monsignor Giovanni Battista Montini visited the Abbey of Maria Laach in August of 1928 during a journey that had reached France, Belgium and Germany. Cf. G. B. Montini, *Lettere ai familiari: 1919–1943*, vol. II, *1928–1943*, ed. Nello Vian (Rome: Studium, 1986), 556.

[121] Ildefonso Herwegen (1874–1946), German Benedictine, began his novitiate in the Abbey of Maria Laach in 1894, where he was ordained in 1901 and elected abbot in 1913.

[122] Odo Casel (1886–1949), German Benedictine, ordained in 1911, editor of the *Jahrbuch für Liturgiewissenschaft* (1921–1924), from 1922 to 1948 spiritual director of the Abbey in Herstelle (Westphalia). Cf. Arno Schilson, *Theologie als Sakramententheologie: Die Mysterientheologie Odo Casels* (Mainz: Matthias Grünewald, 1982).

[123] Romano Guardini (1885–1968), ordained in 1910. Taught philosophy of religion in Berlin, Tübingen, and Munich. There he was one of the founders of the *Katholische Akademie*. Cf. Hanna Barbara Gerl, *Romano Guardini, 1885–1968: Leben und Werk* (Mainz: Mathias Grünewald, 1985).

[124] Cf. R. Guardini, "Briefe an den Laacher Abt Ildefons Herwegen aus den Jahren 1917 bis 1934," ed. Angelus A. Häussling, O.S.B., in *Archiv für Liturgiewissenschaft* 27 (1985): 205–262, 408–411.

their initiative, three series of scholarly volumes were inaugurated: *Ecclesia Orans*, *Liturgiegeschichtliche Quellen*, and *Liturgiegeschichtliche Forschungen* [*The Praying Church, Sources of Liturgical History, Investigations in Liturgical History*].

Dom Pius Parsch,[125] an Augustinian canon of Klosterneuburg Abbey near Vienna, author of *Das Jahr des Heiles* [*The Church's Year of Grace*] (1923), began to celebrate Mass "facing the people" and to translate liturgical texts into German. The title of his most important work, *Volksliturgie*[126] (1940), which he borrowed from the Jesuit Joseph Jungmann of Innsbruck, expressed the idea of a "people's liturgy" that makes the vertical relationship with God horizontal. The participants in the first "Liturgical Masses" in Klosterneuburg came from the "biblical movement," which in Germany, as in Belgium, merged with the liturgical movement. The nuncio, Eugenio Pacelli, did not conceal his critiques of the new liturgicism: "The so-called movement," he wrote to his superiors upon leaving Germany in November 1929, "exaggerates the value of the liturgy, attempting, so to speak, to replace the essential content of the Catholic faith with exterior forms."[127] In the 1930s also the activities of the Abbey of Maria Laach would be severely criticized by Cardinal Secretary of State Pacelli.[128]

These new ideas had weighty repercussions in the fields of spirituality, pastoral ministry, and even ecclesiology. The reformers tended to disregard the substantial difference between the sacramental priesthood of the ordained and the common priesthood of the laity, so as to attribute a true and proper priestly nature to the community of the faithful; they suggested the idea of a "concelebration" of the priest with the people; they maintained that one had to "participate" actively at Mass by dialoging with the celebrant, to the exclusion of any other legitimate form of attending the Holy Sacrifice, such as meditation, reciting the

125 Pius Parsch (1884–1954), Austrian, Augustinian Canon of the Abbey of Klosterneuburg, ordained in 1905, founder and first editor of *Bibel und Liturgie*.

126 Cf. Pius Parsch, *Volksliturgie, Ihr Sinn und Umfang* (Würzburg: Echter Verlag, 2004).

127 Cited in P. Chenaux, *Pio XII, op. cit.*, 361. Father Max Kassiepe, O.M.I. (1867–1948), in his *Irrwege und Umwege im Frömmigkeitsleben der Gegenwart* (Kevelaer: Butzon-Bercker, 1939), denounced the errors of "liturgism" as being among the first. Next came the critique by August Doerner, *Sentire cum ecclesia* (1941) and the *Memorandum* dispatched to the German bishops in 1943 by the archbishop of Freiburg Conrad Gröber (1872–1948).

128 Pacelli to Abbot von Stotzinger, August 3, 1933, cited in P. Chenaux, *Pio XII, op. cit.*, 361–362.

rosary, or other private devotions; they championed the reduction of the altar to the status of a table; they considered Holy Communion "*extra Missam*" [outside of Mass], visits to the Blessed Sacrament, and perpetual adoration to be forms of extra-liturgical piety; and they gave little or no attention to devotions to the Sacred Heart, Our Lady, and the saints or, more generally, to spirituality and traditional morality. In a word, this was a "reinterpretation" of the doctrine and structure of the Church in order to adapt them to the modern mindset.

In Belgium, the liturgical movement benefited from the development of Catholic Action, especially of the Young Christian Workers movement (*Jeunesse Ouvrière Chretienne*), founded in 1925 by Fr. Joseph Léon Cardijn.[129] Cardijn was a friend of Mont-César Abbey, and when he began to organize large gatherings, he entrusted to the monastery the celebration of Mass, which was supposed to be the central point of the day. "It is certain," Dom Bernard Botte recalls, "that these assemblies of young workers, who said the responses to the priest's prayers, sang the Ordinary of the Mass, and participated in the Offertory and at Communion, advanced the liturgical movement more than many articles."[130]

Towards the end of the Second World War, the Center of Pastoral Liturgy in Paris, headed by Canon Aimé-Georges Martimort,[131] and the Liturgical Institute of Trier, directed by Monsignor Johannes Wagner,[132] came into contact Mont-César Abbey. In 1951, the two centers organized a private meeting at the Abbey of Maria Laach during which, in the absence of any representative of the Roman hierarchy, they addressed for the first time the issue of a radical reform of the Mass. Jungmann, director of the German Liturgical Movement, proposed structural changes even to the canon of

129 Joseph-Léon Cardijn (1882–1967), Belgian, ordained in 1906, consecrated bishop in 1965 and created cardinal that same year.

130 B. Botte, *op. cit.*, 66. Dom Bernard Botte (1893–1980), Belgian Benedictine, was Consultor of the Preparatory Commission for the Sacred Liturgy.

131 Aimé-Georges Martimort (1911–2000), priest of the Diocese of Toulouse, professor at the Institute Catholique of Toulouse. Consultor of the Preparatory Liturgical Commission, conciliar *peritus*.

132 Johannes Wagner (1908–1999), German, ordained in 1932. secretary of the Liturgical Commission of the Episcopal Conference of Fulda (later the German Bishops Conference) from 1946 to 1975. Consultor of the Pontifical Congregation for Divine Worship until 1975.

the Mass at the consecration.[133] The Center for Pastoral Liturgy and Mont-César Abbey then created, under the direction of Dom Bernard Botte, another monk of Mont-César, the Higher Institute of Liturgy in Paris, which the Holy See made equal in rank to the Pontifical Liturgical Institute of Sant'Anselmo in Rome.

On November 20, 1947, the encylical *Mediator Dei* on the sacred liturgy was published.[134] It was intended to correct the deviations in the liturgical movement, developing the papal teaching already begun with *Mystici Corporis.*[135] Pius XII, however, influenced by his confessor Father Bea, and prompted by the perfectionism that characterized his personality, agreed that the biblical movement should advance a projecct of liturgical reform that had been initiated even before *Mediator Dei* with the new Latin version of the Psalms, which had been accomplished by Bea himself. The new translation of the Psalter from Hebrew, started by the Biblicum in 1941,[136] in which the "Christian Latin" of the Vulgate was replaced with an artificial "Ciceronian" Latin, represented the most serious blow dealt to the work of St. Jerome since the times of Lorenzo Valla and Erasmus.

The writer Nino Badano[137] recalls:

> For more than fifteen centuries, in the cloisters, in the abbeys, in the hermits' cells, generations of holy monks had recited the psalms in the words of the Vulgate: then the "Septuagint" [seventy scholars] from Augustin Bea's Biblicum had to come along and propose their

---

[133] Cf. B. Botte, *op. cit.*, 206–207. Joseph Jungmann (1889–1975), Austrian, of the Society of Jesus, ordained in 1913, professor on the theological faculty of the University of Innsbruck, editor of the *Zeitschrift für Katholische Theologie* (1927–1939, 1945–1963), member of the Preparatory Commission, then *peritus* of Vatican Council II. His book *Die Frohbotschaft und unsere Glaubensverkündigung* (Regensburg: Pustet, 1936), was withdrawn from libraries through the intervention of the Holy Office, but was reprinted and reworked in 1963 (Innsbruck: Tyrolia, 1963). About him see *J. A. Jungmann: Ein Leben für Liturgie und Kerygma*, ed. Hans-Bernhard Meyer, S.J. (Innsbruck: Tyrolia, 1975).

[134] Cf. Pius XII, encylical *Mediator Dei* (November 20, 1947), in AAS 39 (1947): 521–600.

[135] Cf. Pius XII, encylical *Mystici Corporis* (June 29, 1943), in AAS 35 (1943): 193–248.

[136] Cf. Schmidt, *Bea*, 102–105. According to the author, it was Pius XII himself who "imposed" on Bea the use of "Ciceronian" Latin (ibid., 102–105).

[137] Nino Badano (1911–1991), editor of *Il Quotidiano* (1950–1964), then of *Il Giornale d'Italia* (1966–1969), and editorialist for *Il Tempo* in Rome for twenty years.

eminently wise philological corrections.... The most surprising thing is that this first profanation of the Psalter was carried out and permitted by Pius XII: an undeniably great pope, but obsessed with a formalistic perfectionism which made him regard as increasingly important the teaching authority of his governance; the mission of teaching with respect to the mission of watching over the flock.... He was the one to order or to tolerate the modification of the Psalter out of a scruple of philological precision that caused him to disregard the inestimable value of tradition."[138]

In 1948 the Commission for Liturgical Reform was appointed,[139] presided over by Cardinal Clemente Micara[140] and then, from 1953 on, by Cardinal Gaetano Cicognani, prefect of the Sacred Congregation of Rites. A young Vincentian priest, Fr. Annibale Bugnini,[141] editor of *Ephemerides Liturgicae*, was appointed secretary. Bugnini himself recalled that during the twelve years of its existence (June 28, 1948 to July 8, 1960) the commission held eighty-two meetings and worked in absolute secrecy. "The commission enjoyed the full confidence of the pope, who was kept abreast of its work by Monsignor Montini and even more, on a weekly basis, by Father Bea, confessor of Pius XII."[142] Practically all the liturgical books were renewed, in particular the Divine Office and the liturgy of Holy Week. Unexpectedly, the decree of the Congregation of Rites *Dominicae Resurrectionis Vigiliam*

---

138 Nino Badano, *I primi giorni della Chiesa e gli ultimi* (Rome: Volpe, 1973), 158–159.

139 Cf. Nicola Giampietro, O.F.M., *Il Card. Ferdinando Antonelli e gli sviluppi della riforma liturgica dal 1948 al 1970* (Rome: Pontificio Ateneo S. Anselmo, 1998); *idem,* "A cinquant'anni dalla riforma liturgica della Settimana Santa," in *Ephemerides liturgicae* 3 (2006): 293–332. On the commission's work, see also Carlo Braga, C.M., *La riforma liturgica di Pio XII: Documenti*, vol. I *La "memoria sulla riforma liturgica"* (Rome: Edizioni Liturgiche, 2003).

140 Clemente Micara (1879–1965), ordained in 1902, in 1920 was appointed apostolic nuncio in Czechoslovakia and consecrated titular bishop of Apaurea, then nuncio in Belgium and Luxemburg (1923–1946). Created cardinal in 1946. pro-prefect of the Congregation of Rites (1950–1953).

141 Annibale Bugnini (1912–1983), of the Congregation of the Mission (Vincentian). Ordained in 1936. secretary of the Sacred Congregation for Divine Worship (1969–1976), titular archbishop of Diocletiana (1972). apostolic pro-nuncio in Iran (1976–1982).

142 A. Bugnini, *The Liturgical Reform (1948–1975)*, English translation (Collegeville, MN: Liturgical Press, 1990), 9.

was published on February 9, 1951, and on November 16, 1955, the decree *Maxima redemptionis nostrae mysteria*[143] on the reform of the Holy Week liturgy. The future cardinal Ferdinando Antonelli had to describe it as "the most important act in the history of liturgy from St. Pius V until today."[144] The whole *ratio* [plan] of this reform—as has been correctly observed—seems to be permeated by a mixture of rationalism and archaeologism that is sometimes fanciful in its contours.[145]

5. The philosophical and theological movement

On August 4, 1879, Leo XIII addressed to the Catholic world the encylical *Aeterni Patris*, in which he proposed the doctrine of St. Thomas as the basis for higher studies in philosophy, singling out Thomism as the first and necessary response to the philosophical errors that threatened the Catholic faith and the natural law itself.[146]

On the philosophical level, the historical-critical method adopted by the modernists was dominated by the principle of immanence, which, while not directly opposing any particular revealed truth, radically changed the very notion of "truth," "religion," and "revelation" and was diametrically opposed to the philosophical system of St. Thomas Aquinas.[147]In the

---

143 Cf. AAS 47 (1955): 838–847. On the major modifications introduced see F. Antonelli, O.F.M., "Importanza e carattere pastorale della Riforma liturgica della Settimana Santa," in *L'Osservatore Romano*, November 27, 1955.

144 F. Antonelli, O.F.M., "La riforma liturgica della Settimana Santa: importanza attualità prospettive," in *La Restaurazione liturgica nell'opera di Pio XII: Atti del primo Congresso Internazionale di Liturgia Pastorale, Assisi-Roma, 12–22 settembre 1956* (Genoa: Centro di Azione liturgica, 1957), 179–197, cited in C. Braga, "'Maxima Redemptionis Nostrae Mysteria' 50 anni dopo (1955–2005)," in *Ecclesia Orans* 23 (2006): 11–36 at 34.

145 Cf. Stefano Carusi, "La riforma della Settimana Santa negli anni 1951–1956," in *Disputationes Theologicae* (http://disputationes-theologicae.blogspot.com/2010/03/la-riforma-della-settimana-santa-negli.html).

146 A collection of the fundamental documents of the magisterium, with extensive commentary, in Santiago Ramirez, O.P., De auctoritate doctrinali S. Thomae Aquinatis (Salamanca: Apud Sanctum Stephanum, 1952).

147 Cf. C. Fabro, "Modernismo," in EC, 8:1188–1196 at 1191–1192. On the philosophical origins of the principle of immanence, cf. *Idem, Introduzione all'ateismo moderno*, 2 vols. (Rome: Studium,

encylical *Pascendi*, Pius X condemned the philosophy of immanence and prescribed that the foundation of seminary studies should be *scholastic philosophy*, by which he meant chiefly (*praecipue*) "*that of Thomas Aquinas.*"[148] In the extensive document *Doctoris Angelici*, issued on June 29, 1914, two months before his death, the pope expressly ordered that scholastic philosophy be placed "at the foundation of sacred studies," specifying once again that he meant the philosophy of St. Thomas Aquinas.[149] "In fact, the key points of the philosophy of St. Thomas must not be viewed as opinions about which it is permissible to debate, taking one side or the other, but as the foundations upon which all science about things natural and divine is based."[150] With a categorical formula (*Nos volumus, iubemus, praecipimus*) [We propose, command, and prescribe], the pope ordered that the *Summa Theologiae* of St. Thomas be reintroduced in theological institutes as a textbook. This essential document was followed, the next month, by the publication of twenty-four Thomistic theses by the Sacred Congregation of Studies,[151] which according to Pius X contained the *"principia et pronuntiata maiora doctrinae S. Thomae"* ["principles and major pronouncements of the doctrine of St. Thomas"].[152]

Full and complete adherence to the philosophy of St. Thomas implied a rejection of all forms of modern philosophy, from Descartes to Kant, down to the currents of idealism, historicism, and evolutionism that had

1969), *passim*. Alberto Caturelli, "El principio de immanencia, la divinización del hombre y el orden temporal," in *Verbo* 253–254 (1987): 249–294.

148 Cf. ASS 40 (1907): 640.

149 Cf. AAS 6 (1914): 338.

150 Ibid., 337–338.

151 Cf. Sacred Congregation of Education and Studies, Declaration (known as the Twenty-four Theses of the philosophy of St. Thomas) dated July 27, 1914, in AAS 6 (1914): 383–386. The Twenty-four Theses were chiefly the work of the Jesuit Guido Mattiussi (1852–1925). "They have been ordered so marvelously that they all depend on the first, which articulates the very foundation of the Thomistic synthesis, namely the real distinction between potency and act" (Réginald Garrigou-Lagrange, O.P., *Sintesi tomistica* [Brescia: Queriniana, 1953], 401). See also Carlo Giacon, S.J., "Per una prima genesi delle XXIV tesi del tomismo specifico," in *Doctor communis* 24 (1981): 175–193; Jésus Villagrasa, L.C., "Il retroscena di una polemica: le XXIV tesi tomistiche," in *Neotomismo e suarezianismo: Il confronto di Cornelio Fabro* (Rome: Ateneo Pontificio Regina Apostolorum, 2006), 35–90.

152 AAS 6 (1914): 383.

appeared at the dawn of the twentieth century. The nucleus of modern philosophy, as Pius had correctly seen, was immanentism, in other words the principle that the source and the measure of being arise from man's consciousness. Twentieth-century neo-scholasticism did not understand, however, the metaphysical subversion entailed in the principle of immanence and often sought a compromise with it. The philosophical "Third Party" was represented by the movement which, after World War I, sought to reconcile scholasticism with the currents of modern thought.[153]In Belgium, the Jesuit Joseph Maréchal,[154]starting in 1912, pointed to Blondel as one of the greatest contemporary thinkers[155]and reinterpreted Thomism in Blondellian fashion.[156]His posthumous work, *Le point de départ de la métaphysique*" [The Point of Departure of Metaphsyics][157] (1947), inaugurated a philosophical trend inaccurately described as "transcendental Thomism,"[158] which established a bridge to the phenomenology of Martin Heidegger. Maréchal had the authoritative support of the Belgian, Cardinal Mercier, who sought to reconcile Thomism with the approaches of modern philosophy, from Descartes to Kant.[159]

---

153 Cf. Eduard Habsburg-Lothringen, *Das Ende des Neuthomismus: Die 68er, das Konzil und die Dominikaner* (Bonn: Nova et Vetera, 2007), 86–94.

154 Joseph Maréchal (1878–1944), Belgium philosopher and psychologist of the Society of Jesus, ordained in 1908. Professor at the University of Louvain.

155 Cf. Joseph Maréchal, S.J., "Science empirique et psychologie religieuse," in *Recherches de Science Religieuse* 3 (1912): 1. The influence of Blondel on Maréchal was studied by A. Millet, "Les 'Cahiers' du P. Maréchal: Sources doctrinales et influences subies," in *Revue néo-scolastique de philosophie* 43 (1945). See also Gerald A. McCool, *From Unity to Pluralism: The International Evolution of Thomism* (New York: Fordham University Press, 1989), 87–113.

156 Cf. Giovanni Moretto, *Destino dell'uomo e Corpo Mistico: Blondel, de Lubac e il Concilio Vaticano II* (Brescia: Morcelliana, 1994), 64. See also Salvatore Nicolosi, "La presenza di Blondel nel Concilio Vaticano II," in Various Authors, *Attualità del pensiero di Maurice Blondel* (Milan: Massimo, 1976), 49–91.

157 Cf. J. Maréchal, S.J., *Le point de départ de la métaphysique* (Bruges-Louvain: Alcan, 1922–1947), 4 vols.

158 "In fact to describe Thomism as 'transcendental' in the Kantian sense is a *contradictio in terminis* because the Thomist transcendental is realist, whereas the Kantian transcendental is irrealist" (Giovanni Cavalcoli, O.P., *Karl Rahner: Il Concilio tradito* [Verona: Fede e Cultura, 2009], 19).

159 Desiré Mercier (1851–1926), ordained in 1874, archbishop of Malines (1906) and cardinal

The error of neo-scholasticism in the 1920s and 1930s was to maintain that a simple restatement of the traditional metaphysical principles would be sufficient to block the revolutionary process of the secularization of society. Very often the neo-scholasticism of those years lacked a theology of history and refused to fight its opponent, fleeing to an intellectual ivory tower. In reality, modernism circulated not only in books but in the entire social structure (art, literature, dress, etc), poisoning every aspect of it. This allowed the nascent "*nouvelle théologie*" ["new theology"] to present itself as a "living" theology and philosophy, connected with history, as opposed to the abstract book learning of scholasticism.

In Belgium, at Tournai, stood the Dominican convent of Le Saulchoir where, from 1932 on, Father Marie-Dominique Chenu was "Regent of Studies."[160] In 1937 an essay by him appeared in draft form, entitled *Une école de théologie, Le Saulchoir,*[161] which claimed to be a "methodological" program to redesign Dominican studies. Chenu criticized anti-modernist theology, in the name of a "Christ of faith" who is known (as the modernists tried to do) in the "Christ of history."[162] To the extent in which historicity is the prerequisite for faith and the Church,[163] theologians had to be able to read "the signs of the times," in other words the manifestation of faith within history.[164]

(1907), was the founder of the neo-Thomistic school of Louvain. Cf. Louis de Raeymaeker, *Le cardinal Mercier et l'Institut supérieur de philosophie de Louvain* (Louvain: Presses Universitaires de Louvain, 1952); R. Aubert, *Le cardinal Mercier, archevêque de Malines, 1906–1962: Un prélat d'avant-garde* (Louvain: Presses Universitaires de Louvain, 1976, 19942).

[160] Marie-Dominique Chenu (1895–1990), French Dominican, studied at the Angelicum in Rome with Fr. Garrigou-Lagrange and was professor of Church History at the Faculty of Saulchoir from 1920 to 1942. At the Council he was the personal expert of Bishop Claude Rolland of Antsirabe (Madagascar). About him, cf. *Jacques Duquesne interroge le Père Chenu: Un théologien en liberté* (Paris: Centurion, 1975); *L'hommage differé au Père Chenu* (Paris: Cerf, 1990); Florent Gaboriau, *Trente ans de théologie française: Dérive et genèse* (Lausanne: L'Âge d'Homme, 2003), 139–152.

[161] Cf. M. D. Chenu, O.P., *Une école de théologie: Le Saulchoir, op. cit.*; reprinted by G. Alberigo as *Le Saulchoir: Una sculoa di teologia, op. cit.* About Le Saulchoir, see E. Fouilloux, *Une Église en quête de liberté, op. cit.,* 124–148.

[162] M. D. Chenu, O.P)., *Une école de théologie, op. cit.*, 61.

[163] Ibid., 42–46.

[164] See also Y. Congar, O.P., "La storia della Chiesa come luogo teologico," in *Concilium* 6 (1970): 103–115.

The French Dominican's "manifesto" was put on the Index of Forbidden Books by a decree of the Holy Office dated February 4, 1942,[165] together with the *"Essai sur le problème théologique"* by his confrère Louis Charlier,[166] and he was removed from his post. His disciples, priests like the Dominican Yves Congar,[167] who was ten years his junior, were convinced from then on that their generation had to "rescue for the Church whatever was of value in the approach of the modernists."[168] Chenu himself, on the other hand, had seen in modernism only a "crisis of growth in the Church."[169] Chenu, Congar, and Henri-Marie Féret,[170] the least well known of the theologians

---

165 Cf. AAS 34 (1942): 37.

166 Louis Charlier (1898–1981), Belgian Dominican, author of an *Essai sur le problème théologique* (Thuillies: Ramgal, 1938) that was placed on the Index on February 4, 1942. About him see *Nouvelle théologie*, 61–69, and the critique by Fr. Marie-Rosaire Gagnebet, O.P., "Un essai sur le problème théologique," in *Revue thomiste* 45 (1939): 108–145.

167 Yves Congar (1904–1995), French Dominican, ordained in 1930, professor of theology at Le Saulchoir until 1937. Described as "father and inspiration of Vatican II" (B. Forte, in *Avvenire*, June 23, 1996), he was, at the age of ninety, invested with the cardinalatial purple in November 1994 by John Paul II. About him see E. Fouilloux, "Frère Yves, Cardinal Congar, dominicain: Itinéraire d'un théologien," in *Revue des sciences philosophiques et théologiques* 79 (1995): 379–404; *Idem,* "Comment devient-on expert au Vatican II? Le cas du Père Yves Congar," in *Le deuxième concile du Vatican,* 307–331; *Cardinal Yves Congar 1904–1995*, ed. André Vauchez (Paris: Cerf, 1999): G. Alberigo, "P. Congar, Dossetti e l'officina bolognese," in *Cristianesimo nella storia* 24 (2003): 154–165; Jean-Pierre Jossua, "Le concile d'Yves Congar," in *Cristianesimo nella storia* 24 (2003): 149–153; A. Melloni, "Congar, Architect of the Unam Sanctam," in *Louvain Studies* 29 (2004): 222–238; Marie-Anne Vannier, "Notes sur Yves Congar et Vatican II," in *Revue des Sciences Religieuses* 77 (2003): 1, 8–10; J. Wicks, "Yves Congar's Doctrinal Service of the People of God," in *Gregorianum* 84 (2003): 499–550; special issue of *Istina* 48/1 (2003) dedicated to *Deux pionniers de l'unité: Yves Congar et Willem Visser't Hooft* (acts of a colloquium in Paris, September 27, 2002), with essays by B. Dupuy, É. Mahieu, K. Raiser, F. Fleinert-Jensen, B. Bobrinskoy, R. Beaupère, and M. Chevallier.

168 Aiden Nichols, O.P., *Yves Congar* (Wilton, CT: Morehouse-Barlow, 1989), 5.

169 M. D. Chenu, *Une école de théologie, op. cit.*, 38.

170 Henri-Marie Féret (1904–1992), French Dominican, professor of Church History at Le Saulchoir, then prior of a Dominican community in Dijon (1958–1964), directed for fifty years, until his death, an "evangelical group" consisting of women who met monthly to study the Holy Bible. During the Council he was advisor of the bishop of Saint-Claude, Claude Fusin. He is the author of a controversial volume *L'Apocalypse de saint Jean: Vision chrétienne de l'histoire* (Paris:

of Le Saulchoir, came to be described as the "Three Musketeers" and met in Rome during the Second Vatican Council.

What the school of Le Saulchoir was to the Dominicans, the school of Fourvière[171] was to the Jesuits, who had a university run by a community of the Society of Jesus in nearby Lyons. The environment of Lyons-Fourvière, was influenced especially by the teaching of Father Auguste Valensin,[172] professor of philosophy in Lyons from 1929 to 1934, a disciple of Blondel and a friend of another prominent figure, who exercised a "hidden" influence in that period: the Jesuit Pierre Teilhard de Chardin.[173] Director of many scientific expeditions and missions and author of many writings, Teilhard had never had permission during his life to publish his works, in which he outlined a philosophical and religious concept incompatible with Christianity. In 1926 he had been suspended from teaching, and the following year the Holy See refused to give the *imprimatur* to his book *Le milieu divin*. In 1933 Rome ordered him to leave Paris, and in 1939 his book *L'énergie humaine* was put on the Index by the Holy Office. "return to the bible" and "renewal of patristic theology" were the slogans used against scholasticism by the Jesuits of Fourvière. Central to their thinking was not a "return to the Church fathers", but rather a theological anthropology based on the philosophy of Blondel and influenced by Teilhard de Chardin.[174]

Correa, 1943). About him, see *Nouvelle théologie*, 57–60.

[171] Cf. E. Fouilloux, "Une 'école de Fourvière'?" in *Gregorianum* 83 (2002): 451–459; Dominique Avon, "Une école théologique à Fourvière," in *Les jésuites à Lyon XVIe-XXe siècle*, ed. E. Fouilloux, Bernard Hours (Lyons: ENS Éditions, 2005), 231–246.

[172] Auguste Valensin (1879–1953), Franch Jesuit, ordained in 1910. Professor of philosophy on the Catholic faculty of Lyons from 1920 to 1934.

[173] Pierre Teilhard de Chardin (1881–1955), French Jesuit, ordained in 1911, scholar of paleontology and the natural sciences, repeatedly censured by the Holy See for his heterodox theses. Cf. Rosino Gibellini, *Teilhard de Chardin: L'opera e le interpretazioni* (Brescia: Queriniana, 1981), with bibliography. On his relations with Blondel, see Christian d'Armagnac, "De Blondel à Teilhard: Nature et intériorité," in *Archives de Philosophie* 21/2 (1958): 298–312; Paul-Henri Coutagne, "Le problème de l'*Action* chez Teilhard et Blondel," in *Maurice Blondel: Une dramatique de la modernité*, Acts of the colloquium in Aix-en-Provence (March 1989), ed. Dominique Folscheid (Paris: Éditions Universitaires, 1990), 188–200.

[174] Another Blondellian like de Lubac was Fr. Henri Bouillard, S.J. (1908–1981), whose work *Conversion et grâce chez saint Thomas d'Aquin* (1944) was among the factors precipitating the polemic about the *"nouvelle théologie"* (M. Pesce, "Un 'bruit absurde,'" *op. cit.*, 306).

The thinker who most directly continued the work of Blondel and Teilhard was Father Henri de Lubac[175] of the Society of Jesus. De Lubac had begun his studies in England and had concluded them in 1928 in Lyons, where he had been named professor of fundamental theology. In the early 1920s he had become acquainted with Teilhard, who decisively influenced his thinking, and he acknowledged in his formation a particular debt to Blondel and Maréchal[176]. Hans Urs von Balthasar, who belonged to the same school, sees in the triad Blondel-Maréchal-de Lubac the "three martyrs of truth"[177] of that time.

Father Jean Daniélou[178], a student of de Lubac at Fourvière, in an extensive programmatic article that appeared in 1946 in the magazine *Études* under the title *"Les orientations présentes de la pensée religieuse"* ["Current trends in religious thought"], discredited, in turn, the philosophy of Thomas

---

[175] Henri de Lubac (1896–1991) entered the Society of Jesus in 1913 and was ordained in 1927. Professor of theology in Lyons, he was a consultor of the Preparatory Theological Commission, then *peritus*. Was created cardinal by John Paul II in 1983. About him cf. J. Guillet, in DHCJ, 2430–2432; Georges Chantraine, S.J., *Le cardinal Henri de Lubac: L'homme et l'oeuvre* (Paris: Lethielleux, 1983) and the volume cited below.

[176] "During my years of philosophy in Jersey (1920–1923), I had read passionately *Action*, the Letter (on apologetics), and various other studies by Maurice Blondel," Henri de Lubac testifies (*Mémoire sur l'occasion de mes écrits* [Paris: Cerf, 2006], 15; English edition *At the Service of the Church: Henri de Lubac Reflects on the Circumstances that Occasioned his Writings* [San Francisco: Ignatius Press, 1993]). About de Lubac's Blondellian approach to religious philosophy, see, among other studies, Antonio Russo, *Henri de Lubac: teologia e dogma nella storia: L'influsso di Blondel* (Rome: Studium, 1990); E. Fouilloux, *Une Église en quête de liberté, op. cit.*, 174–181; G. Moretto, *Destino dell'uomo e corpo mistico, op. cit.*; Gianfranco Coffele, *Apologetica e teologia fondamentale da Blondel a de Lubac* (Rome: Studium, 2004).

[177] Hans Urs von Balthasar, Henri de Lubac: Sein organisches Lebenswerk (Einsiedeln: Johannes Verlag, 1976); English translation The Theology of Henri de Lubac: An Overview (San Francisco: Ignatius Press, 1991). Hans Urs von Balthasar (1905-1998), Swiss theologian of the Society of Jesus, which he left in 1950. Created cardinal in 1988, but died before the consistory.

[178] Jean Daniélou (1905–1974), French Jesuit, ordained in 1938, professor of ancient history of Christianity at the Institut Catholique in Paris, conciliar *peritus*. Was created cardinal in 1969. In 1972 was elected a member of the Académie Française. It caused a sensation when he died unexpectedly on June 21, 1974, in the house of a Parisian prostitute. About him see Donato Valentini, *La teologia della storia nel pensiero di Jean Daniélou, con bibliografia generale dal 1936 al 1968* (Rome: Pontificia Università Lateranense, 1970); P. Duclos, in DHCJ, 1044–1046 with bibliography.

Aquinas, asserting that "the notion of history is foreign" to it, whereas, on the contrary, "the major patristic systems are founded precisely on it,"[179] and he looked forward to the day when contemporary theology would use psychology and religious phenomenology to recover the historical sense and contact with life. Moreover he described modernism as "an unfortunate expression of authentic needs,"[180] assigning responsibility for its birth to a "rupture between theology and life" within traditional Catholic thinking.

In 1942 de Lubac and Daniélou founded two series of volumes: *"Sources chrétiennes,"*[181] to promote the study of the fathers of the Church in implicit opposition to scholasticism, and *"Théologie,"* in which they proposed revisiting theological questions with the historical-critical method.

The publication, in 1938, of de Lubac's book *Catholicisme*, in the series *"Unam Sanctum"* edited by Father Congar, expressed the "fraternity" that linked the two most heterodox schools at the time: the Jesuit school of Fourvière and the Dominican school of Le Saulchoir. Nonetheless, while Chenu wanted to make Le Saulchoir the ideological school, de Lubac disputed the existence of "a mythical school of Fourvière."[182]

Corresponding to the "*nouvelle théologie*" was the idea of a "*nouvelle Chrétienté*" [new Christendom] developed during the same years by the French philosopher Jacques Maritain.[183] In the apostolic letter *Pervenuti all'anno vigesimoquinto* (1902),[184] Leo XIII traced the lines of the revolutionary

---

179 J. Daniélou, S.J., "Les orientations présentes de la pensée religieuse," in *Études* 249 (1946): 5–21 at 10.

180 Ibid., 7.

181 Cf. E. Fouilloux, *La collection "Sources chrétiennes": Éditer les Pères de l'Église au XXème siècle* (Paris: Cerf, 1995).

182 H. de Lubac, S.J., *Entretien autour de Vatican II* (Paris: Cerf, 1985), 12. For an abridged English translation, see *De Lubac: A Theologian Speaks* (Los Angeles: Twin Circle Pub. Co., 1985).

183 Jacques Maritain (1882–1973), disciple of the philosopher Henri Bergson, converted to Catholicism in 1906, together with his wife Raissa, an ethnically Russian Jew. After being close to *Action Française*, he parted ways with Maurras, touting himself as the new *maître à penser* [master thinker] of the Catholic world. After spending the war years in America, he was nominated French ambassador to the Holy See (1944–1948), only to return to America as a professor at the University of Princeton. About him see, *e.g.* Guillaume de Thieulloy, *Le chevalier de l'absolu: Jacques Maritain entre mystique et politique* (Paris: Gallimard, 2005).

184 Cf. Leo XIII, apostolic letter *Annum Ingressi* (March 19, 1902), marking the twenty-fifth

process that ran from protestantism, through the French Revolution, down to communism. The overturning of Leo XIII's philosophy of history came about with the work by Maritain, *Integral Humanism*[185] (1936), which had as much influence, above all on the laity, as *Action* by Blondel.[186] Father Meinvielle, in his book *De Lamennais à Maritain*, published in 1945, pointed out the almost verbatim coincidence between the "social Christianity" of Lamennais and the "new Christendom" of Maritain.[187] For Christian civilization, Maritain wanted to substitute a secular *civitas humana* understood as "a temporal regime or … an age of civilization whose animating form would be Christian and which would correspond to the historical climate of the epoch into which we are entering."[188] At the basis of this philosophy of history, which looked for a hypothetical "third way" between "the medieval conception" and the "liberal" one,[189] there was the deterministic thesis of the irreversibility of the modern world and

---

anniversary of his pontificate. English translation in *Papal Pronouncements: A Guide, 1740–1978*, 2 vols., ed. Claudia Carlen, IHM (The Pierian Press, 1990).

[185] Cf. J. Maritain, *Humanisme intégral: Problèmes temporels et spirituels d'une nouvelle chrétienté* (Paris: Aubier-Montaigne, 1936); reprinted in *Oeuvres complètes* (Fribourg: Éditions Universitaires, 1984), 6:293–642; English edition in *The Collected Works of Jacques Maritain*, ed. Ralph McInerny et. al., vol. 11, (Notre Dame, IN: University of Notre Dame Press, 1996), 143–345. Louis Salleron, in the *Revue Hebdomadaire* on August 22, 1936, (reprinted as "Humanisme intégral? M. Jacques Maritain, marxiste chrétien," in *L'Ordre Français* 176 [1973]: 11–24), as early as 1936 denounced Maritain's dialectic as "purely Marxist" (ibid., 21). For a critical analysis of the thought of the French philosopher, see also Julio Meinvielle, *De Lamennais à Maritain* (Buenos Aires: Theoria, 1945, 19672); Leopoldo Palacios, *El mito de la nueva cristianidad* (Madrid: Speiro, 1952); and the articles in *Civiltà Cattolica* by Antonio Messineo, S.J.: "Evoluzione storica e messaggio cristiano," q. 2433 (1952): 253–263; "Laicismo politico e dottrina cattolica," q. 2443 (1952): 18–28; and "Umanesimo integrale," q. 2549 (1956): 449–463.

[186] Cf. Jean-Hugues Soret, *Philosophes de l'Action catholique: Blondel-Maritain* (Paris: Cerf, 2007).

[187] J. Meinvielle, *De Lamennais à Maritain, op. cit.* "My book is entitled *From Lamennais to Maritain* and not *Lamennais and Maritain*," wrote Meinvielle to Fr. Garrigou-Lagrange, "because I do not want to compare the two men but rather point out that both men held exactly the same error that had been condemned in the last century" (J. Meinvielle, *Correspondance avec le R. P. Garrigou-Lagrange à propos de Lamennais et Maritain* [Buenos Aires: Nuestro Tiempo, 1947], 39).

[188] J. Maritain, *Integral Humanism, op. cit.*, 236 (see the fuller treatment on pages 233–284).

[189] Ibid., 261.

the Marxist postulate of "the historical role of the proletariat."[190] Despite Maritain's declared adherence to the principles of Thomism, his philosophy on history and his sociology converged with the neo-modernism that was flourishing among the young religious of the Jesuit and Dominican orders. In a letter to Maritain, Father Chenu mentioned the "profound shock" that he had experienced while reading Maritain's book, which from then on had constantly "nourished" him.[191]

Maritain had an enormous influence in Latin America, where he traveled for a series of conferences in the 1930s, in the United States, where he stayed from 1940 to 1945, and in Rome, where he served as the ambassador of France to the Vatican from 1945 to 1948.[192] One expression of the reversal of perspectives in the relationship between the Church and the world was the pastoral letter published by Cardinal Emmanuel Suhard, archbishop of Paris, during Lent of 1947. The cardinal interpreted the crisis of his own time as a crisis of youth and growth that collided with all the structures of the human order, and he foresaw a time of "day-break" for the Church.[193]

6. The ecumenical movement

The biblical-liturgical movement and the philosophical and theological tendencies merged into a broader "ecumenical" movement, which was also characterized by a strong anti-Roman sentiment. Unlike the preceding movements, ecumenism originated outside of the Catholic Church, specifically in the environment of the protestant missions, where the multiplicity of denominations created major problems in proselytizing.[194] The 1920 conference in Edinburgh was the beginning of two movements,

---

190 Ibid., 299–301.

191 Letter dated March 3, 1947, in P. Chenaux, *Paul VI et Maritain: Les rapports du "montinianisme" et du "maritainisme"* (Brescia: Studium, 1994), 80.

192 Cf. Roberto Fornasier, *Jacques Maritain Ambasciatore: La Francia, la Santa Sede e i problemi del dopoguerra* (Rome: Studium, 2010).

193 Cf. E. Suhard, *Essor ou déclin de l'Église* (Paris: Lahure, 1947). Emmanuel Célestin Suhard (1874–1949), ordained in 1897, bishop of Bayeux in 1928, archbishop of Reims from 1930 on, created cardinal in 1935, archbishop of Paris in 1940.

194 Cf. Ruth Rouse and Stephen C. Neil, *A History of the Ecumenical Movement*, 3 vols. (Philadelphia: Westminster Press, 1967–1970).

"Faith and Order" and "Life and Action," which resolved to seek the path to ecumenical union among the (protestant) churches in the areas of doctrine and action respectively. The Catholic Church never participated in these initiatives. On July 4, 1919, the Holy Office extended the prohibition by Pius IX (1864) against participating in "public or private conferences organized by non-Catholics, which aim to promote the union of all groups that call themselves Christian."[195]

Gradually, however, the protestant ecumenical aspirations made their way into the Catholic Church, finding one of their first exponents in Baron Friedrich von Hügel,[196] whose letters to his Anglican niece formed, as Georges Tavard writes, "a model of ecumenical correspondence."[197] Hügel was, as Loisy put it, an important "connecting agent"[198] among various circles and currents of modernism, "the intermediary link between German, English, and Italian society, between the ideas of the philosophy of action and those of historical immanence,"[199] but his initiatives did not have the authority of those promoted in Belgium during the 1920s.

Between 1921-26, at the initiative of Lord Halifax[200] and the French Vincentian Father Fernand Portal,[201] several unofficial meetings were held

---

[195] Decree *De Participatione catholicorum societati "ad procurandam christianitatis unitatem,"* in AAS 11 (1919): 309.

[196] Friedrich von Hügel (1852–1925), Austrian but born in Italy, was one of the key figures of modernism. About him see J. P. Whelan, article in DSp 7:852 ff., with an extensive bibliography; John J. Heaney, *The Modernist Crisis: Von Hügel* (London: G. Chapman, 1969); *Baron Friedrich von Hügel: Selected Letters, 1896–1924*, ed. Bernard Holland (London: Dent, 1928).

[197] Georges Tavard, *Petite histoire du mouvement oecuménique* (Paris: Éditions Fleurus, 1960), 159.

[198] Cf. Maurice Nédoncelle, *La pensée religieuse de Friedrich von Hügel* (Paris: Vrin, 1935), 14.

[199] Giuseppe Prezzolini, *Cos'è il modernismo* (Milan: Treves, 1908), 75.

[200] About Charles Lindley Wood, Lord Halifax (1839–1934), cf. John Gilbert Lockhart, *Charles Lindley Viscount Halifax*, 2 vols. (London: Geoffrey Bless, 1935–1936); J. Guitton, *Trois serviteurs de l'unité chrétienne: le P. Portal, lord Halifax, le cardinal Mercier* (Paris: Cerf, 1939); Albert Gratieux, *L'amitié au service de l'union: Lord Halifax et l'abbé Portal* (Paris: Bonne Presse, 1951).

[201] Fernand Portal (1855–1926), ordained in the Congregation of the Mission (Vincentians) in 1880, in 1908 left his position as superior of the university Seminary of Saint Vincent de Paul because he was suspected of modernism. Cf. F. Portal, *Refaire l'Église de toujours: Textes présentés par Régis Ladous* (Paris: Nouvelle Cité, 1977); Hyppolyte Hemmer, *M. Portal, prêtre de la Mission de Paris* (Paris: Bloud & Gay, 1947); Régis Ladous, *Monsieur Portal et les siens (1855–1926)*, preface by Emile Poulat (Paris: Cerf, 1985).

in Belgium between Catholics and Anglicans which came to be known as the "Malines Conversations," since those meetings took place in the residence of Cardinal Mercier who sponsored them.[202] Participating actively in these talks was Dom Lambert Beauduin, who, after having promoted the liturgical movement, embarked on the ecumenical movement, founding the Monastery of Chevetogne in Amay-sur-Meuse in Belgium in 1925. His monks would have to "de-Romanize" themselves and be open to the "dialogue" with the Anglicans and with the "Orthodox" schismatics.[203] The monastery's academic journal, with the significant title of *Irénikon*, was the hub for propagating these ideas. "The Malines Conversations left their mark on our generation," Cardinal Suenens recalls. "In the course of the meetings, Cardinal Mercier read the famous *Memorandum* on 'The Anglican Church, united but not absorbed,' written by Dom Lambert Beauduin, OSB, who later founded the ecumenical monastery of Amay."[204]

After a stay at Amay in 1932, Paul Couturier,[205] a priest from Lyons, discovered his "ecumenical vocation." In 1908, Lewis Wattson,[206] an Anglican convert to Catholicism, had popularized an "octave" of prayer for the return of the separated brethren to the Church. Father Couturier, after a stay at the abbey in Amay-sur-Meuse, decided to introduce into his community *The Octave for Unity*, the purpose being not to pray for the return of the

---

202 Cf. R. Aubert, "Les Conversations de Malines: Le Cardinal Mercier et le Saint-Siège," in *Bulletin de la Classe des Lettres et des Sciences Morales et Politiques* 3 (1967): 87–159, reprinted in *Le cardinal Mercier (1851–1926): Un prélat d'avant-garde*, Publications by Prof. Roger Aubert collected on the occasion of his 80th birthday, ed. Jean-Pierre Hendrickx, Jean Pirotte, and Luc Courtois (Louvain: Presses Universitaires de Louvain, 1994), 393–452; E. Fouilloux, *Les catholiques et l'unité chrétienne du XIXe au XXe siècle: Itinéraires européens d'expression française* (Paris: Le Centurion, 1982), 125–158.

203 Cf. L. Bouyer, *op. cit.*, 133–135.

204 L.-J. Suenens, *Memories and Hopes* (Dublin: Veritas, 1992), 73.

205 Paul Couturier (1881–1953), ordained in 1906, was one of the chief promoters of twentieth-century Catholic ecumenism. Cf. the apologetic biographies by Maurice Villain, *L'abbé Paul Couturier, apôtre de l'unité chrétienne* (Tournai: Casterman, 1957), and Pierre Michalon, *L'abbé Paul Couturier: Apôtre de l'unité chrétienne* (Paris: Nouvelle Cité, 2003).

206 Lewis Thomas Wattson (1863–1940). Son of an Episcopalian pastor and himself a pastor (as of 1886), founder of the Congregation of the Franciscan Friars of the Atonement, a protestant religious community dedicated to ecumenical activity. In 1909 he converted to Catholicism together with his community, which was recognized by the Holy See as a religious congregation; the following year he was ordained a priest.

separated brethren, as had been done in the Church until then, but rather to create a new spiritual "unity" among the various denominations: ecumenism was for him a "convergence" towards Christ, in whom all Christians would be able to meet, regardless of their church affiliation.[207]

The encylical by Pius XI, *Mortalium animos*, dated January 6, 1928,[208] which can be considered the pontifical act of greatest doctrinal importance since *Pascendi*, radically critiqued the false notions of unity of those who interpreted the Christ's words: "that all may be one.... there will be one fold and one shepherd" (John 17:21; 10:16) as if in these words "Christ Jesus merely expressed a desire and prayer, which still lacks its fulfillment."[209] Against the false ecumenism of the so-called "pan-Christians", Pius XI reaffirmed that "the union of Christians can only be promoted by promoting the return to the one true Church of Christ of those who are separated from it, for in the past they have unhappily left it. To the one true Church of Christ, we say, which is visible to all, and which is to remain, according to the will of its author, exactly the same as he instituted it."[210] Pius XI then recalled the clear affirmations of Lactantius: "The Catholic Church is alone in keeping the true worship. This is the fount of truth, this the house of faith, this the temple of God: if any man enter not here, or if any man go forth from it, he is a stranger to the hope of life and salvation."[211]

The research of Johan Ickx in the Secret Vatican Archives has shown that the encylical of Pius XI intended to attack not only the Malines Conversations between Catholics and Anglicans and the overtures to the Greek schismatics by Dom Beauduin, but also the birth of a "German High Church" which proposed to blend into one ecumenical church, the so-called three major Christian confessions: protestantism, Catholicism, and the Greek Orthodox Church.[212]

---

207 Cf. Sandro Spinauti, *Ecumenismo* (Rome: Centro "Ut unum sint," 1982), 59–63.

208 *Mortalium animos* are the first words of the encylical by Pius XI dated January 6, 1928, *De vera religionis unitate favenda* [On promoting true unity of religion] (AAS 20 [1928]: 5–16; EE 5:300–321), published a few months after the negative reply by the Congregation of the Holy Office to the *dubio* as to whether Catholics are allowed to participate in pan-Christian congresses (July 8, 1927, in AAS 19 [1927]: 278).

209 Pius XI, encylical letter *Mortalium animos, op. cit.*, 309.

210 Ibid., 317.

211 Lactantius, *Divinae Institutiones*, 4, 30, 11–12, cited in Pius XI, *Mortalium animos, op. cit.*, 319.

212 Cf. Johan Ickx, "L'enciclica 'Mortalium animos' (1928): sfide storiografiche in base al nuovo

In that same year, in 1928, Dom Beauduin was removed from his position as prior of the monastery in Amay and then transferred to the one in En-Calcat (France). The ecumenical movement within the Catholic Church followed other paths, however. In Paris some private meetings were held between Catholics, Orthodox, and protestants so as to seek common ground on theological and philosophical topics. The meetings revolved especially around the already prestigious figures of Jacques Maritain and Nicolai Berdyaev,[213] who starting in 1929 formed a French-Russian circle of interdenominational meetings.[214] Participating in the meetings was the young Dominican priest Yves Congar, who wrote two books based upon them: *Chrétiens désunis* (1937)[215] and *Esquisses du mystère de l'Eglise* (1941).[216]

Chrétiens désunis, the first volume in a new series "Unam Sanctam", founded by the Parisian publishing house du Cerf, proposed a new "Catholic ecumenism" which cleverly mixed propositions that in and of themselves were orthodox (that the dissident churches have preserved some principles of the true Church, and souls can be sanctified within those denominations, despite them) with others that were obviously

materiale archivistico della Santa Sede," in *La sollecitudine ecclesiale di Pio XI alla luce delle nuove fonti archivistiche,* Acts of the International Study Congress, Vatican City, February 26–28, 2009, ed. C. Semeraro (Vatican City: Libreria Editrice Vaticana, 2010), 320–327.

[213] Nicolai Berdyaev (1874–1948) had founded the Saint Sergius Institute in Paris with Sergei Bulgakov (1871–1944) and Semen Frank (1877–1950), where "orthodoxy" was reinterpreted in a mystical-pantheistic key. Cf. Olivier Clément, *Berdaijev: un philosophe russe en France* (Paris: Olivier Clément Publisher, 1991).

[214] Cf. Catherine Gousseff, "Une intelligentsia chrétienne en exil: les orthodoxes russes dans la Frances des années 20," in *Intellectuels chrétiens et esprits des années 1920,* ed. Pierre Colin (Paris: Cerf, 1997), 115–138; Antonella Cavazza, "L'idea di 'sobornost' da A. S. Chomjakov al Concilio Vaticano II: Messa a fuoco del problema," in *Vatican II in Moscow,* 129–144 at 130–132; see also J. Famerée, *L'ecclésiologie d'Yves Congar avant Vatican II: histoire et Église: Analyse et reprise critique* (Louvain: Presses Universitaires de Louvain, 1992).

[215] Cf. Y. Congar, O.P., *Chrétiens désunis: Principes d'un oecuménisme catholique* (Paris: Cerf, 1937); English edition: *Divided Christendom: a Catholic study of the problem of reunion* (London: G. Bles, 1939).

[216] Cf. Y. Congar, O.P., *Esquisses du mystère de l'Église* (Paris: Cerf, 1941); printed in English together with another volume by the same author as *The Mystery of the Church: Studies by Yves Congar* (Baltimore: Helicon Press, 1960).

heterodox (the separated churches *are* true churches, although not to the same extent as the Catholic Church, and one can be sanctified in them and *because of them*).[217]

In 1932 Congar had met and struck up relationships with Fr. Couturier and Dom Beauduin.[218] "Fr. Couturier," Congar recalls, "developed in me a vision of a church of inspiration that had a rather Bergsonian inspiration: there was within the Church an impulse of life; there was something that corresponded to matter, interpreted as 'fallen spirit.'"[219] Couturier's "evolutionist" vision, which fascinated Congar, is not surprising, given that Couturier himself was an outspoken admirer of Teilhard de Chardin, at whose wellspring he nourished his ecumenism.[220] Congar became a frequent visitor to the monastery in Chevetogne, which from the 1940s on was a center for "ecumenical days" organized above all by Dom Olivier Rousseau.[221] The Catholic ecumenists of the forties and fifties claimed to extend the concept of the Mystical Body to all the Christian churches, intending it in the broad and "pneumatic" sense, regardless of the legal and institutional dimension of the Catholic Church.[222] Congar, in particular, was influenced by the German theologian Johann-Adam Möhler,[223] whose

---

217 Cf. Claude Barthe, *Trouvera-t-il encore la foi sur la terre? Une crise de l'Église, histoire et questions* (Paris: François-Xavier de Guibert, 20063), 51–52.

218 Cf. Y. Congar, O.P., *Une passion: l'unité; Réflexions et souvenirs 1929–1973* (Paris: Cerf, 1974), 20–23.

219 Ibid., 23.

220 One of Couturier's favorite texts was *Le Milieu Divin* by Teilhard de Chardin, of which he distributed handwritten copies even before its publication. Cf. Teresa Burke, C.P., "The Abbé Paul Couturier, Pioneer of Spiritual Ecumenism," in *The Unity of Christians: the vision of Paul Couturier*, special issue of *The Messenger of the Catholic League* 280 (2003–2004): 1.

221 Olivier Rousseau (1898–1984), Belgian, monk of the Abbey of Chevetogne, editor of the review *Irénikon*. One of the participants in these meetings, Father Emmanuel Lanne, recalls for example, the 1945 conference on the concept of the "people of God" in ecclesiology, at which Charles Moeller, Gustave Thils, Yves Congar, and Jérôme Hamer spoke, all of whom were to be participants at Vatican II (E. Lanne, "Il ruolo del monastero di Chevetogne al Concilio Vaticano II," in *Cristianesimo nella storia* 27 [2006]: 517–518).

222 Cf. for example Erich Przywara, "Corpus Christi mysticum: Eine Bilanz," in *Zeitschrift für Aszese und Mystik* 15 (1940): 197–215.

223 Johann-Adam Möhler (1796–1838), German, ordained in 1819, professor of Apologetics and

major work *Die Einheit in der Kirche* [Unity in the Church] he published in French in 1938 in the series "Unam Sanctam." The book emphasized the role of the Holy Spirit as the vital principle of the Church, according to the principle that "the whole constitution of the Church is nothing other than embodied love."[224]

Among Couturier's disciples was also a young Swiss Calvinist, a student of theology, Roger Schutz,[225] who with his fellow student Max Thurian[226] founded the Taizé Community in 1949, not far from the ruins of the Benedictine Abbey of Cluny, in France.[227] Through the apostolic nuncio in Paris, Archbishop Roncalli, they obtained authorization from the Holy See to celebrate their liturgies in the Catholic Church in the little village of Taizé, which had been closed since the French Revolution, thus inaugurating a new "ecumenical" liturgy.

Pius XII in *Orientalis Ecclesia*, dated April 9, 1944,[228] stressed that there is only one path to unity: return to the one, true, visible Church of Christ, which is the Roman Catholic Church. The Instruction *Ecclesia Catholica* of the Sacred Congregation of the Holy Office, dated December 20, 1949, recommended that the clergy "avoid allowing Catholic teaching (whether dogma or truth connected with dogma) to become conformed with or accommodated to the teachings of the dissidents, for the sake of a so-called 'irenic' spirit, to such an extent…that the fullness of Catholic doctrine

---

Church History in Tübingen and Munich. His greatest work is *Die Einheit in der Kirche oder das Prinzip des Katholizismus dargestellt im Geiste der Kirchenväter der drei ersten Jahrhunderte* 1825); English edition *Unity in the Church, or The Principle of Catholicism, Presented in the Spirit of the Church Fathers of the First Three Centuries*, translated and edited by Peter C. Erb (Washington, D.C.: Catholic University of America Press, 1996). About him see the article by Harald Wagner in TRE 23:140–143 with bibliography.

[224] J. A. Möhler, *L'Unité dans l'Église* (Paris: Cerf, 1938), 206. See also Philippe Bourrat, "Ce que Lumen gentium doit à Möhler," in *L'unité spirituelle du genre humain*, 65–89.

[225] Roger Schutz (1915–2005), Swiss Reformed pastor, founder and prior of the Ecumenical Community of Taizé. Guest of the Secrtariat for Promoting Christian Unity at Vatican Council II.

[226] Max Thurian (1921–1996), Swiss Reformed pastor, vice-prior of the Community of Taizé. Guest of the Secretariat for Promoting Christian Unity at the Council, was ordained a priest of the Catholic Church in 1987.

[227] Cf. Y. Chiron, *Frère Roger*, (Paris: Perrin, 2008); 64–65.

[228] Cf. Pius XII, encylical letter *Orientalis Ecclesia*, in DRM 6:325–340.

suffers and its genuine and certain meaning is obscured."[229] Opposed to this perspective was the vision of the various protestant currents which, after having joined together at the pan-Christian assembly in Amsterdam, gave birth in 1948 to the World Council of Churches (WCC). In July 1950, in Toronto, the WCC drew up an "ecumenical paper" which presupposed the idea of an "ecumenical church" that resulted from overcoming the individual Christian denominations, none of which, alone, possessed truth in its entirety.[230] Hence the eschatological conception of a Church as "people of God" journeying toward full unity in a future Church which would be the synthesis of all the present denominational churches. The aspirations of protestant ecumenism were welcomed sympathetically in *"nouvelle théologie"* circles, which were inclined to relativism and historicism. These tendencies were reinforced by a psychological attitude that dominated secular and Catholic intellectual circles that had an unconditional trust in the idea of "progress."

7. A secret society inside the Church?

We have attempted to trace the main lines of the ferment of ideologies that were developing within the Church in an apparently spontaneous manner, without order or direction, as had already occurred during the era of modernism. St. Pius X, however, with the encylical *Pascendi*, had endeavored to reduce *ad unum* [to one principle] the volcanic movement that was spreading right before his eyes. Three years after *Pascendi*, in the motu proprio *Sacrorum antistitum* dated September 1, 1910, he had also advanced the hypothesis that the movement had a unified underground organization, so as to form a veritable "secret society" within the Church:

> We think that no bishop is unaware that that most crafty class of men, the modernists, although unmasked by the encylical letter *Pascendi dominici gregis*, has not renounced their plans to disturb the peace in the Church. *Indeed, they have not ceased to ensnare new associates and to admit them to their clandestine group, and with them to inject into the veins of Christian society the poison of their opinions, by means of*

[229] Suprema Sancta Congregatio Sancti Officii, Instructio *De motione ecumenica* (December 20, 1949), in AAS 42 (1950): 142–147 at 143.

[230] Cf. Maurizio Gordillo, "Ecumenismo" in EC 5:63–65 at 63.

> *books and commentaries published anonymously or under assumed names.* If you consider attentively this height of audacity which has caused Us such great sorrow, after rereading Our aforementioned letter, it will readily appear that men of this sort are none other than those described therein, enemies who are the more to be feared the closer they are, abusing their ministry and putting poisoned food on hooks to waylay the unwary, circulating their specious doctrine that contains the summary of all errors.[231]

The words of St. Pius X do not appear exaggerated to the historian. Secrecy and dissimulation in fact characterized the modernists, as it had happened before with the Italian heretics of the 1500s.[232] "Knowing how to conceal one's own artillery is one of the essential principless of modern warfare. It was also one of the distinctive characteristics of the modernist movement: combining direct attacks against dogmas with the utmost variety of subterfuges," observed Jean Rivière,[233] recalling the advice given from his deathbed by Fogazzaro's fictional "saint": "Never publish writings about difficult religious question in order to sell them, but rather distribute them prudently, and never put your name on them."[234]

"The frequent duplicity of the modernists," writes Fogazzaro's biographer, Tommaso Gallarati Scotti, "is one of the dark sides on which future history will have to pass judgment. The mere phenomenon of anonymity certainly does not appear in a sympathetic light to the impartial eye. This is because a man does not disguise his name without profound humiliation, yet modernism tolerated this deceit in its most complex forms. The movement, which wanted to be a great purifying breath of fresh air in the Church, a reaffirmation of manly sincerity as opposed to corrupt ecclesiasticism,

---

231 Pius X, motu proprio *Sacrorum antistitum, op. cit.*, 655. The sentence printed in italics, which in Latin reads: *"Haud enim intermiserunt novos aucupari et in clandestinum foedus ascire socios, cum iisque in christianae reipublicae venas opinionum suarum virus inserere, editis libris commentariisque suppresso aut mentito scriptorum nomine,"* was deleted from the Italian translation of the text published by Ugo Bellocchi, in Bellocchi, vol. VII, *San Pio X (1903–1914)*, 415–441 at 425.

232 Cf. Delio Cantimori, *Umanesimo e religione nel rinascimento* (Turin: Einaudi, 1980), 207–208; Carlo Ginzburg, *Il nicodemismo: Simulazione e dissimulazione religiosa nell'Europa del '500* (Turin: Einaudi, 1970); R. de Mattei, *A sinistra di Lutero, op. cit.*, 84–85.

233 Cf. Jean Rivière, *Le modernisme dans l'Église* (Paris: Letouzey et Ané, 1929), 484–485.

234 Antonio Fogazzaro, *Il Santo* (Milan: Mondadori, 1941), 282.

adapted itself to these forms of worldly prudence whereby it was thought possible and permissible to be two contradictory things."[235]

With regard to the condemnation contained in *Pascendi*, the modernists' attitude was similar to that of the Jansenists in the aftermath of the condemnation of Jansen's propositions and the papal Bull *Unigenitus* of 1713: they denied that the condemned propositions applied to them, asserting that the modernism condemned in the encylical was a figment of the imagination.[236]

An "insider" like the French ex-Benedictine Albert Houtin, in describing the plan of modernism, foresaw that the innovators would not leave the Church, not even if they had lost the faith, but would remain as long as possible to propagate their ideas.[237] "It is in this sense that it was agreed around 1903 and was still written in 1911, that no true modernist, whether layman or priest, would be able to abandon the Church or thc cassock, because otherwise he would then cease to be a modernist in the lofty sense of the term";[238] "at the same time as the *Delenda Carthago* ['Carthage must be destroyed', an ancient Roman political slogan], why not carry out the *Dissolvenda* ['It must be dissolved']?"[239]

"Until now," Ernesto Buonaiuti explained in turn, "they wanted to reform Rome without Rome, or even against Rome. Rome needs to be reformed with Rome; they have to act so that the reform passes through the hands of those who need to be reformed. This is the true and infallible method; but it is difficult. *Hic opus, hic labor* [This is laborious work]."[240] From this perspective, modernism proposed to

---

[235] Tommaso Gallarati Scotti, *Vita di Antonio Fogazzaro* (Milan: Baldini e Castoldi, 1920), 496–497; the passage is quoted also by E. Poulat in his *Histoire, dogme et critique de la crise moderniste* (Paris: Casterman, 1962), 621.

[236] Buonaiuti accepts the parallel and speaks about "a certain close correspondence that upon objective examination reveals that the two movements are connected as ideas more than one might be led to think at first glance" (E. Buonaiuti, *Storia del cristianesimo* [Milan: Dall'Oglio, 1943], 3:617).

[237] Cf. Albert Houtin (1867–1926), *Histoire du Modernisme catholique* (Paris, self-published, 1913), 116–117.

[238] Ibid., 122.

[239] Ibid., 116.

[240] Cf. E. Buonaiuti, *Il modernismo cattolico* (Modena: Guanda, 1943), 128.

transform Catholicism from within, leaving intact, as much as possible, the external trappings of the Church. "The external worship," Buonaiuti continues, "will last forever like the hierarchy, but the Church, as the teacher of the sacraments and of her sacred orders, will modify her hierarchy and her worship according to the times: she will make it simpler, freer, and thus more spiritual; that way she will become a form of protestantism; but an orthodox protestantism that is gradual and not violent, aggressive, revolutionary, or insubordinate; a protestantism that will not destroy the apostolic continuity of ecclesiastical ministry or the very essence of worship."[241]

"Rome," George Tyrrell had asserted, "cannot be destroyed in a day, but it is necessary to make it fall into dust and ashes gradually and inoffensively; then we will have a new religion and a new decalogue."[242]

The existence of this underground stream that flowed in the Church was confirmed in 1978 when a hitherto unknown document was published, entitled *Out of the Depths: The Testament of Faith of Don Primo Vannutelli*, a Roman priest who died in Rome on April 9, 1945,[243] in the community of the Oratorian Fathers. Don Vannutelli, after having been a modernist, had officially "rejoined the ranks" by taking the prescribed anti-modernist oath. According to the executor of his will, Francesco Gabrieli, "his place is among those modernists who remained in the Church after the condemnation, who submitted to her discipline while keeping their inmost convictions in their heart...."[244] Listening to this voice coming from underground and comparing it to the Nicene Creed, the whole edifice of the faith "crumbles," according to Gabrieli: "the divine filiation [sonship] of Jesus, his virgin birth, his miracles, his resurrection,

---

241 Ibid., 130.

242 G. Tyrrell, *Lettres de Georges Tyrrell à Henri Brémond, op. cit.*, 287.

243 "Il testamento di fede di don Primo Vannutelli," ed. Francesco Gabriele, in Centro Studi per la Storia del Modernismo, *Fonti e Documenti* 7 (1978): 119–253. Don Primo Vannutelli (1885–1945) came from a family that had already given two cardinals to the Church in his brothers Serafino (1834–1915) and Vincenzo (1836–1930). Ordained in 1909, he lived until his death with the Oratorians of St. Philip Neri at the Chiesa Nuova in Rome. Cf. Federico Battistretta, *Trittico eretico: Sentieri interrotti del Novecento religioso: Ernesto Buonaiuti, Primo Vannutelli, Ferdinando Tartaglia* (Novara-Milan: Millenia, 2005), and F. Ricossa, "Un 'profeta' modernista: Il testamento di don Primo Vannutelli," in *Solidatium* 64 (2010): 14–22.

244 Presentation by F. Gabrieli, in "Il testamento di Fede," *op. cit.*, 125.

the Trinity.... The dogmatic structure of Christianity, or at least Roman Catholicism, goes to pieces as a result...."[245]

Don Primo Vannutelli articulates his profession in the new Church as follows:

> Careful studies conducted for centuries, by men of many nations, with various mentalities, including several by your sons, have shown that according the older gospels Jesus did not know that he was the *Logos* of God, was God with the Father, and had been so before the creation of the world. In those accounts Jesus never gives himself these titles. He was a great prophet, the servant and son of God, sent to do a great work, but was not fortunate like Moses or Muhammad, or Francis of Assisi: when he was alive, his people were expecting a Messiah.... It does appear that Jesus himself considered himself the Messiah: but he never said that he was the *Logos* of God, God co-equal with the Father.
>
> And if someone who reads these pages were to ask me: 'What remains then of Christianity, if Jesus is not God?', I would tell him right away: "Very little remains: God, and the longing and joy of the universe." "But then, what will distinguish a Christian from a Jew and from a Muslim now?" Would you be saddened if nothing really distinguished us? If in the Father's love we were all of one mind and one heart? If, with all the causes of discord among men, we did not add what ought to be the cause of love? If the truth, which is one, were to unite us?[246]

While denying the divinity of Christ and the divine constitution of the Church, the Roman priest theorized that it was necessary not to leave it, patiently awaiting its inevitable historical transformation. The means of furthering this process were, for him, freedom of discussion and of research and change in the liturgy. The reform, in order to be radical, "would have to be reform of the rites, not openly of the dogmas."[247]

Primo Vannutelli had remained an unbeliever who performed his ministry in one of the most beautiful churches in Rome, the new Church, where he lived completely in harmony with Father Giulio, the future Cardinal

---

245 Ibid., 124.

246 Ibid., 244–245, 246, 247.

247 Ibid., 251.

Bevilacqua, and Father Caresana,[248] superior general of the congregation, without anyone noticing his duplicity.

It is legitimate to ask whether the movement attacked by St. Pius X remained inactive after the death of the pope or instead tried to regroup under the shadow of the "Third Party" that guided the destiny of the twentieth-century Church during the twenties and thirties.[249] What is certain is that during those same years, while new heterodox tendencies were developing in all areas of Catholic doctrine, anti-modernism disappeared and there was no reaction to counteract the errors that were being propagated in the Church. Modernism survived but anti-modernism dissolved in the illusion that the worst had been overcome. The voices of denunciation and alarm were rare and isolated, often dismissed haughtily as remnants of "integrism," even during the pontificate of Pius XII, which was much less "repressive" than one might imagine. This is why we propose to highlight some of these voices of alarm coming from different cultural and geographic areas during a fifteen-year time span, but sharing the same love for the Roman Church.

---

[248] Paolo Caresana (1882–1973), Oratorian, was from 1934 until 1958 confessor of Giovanni Battista Montini and his spiritual director (cf. the correspondence: P. Caresana – G. B. Montini, *Lettere: 1915–1973*, ed. Xenio Toscani [Rome: Studium, 1998], which also reveals Monsignor Montini's ties with Don Primo Vannutelli, 113–115).

[249] Historians ignore the problem raised by St. Pius X and present modernism as a current of thought that sprang up spontaneously from the unstoppable course of history. Anyone who takes seriously the pontiff's words can do no less than to ask himself the question that Jean Madiran raises: "On what date did the secret association of modernists cease to exist? One cannot even ask whether by chance it was not later 'reconstituted'; in order to 'be reconstituted' it must have ceased to exist: but no one knows whether and when it was dissolved. But not only does everyone not know the answer; they pretend to be unaware of the question" (J. Madiran, *L'intégrisme, op. cit.*, 250, and more generally, 247–277).

8. The reactions to neo-modernism during the pontificate of Pius XII

a) Plinio Corrêa de Oliveira: in defense of Catholic Action

With regard to the new heterodox tendencies that were beginning to spread in the Church, the first cry of alarm came unexpectedly from Latin America, where progressivism had arrived during the thirties via the central European liturgical movement[250] when a Benedictine monk from Germany, Martin Michler,[251] had started his liturgical apostolate in conjunction with Brazilian Catholic Action.[252]

In Brazil, Plinio Corrêa de Oliveira,[253] who was a little more than thirty years old, was the most visible representative of the catholic movement.

---

[250] Cf. José Ariovaldo da Silva, O.F.M., *O Movimento litúrgico no Brasil* (Petrópolis: Editora Vozes, 1983); see also Clemente Isnard, O.S.B., "Reminiscências para a História do Movimento litúrgico no Brasil," appendix in B. Botte, O.S.B., *O Movimento litúrgico: Testemunho e recordações* (San Paolo: Edicões Paulinas, 1978), 208–209.

[251] Dom Martin Michler (1901–1969) was a Benedictine at Neusheim, at Maria Laach, and at San Anselmo in Rome, and was thus influenced by Romano Guardini, and also by Dom Beauduin and Dom Odo Casel. Cf. J. A. da Silva, O.F.M., *op. cit.*, 40–58; Clemente Isnard, O.S.B., "O papel de dom Martin Michler no Movimento Carólico brasileiro," in *A Ordem* 36 (1946): 535–545.

[252] On July 11, 1933, the first dialogue Mass was celebrated *versus populum* in Brazil. Cf. J. A. da Silva, O.F.M., *op. cit.*, 41–42 and C. Isnard, O.S.B., "Reminiscências," *op. cit.*, who recalls "in the main hall, he [Dom Michler] prepared an altar for the celebration of Mass. But, to our great surprise, instead of placing the table against the wall, he put in the middle of the hall and arranged a semicircle of chairs, saying that he was about to celebrate facing us. It was the first Mass celebrated in Brazil facing the people!" (218).

[253] Plinio Corrêa de Oliveira (1908–1995), Brazilian, historian and man of action, deputy to the Constitutional Assembly (1933), professor of Modern and Contemporary History at the University of Sao Paulo, editor of the weekly newspaper *O Legionario* (1933–1947), founder in 1960 of the *Sociedade Brasileira de Defesa da Tradição, Familia e Propiedade* [Society for the Defense of Tradition, Family and Property, "TFP"], which then spread throughout the world. About him see R. de Mattei, *The Crusader of the Twentieth Century: Plinio Corrêa de Oliveira*, with a preface by His Eminence Alfons Maria Cardinal Sticker, S.D.B. (Trowbridge: Cromwell Press, 1998). See also Various Authors, *Plinio Corrêa de Oliveira dez anos depois…*, Associação dos Fundadores da TFP (Sao Paulo, 2005); M. Introvigne, *Una battaglia nella notte, op. cit.*, and the doctoral thesis of Rodrigo Coppe Caldeira, *O influxo ultramondano no Brasil: O pensamento de Plinio Corrêa de Oliveira* (Belo Horizonte, 2005).

In 1932, at the age of twenty-four, he had promoted the formation of the Catholic Electoral League and the following year had been elected on its slate to the Constitutional Assembly as its youngest deputy and the one with the most votes in the whole country. He edited the Catholic weekly *O Legionario* and in 1940 had been one of the founders of Catholic Action of Sao Paulo, of which he had been appointed president of the interdiocesan council. In June 1943 his book entitled *In Defense of Catholic Action*[254] was published with a preface by the nuncio, Benedetto Aloisi Masella,[255] and with the *imprimatur* of the Archdiocese of Sao Paulo. The work, divided into five parts, was the first thoroughgoing refutation of the deviations that were lurking within Catholic Action in Brazil and, upon reflection, in the world, especially with regard to the liturgy, spirituality, and methods of the apostolate and lay activity.[256]

From the viewpoint of the interior life, the liturgical ideas that were spreading seemed to include a "new asceticism," connected with a specific "grace of state-of-life" peculiar to Catholic Action. The liturgy, according to the new theses, would exert on the faithful a mechanical or magical action such as to render superfluous any effort at collaboration between man and God.[257] The more common devotional practices and any effort of the will, from an examination of conscience to making the Spiritual Exercises of Saint Ignatius, were systematically discouraged, because they were considered useless and outmoded. The origin of these errors, according to the author, was found in the spirit of independence and of pleasure-seeking that tried to liberate man from the burden of the sacrifices imposed by the work of sanctification: indeed, "with the spiritual battle eliminated, the life of a Christian appears to them as an uninterrupted series of spiritual pleasures and consolations."[258] Plinio Corrêa de Oliveira recorded in this regard the words of Pius XI in the letter *Magna equidem* dated August 2, 1924:

---

[254] Cf. P. Corrêa de Oliveira, *Em defesa de Ação Catolica* (Sao Paulo: Ave Maria, 1943).

[255] Benedetto Aloisi Masella (1879–1970), ordained in 1902, titular archbishop of Caesarea (1927) and apostolic nuncio in Brazil (1927–1945). Created cardinal in 1946.

[256] Cf. R. de Mattei, *The Crusader of the Twentieth Century, op. cit.*, 69–101.

[257] Cf. P. Corrêa de Oliveira, *Em defesa de Ação Catolica, op. cit.*, 94.

[258] Ibid., 97.

> The unrestrained desire for pleasure, by weakening the strength of the soul and corrupting morals, gradually destroys the conscience of duty. In fact today there is an increasing number of people who, attracted by the pleasures of the world, abhor nothing more strongly, nor avoid anything with greater attention, than the sufferings that arise or the voluntary afflictions of the body or soul and they normally behave, according to the words of the Apostle, as enemies of the cross of Christ. Now nobody can obtain eternal beatitude if he does not renounce himself, if he does not pick up his cross and follow Jesus Christ.
>
> [English transl. in R. de Mattei, *Crusader of the Twentieth Century, op. cit.*, 86].

At the end of a long list of points concerning deviations in the teachings and the mentalities in Catholic Action circles, Plinio Corrêa de Oliveira concluded:

> All of these are connected, proximately or remotely, to the following principles: a negation of the effects of original sin; the resulting concept of grace as the exclusive factor in the spiritual life; and a tendency to separate oneself from authority, in the hope that order will result from a free, vital and spontaneous combination of intellects and wills.[259]

The book was the first denunciation of progressivism which, although it originated in Europe, used Latin America as its "laboratory." Its publications contributed to the awakening of the slumbering majority and put them on guard against incipient progressivism. Its analysis was shared in Rome, so much so that in 1947 the two priests who had supported Plinio Corrêa de Oliveira, Father Geraldo de Proença Sigaud[260] and Don Antonio de Castro Mayer,[261] after having been "purged" by the Brazilian ecclesiastical

---

[259] Ibid., 337.

[260] Geraldo de Proença Sigaud (1909–1999), Brazilian, member of the Congregation of the Divine Word, earned a degree in theology at the Gregorian University in Rome, where he was ordained on March 12, 1932. On May 1, 1947, he was consecrated bishop of Jacarezinho in Paranà (1947–1961); then he was metropolitan archbishop of Diamantina (1961–1980), carrying out a variety of pastoral activities that made him well known throughout the country.

[261] Antonio de Castro Mayer (1904–1991), Brazilian, earned a degree in theology at the Gregorian University in Rome, where he was ordained on October 30, 1927. Assistant general of Catholic

hierarchy, were unexpectedly "promoted" by the Roman authorities: Father Sigaud was appointed bishop of Jacarezinho and Monsignor De Castro Mayer—coadjutor bishop with the right of succession of the bishop of Campos, whom he succeeded the following year. The two Brazilian bishops would play, in close collaboration with Plinio Corrêa de Oliveira, an important role in the future conciliar assembly.

b) Father Réginald Garrigou-Lagrange: where is the new theology going?

Father Réginald Garrigou-Lagrange,[262] a scholar of philosophy, theology, asceticism, and mysticism, was one of the keenest theological minds of his time. In 1909 he had been called to Rome by the master general of the Dominicans, Giacinto Cormier,[263] to teach at the International Angelicum College, which had just been founded, and there he lavishly devoted all his efforts until 1960, when he ended his academic activity and retired to the Dominican convent of Santa Sabina. In all his published work, Father Garrigou-Lagrange contrasts the reality notion of truth with that of pragmatism and evolutionism, which characterized the "philosophy of action." In 1946 an important article by him was published on the topic

Action of Sao Paulo (1940), then vicar general of the Archdiocese (1942–1943). On May 23, 1948 he was consecrated coadjutor bishop of Campos with the right of succession. He governed the Diocese of Campos as bishop until 1981. With Archbishop Marcel Lefebvre he participated in the episcopal consecrations in Ecône on June 30, 1988, whereby he incurred excommunication *latae sententiae*.

262 Réginald Garrigou-Lagrange (1877–1964), French Dominican, ordained in 1902, from 1909 to 1960 professor of theology at the Angelicum. Cf. the immense bibliography in *Angelicum* 42 (1965): 200–272. About him: Louis Jugnet, "Le Révérend Père Garrigou-Lagrange métaphysicien," in *La Pensée catholique* 91 (1964): 40–45; M. R. Gagnebet, O.P., "L'oeuvre du P. Garrigou-Lagrange: Itinéraire intellectuel et spirituel vers Dieu," in *La Pensée catholique* 98 (1965): 33–52; Innocenzo Colosio, O.P., "Il P. Maestro Réginald Garrigou-Lagrange: Ricordi personali di un discepolo," in *Rivista di Ascetica e Mistica* 9 (1964): 226–240; Benoît Lavaud, "Le Père Garrigou-Lagrange: in Memoriam," in *Revue Thomiste* 64 (1964): 181–192.

263 Giacinto Enrico Maria Cormier (1832–1916), Dominican, ordained in 1856, provincial of the order for France (1865–1878), from 1891 to 1896 he was the assistant of the master general for the French language and then procurator general under Master General Frühwirth (1896–1904). In the General Chapter of 1904 he succeeded him as master general. He was beatified by John Paul II in 1994.

"Where is the New Theology Leading Us?" in which he underscored the danger of the new definition of truth understood no longer as "conformity of the intellect to reality," but as "conformity of the mind to life."

> It is very dangerous to say: "Ideas change, the affirmation remains." If even the idea of truth is changing, the affirmations do not remain true in the same way, nor according to the same meaning. Then *the meaning of the councils* is no longer maintained, as one would have wished.
>
> Unfortunately, the new definition of the truth is spreading among those who forget what Pius X said: "We admonish professors to bear well in mind that they cannot set aside St. Thomas especially in metaphysical questions, without grave disadvantage. A small error in principle, says Aquinas, is a great error in conclusion" (encylical *Pascendi*). This is even more true if one disdains all metaphysics, all ontology, and tends to replace the philosophy of being with the philosophy of the phenomenon or of becoming or the philosophy of action.
>
> Is it not perhaps the new definition of truth that is offered in the new definition of theology? "Theology is no more than a spirituality or religious experience which has found its intellectual expression." And what are we to think about assertions such as these: "If theology can help us to understand spirituality, spirituality will, in turn, in many cases, explode our theological categories and will oblige us to formulate different types of theology.... For each great spirituality corresponded to a great theology." Does this mean that two theologies can be true, even if their fundamental theses are opposed and contradictory? The answer will be no if one keeps to the traditional definition of truth. The answer will be yes if one adopts the new definition of truth, conceived not in relation to reality and its immutable laws, but relative to different religious experiences. These definitions seek only to reconcile us to modernism....
>
> Whither the new theology? It returns to modernism. Because it accepted the proposition which was intrinsic to modernism: that of replacing, as if it were illusory, the traditional definition of truth: *adaequatio rei et intellectus* (the adequation of intellect and reality), with the subjective definition: *adequatio realis mentis et vitae* (the adequation of the real intellect and life).... The truth is no longer the conformity of judgment to extra-mental (objective) reality and its immutable laws, but the conformity of judgment to the exigencies of action, and of human life which is evolving continually. The philosophy of being or

> ontology is replaced by the philosophy of action, which defines truth no longer in terms of being but of action. Thus is modernism reprised: "Truth is no more immutable than man himself, inasmuch as it is evolves with him, in him, and through him (Denz. 2058)." Therefore Pius X said of the modernists, "they pervert the eternal concept of truth (Denz. 2080)."[264]

c) Monsignor Joseph Clifford Fenton: a "Roman" voice in the United States

In the United States, in the early forties, the voice that was most faithful to the Roman magisterium was that of Joseph Clifford Fenton,[265] a young theologian who in 1944 became editor-in-chief of *The American Ecclesiastical Review*, the academic journal of the Catholic University of America in Washington, D.C.

In 1943 the encylical *Mystici Corporis*[266] by Pius XII tried to put an end to the "ecclesiological Babel"[267] about the concept of the "Mystical Body," a notion that went back to Vatican Council I, but which the *"nouvelle théologie"* used as a crowbar to introduce a new "pneumatic" vision of the Church. Fenton, who was an excellent ecclesiologist, devoted many studies to the necessity of the Catholic Church in order to attain salvation[268] and

264 R. Garrigou Lagrange, O.P., "La nouvelle théologie où va-t-elle?" in *Angelicum* 23 (1946): 126–145 at 130–131, 143. English translation by *Catholic Family News* at http://cfnews.org/gg-newtheo.htm, emended.

265 Joseph Clifford Fenton (1906–1969), ordained in 1930, was professor of theology at the Catholic University of America and editor of *The American Ecclesiastical Review* (1944–1966). The Holy See showed great appreciation for his services, appointing him master of ceremonies (1951), honorary prelate (1954), and apostolic protonotary (1963). He was part of the Pontifical Roman Academy of Theology and was a consultor of the Congregation of Seminaries and Universities. He is credited, among other works, with an excellent study on ecclesiology: "Scholastic Definitions of the Catholic Church," in *The American Ecclesiastical Review* 111 (1944): 59–69, 131–145, 212–228.

266 Pius XII, encylical *Mystici Corporis* (June 29, 1943), in AAS 35 (1943): 200–248.

267 Cf. B. Gherardini, "L'enciclica *Mystici Corporis* (29 giugno 1943), in *L'eredità del Magistero di Pio XII*, ed. P. Chenaux (Rome: Lateran University Press-GBP, 2010), 203–217 at 204.

268 Cf. J. C. Fenton, "Extra Ecclesiam nulla salus," in *The American Ecclesiastical Review* 110 (1944):

to the problem of relations between church and state, which was very sensitive in the United States. On these topics, he came into conflict with Father John Courtney Murray,[269] a progressively oriented Jesuit from New York, who edited the journal *Theological Studies*. A follower of Maritain, Murray called into question the traditional principle *extra Ecclesiam nulla salus*[270] and cited the First Amendment of the American Constitution to justify religious liberty in church-state relations.[271]

The New York Jesuit established ties with Archbishop Montini, whom he knew in the fifties, while Fenton was greatly esteemed by Cardinal Ottaviani, who in 1960 called him to Rome as an expert of the Preparatory Theological Commission of Vatican II. The two theologians were almost exact contemporaries (Murray had been born in 1904, Fenton in 1906) and died, relatively young, at almost the same time (the former in 1967, the latter in 1969). They represented the two contrasting souls of American Catholicism.[272]

One of the basic themes that recur in Fenton's articles in *The American Ecclesiastical Review* during those years is a critique of those who sought

---

300–306; *Idem*, "The Meaning of the Church's Necessity for Salvation," *ibid.* 124 (1951): 124–143, 203–221, 290–302.

[269] John Courtney Murray (1904–1967), American Jesuit ordained in 1933. After studying in Rome he taught from 1937 until his death at Woodstock College and edited the journal *Theological Studies* (1942–1967). In 1955 he had had to stop writing about religious liberty on orders from Rome. The personal expert of Cardinal Spellman, he was appointed a *peritus* of the council during the second session. See the article "Murray" by W. J. Burghard, with bibliography, in DHCJ, 2774–2775, and Donald E. Pelotte, *John Courtney Murray: Theologian in conflict* (New York: Paulist, 1975), with a bibliography on Fenton and Murray; Dominique Gonnet, "L'apport de John Courtney Murray au schéma sur la liberté religieuse," in *Les Commissions conciliaires*, 205–215.

[270] "No salvation outside the Church." See the presentation of this principle made in 1907 by Father Édouard Hugon, O.P. (1867–1929), *Hors de l'Église, point de salut* (Clovis, reprinted 1995). For an "updated" discussion of the same principle, see "Giacomo Canobbio, *Nessuna salvezza fuori della Chiesa? Storia e senso di un controverso principio teologico* (Brescia: Queriniana, 2009).

[271] See for example "Contemporary Orientations of Catholic Thought on Church and State in the Light of History," in *Theological Studies* 10 (1949): 177–234.

[272] On the antithesis between the positions of Monsignor Fenton and Fr. Murray, cf. Michael Davies, *The Second Vatican Council and Religious Liberty* (Long Prairie, MN: The Neumann Press, 1992). The book is dedicated to the memory of Monsignor Fenton. See also Gerald P. Fogarty, "The Council Gets Underway," in HVT 2:69–106, esp. 91–93.

to exploit the encylical *Mystici Corporis* by Pius XII so as to develop the "charismatic" dimension of it. He wrote:

> The *funestus error* reproved by the sovereign pontiff exists in Catholic theological literature under the guise of teaching on the body and soul of the Church. Some authors have described the soul of the Catholic Church as an invisible, spiritual society, and then designated the existing and visible Church as the *body*, the counterpart of that soul. The invisible or spiritual Church is presented as a society of good men and women in a state of grace, bound together by ties of faith and charity. According to those who have used the distinction rejected in the *Mystici Corporis* this soul of the Church is a *society* which exists even outside the membership of the visible Church. It is distinct from the Church of which the Roman pontiff is the visible head, and yet it is in some way connected with it....
>
> The distinction condemned by the Holy Father is used ordinarily to explain the connection between non-Catholics who are saved and the Catholic Church. Such a connection must exist, since the Church is necessary for the attainment of the beatific vision. To obviate what seemed to them a difficulty, some writers postulated the existence of a social organism of men and women who possess charity. This invisible Church or soul of the Church was depicted as wider in extent than the visible society, distinct from it, yet in some manner belonging with it. The body and the soul were presented as parts of that universal Church to which a person had to belong in order to be saved.
>
> Once and for all, the *Mystici Corporis* has stigmatized such an hypothesis as erroneous. There is no Church of God in this world in any way distinct from the one visible society which Jesus Christ instituted during the days of his earthly sojourn, and which he placed under the supreme and visible direction of St. Peter and his successors. Furthermore there is no society in this world composed only and entirely of persons in the state of grace. The just on earth are not organized into any society, made up exclusively of their own number.[273]

Against the new "ecumenist" ecclesiologists, Fenton reiterated the classic

[273] J. C. Fenton, "The use of the terms Body and Soul with Reference to the Catholic Church," in *The American Ecclesiastical Review* 110 (1944): 48–57 at 48–49.

and unsurpassable definition of the Church by St. Robert Bellarmine in *De Ecclesia militante*:

> To our way of thinking, the Church is only one, not two, and this one true Church is the community of men gathered by their profession of the same Christian faith, and their communion in the same sacraments, under the government of legitimate pastors, especially of the one vicar of Christ on earth, the Roman pontiff.... The difference between our definition and all the others is that all the other definitions require internal virtues in order to determine that someone is in the Church, and they thereby make the true Church invisible; we, on the other hand, also believe that all the virtues are found in the Church (faith, hope, charity, and the rest), nevertheless, in order that someone may be said, in a certain way, to be a member of the true Church about which the scriptures speak, we do not think that any interior virtue is required, but only the external profession of faith and the communion of the sacraments—things that the senses can perceive. The Church is, indeed, a group of men as visible and palpable as is the group of the Roman people, or the Kingdom of France, or of the Republic of Venice.[274]

Monsignor Fenton realized that within the Church a decisive conflict was in the making between the heirs of modernism and those of the "integralism" of the era of St. Pius X. In 1949, commenting on the pastoral letter of Cardinal Suhard, Monsignor Fenton explained the nature of the two currents which, ten years later, would oppose each other at the council.

> An incautious reader of Cardinal Suhard's pastoral [letter] might possibly come to the dangerously false conclusion that modernism and integralism, as we know them, are two contrary false doctrines, the one, as it were, to the left, and the other to the right, of genuine Catholic teaching. Nothing, of course, could be farther from the truth. Modernism, in the technical language of Catholic doctrine, is the name applied to the definite series of errors condemned in the decree *Lamentabili sane exitu*, in the encyclical *Pascendi dominici gregis*,

---

[274] Robert Bellarmine, "De Ecclesia militante," in *De Controversiis*, chapters I and II (Naples: Giuliano, 1857), 2:73–75 at 75. [English translation from the Latin with reference to the Italian.]

> and in the motu proprio *Sacrorum antistitum*. Pope Pius X spoke of modernism as "a conglomeration of all the heresies.'"[275]
>
> Integralism, on the other hand, is essentially the teaching or the attitude of those who worked for the presentation of an integral Catholicism, of Catholic dogma set forth accurately and in its entirety. Most frequently the name of integralism was applied to the doctrine and the viewpoint of those Catholic writers who entered into controversy against the modernists during the first decade of the present century. Understood in this fashion, integralism was nothing else than the contradiction of heretical modernism. It was thus basically only the exposition of Catholic truth.[276]

Unlike modernism, and apart from possible exaggerations, integralism, Fenton emphasized, is not a heresy.

> We must not forget the fact that modernism, as such, is a definite heresy or collection of heretical teachings, while integralism, as such, is nothing of the sort. The true Catholic teaching is not to be found at any half-way point between the teachings of such as Tyrrell and Loisy and the doctrines of the Catholic authors who opposed them. In opposing the dicta condemned in the *Lamentabili*, the *Pascendi*, and the *Sacrorum antistitum*, the great Catholic authors of a generation ago were perfectly justified. If, as is usual in our own country, the name of integralism is applied to this specifically anti-modernistic teaching, then integralism is nothing more than a statement of Catholic truth, implied in a denial of errors which are incompatible with the divine message of the Catholic Church.[277]

Fenton and Murray would meet again to fight one last battle shortly before their death, in the council hall.

---

[275] *Pascendi, op. cit.*, par. 39. Cf. *Codicis iuris canonici fontes* (Vatican City: Typis Polyglottis Vaticanis, 1933), 3:713.

[276] "Two Currents in Contemporary Catholic Thought," in *The American Ecclesiastical Review* 119 (1948): 293–301 at 297.

[277] Ibid., 298.

d) Father José Antonio de Aldama: modernism has not disappeared

The Spanish Jesuit José Antonio de Aldama[278] was one of the most renowned Mariologists of the twentieth century. He belonged to a deeply Christian family, in which all his siblings consecrated themselves to God: Antonio María and Borja became Jesuits, whereas their two sisters became Daughters of the Sacred Heart. His parents, the Count of Aldama and the Marquesses of Ayala, decided to follow the same path: his father was ordained a priest in Granada on December 24, 1929, and the following day bestowed the habit of a Salesian nun on his wife in Siviglia; on January 5, 1930, he entered the Society of Jesus in Loyola, where he died one month later, assisted spiritually by his son, in whose presence he took his vows *"in articulo mortis"* [on the point of death].

Father de Aldama was a professor of dogmatic theology at the Gregorian University, the Pontifical University of Salamanca, and the theology faculty of Granada, of which he became the rector. In an incisive article that appeared in the theological review *Salmaticensis* in 1956, he drew a parallel between the attitude of Pius X toward modernism and that of XII toward the "new theology."

> There is a theological affinity between Pius X and Pius XII, a similarity in doctrinal comportment, a great similarity in their historical situations, which cause these two names and these two extremely keen figures to remain forever in the vital development of Catholic theology.[279] These two outstanding figures, who at the beginning and in the middle of the twentieth century immortalized the Chair of Saint Peter with their magisterium, are historically united in their valiant defense of the treasure of the faith and of the deposit of revelation, which was totally

[278] Padre José Antonio de Aldama (1903–1980), Spanish Jesuit, ordained in 1929, professor, then rector at the University of Granada; see his works *Virgo Mater: estudios de teología patrística* (Granada: Facultad de Teología de Granada, 1963); *De questione mariali in hodierna vita Ecclesiae* (Rome: Pontificia Academica Mariana Internationalis, 1964). About him, see Cándido Pozo, S.J., *El p. José Antonio de Aldama, s.j. como teólogo* (Granada: Facultad de Teología de Granada, 1980); *Idem*, "In memoriam," in *Scripta de Maria* 3 (1980): 11–30; Francisco de P. Sola, "En la paz de Cristo: P. J. De Aldama, Mariologo eminente," in *Ephemerides Mariologicae* 30 (1980): 253–258.

[279] Cf. J. A. de Aldama, S.J., "Pio XII y la teología nueva," in *Salmanticensis* 3, (1956): 303–320 at 303.

threatened, not in one truth or in one dogma, but in its entirety, in its ideological interpretation, in its rational foundations. Pius X raised his voice resoundingly against what he called "the collection of all heresies"; Pius XII raised his voice in no less resounding tones against the new opinions "that threaten to destroy the foundations of Catholic doctrine." In both cases it was not a matter of one particular error, there was no attack on one specific dogma. The dangers were decidedly greater, inasmuch as they pertained to the deposit of revelation itself and to its human exposition in dogma and theology.

Naturally we are alluding to modernism and to the new theology; to the encylical *Pascendi*, including the appended documents, and to the encylical *Humani generis*, with the various papal actions that prepared for it....[280]

Pius XII has described for us the doctrinal confusion of the thinkers who are far from the Church, allowing us to know their chief ideological orientations: an evolutionism that they claim to "extend to the origin of all things, ... boldly entertain[ing] the monistic and pantheistic theory that the whole world is subject to continuous evolution"; an existentialism that "neglects the immutable essence of things" and "is concerned only with the 'existence' of individual things" and "is either atheistic or at least disputes the value of metaphysical reasoning"; and an historicism that "attends only to events of human life, and razes the foundations of all truth and absolute law."

Amidst the agitation of these errors, Pius XII, supreme teacher and august custodian of the revealed deposit, has denounced in the promoters of the new theology their imprudent effort to assimilate our theological thought and to adapt it to their own. He too has spent himself in condemning this attempt to "express dogma in the terms of modern philosophy, whether of 'immanence' or of 'idealism,' or 'existentialism,' or of any other system." He too has unmasked the absurdity of believing, with an evolutionist and historicist notion of dogma, that "the mysteries of faith can never be expressed by notions that are adequately true, but only by so-called 'approximative' notions, always changeable, by which truth is indicated to a certain degree, but is also necessarily deformed.'"[281]

---

[280] Ibid., 304.

[281] Ibid., 311.

On this point the theologian from Granada critiqued the forecasts of one of his illustrious confrères, Father Léonce de Grandmaison,[282] who in 1923 had ruled out the possibility that the Church could ever go through a new modernist crisis. Grandmaison's judgment, according to Fr. de Aldama, was based on reasons which, "if they are reargued today in the historical presence of the new theology, seem to us to lead precisely to the opposite conclusion."

> According to Fr. Grandmaison the fact that the modernist errors are better known today prevents us from repeating them. Modernism was not the result of a rebellion, but came about based on the facts, as a result of the impact with the difficulties that the sciences, history, and exegesis presented for faith and theology. Theologians, defenseless with their superficial theology, full of the anxiety that prevailed, sensing the desires for independence and distrust toward the Church in an atmosphere saturated with evolutionism, were not able to control themselves and succumbed to the modernist temptation. The description is exactly right. But would it be forcing the issue to apply it to the creators of the new theology?
>
> Another decisive element diminishing the likelihood of a new modernism was, according to Fr. Grandmaison, the progress that religious education had recently achieved, setting itself on a par with the general education. He considered those who had begun seriously and who had really been fascinated by the scholastic teaching to be immune to the excessive and all-encompassing taste for what is modern that causes modernism. Exactly, once again. But this is precisely what was lacking and we saw it. Notwithstanding the recommendations by Pius X and Pius XI promoting scholasticism, he had not dedicated his studies and his attention to the theological circles nor to the difficulties of modernism, despite the enormous efforts of Leo XIII. And although our religious education has managed to advance to the point of reaching the level of the general education, it has not succeeded in becoming a religious education with solid foundations, precisely because it omitted the serious study of scholastic philosophy.
>
> What could be said about the final consideration that convinced Fr. Grandmaison to deny the probability of a new modernist crisis?

[282] Léonce de Grandmaison (1868–1927), French Jesuit, professor of theology, then editor of *Études* and founder of *Recherches de science religieuse*. About him see Jules Lebreton, *Le Père Léonce de Grandmaison* (Paris: Beauchesne, 1932).

> Is it true that, since Catholics have labored so much at the scientific study of the sources and of positive theology, young people seeking knowledge no longer have had to go to the sources fouled by heterodox writers, as they did during the modernist era? Are we not witnessing instead a concoction of ideas, concerns, and methods, in which the boundaries between the heterodox writers and the orthodox remain so blurred that they can be discerned only with difficulty?
>
> Given these facts, the considerations that Fr. Grandmaison expressed thirty years ago with good will and excessive optimism are evidently inconsistent with them. History does not seem to have proved him right. And history prevails.[283]

e) Father Antonio Messineo: the relation between modernism and progressivism

In the same year in which Father de Aldama was developing these lucid reflections, one of his confrères, Father Antonio Messineo,[284] in three articles published by *Civiltà Cattolica*, combined with equal acumen the state of mind and the doctrinal tendencies of the new theologians under the category of "progressivism," thus establishing their relation with modernism.[285] Father Messineo was a Sicilian Jesuit with a very lively intellect and a solid spirituality, who was part of the select group of editors *ad vitam* [for life] of *Civiltà Cattolica*, the review considered to be the

283 J. A. de Aldama, S.J., "Pio XII y la teología nueva," *op. cit.*, 316.

284 Antonio Messineo (1897–1978), of the Society of Jesus, ordained in 1930, was from 1931 until his death one of the best qualified writers for *Civiltà Cattolica* in the field of social sciences, morality, and international law. He represented the Holy See at the International Conference in Vienna (1968–1969). Among his works see *La nazione* (Rome: La Civiltà Cattolica, 1942), and *Il diritto internazionale nella dottrina cattolica* (Rome: La Civiltà Cattolica, 1942). About him, see Domenico Mondrone, S.J., "Ricordo del padre Antonio Messineo," in *Civiltà Cattolica* q. 4071 (1978): 468–473.

285 See *Civiltà Cattolica*: "Il progressismo contemporaneo," q. 2537 (1950): 494–506; "Lo storicismo progressista," q. 2541 (1956): 225–238; "Il provvidenzialismo progressista," q. 2543 (1956): 462–474. The series was completed by the compelling summary: "L'umanesimo e gli umanesimi," q. 2545 (1956): 17–29.

unofficial mouthpiece of the Holy See. The following lines certainly had the approval of Pius XII.

> Modern progressivism, if it is not essentially modernism with a new coat of varnish, can be compared very well to that current of thought, of which it seems to some people, perhaps not at all mistakenly, to be an offspring. Modernism claimed to renew dogma, while emptying it of its transcendent content, after having submerged it in the fluctuating waves of historicist relativism; it appealed to subjectivism and with the yardstick of feelings tried to establish the truth and to attain union with the divinity; it was altogether rationalistic and skeptical about the powers of reason and above all anti-authoritarian, and along these tracks it proceeded to a radical revision, destroying a whole past of glorious and fruitful doctrinal speculation, so as to adapt to so-called modern thought and to the supposed demands of contemporary intellectual progress. Progressivism, truly, carried imprinted upon itself some of the connotations just described. It is historicist…, believes in the unceasing evolution of the truth and of institutional forms, in which the life of the Church and civil social life is framed; it is rationalistic, humanitarian, and naturalistic, and claims, just as modernism did, to revise, from the ground up, the theoretical attitudes and the practical teachings that are the accumulated patrimony of a long series of years and of fruitful experiences in thought and in practice. In its statements it maintains a bearing of superior self-sufficiency, as the qualified, independent interpreter of the demands of the intellectual and social life of the present time, which supposedly only its own promoters understand fully, whereas the hierarchy and the teachers who still firmly adhere to the traditional positions are allegedly out of touch and, if not obtuse, at least misguided by a reactionary, deadening conservatism.
>
> The progressive knows, understands, judges by a criterion of his own, which then turns out to be nothing other than the fluctuating criterion of a relative truth, which varies in different periods of history, and for the present time is merely so-called modern thinking, modern society, modern spiritual tendencies, in a word: so-called modern progress. Hence it derives its name, which expresses both its tendency to adaptation thereto and the drive to proceed further in its reform of principles and practice, according to the guidelines set out by the same.[286]

---

[286] A. Messineo, "Il progressismo contemporaneo," *op. cit.*, 498–499.

Fr. Messineo moreover lucidly described the drift toward Marxism in Catholic progressivism.

> Not least among the features that characterize modern progressivism is its remarkable sympathy toward communism and Marxism in general. It is led to this not only by the irenicism that was mentioned earlier, and the resulting desire to enter into conversation with all the modern currents of thought, but also by an at least partially positive evaluation of the Marxist ideology. The eye of the progressive is invariably turned toward the left, because in the approaches of the currents that are aligned on that side, due to a visual handicap [*deformazione*] that has been confirmed in his mind, he believes that he is discovering contacts and resemblances with the approaches of his own religious creed and of his moral and social convictions.
>
> With regard to communism, the progressive deplores the materialistic substratum of the ideology on which its logically consistent atheism is based, but, having made this reservation that is indispensable in order to salvage the Christian faith, he accepts its postulates and makes them his own, not ruling out a possible collaboration in order to carry them out. Communism, he asserts, is from now on a force, a movement in history, a mainspring propelling modern society, and therefore it is necessary to value it for what it is and to reconcile Christian thinking with it. The Manichaean division, as it is called, between a world that is entirely bad and a world in which only good is to be found, must be overcome through mutual understanding, so as not to place ourselves outside the cycle of history and in order to smooth differences with peacemaking. The encounter is possible, he adds, around the nucleus of Christian values that communism also supposedly conveys, although they are deformed by its ideological superstructures.
>
> Therefore the progressive is the man of détente, a convinced supporter of the outstretched hand, a promoter of dialogue with Marxist currents of thought, when he is not an outright follower or supporter thereof, without however adhering to them as a fellow traveler, on account of some remaining split between his vision of the world and the one propagated by communism. Sometimes he does not dare to press on to those limits, but, while he rejects communism as such, in front of which he finds a barrier set up by the explicit teaching of the Church, he does not hesitate to regard other Marxist currents of thought as welcome allies, with which he would gladly walk together on the political and social plane.

> The strange thing is that, while progressivism claims to overcome the Manichaean distinction between communism, Marxism, and Christianity, by way of understanding and coexistence based on détente, it introduces this selfsame irreconcilable opposition between Christianity and those currents of thought that it brands with the contemptuous name of the reactionary right. In its view the principle of evil has been concentrated in the right, a dark pit of reactionary forces lying in ambush, into which he throws, with an irrevocable judgment, whatever is contrary to progressive ideas and tendencies.[287]

9. Between false reforms and true revolution

The pages that we have quoted, to which others could be added, demonstrate how, faced with the resurgence of modernism, there was no lack of worried voices to cry the alarm. Most of the shepherds of the Church, while faithful to orthodoxy, inclined however toward optimism. In the fifties, the Catholic Church found itself at an historical crossroads: World War II had been the tragic outcome of a process in which human society had drifted away from the religious and moral order—a process that Pius XII had denounced in his encylicals and his radio messages. The major alternative that the world now faced was either a return of societies to Christ or else a de-Christianization that would result in a catastrophe worse than the Second World War, because it would strike not the bodies of human beings but rather their souls. Indeed, Pius XII had warned, "at the head of the road which leads to the spiritual and moral bankruptcy of the present day stand the nefarious efforts of not a few to dethrone Christ; the abandonment of the law of truth which He proclaimed and of the law of love which is the life breath of his kingdom. In the recognition of the royal prerogatives of Christ and in the return of individuals and of society to the law of his truth and of his love lies the only way to salvation."[288]

In the Church solid doctrine was not lacking: the magisterium of Pius XII was an encyclopedic *corpus* [body of work] that embraced all areas of faith and morals, competently addressing scientific, technical, and

---

[287] Ibid., 503–505.

[288] Pius XII, encylical *Summi Pontificatus*, in DRM, 3:435–467 at 441.

professional questions.[289] Pope Pacelli had given impetus to the compilation of an Italian *Enciclopedia Cattolica* that included contributions from the leading specialists, offering a *summa* of doctrine and information that took its place alongside the great French *Dictionnaire de Théologie Catholique*.[290] To this teaching, which spread throughout the world from the See of Peter, magnificent ceremonies gave a splendor that was unprecedented in history. When the naves of Saint Peter's resounded with the chants of the liturgy according to the ancient Roman Rite and the pope, blessing the crowds, advanced in the basilica seated between feather fans on his portable throne, escorted by the noble guardsmen in their red uniforms, the imagination was stuck by the spectacle of the beauty of the truth.

Many errors, as we have seen, were lurking nevertheless within the Church. Modernism, during the pontificate of Pius X, had been engulfed, but it continued to run like an underground stream within the ecclesial body. The movements of biblical, liturgical, philosophical, and ecumenical "reform" that developed starting in the twenties formed a subterranean network that brewed beneath the surface.

During the years of the second post-war period of the twentieth century, after the tragedy of World War II, a spirit of hedonistic materialism was spreading and penetrated the Church herself. After so many sufferings, an illusion took hold on some men of the Church: the illusion that the moment had arrived to abandon the cross, which had been carried for too long a time, and to find relief in the words of peace and well-being pronounced by the world. The illusion that it was possible to bring about an earthly society, inspired by the world's values, was the chief temptation that presented itself to the clergy in the 1950s, while the pontificate of Pius XII was coming to a close. Furthermore, even when the pastors of the Church reaffirmed the traditional principles of faith and morals, their lives did not always conform to those principles. The Church needed

---

[289] Pius XII signed forty-three encylical letters, which deal with a wide variety of topics; equally important are his radio messages. Cf. EE 6 (2002). For an overall view of the Pacellian *corpus*, see J. Chelini, *L'Église sous Pie XII, op. cit.*, 2:158–224; Vitaliano Mattioli, *L'eredità di Pio XII* (Verona: Fede e Cultura, 2008); *L'eredità del Magistero di Pio XII*, ed. P. Chenaux, *op. cit.*

[290] The *Dictionnaire de Théologie Catholique* was started at the beginning of the twentieth century with Jean-Michel Alfred Vacant (1852–1901) as editor-in-chief, and continued under the direction of Eugène Mangenot (1856–1922) with the cooperation of a large number of authoritative collaborators. It was published in Paris by Letouzey and Ané (1902–1950) in thirty volumes. The *Enciclopedia cattolica* was published in Vatican City from 1948 to 1954 in twelve volumes.

more consistency between the integrity of her doctrine and the holiness of her members, starting with her own hierarchy. Certainly it was necessary to condemn errors, but also to reawaken souls to repentance, to prayer, to the reception of the sacraments, to devotion to the Virgin Mary. The most devout souls were aware of this situation, as is evident from the correspondence during those years between two religious who have now been raised to the honors of the Altars: Don Giovanni Calabria,[291] founder of the Poor Servants of Divine Providence, and Cardinal Ildefonso Schuster,[292] archbishop of Milan.

"For years," Don Calabria wrote to Cardinal Schuster, "with growing insistence I have heard resounding in the depths of my the lament of Jesus: O my Church!"[293] For his part, when in 1953 Our Lady wept at Syracuse, the archbishop of Milan commented: "Even the Most Blessed Virgin is weeping about the troubles of the Church and about the chastisement that looms over the world."[294]

Saint Giovanni Calabria in turn said that he was convinced that:

> The clergy of our times is called to exert a powerful influence on the people, to begin a new work of spiritual, intellectual, and moral civilization. Everything requires self-denial, heroism, sanctity; to suffer for justice; for precisely this we were called to serve in God's ranks, *in sortem Domini vocati.*
>
> We priests are either saints who can save the whole world, or else we are bad and can ruin it for centuries and centuries. Who gave Christianity to the earth? The heroism of the holy popes, bishops, and priests. Who tore the garments of the Church? Arius, Photius, Luther. "Your nation and the chief priests handed you over to me" (Jn 18:35), said Pilate to Jesus in chains. It is a statement that makes one tremble.

---

[291] Giovanni Calabria (1873–1954), ordained in 1901, founded the Poor Servants of Divine Providence, a congregation that was approved by the bishop of Verona in 1932 and by Pius XII in 1949. He was canonized by John Paul II in 1999.

[292] Alfredo Ildefonso Schuster (1880–1954), ordained in 1904, became a Benedictine monk and in 1918 abbot of Saint Paul's Outside the Walls in Rome. He was appointed by Pius XI archbishop of Milan and was created cardinal in 1929. He was beatified by John Paul II in 1997.

[293] Letter from Don Giovanni Calabria to Cardinal Schuster dated November 21, 1948, in *L'epistolario card. Schuster – don Calabria (1945–1954)*, ed. Angelo Majo and Luigi Piovan (Milan: NED, 1989), 30.

[294] Letter from Cardinal Schuster to Don Calabria dated October 6, 1953, in *L'epistolario, op. cit.*, 160.

> We read that in 1790 in the Christian world there were more than seven thousand convents of Franciscans alone, with one hundred thousand religious, not counting the women. Add the religious of all the other orders and congregations; set aside the priests of the secular clergy, who were extremely numerous then. With such a great number of defenders, how can one explain the disaster of the French Revolution that was unleashed even against the Church?
>
> And yet with only twelve men Jesus went forth to conquer the world. But they were saints![295]

The two religious were keenly aware of the Church's need for a profound work of reform, which would have to start with the sanctification of the clergy. Holiness of life is required of every baptized person, but especially for those who receive Holy Orders and administer the sacred mysteries. Holy bishops and priests are the ones who make Christian society holy, whereas if the clergy's living testimony of sanctity diminishes, souls drift away and it leads to the de-Christianization of entire countries and nations.

In the history of the Church the movements of true reform, such as those of the eleventh or the sixteenth centuries (the latter artificially divided into two phases of "Catholic Reform" and "Counter-Reformation"), were characterized on the one hand by the recuperation of the role of the papacy and of the Church's authority, and on the other hand by a heroic movement toward asceticism and a profound spirit of penance and prayer. The path marked out by the "innovators" was different.

In a book entitled *True and False Reform*,[296] Fr. Yves Congar presented as "true" a "reform" of the Church that would prove to be, more than a true reform, a genuine revolution. To the Dominican theologian we owe one of the first articulations of the formula of the "primacy of the pastoral," which introduced the distinction between dogmas and their formulation, as though the expression of doctrine could change without affecting the content. The modernist reform of "faith without dogmas" was

---

[295] G. Calabria, *Apostolica vivendi forma* (Verona: Regnum Dei Editrice, 1958), 61, 113.

[296] Y. Congar, O.P., *Vraie et fausse réforme dans l'Église* (Paris: Cerf, 1950); English transl. *True and False Reform in the Church* (Collegeville, MN: Liturgical Press, 2011). On the repercussions of this book, see E. Fouilloux, "Recherche théologique et magistère romain en 1952: Une 'affaire' parmi d'autres," in *Recherches de science religieuse* 71 (1983): 269–286. See also A. B. Simoni, "Da *Vera e falsa riforma nella Chiesa* all'aggiornamento del Vaticano II," in *Rivista di ascetica e mistica* 30/1 (2005): 145–179.

now replaced by a non-dogmatic formulation of the faith,[297] which counted on changing the faith itself, without appearing to touch doctrine. Congar cultivated "the power and ambivalence of original thinking,"[298] asserting that "there is no vital thinking which isn't also dangerous."[299] "There are no active seeds that are not mixed in with germs as well."[300] Since killing the bacteria would mean killing other living seeds, in his opinion it was better to allow both to thrive. The condemnation of errors by the Church, from medieval heresies down to modernism, allegedly squandered the positive approaches present in them: the Church would have done better to let those errors live and spread.[301] With this attitude he proposed the change the Church from within, through "a reform without schism."[302] "We don't need to create *another church*," he explained; "what we need to some degree is a church that is *other*."[303]

The "true reform" that the Church needed in the mid-twentieth century was something quite different. It was nothing other than the "law of restoration" enunciated by Pope Leo XIII, who maintained that "when an organic being withers and declines, this results from the cessation of the influence of the causes that gave it form and continuance; and there is no doubt that in order to make it sound and flourishing again, it is necessary to restore to it the vital influences of those same causes."[304]

Pius X himself, who is presented as a "reactionary" and "anti-reformist" pope, had set out the plan for an authentic reform modeled on that of St. Charles Borromeo, in the encylical *Editae saepe* dated May 26, 1910.[305] He pointed to the archbishop of Milan as "a model for both clergy and people in these days. He was the unwearied advocate and defender of

---

297 Cf. C. Barthe, *op. cit.*, 54.

298 Y. Congar, O.P., *True and False Reform in the Church, op. cit.*, 205 (French text 238).

299 Ibid., 204 (FT 236).

300 Ibid., 204 (FT 237).

301 Ibid., 208–212 (FT 241–246).

302 Ibid., 213 (FT 247).

303 Ibid., 218 (FT 251).

304 Leo XIII, apostolic letter *Annum ingressi, op. cit.*, p. 1911.

305 Saint Pius X, encylical *Editae saepe, De S. Caroli Borromaei apostolica activitate et doctrina*, English text at Vatican website.

the true Catholic reformation, opposing those innovators whose purpose was not the restoration, but the effacement and destruction of faith and morals."[306] In the sixteenth century, as at the beginning of the twentieth, "a continual battle was being waged against errors. Human society, going from bad to worse, was rushing headlong into the abyss. Then those proud and rebellious men came on the scene who are "enemies of the cross of Christ.... These men were not concerned with correcting morals, but only with denying dogmas. Thus they increased the chaos. They dropped the reins of law, and unbridled licentiousness ran wild. They despised the authoritative guidance of the Church, and... tried to destroy the Church's doctrine, constitution, and discipline."[307]

Whereas modernism proposed "a universal apostasy even worse than the one that threatened the age of Charles; it is worse, We say, because it stealthily creeps into the very veins of the Church,"[308] St. Pius X contrasted it with an authentic reform that had its own point of reference in the preservation and transmission of Catholic truth.

> The errors appear in many forms and the enticements of vice wear different dresses. Both cause many, even among our own ranks, to be ensnared, seducing them by the appearance of novelty and doctrine, or the illusion that the Church will accept the maxims of the age. Venerable Brethren, you are well aware that we must vigorously resist and repel the enemy's attacks with the very weapons Borromeo used in his day. Since they attack the very root of faith either by openly denying, hypocritically undermining, or misrepresenting revealed doctrine, we should above all recall the truth Charles often taught. "The primary and most important duty of pastors is to guard everything pertaining to the integral and inviolate maintenance of the Catholic faith, the faith which the Holy Roman Church professes and teaches, without which it is impossible to please God."
>
> ...With Charles we must be mindful "of the supreme zeal and excelling diligence which the bishop must exercise in combating the crime of heresy."[309]

---

[306] Ibid., par. 5.

[307] Ibid., par. 9.

[308] Ibid., par. 18.

[309] Ibid., pars. 21–22.

Firmness of doctrine must be matched with the ardor of charity. Indeed, true reformers, Pope Sarto recalled, "They do not kill the blossom in saving the root. That is to say, they do not divorce faith from holiness. They rather cultivate both of them, enkindling them with the fire of charity, 'which is the bond of perfection' (Col 3:14)."[310]

There was and there is no other reform possible for the Church besides that doctrinal and moral integrity in which thought and life find their consistent harmony. But a different path would be traveled in the twenty years that followed the death of Pius XII.

---

310 Ibid., par. 29.

II
Toward the Council

1. The death of Pius XII: the end of an era?

During the night of October 18, 1958, at Castel Gandolfo, Pius XII, Eugenio Pacelli, who had governed the Church for nineteen years, breathed his last. "Rome awoke immersed in grief," wrote the Vaticanist Benny Lai. "Until dawn the bells of Castel Gandolfo tolled the death, desolately alone; but before the sky was tinged with reddish hues, the bells of the city responded in kind."[1]

Pius XII was buried on October 13 in the grotto of Saint Peter's basilica, after a solemn funeral rite in the presence of twenty-two cardinals. "During the days of Hitler and Stalin, of iron and fire, of the secret police and the concentration camps," wrote Indro Montanelli in *Corriere della Sera*, "the new pope, a spiritual figure, was the one best suited to repudiate their example and their propaganda and to remind humanity about the eternal when it seemed to have lost all concept of it." "The vacuum that he leaves," added Montanelli, "is perhaps even greater than the office that he held."[2] About two million of the faithful flocked to Rome to pay homage

---

[1] Benny Lai, *Il "mio" Vaticano: Diario tra Pontefici e cardinali* (Soveria Mannelli: Rubbettino, 2006), 142.

[2] Indro Montanelli, "Un'apparizione," in *Corriere della Sera*, October 10, 1958.

to the pope who with such great dignity had personified the Church in a tempestuous hour in history. There was a pervasive feeling that his death signaled the end of an era, symbolized by his high-priestly figure. "May God preserve for us the Holy Father, Pius XII," Cardinal Shuster had written in 1951, "because from now on I pity his successor. The storm is raging, and who would dare take command of the ship?"[3]

In the first ten issues of the weekly *L'Espresso* in 1958,[4] the "defrocked" journalist Carlo Falconi[5] had launched a massive attack on the Vatican curia,[6] dominated, in his view, by a conservative "Pentagon" composed of Cardinals Nicola Canali,[7] Clemente Micara, Alfredo Ottaviani,[8] Adeodato Piazza,[9] and Giuseppe Pizzardo.[10] On the opposing side Falconi identified

---

[3] Letter from Cardinal Schuster to Don Calabria dated July 20, 1951, in *L'epistolario, op. cit.*, 93.

[4] The articles of Carlo Falconi, which originally appeared between January and March, were later collected and developed in the volume *Il Pentagono Vaticano* (Bari: Laterza, 1958).

[5] Carlo Falconi (1915–1985), ordained in 1938, left the Church in 1949 and dedicated himself to journalism, collaborating especially with the secularist weekly paper *L'Espresso*.

[6] In 1952 *Schleifung der Bastionen* by H. U. von Balthasar had appeared, which in its title seemed to outline a program. Translated into English as *Razing the Bastions* (San Francisco: Ignatius Press, 1993).

[7] Nicola Canali (1874–1961), ordained in 1900, substitute of the Secretary of State (1908–1914), assessor of the Holy Office (1926), created cardinal in 1935, and subsequently held various administrative positions in the curia. He was the most faithful student and disciple of Cardinal Raphael Merry del Val.

[8] Alfredo Ottaviani (1890–1979), ordained in 1916, secretary of the Sacred Congregation for Extraordinary Ecclesiastical Affairs (1928–1929) and substitute to the Secretary of State (from 1929 on). In 1935 he entered the Holy Office as an assessor. Created cardinal in 1953, he worked side by side with Cardinal Pizzardo as pro-secretary of that "Supreme Congregation" and on November 7, 1959, became its secretary. Cf. Grootaers, *I protagonisti*, 195–207; Emilio Cavaterra, *Il Prefetto del Sant'Uffizio: Le opere e i giorni del cardinale Ottaviani* (Milan: Mursia, 1990).

[9] Adeodato Piazza (1895–1957), Carmelite, ordained in 1908, bishop of Benevento (1930), created cardinal in 1937.

[10] Giuseppe Pizzardo (1877–1970), ordained in 1903, substitute of the Secretary of State (1921–1929), bishop of Nicaea and secretary of the Sacred Congregation of Ecclesiastical Affairs (1929–1939), was created cardinal by Pius XI in 1937 and appointed by Pius XII in 1939 prefect of the Sacred Congregation of Seminaries and Studies, a post that he held until 1967. From 1951 to 1959 he was also secretary of the Holy Office.

the main exponents of the progressive, anti-curial faction as Cardinal Giacomo Lercaro,[11] archbishop of Bologna, Cardinal Giuseppe Roncalli,[12] patriarch of Venice, and the archbishop of Milan, Giovanni Battista Montini, who was not yet a cardinal. In the space of five years two of them would ascend to the papal throne.

Perhaps in no other moment can earth meet heaven as it does in a conclave. The Church, in its noblest part, the cardinals, is joined together to elect the vicar of Christ, the one who is destined to epitomize in his own person the Church itself, to lead it and to govern it. The moment is so exalted that Christ promised the Church to assist her in this choice, in particular with the Holy Spirit, who illumines and sanctifies the Church with his grace. As with every grace, however, the one due to the extraordinary intervention of the Holy Spirit presupposes man's full compliance and cooperation. This cooperation may be opposed by the human desires and interests of the churchmen who are gathered in the conclave, who therefore prepare themselves with special ceremonies to receive the life-giving influence of the Holy Spirit.

Along these lines, Father Dolindo Ruotolo wrote to a priest friend of his on October 25, 1958: "Today the conclave begins for the election of the successor of Pius XII. It is necessary to pray because the election of

---

[11] Giacomo Lercaro (1891–1976), ordained in 1914, archbishop of Bologna from 1952 to 1968, created cardinal in 1953. Was nominated in 1963 by Paul VI as one of the four moderators of the council. See the (hagiographical) volumes, *Giacomo Lercaro: Vescovo della Chiesa di Dio (1891–1976)*, ed. Angelina Alberigo (Genoa: Marietti, 1991); *Araldo del Vangelo: Studi sull'episcopato e sull'archivio di Giacomo Lercaro a Bologna 1952–1968*, ed. Nicola Buonasorte (Bologna: Il Mulino, 2004); as well as Grootaers, *I protagonisti*, 157–171.

[12] Angelo Giuseppe Roncalli (1881–1963), of the diocesan clergy of Beramo. Ordained in 1904; titular archbishop of Areopoli (1925); apostolic visitator (1925–1931) and apostolic delegate in Bulgaria (1931–1934); titular archbishop of Mesembria (1934); apostolic delegate in Turkey and Greece (1934–1944); nuncio in France (1944–1953); in 1953 was created cardinal and patriarch of Venice (1953–1958). Elected supreme pontiff with the name John XXIII (1953), beatified by John Paul II (2000). Besides the historical *Positio*, see the hagiographical but well-documented biography by Marco Roncalli: *Giovanni XXIII: Angelo Giuseppe Roncalli: Una vita nella storia* (Milan: Mondadori, 2007). For a critical interpretation that one cannot always share, see the series of twenty-three articles on "Il Papa del Concilio" by Don Francesco Ricossa that appeared in *Sodalitium* between 1990 and 1999. Bibliography on him in G. Alberigo, "Il Pontificato di Giovanni XXIII," in *SC, La Chiesa del Vaticano II*, XXV/I:15–16 and F. Traniello, article in EP, 646–657.

the pope is accomplished by the Holy Spirit, but it happens through the cardinals. They are free to choose the one whom they elect, but their human views can interfere with the inspiration of the Holy Spirit. Therefore it is necessary to pray so that there will be no such interference."[13]

2. The 1958 conclave

a) The "great maneuvers"

The conclave opened the afternoon of October 24, 1958.[14] The number of cardinals present was fifty-one, of which eighteen were Italian, and eleven of them served in the Roman curia. It was impossible for two of the cardinals to participate in the election because they were detained by the respective communist governments: Joseph Mindszenty,[15] archbishop of Budapest, who had taken refuge in the American embassy after the Hungarian revolt in 1956, and Alojzije Stepinac,[16] archbishop of Zagreb,

---

[13] D. Ruotolo, letter to Monsignor Giacomo Cicconardi dated October 25, 1958, in *Letter a sacerdoti: Anni 1958–1959* (Naples: Apostolato Stampa, 1999), 32.

[14] On the 1958 conclave, cf. M. Roncalli, *Giovanni XXIII, op. cit.*, 417–432; Giancarlo Zizola, *Il Conclave: Storia e segreti: L'elezione papale da san Pietro a Giovanni Paolo II* (Rome: Newton Compton, 1993), 216–227.

[15] József Mindszenty (1892–1975), Hungarian, ordained in 1915, bishop of Veszprím in 1944, archbishop of Esztregom and primate of Hungary from 1945 to 1973, was created cardinal in 1946 by Pius XII. Arrested by the communist government in 1948 and accused of treason and conspiracy, he was sentenced to life imprisonment. Freed in 1956 by the Hungarian revolt, he lived in the American embassy in Budapest. Removed by Paul VI from his office, he took refuge in the West where he continued his activity on behalf of the Church of Silence. His process of beatification has been introduced. See his *Memoirs* (New York: Macmillan, 1974). See also Bela Fabian, *Cardinal Mindszenty: the Story of a Modern Martyr* (New York: Charles Scribner's Son, 1949).

[16] Alojzije Stepìnac (1898–1960), Croatian, ordained in 1930, in 1933 was appointed by Pius XI coadjutor Bishiop of Zagreb and, in 1937, successor to Archbishop Anton Bauer. When the communists seized power, he was arrested (September 18, 1946) and condemned to sixteen years of hard labor for his alleged collaboration [with the enemy]. He was created cardinal by Pius XII in 1953, but the Tito regime, while commuting his imprisonment to strict house arrest, never allowed him to travel to Rome. He died on February 8, 1960, probably as the result of poisoning. He was beatified by John Paul II on October 3, 1998. The best historical documentation is collected in

who had been condemned to hard labor and then to house arrest by the Tito regime. Both were important symbols of the Catholic Church's resistance to the communist persecution in Eastern Europe. Moreover in the days preceding the conclave, two cardinals died: the American Edward Mooney,[17] archbishop of Detroit, and the Italian Celso Costantini,[18] a leader in the diplomatic life of the Church. The archbishop of Milan, Montini, the ideal candidate of the progressive line-up who had strong support, did not participate in the conclave since he had not been created a cardinal by Pius XII, perhaps at the very end to prevent his election. His concern was a short, transitional pontificate that would allow him to receive the red hat and participate in the next conclave. Among the names that circulated were those of the Cardinals Ottaviani, Ruffini, and Siri,[19] who were of the same mind as Pius XII. But Siri was too young and Ottaviani and Ruffini, who were considered too idiosyncratic to be elected, were betting on Cardinal Benedetto Aloisi Masella, or alternatively on Cardinal Gregorio Agagianian.[20] Silvio Negro, the Vatican correspondent

---

volume III of the acts of the beatification process: *Beatificationis et canonizationis Servi Dei Aloysii Stepinac, S.R.E. Cardinalis, Zagabrien Archiepiscopi (1898–1960)* (Rome: Tipografia Guerra, 1996).

17 Edward Aloysius Mooney (1882–1958), from the United States, ordained in 1909, titular archbishop of Irenopolis in Isauria in 1926, archbishop of Rochester in 1933 and of Detroit in 1937, created cardinal in 1946.

18 Celso Benigno Luigi Costantini (1876–1958), ordained in 1899, titular bishop of Hierapolis in Phrygia in 1921, titular archbishop of Theodosiopolis in Arcadia in 1922, secretary of the Congregation for the Propagation of the Faith in 1935, created cardinal in 1953.

19 Giuseppe Siri (1906–1989), studied at the Gregorian, in Rome, where he was ordained in 1928. In 1944 Pius XII consecrated him titular bishop of Liviade, as auxiliary of Cardinal Pietro Boetto, upon whose death he succeeded him as archbishop of Genoa in 1946. Created cardinal in 1953, he then became president of the Italian Episcopal Conference from 1959 to 1965. Upon completing his 75th year, he sent to John Paul II his letter of resignation from the government of the diocese, but was kept in it until July 6, 1987. About him see, among other works, B. Lai, *Il Papa non eletto: Giuseppe Siri cardinale di Santa Romana Chiesa* (Rome: Laterza, 1993); N. Buonasorte, *Siri: Tradizione e Novecento* (Bologna: Il Mulino, 2000); Various Authors, *Siri: La Chiesa, l'Italia*, ed. Paolo Gheda (Genoa-Milan: Marietti 1820, 2009).

20 Grégoire-Pierre Agagianian (1895–1971), Armenian, ordained in 1917. Armenian patriarch of Cilicia from 1937 to 1962, created cardinal in 1946, prefect of the Congregation for the Propagation of the Faith from 1958 to 1970, member of the Central Preparatory Commission of the council and then moderator.

from *Corriere della Sera*, mentioned as the youngest of the likely candidates the sixty-three-year-old patriarch of the Armenians, Agagianian, who had been born in the Caucasus but had always lived in Rome, spoke Italian with a Roman accent, having been educated in Italy, and was thoroughly acquainted with the curia and a man of exemplary piety.[21]

As with every conclave in history, the one following the death of Pius XII also was subject to political pressures and attempts at interference. The most intrusive diplomatic campaign was conducted by France, then ruled by General De Gaulle, which did not renounce its Gallican traditions. De Gaulle had instructed his Ambassador to the Holy See, Roland de Margerie, to do everything possible to prevent the election of either Ottaviani or Siri, who were considered to be "reactionaries" and in league with Pius XII, the pope who beatified Innocent XI, the champion of the Holy See's resistance to King Louis XIV.[22] The "French party," headed by Cardinal Deacon Eugene Tisserant,[23] had a favorable view of Roncalli, the patriarch of Venice, who had become well-known in France for his joviality and independence of judgment. As Cardinal Silvio Oddi[24] later recounted, "Roncalli went into the conclave quite sure that he would become the pope, and did not hesitate to communicate his near-certainty to several

[21] Cf. Silvio Negro, "Possibile non probabile che venga eletto uno straniero," in *Corriere della Sera*, October 10, 1958.

[22] Cf. Poswick, *Journal*, 162. See more generally A. Melloni, "Governi e diplomazie davanti all'annuncio del Vaticano II," in Matthijs Lamberigts and Claude Soetens, eds., *À la veille du Concile Vatican II: Vota et réactions en Europe et dans le catholicisme oriental* (Louvain: Bibliotheek van de Faculteit der Godgeleerdheid, 1992), 214–275.

[23] Eugène Tisserant (1884–1972), French, ordained in 1907. Created cardinal in 1936, was secretary of the Congregation for Oriental Churches from 1936 to 1959, prefect of the Congregation for Ceremonies from 1951 to 1967, librarian and archivist of the Holy Roman Church from 1957 to 1971. In 1962 he was elected a member of the Académie Française. During the council he was dean of the Board of Presidency.

[24] Silvio Oddi (1910–2001), ordained in 1933, was consecrated bishop by Roncalli himself in Piacenza on September 27, 1953, after having taken part in the Parisian experience for three years. apostolic delegate to Jerusalem and in Palestine (1953), then internuncio to the Republic of Egypt (1957). In May 1962 was appointed nuncio in Belgium where he remained until 1969. In that same year he was created cardinal by Paul VI. In 1979 John Paul II appointed him prefect of the Congregation for the Clergy.

friends."[25] In his diary he wrote on October 15: "Today I have butterflies in my poor stomach. Some furtive encounter which however did not disturb my tranquility"[26]. Roncalli was associated with neither the progressives who leaned toward Montini nor the curial conservatives; he was advanced in age and could thus guarantee a transitional pontificate.[27] Many votes from both factions finally went to him, who, according to some indiscrete leaks, allegedly won thirty-six of them, surpassing the [required two-thirds] majority of thirty-five after eleven rounds of voting.[28] "On the eleventh ballot there I was, elected pope" Angelo Roncalli would write in his diary, "one would say as in a dream, and it is, next to death itself, the most solemn event in my poor life.[29]

b) The election of John XXIII

In the afternoon of October 28, 1958, Cardinal Canali announced to the crowd gathered in St. Peter's Square that Angelo Giuseppe Roncalli, the seventy-six-year-old patriarch of Venice, had been elected to the papal throne with the name of John XXIII, an unexpected name that had not been used since long-ago—1415 when a John XXIII had been deposed as an anti-pope.

Cardinal Tisserant confirmed that the French cardinals had been the ones most responsible for Roncalli's election. "They were interested in solving the problem of the worker-priests and Roncalli had assured them that the issue would be resolved."[30] Like the Quai d'Orsay, the Kremlin, too, appeared to be satisfied with his election." The party archives in Moscow record many positive comments about the fact that the new pope comes

---

25 Lucio Brunelli and S. Oddi, *Il tenero mastino di Dio: memorie del Cardinale Silvio Oddi* (Rome: Progetti museali, 1995), 114.

26 John XXIII, *Pace e Vangelo: Agende del Patriarca*, 752–753.

27 "Angelo Giuseppe Roncalli, transitional pope," noted the young but well-informed Vaticanist Benny Lai on October 28, 1958 (*Il "mio" Vaticano, op. cit.*, 166).

28 Cf. G. Zizola, *Il Conclave: Storia e segreti, op. cit.*, 222; M. Roncalli, *Giovanni XXIII, op. cit.*, 428.

29 John XXIII, *Pace e Vangelo: Agende del Patriarca*, 768–770 at 769.

30 G. Zizola, *Il Conclave: Storia e segreti, op. cit.*, 217. On worker priests, cf. E. Poulat, *Naissance des prêtres ouvriers* (Casterman, 1965).

from a peasant family, but also about the 'political' fact that Roncalli had been apostolic nuncio to Sofia and Ankara, and Pontifical Representative to Athens ... he always knew how to carry out his duties" in such a manner that Montini, during the time when he was with the secretariate of state, had transferred him to the nunciature in Paris, where he had won the confidence of General De Gaulle, and from Paris, by way of the Russian diplomat Bogomolov, "he found the road to Moscow."[31]

The election of Cardinal Roncalli was therefore a compromise, as was evident from his first papal appointments. On November 4, shortly before the beginning of his coronation ceremony, John XXIII announced, in a handwritten note to Archbishop Montini, the latter's imminent cardinalatial appointment: "My dear Excellency, I am about to ascend to the throne of St. Peter with great ceremony. . . Then I will announce the consistory in which the names of Archbishop Montini and Monsignor Tardini will figure prominently. But that will be next week, and meanwhile [there must be] absolute secrecy."[32]

On November 17 the newly-elected pope entrusted to Monsignor Domenico Tardini[33] the office of Secretary of State, which had been vacant for fourteen years, and announced the next consistory. First on the list of the new cardinals, twenty-three in all, was the name of the archbishop of Milan, Giovanni Battista Montini. Tardini and Montini, both of whom had strong personalities, represented two parallel and, in a certain respect, opposite lines within the curia. They both had had the title of secretary for Extraordinary Affairs and substitute for Ordinary Affairs, then, from 1953 on, they were pro-secretaries of state, but then in 1954 their two paths had diverged.[34]

---

[31] Viktor Gaiduk, "Vaticano e Cremlino: A proposito della presa di coscienza dell'ingresso nell'era nucleare: crinale apocalittico della storia," in *Vatican II in Moscow*, 13–34 at 24.

[32] John XXIII, *Lettere del pontificato* (Cinisello Balsamo: San Paolo, 2004), 67.

[33] Domenico Tardini (1888–1961), ordained in 1912, undersecretary of the Sacred Congregation for Extraordinary Ecclesiastical Affairs (1929), substitute of the Secretary of State (1935), pro-Secretary of State (1944) and finally Secretary of State of John XXIII in November 1958. On the same day he was appointed titular archbishop of Laodicea of Syria and created cardinal. Cf. Giulio Nicolini, *Il cardinale Domenico Tardini* (Padua: EMP, 1980); Carlo Felice Casula, "Il cardinale Domenico Tardini," in *Le deuxième Concile du Vatican*, 207–227.

[34] Cf. Robert A. Graham, S.J., "Montini Substitute Secretary of State (in tandem with Domenico Tardini)," in *Paul VI et la modernité* (Rome: École Française de Rome, 1984), 67–82.

If the support given by the conservatives in the conclave to Cardinal Roncalli was due to the notion that they would have in him a malleable, "transitional" pope, that was undoubtedly an error of judgment. Cardinal Roncalli, behind the *bonhomie* [good-natured, easy-going friendliness], had a very strong personality and was sometimes stubborn. "I do not fear adversity and do not refuse sufferings" he wrote after the first month of his pontificate. "I feel that I am the last of all, but I have in mind a plan of action that is not frantic, but well thought out.[35]

The young German theologian Hans Küng[36] was among those who seemed unsurprised by the election. His doctoral adviser, Louis Bouyer,[37] had long since predicted to him that Roncalli would be the future pope. Why? Because, Bouyer replied, he was "jovial, pious, and not all that intelligent."[38] Roger Poelman, a disciple of Dom Lambert Beauduin, recounts in his turn a conversation that he had with the latter during the final illness of Pius XII. Beauduin: "I'm telling you in advance: he will die very soon. His successor will be Roncalli." Poelman: "That fat nuncio to Paris?" Beauduin: "Well, you will see. He will hold a council and will do so in an ecumenical perspective."[39] Cardinal Suenens also records in his memoirs the words of Dom Beauduin: "If Roncalli is made pope, we shall have a council."[40]

---

[35] Previously-cited memorandum dated November 28, 1958, in *Ioannis XXIII: Biografia documentata*, pars IV, p. 2669.

[36] Hans Küng (1928–), Swiss theologian, ordained in 1954, professor at the University of Tübingen from 1962 to 1996, was appointed an "expert" of the council in 1962. In 1979 the Holy See revoked his authorization to teach Catholic theology because of his heterodox positions.

[37] Louis Bouyer (1913–2004), French theologian. A Lutheran pastor who converted to Catholicism, he became a priest of the Oratory in 1944 and taught at the *Institut Catholique* in Paris until 1963.

[38] Küng, *My Struggle*, 171.

[39] Cited in Jacques Mortiau and R. Loonbeek, *Com Lambert Beauduin visionnaire, op. cit.*, 251. Cardinal Roncalli for many years was a friend of Dom Beauduin, whom he had met in Rome (1925), Sofia (1929), Istanbul (1930), and Paris from 1944–1953. Cf. Sonya Quitslund, *Beauduin: A Prophet Vindicated* (New York: Newman, 1973), 54–55, 148, 167, 191, 200–201, 228, 237–253, and Francesca Della Salda, *Obbedienza e pace: il vescovo A. G. Roncalli fra Sofia e Roma* (Genoa: Marietti, 1989), 36–40 and *passim*.

[40] Suenens, *Memories and Hopes*, 74.

3. Angelo Roncalli: conservative or revolutionary. Roncalli the enigma.

Angelo Giuseppe Cardinal Roncalli, born in Sotto il Monte (Bergamo) on November 25, 1881, to a peasant family, had had a difficult life. The suspicion of modernism had hung over his life as a young priest on account of his relationship with Ernesto Buonaiuti. At his priestly ordination in the church of Santa Maria in Montesanto on August 10, 1904, he had been assisted by Buonaiuti, a fellow student in the seminary.[41] He had not been insensitive to the demands of modernism, but without intending "to hazard propositions which might differ in the slightest degree from the right judgment of the Church."[42]

After his priestly ordination, he was recalled to Bergamo as secretary to the new bishop, Giacomo Radini Tedeschi,[43] who was also "open" to the suggestions of modernism. Cardinal Gaetano De Lai, [44] prefect of Sacred Congregation of the Consistory, in June of 1914, having learned that on some occasions the young Father Roncalli had demonstrated "proclivities toward that broad current of thought that tends to diminish the importance of traditions and the authority of the past," he had exhorted him to "free yourself from the gloomy allure of certain books and certain authors."[45]

---

[41] Roncalli recalls Buonaiuti as follows in his remembrances: "He was beside me, between Don Nicola Turchi and myself; he had assisted me and was holding the missal between the two of us. Excommunicated in 1921, declared *vitandus* [shunned] in January 1926, died on April 20, 1946, Holy Saturday. Therefore he died at the age of 65: *in luce et in Cruce*. His admirers wrote about him that he was a profoundly and intensely religious mind, clinging to Christianity with every fiber, bound with unbreakable bonds to his beloved Catholic Church. Naturally there was no clergyman to bless his remains; no churchyard that would receive his burial" (cited in Stefano Trinchese, "Roncalli e i sospetti di modernismo," in *Il modernismo tra cristianità e secolarizzazione* [Urbino: Quattroventi, 2000], 727–770 at 749).

[42] John XXIII *Journal of a Soul*, transl. by Dorothy White (New York: McGraw-Hill, 1965), 144.

[43] Giacomo Maria Radini Tedeschi (1857–1914), ordained in 1879, bishop of Bergamo from 1905 to 1914, had to defend himself against suspicions of modernism. Cf. the correspondence of Pius X and Giacomo Maria Radini Tedeschi in Alejandro M. Diéguez and Sergio Pagano, *Le carte del "sacro tavolo": Aspetti del pontificato di Pio X dai documenti del suo archivio privato* (Vatican City: Archivio Storico Vaticano, 2006), 283–292.

[44] Gaetano De Lai (1853–1928), ordainted in 1876, created cardinal in 1907, secretary of the Consistorial Congregation from 1908 to 1928.

[45] Document in S. Trinchese, *op. cit.*, 764. On this case, cf. Mario Benigni, *Papa Giovanni XXIII:*

Like his bishop Radini Tedeschi, Roncalli, while remaining aloof from the modernist movement, nevertheless dissented, albeit privately, from the anti-modernist attitude of St. Pius X.[46]

Radini Tedeschi died on August 22, 1914, two days after Pius X, and Roncalli spent the years of the Great War as a military chaplain. He was than summoned to work in Rome at the *Propaganda Fide* [Congregation for the Propagation of the Faith], and in 1925 he was consecrated a bishop and appointed apostolic visitor to Bulgaria, one of the less important centers of Vatican diplomacy, where his promotion to apostolic delegate was delayed, and the mission seemed to him to last too long.[47] His diplomatic career continued as apostolic delegate in the Turkey of Kemal Atatürk (1935-1944) and then as nuncio in France (1945-1953). Paris was a prestigious center, but the Holy See had wished to entrust it to a second-string diplomat, chosen from among the apostolic delegates rather than from among the nuncios, as a form of "revenge" against the French government, which had forced the Vatican to withdraw the previous nuncio, Valerio Valeri,[48] who had been accused of sympathy for the Vichy regime.[49] The nunciature of Paris therefore opened to Roncalli the path to the Sacred College. Roncalli was created a cardinal in 1953 and was assigned, at seventy-two years of age, to the patriarchal see of Venice, the same one that had been governed by Pius X before he ascended to the papal throne.[50] The distinctive note

Chierico e sacerdote a Bergamo 1892–1921 (Milan: Glossa, 1998), 271–275.

[46] Cf. M. Roncalli, *op. cit.*, 84–114.

[47] Cf. A. Roncalli, *Lettere alla famiglia*, ed. Emanuele and M. Roncalli (Milan: Rusconi, 1989), letter dated December 21, 1929, p. 120.

[48] Valerio Valeri (1883–1963), ordained in 1907, archbishop of Ephesus in 1927, apostolic nuncio in Rumania in 1933 and in France in 1936, created cardinal in 1953.

[49] Concerning Paris, cf. E. Fouilloux, "Straordinario ambasciatore? Parigi 1944–1953," in Alberigo, *Papa Giovanni*, 67–95 at 71; *Idem*, "Le nonce Roncalli et l'Église de France," in *L'ora che stiamo attraversando*, 213–226; A. Riccardi, "Angelo Giuseppe Roncalli, un diplomatico vaticano," in Various Authors, *Un cristiano sul trono di Pietro: Studi storici su Giovanni XXIII* (Gorle [BG]: Servitium, 2003), 177–251. According to Riccardi, Archbishop Roncalli "was considered by his superiors—particularly by Tardini himself—as an original, ingenuous character" (ibid., 250).

[50] On his years in Venice, see G. Vian, "Il patriarca Roncalli attraverso le sue agende veneziane," in *Rivista di Storia e Letteratura Religiosa* 2 (2009): 369–394. In his 1955 Christmas message, the patriarch of Venice had written: "We turn especially to you, dear young people, who are so honest,

of his five years of governing the diocese was a pastoral style marked by optimism about the present, even "faced with the specter of the triumph of atheistic and materialistic Marxism," as he reaffirmed in his pastoral letter for Lent of 1955, "For a Pastoral Renewal."[51]

The figure of Angelo Roncalli still remains, in a certain respect, a "mystery." One could not attribute to the patriarch of Venice, who ascended to the papal throne, either a "progressive" or a "conservative" vision, like those that were clearly emerging at the threshold of the sixties. His mindset and his religious sensibilities made him a "conservative," but his "humanity" impelled him to make gestures that broke with tradition and to embrace "novelties" of a pastoral sort. The revolutionary character of his pontificate must be sought, not so much in his ideology, as in his way of life, in an earthly "humanity," even though, as Melloni observes, "the human element of Roncalli has nothing in common with the 'anthropological revolution' of the theology of the sixties and with its late twentieth-century pastoral or outrightly political byproducts."[52]

The pontificate of Angelo Roncalli, like his previous life, did not unfold along the lines of a consistent plan, but had a certain impromptu character guided by a "love of life" and a natural optimism which had, as its psychological rather than ideological consequence, the idea of "adaptation," or as they would say later, of *"aggiornamento"* ["updating"]. Roncalli, as Alberigo points out, until the late thirties, never tired of saying that "it is necessary to adapt the effective forms [of prayer, the sacraments] to the

---

generous, and well-intentioned. Do not allow yourselves to be enchanted by vain words. We who are speaking to you were also young like you. A half-century ago extremely dangerous and serious questions of a doctrinal nature were causing agitation in the Church. They were a temptation for our soul, which was however fervently seeking the good, the best. The grace of our Lord, experience, the guidance of Holy Church made us wise, preserving us from the laxity and openness of that time. Saint Pius X, the great Venetian pope, swept the horizon clean of errors and saved the Church" (Christmas message of the patriarch dated December 14, 1955,) in *Bollettino ecclesiastico Diocesi di Vittorio Veneto* 1 (1955): 19–21.

[51] A. Roncalli, *Scritti e discorsi* (Rome: Edizioni Paoline, 1959–1962), 2:28–42.

[52] A. Melloni, "Roncalli: Fare storia di un cristiano così," in *L'ora che il mondo sta attraversando: Giovanni XXIII di fronte alla storia*, Acts of a conference in Bergamo (November 20–21, 2008), edited by Grado Giovanni Merlo and Francesco Mores (Rome: Edizioni di Storia e Letteratura, 2009), 41.

circumstances of times and places."[53] The idea that one could be freed from the ancient forms without distorting the essence of doctrine, contained in embryo the "spirit" of Vatican II.

4. Toward the Second Vatican Council

a) How the idea of the council was born

The bomb exploded just three months after his election. On January 25, 1959, in the Capitular Hall of the Abbey of St. Paul's Outside the Walls, John XXIII told a group of cardinals who were present, and the whole world, his proposal to convoke an ecumenical council.[54] The pope was baffled by the "impressive, devout silence" of those present, which manifested their uncertainty and perplexity.[55] Joseph Cardinal Siri, archbishop of Genoa, had the same reaction when he heard the news on the radio while on a pastoral visit in a small town in the Diocese of Liguria. "Only when he returned to the archiepiscopal palace did the cardinal confide to his secretary his surprise and foreboding.... His anxieties were born of the fear that the innovational theological trends that had cropped up in the area of France and Germany after the war, together with the commotion in biblical studies, could increase by exploiting the conciliar event."[56]

One consideration is necessary at this point. In the last five centuries of the second millennium, only two councils had been held; Trent and

---

[53] G. Alberigo, "L'ispirazione di un Concilio ecumenico: le esperienze del cardinale Roncalli," in *Le deuxième Concile du Vatican*, 81–99 at 92.

[54] AD I-I:3–6. Cf. Alexandra von Teuffenbach, "L'annuncio del Concilio cinquanta anni fa: Una lettura nell'ambito della Chiesa," in *Alpha Omega* XII/3 (2009): 399–446.

[55] John XXIII, DMC, 4:259. The future Cardinal Giacomo Biffi, recalling the convocation of Vatican II, notes in his autobiography: "We were all astonished.... The pope, as was right, attributed this decision to an 'unexpected illumination from on high.' Councils however had always been prompted by the need to define some article of faith and to combat some heresy; tasks that John XXIII quickly ruled out. But then, I wondered, on the level of human psychology what had been his motives? Carefree as I was, I came to think that his reasons were, at least unconsciously, 'esthetic reasons'..." (*Memorie e digressioni di un italiano cardinale* [Siena: Edizioni Cantagalli, 2007], 156).

[56] B. Lai, *Il Papa non eletto, op. cit.*, 179.

Vatican I. The convocation of an assembly of such vast importance is a decision that cannot be made hastily or carelessly, but rather presupposes deep reflection and broad consultation. That is what happened when both Pius XI and Pius XII had examined the possibility of resuming the First Vatican Council, only to put aside the idea. It is not easy for the historian to understand how John XXIII could have taken on such an engrossing responsibility with such lightning speed, only three months after his election, unless one supposes that he had a special illumination from the Holy Spirit; there is no evidence of that either in his *Journal of a Soul* or in the pope's private memoranda. It is not surprising therefore that the cardinals reacted with stunned silence to the tranquil assuredness with which the newly-elected pope announced to them an event destined to change history. The astonishment was so widespread that an echo of it could be found even in John XXIII, who in a note on September 16 went so far as to write, "I was the first to be surprised at my proposal."[57]

The Secretary of State, Cardinal Tardini himself, learned of the news only a few days prior, presumably January 20, although in the pontiff's diary the same event is recorded twice under two different dates, January 15 and 20. What is certain is that Tardini energetically approved the initiative, perhaps under the illusion that he would hold the reins, but above all in the spirit of service that motivated him. John XXII recalls it as follows:

> In an audience with Secretary of State Tardini, for the first time, and, I would say, as though by chance, I happened to mention the word "council," as if to say what the new pope could propose as an invitation to an enormous movement of spirituality for Holy Church and for the whole world. I actually feared that the response would be a smiling, discouraging grimace. Instead, with a light touch, the cardinal—who had been pale-faced and wan—snapped to attention with an unforgettable exclamation and a flash of enthusiasm: "Oh! Oh? That's an idea, right? Is that just a great idea?"[58]

---

[57] John XXIII, *Journal, op. cit.*, 326. According to Monsignor Capovilla he spoke with Tardini about it only on January 20, 1959 (*Giovanni XXIII: Nel ricordo del Segretario Loris F. Capovilla*, interview by M. Roncalli with unpublished documents [Cinisello Balsamo: San Paolo, 1994], 60).

[58] John XXIII, *Pater Amabilis: Agende del Pontefice*, 25. On January 15 the pontiff reported, "In my conversation with Tardini, the Secretary of State, I wanted to find out what he thought about the idea that came to me of proposing to the members of the Sacred College [of Cardinals] ... the plan for an ecumenical council to be convened *omnibus perpensis* [after weighing everything carefully]

Domenico Tardini, who had spent most of his life in the secretariat of state, where he had started in 1921 as the aide who took the minutes, was a "Roman priest" to the core, pragmatic and witty, but not without a genuine priestly spirit. Until his death on July 30, 1961, he had a sincere and loyal relationship with the pope, which was nicely summed up in a personal note: "Whatever Your Holiness wants. Don't conceal anything from me."[59] Tardini however was not a fool, and one cannot rule out the possibility that with these words of his he intended to lend support to what he himself had already agreed on with the curial Cardinals Ottaviani and Ruffini.

b) The "Estates General" of the Church?

Cardinals Ottaviani and Ruffini were mistakenly persuaded that they could "control" the strong personality of John XXIII. Their erroneous idea was accompanied by another: that they could keep the council under the control of the Roman curia and that the former would reaffirm the traditional teaching of the Church and prevent errors from creeping in. A much different forecast had been made by another illustrious representative of the Roman school of theology, Cardinal Louis Billot,[60] when questioned by Pius XI on the subject. When Pope Ratti in 1923 had started consultations to examine the possibility of reopening the Vatican Council, which had been interrupted in 1870 by the Franco-Prussian War and the invasion of Rome, the French cardinal had replied that he thought it would be dangerous to convoke a council since

---

at the proper time: with the participation of all the Catholic bishops of every rite and region of the world. I was rather hesitant and uncertain. The immediate response was the most joyful surprise that I could have expected. Oh! But this is a luminous and holy idea. It comes right from heaven, Holy Father, it is necessary to cultivate it, develop it, and spread it. It will be a great blessing for the entire world" (ibid., 23–24).

[59] In G. Nicolini, *op. cit.*, 176.

[60] Louis Billot (1846–1931) of the Society of Jesus, French, ordained in 1869, held the chair of dogmatic theology at the Gregorian from 1885 to 1911, when he was created cardinal. Following the condemnation of Action Française by Pius XI in 1927, he resigned from his cardinalatial rank. About him see Henri Le Floch, C.S.Sp, *Le cardinal Billot lumière de la théologie* (Paris: Beauchesne, 1947); Jules Artur, "Les enseignements du cardinal Billot," *La Pensée catholique* 150 (1974): 76–81; P. Duclos, "Billot," in DHCJ, 450.

> it would impossible to conceal the existence of profound differences, within the episcopacy itself, on social, political and economic questions, and their relations with morality and the rule of faith. Because of their complexity, these questions will be presented under different aspects depending on the country, and they will give rise to discussion that will run the risk of being extended and prolonged indefinitely.

Cardinal Billot continued:

> So here we have the most important reason that would seem to me to militate absolutely against the idea. The resumption of the council is desired by the worst enemies of the Church, that is, by the modernists, who are already prepared—as the most certain information testifies—to take advantage of the general situations in the Church in order to start a revolution, the new French Revolution of their hopes and dreams. It is useless to say that they will not succeed, but we will relive the sorrowful days of the end of the reign of Leo XIII and the beginning of the pontificate of Pius X; we will see even worse, and it will be the total destruction of the happy fruits of the encylical *Pascendi* which had reduced them [*i.e.* the modernists] to silence.[61]

Billot's foresight was based on an obvious reason. When he was writing in the 1920s, the wounds were not yet healed following the surgery performed by Pius X to extirpate the disease of modernism from the body of the Church. The proclamation of the Roman primacy in 1870 at the same time made it less necessary for the council to endorse the decisions of the pontiffs. A council, by its nature a large assembly, far from reinforcing the primacy, would have inevitably set the stage for a dialectic between the Roman pontiff and the vast and uncontrollable episcopate, weakening the strength and prestige of Rome's authority. There was a danger that national episcopal blocks would form, which the Church had always tried to avoid because of her universal vocation. What Billot could not foresee, however, was something worse: the explosion of a conflict, not between the pope and the Roman curia on the one hand

---

[61] Caprile, 5:681–701 at 688. Father Caprile examines twenty-six letters and three memoranda written by the cardinals of the curia on the topic of the reopening of Vatican Council I. Strongly negative evaluations were expounded also by Cardinal Frühwirth and Cardinal Boggiani.

and the bishops on the other, but rather between the council fathers, or at least a part of them, and the Roman curia, while the pope would keep for himself the role of "mediator" between the two parties. This was exactly what happened.

c) Cardinals Ottaviani and Ruffini suggest the council

Pius XII also thought highly of the idea of convoking a great ecumenical council to continue the work of Vatican I.[62] In the audience on March 4, 1948, granted to Alfredo Cardinal Ottaviani, assessor of the Holy Office, Pius XII spoke for the first time about whether it would be opportune to resume Vatican I. The idea had come from Ernesto Cardinal Ruffini,[63] the archbishop of Palermo, in an earlier audience on February 24, 1948. "At the feet of Pius XII," he recounted, eleven years after receiving the purple hat, "I, the last of the priests, dared to ask for an ecumenical council. It seemed to me to that it was urgently required by the circumstances and that there would be as much material to deal with as the Council of Trent had. The venerable pontiff did not reject the proposal; he did not even take note of it, as he was accustomed to do in important matters...."[64] A special commission was then created, with Cardinal Ottaviani presiding, which started its work on March 15, 1948. In the minutes of the first meeting of the commission we read that Cardinal Ottaviani said that he had described to the Holy Father "the need to clarify and define several doctrinal points, given the heap of errors that are becoming widespread in philosophical and theological, moral and social matters."[65] In February 1949 the pope

---

[62] Cf. "Relazione sui primi lavori fatti in S. Offizio dal 1948 al 1951," in ASV, Conc. Vat. II, Busta 682, fasc. 1, 10 ff.

[63] Ernesto Ruffini (1888–1967), ordained in 1910, appointed archbishop of Palermo on October 11, 1945, created cardinal in 1946. About him see Angelo Romano, *Ernesto Ruffini: Cardinale arcivescovo di Palermo (1946–1967)*, Studi del Centro A. Cammarata (Caltanissetta-Rome: Salvatore Sciascia Editore, 2002); Francesco Michele Stabile, "Il Cardinale Ruffini e il Vaticano II: Lettere di un 'intransigente,'" in *Cristianesimo nella Storia* 11 (1990): 183–196; Grootaers, *I protagonisti*, 217–229.

[64] Cited in Gian Franco Svidercoschi, *Storia del Concilio* (Milan: Ancora, 1967), 23.

[65] *Relazione sui primi lavori, op. cit.*

appointed a Special Preparatory Commission which had as its president Archbishop Francesco Borgongini Duca,[66] apostolic nuncio in Italy, and as secretary, the Jesuit Pierre Charles,[67] professor of theology at Louvain. The commission held numerous meetings in absolute secrecy between 1949 and January 4, 1951, the date of the last meeting. In its deliberations two different ways of conceptualizing the event developed. Some wanted the council to be very brief, not more than a month, and to deal only with well-defined material, about which agreement would be unanimous, even by "acclamation" [rather than a numerical vote], demonstrating to the world the unity and solidarity of the Church. Others had in mind a long preparation and an equally long proceeding with complete freedom of discussion left to the council fathers, so as not to give the impression that the assembly was being "directed" by the Roman curia.[68] Faced with these differing opinions, which foreshadowed a conflict, Pius XII preferred to set aside the project, not unlike what his predecessor Pius XI had done.

The same Cardinals Ottaviani and Ruffini, who had suggested the idea of a council to Pius XII in 1948,[69] stated that in his cell at the conclave, they were the first to suggest to the newly-elected John XXIII that he convene the twenty-first universal council of the Church.[70]

In an interview published by the weekly *Epoca*, Cardinal Ottaviani was asked, among other things: "When John XXIII announced the council, what was your reaction?" Ottaviani replied:

> He had spoken about it to me from the moment of his election. Or rather, to be more precise, it was I who visited him in his little room at the conclave on the eve of the election. Among other things I told him, "Your Eminence, it is necessary to think about a council." Cardinal Ruffini, who was present at the conversation, was of the same mind.

[66] Francesco Borgongini Duca (1884–1954), ordained in 1906, titular archbishop of Heraclea and apostolic nuncio in Italia in 1929, created cardinal in 1953.

[67] Pierre Charles (1883–1954), Belgian theologian, of the Society of Jesus, ordained in 1910. Professor of dogmatic theology in Louvain, specialist in missiology.

[68] Cf. *Relazione sui primi lavori, op. cit.*; G. F. Svidercoschi, *op. cit.*, 25–26.

[69] Cf. A. von Teuffenbach, "L'annuncio del Concilio," *op. cit.*, 416–417.

[70] Cf. the Ottaviani Deposition in *Ioannis XXIII: Positio*, II/1:238; see also Emilio Cavaterra, *Il prefetto del Sant'Ufficio, op. cit.*, 5–6.

> Cardinal Roncalli adopted this idea and later had this to say: "I have thought of a council from the moment when I became pope." It's true, he welcomed our suggestion."[71]

Surely, as the historian Father Huber Jedin[72] recalls, the unexpected announcement "caused a lot of fanfare in the Church and perhaps even greater excitement outside the Church."[73] It was a surprise to the bishops throughout the world, as Rocco Caporale documents in his volume of interviews with the protagonists at the council. One of them, Archbishop Thomas Roberts,[74] summarizes the thought of the majority: "I never even dreamed of [a council] and never met anybody who did."[75]

The news reached Bishop de Proença Sigaud of the diocese of Jacarezinho, while he was in Sao Paolo, attending a week of anticommunist studies organized by Prof. Plinio Corrêa de Oliveira. Bishop Sigaud, on reading it in the newspaper, turned to Professor de Oliveira and said: "Well, Plinio, it's true: they're convening a council." Plinio: "Dom Sigaud, I'm astonished: this will be the Estates General of the Church! It is the beginning of the revolution in the Church." "No," Sigaud replied, "the pope will manage to change the minds of all of the bishops and everything will turn out well. Nothing [untoward] will happen."[76]

---

[71] Caprile, 5:702.

[72] Hubert Jedin (1908–1980), German, ordained in 1924, Church historian, professor at the Universities of Breslau and Bonn, was appointed an expert at the council in 1962.

[73] Hubert Jedin, "Il Concilio Vaticano II sotto il profilo storico," conference given in several places between 1959 and 1962, reprinted in *Chiesa della fede, Chiesa della storia*, Ital. transl. (Brescia: Morcelliana, 1972), 108.

[74] Thomas Roberts (1893–1976), English, ordained in 1925 in the Society of Jesus, archbishop of Bombay (1937–1950), then of Sugdaea (1950–1970).

[75] Cited in Wilde, 13.

[76] A-IPCO, Meeting on September 9, 1989. A similar exchange of remarks, recalled by Jacques Trémolet de Villers, took place in those same days in France. Archbishop Marcel Lefebvre turned to his friend Jean Ousset (1914–1994), the founder of the publication *Cité Catholique*, with these words: "I have great news to tell you … there will be a council!" "Pardon me, *Monseigneur*, if I do not share your enthusiasm. If you ask me, that is not good news." "What? My dear Ousset, this council will be the council of the *Cité Catholique*!" "*Monseigneur*, when the kingdom is tottering on every side, one does not call together the Estates General!" [an allusion to France in 1789] (cited

d) What does "ecumenical" council mean?

From the beginning the Second Vatican Council was called an "ecumenical" council. But what did this term mean? The existence of an "ecumenical" movement with its origin in protestantism could suggest the idea of a great council for the reunion of all Christians, like the Council of Florence in 1439. "But it is beyond all doubt," Jedin stated on the eve of the opening of the council, "that from the beginning the pope had not attached this meaning to it. He was simply keeping with the terminology of the Church, which appears to be fixed in canon law, in which the chapter that deals with the universal council is entitled *de Concilio Oecumenico*."[77]

The Catholic Church understands herself to be the only Church of Christ, and Pope John could only have been thinking about a great universal council of the Catholic Church.[78] In its logical sense, the Second Vatican Council would be "ecumenical" because the Catholic Church has already recognized twenty such councils as "ecumenical," or "general," or rather "universal." "The ecumenical council," Father Charles Boyer[79] explained in *L'Osservatore Romano*, "has a well defined meaning in the Roman Catholic Church: It is the assembly of all the bishops of the Catholic Church convoked by the Roman pontiff in order to consider questions concerning faith and morals. Its *de facto* universality is constituted by the presence of Catholics from all over the world, while its *de jure* universality consists of the fact that the Church is instituted to gather to itself all men without exception."[80]

---

by M. Introvigne in "Jean Ousset e la *Cité Catholique*: A cinquant'anni da *Pour qu'il règne*," in *Cristianità* 355 [2010]: 9–61 at 48–49).

[77] H. Jedin, *Il Concilio Vaticano II, op. cit.*, 66–87 at 66.

[78] A. von Teuffenbach, "L'annuncio del Concilio," *op. cit.*, 434–435; *Idem, Die Bedeutung des "subsistit in" (LG 8): Zum Selbstverständnis der katholischen Kirche* (Munich: Herbert Utz Verlag, 2002): 184–201.

[79] Charles Boyer (1884–1980), French Jesuit, ordained in 1916. Professor of theology at the Gregorianum until 1962, he was the founder of the Unitas Center and of the journal by the same name, created in 1946. He was appointed a member of the Secretariat for Unity in 1960, then expert at the council in 1962. From 1935 until his death he was secretary of the Pontifical Academy of St. Thomas and editor of the review *Doctor Communis*. Cf. Luigi Bogliolo, "Il padre Carlo Boyer s.j., Segretario dell'Accademia di S. Tommaso dal 1934 al 1980," in *Doctor Communis* 35 (1982): 3–14; H. de Gensac and P. Duclos, "Charles Boyer," in DHCJ, 515–516.

[80] *L'Osservatore Romano*, April 6–7, 1959.

In addressing the parish priests of Rome, John XXIII affirmed his desire to address all the Christian churches, in order to "tell them to end their disagreements and to come back together, without judging history in great detail to see who was wrong and who was right."[81] He did not intend thereby to give expression to a new "ecumenical theology," but rather to emphasize the new "pastoral" aspect that the impending council was to have.

In the encylical *Ad Petri cathedram*, dated June 29, 1959, which can be considered the document stating the program for his pontificate,[82] the pope made clear that the Roman Church already possesses full unity,[83] and he delineated the two principal purposes of the upcoming council in these terms: *"ut ad catholicae Fidei incrementum et ad rectam cristiani populi morum renovationem deveniatur"*[84]—the growth of the faith and the renewal of morality in the lives of the Christian people, as has been the tradition of every council of the Catholic Church. In the address on November 14, during the preparatory phase of the council, the pope reaffirmed that "in the modern era, rather than one point or another of doctrine and discipline… it is a question of reemphasizing the value and greatness of human and Christian thought and life, of which the Church is the repository and teacher through the ages."[85]

And although the World Council of Churches (WCC), through the initiative of its secretary general, the Dutch Pastor W. A. Visser't Hooft,[86] as of January 27, 1959, expressed a "very particular" interest because of John XXIII's reference to the unity of all Christians, in the autumn of that same year Cardinal Secretary of State Tardini, declared that there was no

---

[81] Caprile, I/1:107; G. F. Svidercoschi, *op. cit.*, 39 ff.

[82] The first encyliencyclical was followed, between August and November, by another three: *Sacerdotii nostri primordia* (August 1959) on the priesthood, on the centennial of the death of the holy "Curate of Ars"; *Grata recordatio* (September), dedicated to the recitation of the Rosary for the missions for peace; and *Princeps pastorum* (November) on the theme of the missions.

[83] AAS 51 (1959): 497–531.

[84] John XXIII, DMC, 1:818.

[85] *L'Osservatore Romano*, November 15, 1959.

[86] Willem Visser't Hooft (1900–1985), Dutch pastor, was the first secretary of the World Council of Churches (1948–1966). Cf. W. A. Visser't Hooft, *Pionnier de l'oecuménisme Genève-Rome: Textes présentés par Jaques Maury* (Paris: Cerf, 2001).

plan to invite non-Catholic ecclesial communities to the council, while not ruling out the possibility of admitting some "observers." It was only in the following months that the "ecumenical movement" succeeded in leaving its own imprint on the council.

e) Archbishop Pericle Felici, Secretary General of the Council

On May 16, 1959, John XXIII established an Ante-Preparatory Commission,[87] presided over by Cardinal Secretary of State Tardini, to whom was assigned the task of organizing the upcoming council. As secretary of this planning body he called on Archbishop Pericle Felici,[88] who had been a jurist for forty-eight years; in the *History of Vatican II* by Alberigo he is described as "an obscure auditor of the Rota."[89] Born in Segni in Ciociaria [in 1911], Archbishop Felici had been ordained at the age of only twenty-two, with an exceptional dispensation granted by Pius XII. After having brilliantly completed his studies of Canon Law, at the age of twenty-seven he was appointed rector of the Pontifical Roman Seminary for Canon Law Studies. From 1943 on he taught moral theology at the Lateran Athenaeum and in 1947 he was appointed an auditor of the Roman Rota. From the beginning, despite many differences that cropped up with his younger collaborator, Tardini preferred to leave the initiative to Felici, who also had a strong personality and conducted business with a sure hand. His activity as secretary general of the council was destined to influence decisively the course of events.[90]

---

[87] Cf. AD I-I:22–23.

[88] Pericle Felici (1911–1982), ordained in 1933, titular archbishop in 1960, created cardinal in 1967, then president of the Pontifical Council for Legislative Texts (1967) and prefect of the Supreme Tribunal of the Apostolic Signatura (1977). Cf. Riccardo Burigana, "Pericle Felici," in DBI 46 (1966): 69–74. On his role in the council, see *Actes et acteurs*, 301–313; Grootaers, *I protagonisti*, 115–133.

[89] G. Alberigo, "The Announcement of the Council: From the Security of the Fortress to the Lure of the Quest," in HVT 1:1–54, at 46.

[90] Cf. Grootaers, *I protagonisti*, 115–132. The Ante-preparatory Commission was made up of the secretaries of the seven Roman congregations: Propaganda Fide (Pietro Sigismondi), the

On June 15, 1959, Cardinal Tardini wrote a letter to the entire Catholic hierarchy, which was called by law to take part in the ecumenical council (cardinals, patriarchs, archbishops, bishops of dioceses and titular bishops, abbots and prelates *nullius*, vicars and apostolic prefects), and also to the superiors general of the exempt religious orders and of the non-exempt congregations, to the dicasteries of the Roman curia and to the theological faculties of the Catholic universities, asking them to communicate "the critiques [*sic; pareri* = opinions, advice], suggestions, and wishes which your pastoral concern and your zeal for souls urges you to offer in connection with matters and subjects for possible discussion at the coming council."[91] This consultation sought input from 2,700 individuals and sixty-two communities and institutions. Such a procedure, Philippe Levillain remarks, constituted a "democratic turn" in the preparation of the council, as compared to the methods used in organizing the first Vatican Council.[92] The preceding council had actually established a procedure whereby the pope was the one who posed the questions to the council, leaving to the bishops only the possibility of expressing their opinion by their vote. Now instead the initiative was in fact transferred to the bishops of the whole world, and they did not hesitate to make use of it.

On July 14 John XXIII informed Cardinal Tardini that the name of the next council would be Vatican II. It was to be therefore a new council and not a resumption and completion of Vatican I.

Congregation for Extraordinary Ecclesiastical Affairs (Antonio Samoré), for the Discipline of the Sacraments (Cesare Zerba), for the Council (Pietro Palazzini), for Religious (Arcadio Larraona), for Seminaries and Universities (Dino Staffa); the pro-secretary of the Congregation for Rites (Enrico Dante), the assessors of the Consistorial Congregation (Giuseppe Ferretto) and of the Congregation for the Oriental Churches (Acacio Coussa) and the commissary of the Holy Office (Paul Philippe). Their task was to collect the documents for the "proximate preparation" of the conciliar work, to sketch the general lines of the topics to be treated, to suggest the composition of the various organizations destined to take care of the detailed preparation of the business. This weighty activity took place in five sessions over the course of eleven months, between May 1959 and April 1960.

[91] É. Fouilloux, "The Antepreparatory Phase: The Slow Emergence from Inertia," in HVT 1:55–166, citation at 94.

[92] Philippe Levillain, *La mécanique politique de Vatican II: La majorité et l'unanimité dans un concile*, Preface by René Rémond (Paris: Beauchesne, 1975), 37.

5. John XXIII and "the signs of the supernatural" in the Church.

a) "Fatima is not concerned with the years of my pontificate"

John XXIII spent the month of August 1959 in Castel Gandolfo. There, on the 17th of the month, according to the testimony of his personal secretary,[93] who was present,[94] the pope received from the hands of Father Paul Philippe,[95] Commissioner of the Holy Office, the sealed envelope that contained the Third Secret of Fatima. "He said that he opened and read the letter the following Thursday [August 21], in the presence of his confessor Monsignor Cavagna,[96] so he was not in a hurry. He read it but since here and there the text was a bit difficult to understand because of the Portuguese dialect in which it was written, he had it translated by Monsignor Paolo Tavares,[97] an official of the Secretariat of State (later the bishop of Macao). I was present. Also present were the heads of the Secretariat of State and the Holy Office and others, for example Cardinal Agagianian."[98]

The message that had been revealed to the three little shepherds of Fatima, which as Cardinal Bertone has written, "undoubtedly the most prophetic of modern apparitions,"[99] consists of three distinct parts. The first

---

[93] Loris Capovilla, born in 1915, ordained in 1940, was the private secretary of John XXIII and then an expert at the council in 1964. He was bishop of Chieti from 1967 to 1971.

[94] *Giovanni XXIII nel ricordo del Segretario Loris F. Capovilla, op. cit.*, 113–117.

[95] Paul Philippe (1905–1984), French Dominican, ordained in 1932. Member of the Holy Office from 1955 to 1959, then secretary of the Congregation for Religious. Member of the Ante-preparatory Commission. Consecrated bishop in 1962, he was appointed member of the Commission for Religious during the first session. Created cardinal in 1973, pro-prefect of the Congregation for Oriental Churches from 1973 to 1980.

[96] Alfredo Maria Cavagna (1879–1970), ordained in 1902, bishop of Tio in 1962.

[97] Paulo José Tavares (1920–1973), Portuguese, ordained in 1943, bishop of Macao (China) from 1961 until his death.

[98] *Giovanni XXIII nel ricordo del Segretario Loris F. Capovilla, op. cit.*, 115.

[99] Congregation for the Doctrine of the Faith, "The Message of Fatima," *L'Osservatore Romano*, English weekly edition, special insert n. 26 (1649) (28 June 2000), from the introduction. The CDF document includes the three parts of the "secret" in the version written by Sister Lucia (pages III-IV), a presentation by the secretary of the congregation, Archbishop Tarcisio Bertone, SDB

is the dramatic vision of hell, into which innumerable souls fall.

> Our Lady showed us a great sea of fire which seemed to be under the earth. Plunged in this fire were demons and souls in human form, like transparent burning embers, all blackened or burnished bronze, floating about in the conflagration, now raised into the air by the flames that issued from within themselves together with great clouds of smoke, now falling back on every side like sparks in a huge fire, without weight or equilibrium, and amid shrieks and groans of pain and despair, which horrified us and made us tremble with fear. The demons could be distinguished by their terrifying and repulsive likeness to frightful and unknown animals, all black and transparent. This vision lasted but an instant. How can we ever be grateful enough to our kind heavenly Mother, who had already prepared us by promising, in the first apparition, to take us to heaven. Otherwise, I think we would have died of fear and terror.[100]

In the second part, Our Lady predicted the end of the First World War, the outbreak of a new war, and the spread of communism if the world did not convert, but also the remedy for the salvation of mankind: devotion to her Immaculate Heart.

> We then looked up at Our Lady, who said to us so kindly and so sadly:
>
> "You have seen hell where the souls of poor sinners go. To save them, God wishes to establish in the world devotion to my Immaculate Heart.
>
> "If what I say to you is done, many souls will be saved and there will be peace. The war is going to end: but if people do not cease offending God, a worse one will break out during the pontificate of Pius XI. When you see a night illumined by an unknown light, know that this is the great sign given you by God that he is about to punish the world for its crimes, by means of war, famine, and persecutions of the Church and of the Holy Father.

(pp. V-VI), and a theological commentary on the third part of the "secret" by the prefect of the congregation, Cardinal Joseph Ratzinger (pp. VII-VIII).

100 "First and Second Part of the "Secret' according to the version presented by Sister Lucia in the 'Third Memoir' of 31 August 1941 for the bishop of Leiria-Fatima," in Congregation for the Doctrine of the Faith, *The Message of Fatima, op. cit.*, III.

> "To prevent this, I shall come to ask for the consecration of Russia to my Immaculate Heart, and the Communion of reparation on the First Saturdays. If my requests are heeded, Russia will be converted, and there will be peace; if not, she will spread her errors throughout the world, causing wars and persecutions of the Church. The good will be martyred; the Holy Father will have much to suffer; various nations will be annihilated. In the end, my Immaculate Heart will triumph. The Holy Father will consecrate Russia to me, and she shall be converted, and a period of peace will be granted to the world."[101]

The third part of the message is a mysterious vision in which the pope, bishops, religious, and lay people tragically meet their deaths.

> After the two parts which I have already explained, at the left of Our Lady and a little above, we saw an angel with a flaming sword in his left hand; flashing, it gave out flames that looked as though they would set the world on fire; but they died out in contact with the splendor that Our Lady radiated towards him from her right hand: pointing to the earth with his right hand, the angel cried out in a loud voice: "Penance, Penance, Penance!" And we saw in an immense light that is God: "something similar to how people appear in a mirror when they pass in front of it" a bishop dressed in white "we had the impression that it was the Holy Father." Other bishops, priests, men and women religious going up a steep mountain, at the top of which there was a big cross of rough-hewn trunks as of a cork-tree with the bark; before reaching there the Holy Father passed through a big city half in ruins and half trembling with halting step, afflicted with pain and sorrow, he prayed for the souls of the corpses he met on his way; having reached the top of the mountain, on his knees at the foot of the big cross he was killed by a group of soldiers who fired bullets and arrows at him, and in the same way there died one after another the other bishops, priests, men and women religious, and various lay people of different ranks and positions. Beneath the two arms of the cross there were two angels each with a crystal aspersorium in his hand, in which they gathered up the blood of the martyrs and with it sprinkled the souls that were making their way to God.[102]

---

[101] "First and Second Part of the 'Secret'...," *ibid.*

[102] "Third part of the 'secret'," translated from the original, in Congregation for the Doctrine of the Faith, *The Message of Fatima, op. cit.*, IV. The contents of the Third Secret are currently the subject

It was expected that this last part, which was not made public by the Holy See until June 26, 2000, would be revealed in 1960. In the United States, the Blue Army[103] had launched an intensive campaign focused on the imminent revelation of the Third Secret, and there was great expectation of this event in public opinion and in the mass media.

The world was going through a difficult historical hour. The announcement by John XXIII that he intended to gather all the bishops of the world in a council had been preceded only a few weeks earlier by the entrance of Fidel Castro's troops into Havana. The Cuban revolution had confirmed the existence of a plan for the worldwide expansion of communist imperialism. Less than three years later, with the international crisis between the United States and the Soviet Union, following the decision of the Kremlin to install its missiles in Cuba, the world would find itself on the brink of a nuclear war. The message of Fatima reminded anyone who professed an unfounded optimism concerning the historical course of events about the tragedy of the moment and showed the way to confront it. Reading the text [of the Third Secret] did not startle the pope, who did no more than dictate to Monsignor Capovilla a note testifying "that the pope had looked over the contents of the letter and left for others

---

of a controversy that finds expression in the book by Antonio Socci, *The Fourth Secret of Fatima* (Fitzwilliam, NH: Loreto Publications, 2009), and the book by Cardinal T. Bertone with Giuseppe De Carli, *The Last Secret of Fatima*, (New York: Doubleday, 2008), and *Idem, L'ultima veggente di Fatima: I miei colloqui con suor Lucia* [The Last Visionary of Fatima: My Conversations with Sister Lucia] (Milano: Rizzoli, 2007). For a balanced summary of the issue, see: A. A. Borelli Machado, "Riflessioni amichevoli per chiarire una polemica," in *Lepanto* 174 (2007): 2–24.

[103] The Blue Army was formed in 1947 in the Diocese of Newark, New Jersey (USA), through the work of a priest, Father Harold Colgan, who was seriously ill but completely recovered the next day and then learned about the message of Our Lady of Fatima from a magazine. So he began to organize the spread of the message and the "pilgrimage" of a statue of Our Lady of Fatima. The initiative began to spread in the United States and in the world also through the work of a fervent layman, the journalist and writer John Mathias Haffert (1915–2001), who through *Soul Magazine* and pilgrimages to Fatima publicized the movement everywhere, so that on May 13, 1950, Father Colgan brought to Fatima a microfilm on which were recorded the names of millions of devotees who had enrolled to that date. After many pilgrimages were made from Italy to Fatima, the plan for a *peregrinatio* of the image of Our Lady of Fatima through the main cities of the Italian provinces was carried out, concluding in Catania, on the occasion of the National Eucharistic Congress, with the consecration of Italy to the Immaculate Heart of Mary on September 13, 1959.

— his successor? — the task of commenting on it."[104] Father Alonso, the foremost expert on Fatima, who probably learned this from one of those present at Castel Gandolfo, recounts that, after having read the message, the pope said: "This does not concern the years of my pontificate."[105] The instruction from the ecclesiastical authorities was the one transmitted by Father Giovanni Caprile in the pages of *Civiltà Cattolica*: "Neither terrors, nor alarmist statements, nor 'sensationalism' nor morbid curiosity."[106] The reasons why Pope Roncalli decided to postpone the publication of the Third Secret are obvious: There was a shrill contrast between "the prophecy of doom" of the message of Fatima and the optimistic outlook on the future of the new pontiff, who inaugurated the Second Vatican Council.[107] The existence of this contrast between two "prophetic visions" helps us to understand the events of the following years.

Later that year on September 13, Italy was consecrated to the Immaculate Heart of Mary during a solemn ceremony that took place in Catania with 300,000 people present from all over the Italian peninsula. On that occasion the pilgrim statue of Our Lady of Fatima arrived from Portugal and travelled to 150 cities in Italy, amidst extraordinary fervor.[108]

---

[104] L. Capovilla, *Giovanni XXIII nel ricordo del Segretario Loris F. Capovilla, op. cit.*, 115.

[105] J. M. Alonso, C.F.M., *La vérité sur le secret de Fatima* (Paris: Téqui, 1979), 106. See also Frére Michel de la Sainte Trinité, *The Whole Truth about Fatima, op. cit.*, 3:578–591; Frére François-Marie des Anges, *Fatima, joie intime: Évenement Mondial* (Parres-les Vaudes: Contre-Réforme, 1991), 295 ff.

[106] G. Caprile, S.J., "Fatima e il suo 'segreto' non svelato," in *Civiltà Cattolica*, q. 2640 (1960): 614–618. Giovanni Caprile (1917–1993) of the Society of Jesus, editor of the *Civiltà Cattolica* from 1953 until his death, chronicler of the council in that publication. Cf. Anon., "In ricordo del padre Giovanni Caprile," in *Civiltà Cattolica* q. 3430 (1993): 365–368.

[107] The historian Giorgio Rumi, who approved the decision of John XXIII, testified that the latter had failed as a prophet in these words: "Today we know that communism would fall. But then Roncalli could not foresee it with certainty; on the contrary, communism was very strong" (Interview with Paolo Conti, "Gli intellettuali cattolici: Giovanni XXIII fece bene a non divulgare il segreto," in *Corriere della Sera*, May, 14, 2000).

[108] One of the final stages of the itinerary of the Pilgrim Statue of Our Lady was San Giovanni Rotondo, where it arrived on August 5, 1959, and Padre Pio, who at that moment was seriously ill, unexpectedly regained his strength. Cf. Y. Chiron, *Padre Pio le stigmatisé* (Paris: Perrin, 1991), 254–260.

In his radio address, John XXIII did not make any reference either to Fatima or to its secret.[109]

b) John XXIII and Padre Pio

The Christian historian cannot ignore the manifestations of divine action in human affairs. The supernatural does not manifest itself only in apparitions or extraordinary visions, but also in the ordinary lives of the saints, which constitutes one of the principal expressions of God's presence in history. Dom Guéranger writes: "In his infinite justice and mercy, God bestows saints on various times, or else decides not to grant them so that, if it is permissible to speak in this way, one must consult the thermometer of sanctity in order to test whether the condition of an era or a society is normal."[110] The twentieth century, in comparison with other epochs, was lacking in saints. And yet one charismatic figure seemed to encompass within himself a large share of the extraordinary gifts that were missing in his time. This figure was Padre Pio of Pietrelcina,[111] the stigmatist of San Giovanni Rotondo, who became the center of a network of prayer groups scattered throughout the world.

The stigmatist of Pietrelcina was subject to misunderstandings and calumnies, for which he had to suffer humiliating canonical investigations. Among these was one promoted by John XXIII, who sent Monsignor Carlo Maccari,[112] then secretary of the vicariate of Rome, as apostolic visitator

---

[109] Cf. Radio message at the conclusion of the 16th National Eucharistic Congress, DMC 1:432–437.

[110] P. Guéranger, O.S.B., "Le sens chrétien de l'histoire," in *Essai sur le naturalisme contemporain* (Éditions Delacroix, 2004), 365–402 at 377.

[111] Saint Pio of Pietrelcina, in the world Francesco Forgione (1887–1968), made his solemn vows in 1907 in the Capuchin order, taking the name Pio, and was ordained in 1910; in 1916 he was assigned to the convent of San Giovanni Rotondo, where in 1918 he received the visible stigmata of the Passion of Christ that remained open and bleeding for fifty years. He was beatified (1999) and canonized (2002) by John Paul II. About him see *Sipontina Beatificationis et canonizationis Servi Dei Pii a Pietrelcina Positio Super Virtutibus*, vol. I/1 (Vatican City, 1997).

[112] Carlo Maccari (1913–1997), ordained in 1936, bishop of Emmaus in 1961, archbishop of Mondovi in 1963, of Ancona and Numana in 1968, bishop of Osima and Cingoli in 1972.

to San Giovanni Rotondo from July 13 to October 2, 1960. That period would be remembered as the time of harshest persecution for the saint of Pietrelcina.[113] Pope Roncalli's mistrust was surprising, especially in light of a movement that was gathering crowds of pilgrims around Padre Pio.

In 1971 the Postulator of the cause for the beatification of Padre Pio, Father Bernardino da Siena, turned to Monsignor Capovilla in order to find out what John XXIII had thought about Padre Pio. The response was evasive.[114] From the documentation of the *Positio* of the process emerges the essential lack of comprehension on the part of John XXIII for the spiritual figure of Padre Pio of Pietrelcina,[115] who was then beatified and canonized by John Paul II.

6. The "vota" of the council fathers

a) Like the "cahiers de doléance" of the French Revolution

During the summer of 1959, in response to Cardinal Tardini's request for opinions, the *"vota"* or recommendations from the bishops, the superiors of religious orders, and the Catholic universities arrived. The compilation of this enormous quantity of material began in September and concluded in late January of 1960. The approximately three thousand letters that were sent in fill the eight volumes of the *Acta et documenta concilio Vaticano II apparando.*[116]

---

[113] Cf. Francobaldo Chiocci, *I nemici di Padre Pio* (Roma: Edizioni Reporter, 1968); Marco Tosatti, *Quando la Chiesa perseguitava Padre Pio* (Casale Monferrato: Piemme, 2005). The canonical visit took place at the request of Father Clemente from Milwaukee, superior general of the Capuchin order, who was involved in the bankruptcy of the banker Giovanni Battistas Giuffré. The intermediary between the Capuchins who were against Padre Pio (who set up microphones in the parlor of the convent) and the Holy Office was the Roman priest Don Umberto Terenzi (1900–1974), from 1932 on rector of the Shrine of Divine Love.

[114] Cf. *Servi Dei Pii a Pietrelcina Positio, op. cit.*, 229–243.

[115] Cf. ibid., 243–251. See also the tendentious but well-documented book by Sergio Luzzatto, *Padre Pio: Miracoli e politica nell'Italia del Novecento* (Turin: Einaudi, 2007), 364–387. A contrary view in Fabrizio Cannone, "Padre Pio: lettura critica di una lettura critica," in *Nova Historica* 9 (2010): 152–169.

[116] The compilation of the *vota* is published in *Acta et documenta Concilio Oecumenico Vaticano*

A careful examination of the *"vota"* allows the historian today, as it allowed the pope, the curia, and the Preparatory Commission then, to get a picture of the *"desiderata"* of the worldwide episcopate on the eve of the council.

The requests of the future council fathers, considered as a whole, do not express the desire for a radical turn, much less for a "revolution" within the Church.[117] Although the anti-Roman tendencies of some bishops emerge clearly in some responses, such as those of Cardinal Alfrink,[118] archbishop of Utrecht, generally the fathers were looking forward to a moderate "reform" along traditional lines. The majority of the *vota* asked for a condemnation of modern evils, both inside and outside the Church, above all of communism, and for new doctrinal definitions, in particular regarding the Blessed Virgin Mary. In the recommendations of the British episcopate for example, there is a denunciation of the evils of contemporary society, but no call for radical reform;[119] even among the French episcopate, which was considered to be one of the most progressive, many demanded the condemnation of Marxism and communism, and a solid minority asked for the definition of the dogma of Mary as Mediatrix.[120] As for the Belgian bishops, Claude Soetens, who examined their *"vota,"* emphasizes "the rather disappointing character" of their proposals, "which were hardly apt to bring about a true ecclesiastical renewal," confirming the impression of those who have pointed out the discrepancy between the responses of

---

II apparando – Series I (Antepraeparatoria), op. cit. Out of 2,594 future council fathers, 1,988 responded, or 77% (cf. E. Fouilloux, "The Antepreparatory Phase," *op. cit.*, 97).

[117] An overall examination of the *Vota* in *À la veille du Concile Vatican II, op. cit.*, and also in *Le deuxième Concile du Vatican*, 101–177. For the Italian prelates, see Mauro Velati, "I 'consilia et vota' dei vescovi italiani," in *À la veille du Concile Vatican II, op. cit.*, 83–97; Roberto Morozzo della Rocca, "I 'voti' dei vescovi italiani per il Concilio," in *Le deuxième Concile du Vatican*, 119–137.

[118] AD I-II/2:509–516. Bernard Jan Alfrink (1900–1987), Dutch, ordained in 1924, archbishop of Utrecht from 1955 on, created cardinal in 1960, member of the Preparatory Commission and of the Board of Presidency. Cf. Fabrizio de Santis, *Alfrink, il cardinale d'Olanda* (Milan: Longanesi, 1969); Antonius Hendrikus Maria van Schaik, *Alfrink: Een biografie* (Amsterdam, Authos, 1997). On his role at the council, cf. *Actes et Acteurs*, 522–553.

[119] Cf. Solange Dayras, "Les voeux de l'épiscopat britannique: Reflets d'une église minoritaire," in *Le deuxième Concile du Vatican*, 139–153.

[120] Cf. Yves-Marie Hilarie, "Les voeux des évêques français après l'annonce du Concile," in *Le deuxième Concile du Vatican*, 101–117 at 102.

the bishops to the consultation in 1959 and their subsequent attitude during the council.[121]

The Italian bishops, the largest contingent, would have wanted the council to proclaim the dogma of "the universal mediation of the Blessed Virgin Mary."[122] They also called for the definition of a second dogma, the Kingship of Christ, as opposed to the prevailing secularism.[123] Moreover many asked that the council condemn various doctrinal errors: ninety-one would have liked to see the condemnation of communism repeated, fifty-seven spoke out against atheistic existentialism, forty-seven against moral relativism, thirty-one against materialism, and twenty-four against modernism.[124] Giovanni Turbanti points out that: "In the thousands of letters that arrived in Rome from all over the world, communism appeared as the most serious error that the council would have to condemn. A good 286 bishops mentioned it. To these should be added the numerous references to socialism, materialism, and atheism."[125] In the *Summary Report*, too, which recaps the *"vota"* of the bishops country by country and was compiled by the secretary general of the Preparatory Commissions, communism appeared as the error that the council would have to condemn first and foremost.[126]

There is an interesting analogy between the *"vota"* of the council fathers and the *Cahiers de doléance* ["Lists of grievances"] that were drawn up in France, with a view to the Estates General of 1789. Before the French Revolution no *"Cahier de doléance"* set out to subvert the foundations of the *Ancien Régime*, and in particular the monarchy and the Church. The historian Armando Saitta emphasizes that "Not one *cahier* was worded as

---

[121] Cf. C. Soetens, "Les 'vota' des évêques belges en vue du Concile," in *À la veille du Concile Vatican II, op. cit.*, 38–52 at 49.

[122] Roberto Morozzo della Rocca, "I 'voti' dei vescovi italiani," *op. cit.*, 127.

[123] Ibid.

[124] Cf. ibid., 119–137.

[125] G. Turbanti, "Il problema del comunismo al Concilio Vaticano II," in *Vatican II in Moscow*, 147–187 at 149.

[126] Ibid., 150. We should mention the recommendations of the Catholic universities, such as the *votum* of the Athenaeum *De Propaganda Fide* in Rome, which presents a long and in-depth study of the Stigmatine Father Cornelio Fabro on the origin and nature of contemporary atheism (Cf. *De atheismo positivo seu constructivo ut irreligiositatis nostri temporis fundamenta*, AD I-I/1:452–463).

if the Estates General should have the task of abolishing all preexisting authority and to create or recreate it *ex-novo.*"[127] What was being requested was a moderate reform of institutions, not their subversion, as unexpectedly happened, when the Estates General met. Likewise in the case of Vatican II, Father O'Malley concludes, "in general, the responses requested a reinforcement of the *status quo*, a condemnation of modern evils, both inside and outside the Church, and other doctrinal definitions, especially connected with the Blessed Virgin Mary."[128]

The council did not heed the requests that emerged from the *"vota"* of the council fathers, but rather favored the claims of a minority which, from the outset, managed to put itself in charge of the assembly and to orient its decisions. This is what emerges indisputably from the historical data.

b) Bishop de Proença Sigaud: the council between revolution and counter-Revolution.

Among the *"vota"* that arrived in Rome, there is one that stands out for the fullness of the picture that it presents, for the evils that it denounces, and for the remedies that it proposes. It is the recommendation of the bishop of Jacarezinho, Geraldo de Proença Sigaud, who in 1961 would be elevated by John XXIII to the rank of archbishop of Diamantina. The document by Bishop Sigaud[129] clearly reveals the inspiration, and perhaps even the hand, of Plinio Corrêa de Oliveira, whose most famous article entitled "Revolution and Counter-Revolution"[130] had just appeared in 1959 in issue number 100 of the review *Catolicismo.*

Bishop de Proença Sigaud in his *votum*, like Corrêa de Oliveira, used the terms "Revolution" and "Counter-Revolution" in precisely the same sense that had been given to them since the French Revolution by the papal magisterium and by the productive strain of Catholic thought that

---

[127] Armando Saitta, *Costituenti e Costituzioni della Francia rivoluzionaria e liberale (1789–1875)* (Milan: Giuffrè, 1975), 3.

[128] John W. O'Malley, *Vatican II: Did Anything Happen?, op. cit, 4.*

[129] AD I-II/7:180–195.

[130] Cf. P. Corrêa de Oliveira, "Revolução e Contra- Revolução," in *Catolicismo* 100 (April 1959): 1–12. English translation cited.

has been described as "counter-revolutionary":[131] a religious and moral clash rooted in the decline of medieval Christianity. This was the perspective from which the Brazilian bishop denounced the penetration [into the Church] of the principles and the spirit of the so-called "revolution of the priests and the Christian people." He wrote:

> Just as once the principles, the teachings, the spirit and the love of the ancient pagan world entered into medieval society and caused the pseudo-reforms [of the Renaissance], many clerics [today] do not yet understand the errors of the revolution, and still do not oppose them. Others among the clergy love the revolution as an ideal principle, they spread it, they collaborate with it, they obstruct the adversaries of the revolution, denigrating and impeding their apostolate. Many pastors remain silent. Others have embraced the errors and the spirit of the revolution, and favor them openly and secretly, as did the priests at the time of the Jansenism. Whoever accuses them and refutes their errors is persecuted by their colleagues, and are called "Integrists." From the seminaries of Rome itself seminarians come back full of the ideas of the revolution. They call themselves "Maritainians," "followers of Teilhard de Chardin," "socialist Catholics," or "evolutionists." Rarely is a priest who opposes the revolution elevated to the episcopacy; those who favor it—frequently.

According to the bishop of Jacarezinho, the situation of the Catholic Church in 1959 was already serious because of the infiltration of neo-modernists.

> . . . In my humble opinion, if the council wants to attain beneficial results, it must in the first place consider the current state of the Church, which like Christ, is experiencing a new Good Friday, handed over defenseless to her enemies, as Pius XII said to the Italian youth. It is necessary to see the mortal combat being waged against the Church in every field, to know the enemy, to discern the strategy and tactics of the battle, its logic, to see clearly the psychology and dynamics of it, so as to interpret accurately the individual conflicts and to organize the counterattack and conduct it confidently.

---

131 R. de Mattei, *The Crusader of the Twentieth Century, op. cit.*, 102–140, with the related bibliography.

> Our ruthless enemy of the Church and of Catholic society has been active in this conflict for five centuries now and with slow, systematic, and deadly progress has subverted and destroyed almost the entire Catholic order, that is, the city of God, and is striving to build the city of man in its place. His name is revolution. What does he want?
>
> To build the whole structure of human life, a society and a humanity without God, without the Church, without Christ, without revelation, relying only on human reason, on sensuality, greed, and pride. To this end it is necessary to subvert, destroy, and supplant the Church down to its foundations.
>
> In our days this enemy is more active than ever; indeed, he is sure of his victory in the coming years. Even so, many Catholics leaders dismiss what I say as the dreams of a sick imagination. They behave as the men of Constantinople behaved in the years before their defeat: being blind, they did not want to see the danger.[132]

Bishop de Proença Sigaud then analyzed the anti-Christian forces at work: communism, Freemasonry and international Judaism (while reiterating the Church's condemnation of anti-Semitism), stressing the role of the disordered passions in the revolutionary process.

> The revolutionary process begins at the end of the Middle Ages, continues with the pagan Renaissance, and made great strides during the pseudo-Reformation. During the French Revolution it destroyed the political and social foundation of the Church. During the conquest of the Papal States it thought that it was destroying the Holy See. With the confiscation and secularization of the properties of religious orders and dioceses it dispersed the patrimony of the Church. With modernism it created an extremely serious internal crisis, and most recently with communism it created a decisive instrument for banishing the Christian name from the earth.
>
> The greatest strength of the revolution comes from its cunning use of human passions. Communism created the science of revolution, and its most basic weapons are: unbridled human passions, methodically stirred up.
>
> The revolution uses two vices as forces to destroy Catholic society and to build an atheistic society: sensuality and pride. These strong,

[132] AD I-II/7:181–182.

> disordered passions are directed scientifically to a specific end, and they are submitted to the iron discipline of their masters in order to raze the city of God to its foundations and to build the city of man. They even welcome dictatorship and promote poverty so as to construct the social order of the Antichrist.[133]

The Brazilian bishop then established several principles to counteract this process.

> a. The condemnation of these perverse doctrines is absolutely necessary but is not sufficient.
>
> b. An organized campaign is necessary against these errors and against their proponents and those who spread errors. Such an organized campaign, like a well-ordered and methodical army, is easy to accomplish today because of advances in communications with the Holy See. However the clergy, the religious orders, our schools, and the laity are not being deployed systematically in this campaign. There is the lack of organized resistance against those ideas and those individuals.
>
> c. An organized campaign must strike also against disguised forms of revolution and its errors and spirit, which spread revolution along with its spirit. These forms generally have two characteristics:
>
> 1. They are logical consequences of errors, or psychological expressions of a false principle, applied to a very specific field.
>
> 2. The matter is presented in such a way that a less well-informed Catholic does not grasp the malice of the teaching.
>
> 3. Although the evil of the teaching is not perceived, the Catholic retains the perverse principle in his soul in a latent and active way, and without noticing it gradually becomes imbued with this principle, and with the spirit of the revolution.[134]

The bishop of Jacarenzinho considered it necessary to reissue the *Syllabus* of Pius IX, including in it the errors of socialism and those of Marc Sangnier

---

[133] AD I-II/7:184–185. For Plinio Corrêa de Oliveira too, the most profound cause of the revolutionary process is an explosion of pride and sensuality, which has animated a long series of cause and effects in the deepest regions of the soul and of Western culture (*Revolution and Counter-Revolution, op. cit., passim*).

[134] AD I-II/7:185.

and the "*Sillon*";[135] "the entire social heresy of Maritain,"[136] the idolatry of democracy; the idols of the Christian Democrats; the errors of liturgicism; the errors of Catholic Action regarding the priesthood of the laity, the errors concerning obedience and religious vows; the errors of communism concerning property, and universal pantheistic evolutionism."[137]

In his comprehensive treatment Bishop de Proença Sigaud then went on to describe the enemy's "Trojan Horse strategy"; he identified several characteristic points that the latter employed to dissolve Catholic principles and morality: "the doctrine of the lesser evil"; "adaptation to non-Catholics"; "collaboration with non-Catholics"; the myth of "good faith"; "dancing"; "fashions"; "beauty pageants"; provocative "cinema"; the circulation of bad books.[138]

Bishop Sigaud hoped for a "science of Counter-Revolution" that would help to strike hard at the errors inside and outside of the Church.

> The conspiracy of the revolution is united and organized. Such a conspiracy must be fought likewise with a unified, organized campaign....
>
> It seems to me that a Catholic strategy must be created with a centralized battle plan against the revolution worldwide, and that Catholics must be enlisted in it. Then there would be hope for the dawn of a truly better world. It is appropriate that the Holy See should

---

135 *Le Sillon* [The Furrow], the first historical expression of the Christian Democratic movement, founded by Marc Sangnier (1873–1950), was condemned by St. Pius X in 1906 with the letter *Notre charge apostolique* dated August 25, 1910 (in AAS 2 [1910]: 607–633). Cf. Emmanuel Barbier, *Les erreurs du Sillon: Histoire documentaire* (Paris: Lethielleux, 1906), and from a "Sillonist" perpective, Jean de Fabrègues, *Le Sillon de Marc Sangnier: Un tournant majeur du mouvement social catholique* (Paris: Perrin, 1964).

136 AD I-II/7:186. "One condemnation that is absolutely necessary is of Jacques Maritain. His errors have caused extremely serious harm to the Church, especially in Latin America. The young clergy is ruined by it. The damage of the errors of the 'Christian Democratic' Party is derived from Maritain's ideas. The political agitations in America are said to be provoked by his disciples. The Catholics say: 'The Vatican approves of Maritain, in fact he was ambassador of France to the Holy See.' The bishops call themselves 'Maritainists.' In the Catholic universities of Brazil his teachings dominate. Rome however is silent" (ibid., 189).

137 AD I-II/7:186.

138 Ibid., 186–189.

direct this "offensive." Those members of the clergy and the laity who have already been proven in the counter-revolutionary battle should make up the "officer corps" of this army. A true science of counter-revolutionary warfare must be created, just as there is a science of revolutionary warfare.

The Catholic battle against the Church's enemies often seems to me to be a battle of the blind against the sighted. We are ignorant of their goal, their method, their dynamics, strategy, and weapons....

The power of the Holy See is immense. If the faithful were enlisted and assembled, and were deployed energetically, clearly, methodically, in a truly worldwide battle, under the guidance of the Roman pontiff, the triumphal march of the revolution would be interrupted and the reign of the Sacred Heart of Jesus would be established. "To restore all things in Christ." ...

For many Catholics there is a strong temptation to treat communism in the same way liberalism was treated by the Church in the last century, and is still treated in our time....

Cooperation with communism will always have as its outcome the ruin of the Church.

The solution to today's problems is not to be found primarily in international conferences, but in the new Christianization of morals. If God and his Christ were placed at the foundation of individual, familial, and national life, the very forces of nature would require natural solutions, which would have to be assisted by human intellect and good will....

If the ecumenical council presented a positive plan for counter-revolutionary action and the building up of Christianity, including specific details, and called Catholics together for that purpose, I think that there would be the dawn of the Reign of the Sacred Heart of Jesus and of the Immaculate Heart of Mary."[139]

---

[139] AD I-II/7:191–195. "With liberalism," he explained, "coexistence is possible. 1) Liberalism did not prevent the Church from teaching her doctrine, and did not oblige her to teach liberal doctrine. 2) Liberalism allowed the condemnation of its errors. However under the communist regime neither of these two things happens." Instead, "the opposition of communism to the Catholic Church is essential, radical, continual, total" (Ibid., 192).

7. Italy "opens" to the Left

The "ante-preparatory" phase was followed by the actual "preparatory" phase of the council.

The pope, in his motu proprio *Superno Dei nutu*[140] (June 5, 1960), entrusted the task of preparing the working "schemas" that were to be submitted to the council to ten commissions (Theological Commission; Commission for Bishops and for the Government of Dioceses; for the Discipline of the Clergy and of the Christian Peoples; for Religious; for the Discipline of the Sacraments; for the Sacred Liturgy; for Seminaries Studies and Catholic Education; for Eastern Churches; for the Missions; for the Lay Apostolate). These commissions corresponded, with the exception of the Commission for the Lay Apostolate, to the Congregations of the Roman curia. Three secretariats were established also, one for the means of communication, one for economic and social aspects, and one for the union of Christians. A Central Preparatory Commission composed of cardinals, bishops, and superiors of religious orders, would coordinate and evaluate the work of the commissions. This commission at first was made up of seventy-four members plus its secretary, Pericle Felici, with the pope presiding. Thirteen cardinals were appointed to head the ten commissions and the three secretariats that were to prepare the schemas. Cardinal König, who represented the Austrian hierarchy within the Central Commission, wrote that the large majority of the members of the commission had no reformist ambitions but were inclined to present at the council the major themes of traditional theology.[141]

The year 1961 was almost entirely occupied with the work of the commissions and the secretariats, which was finished on June 11, 1962. On July 13, three months before the opening of the council, John XXIII ordered that the first seven schemas be sent to all of the council fathers as the basis for discussion by the General Congregations.

On July 20, 1961, the Secretary of State, Cardinal Tardini died. His death was described as "the second death of Pius XII."[142] John XXIII, ever since his election, had cleared every initiative with Tardini, and Tardini had defended him against the increasing pressures from the central European

140 AD I-I:93–99.

141 Cf. F. König, *Chiesa dove vai? Gianni Licheni interroga il cardinale Franz König* (Rome: Borla, 1985), 20.

142 C. Barthe, *op. cit.*, 94.

hierarchy. Cardinal Amleto Cicognani,[143] who succeeded him, was a much less colorful figure. The Secretary of State was in fact guided by Archbishop Angelo Dell'Acqua,[144] whom many considered Cardinal Montini's representative in Rome, while the role of the pope's "personal secretary," the Venetian Monsignor Loris Capovilla, was growing in importance. The ex-priest Carlo Falconi, explaining in the March 4, 1962, issue of *L'Espresso* the reasons that had prompted the pope to accept this "opening to the left," attributed to Monsignor Capovilla "most of the responsibility for the attitude of John XXIII." "Capovilla, it is commonly said, was in fact the point man of the left, if not the veritable standard-bearer of the opening to the left, in the Vatican City State. Even Montini's agent, Angelo Dell'Acqua, would follow him by many lengths."[145]

During the month of September the Soviet press (TASS, *Pravda*, and *Izvestia*) highlighted the September 10 radio message by John XXIII on peace,[146] which Khrushchev characterized as the sign of a change in the Holy See's policy with respect to the Eastern European countries. This was the climate in which Krushchev sent a message congratulating the pope on his eightieth birthday: a message that received worldwide coverage and showed the Soviets' willingness to establish permanent diplomatic relations with the Holy See.[147] The initiative for the birthday greetings seems to have come from a Roman cleric, Monsignor Giuseppe De Luca,[148] who had

---

[143] Amleto Giovanni Cicognani (1883–1973), ordained in 1905, was apostolic delegate in the United States for twenty-five years (1933–1969). Created cardinal by John XXIII, he was secretary of the Congregation for the Oriental Churches from 1959 to 1961, and in August of that year, at the death of Cardinal Tardini, he became Secretary of State.

[144] Angelo Dell'Acqua (1903–1972), ordained in 1928. Substitute of the Secretariat of State for ordinary affairs from 1952 to 1967, created cardinal in 1967 and, the following year, vicar general of Rome.

[145] [A horse-racing metaphor.] Cited in Mario Tedeschi, *I pericoli del Concilio* (Milan: Il Borghese, 1962), 93–94. On February 22, 1962, *Il Borghese*, edited by Tedeschi, launched a harsh attack on Monsignor Capovilla, in an article signed with the pseudonym *"Il bussolante"* [one who charts a course with a compass], entitled "Il potente monsignore."

[146] Cf. John XXIII, DMC 3:662–666.

[147] Cf. R. Burigana, "Il Partito comunista e la Chiesa," in *Vatican II in Moscow*, 188–226 at 201.

[148] Giuseppe De Luca (1898–1962), ordained in 1921, between 1942 and 1954 functioned as a mediator between representatives of the curia and the Italian political world. About see the article by Gabriele De Rosa in DBI 38: 347–353.

established an informal but direct channel of communication between the secretary of the Italian Communist Party, Togliatti, and the Vatican.[149]

On December 7 1958, three days after his coronation, John XXIII had received Cardinal Giuseppe Siri, informing him of his desire to replace promptly the leaders of Catholic Action, including its president Luigi Gedda,[150] the chief architect of the anti-communist victory of 1948. Simultaneously, the pope decided to reorganize the Italian Episcopal Conference (CEI), entrusting the presidency to Siri.[151] The young Siri was, as Gianni Baget Bozzo recalls, "the best theologian of the younger generation in Italy."[152] His vision of the Church and of society was antithetical to that of Cardinal Montini,[153] who had never shared Pius XII's vision of Italian politics,[154] with whom he had somehow collaborated closely as substitute Secretary of State. Pope Pacelli, who looked forward to a rebirth of a Christian Italy, did not approve of the "non-denominational character" of De Gaspari's Christian Democrats,[155] while Montini conceived of the

---

[149] R. Burigana, "Il Partito comunista e la Chiesa," *op. cit.*, 200–201; Luisa Mangoni, *In partibus infidelium: Don Giuseppe De Luca, il mondo cattolico e la cultura italiana del Novecento* (Turin: Einaudi, 1989), 397–398.

[150] Luigi Gedda (1902–2000), central president of the Italian Youth division of Catholic Action from 1934 to 1946, then general president of the whole association from 1952 to 1959, was one of the chief architects of the electoral success of the Christian Democrats in the elections of 1948, thanks to the "Civil Committees" that he organized.

[151] Cf. A. Riccardi, "La Conferenza episcopale italiana negli anni Cinquanta e Sessanta," in Various Authors, *Chiese italiane e Concilio: Esperienze pastorali nella Chiesa italiana tra Pio XII e Paolo VI* (Genoa: Marietti, 1988), 35–59; P. Gheda, "La Conferenza episcopale italiana e la preparazione del Concilio Vaticano II," in *La PUL e la preparazione del Concilio*, ed. P. Chenaux, Acts of an International Study Convention, Vatican City, January 20, 2000 (Rome: Mursia, 2001), 99–119.

[152] Gianni Baget Bozzo, "Don Camillo Siri," in *Panorama* (September 26, 1993): 120.

[153] Cf. P. Gheda, "Siri e Montini," in *Siri, La Chiesa, l'Italia, op. cit.*, 3–95.

[154] Cf. Pietro Scoppola, *La proposta politica di De Gasperi* (Bologna: Il Mulino, 1977); see also A. Riccardi, "Chiesa di Pio XII o chiese italiane?" in *Le chiese di Pio XII*, ed. A. Riccardi (Rome-Bari: Laterza, 1986), 21–52; *Idem,* "La Chiesa cattolica in Italia nel secondo dopoguerra," in G. De Rosa, ed., *Storia dell'Italia religiosa: L'età contemporanea* (Rome: Laterza, 1995), 335–339; *Idem, Pio XII e Alcide De Gasperi: Una storia segreta* (Rome-Bari: Laterza, 2003).

[155] Cf. Dario Composta, "I Cattolici di ieri e di oggi di fronte alla morale politica," in Various Authors, *Questione cattolica e questione democristiana*, ed. Danilo Castellano (Padua: CEDAM, 1987), 1–98.

Christian Democrats as a secular party and approved of its new political course,[156] supporting the left-wing Amintore Fanfani, who at the Congress of Florence in October 1959 prevailed on the Christian Democrats to renounce forever the support of the right-wing parties. The overture to the socialists appeared to be a logically consistent transition.[157]

In the early 1950s, Archbishop Montini, then Pro-Secretary of State, in a long and lively conversation with the archbishop of Genoa, had maintained "that a socialist experiment in Italy was inevitable." Siri had retorted sternly in these words: "Naturally, Your Excellency, if in your present position, with the status that you have, you think such an idea possible and support it, certainly you will find people who will follow it, and will make sure that it comes true. But remember that you will always find me on the opposite side."[158]

The Italian Episcopal Conference, headed by Siri, had a different approach from that of the Secretariat of State, where Archbishop Angelo Dell'Acqua supported Fanfani,[159] but it converged with the approach of the conservatives in the Roman curia. The May 18, 1960, issue of *L'Osservatore Romano* had published, under the significant headline "Firm Principles," an article written by Cardinal Ottaviani with Siri's assent, which claimed that the Catholic hierarchy had the right and duty to guide the faithful not only on the level of ideas but also on the level of political action."[160]

The street violence unleashed by the Communist Party of Genoa, in July 1960, effectively brought down the Prime Minister Fernando Tambroni, who was abandoned by his own party. The Fanfani government of the

---

[156] "The Maritainian roots of Montini's project led him to distinguish between a party with a Christian inspiration and a Catholic denominational party: the latter hypothesis was unacceptable" (N. Buonasorte, *Siri: Tradizione e Novecento, op. cit.*, 176); see also G. Baget Bozzo, "Maritain e la politica dei cattolici in Italia," in *Renovatio* XI/4 (1976): 539–548.

[157] Between 1954 and 1962, according to Gianni Baget Bozzo, "the explicit form of the Christian Democrats as a Christian party wasted away" (*Idem, Il partito cristiano e l'apertura a sinistra: La Dc di Fanfani e di Moro 1954–1962* [Florence: Vallecchi, 1977], 3).

[158] Conversation of Cardinal Siri with Benny Lai on April 12, 1985, in B. Lai, *Il Papa non eletto, op. cit.*, 98.

[159] Cf. Sandro Magister, *La politica vaticana e l'Italia 1943–1978* (Rome: Editori Riuniti, 1979), 203–204.

[160] See: Gaetano Quagliariello, "Il card. Giuseppe Siri e il quadro politico italiano," in *Siri, la Chiesa, l'Italia, op. cit.*, 238–253.

"parallel convergences" inaugurated, on July 26, the political "turn" to the left.[161] From then on, as Gianni Baget Bozzo observes, a "dual language" was created: the Christian Democrats would refer to the Church as "the Catholic electorate" and the Church would refer to the Christian Democratic Party as the "Christian party."[162] According to the Christian Democratic formulation, however, the Church was to be subordinated to the Party. The latter became the "guide of the "Catholic electorate" toward the "maturity" of political democracy.[163]

Moro, like the socialist Pietro Nenni, continued to borrow the ideas of "structural reform" and "planning policy"—considered indispensible for the transition to socialism—from the encylical of John XXIII, *Mater et Magistra*,[164] which had been published on May 15, 1961, and, as the Italian commentator Sandro Magister recalls, was interpreted "as an implicit free pass to ford the stream from the Christian Democratic Party to the shores of the center-left."[165]

Around the middle of 1961, moreover, the United States dropped its previous hostility toward the center-left in Italy.[166] In June 1961 Kennedy assured Fanfani, who was visiting Washington, that the White House would follow with watchful "sympathy" the Italian change of direction.[167] "The attempts by the president of the CEI, Cardinal Siri, to block this maneuver, came to naught. Moro turned directly to the pontiff, bypassing the Italian episcopate and obtaining from him his complete agreement."[168] In his speech on January 27 1962, Moro spoke theoretically about the

---

[161] Cf. Luciano Radi, *La Dc da De Gasperi a Fanfani* (Soveria Mannelli: Rubbettino, 2005), and Vincenzo La Russa, *Amintore Fanfani* (Soveria Mannelli: Rubbettino, 2006).

[162] Cf. G. Baget Bozzo, *Il partito cristiano e l'apertura a sinistra, op. cit.*, 5.

[163] On the itinerary of the Christian Democrats, see R. de Mattei, *Il centro che ci portò a sinistra* (Rome: Fiducia, 1994).

[164] John XXIII, encyliencyclical *Mater et Magistra* (May 15, 1961), in DMC 3:687–752.

[165] Sandro Magister, *La politica vaticana, op. cit.*, 261.

[166] Cf. Giuseppe Tamburrano, *Storia e cronaca del centro-sinistra* (Milan: Rizzoli, 1990), 74–78; R. de Mattei, "I padrini dell'Italia rossa," in *Cristianità* 14 (1975): 8–9.

[167] Arthur M. Schlesinger, *A Thousand Days: John F. Kennedy in the White House* (Greenwich, CT: Fawcett Publ., 1965), 802.

[168] On the relation between Moro and the Italian hierarchy, see, among other sources, Augusto D'Angelo, *Moro, i vescovi e l'apertura a sinistra* (Rome: Studium, 2005).

Catholic party becoming autonomous and non-denominational, thus establishing the "opening to the left," but without describing any specific program for it.[169]

8. The "Roman Party" takes sides

a) The "Roman school of theology"

The strategy of De Gaspari, who had initiated Italy's political shift to the left, had been vigorously opposed by the "Roman Party," the name by which Andrea Riccardi designated the ecclesiastical current of thought that had Archbishop Roberto Ronca[170] as its most active proponent during the fifties. His ecclesiastical career had run parallel to that of Archbishop Giovanni Battista Montini, whose position he had assumed as chaplain to the Italian Catholic University Federation (FUCI), and, as in the case of Cardinal Siri, his vision of the Church and of society was antithetical to that of Montini, whom he accused of having a "modernist sensibility."[171]

---

[169] Cf. Andrea Tornielli, *Paolo VI: L'audacia di un papa* (Milan: Mondadori, 2009), 261. Tornielli cites a note penned by Fanfani in his diary on March 27, 1962, in which it seems that John XXIII is giving a "green light" to the center-left.

[170] Roberto Ronca (1901–1977), ordained in 1928, in September 1929 was promoted to vice-rector of the Pontifical Major Seminary of Rome and in September 1933, rector of the same seminary. Then he was founder of the civic-political movement *Unione Nazionale Civiltà Italica* (1946–1955) and in 1949 of the men's and women's religious Congregation of the Oblates of Our Lady of the Rosary. In 1948 he was consecrated titular archbishop of Lepanto. In February 1962 he was appointed by John XXIII chief inspector of the chaplains of Italian prisons. He figures centrally in the study by A. Riccardi, *Il "partito romano", politica italiana, Chiesa cattolica e curia Romana da Pio XII a Paolo VI* (Brescia: Morcelliana, 1983, 20072), and is the object of research by Giuseppe Brienza, *Identità cattolica e anticomunismo nell'Italia del dopoguerra: La figura e l'opera di mons. Roberto Ronca* (Crotone: D'Ettoris, 2008), which deals especially with his role in the years 1940 and 1950. See also the booklet by R. Ronca himself (edited by G. Brienza), *Lavorare e sacrificarsi per la gloria di Maria* (Chieti: Amicizia Cristiana, 2010).

[171] Cf. A. Riccardi, *Il "partito romano," op. cit.*, 254, in which he tells of having met Archbishop Ronca in 1975 and of asking his opinion about Cardinal Montini, who had become Pope Paul VI. "He replied harshly: 'Montini, *salva reverentia* [with all due respect]—he was at that moment pope—was always a sinister individual.' Amazed by such a harsh judgment by a bishop with regard

At the age of only thirty-two, Ronca had been appointed rector of the Pontifical Roman Major Seminary, forming hundreds of alumni for the priesthood during his years as rector (1933-1948). He had then been promoted and for ten years (1946-1955) directed the "National Union for Italian Civilization" (*"Unione Nazionale Civiltà Italica"*), a Catholic, anti-communist civic-political movement, which distinguished itself by its training and publicity efforts before, during, and after the elections of April 18, 1948. Following the April 18 victory, Ronca was elevated on June 21, 1948, to the episcopal dignity with the title of archbishop of Lepanto. During the fifties, the "Roman Party" of Ronca had been the organized voice of the curia, or at least of that part of it that was more faithful to the line taken by Pius XII.

Circling the wagons around the curia was a top-level theological movement, which had its most authoritative mouthpiece in the journal *Divinitas*, edited by Monsignor Antonio Piolanti,[172] the rector of the Lateran University.[173] Despite its privileged relations with the Lateran, *Divinitas* accepted articles by the leading Roman theologians from the various religious orders, colleges and universities. Many of them were associated with the Congregation of the Holy Office and became members and consulters of the Preparatory Theological Commission for the

---

to the pope, I asked him in what sense he was sinister, and he laconically replied, 'in the sense of *sinistra* [the political left] he is *sinistro*'" (ibid., 257).

[172] Monsignor Antonio Piolanti (1911–2001), ordained in 1934, was professor of theology at the Urbanian and Lateran Universities; he was rector of the latter from 1957 to 1969. vice-president of the *Pontificia Accademia S. Tommaso d'Aquino* and Postulator of the Cause of Beatification of Pius IX. During the preparation for the council he was a member of the Theological Commission and subsequently a conciliar *peritus*. Cf. Costantino Vona, in PUL, 91–92; Enrico Bini, "Bibliografia degli scritti di mons. Antonio Piolanti," in *Divinitas* 34 (2002): i-xxxvi; R. M. Schmitz, "Prälat Prof. Dr. Antonio Piolanti (1991–2001): Zu Ehren eines grossen Vertreters der Römischen Schule," in *Doctor Angelicus* 2 (2002): 15–24.

[173] Shortly before the council, with the motu proprio *Cum inde* dated May 17, 1959, John XXIII elevated the Lateran Athenaeum to a Pontifical University. The Lateran University, "the University of the Pope" (cf. art. 1 of its Statutes) made use of two academic journals, *Divinitas* (1957) and *Aquinas* (1958), the common mouthpiece of the Faculty of Theology and the Pontifical Roman Theological Academy, with Monsignor Antonio Piolanti as editor-in-chief.

Council.[174] The point of reference for them was Thomistic philosophy,[175] which had been cited again as an example by the encylical *Aeterni Patris* of Leo XIII and was represented at the Lateran by internationally renowned professors such as Stigmatine Father Cornelio Fabro[176] and Piolanti himself, who had organized international congresses on St. Thomas Aquinas.

The number of professors from the Lateran who took part in the work of the preconciliar phase was significant. Many seminary instructors worked on the Preparatory Theological Commission, or on other commissions, among them (besides the rector Piolante and Father Fabro) Monsignor Ugo Lattanzi,[177] Fathers Umberto Betti, [178] and Agostino Trapè[179] of the Medieval Patristics Institute, Monsignor Salvatore Garofalo,[180]

---

174 Cf. E. Fouilloux, "Théologiens romains et Vatican II (1959–1962)," in *Cristianesimo nella storia* 15 (1994): 373–394.

175 "No one who thinks in a Catholic way can set aside the encylical encyclical *Aeterni Patris* (August 4, 1879) by Leo XIII. This encylicalencyclical is insurmountable" (G. Siri, "Ortodossia: cedimenti compromessi," Pastoral letter dated July 7, 1961, in *Il primato della verità: Lettere pastorali sull'ortodossia* [Pisa; Giardini, 1984], 36).

176 Cornelio Fabro (1911–1995), ordained in 1935 in the Stigmatine order. Professor of philosophy at various universities, member of the Preparatory Commission and *peritus* at Vatican Council II. About him see, *inter alia*, Rosa Goglia, *Cornelio Fabro: Profilo biografico, cronologico, tematico da inedtit, note di archivio, testimonianze* (Rome: Edivi, 2010).

177 Ugo Lattanzi (1899–1971), ordained in 1924, head of the department of biblical theology (1934) and then professor of dogmatic theology (1954) at the Lateran University, dean of the Faculty of Theology (1963), consultor of the Preparatory Theological Commission, conciliar *peritus.*

178 Umberto Betti (1922–2009), Franciscan, ordained in 1946, professor at the Antonianum, consultor of the Preparatory Theological Commission, *peritus* of Cardinal Florit, rector of the Lateran University from 1991 to 1995.

179 Agostino Trapé (1915–1987), of the Augustinian order, of which he was general superior, ordained in 1937, professor of patrology at various Roman universities. Member of the Preparatory Theological Commission, was appointed *peritus* at the council in 1962.

180 Salvatore Garofalo (1911–1998), ordained in 1933, professor of biblical exegesis and then rector in the Pontifican Urbanian University, conciliar *peritus.*

Don Roberto Masi,[181] Monsignor Francesco Spadafora,[182] Father Charles Boyer, and others.[183]

Among the various athenaeums, Catholic universities and ecclesiastical faculties that were extensively consulted during preparations for the council, the *votum* [formal written evaluation] of the Lateran University stood out not only for its quality but also for its volume (273 pages) and for the number of those who contributed to its composition (a good twenty-seven professors belonging to the faculties of theology, canon law, and philosophy).[184] The journal *Divinitas*, edited by Piolanti himself, produced two special issues dedicated to the impending council; the first, which appeared in 1961 with the title *Magisterium et theologia*, emphasized the role of the Church's magisterium; the second, entitled *Symposium theologicum de Ecclesia Christi*, published in 1962, proposed "to reject the aberrations that are circulating even within the field of Catholic theology, and to shed light on the way toward a correct solution."[185]

During the Lateran University's week in preparation for the council, Monsignor Antonio Piolanti proposed a council that would condemn the

---

181 Roberto Masi (1914–1969), ordained in 1930, professor of sacramental theology at the Lateran. Conciliar *peritus*.

182 Francesco Spadafora (1913–1997), ordained in 1935, professor of sacred scripture at the Marianum and, from 1956 on, at the Pontifical Lateran University. Was secretary of the Italian Biblical Association and founded the *Rivista biblica* and edited it for five years. Participated in Vatican Council II as a member of the Preparatory Commission for Studies and Seminaries. About him see "In memoria di mons. Francesco Spadafora," in *Sì sì no no* 5 (2007): 1–2.

183 Férmina Álvarez Alonso, "La posizione del Laterano sui problemi ecclesiologici nella fase preparatoria del Concilio," in *L'Università del Laterano e la preparazione del Concilio Vaticano II*, ed. P. Chenaux (Mursia: PUL, 2001), 78–79. The Lateran's Patristic-Medieval Institute included instructors such as Monsignor Andrea Combes and Fathers Carlo Balić, O.F.M., Umberto Betti, O.F.M., Charles Boyer, S.J., Cornelio Fabro, C.S.S., Louis Gillon, O.P., Bonaventura Mariani, O.F.M., Michel Guérard des Lauriers, O.P., Gabriele Maria Roschini, O.S.M., Pawel Siwek, S.J., Agostino Trapé, O.S.A., Alberto Vaccari, S.J. Some of these instructors collaborated with the *Cattedra San Tommaso*, launched on March 10, 1963, with the support of other illustrious scholars, such as Father Philippe de la Trinité, O.C.D., president of the Carmelite Theological Faculty, Étienne Gilson, of the *Académie Française*, Nicola Petruzzellis, from the University of Naples, and the Dominican Santiago Ramírez from the Pontifical University of Salamanca.

184 AD I-IV/1:171–442.

185 Cf. F. Álvarez Alonso, *op. cit.*, 67–80.

errors of the modern world, along the same lines as what Father Gabriel Maria Roschini,[186] head of the theology faculty at the Marianum, had done on December 6, 1959, when he sent to Archbishop Felici a well organized study with the significant title *Collection of Contemporary Theological Errors,*[187] in which he expressed the hope that the council would issue a new *Syllabus against the Principal Errors of our Age.*[188]

The Lateran was heir to the glorious "Roman school of theology," that was born during the pontificates of Gregory XVI (1831-1846) and Pius IX (1846-1878) and was exemplified by great theologians like Giovanni Perrone,[189] who can be considered its founder, and Louis Billot, who was its greatest disciple from the late nineteenth century into the twentieth, having taught for forty-two years at the Gregorianum.[190] In the field of

---

[186] Gabriele Maria Roschini (1900–1977), of the Servants of Mary, whom Stefano De Fiores describes as "the most famous manualist Mariologist of our century" (*Maria Madre di Gesù* [Bologna: Dehoniane, 1993], 376), was master of Sacred Theology in his order, consultor of the Supreme Congregation of the Holy Office, founder of the journal *Marianum* (1939), promoter and first president of the Marianum Faculty of Rome. Among his works are a four-volume *Mariologia* in Latin (Rome, 1941–1948); *La Madonna secondo la fede e la teologia*, 4 vols. (Rome: F. Ferrari, 1953–1954); *Maria Santissima nella storia della salvezza: Trattato completo di mariologia alla luce del Concilio Vaticano II* (Isola del Liri: Pisani Editore, 1969), 4 vols. A non-exhaustive bibliography can be found in Giuseppe Maria Besutti, "Bibliografia di P. Gabriele M. Roschini, O.S.M.," in *Marianum* 41 (1979): 1–63. This 587–page issue of the journal compiles the studies offered in his memory. See also "Atto accademico nel venticinquesimo della morte di Fra Gabriele M. Roschini o.s.m., primo preside della Facoltà († Roma, 12 settembre 1971)," in *Marianum* 64 (2002): 547–606; Pietro Parrotta, *La cooperazione di Maria alla redenzione in Gabriele Maria Roschini* (Pregassona: Eupress, 2002).

[187] G. Maria Roschini, O.S.M., *Silloge degli erroro teologici contemporanei: Con appendice sul "Magistero ecclesiastico"* (Rome: Facoltà Teologica "Marianum," 1959).

[188] Roschini to Felici, December 6, 1959, in ASV, Conc. Vat. II, busta 259, fasc. 15, f. 1.

[189] Giovanni Perrone (1794–1876), ordained in 1827 in the Society of Jesus, professor at the Roman College. His chief work, *Praelectiones theologicae* I-IX (Rome: Typis Collegi Urbani, 1835–1842), went through thirty editions and it a theological classic.

[190] One should also include in the "Roman School" in the broad sense Fathers Carlo Passaglia (1812–1887), Clemens Schrader (1820–1875), Johann Baptist Franzelin (1816–1886) of the Society of Jesus, illustrious Dominicans such as Fathers Tommaso Maria Zigliara (1833–1883), Zefirino Gonzales (1831–1894), Alberto Lepidi (1838–1922), Reginald Garrigou-Lagrange, and theologians who never taught in Rome but absorbed its spirit, such as Matthias Scheeben

Public Law, its most eminent representative in the nineteenth century was Cardinal Camillo Tarquini,[191] whose principal work *Juris publici ecclesiastici institutiones* had gone through more than thirty editions. Other descendants of this same school were Cardinal Felice Cavagnis,[192] Father Felice Maria Cappello,[193] and Cardinal Alfredo Ottaviani. There was a saying then in Rome: *"Tarquini genuit Cavagnis autem Cavagnis genuit Cappello et Ottaviani"* ["Tarquini begot Cavagnis, Cavagnis begot Cappello and Ottaviani"].[194]

A few days after Tardini's death on August 13, Cardinal Nicola Canali also died, who was the most faithful heir of the pontificate of St. Pius X and the "strong man" of the Vatican "Pentagon." From now on it was destined to be represented by Cardinal Ottaviani alone, who in 1935 had replaced Canali as assessor at the Holy Office and later became its secretary. The "Roman Party" now found in him its best qualified exponent.[195]

(1835–1888), Hugo Adalbert Hurter (1832–1914), Heinrich Denzinger (1819–1883), Joseph Hergenröther (1824–1890), the first Cardinal-prefect of the Vatican Archives; cf. Heribert Schauf, *Carlo Passaglia und Clemens Schrader: Beitrag zur Theologiegeschichte des neunzehnten Jahrhunderts* (Rome: Pontifical Gregorian University, 1938); W. Kasper, *Die Lehre von der Tradition in der Römischen Schule* (Freiburg: Herder, 1962); K. H. Neufeld, "'Römische Schule': Beobachtungen und Überlegungen zur genaueren Bestimmung," in *Gregorianum* 63/64 (1983): 677–699; B. Gherardini, *Quod et tradidi vobis: La tradizione vita e giovinezza* (Frigento [AV]: Casa Mariana Editrice, 2010).

[191] Camillo Tarquini (1810–1874), ordained in 1833, member of the Society of Jesus in 1837, professor of Canon Law for twenty years at the Roman College, created cardinal in 1873 by Pius IX. See his famous *Iuris Ecclesiastici publici institutiones* (Rome, 1862).

[192] Felice Cavagnis (1841–1906), ordained in 1863, pro-secretary of the Roman curia in 1893, created cardinal in 1901. Was also an eminent philologist and archaeologist.

[193] Felice Maria Cappello (1879–1962), theologian and canonist of the Society of Jesus, ordained in 1902, professor of Canon Law at the Gregorianum from 1920 to 1959. His cause for beatification was introduced (1998). See his *Summa Iuris publicis ecclesiastici* (Rome, 1923). See the biographical profile by D. Mondrone, *Il confessore di Roma: padre Felice M. Cappello* (Rome: La Civiltà Cattolica, 1962).

[194] G. Martina, "The Historical Context...," *op. cit.*, 49.

[195] Cf. A. Riccardi, *Il "partito romano," op. cit.*, 45–46 and *passim*.

b) The Theological Commission's "Profession of Faith"

The Theological Commisssion,[196] presided over by Cardinal Alfredo Ottaviani, was the most important conciliar commission because of its exclusive competence in doctrinal matters. As secretary of the Congregation of the Holy Office, which was known as *"la Suprema"* because of the preeminent role that it played in defending the purity and integrity of the faith, Ottaviani, son of a baker from Trastevere, was, like his school-mate Tardini, a genuine "Roman of Rome." His public persona was that of the inflexible guardian of the doctrine of the faith, but his doctrinal firmness was inseparable from his personal warmth, well known by the children of Rione Borgo and of the Aurelio district, where he ministered zealously and generously for years.

The secretary of the Theological Commission was the Dutch Jesuit Sebastian Tromp,[197] a professor at the Gregorianum, who had also been visitator of the Catholic University of Nijmegen, and of the Dutch seminaries, and in the Netherlands he was regarded with distrust on account of his *"romanità."* He in turn had an excellent collaborator in Father Heribert Schauf.[198] Pope John had entrusted to the Theological Commission the task of investigating *"quaestiones ad Scripturam sacram, sacram Traditionem, fidem moresque spectantes"*[199] ["questions concerning sacred scripture, sacred tradition, and faith and morals"]. Collaborating as

---

[196] See also R. Burigana, "Progetto dogmatico del Vaticano II: la Commissione teologica preparatoria," in *Verso il Concilio Vaticano II (1960–1962): Passaggi e problemi della preparazione conciliare*, ed. G. Alberigo and A. Melloni (Genoa: Marietti, 1993), 141–206.

[197] Sebastian Tromp (1889–1975), Dutch Jesuit, ordained in 1922, professor of theology at the Gregorianum from 1929 to 1967, member of the Pontifical Academy of Theology (1956), author of many works, among them the fundamental *Corpus Christi quod est Ecclesia*, 4 vols. (Rome, 1937–1972). secretary of the Preparatory Theological Commission and then of the Doctrinal Commission. Conciliar *peritus*. Cf. G. Barjen, "Tromp," in DHCJ, 3842–3843.

[198] Heribert Schauf (1910–1988), German, ordained in 1935, professor of Canon Law at Aachen, member of the Preparatory Theological Commission, conciliar *peritus*. Cf. *Geist und Kirche: Studien zur Theologie im Umfeld der beiden Vatikanischen Konzilien: Gedenkschrift für Heribert Schauf*, ed. Herbert Hammans, Hermann-Josef Reudenbach, and Heino Sonnemans (Paderborn: Verlag Ferdinand Schöningh, 1991).

[199] Cf. J. A. Komonchak, "The Struggle for the Council During the Preparation of Vatican II," in HVT 1:167–356, at 227–236.

members of this commission were the greatest Roman theologians: Philippe de la Trinité,[200] Luigi Ciappi, Marie-Rosaire Gagnebet,[201] and Franz Xavier Hürth.[202]

The Theological Commission considered it necessary to open the council with a *Formula nova professionis fidei*, a new formula of faith that would combine the Tridentine profession with the anti-modernist oath.[203] The text, approved by the pope, was sent by Cardinal Ottaviani to the Central Preparatory Commission on November 8, 1961.[204] It consisted of eighteen points that reaffirmed the traditional Catholic truths, condemning a series of errors such as: secularism, the denial of the Catholic Church as the one Church, the denial of the difference between the universal priesthood and the hierarchical priesthood, minimalism in Mariology, and the abandonment of the doctrine of hell. The *Formula fidei* was displeasing to the Central Commission, however, which considered it excessively "defensive" and set it aside. It is worth trouble to reread today at least the final points in this *Formula fidei* in order to appreciate its pellucid clarity and striking relevance.

> I acknowledge with sincere faith original sin, through which all men have sinned in their first father, Adam, (as a) sin strictly speaking that is transmitted by generation and belongs to each individual.
>
> I acknowledge as absolutely certain signs the external proofs of revelation, and first of all the miracles and the prophecies, through which without any doubt it is demonstrated that the Christian religion has a divine origin, and I maintain that even today it is suited to the

200 Philippe de la Trinité (1908–1977), French Discalced Carmelite, ordained in 1934. Entered the Holy Office in 1952 and as of the following year also headed the theology faculty of his order.

201 Marie-Rosaire Gagnebet (1904–1983), French Dominican, professor of theology at the Angelicum (1935), then consultor of the Holy Office (1964), member of the Preparatory Theological Commission, conciliar *peritus*.

202 Franz Hürth (1880–1963), German Jesuit, ordained in 1905. Professor at the Gregorianum, then *peritus* in 1962.

203 Cf. "Formula Nova Professionis Fidei (Secunda Congregatio: 9 novembre 1961)," in AD, II-II/1:495–497. Antonino Indelicato, "La 'Formula nova professionis fidei' nella preparazione del Vaticano II," in *Cristianesimo nella storia* 7 (1986): 305–340.

204 Cf. A. Indelicato, *Difendere la dottrina o annunciare l'Evangelo: Il dibattito nella Commissione centrale preparatoria del Vaticano II* (Genoa: Marietti, 1992).

human intellect. I also maintain that the Church itself, considered *per se*, on account of its universal unity, its sublime holiness, its inexhaustible fruitfulness in all good things, its marvelous diffusion, and its invincible firmness, is a perpetual reason for belief and an indisputable testimony to its divine inheritance.

I sincerely accept the doctrine of the faith handed down to us by the apostles by way of the orthodox fathers with the same meaning and with the same expressions. Therefore, even though the Church grows in its understanding of revealed truth, I nevertheless reject as heretical the opinion of the evolution of dogmas which with the passage of time take on a different meaning from the one that the Church taught once and for all.

I hold that the deposit of faith, that is to say, the word of God written or handed down by the apostles, is complete. I firmly hold that sacred scripture, free of all error, must be explained with the guidance of the magisterium of the faith, according to the norm of tradition and according to the analogy of the faith.

I profess that faith is not just an obscure religious sentiment or just an opinion of the mind, but a true assent of the intellect to the truth, received from outside by hearing, through which we believe what has been revealed and testified by a personal God, because of the authority of God who is supremely truthful, and in believing in him we offer the full submission of our intellect and will, with the inspiration and the help of God's grace.

I profess without any doubt all of the other truths defined and proclaimed by the ecumenical councils and above all by the sacred Council of Trent and the First Vatican Ecumenical Council, particularly with regard to the primacy of jurisdiction of the Roman pontiff and his infallible magisterium, and so I condemn and reject what has been condemned and rejected in those same councils and in the encylical letters, especially *Pascendi* and *Humani generis*.

This true Catholic faith, apart from which no one can be saved, I now profess freely, and I sincerely uphold it, and I will strive so that it may be preserved whole and inviolate by me and by those who are subject to me, until the final breath of my life, with utmost firmness and absolute constancy, with the help of God. And so I myself, N., in the presence of God and of Jesus Christ, who will judge me worthy of eternal life or everlasting punishment, do promise, vow, and swear.[205]

---

205 A. Indelicato, "La 'Formula nova professionis fidei,'" *op. cit.*, 497.

The prominence of the role assigned to the Theological Commission, presided over by Cardinal Ottaviani, was clear to everyone. On the other hand nobody ascribed great importance to the creation of the secretariat for Promoting Christian Unity, a new organization presented as a simple "service," like other recently instituted press and administrative services. In reality, this secretariat, entrusted to Cardinal Augustin Bea, was destined to become the most powerful engine of the opposition to the Theological Commission and to the doctrinal line set by the Roman curia.

9. Cardinal Bea appears on the scene.

a) The Secretariat for Promoting Christian Unity

Among the eight cardinals appointed by John XXIII in the Consistory of December 14, 1959, was Father Augustin Bea, now eighty years old, the former confessor of Pius XII and the former rector of the Pontifical Biblical Institute in Rome. When Roncalli created him cardinal, Augustin Bea was already "old, stoop-shouldered, his long face full of creases and wrinkles, and somewhat bent over," as Benny Lai described him,[206] and his life, according to his biographer, seemed to be headed toward a "peaceful sunset."[207] In November 1959, the archbishop of Paderborn, Lorenzo Jäger,[208] had presented to the new cardinal the plan for the creation of a "Pontifical Commission to promote the unity of Christians."[209] Bea, on March 11, 1960, presented in turn a petition to the pope, who welcomed it in a surprisingly speedy manner, receiving him in audience two days later. John XXIII said that he was thoroughly in agreement, and merely changed the name of the new organization. "Commissions," he said to Bea, "have their own tradition. Let us call this new organism a secretariat. That way you will not be connected to any tradition; you will be freer."[210]

---

[206] Cf. B. Lai, *Vaticano Aperto* (Milan: Longanesi, 1968), 178–179.

[207] Schmidt, *Bea*, 309–318.

[208] Lorenzo Jäger (1892–1975), German, ordained in 1922, archbishop of Paderborn from 1941 to 1973, created cardinal in 1965. Member of the Secretariat for Promoting Christian Unity.

[209] Cf. Schmidt, *Bea*, 342–348.

[210] Ibid., 348.

On June 5, 1960, the pope appointed Bea president of the newly created secretariat for Promoting Christian Unity, a post that the German cardinal held until his death and that made him the key figure in the development of ecumenism in the Catholic Church. The appointment signaled a change not only in the life of the cardinal, who unexpectedly recovered his health and strength, but above all in the history of the Church. It can be considered, after the appointment of Cardinal Montini, the most important appointment of John XXIII's pontificate.

On September 23, 1960, the secretariat opened its headquarters at *Via dei Corridori* 64. The Dutch priest Johannes Willebrands[211] was named the secretary of the organization. Thirty years younger than Bea, Willebrands was his closest collaborator and was continuously at his side, until the German Jesuit's death on November 16, 1968. After Bea, the *"spiritus rector"* ["guiding spirit"] of the secretariat, as Hans Küng observed, would be precisely Willebrands.[212] Thus was born, officially as well, the "duo" Bea-Willebrands, president and secretary of the newly minted ecumenical organization.[213]

The first step taken by the secretariat was a meeting, held in secrecy at the Saint Fidelis Center in Milan, between Bea and Visser't Hooft, secretary general of the World Council of Churches (WCC, founded in 1949), in order to establish the outline for a collaboration between the two organizations. Willebrands, president of the St. Willibrord Association and personal advisor to the archbishop of Utrecht on ecumenical issues, had long since had ties with Willem Visser't Hooft, who was also Dutch. With regard to the plan for that meeting, Bea related that he had previously asked John XXIII whether he thought it opportune to make contact with the WCC. "The matter does not seem ripe to me," the pope replied. "For my part," the cardinal declares, "I drew the conclusion that it was therefore necessary to make it ripen."[214]

---

[211] Johannes Willebrands (1909–2006), Dutch, ordained in 1934, secretary of the Secretariat for Promoting Christian Unity, conciliar *peritus* and then titular bishop of Mauriana (1964). Created cardinal on April 28, 1969, succeeded Cardinal Bea as president of the secretariat and then Cardinal Alfrink as archbishop of Utrecht from 1975 to 1983.

[212] Küng, *My Struggle*, 184.

[213] Cf. Salvatore Campo, "I cardinali Bea e Willibrands: il loro ruolo 'ecumenico' nel Vaticano II," in *Istituto Paolo VI* 52 (2006): 60–68. Willebrands was assisted by two collaborators: the Frenchman Jean-François Arrighi and the American Thomas Stransky.

[214] Schmidt, *Bea*, 361.

The creation of the new organization was a genuine turning point because it took away from the Holy Office the responsibility for relations between Catholics and other Christians, and above all because it turned on its head the traditional Roman attitude towards heretics and schismatics.[215] Around Bea and Willebrands a congenial team formed which during the preparatory period of the council held various meetings in the religious house of the Pious Union of St. Paul, in the Castelli Romani [the suburban hills south of Rome]. Monsignor Jean-François Arrighi,[216] one of their young collaborators, recalled that "During those days of intense work, a spirit of fraternity developed, which was one of the most important characteristics of the Secretariat for Unity."[217]

Bea and his collaborators had ambitious ideas, which went far beyond the essentially "informative" task entrusted by John XXIII to the Secretariat for Promoting Christian Unity. The principal way in which the secretariat sought to influence the preparatory work was by forwarding to the other commissions documents that emphasized the negative consequences that the schemas being drafted could have on ecumenism. The secretariat was therefore a crypto-commission that cut across all the others and arrogated to itself a directly theological competence, branching out into sub-commissions on many fundamental topics such as the relation of non-Catholic baptized Christians with the Church; the hierarchical structure of the Church; the priesthood of all believers; the laity; religious liberty; the word of God in the Church; liturgical questions; mixed marriages; the ecumenical movement. The documents from the Theological Commission and those with an opposing orientation from the Secretariat for Promoting Christian Unity would arrive together at the Central Commission, provoking vehement polemics and discussions within it: one typical case was the topic of religious liberty.

---

[215] Cf. G. Alberigo, "Il pontificato di Giovanni XXIII," *op. cit.*, 27–28; S. Schmidt, "Giovanni XXIII e il Segretariato per l'unione dei cristiani," in *Cristianesimo nella storia* 8 (1987): 95–117; M. Velati, "'Un'udienza a Roma': La nascita del Segretariato per l'Unità dei Cristiani (1959–1960)," in *Il Vaticano II fra attesa e celebrazione*, 74–118.

[216] Jean-François Mathieu Arrighi (1918–1998), French, ordained in 1948, vice-president of the Pontifical Council for the Family and bishop of Vico Equense in 1985.

[217] Cited in Caprile, 5:716.

b) Bea and Ottaviani square off

On June 19, 1962, the next to last day of the final session, Cardinals Ottaviani and Bea came into direct conflict. Two schemas were presented: one from the Theological Commission and the other from the Secretariat for Promoting Christian Unity. Bea, in presenting his schema, asserted that it was focused on non-Catholics and corresponded to the *"aggiornamento"* of current living conditions in the Church desired by the pope.[218] Ottaviani vehemently retorted that the secretariat had no right to deal with the question, for which the Theological Commission was competent.

Archbishop Marcel Lefebvre[219] recalls this episode, of which he was a eyewitness:

> I must relate to you a minor incident that occurred in 1962, when I was a member of the Central Preparatory Commission of the council. We held our meetings in the Vatican, but the last one was dramatic. Among the papers given to the Central Commission there were two on the same subject: one came from Cardinal Bea, president of the Commission for Unity, and the other from Cardinal Ottaviani, president of the Theological Commission. When we had read them, when I myself had read the two schemas, I said: "It is very strange that there are two completely different points of view on the same subject, that is, religious liberty or the Church's attitude toward other religions." Cardinal Bea's was entitled *De libertate religiosa*; Cardinal Ottaviani's—*De tolerantia*

---

[218] Cf. AD II-IV:689.

[219] Marcel Lefebvre (1905–1991), of the Congregation of the Holy Spirit. Ordained in 1929, titular bishop of Antedonia (1947); apostolic vicar of Dakar (1948–1955); titular archbishop of Arcadiopoli in Europa (1948); apostolic delegate for French Africa (1948–1959); archbishop of Dakar (1955–1962); bishop of Tulle (1962), then of Sinnada in Phrygia (196–1970); superior general of the Congregation of the Holy Spirit (1962–1969). In 1970, founded the Priestly Society of Saint Pius X in the Diocese of Fribourg, Switzerland, with the approval of Bishop François Charrière, the local Ordinary. In 1974 began the dispute with the Holy See that would lead to his suspension *a divinis*, following priestly ordinations that he celebrated on June 29, 1976, and to his excommunication *latae sententiae*, after he consecrated four bishops on June 30, 1988 (AAS 80 [1988]: 1495–1498). The excommunication of the four bishops was revoked by Benedict XVI on March 10, 2009. Concerning him see, among other works, Bernard Tissier de Mallerais, *Marcel Lefebvre: The Biography* (Kansas City, MO: Angelus Press, 2004); Cristina Siccardi, *Mons. Marcel Lefebvre: Nel nome della Verità* (Milano: Sugarco, 2010).

> *religiosa*. Do you see the difference, the profound difference? What was happening? Why two completely different schemas on the same subject? At that moment during the meeting, Cardinal Ottaviani stood up and, pointing with his finger, said to Cardinal Bea: "Eminence, you did not have the right to compose this schema, you did not have the right to do it because it is a theological schema and therefore within the competence of the Theological Commission." And as Cardinal Bea stood up he said: "Excuse me, but I did have the right to compose this schema as president of the Commission on Unity; if anything concerns unity, certainly religious liberty does." He added, turning to Cardinal Ottaviani, "I radically oppose what you say in your schema *De tolerantia religiosa*." … It was the final session of the Central Commission, and we could clearly perceive, on the eve of the council, displayed in front of us, the whole battle that would take place during the council. This means that these things had already been prepared before the council. Cardinal Bea certainly did not compose his schema *De libertate religiosa* without having reached an agreement with other cardinals.[220]

To get around the doctrinal obstacles, the secretariat proposed a new "para-diplomatic" way of expressing the faith, which consisted of couching dogmatic topics in contemporary terms without addressing them from a dogmatic perspective, but rather leaving them vague in the name of the primacy of the pastoral approach.[221]

The secretary for Promoting Christian Unity expanded his role, moreover, through the influence that he exerted on the "mixed commissions." Most of these commissions in fact duplicated the curial dicasteries and were composed of bishops who were faithful to Rome. While the Theological Commission rejected all interference by Bea's secretariat in the composition of the schemas, other commissions agreed to form "mixed commissions" with the Secretariat for Promoting Christian Unity, for instance the Commission for the Discipline of the Sacraments. The best collaboration occurred with the Liturgical Commission, whose secretary was Father Annibale Bugnini. Bea's secretariat asked, in February 1961, for "the widest

---

220 M. Lefebvre, *Le Coup de maître de Satan: Ecône face à la persécution* (Martigny: Éditions Saint-Gabriel, 1977). Citation translated from the Italian edition: *Il colpo da maestro di Satana* (Milan: Il Falco, 1978), 12–15.

221 Cf. C. Barthe, *op. cit.*, 97–98.

possible use of the vernacular."[222] In April Bea himself intervened: "We must strongly oppose the idea that [liturgical] Latin is a sign of unity. It is more a sign of uniformity than a sign of unity."[223]

On October 22, eleven days after the opening of the council, John XXIII elevated the Secretariat for Promoting Christian Unity to the rank of a commission. This new status gave the organization the right to present schemas to the General Assembly and to correct them. Its role would be decisive.

10. The biblical controversy

a) Monsignor Romeo's cry of alarm

The Pontifical Biblical Institute, directed by Father Bea, had become one of the principal centers for the dissemination of the new rationalistic exegesis. In fact, as the historian Mauro Pesce points out, from the 1930s to the 1960s, impelled by Bea, historical exegesis managed to bring about "profound changes in Catholic theological thought, without even directly venturing a reform of theology as such."[224] Bea's work was continued by Father Ernest Vogt,[225] who in 1949 succeeded Father Bea as head of the Biblical Institute.[226] Monsignor Francesco Spadafora recalls that at the Biblicum there was at that time the atmosphere "of a mystery religion," in which the devotees of the "innovations" considered themselves the custodians of truths unknown to the others, which it was necessary however to spread by any and all means. The watchword was the dialectical juxtaposition between a retrograde or "rigid" biblical school and a modern

[222] J. A. Komonchak, "The Struggle for the Council During the Preparation of Vatican II," *op. cit.*, 220.

[223] Ibid.

[224] M. Pesce, "Esegi storica … da Leone XIII a Pio XII," *op. cit.*, 286 .

[225] Ernest Vogt (1903–1984), Swiss Jesuit, ordained in 1933. Rector of the Biblical Institute from 1949 to 1963. Appointed consultor of the Preparatory Theological Commission in early 1961.

[226] Cf. F. Spadafora, *La nuova esegesi: Il trionfo del modernismo sull'Esegesi Cattolica* (Sion: Éditions Les Amis de saint François de Sales, 1996), 63–70. See also *Idem, Razionalismo: Esegesi cattolica e Magistero* (Rovigo: Istituto padano di Arti Grafiche, 1961).

or "broad-minded" school, which the encylical by Pius XII, *Divino afflante Spiritu* (1943), allegedly had "canonized." The manifesto of this "new way" appeared to be the article by the Jesuit Luis Alonso Schökel,[227] "Whither Catholic Exegesis?" which was published in 1960 in the August 27 issue of *Civiltà Cattolica*,[228] in which the author described the existence of a "strict" school which should be considered outmoded, and a "broad" school that was now predominant in the field of exegetical studies. According to the innovators, the encylical of Pius XII represented a moment of discontinuity with the encylical *Providentissimus* of Leo XIII, of which it celebrated the fiftieth anniversary, and supposedly had opened up "a new and fuller way"[229] in biblical studies. Schökel reiterated the thesis of his confrère at the Biblicum, Stanislas Lyonnet,[230] who had been a professor at Fourvière from 1938 to 1943 and was connected with the *"nouvelle théologie."* He dismissed original sin, repeating the rationalist exegesis which maintains that the Pauline verse, "death spread to all men because all men sinned", (Rom 5:12) should be understood to refer, not to original sin, but rather to the personal sins of each individual. Monsignor Spadafora, in a detailed article in the review *Divinitas*,[231] demonstrated that Lyonnet, besides presenting inconsistent philological arguments, did not take into account at all the infallible magisterium of the Church. These critiques were deemed excessive, but it is no accident that one of Lyonnet's students, the Dutch

---

[227] Luis Alonso Schökel (1920–1998), Spanish Jesuit, professor of sacred scripture at the Biblicum from 1957 on.

[228] Cf. L. A. Schökel, S.J., "Dove va l'esegesi cattolica?" in *Civiltà Cattolica*, q. 2645 (1960): 449–460.

[229] Ibid., 455–456.

[230] Stanislas Lyonnet (1902–1986), French Jesuit, ordained in 1934. Professor of sacred scripture at Fourvière (1938) then of exegesis at the Biblical Institute. He had to interrupt his teaching career at the request of the Holy Office from 1962 to 1964. Cf. Albert Vanhoye, "In memoriam," in *Rivista Biblica* 68 (1987): 141–142. See his "Le péché originel et l'exégèse de Rom. 5,12–14," in *Recherches des Sciences Religieuses* 44 (1956): 63–84; "L'attualità della Lettera di San Paolo ai Romani e il problema ecumenico," in *Civiltà Cattolica* q. 2596 (1958): 365–377.

[231] Cf. F. Spadafora, "Rm. 5,12: esegesi e riflessi dogmatici," in *Divinitas* 4 (1960): 289–298. See also B. Mariana, O.F.M., "La persona di Adamo e il suo peccato originale secondo San Paolo 5, 12–21," in *Divinitas* 2 (1958): 486–519.

Jesuit Piet Schoonenberg,[232] was the author in 1968 of a study on original sin, in which he compounded his teacher's secularizing theses,[233] in exactly the sense explained by Spadafora. The recommendations presented on behalf of the Pontifical Biblical Institute by its rector Ernest Vogt, on April 24, 1960, to the Ante-Preparatory Commission, on the other hand, called into question the historicity and inerrancy of the gospels[234] and took up a line of thought quite different from the one indicated by the magisterium.

In early January 1960, Monsignor Antonino Romeo,[235] of the Sacred Congregation for Seminaries and Universities, launched in the pages of *Divinitas* a thoroughgoing attack against the Biblical Institute.[236] Monsignor Romeo was an energetic, slender prelate, who since the 1930s had worked at the congregation of which Cardinal Ruffini had been the secretary. His article denounced, for the first time, the existence of a conspiracy hatched by the neo-modernist circles that were operating within the Church.[237] Monsignor Romeo described it as

---

[232] Piet Schoonenberg (1911–1999), Dutch Jesuit, ordained in 1939, student at the Biblical Institute, professor of dogmatic theology at the University of Nijmegen (1964–1979). About him, see *Nouvelle théologie*, 126–138.

[233] Cf. P. Schoonenberg, "Der Mensch in der Sünde," in *Mysterium Salutis: Grundriss heilsgeschichtlicher Dogmatik*, ed. J. Feiner and M. Löhrer, vol. II *Die Heilsgeschichte vor Christus* (Einsiedeln-Zürich-Cologne: Benziger, 1967), 845–941.

[234] Cf. AD I-IV/1:125–136. Concerning the incident, cf. F. Spadafora, *La nuova esegesi, op. cit.*, 91–115.

[235] Antonino Romeo (1902–1979), ordained in 1924, from 1938 to 1972 was in Rome as a study assistant with the Sacred Congregation for Seminaries of Universities. He is the author of, among other things, many articles in the *Enciclopedia Cattolica* and the *Dizionario biblico* edited by Monsignor Francesco Spadafora. About him see Andrea Dalledonne, "La morte di mons. Antonino Romeo: una grave perdita per la Chiesa cattolica," in *Implicazioni del tomismo originario* (Genoa: Quadrivium, 1981), 67–71. On this question, cf. R. Burigana, "La querelle tra il Laterano e l'Istituto Biblico," in *L'Università del Laterano, op. cit.*, 50–66.

[236] Cf. A. Romeo, "L'Enciclica 'Divino afflante Spiritu' e le 'opiniones novae,'" in *Divinitas* 4 (1960): 385–456.

[237] A documented reconstruction of the polemic in Anthony Dupont and Karim Schelkens, "Katholische Exegese vor dem Zweiten Vatikanischen Konzil (1960–1961)," in *Zeitschrift für katholische Theologie* 1 (2010): 1–24.

> a group that is agitating tirelessly to open ever larger breaches in the superhuman edifice of the Catholic faith, under the pretext that today only what is new should be of interest, since the gospel to be acknowledged is not the one of the past, but the one of the future, and the Church that we must obey is not the one that we know, but the Church of the future.[238]
>
> . . . Thus they have arrived today at the "new theology" inspired by the slogans of the moment, at the "new" morality which tries to satisfy human passions and abolish the notion and the sense of sin, at the "new history" which validates historicism or the triumph of fact, at the "new law" which proclaims the liberty of evil and of those who are powerful enough to be able to allow themselves anything, at the "new psychology" based on pan-sexual psychoanalysis, at the "new pedagogy" which satisfies every instinct, at the "new sacred art" which exalts the surrealism and conceptualism of charlatans. The word "principles", which once was used so much, is disappearing from circulation.... Founded on the double myth of human liberty and human progress, that two-fold gnostic postulate that deifies the fleeting contingency of our individual value and of our eternal collective flow toward an unknown future, making it the surrogate for the Absolute, today's progressivists transform religion and science into an unending search, without defining the purpose, the object, and the "constants" that every faith and every science must also pre-establish for itself. Thus we can observe the triumph of indeterminacy, that is, of relativism and, basically, of denial.[239]

It should be noted that Monsignor Romeo not only was a renowned Biblical scholar but also had deep knowledge of the *"mysterium iniquitatis."* He is credited, among other writings, with the articles on "Antichrist" and "Satanism" in the Italian *Catholic Encyclopedia*, in which he demonstrated a penetrating theological knowledge of the forces of evil at work in history. The lines that we have cited and those that follow earned him the accusation of being a "visionary," but today they appear to us to have prophetic power. So he continued:

---

238 A. Romeo, "L'Enciclica 'Divino afflante Spiritu,'" *op. cit.*, 444.

239 Ibid., 447, 449.

> Such a relentless activity by termites moving about in the shadows, in Rome and in all parts of the world, compels us to guess the active presence of a complete plan to surround and break down the doctrines that form and nourish the Catholic faith. More and more evidence, from various quarters, attests to a gradual accomplishment of a large-scale progressive maneuver, directed by extremely capable and ostensibly devout "captains," which tends to remove from our midst the Christianity hitherto taught and lived out for nineteen centuries, so as to replace it with a Christianity "of modern times."
>
> The religion taught by Jesus and the apostles, and intensively put into practice in the lives of St. Augustine, St. Benedict, St. Dominic, St. Francis, and St. Ignatius of Loyola, is feverishly corroded so that it disappears, in order to impose in its place a new religion, the religion longed for by the gnostics of all times, which here and there is already called "Christianity adapted to modern times." Christianity "of modern times" will be based on the cosmic divinity and on human rights; it will have as the dogmas of its "Credo" evolutionist monism and unending progress, unlimited human liberty and universal equality, with traces of scientific, theosophical, or occultist "faith" that will vary according to the circumstances. It will have as its obligatory morality "adaptation," in other words, "conformism," with the prohibition of any "frustration" and the obligation to satisfy all instincts and impulses; the ultimate finality of eternal life will be dismissed and "earthly realities" will take its place, which the "obscurantism" of nineteen centuries had put into quarantine but which today have been "rehabilitated" with great zeal. In this "new" Christianity, Jesus, the apostles, the definitions and directives of the Church's magisterium for nineteen centuries, will remain only as memories, with a merely "historical and apologetic" value: links in the unfailing evolution that will conclude only when man, having become the most perfect Being, will be reabsorbed into the infinity of the Universe.[240]

Monsignor Romeo's pessimism was shared by a theologian with whom he had established an immediate understanding: Monsignor Joseph Fenton, the editor *The American Ecclesiastical Review*, who had been called on by Cardinal Ottaviani to be part of the Theological Commission. Fenton was one of those who most clearly discerned the gravity of the situation.

---

240 Ibid., 468–469.

"Humanly speaking," he noted in his *Diary* on December 24, 1960, "there is no possibility of converting any of those who are opposed to us."[241]

b) Cardinal Ruffini enters the fray

The controversy over biblical studies continued in the following months, until the Holy Office intervened: after hearing both sides of the issue, it condemned the Jesuit Stanislas Lyonnet and his confrère Max Zerwick,[242] sending them away from Rome and forbidding them to teach.[243] On June 20, 1961, a *Monitum* of the Holy Office was published which noted the diffusion of "judgments and opinions" that compromised the authentic historical and objective truth of sacred scripture and admonished exegetes always to treat the sacred books with due discretion.[244] A few days later, June 28, the *Life of Jesus* by the French priest Jean Steinmann was put on the Index of Forbidden Books. On August 24, Cardinal Ruffini criticized recourse to literary genres interpreting the Bible in an article in *L'Osservatore Romano*[245] that Cardinal Pizzardo sent to the rectors of all the diocesan seminaries in Italy, asking them to bring it to the attention of their professors.

---

241 Fenton, *Diary*, 17. In October 1962 Monsignor Fenton published an article entitled "The Virtue of Prudence and the Success of the Second Ecumenical Vatican Council," in which he stated, among other things: "It is possible that the council might act other than with the fullness of supernatural prudence. It is possible that, seen in its perspective, it might not be completely successful" (in *The American Ecclesiastical Review* 147/4 [1962]: 255–265 at 265).

242 Max Zerwick (1901–1975), German, ordained in the Society of Jesus in 1931, professor of exegesis at the Biblical Institution from 1953 on. Cf. Carlo Maria Martini, "In memoria di P. Max Zerwick," in *Rivista Biblica* 56 (1976): 444–445.

243 In 1963 Paul VI, who had just been elected, called him to Rome and reinstated him as an instructor at the Pontifical Biblical Institute.

244 Cf. AAS 9 (1961): 507.

245 Cf. Ernesto Ruffini, "Generi letterari e ipotesi di lavoro nei recenti studi biblici," in *L'Osservatore Romano*, August 24, 1961; reprinted in *Idem, Conferenze bibliche* (Rome: Ancora, 1966), 222–224. Monsignor Fenton arranged for the publication of Cardinal Ruffini's article in English as "Literary Genres and Working Hypothesis in Recent Biblical Studies," in *The American Ecclesiastical Review* 145 (1961): 362–365.

Cardinal Ruffini wrote:

> We are witnessing a flood of publications, conferences, meetings in which very often hazardous judgments and disconcerting interpretations prevail. One of the topics more often treated and discussed is that concerning *literary genres*, or—as they say today for the New Testament, using an expression translated from the German—the "method of the history of forms [*Formgeschichte*]." The principle that to know the literal sense of a particular writing it is necessary to know clearly beforehand the form or genre which the writer wished to use is not something enunciated only today. Everyone can understand that a sapiential book is quite different from a legislative text, that an apocalyptic book, written after the events, is very different from a collection of prophecies in the strict sense, and that poetry is not read like a history....
>
> The fever which in recent years has been enkindled from day to day around the literary genres of the inspired books, not excluding the gospels, is caused partly by comparisons with documents, always very scarce, of ancient Oriental literatures, but above all by an hypercritical spirit which prescinds completely from the traditional teaching of the Church, and from the interpretation of the faithful, which is its genuine echo. In this way more or less explicitly some—unfortunately even ecclesiastics—have reached the point of eliminating from the historical level most important passages such as, for example the narratives of the first few chapters of Genesis and of the gospels....
>
> The limits of an article do not allow us to go into details. To these new exegetes, who call themselves, and pretend to be, Catholics, we put this question: How can you claim that the Church, *Mater et Magistra* [Mother and Teacher], to whom it pertains to judge the true sense of sacred scripture—as we have sworn many times before the altar (cf. the *Profession of the Catholic Faith* [at the beginning of the *Codex Iuris Canonici* and the Formula of the Oath against Modernism in *AAS* [1910]: 669-672)—has, for nineteen centuries, presented the divine book to her children without knowing its literary genre, which is the key to exact interpretation? Such an absurdity gets worse when one bears in mind that not a few of the above-mentioned hypercritics not only advance new applications of the theory of literary genres to the inspired books, but leave a definitive clarification of them to the future, when the manner of speaking and of writing used by the ancients, especially the Orientals, will become better known through

> the study of history, archeology, ethnology, and the other sciences. Some, realizing the enormous difficulty of harmonizing such a doctrine, which we would call revolutionary, with the voice of conscience and the instructions of the ecclesiastical authority, have begun to appeal to the method used legitimately in physics and natural sciences: that of the *working hypothesis*.
>
> It is well known that the experimental sciences are in continuous development. Many aspects are still unknown and phenomena not yet explained. The learned scholars, with the intention of leveling the way which leads to the discovery of truths, formulate hypotheses, which, being only provisory—intermediate stations, as it were—are wont to be called *working hypotheses*, that is, hypotheses which form the groundwork for future research. But to speak of working hypotheses which are, in our case, ill-concealed negotiations of the historicity, with reference for example to the Annunciation of the Archangel Gabriel to the Blessed Virgin Mary (Lk 1:26-28), and to the promise of the primacy to St. Peter (Mt 16:17-19), which they represent as imitations of pre-existing patterns or as later elaborations of Christian thought, is to overturn Catholic exegesis and is a heretical attempt against the truths, even held—beginning from the first fathers of the Church—as corresponding to historical realities.
>
> We never would have thought that we could reach such a point! St. Jerome said of his times that the Christian world awoke to find itself Arian (an heresy then widespread). What would be the reaction of St. Pius X—who energetically condemned modernism—in the face of errors which revive it and render it more insidious, because accredited by men for many reasons worthy of particular consideration?"[246]

Writing to Cardinal Ottaviani on May 19 of the same year, Ruffini expressed himself in no uncertain terms: "I told him time and again and I repeat: modernism, condemned by St. Pius X, today is being spread freely in ways that are even more serious and deleterious than was the case then."[247] The archbishop of Palermo continued: "Your Eminence, in looking at the situation around me, I am sometimes deeply discouraged, and if I manage to lift my spirits again it is because I trust in the help that Jesus promised to His Church: 'I am with you all days even to the end of time.' I hope that

---

246 *The American Ecclesiastical Review* 145 (1961): 362–365.

247 Letter from Ruffini to Cardinal Ottaviani dated May 9, 1961, in F. M. Stabile, *op. cit.*, 115.

the upcoming ecumenical council defines once and for all what is meant by inspiration, biblical inerrancy, and bible history, and determines to what extent the scientific interpretation of sacred scripture may depart from the traditional one."[248]

Cardinal Ernesto Ruffini, whose birthplace was Mantua, was seventy-two years old, but his sturdy build, his vivacious spirit, and the energy that he put into everything he did, augured that he would be a protagonist in the conciliar debates.[249] His career began "in the chair," when he was appointed professor of Biblical Studies at the Lateran University by Pope Pius X in 1913, at only twenty-five years of age. In 1928, appointed by Pius XI as secretary of the Sacred Congregation for Seminaries and Universities, he had prepared the reform of ecclesiastical studies that culminated in the apostolic constitution *Deus scientiarum Dominus*,[250] issued by the pope on Pentecost of 1931. Pope Pius XI himself wanted him to be rector of the Lateran University, and Pius XII appointed him archbishop of Palermo in 1945 and created him cardinal in 1946. On account of his erudition and theological solidity Cardinal Ruffini was one of the chief points of reference during the difficult moment of transition from the pontificate of Pius XII to that of Pope Roncalli.

For his part John XXIII maintained an ambivalent attitude about the controversy. On the one hand he seemed to express trust vis-à-vis the Biblicum, appointing its rector Ernest Vogt to the Theological Commission; on the other hand, right on the eve of the conciliar assembly, in a speech given to a gathering of the Italian Biblical Association that had been convened by Monsignor Romeo, the pope stressed the right of the Church to supervise the work of biblical scholars, in their study and transmission of revealed truth.[251]

---

[248] Ibid., 116. In a conference held in Assisi on December 30, 1961, Cardinal Ottaviani reiterated for his part his hopes in the upcoming ecumenical council: "A great beacon which will emit light and heat is about to be lit through the upcoming worldwide assemblies of truth and justice that are about to begin on the Vatican Hill, near the tomb of the prince of the apostles" (A. Ottaviani, "La parola della Croce alla vigilia del Concilio Ecumenico," in *Discorsi di sua em.za il cardinale Alfredo Ottaviani, Segretario della Suprema S. Congregazione del S. Uffizio* [Bastia Umbra: Gruppo studi sociali Luigi Sturzo, 1962], 26).

[249] Cf. the profile by S. Negro in *Vaticano minore e altri scritti* (Vicenza: Neri Pozza, 1963), 344–348.

[250] Pius XI, letter *Deus scientiarum Dominus* (May 14, 1931), in AAS 23 (1931): 241–262.

[251] "One understands then the Church's anxiety with regard to biblical studies. While indeed she has serene confidence in the seriousness of her sons' research, she cannot be content with gathering its

11. Cardinal Bea's ecumenical "tour"

a) Dialog with the "separated brethren"

The progressive ecclesiological tendencies were developing meanwhile within the new "ecumenical" framework. On Sunday, January 22, 1961, Cardinal Bea held a conference the auditorium at the Angelicum on the subject of "The Great Call to the Fold of Christ," in which he said, among other things:

> It is true that schism and heresy as such separate men from the Mystical Body of Christ which is the Church, that is, from full participation in the life that Christ communicates to the Church. But this applies to those who personally and deliberately detach themselves from the Church, not of course to those who in good faith find themselves separated as a result of the heritage received from their ancestors. Besides, all non-Catholic Christians are considered by the Church as "brothers," as "sons," as the objects of her own maternal love; in other words, she considers them as her own subjects and members, although not in the full sense.[252]

That same day, commenting on the visit to Rome of the primate of the Anglican church, Dr. Geoffrey Francis Fisher, in an interview with Father Antoine Wenger[253] for *La Croix*, Bea declared: "This visit is an important episode within the framework of the great work of the unity of all the baptized that the Holy Spirit has been preparing slowly but irresistibly during recent decades."[254]

---

fruits, but must guide its steps, just as it is up to her to ratify its conclusions" (Address to the Biblical Association on September 23, 1962, in DMC, 4:540–545 at 542. See also J. A. Komonchak, "The Struggle for the Council during the Preparation," *op. cit.*, 281.

[252] *L'Osservatore Romano*, January 27, 1961.

[253] Antoine Wenger (1919–2009), French Assumptionist, ordained in 1943. From 1957 to 1973 edited the newspaper *La Croix*, while continuing to teach Catholic theology in Strasbourg. He was a great friend of Cardinal Jean Villot, visiting him every Sunday at four o'clock in the afternoon, from 1973 until the latter's death (January 1979) (A. Wenger, *Vatican II* [Paris: Centurion, 1964–1966], 4 vols.). About him cf. Philippe Levillain, "Il patrologo che scriveva la storia del tempo presente: Ricordo di padre Antoine Wenger," in *L'Osservatore Romano*, May 27, 2009.

[254] *La Croix*, January 24, 1961. See also Roberto Tucci, S.J., "La visita di cortesia del dott. Fischer

Despite his advanced age, Cardinal Bea subjected himself to a frenetic schedule of journeys and contacts.[255] In the month of January 1961 he went to Bern, Basel, Strasbourg, and Paris; in February and March to Heidelberg, Tübingen, Essen, and both West and East Berlin. Then off to Liverpool and London where, for the first time in history, he wore the purple robes of Rome in Lambeth Palace, the "Anglican Vatican," where he was received by the Primate Ramsey, who was just back from Moscow.[256]

From September 26 to 28, 1960, a number of Catholic bishops along with pastors of various protestant denominations had met at Taizé in France "for the purpose of sharing together their concerns about evangelization."[257] Toward the end of October, Pastor Roger Schutz and Pastor Max Thurian of the Taizé Community came to Rome and were received in audience by the Holy Father.[258] On August 4, 1961, in an interview for *France Catholique*, Bea confirmed that he was following with the greatest interest the development of ecumenical centers such as Taizé. "The protestants who are not responsible for the divisions in the Church," he declared, "can aspire to salvation on an equal footing with Catholics. In some way these people are also united to the Church."[259]

One of the chief objectives of Cardinal Bea's ecumenical activities was, from the beginning, the relationship with the patriarchate of Moscow, the state church which in those years was notoriously controlled by the Kremlin. The "patriarch of Moscow and of all the Russians'" at that time was Metropolitan Alexius, who had succeeded Patriarch Sergius in 1945, with whom he shared a political-religious vision: Moscow, the "third Rome," would have to become simultaneously the world capital of the proletariat and the universal capital of Christianity.[260] As of

a S.S. Giovanni XXIII," in *Civiltà Cattolica*, q. 2650 (1960): 337–353.

255 Cf. C. Falconi, "Perché Bea viaggia tanto," in *L'Espresso*, August 26, 1962.

256 Cf. Schmidt, *Bea*, 370–372.

257 *La Croix*, October 26, 1960.

258 Caprile, I/2:2.

259 Ibid., I/2:166.

260 About Alexius I (1877–1970) cf. Jean G. H. Hoffmann, "Alexeij Patriarche de Moscou et de toutes les Russies," in *Résistances en Union Soviétique: Les Cahiers de "Tant qu'il fait jour"* (Paris, 1971), 56–81.

January 31, 1959, Yuri Zhukov, president of the State Committee for Foreign Cultural Relations of the Council of Ministers of the U.S.S.R., had prepared a note for the Central Committee about the upcoming ecumenical council. In his proposal to the party, he suggested, 1) that they organize interdenominational meetings "for peace"; 2) that they make all the churches subject to the U.S.S.R. join the World Council of Churches, starting with the Moscow patriarchate; 3) finally that they arrange for Russian Orthodoxy to push for the convocation of a pan-orthodox council during the year 1961.[261] Zhukov's great fear was that the Vatican might establish a relationship directly with the patriarch of Constantinople, thus isolating the Kremlin politically. Instead he would try to "ditch" Constantinople so as to allow Moscow to establish a privileged bond with the Vatican of John XXIII.

The campaign suggested by Zhukov was carried out according to the prearranged plan. During the course of the "Pre-Synod" of the Orthodox world that took place in Rhodes from September 24 to October 1, 1961, the two Orthodox patriarchs, of Constantinople and of Moscow, found a basis for unity and together decided to inaugurate "amicable relations" with the Catholic Church and the other Christian churches. From November 18 to December 15 of the same year the third meeting of the World Council of Churches was held in New Delhi. The representatives of the Muscovite Patriarch Alexius, after being put back into circulation in the Christian "circuit," obtained the rights of "citizenship." This facilitated the start of conversations aimed at obtaining for them an invitation to the council, with the status of "observers."[262] Thanks to the entrance of the patriarchate of Moscow into the World Council of Churches, the Soviet government could now infiltrate its informants into a privileged international religious assembly. On the occasion of his ninetieth birthday, Patriarch Alexius received the "Red Flag of Labor" as a reward for his "extraordinary contribution to the defense of peace."

It should be noted also that in 1961 the Berlin Wall had been erected, and in the same year, the famous Ilitchev Report had been published in the

---

[261] Cf. A. Melloni, *L'altra Roma: Politica e S. Sede durante il Concilio Vaticano II (1959–1965)* (Bologna: Il Mulino, 2000); Alfredo Roccucci, "Russian observers at Vatican II: The 'Council for Russian Orthodox Church Affairs' and the Moscow patriarchate between anti-religious policy and international strategies," in *Vatican II in Moscow*, 45–69, at 50–51; M. Velati, "La Chiesa ortodossa russa tra Ginevra e Roma negli anni del Concilio Vaticano II," *Ibid.*, 91–110.

[262] Cf. M. Tedeschi, *op. cit.*, 47–57.

Soviet Union, in which the communist ideologue gave detailed instructions for conducting an effective war against religion and for spreading militant atheism.[263] This document, which was binding on states with communist regimes, was confirmed by the guidelines contained in the plan of the Communist Party of the U.S.S.R. adopted during its 22nd Congress on October 31, 1961.[264]

Between February and July of 1962 the secretary for Promoting Christian Unity Willebrands undertook numerous trips in order to ensure that the council would have an "ecumenical presence." There were no problems with the protestant communities, starting with the Anglican Church, nor with the "non-Chalcedonic" Churches, like the Coptic Church of Egypt, the Orthodox Syrian Church, the Ethiopian Orthodox Church, and the Armenian Church. The major difficulties were rather with the other Orthodox Churches. Cardinal Bea addressed himself to Patriarch Athenagoras of Constantinople,[265] proposing that he send a delegation that would represent also the patriarchates of Moscow, Sofia, Bucharest, and Belgrade, and asking him to act as a channel for communicating with the other patriarchs. However when Athenagoras forwarded the invitation to the council to the patriarch of Moscow, the latter responded with a solemn *"non possumus"* with regard to what he considered an internal affair of the Catholic Church.[266]

---

[263] Cf. Leonid Ilitchev, *L'educazione atea: Rapporto alla Commissione ideologica del P.C.U.S.* (Rome: ICAS, 1964).

[264] Cf. Giovanni Codevilla, *Le comunità religiose nell'URSS: La nuova legislazione sovietica* (Milan: Jaca Book, 1978), 11–12.

[265] Athenagoras (1886–1972), ecumenical patriarch from 1948 until his death. About him see Valeria Martano, *Athenagoras il patriarca (1886–1972): Un cristiano fra crisi della coalizione e utopia ecumenica* (Bologna: Il Mulino, 1996).

[266] The article entitled "Non possumus" ["We cannot"] appeared in the review of the Moscow patriarchate, *Zurnal Moskovskoj Patriarchii* on June 6, 1961; French transl. in *Istina* 10 (1964): 503–506. Cf. José Oscar Beozzo, "The External Climate," in HVT 1:357–404 at 403; A. Wenger, *Les trois Rome: L'Église des années Soixante* (Paris: Desclée de Brouwer, 1991), 80.

b) The meeting in Metz

Notwithstanding this setback, in August of 1962 a secret meeting was held in Metz[267] between Cardinal Tisserant and the new Orthodox archbishop of Yaroslavl, Nikodim.[268] An agreement was reached on that occasion stipulating that the patriarchate of Moscow would welcome the papal invitation, while the pope was to guarantee that the council would refrain from condemning communism.

The meeting in Metz has been ignored or called into question by some historians, but Serge Bolshkoff, in his unpublished memoirs about Cardinal Tisserant,[269] and Dom Emmanuel Lanne,[270] who had access to them, have offered a documented reconstruction of it.[271]

The Central Committee of the World Council of Churches (WCC) had met in Paris in early August of 1962. The Vatican was represented by Monsignor Willebrands, who on August 11 met with Nikodim, who

---

267 Cf. J. Madiran, *L'accord de Metz ou pourquoi notre Mère fut muette* (Versailles: Via Romana, 2006).

268 Nikodim, whose secular name was Boris Georgievic Rotov (1929–1978), archbishop of Yaroslavl (1960–1963), Metropolitan of Minsk (1963), then of Leningrad (1963–1967) and Novgorod (1967–1978), then Exarch of Western Europe (1974–1978). Died of a heart attack in the Vatican on September 5, 1978, while he was being received in an audience by John Paul I. It has been documented, based on archival research, that the World Council of Churches was an organization extensively infiltrated by agents of the Kremlin and that Metropolitan Nikodim, who succeeded in becoming one of its presidents, was a KGB agent (cf. Gerhard Besier, Armin Boyens, and Gerhard Lindemann, *Nationaler Protestantismus und Ökumenische Bewegung: Kirchliches Handeln im kalten Krieg (1945–1990)* [Berlin: Dunker und Humblot, 1999]).

269 Cf. Serge Bolshkoff, *Le cardinal Tisserant (1884–1974*, (typescript, Hauterive, 1984), 15–17.

270 Cf. Emmanuel Lanne, O.S.B., "La perception en Occident de la participation du patriarcat de Moscou à Vatican II," in *Vatican II in Moscow*, 111–117. See also "Le 'non possumus' du patriarcat de Moscou," in *Istina, op. cit.*

271 Documentary verification is found also in the archive of Cardinal Tisscrant, where there is a letter dated August 22, 1962, in which the French prelate writes to Serge Bolshkoff, informing him of the meeting with Nikodim (Tisserant to Bolshkoff, August 22, 1962, Archive of the Association Amis Card. Tisserant, "Bolshkoff Serge," doc. V-3, cited in A. Tornielli, *Paolo VI, op. cit.*, 303). On this incident see also Tommaso Ricci, "Chiesa e comunismo: Quella 'svista' del Concilio," in *30 Giorni* 8–9 (1989): 56–63, and *Idem,* "Il mistero del patto Roma-Mosca," in *30 Giorni* 10 (1989): 275–280.

represented the Russian Orthodox Church, which had just been admitted to the WCC the preceding year in New Delhi. Nikodim immediately addressed the problem of the participation of Orthodox observers at the council and insistently asked Willebrands to handle the problem directly with Moscow.[272] In the meantime Bolshkoff, a writer connected with the monastery of Chevetogne, arranged a meeting on August 18 in Metz, in Alsace, in which Nikodim, Cardinal Tisserant, and the Orthodox archbishop of Brussels, Basile Krivochéine[273] participated.

Meanwhile, through the Soviet ambassador to Ankara, contacts were developed between the Kremlin and the apostolic delegate in Turkey, Archbishop Francesco Lardone,[274] in order to obtain the Moscow government's consent to the participation of the Russian Catholic bishops at the council.[275] Monsignor Willebrands made a secret trip to Moscow from September 27 to October 2, 1962, to dispel the Kremlin's anxieties about the council's attitude toward communism.[276] On his return to Rome, Cardinal Bea dispatched the official invitation to the patriarchate. On October 10, the eve of the opening of the council, Patriarch Alexius and his synod sent an official telegram of acceptance, and the Russian observers, Archpriest Vitalij Borovoij and Archimandrite Vladimir Kotlyarov, arrived in Rome in the afternoon of October 12.

Meanwhile in Constantinople, Patriarch Athenagoras, still in the dark about the secret negotiations and convinced that the Russian Church would not be sending observers, convened his synod and, although personally inclined to accept the pope's invitation, announced that it was impossible

---

[272] J. Willebrands, "La rencontre entre Rome et Moscou: Souvenirs," in *Vatican II in Moscow*, 331–338 at 333–335.

[273] Basile Krivochéine (1900–1985), Orthodox archbishop of Brussels.

[274] Francesco Lardone (1887–1980), ordained in 1910, archbishop of Rize (1949) and apostolic nuncio to Haiti and for the Dominican Republic (1949–1953), then in Peru (1953–1959), whereas Turkey would be his final destination as apostolic internuncio (1959–1966). On his public persona, cf. Giuseppe Tuninetti, *Monsignor Francesco Lardone (1887–1980): Il Nunzio Apostolico precursore della Ost-Politik* (Savigliano: L'Artistica Savigliano, 1997).

[275] A. Riccardi, *Il Vaticano e Mosca 1940–1990* (Rome-Bari, Laterza, 1993), 232–238.

[276] Cf. the Report of the visit to Moscow on October 7, 1962, cited in P. Chenaux, *L'Église catholique et le communisme en Europe (1917–1989): De Lénine à Jean Paul II* (Paris: Cerf, 2009), 256–257; J. Willebrands, "La rencontre," *op. cit.*, 336–338.

to send observers to Rome so as not to offend pan-Orthodox unity.[277] Thus the patriarchate of Moscow had very cleverly displaced the patriarchate of Constantinople through the new network of relations with the Vatican. Bea's biographer states: "Painful recriminations among the Orthodox followed, and also against the secretariat, as if it had tried to divide Orthodoxy."[278] In fact, only the meeting between Paul VI and Athenagoras in January 1964 managed to defuse the situation and make possible the participation of observers from the Orthodox Churches starting with the third session of the council. As Komonchak emphasizes: "The decision to invite non-Catholics as observers was one of the most important decisions made during the preparatory period, with consequences for the character the council would assume and the work it would carry out that far surpassed the expectations of even the most optimistic. In more ways than one, their presence at the council marked 'the end of the Counter-Reformation.'"[279]

c) Communism at the council

The magisterium of the Catholic Church had spoken out repeatedly against communism in terms clearly condemning it, in particular in the encylical of Pius XI, *Divini Redemptoris* dated March 19, 1937,[280] and in the encylical of Pius XII, *Ad Apostolorum Principum* dated June 29, 1958.[281] A decree of the Holy Office in April 1959 had confirmed the validity of the excommunication dated January 7, 1949, incurred by any sort of collaboration with communism.[282] John XXIII, however, did not agree with the 1949 document, as he confided to several interlocutors, among them

---

277 Cf. José Oscar Beozzo, "The External Climate," *op. cit.*, 404.

278 Schmidt, *Bea*, 382. The Greek-Orthodox Metropolitan Jakovos (1911–2005) of the two Americas went so far as to accuse the Vatican of having used the council to divide and weaken Orthodoxy (A. Wenger, *Vatican II, op. cit., Première Session*, 222–265).

279 J. A. Komonchak, "The Struggle for the Council During the Preparation," *op. cit.*, 326. Cf. also Y. Congar, O.P. "Le rôld des 'Observateurs' dans l'avancée oecuménique," in *Le Concile Vatican II: Son Église, Peuple de Dieu et Corps du Christ* (Paris: Beauchesne, 1984), 90–98.

280 AAS 29 (1937): 65–106.

281 AAS 50 (1958): 601–614.

282 AAS 41 (1949): 34.

Monsignor Parente ("basically, the communists are seeking justice and are sick people.")[283]

According to the bishops' *vota* [written recommendations] that had arrived in Rome for the council, communism appeared as the most error to condemn.[284] In the ante-preparatory phase of the council, a good 378 bishops had requested that it deal with modern atheism and, in particular, with communism, identifying remedies with which to confront the danger.[285] The Vietnamese archbishop of Hué, Ngô-Dinh-Thuc,[286] for example, described communism as "the problem of problems,"[287] the most important question of the moment. Archbishop Ngô-Dinh-Thuc, speaking in the commission on the topic of communism, had declared:

> Our Central Preparatory Commission has until now examined many problems, but communism seems to me to be the problem of problems; indeed, it concerns the very existence of Christianity, which communism has put in the utmost danger. To discuss other problems without giving priority to solving the problems that arise from communism would be to follow the example of the theologians of Constantinople who were bitterly debating about the sex of the angels while the Mohammedan army threatened the very walls of the city. The sorrowful condition of the Church in China perhaps is the result of our lack of preparation. However, with regard to the countries

[283] Cited in A. Riccardi, "Dalla Chiesa di Pio XII alla Chiesa giovannea," in Alberigo, *Papa Giovanni*, 135–174 at 151.

[284] On the relations between the Church and communism during the council cf. Wiltgen, 272–278; A. Wenger, *Vatican II, op. cit.* 1:187–346 and 2:297–316; P. Levillain, *La mécanique politique, op. cit.*, 361–439; Vincenzo Carbone, "Schemi e discussioni sull'ateismo e sul marxismo nel Concilio Vaticano II: Documentazione," in *Rivista di Storia della Chiesa in Italia* 44 (1990): 10–68; A. Riccardi, *Il Vaticano e Mosca, op. cit.*, 217–304; Giovanni Turbanti, "Il problema del comunismo al Concilio," in *Vatican II in Moscow*, 147–187; P. Chenaux, *L'Église catholique et le communisme en Europe* (Paris: Cerf, 2009), 239–267.

[285] Cf. V. Carbone, "Schemi e discussioni sull'ateismo e sul marxismo," *op. cit.*, 11–12.

[286] Pierre Martin Ngô-Dinh-Thuc (1897–1984), Vietnamese, ordained in 1925. archbishop of Hué (Vietnam) from 1960 to 1968. Member of the Commission for the Missions during the first session. After the council, he ordained several bishops on his own initiative and was excommunicated by Paul VI.

[287] AD II-II/3: 774–776.

> that are presently in the hands of communists, for example Laos and Vietnam, it seems to me that the Catholics, and above all the bishops of the Catholic world, must not limit their concern to saying a few prayers, but can offer very powerful help by arousing public opinion among their fellow countrymen on behalf of the oppressed nations. We are all stupefied by the silence of the Catholic world with regard to the agony of the most unfortunate Laotian people and the passion that the Vietnamese people are going through, while in the meantime one hears everywhere the voice of the communists and of their accomplices who live in the democratic nations, of which some are Catholic, who prefer to howl with the wolves: the voice, I say, of those who condemn the victims and glorify the executioners.[288]

In the subsequent preparatory phase, the topic of communism was assigned to the Doctrinal Commission with these instructions: "Let the Catholic doctrine be explained in its entirety, and the principal contemporary errors rejected, namely, naturalism, materialism, communism, and secularism."[289] The Theological Commission however did not address the issue. Three other commissions dealt with it instead under the pastoral aspect: the Commission for Bishops and the Governance of Dioceses,[290] which accepted a document condemning communism (with three dissenting votes, among them Cardinal Tisserant's);[291] the Commission for the Discipline of the Clergy and the Christian People, which was evasive, replacing the term "communism" with the more generic term "materialism"; and the Commission for the Lay Apostolate, which also approved a generic, ambiguous document. Also in the work of the Central Commission, which sifted through the proposals submitted by the Preparatory Commissions, the subject did not attract much attention. Cardinal Montini, for example, used very cautious words, asking whether the reason for the spread of communism should not be sought in the errors of the Church herself, and Cardinal Alfrink asked for a distinction between communism's ends and its means, because to some extent the ends

288 AD II-II/3:775.

289 AD II-II/1:408.

290 AD II-II/3:761–842.

291 AD II-II/3:777–790.

could be considered just.[292] During the first session of the council, Cardinal Tisserant, who presided over the mixed sub-commission responsible for the schema *De cura animarum*, insisted that the word *communismus* be removed from the draft and, according to Giovanni Turbanti, intervened also for the deletion of the paragraphs denouncing the persecutions in communist countries.[293]

On November 2, 1962, Plinio Corrêa de Oliveira met with Cardinal Tisserant and found him, despite his eighty years, "lucid, calm, and lively."[294] The Cardinal confided to him that he had participated in the negotiations with the schismatic Russian Orthodox: "Moscow demanded that no one speak against communism in the council, and Rome agreed," he said, adding that he thought it "possible to speak against materialism and atheism without mentioning communism; in this way the council, which deals only with religion, could accomplish its mission perfectly." Besides, he asserted, "Who could ever speak against taking from the rich so as to give to the poor?" For this reason, in his opinion, the Holy See had accepted the Kremlin's conditions. In the course of the conversation, conducted in French, Tisserant praised Cardinal Stefan Wyszyński, described Cardinal Mindszenty as a *"pauvre imbecile,"* and declared that it was more difficult to convert a schismatic monarchist than an atheist communist, because "the first accepts only the Tsar as his master, while the second harbors no anti-Roman preconceptions."[295]

Cardinal Mindszenty had remained the last symbol of ecclesiastical resistance to communism, after the death of Cardinal Alojzije Stepìnac, who had died of poisoning on February 10, 1962. Until then the position of these two pillars of the Church was identical to the instructions issued by the Holy See. In the early sixties, however, both the international and the ecclesiastical picture appeared to have changed.[296]

---

[292] G. Turbanti, "Il problema del comunismo al Concilio," in *Vatican II in Moscow*, 155.

[293] Ibid., 159.

[294] Maranhão Galliez, *Diario*, November 2, 1962.

[295] Ibid. The meeting, reported by Murillo Maranhão Galliez, was confirmed several times by Plinio Corrêa de Oliveira (A-IPCO, Meeting on September 28, 1980).

[296] Cf. A. Riccardi, *Il Vaticano e Mosca, op. cit.*, 151–158. On October 3, 1956 Stepìnac wrote to Father Sakač: "A battle of life and death is being waged and it is not possible to retreat if we do not want to betray God. Bloody communism, too, knows very well that it will be destroyed down to its roots as soon as the opportunity presents itself to the people. There is no longer any power

12. The battle for the liturgy

a) Latin is the language of the Church

If the Theological Commission represented the bastion of tradition, the vanguard of progressivism was centered in the Liturgical Commission. The commission had as its president the prefect of the Congregation of Rites, Gaetano Cicognani, with Father Annibale Bugnini as secretary, both of them authors of the reform of the liturgical books started by Pius XII.[297] Many of the most important figures of the liturgical movement participated in the commission: Father Cipriano Vagaggini,[298] Dom Bernard Capelle,[299] Dom Bernard Botte, Father Antoine Chavasse,[300] Father Pierre Jounel,[301]

---

on earth capable of rehabilitating communism in the eyes of the masses, so odious, indeed, it has made itself with its bloody violence, its pillaging, its lies, its intrigues and inhumane acts, which are unparalleled in world history. A true, living image of hell! I have already said several times: if hell for all eternity were nothing other than what we are experiencing today, it would be a horrible, insupportable thing. And yet in the West there are still naïve individuals who play with fire and in their naïveté believe in the possibility of coexistence with bloody communism. They do not know that it is the living image of hell, a true *"mendacium incarnatum"* ["falsehood in the flesh"]. Our head of state on one occasion defined communism as a superior type of democracy. I agree, but on one condition, that you add one syllable to the word democracy, so that it reads 'demonocracy,' since only a superior being like a demon could have invented such great torments for unhappy humanity, and not a normal human brain" (A. Stepinac, letter dated October 3, 1956 to Fr. Stjepan Sakač, S.J., in *Positio, op. cit.*, 3:1257).

297 On the work of the Preparatory Commission, see among other authors, B. Botte, *Il movimento liturgico, op. cit.*, 167–189, and A. Bugnini, *The Reform of the Liturgy, op. cit.*, 14–28.

298 Cipriano Vagaggini (1909–1999), monk of the Camaldolese Congregation of the Order of Saint Benedict. Ordained in 1934, studied at the Pontifical Institute of St. Anselm, of which he became the dean.

299 Bernard Capelle (1884–1961), Belgian, monk of Maredsous, editor of the *Revue Bénédictine*, from 1928 on abbot of Mont César. Cf. F. Vanderbrovck, "Dom Bernard Capelle (1884–1961)," in *Ephemerides Liturgicae* 76 (1962): 43–49.

300 Antoine Chavasse (1909–1983), French, ordained in 1934. Professor on the Catholic Faculty of Theology in Strasbourg. Liturgist, was appointed member of the Preparatory Commission on the Liturgy, then expert at the council.

301 Pierre Jounel (1914–2004), French priest, professor at the Institut Catholique in Paris. Cf.

canon Aimé-George Martimort, Father Josef Andreas Jungmann, and Father Romano Guardini. The preparatory liturgical schema was consistent with the causes that the liturgical movement had been promoting since the thirties. It assigned absolute primacy to the "pastoral" dimension and hoped for a renewal of the liturgy focused on the "active participation" of the faithful.[302]

One of the objectives of the liturgical movement had always been the replacement of Latin with the vernacular. It is no coincidence that the first topic the commission addressed was precisely the use of Latin in the liturgy and in ecclesiastical studies. The new pope, however, was not very receptive to this "reform."

On March 25, 1961, *L'Osservatore Romano* published a front-page article signed with three stars and entitled "Latin, Language of the Church," which vigorously defended the necessity for the Church to have a language that was "universal, unchangeable, and not vernacular." The article fully developed and articulated the statement of St. Pius X that "With good reason the Latin language is called and is the proper language of the Church"[303] and also the passage by Pius XI in his letter *Officiarum Omnium* dated August 1, 1922, in which he says that the Church "requires by her very nature a language that is universal, unchangeable, and not vernacular."[304] It is worth quoting the basic arguments of the article, to which no convincing answer has ever been given:

> The first requirement of the Church's language, the pope teaches, is that it be universal. Within the framework of the ecclesiastical institution, it should serve to put the center of the Church in immediate, secure, and equal contact with all of the radii that are directed toward that center. Although in speeches addressed on solemn occasions to this or that particular people the popes gladly use the respective national languages, whenever they must turn to the universal Catholic family,

---

N. Giampietro, "In memoriam: Mons. Pierre Jounel 1914–2004," in *Ephemerides Liturgicae* 119 (2005): 83–86; Pierre Jounel, "L'élaboration du missel de Vatican II: Souvenirs personnels," *Ibid.*, 87–113.

[302] Cf. Maria Paiano, "Il dibattito sui riflessi dell'antisemitismo nella liturgia cattolica," in *Studi storici* 41 (2000): 134–135.

[303] Pius X, letter *Vehementer sane: Ad episcopos universos* (July 1, 1908), in Ench. Cle., 470.

[304] Pius XI, letter *Officiorum omnium* (August 1, 1922), in AAS 14 (1922): 449–458.

however, the use of one or another modern language that is proper to a specific community would result in preferential treatment of that particular community, to the detriment of the others. The Church, in the words of St. Paul, proclaims: *"ubi non est gentilis et iudaeus... barbarus et Scyta, servus et liber"* ["where there is neither Gentile nor Jew...barbarian nor Scythian, slave nor freeman"] (Col 3:11; Gal 3:28; Rom 10:12), and she will never place the weight of the eternal values of which she is the custodian on one plate of the scales so as to favor the earthly interests of one people to the detriment of others. The Church will never force nations that are less powerful politically or culturally to bow to the stronger ones, like the sheaves in Joseph's prophetic dream (Gen 37:6 ff). Hence the use of Latin, a language which does not belong to any people and neither favors nor disfavors anyone with partiality; and thereby it fulfills an essential condition that a universal language must have in the Christian order.

The use of Latin by the Church is not limited to the negative function of eliminating partiality and resentments. It allows priests throughout the world to understand readily, precisely, and uniformly the supreme pontiff's magisterial, legislative, and exhortative acts; it enables them to follow in the *Acta Apostolicae Sedis* the ordinances of the Roman dicasteries; it gives them direct access, during their studies and afterwards, to the works of the Church fathers and of the great teachers; it establishes the use of an exact, unchangeable, and universal terminology, and that widespread competency which is fundamental to science of being able to go to the original sources; a rapid comprehension of the liturgical texts; and finally, the community of a higher culture that enriches but does not minimize the national cultures. All of these ties combined contribute to strengthen the unity of all of the members of the Church, of the priestly order first and foremost, and by means of them all the faithful as well. Pius XI (apostolic letter *Officiorum omnium*, August 1, 1922) said: "It is by a providential disposition that Latin furnishes to the more cultured Christians in every nation a powerful bond of unity permitting them to know more profoundly things pertaining to Mother Church, and to be able to have a closer union with the head of the household." Pius XII summarized and agreed: "The Latin language is a precious bond of the Catholic Church."

Besides the requirement of an attitude of ethnic and geographic universality, the Church's language, the supreme pontiff says, must possess the attribute of immutability. "The Church, which must last until the end of time, requires, by her very nature, a language that is unchangeable." It is a fact that living languages are in continuous flux; and the more the peoples who speak them participate in the movements of history, the more their languages change. In periods of great upheaval, intervals on the order of a decade are enough to change the face of a language. And the alteration is even greater, naturally, if it is a matter of centuries. Which of the modern highly cultured nations does not need dictionaries in order to read their own classics from four, five or six hundred years ago? Now, if the Church today had to fit the deposit of her truths into the changeable mold of the modern languages, of a few or many modern languages, without one of them having greater authority over the others, it would necessarily follow that the formulation thereof would be subject to distortion from many quarters and of unequal effect. Nor would there be any longer a unique and unalterable standard in which the individual standards could seek the norm. These are obvious facts that modern linguistics, in highlighting the diachronic aspect in the life of languages, has abundantly pointed out and defined. Latin, in contrast, being exempt from the changes caused by daily use by a large population in the midst of tumultuous history, lives in a sphere of crystal clarity and precision. The semantic modifications that it underwent as a popular, living language have ceased definitively; the changes in meaning that are due to doctrinal developments, polemics, and controversies, are now clearly identified and have no troublesome influence on the definitions of right doctrine.

The third requirement of the Church's language, the supreme pontiff continues, is that it not be vernacular. No one thinks that the Church, which prays to the Lord that he might "look favorably on the tribulations of the people, the dangers to the nations, the groans of prisoners, the misery of orphans, the needs of exiles, the abandonment of the weak, the hopelessness of the sick, the decline of the elderly, the yearnings of the young, the vows of virgins, the lamentations of widows" (*Roman Breviary*, "Preparation for Mass," Wednesday), and that this troubled humanity might draw upon the words of its divine founder: "You are all brothers" and from Paul's comment: "In Christ there is no longer barbarian or Scythian, slave or freeman," no one will think that the Church will let herself be swayed by Horatian rhetoric addressed to the *"profanum vulgus."* The *"vulgus"* are the masses immersed in everyday life, with their interests and passions. And although the Church on the one hand learns and also uses the obscure dialect of a small tribe in

> the Congo or the Amazon, in order to evangelize these children whom Christ has entrusted to her, on the other hand she senses the need and the obligation to entrust the sacred deposit of her truths to a language that neither identifies with this or that language of a particular people, nor is generally found at the level of the passions or of partial interests. These requisite qualities of loftiness she find also in Latin, which is therefore "a strong-box of incomparable excellence" (Pius XII, Address *Magis quam*) for her eternal and immutable truths. If Latin had not been offered by providence at the beginning of her long history, the Church would have had to search for a language that possessed the three required characteristic that Pope Pius XI specified. "Since Latin fully satisfies the threefold requirement," the pontiff concludes, "We maintain that it was arranged by divine providence that it should place itself admirably in the service of the teaching Church" (apostolic letter *Officiorum omnium*).
>
> The pith and the substance of the reasons why the Church is attached to Latin are thus essentially religious. As an institution that is universal in space and indefectible in time, she needs a linguistic means that establishes communication between the hub and the spokes, past, present and future: a language that expresses the truth clearly and is incorruptible in these changing times and beyond the reach of the troubled waters of the passions.[305]

b) John XXIII removes the heads of the Liturgical Commission

Even more significant was the apostolic letter that John XXIII sent on December 7 of that same year to the strongest defender of Latin on the Liturgical Commission, Monsignor Higini Anglès,[306] director of the Pontifical Institute for Sacred Music. The pope praised the institute's work

---

305 *L'Osservatore Romano*, March 25, 1961.

306 Cf. Higini Anglès, "Il prossimo Concilio Ecumenico e la Musica sacra," in *Bollettino degli Amici del Pontificio Istituto di Musica Sacra* 11 (1959). Monsignor Higini Anglès (1888–1969), Spanish, in recognition of his achievements as an eminent musicologist, was appointed by Pius XII in 1948 as president of the Pontifical Institute of Sacred Music in Rome, and also domestic prelate of His Holiness and consultor of the Sacred Congregation of Rites. Cf. *Sub tuum Praesidium confugimus: Scritti in memoria di mons. Higini Anglès* (Rome: Pontificio Istituto di Musica Sacra, 2002).

in defense of sacred music, declaring that "in solemn liturgies, whether in the large churches distinguished for their magnificence, or in the little churches of the country towns, it will always be legitimate to keep alive the royal scepter and the noble empire of the Latin language."[307]

Aware of the opposition, Bugnini formed a group of ten *periti*, who met secretly at the Domus Mariae from October 11 to 13, 1961, in order to speed up the revision of the schema.[308] On February 22, 1962, however, the pope signed the apostolic constitution *Veterum sapientia*,[309] which was a firm and unexpected response to those who supported the introduction of the vernacular into the liturgy. In this document John XXIII underscored the importance of the use of Latin, "the living language of the Church," and recommended that the most important ecclesiastical disciplines should be taught in Latin (no. 5) and that aspirants to the priesthood, before undertaking their ecclesiastical studies, "shall be given a sufficiently lengthy course of instruction in Latin by highly competent masters" (no. 3). The pope prescribed for all the ministers of the Catholic Church, both secular and religious clerics, "the study and the use" of the Latin language. "We ... are fully determined to restore this language to its position of honor, ... so as to ensure that the long-standing and uninterrupted use of Latin be maintained and, where necessary, restored."

That same day the pope named the new prefect of the Congregation for the Rites, Cardinal Arcadio M. Larraona,[310] as president of the Preparatory

---

307 AAS 53 (1961): 812.

308 Cf. A. Bugnini, *The Reform of the Liturgy, op. cit.*, 19–20.

309 Cf. AAS 54 (1962): 129–135. Cf. G. M. Roschini, O.S.M., *La Chiesa e la lingua latina: Considerazioni sulla costituzione apostolica "Veterum Sapientia" di S.S. Giovanni XXIII* (Rome, 1962); Alfons M. Stickler, "A 25 anni dalla costituzione apostolica 'Veterum Sapientia' di Giovanni XXIII: Rievocazione storica e prosopettive," in *Salesianum* 2 (1988): 367–377. A. Melloni, "Tensioni e timori nella preparazione del Vaticano II: La *Veterum Sapientia* di Giovanni XXIII (22 febbraio 1962)," in *Cristianesimo nella storia* 11 (1990): 275–307. *Idem*, "Contesti, fatti e reazioni attorno alla *Veterum Sapientia* di Giovanni XXIII," in *Rivista liturgica* 89/3 (2002): 391–407.

310 Arcadio Larraona (1887–1973), Spanish, member of the Missionary Sons of the Immaculate Heart of Mary (Claretians), ordained in 1911. Professor of Law at the Lateran and Urbanian Universities, in 1950 secretary of the Congregation for Religious. Created cardinal in 1959, was appointed prefect of the Sacred Congregation of Rites on February 12, 1962, and consecrated bishop on April 19 of the same year. The biography by Basilio Frisón, *Cardenal Larraona* (Madrid: Istituto teológico de Vida Religiosa, 1979), is surprisingly evasive concerning Larraona's role in the council. See instead "Il cardinal Arcadio

Commission, replacing Cardinal Cicognani, who passed away on February 5. If the selection of Larraona, a distinguished Spanish canonist who was deeply attached to the Roman See, was significant, then even more so was the replacement of Bugnini himself by Father Ferdinando Antonelli[311] in October 1962 on the eve of the opening of the council. Of all the secretaries of the preparatory commissions, only Bugnini was not reappointed secretary [of the corresponding conciliar commission] and he was dismissed from his professorial chair in Liturgical Studies at the Lateran University.[312]

With these measures John XXIII clearly showed that he was not happy with the direction taken by the Liturgical Commission. However, despite the explicit instructions in *Veterum Sapientia* the constitution was ignored. The order for the gradual dismissal of professors who were unable to speak Latin is one proof of this: the instructors at the pontifical universities in fact threatened to resign *en masse*, creating an embarrassing situation for the governing boards, who could never have replaced them in a timely fashion.[313]

13. The progressives declare war

Between 1961 and 1962 many Roman theologians, such as Father Raimondo Spiazzi,[314] and Father Sebastian Tromp[315] took to the field to correct the false interpretations of the council that were making the rounds.

Maria Larraona (1887–1973), edited by Fermina Álvarez Alonso, in *Centro Vaticano II, "Ricerche e documenti"* vol. I, no. O (January 2000): 28–41. See the biographical profile in PUL, 278–279.

[311] Ferdinando Antonelli (1896–1993), Franciscan, ordained in 1922. secretary of the Commission for the Liturgy and expert at the council, then secretary of the Congregation for Divine Worship and the Discipline of the Sacraments from 1965 to 1969. Was created cardinal in 1973.

[312] Cf. Reiner Kaczynski, "Toward the Reform of the Liturgy," in HVT 3:192–256 at 235.

[313] Cf. Mauro Gagliardi, *Introduzione al Mistero Eucaristico: Dottrina, liturgia, Devozione* (Salerno: Edizioni San Clemente, 2007), 352–353. In implementing the apostolic constitution *Veterum Sapientia*, the *Pontificium Institutum Altioris Latinitas* was founded on February 22, 1962, as part of the Pontifical Salesian University in Rome.

[314] Cf. Raimondo Spiazzi, O.P., "Il senso del Concilio," in *L'Osservatore Romano*, May 21, 1959. Raimondo Spiazzi (1918–2002), Dominican theologian, ordained in 1944, taught at the Angelicum and at the Lateran.

[315] Cf. S. Tromp, S.J., "De futuro Concilio Vaticano II," in *Gregorianum* 43 (1962): 5–11.

Father Luigi Ciappi,[316] master of the Sacred Apostolic Palace, in an article published in the magazine *Divinitas* entitled "The expectations of theology with regard to Vatican Council II," recalled the multifarious errors condemned by Pius XII (atheism, religious and moral agnosticism, atheistic secularism, progressivism, false humanism, immanentism, dogmatic relativism, evolutionism, etc.) and wrote:

> Well then, will the council fathers have to regard as dead and buried now these errors, not to mention the heresies, denounced by Pius XII? Might we perhaps hope for a solemn intervention by the whole body of the teaching Church that would confirm and complement the condemnations of the errors that are still lurking around, like pernicious weeds, in the vineyard of Christ, while sparing those who err, and even multiplying our paternal invitations, so as to bring them back onto the right path? This, I think, is the wish of many theologians.[317]

Although the majority of the council fathers saw the council as an occasion to renew the Church and to give new impetus to her activities, a minority of them wanted to seize the opportunity during this conciliar event to bring about a radical transformation of the ecclesiastical structures. This was the thesis of the volume by the young German theologian, Hans Küng, published in 1960 in Fribourg with the title *Council and Reunion: Renewal as a Call to Unity*.[318] The volume, which included a preface by Cardinal König,[319] was translated in 1961 into English, French, and Dutch.

---

[316] Mario Luigi Ciappi (1909–1996), Dominican theologian, ordained in 1932, master of the Sacred Palace (1955), consultor to the Congregation of the Holy Office, member of the Preparatory Theological Commission, appointed an expert in 1962. Was created cardinal in 1977.

[317] L. Ciappi, O.P., "Le attese della teologia di fronte al Concilio Vaticano II," in *Divinitas* 2 (1961): 494–502 at 499.

[318] Cf. Hans Küng, *Konzil und Wiedervereinigung: Erneuerung als Ruf in die Einheit*, with a Foreword by Cardinal Franz König (Vienna: Herder, 1960). "In expounding these ideas," Father Roberto Tucci wrote about Küng in the printed review *Civiltà Cattolica*, "a sincere love of the Church animates him, and he sets forth his viewpoints very frankly" (Caprile, I/2:43).

[319] Franz König (1905–2004), Austrian, ordained in 1933, coadjutor bishop of Sankt Pölten (1952), archbishop of Vienna from 1956 to 1985. Member of the Preparatory Commission and the Doctrinal Commission. Created cardinal in 1985, president of the Secretariat for Non-believers in 1965. Cf. Grootaers, *I protagonisti*, 145–157.

Ten thousand copies of the French edition were printed, which had a second preface by Cardinal Liénart,[320] archbishop of Lille. On June 8, 1962, *Time Magazine* published an article about the book with the headline "A Second Reformation, for Both Catholics and protestants," illustrated with three photographs with Hans Küng between Luther and Pope John.[321]

Küng, who was in his early thirties, had studied at the Gregorianum and then had been in Münster the assistant of Prof. Hermann Volk,[322] who was later bishop of Mainz. His volume theorized that the biblical-liturgical movement would converge with the ecumenical movement to "renew" the Church from within by transforming her structures. The Dominican Yves Congar, the chief exponent of the ecumenical movement, had very clearly in mind the strategy to follow: the involvement of public opinion was necessary to promote the more daring demands expressed by Küng:

> A number of us at once saw in the council an opening for the cause, not only of unionism, but also of ecclesiology. We saw in it an opportunity, which needed to be exploited to the maximum, of hastening the recovery of the values of episcopacy and *Ecclesia* in ecclesiology, and of making substantial progress from the point of view of ecumenism. Personally, I have endeavoured to urge public opinion to expect and to ask for a great deal. I have kept saying everywhere that it would pass perhaps no more than five per cent of what we wanted. All the more reason, therefore, to maximize our requests. Christian public opinion must force the council to exist in fact, and to achieve something.[323]

In a conference during the study days sponsored by *Informations catholiques internationales* in 1961, Congar's confrère and teacher, Marie-Dominique Chenu, proclaimed for his part, that the objective of the

---

320 Achille Liénart (1884–1973), French, ordained in 1907, bishop of Lille from 1928 to 1968. Created cardinal by Pius XI in 1930. Cf. Jean Vinatier, *Le cardinal Liénart* (Paris: Le Centurion, 1978).

321 Küng, *My Struggle*, 263.

322 Hermann Volk (1903–1988), German, ordained in 1927. Professor of dogmatic theology in Münster, bishop of Mainz from March 1962 to 1982, created cardinal in 1973.

323 Congar, *Journal*, 4.

impending council was "the end of the Constantinian era";[324] he explained that this formula was "rather provocative in its suggestive force and even in its indefiniteness," but that it was "beginning to circulate almost everywhere, in Germany and in Italy even more than in France, often proposed by renowned intellectuals, and even by Church authorities."[325] Congar identified a parallel between Chenu's philosophy of history, which was founded on the idea of progress, and the cosmology of Teilhard de Chardin, which was centered on the idea of evolution. According to Congar, "what Teilhard de Chardin intuited for the cosmos as a whole and for its entire history, Chenu intuited for the historical and social dimension of human life."[326] From the perspective of Chenu and Teilhard, the world would have to impregnate the Church with its spirit instead of the Church sanctifying the world.

Teilhard de Chardin died in New York in 1955. On November 15, 1957 a letter from the Holy Office had ordered his works to be withdrawn from Catholic libraries. On June 30, 1962, on the eve of the opening of the council, a *Monitum* of the Holy Office had subsequently condemned his works. But that same year a book by Father de Lubac had been published on *The Religious Thought of Father Teilhard de Chardin*,[327] and an article by Father Daniélou had appeared with the title *"Signification de Teilhard de Chardin,"*[328] in which he exalted Teilhard's "integral humanism."[329] His name fluttered over the impending council and would be an interpretive key thereof.

---

[324] Published in *Un Concile pour notre temps* (Paris: Cerf, 1961), 59–87.

[325] Ibid., 59.

[326] Y. Congar, O.P., "Marie-Dominique Chenu," in *Bliancio della teologia del XX secolo*, ed. R. Vander Gucht (Rome: Città Nuova, 1972) 4:103–122 at 120.

[327] Cf. H. de Lubac, S.J., *La pensée religieuse du Père Teilhard de Chardin* (Paris: Aubier, 1962); Eng. transl. *The Religion of Teilhard de Chardin* (New York: Desclee Co., 1967). The book was followed by many others dedicated to Teilhard: *La prière du P. Teilhard de Chardin* (1964) = *Teilhard de Chardin: the man and his meaning* (1965); *Teilhard missionnaire et apologiste* (1966) = *Teilhard explained* (1968); *Teilhard et notre temps* (1968); *Teilhard postume* (1977).

[328] Cf. Jean Daniélou, S.J., "Signification de Teilhard de Chardin," in *Études* 312 (1962): 145–161.

[329] The Carmelite Philippe de la Trinité responded to it with a closely-argued study of *Teilhard et Teilhardisme* (Rome: Pontificia Università Lateranense, 1962).

a) The central European bishops organize

Under the influence of the biblical-liturgical movement and the ecumenical movement, a new "theology of the episcopate" had taken shape during the decade 1948-1958 in central Europe.[330] This "episcopalist" tendency was adopted in Belgium by the Cardinal Primate Jozef-Ernest Van Roey[331] and in Holland by the Cardinal Primate Bernard Jan Alfrink. A figure who nicely personified this trend was Bishop André-Marie Charue,[332] Ordinary of Namur from 1942 on, who in paying his respects to Cardinal Van Roey in June 1957 emphasized the existence of a "union of the episcopate like that of the Apostles in the College of the Twelve."[333] The formula "government by the Twelve" would have great success at the council.

The position that Cardinal Alfrink was to assume could easily be deduced from three "stages" of his attitude: the *vota* [recommendations] submitted by him in the name of the Dutch hierarchy on December 22, 1959; the pastoral letter of that same episcopate, published on Christmas 1960 and dedicated to the "meaning of the council";[334] his intervention at the Central Preparatory Commission in May 1962 on the role of the bishops in the Church, in which the primate of Holland severely criticized the preparatory schema *De Ecclesia*.

The 1960 pastoral letter signed by the Dutch bishops formally proposed two theses topics for discussion at the next conciliar session: the role of the laity and that of the episcopate. One passage from the pastoral letter declared that "the premature interruption of the First Vatican Council created the impression that the isolated definition of papal infallibility was

---

330 *Actes et Acteurs*, 339–357.

331 Jozef-Ernest Van Roey (1874–1961), Belgium, ordained in 1897, consecrated bishop in 1926, archbishop of Malines (1926–1961), was created cardinal in 1927.

332 André-Marie Charue (1898–1977), Belgium, ordained in 1922, bishop of Namur from 1942 to 1974, member of the Doctrinal Commission, of which he was elected vice-president on December 2, 1963. Cf. J. Coppens "In memoriam de son excellence Mgr André-Marie Charue 1898–1977," in *Ephemerides Theologicae Lovanienses* 54 (1978): 221–235; *Actes et Acteurs*, 367–368, and the introduction by Claude Troisfontained to Charue, *Carnets Conciliaires*, 5–25.

333 Cited in *Actes et Acteurs*, 346.

334 *Le sens du Concile: Une réforme intérieure de la vie catholique: Lettre pastorale de l'épiscopat hollandais* (Bruges: Desclée de Brouwer, 1961).

a complete, self-sufficient truth. In fact this personal infallibility is part of the official infallibility of the worldwide episcopate, which is founded in turn upon the infallibility of the whole community." Archbishop Felici judged it prudent to have the Italian translation of the text by the primate of Holland withdrawn from Catholic libraries,[335] but the latter did not desist from his episcopalist advocacy: in the winter of 1961 Alfrink declared on Dutch television that the primacy of papal infallibility had "come in through the window because of the presence of the Italian troops" that were pressuring the Papal State.[336]

In Belgium the centers propelling progressivism were the University of Louvain and the Benedictine monastery of Chevetogne, founded by Dom Beauduin. After the announcement of the council in 1959, Chevetogne decided to dedicate its annual colloquia to the preparations for the council, choosing as themes: the notion of council (1959), the theme of the local Church (1960), and "the infallibility of the Church" (1961).[337]

On March 19, 1962, Archbishop Léon-Joseph Suenens,[338] the new archbishop of Malines-Brussels, became a cardinal and was received by John XXIII, who asked him to prepare a note for the council. The document was presented to the pope in an audience on May 10, 1962.[339] The following

---

335 Cf. Renzo Trionfera, "Il monsignore in doppiopetto," in *L'Europeo* (July 22, 1962): 40.

336 Cf. Lo Svizzero, *La Pira e la via cattolica al comunismi*(Milan: Edizioni de *Il Borghese*, 1964), 97.

337 Cf. O. Rousseau, "Les journées oecuméniques de Chevetogne (1942–1967)," in *Au service de la parole de Dieu*, Mélanges A. M. Charue (Gembloux, 1969), 451–485. The same Rousseau is to be credited with an article on "La vraie valeur de l'épiscopat dans l'Église" ["The true value of the episcopate in the Church"], in *Irénikon* 29 (1956): 121–250, which had repercussions not only in Belgium but also in Holland and Germany.

338 Léon-Joseph Suenens (1904–1996), Belgium, ordained in 1927, archbishop of Malines-Brussels from 1961 to 1979, created cardinal in 1962, was one of the four moderators of the council appointed in September 1963. J. Grootaers, "Von Johannes XXIII zu Johannes Paul II: Ein Gespräch mit Leo-Joseph Kardinal Suenens," in *Herder-Korrespondenz* 34 (1980): 176–182; *Idem, I protagonisti*, 229–243; *Actes et Acteurs*, 316–319; Leo Declerck and Toon Osaer, "Les relations entre le Cardinal Montini-Paul VI (1897–1978) et le Cardinal Suenens (1904–1996) pendant le Concile Vatican II," in *Istituto Paolo VI* 51 (2006): 47–80 at 54; M. Lamberigts and L. Declerck, "The Role of Cardinal Léon-Joseph Suenens at Vatican II," in *The Belgian Contribution*, 61–217.

339 Cf. M. Lamberigts and L. Declerck, "The Role of Cardinal Suenens," *op. cit.*, 67–68.

day the new cardinal, who was being talked about in Rome as *papabile*,[340] had a long meeting with Cardinal Montini.[341]

During the month of June 1962 Suenens gathered a group of cardinals in Rome, at the Belgian College, to discuss a "plan" for the upcoming council.[342] Participating in the meeting were Cardinals Döpfner, Liénart, Montini, and Siri. Suenens tells of discussing with them a "confidential" document that criticized the schemas previously drawn up by the Preparatory Commissions and suggested that the pope create, "for his personal and private use," a commission limited to a few members, "a sort of brain trust" to respond to the major problems in contemporary pastoral ministry, thus avoiding "the danger of immobility."[343]

> The effort of pastoral renewal has not been felt with the same intensity in different countries. There is the risk that the bishops who have more experience in this area are not sufficiently numerous to make their votes prevail in the council. The experience of what is happening in the Central Commission shows that there is a strong integralist current that is opposed to any pastoral renewal at a certain level. May the Holy Spirit enlighten His Holiness the Pope so that the immobilist tendency, although it appears to be numerically stronger, might not prevail in the final analysis.[344]

In his document, the cardinal primate of Belgium finally launched the watchword: "pastoral council."

> If possible, at the end of this note, I would like to express a wish: that the council might be, *par excellence*, a pastoral council, which is to

340 Poswick, *Journal*, 109.

341 Cf. Giselda Adornato, *Cronologia dell'episcopato de G. R. Montini a Milano, 4 gennaio 1955 – 22 gennaio 1963* (Brescia: Istituto Paolo VI, 2002), 866.

342 L. J. Suenens, "Aux Origines du Concile Vatican II," in *Nouvelle Revue Théologique* 107 (1985): 3–21 at 4; *Idem, Souvenirs et espérances*, 65–80.

343 In a conversation with Benny Lai, Cardinal Siri recalled the episode in these terms: "Suenens maintained that only Cardinal Döpfner appeared to be against his proposal, but that he then accepted the opinion of Liénart, Montini and Siri. That is false; I did not accept anything at all. Suenens is someone who has always liked to play the protagonist" (B. Lai, *Il Papa non eletto*, 183, note 13).

344 L. J. Suenens, *Aux Origines du Concile Vatican II, op. cit.*, 8.

> say an apostolic council. What an immense benefit it would be for the Church if it could define in broad strokes how the whole Church must be in mission, and must be so at all levels: laity, religious, clergy, bishops, and Roman congregations! What a magnificent grace of Pentecost it would be for the Church, as our most beloved head hoped with so much affection and Christian hope![345]

John XXIII followed the line drawn by Suenens in the speech that he gave on September 11, 1962, one month before the opening of the council, putting into circulation the distinction between the Church *ad intra* and *ad extra*. The attitude of the Church *ad extra* concerned her relations with the world. This was the chief innovation of the imminent council.

On the eve of the French Revolution, the "liberal party" already had its local committees, lodges, academies, reading rooms, philosophical and patriotic associations, which created a close-knit organizational network.[346] Vatican II also had an "organizational vigil" with plenty of gatherings, conferences, publications, public and private meetings in which a "strategy" was defined, as it became clear from the frenetic meetings that followed one another in the days immediately preceding the opening of the council.[347]

The primate of Belgium was one of the major protagonists of this strategy. "The perspective taken by the council," Grootaers writes, "is due to a great extent to one man, and that man was Cardinal Suenens."[348] "The collegial tendency within the Belgian church"[349] imprinted on it by his predecessors, Mercier and Van Roey, had prepared him to play that role.

During the month of August the pope received also a petition from the Canadian Cardinal Paul-Emile Léger,[350] the Sulpician archbishop of Montréal. The letter was signed by Cardinals Liénart, Döpfner, Alfrink, König, and Suenens. The document frankly criticized the first seven schemas

---

[345] Ibid.

[346] Cf. Pierre Gaxotte, *The French Revolution* (London and New York: C. Scribner's Sons, 1932).

[347] Cf. Chenu, *Diario*, 57–69.

[348] *Actes et Acteurs*, 316.

[349] Suenens, *Memories and Hopes*, 73.

[350] Paul-Emile Léger (1904–1991), ordained in 1929, archbishop of Montreal (1950–1968), created cardinal in 1953, member of the Central Preparatory Commission and of the Doctrinal Commission.

that were supposed to be discussed by the assembly, asserting that they were not in keeping with the orientation that John XXIII intended to give to the council.[351] "We are no longer in the days of the doctrinal liberalism of 1860, nor of the socialism that set itself up against the Church. We do not have to shut ourselves up in a ghetto. Nor to be content with tossing stones at the communists…," Cardinal Léger said animatedly to Chenu on October 10.[352] The archbishop of Montréal had established a special bond with the Belgian theologian Charles Moeller, with whom he had become acquainted in Canada in 1959. It was thanks to Léger that Moeller, initially present at the council only as a journalist, acquired the status of "expert," as his private advisor.

The council was an extraordinary opportunity for the progressive currents of thought. Since it was by nature an assembly, the event would allow the various tendencies to confront one another on a level of ideological equality and to leave it to the rules of parliamentary procedure to determine the winner of the debates. The council would also prove to be an occasion for heterodox theologians to meet, whereas until then they had been scattered and marginalized within their own religious institutes.

Even before the council, a group of Northern European bishops, assisted by their "experts," had provided themselves with an organizational structure by which to exchange information and to coordinate their initiatives "and if need be the pressures that they would exert on the assembly."[353] Cardinal Heenan, then archbishop of Liverpool, writes in his autobiography that "the English-speaking bishops were quite unprepared for the kind of council the rest of the Northern Europeans were planning."[354] "Looking back," he added, "it is easy to see how psychologically unprepared bishops

---

351 Cf. "Lettre inédite du Cardinal Paul-Emile Léger au Pape Jean XXIII en août 1962," in *Mémoires de Vatican II*, ed. G. Routhier (Montréal, 1997), 93–113; for an evaluation thereof, see G. Routhier, "Les réactions du cardinal Léger à la préparation de Vatican II," in *Revue d'Histoire de l'Église de France*," 80 (1994): 281–302 and "L'itinéraire d'un père conciliaire: Le cardinal Léger," in *Cristianesimo nella storia* 19 (1998): 89–147.

352 Chenu, *Diario*, 69.

353 R. Aubert, "Organizzazione e funzionamento dell'assemblea," in *SC, La Chiesa del Vaticano II*, XXV/I:177.

354 John C. Heenan, *A Crown of Thorns: An Autobiography 1951–1963* (London: Hodder and Stoughton, 1974), 339.

were for what happened during the first session. Many of us arrived in Rome in October 1962 with no idea of the anti-Italian mood of many Europeans."[355]

On October 10, on the eve of the opening of the council, the president of the Italian Episcopal Conference, Giuseppe Siri, noted in his diary: "The trouble, if I may say so, will come as usual from the French-German areas and the respective underbrush, because they have never thoroughly eliminated the protestant pressure and the *Pragmatica Sanctio* [an imperial constitution]; a very capable people, but they do not know how to be responsible for a mistaken history."[356]

The pope did not heed the alarming rumors that reached him, and not only from Roman circles. Optimism was the predominant feature in his temperament. The symptoms of his illness, however, had already begun to appear and, on October 8, 1961, he described himself as "a mortal man eighty years old and weighing 103 kilos [227 lbs]."[357]

Perhaps foreseeing his end, John XXIII seemed to be in a hurry to conclude without problems the assembly that he had convoked. In July 1962 he received in audience Archbishop Pericle Felici, who presented to him the revised and approved conciliar schemas. "The council is done," Pope Roncalli exclaimed enthusiastically, "By Christmas we can conclude!"[358]

---

[355] Ibid., 343.

[356] Siri, *Diario*, 356.

[357] Giovanni XXIII, *Pater Amabilis: Agende del Pontefice*, 267.

[358] Cited in Michele Maccarrone, "Paolo VI e il Concilio: testimonianze," in *Rivista di Storia della Chiesa in Italia* 43 (1989): 101–122 at 101.

III

1962: The First Session

1. The opening of Vatican II

a) The ceremony on October 11

The twenty-first ecumenical council in Church history opened on Thursday, October 11, 1962. The rain fell persistently until the early morning hours, then stopped, and a sunny day was forecast.

The long procession of council fathers went out by the Bronze Door, crossed Saint Peter's Square diagonally, climbed the steps and advanced slowly inside the packed basilica. At its head were superiors of religious orders, abbots general and prelates *nullius*; then the bishops, archbishops, patriarchs, cardinals, and finally, on the gestatorial chair, amidst the crowd's applause, John XXIII. As the procession of fathers strode solemnly, singers chanted the *Credo* and then the *Magnificat*. Each father, on entering the church, took off his white miter, proceeded to the central altar, bowed before the cross in a brief gesture of homage, and went to his place. All told, the procession was about 4 kilometers [2.5 miles] long; almost three thousand dignitaries of the Church took part in it.

The presence of the vicar of Christ and the successors of the apostles, in the incomparable setting of Saint Peter's Basilica, made the ceremony a spectacle that was unique in this world. Never before had the Catholic Church manifested her universal and hierarchical character as at that moment. In this event the Church was fulfilling the divine mandate to proclaim the gospel to all nations (Mt 28:19). Thanks to Italian television, the solemn ceremony was followed by millions of people in every corner of the earth.

There were 2,381 council fathers present. The eldest, Most Rev. Alfonso Carinci,[1] had participated in the choir of Vatican I as a child and celebrated his one-hundredth birthday during the council. The youngest, Alcides Mendoza Castro,[2] a Peruvian, was only thirty-four. Only one-third of the bishops were European, although the more than five hundred fathers from Africa and Asia were mostly of European origin,[3] one-third of them Italian. One hundred forty-six bishops were supposed to arrive from the European communist world, but there were fewer than fifty. Of the Chinese bishops, 144 should have come, but only the forty-four expelled ones were present. No council father from North Korea or North Vietnam was present; illustrious witnesses to the faith such as Cardinal Mindszenty and the metropolitan of Ukrainians, Cardinal Slipyj, were absent. The media kept silent about these glaring absences.

The *Ordo Concilii Oecumenici Vaticani II celebrandi*, approved by the motu proprio *Appropinquante concilio* dated August 6, 1962, and promulgated on October 7 of that year, copied that of Vatican Council I.[4] As in the previous assembly, the plenary meetings of the fathers, called General Congregations, were the solemn moment when the schemas would be discussed and voted on. The approved drafts would be examined chapter by chapter. The members would vote *placet* to express their approval, *non placet* to vote against, or *placet juxta modum* in the case of agreement in

---

[1] Alfonso Carinci (1862–1963), ordained in 1885, titular archbishop, secretary of the Congregation of Rites from 1945 to 1960.

[2] Alcides Mendoza Castro (1928–2003), ordained in 1951, auxiliary bishop of Abancay (Peru), was bishop there from December 1962 to 1967.

[3] On the role of the third world in Vatican II, cf. Henri Teissier, "Vatican II et le Tiers Monde," in *Le deuxième Concile du Vatican*, 755–767, esp. 756–759.

[4] Text of the motu proprio in John XXIII, DMC, 4:939–941. Cf. S. Gómez de Arteche y Catalina, *op. cit.,* 1:35–53.

principle, with written motions for amendments. The amended text was then returned so as to be examined by the general assembly, where it was to be voted on, first chapter by chapter, and then as a whole. For final approval, two thirds of the votes of those present were necessary. The plenary sessions, starting with the celebration of Mass, were to be held in the morning in Saint Peter's Basilica, which was especially equipped to accommodate the more than two thousand fathers. The only language permitted was Latin.

b) John XXIII criticizes the "prophets of doom"

The pope's inaugural address, *Gaudet mater ecclesia*,[5] delivered in Latin and immediately relayed to the whole world by the mass media, was, as Father Wenger observes, the key to understanding the council. "The speech on October 11 was the real roadmap of the council. More than an agenda, it defined a spirit; more than a program, it gave an orientation."[6] The novelty was not so much in the doctrinal realm as in the new, psychologically optimistic approach to relations between the Church and the world: sympathy and "openness". Those who called into question this irenic and optimistic mentality were described by the pope as "prophets of gloom".[7]

John XXIII emphasized he had conceived the council in a "completely unexpected" way (no. 3.1) and then set in motion an intense work of preparation in the belief that, "Illuminated by the light of this council, the Church—we confidently trust—will become greater in spiritual riches and, gaining the strength of new energies therefrom, she will look to the future without fear. In fact, by bringing herself up to date where required,

---

[5] Cf. John XXIII, Address *Gaudet Mater Ecclesia* (October 11, 1962) in AS, I/1, pp. 166–175; "Address Delivered by His Holiness Pope John XXIII at the Solemn Opening of the Second Vatican Council," English edition by Vatican Translations, published in a somewhat simplified form by the National Catholic Welfare Conference, (Washington, D.C., no date), 3–12. Concerning this address, cf. A. Melloni, "Sinossi critica dell'allocuzione di apertura del Concilio Vaticano II Gaudet Mater Ecclesiae di Giovanni XXIII," in Various Authors, *Fede Tradizione Profezia: Studi su Giovanni XXIII e sul Vaticano II* (Brescia: Paideia, 1984), 241–283, and the severe critique of it by Paolo Pasqualucci in *Giovanni XXIII e il Concilio Ecumenico Vaticano II* (Albano Laziale [Roma]: Ichthys, 2008), *passim.*

[6] A.Wenger, *Vatican II*, *op. cit.*, 1:38–39.

[7] John XXIII, *Gaudet Mater Ecclesia*, op. cit., p. 169; Eng., p. 6.

and by the wise organization of mutual co-operation, the Church will make men, families, and peoples really turn their minds to heavenly things." At this point the pope criticized those whom he described as the "prophets of gloom." He said he had listened to persons who,

> though burning with zeal, are not endowed with too much sense of discretion or measure.
>
> In these modern times they can see nothing but prevarication and ruin. They say that our era, in comparison with past eras, is getting worse, and they behave as though they had learned nothing from history, which is, none the less, the teacher of life. They behave as though at the time of former councils everything was a full triumph for Christian doctrine, morals, and proper liberty for the Church.
>
> We feel we must resolutely disagree with those prophets of gloom, who are always forecasting disaster, as though the end of the world were at hand. In the present state of human affairs, in which humanity appears to enter a new order of things, one must rather look to the mysterious plans of divine providence which, through men's efforts and often beyond their expectations, despite human reversals, are wisely directed toward the greater good of the Church.

For John XXIII, the main task of the council was to preserve the magisterium of the Church and teach it "more efficaciously".

> The twenty-first ecumenical council… wishes to transmit the [Catholic] doctrine, pure and integral, without any attenuation or distortion, which throughout twenty centuries, notwithstanding difficulties and controversies, has become the common patrimony of men…. [But our primary duty] is not…a discussion of one article or another of the fundamental doctrine of the Church which has repeatedly been taught by the fathers and by ancient and modern theologians, and which is presumed to be well known and familiar to all.
>
> For this a council was not necessary. But from the renewed, serene, and tranquil adherence to all the teaching of the Church in its entirety and preciseness, as it still shines forth in the acts of the Council of Trent and First Vatican Council, the Christian, Catholic, and apostolic spirit of the whole world expects a step forward toward a doctrinal penetration and a formation of consciousness in faithful and perfect conformity to the authentic doctrine, which, however, should be studied and expounded through the methods of research

> and through the literary forms of modern thought. The substance of the ancient doctrine of the deposit of faith is one thing, and the way in which it is presented is another. And it is the latter that must be taken into great consideration with patience if necessary, everything being measured in the forms and proportions of a *magisterium* which is predominantly pastoral in character.

In regard to errors condemned by the Church in every age, even with the utmost severity, the pope announced a new pastoral attitude:

> Nowadays however, the Spouse of Christ prefers to make use of the medicine of mercy rather than that of severity. She considers that she meets the needs of the present day by more clearly demonstrating the validity of her teaching rather than by condemnations.... That being so, the Catholic Church, raising the torch of Catholic truth by means of this ecumenical council, desires to show herself to be the loving mother of all, benign, patient, full of mercy and goodness toward the children who are separated from her.[8]

The council had been convened, not to condemn errors or make new dogmas but to propose the perennial teaching of the Church in language adapted to the new times. With John XXIII, the pastoral paradigm became the magisterial paradigm *par excellence*.[9] According to Alberigo, this perspective was destined to make Vatican II an *event*, rather than a forum in which to prepare and issue guidelines.[10] The main identity of Vatican II thus appeared to be "*aggiornamento*"[11] or "updating," understood as "a

---

[8] John XXIII, *Gaudet Mater Ecclesiae, op. cit.*, 171–172; Eng., 5–6, 8–9. *Cf.* G. Alberigo, "Dal bastone alla misericordia: Il magistero nel cattolicesimo contemporaneo (1830–1980)," in *Cristianesimo nella storia*, 2 (1981): 487–521, esp. 507–511. This proclamation of the principle of mercy, as opposed to the principle of severity—Romano Amerio comments—"ignores the fact that in the mind of the Church *the condemnation of error is itself a work of mercy*" (R. Amerio, *Iota Unum, op. cit.*, 80).

[9] Cf. G. Ruggieri, "Appunti per una teologia in Papa Roncalli," in Alberigo, *Papa Giovanni*, 245–271, at 265.

[10] Cf. G. Alberigo, "Giovanni XXIII e il Vaticano II," in Alberigo, *Papa Giovanni*, 211–244, at 219.

[11] G. Alberigo, *Transizione epocale, op. cit.*, 769.

rejuvenation of Christian life and of the Church"[12] and the "willingness and readiness to search for a renewed inculturation of the Christian message in new cultures".[13]

This does not mean that Pope John was, as Alberigo contends, deliberately aware of the "epochal" scope of the assembly that he had called for. In fact, he had no idea how long it would take or the nature of the discussion, much less the consequences of the assembly that he had convened.

Many fathers were disconcerted by the unusual tone of John XXIII's allocution. "I understood little of the pope's speech; regarding that little, I immediately had the occasion to perform a great act of mental obedience," Cardinal Siri wrote in his diary.[14]

c) The observers from the Russian Orthodox Church

In the afternoon of October 12, two observers from the Russian Orthodox Church arrived in Rome: the Archpriest Vitalij Borovoij and the Archimandrite Vladimir Kotlyarov, "obviously approved and controlled," as Alberto Melloni admits, "by the party organs and police agencies."[15] Both were more than content with the words of John XXIII, which confirmed the assurances that had been given to the patriarch of Moscow by Cardinal Tisserant and Bishop Willebrands. "The pope's major concern," Borovoij recalls,

> was the insistent desire of the conservative political and clerical circles to use the Church and the council to condemn the communists.... The pope, seeking the unity and peace of all men, rejected those demands, expressing himself directly in his inaugural speech at the council, in which he articulates his "disagreement" [*"dissenso"*] with the prophets of misfortune and his reliance, on the other hand, on the plan of divine goodness that provides for the good of the Church.[16]

---

[12] *Ibid.*

[13] *Ibid.*, 771.

[14] Siri, *Diario*, 357.

[15] A. Melloni, "Chiese sorelle, diplomazie nemiche; Il Vaticano II a Mosca fra propaganda, Ostpolitik ed ecumenismo," in *Vatican II in Moscow*, 1–14 at 8.

[16] Vitalij Borovoij, "Il significato del Concilio Vaticano II per la Chiesa ortodossa russa," in *Vatican*

Borovoij then expresses his gratitude to the secretariat of Cardinal Bea, in terms that implicitly confirm the very close ties between the patriarchate of Moscow and the Kremlin: "The Secretariat for Unity and the leaders of the council," he testifies, "were always ready to defend the observers and the dignity of the Russian Orthodox Church in cases of seriously anti-Muscovite, anti-Russian, or anti-Soviet actions, as well as in cases of maneuvers organized by the ultra-conservative or ultra-national-chauvinist forces, whether inside or on the fringes of the council."[17]

Journalists, too, were a privileged channel of contacts between the Kremlin and the Vatican.[18] Among the first of these was Anatolij Krassikov, who was officially accredited at the Vatican on behalf of the Soviet news agency Tass. The correspondent's first report, in a tone that was unexpectedly favorable toward the Vatican, was published by the Soviet organ on October 11 and was reprinted the following day by *Izvestiya*, which was edited by Khrushchev's son-in-law, Adzhubey.[19]

2. The break with council procedures: the session on October 13

The first General Congregation of the Second Vatican Council opened on Saturday, October 13, beneath torrential rain. The day's agenda provided that the assembly would elect its representatives (sixteen out of twenty-four) on each of the ten commissions that were delegated to examine the schemas drawn up by the Preparatory Commission. The council fathers had received three printed hand-outs, prepared by the general secretariat.

II in Moscow, 73–89 at 77.

[17] *Ibid.*, 79. In Italy *L'Unità* devoted considerable space to the presence of the two Russian observers: coverage "justified by the political value that the Italian Communist Party attributed to their participation: an explicit acknowledgment of the importance attributed to the council by the Communist Party of the Soviet Union as well; without their authorization the two could not have traveled to Rome, and the implicit agreement reached between the two churches that the council would not make any statement against communism." R. Burigana, "Il Partito comunista italiano e la Chiesa," in *Vatican II in Moscow*, 205.

[18] Cf. Nicolaij A. Kovalskij, "Vatican II and its Role in the History of the Twentieth Century," in *Vatican II in Moscow*, 303–312 at 309–310.

[19] Cf. Anatolij Krassikov, "The Second Vatican Council in the context of Relations between the USSR and the Holy See," in *Vatican II in Moscow*, 313–330 at 314.

The first contained a complete list of the fathers, who were all eligible, unless they already held other positions. The second indicated the names of those who had taken part in the deliberations of the various commissions of the council; the third consisted of ten pages, each of which had sixteen numbered blank spaces. The council fathers would be able to write in the names of the preselected representatives, for a total of 160 names.

At the opening of the session, however, there was an unexpected scene: Cardinal Achille Liénart, archbishop of Lille, one of the nine presidents of the assembly, addressed Cardinal Tisserant, who was presiding over the proceedings, in a low voice in these words: "Your Eminence, it is really impossible to vote this way, without knowing anything about the most qualified candidates. If you allow me, I ask to take the floor." "Impossible," Tisserant replied. "The order of the day does not provide for any debate. We are meeting simply to vote; I cannot give you the floor."[20]

Cardinal Tisserant's reply was in keeping with the rules, since the congregation was convened to vote and not to decide whether or not to vote. But the archbishop of Lille, not satisfied, grabbed the microphone and read a text stating that the fathers were not yet acquainted with the possible candidates and that it was necessary to consult the national conferences before being able to vote for the commissions. "Since there are forty-two episcopal conferences in the world, which are enumerated in the *Annuario Pontificio* [papal almanac], we ask that the presidents of these commissions convoke the members of the conference and ask them for the names of their colleagues whom they recommend as the best suited for the work of the commissions."[21]

While some applause arose from the assembly, a figure stood up from the bench of the Presidency itself: Cardinal Frings,[22] who asserted that he spoke on behalf of Cardinals Döpfner[23] and König also, and expressed

---

[20] A. Liénart, *Vatican II* (Lille: Facultés Catholiques, 1967), 67; Wiltgen, 16–17.

[21] AS I/1:207.

[22] AS I/1:208. Josef Frings (1887–1978), a German, ordained in 1910, archbishop of Cologne from 1942 to 1969. He was created cardinal by Pius XII in 1946. A member of the Preparatory Central Commission and of the Board of Presidency. Cf. Norbert Trippen, *Josef Kardinal Frings*, vol. I: *Sein Wirken für das Erzbistum Köln and für die Kirche in Deutschland* (Paderborn-Monaco: F. Schöningh, 2003); vol. II: *Sein Wirken für die Weltkirche und seine letzten Bischofsjahre* (2005).

[23] Julius Döpfner (1913–1976), German, ordained in 1939. Created cardinal in 1958, archbishop

his firm support for the request of his French colleague. The applause increased, and Cardinal Tisserant moved to close the session and to report to the Holy Father what had happened. Cardinal Suenens emphasized in his memoirs the revolutionary significance of the happening. "This was indeed a brilliant and dramatic turn of events, an audacious infringement of existing regulations! … To a large extent, the future of the council was decided at that moment. John XXIII was very pleased."[24]

The *"Blitzkrieg"*[25] had been carefully coordinated. In the night between October 12 and 13, at the French Seminary of Santa Chiara, Archbishop Garrone[26] and Bishop Ancel[27] had prepared a text, which had then been entrusted to Cardinal Joseph-Charles Lefebvre,[28] archbishop of Bourges, so that he might in turn deliver it to Cardinal Liénart to read at the beginning of the General Congregation.[29] Cardinal Lefebvre had handed it over to Liénart that very morning, the 13th, at the entrance to Saint Peter's Basilica.[30]

The first session of the Second Vatican Council had lasted less than fifty minutes. Bishop Luigi Borromeo[31] wrote in his *Diary*: "And so they

---

of Munich and Friesing from 1961 to 1976. See Grootaers, *I protagonisti*, 103–114.

24 Suenens, *Memories and Hopes*, 68.

25 So it was described by M. Davies in *Pope John's Council* (Devon: Augustine Publishing Company, 1977), 23–32.

26 Gabriel-Marie Garrone (1901–1994), French, ordained in 1925. archbishop of Toulouse from 1956 to 1966, created cardinal in 1967, pro-prefect and then prefect of the Congregation of Seminaries and Universities (which became the Congregation for Catholic Education in 1967) from 1966 to 1990 and president of the Pontifical Council for Culture from 1982 to 1988. Cf. Grootaers, *I protagonisti*, 133–144.

27 Alfred Ancel (1898–1984), French, ordained in 1923, auxiliary bishop of Lyons from 1947 to 1973. Cf. Olivier de Berranger, *Un homme pour l'Évangile: Alfred Ancel 1898–1984* (Paris: Le Centurion, 1988).

28 Joseph-Charles Lefebvre (1892–1973), French, ordained in 1921, from 1936 to 1938 vicar general of Poitiers, appointed archbishop of Bourges in 1943, then cardinal in 1960. Not to be confused with his cousin, Archbishop Marcel Lefebvre.

29 Cf. Andrea Riccardi, "The Tumultuous Opening Days of the Council," in HVT 2:1–68, at 30–32; P. Levillain, *La mécanique politique, op. cit.* 188–189.

30 A. Liénart, *Vatican II, op. cit.*, 66–67.

31 Luigi Carlo Borromeo (1893–1975), ordained in 1918, bishop of Pesaro from 1952 to 1975.

inconvenienced three thousand persons to walk to Saint Peter's in the rain, to hear someone tell them that the three thousand bishops do not know one another and have to go back home to see to it that they get somewhat acquainted."[32] "It is difficult to account for the astonishment and uneasiness created by this turn of events," Cardinal Siri recorded for his part.[33] While leaving the council hall, one Dutch bishop turned to a priest friend and remarked, "That was our first victory!"[34] The council opened therefore with an act of force. All the observers recognize in it the turning point of the conciliar assembly.[35]

3. A new organizational form: the episcopal conferences

One immediate consequence of Cardinal Liénart's gesture was the introduction of a new organizational form, which would prove to be crucial in the pursuit of the business: the entrance of the episcopal conferences into the conciliar dynamics.[36] As Liénart had demanded in his motion, they were called on to suggest, by October 15, lists of new nominees for the commissions. Their role in the council thus became sanctioned officially. One of the first episcopal conferences, a model of the others, had been, in the early 1950s, the Brazilian conference (CNBB), which came into being through an initiative by Bishop Helder Câmara,[37] with the support of the nuncio Armando

---

Member of the Commission for Religious.

[32] Borromeo, *Diario* (October 13, 1962), 120.

[33] Siri, *Diario*, 360.

[34] Wiltgen, 17.

[35] Thus for example Wilde, 18–19: "The importance of Liénart's motion cannot be overstated." The significance of the episode is downplayed, however, by G. Caprile, "La seconda giornata del Vaticano II 25 anni dopo," in *Civiltà Cattolica*, 3293 (1987): 382–390.

[36] Wilde, 19; A. Riccardi, "The Tumultuous Opening Days of the Council," 32–34.

[37] Helder Pessoa Câmara (1909–1999), Brazilian, ordained in 1931. Auxiliary bishop of Rio de Janeiro from 1952 to 1964, then archbishop of Olinda e Recife. Before arriving at ultra-progressive positions, he had been secretary in the 1930s of the integralist movement led by Plinio Salgado (1895–1975).

Lombardi[38] and of Archbishop Montini, then at the secretariate of State. It had served as the model for CELAM, the Council of Latin American Bishops, which met annually to discuss the shared problems of that continent.

Some conferences, such as those of Italy, Spain, Portugal and, to some extent, the United States, the United Kingdom, Ireland, and Australia, remained more faithful to tradition; those of central Europe (Germany, France, Holland and Belgium), in contrast, formed a block that was aligned with progressive positions, with the decisive contribution of the French bishops,[39] who, with 171 fathers, constituted the most numerous group after the Italian episcopate (367) and the American bishops (216). At the head of the French council fathers was a group of "democratic" cardinals who had been appointed bishops by Pius XI to change the "integralist" trend imposed by St. Pius X after the separation of Church and state:[40] Cardinal Feltin,[41] consecrated a bishop in 1972, Cardinal Liénart, in 1928, and Cardinal Gerlier,[42] in 1929. The three prelates, together, had made a trip to Rome in 1953 to plead the cause of the "worker priests."[43] Among the more progressive French bishops was the coadjutor of Strasbourg, Léon-Arthur Elchinger,[44] who set about establishing close cooperation with the German episcopate.

---

38 Armando Lombardi (1905–1964), ordained in 1928, titular archbishop of Caesarea of Philippi (1950) and apostolic nuncio in Venezuela (1950–1954) and Brazil (1954–1964).

39 Cf. Alain Michel, "L'épiscopat français au deuxième Concile du Vatican, » in *Le deuxième Concile du Vatican*, 281–296.

40 Cf. C. Barthe, *op. cit.*, 37. See also Marc Minier, *L'épiscopat français du ralliement à Vatican II* (Padua : Antonio Milani, 1982); Yves-Marie Hilaire, "Le renouvellement de l'épiscopat, " in Gerard Cholvy and Y. M. Hilaire, *Histoire religieuse de la France contemporaine (1930–1988)* (Toulouse : Privat, 1988), 19–23; Marcel Albert, *Die Katholische Kirche in Frankreich in der Vierten und Fünften Republik* (Freiburg im Breisgau: Herder, 1999).

41 Maurice Feltin (1883–1975), French, ordained in 1909. Bishop of Tarbes and Lourdes in 1929, then archbishop of Paris from 1949 to 1966, created cardinal in 1953.

42 Pierre-Marie Gerlier (1880–1965), French, ordained in 1921, archbishop of Lyons from 1937 until his death. Created cardinal in 1937.

43 Cf. J. Vinatier, *Le cardinal Liénart, op. cit.*, 150 ff.

44 Léon-Arthur Elchinger (1908–1998), French, ordained in 1931. Auxiliary bishop of Strasbourg (1957–1967), then bishop of the same diocese from 1967 to 1984. Bernard Xibaut, *Mgr Léon-Arthur Elchinger: Un évêque français au Concile* (Paris: Cerf, 2009).

The central European conferences were the first to play the new role assigned to them, associating themselves with those from Latin America and the "missionary" countries of Africa and Asia.

According to Melissa Wilde:

> Though many heralded Liénart's decision to intervene on that first day of the council as an impulsive act that was the work of the Holy Spirit, in actuality it was just the first and most public part of a larger progressive plan to circumvent the curia's domination of the council. The second, and perhaps even more important, part of the plan was the result of French leaders' alliances with key Latin American bishops Manuel Larraín and Helder Câmara, both vice presidents of CELAM."[45]

In a turbulent atmosphere, thirty-four electoral lists were approved, but the central European one appeared to be the best organized and most representative. On October 16, as he opened the second General Congregation, Cardinal Ottaviani proposed a procedural change that would have been able to thwart the coup,[46] but among those who opposed him was Cardinal Ruffini,[47] with whom he had not coordinated his efforts in advance. In contrast, the carefully organized progressive machine fully accomplished its objective: not a numerical triumph, but the end of the curia's supremacy in the conciliar assembly.[48]

A second procedural novelty came about on October 20, during the third General Congregation when, at the opening of the session, the secretary general announced that the pope, at the proposal of the council presidency, had suspended the application of article 39 of the *Ordo Concilii*, which required an absolute majority for two ballots and a relative majority for the third. The sixteen council fathers who received the most votes for the various commissions would be elected.[49]

At this point success was assured. The results of the elections were enormously satisfying for the "international" list, which the correspondent

---

[45] Wilde, p. 19.

[46] AS I/1:211–212.

[47] *Ibid.*, 213.

[48] Cf. C. Barthe, *op. cit.*, 106–107.

[49] Cf. AS I/1:223.

from *Le Monde*, Henri Fesquet, described as the "Common Market"[50] and the Divine Word Father Ralph Wiltgen as "the European alliance": out of 109 candidates who had been presented, 79 were elected. The Rhine, as Wiltgen observed, in a turn of phrase that was destined to go down in history, "had begun to flow into the Tiber."[51] The French and the Germans, a worried Cardinal Siri noted, "put on airs as though they were the bosses.... Our list was scrapped, the list belonging to Germany and France, which had the help of the Secretariat of State, won."[52]

The October 28 issue of *L'Espresso* published an article signed by Carlo Falconi and entitled "Toward the new theology: The council fathers who favor renewal prevail" with a photo of Cardinals Liénart and Frings, presented as two "heroes" of the conciliar renewal.[53] Liénart, who was then seventy-eight years old, was the president of the French Episcopal Conference, while Frings, seventy-five, was the head of the Conference of German Bishops. Fesquet, writing for *Le Monde*, noted the cardinals "whose names recur most frequently as likely to influence the council in a special way...[:] Cardinals Koenig [König], archbishop of Vienna; Frings, archbishop of Cologne; Döpfner, archbishop of Munich; Alfrink, archbishop of Utrecht; Paul Emile Léger, archbishop of Montreal; Montini, archbishop of Milan; Bea, president of the Secretariat for Promoting Christian Unity; Suenens, archbishop of Malines-Brussels and primate of Belgium; and Liénart, bishop of Lille."[54] The Franco-German coalition, with slightly shifting contours, Gilles Routhier notes,[55] usually included the prelates Suenens, Liénart, Alfrink, Montini, Lercaro, Frings, Döpfner, König. To this group it was necessary to add Cardinals Léger, the only

---

[50] Fesquet, *Drama*, 27.

[51] Wiltgen, 19. Cf. S. Gómez de Arteche y Catalina, *op. cit.*, vol. I, lib. II, t. II, pp. 309–315.

[52] Conversation of Cardinal Siri with Benny Lai on May 17, 1988, in B. Lai, *Il Papa non eletto, op. cit.*, 187.

[53] Cf. Francis X. Murphy, who was the author, under a pseudonym, reprinted today in *Letters from Vatican City: Vatican Council II (First session): Background and Debates* (London: Faber & Faber, 1963), 60–94. One week earlier, on October 20, an article along the same lines had appeared in *The New Yorker* entitled "Letter from Vatican City."

[54] Fesquet, *Drama*, 27.

[55] Cf. Gilles Routhier, "Finishing the Work begun: The Trying Experience of the Fourth Period," in HVT 5:49–184 at 126, note 309.

North American, Bea as a spokesman of the curia, and Maximos IV[56] as a representative of the Eastern bishops.

Riding on this wave of success, Cardinals Suenens and Döpfner pushed on still further: they asked the pope to allow the bishops to participate in the General Congregations in clothing that was less demanding than their episcopal vestments and to cancel the celebration of Mass at the beginning of the sessions, so as to expand the time for discussion. The central European requests were supported by Cardinal Montini, whom Ambassador Poswick described as "one of the rare Italian cardinals inclined to support the council's liberal wing,"[57] but John XXIII was rigid this time and preferred to follow the advice of Cardinal Siri who, when asked by the pontiff to express an opinion, declared that he was against both abandoning the vestments and the suggestion to do without Mass, given that the council—he said—"perhaps needed prayers more than it needed to think."[58]

In those days Bishop Borromeo of Pesaro pointed out "the sourness of almost all the foreign cardinals against the liturgy of the Roman rite and its language, and the slackness of the Italians, who hardly react or at least have not yet begun to react."[59]

4. The "message to the world"

At the beginning of the third General Congregation on October 20, a "Message to the World," the first version of which had been composed by Father Chenu, was approved by a show of hands.[60] While not strictly

---

[56] Maximos IV Saigh (1878–1967), Syrian, ordained in 1905. Melkite patriarch of Antioch. Cf. *Discorsi di Massimo IV al Concilio: Discorsi e note del patriarca Massimo IV e dei vescovi della sua Chiesa al Concilio Vaticano II* (Bologna: Edizioni Dehoniane, 1968); Grootaers, *I protagonisti*, 171–183; O. Rousseau, "Le patriarche Maximos IV (1878–1967)," in *Revue Nouvelle* 47 (1968): 64–70; M. Villain, "Un prophète: le Patriarche Maximos IV," in *Nouvelle Revue Théologique* 90 (1968): 50–65; Emilios Inglessis, *Maximos IV: L'Orient conteste l'Occident* (Paris: Cerf, 1969).

[57] Poswick, *Journal*, 263.

[58] Deposition of Cardinal Siri in *Ioannis XXIII: Positio*, II/1:1131; see also B. Lai, *Il Papa non eletto, op. cit.* 188–189.

[59] Borromeo, *Diario* (October 24, 1962), 129.

[60] AS I/1:230–232; the approved text is printed *ibid.*, 254–256; Ital. transl. in Caprile, 2:49–51.

speaking an act of the council, it was the first public manifestation of the council fathers. "In conducting our work," they proclaimed, "we will give major consideration to all that pertains to the dignity of man and contributes to true brotherhood among peoples."[61]

Among the few contrary voices was that of Cardinal Heenen,[62] archbishop of Liverpool, who said:

> I maintain that it is not yet the time to send a message to all mankind, and it would seem sad to me that the first message should be so vague and wordy. It is certain that the newspapers will publish almost nothing of this message. I maintain that it would be better to wait a bit, until, after the discussions, there is something truly interesting to say to all mankind, something that could then attract the world's attention. Indeed, the world expects from us a little word of compassion and hope, to comfort the souls that are full of anxiety for fear of a nuclear war, and we must say something in the name of those fathers who are not with us, because of persecution, and a word of compassion for the Christian peoples who happen to be under communism, and to them also we must send a word for the consolation of their souls.[63]

The message had little coverage in the press, as Heenan had foreseen, but it did indicate a line of policy. The Soviet news agency Tass reported, without comment, the passage from it that said, "There is no man who does not detest war and who does not ardently desire peace," and the sentence that said that the ecumenical council in its work would particularly take into account "all that pertains to the dignity of man and all that contributes toward the real brotherhood of nations."[64]

On the other hand, fifteen Eastern-rite Catholic bishops in exile, so-called "Uniates," who had rejoined Rome at the Union of Brest in 1596, refused to be associated with the message because it did not reflect

---

The message was published in *L'Osservatore Romano* on October 21 and 22–23, 1962.

[61] Caprile, 2:50.

[62] John Heenan (1905–1975), English, ordained in 1930. Archbishop of Liverpool from 1957 to 1963, then of Westminster from 1963 until his death. Created cardinal in 1965. Member of the Secretariat for Promoting Christian Unity.

[63] AS I/1:237.

[64] Fesquet, *Drama*, 31.

the dramatic situation imposed by communism on the Church in the countries of Eastern Europe and the Far East.[65] On November 23 they made public the text of a declaration drawing the world's attention to the absence from the council of their Metropolitan Josyf Slipyj,[66] who had been deported to Siberia more than seventeen years previously, the only survivor of the eleven Ukrainian bishops sent to the *gulag*, while participating in the conciliar assembly there were two observers from the patriarchate of Moscow, which was described as "a docile, useful instrument in the hands of the Soviet government."[67] Two days after the publication of this document, during a press conference on November 23, Bishop Willebrands, on behalf of the Secretariat for Promoting Christian Unity, defended the Russian observers, who had "manifested a sincerely religious and ecumenical spirit," and regretted the communiqué of the Ukrainian bishops.[68] On February 9 of the following year, Cardinal Slipyj was suddenly released and arrived in Rome.

In the same days in which the council addressed its "Message to the World," an international crisis broke out that brought humanity to the brink of World War III. The photo-reconnaissance of American "air spies"

---

[65] Among them Ivan Bucko (1891–1974), Ukrainian, ordained in 1915, consecrated bishop by Archbishop Andrej Sheptytskyj (1865–1944) in 1929, then emigrated to the United States. Auxiliary bishop of Philadelphia for the Ukrainian Catholics (1940–1945), then titular archbishop of Leucas; worked in Rome in the curia from 1953 on.

[66] Josyf Slipyj (1892–1984), of the Metropolitan Archeparchy of Lviv (Ukraine). Ordained in 1917, titular archbishop of Serre (1939), in 1944 succeeded Archbishop Andrej Sheptytskyj as metropolitan archbishop of Lviv. Arrested in 1945, deported to a labor camp in Siberia, where he spent eighteen years (1945–1963). Was created cardinal by Paul VI on February 22, 1965. On the plight of the Ukrainian and Ruthenian Churches, see Albert Galter, *The Red Book of the Persecuted Church*, (Westminster, MD: The Newman Press, 1957), and *Cristiani d'Ucraina: Un popolo dilaniato ma indomabile* (Rome: Aid to the Church in Need, 1983); D. Pavlo Vyshkovskyj, O.M.I., *Il martirio della Chiesa cattolica in Ucraina* (Rome: Luci sull'Est, 20097). About Cardinal Slipyj, see Monsignor Ivan Choma, *Josyf Slipyj "Vinctus Christi" et "Defensor Unitatis,"* (Rome: Universitas Catholica Ucrainorum S. Clementis Papae, 1997); *Idem, Josyf Slipyj: Padre e confessore della Chiesa Ucraina martire* (Rome: Aid to the Church in Need, 1990); see the Italian translation of the cardinal's *Testament* in *Quaderni di Cristianità* I/2 (1985): 26–44.

[67] G. F. Svidercoschi, *Storia del Concilio, op. cit.* 164–165.

[68] Text of the communiqué in Caprile, 2:202. See also *L'Osservatore Romano*, November 24, 1962.

over the island of Cuba verified the existence of medium-range missiles, installed by the Kremlin, that were capable of striking a large part of American territory. On October 22 President Kennedy enacted a naval blockade around the island. The next day a Soviet fleet was deployed in Cuban waters in position to attack. After an exchange of messages between Kennedy and Khrushchev, the crisis was resolved with a compromise: withdrawal of the missiles by the Russians and a guarantee of Cuban independence by the U.S.A., which lifted the blockade.[69]

5. The progressives at the council

a) The party of the theologians

The group dynamics that were taking shape during the first weeks were not those of Vatican I, but rather of the Council of Constance (1414-1418), which was perhaps, as Alois Dempf mentions, the first parliamentary experiment in history carried out within the Church.[70] In the hall, interest groups and "parties" were forming along doctrinal but also national lines. Indeed, in order to give more weight to their interventions, the council fathers spoke in the name of groups of the same geographical and linguistic area.

The work of the bishops was conducted in two different settings: in the General Congregation and in the commissions. On weekday mornings the General Congregations assembled all the fathers in Saint Peter's Basilica. There one registered to speak in order of dignity: first the cardinals, then the patriarchs, the archbishops and finally the bishops and, within each category, in order of seniority. In the afternoon the work of the fathers was conducted in the commissions, which included however only one third of the total

---

[69] Cf. Michel Tatu, *Power in the Kremlin: from Krushchev to Kosygin* (New York: Penguin, 1974), 230–297; Michael R. Beschloss, *The Crisis Years: Kennedy and Krushchev, 1960–1963* (New York: Harper & Collines, 1991).

[70] Cf. Alois Dempf, *Sacrum Imperium* (Oldenburg, 1929), Ital. transl. (Firenze: Le Lettere, 1988), 105. Even the historian Ludwig von Pastor admits this parliamentary transformation, describing the various "parties" formed within the Council of Constance: *The History of the Popes, from the close of the Middle Ages* (Wilmington, NC: Consortium, 1978 ff.), 1:205–206.

number of bishops. Also conducted in the afternoon were informal meetings and gatherings in which the bishops were joined by their collaborators.

The council fathers were accompanied by "experts": the official ones, or *"periti,"* who attended the General Congregations, without a right to vote, and the private ones who were invited by some bishops as advisers.[71] The official *periti* could, of course privately, accompany and assist one or more bishops who requested their advice. They were responsible for composing and reworking the schemas and, often, for preparing the interventions of the fathers. Often the "experts" did not limit themselves to that role but sought to influence the work of the commissions, through articles, conferences and texts circulated outside the assembly. On the eve of the opening of the council, John XXIII had appointed 201 *periti*; at the end of the council, counting also the private experts, their number exceeded five hundred. Many of these theologians had been suspected of heterodoxy during the pontificate of Pius XII, such as Fathers Congar, Daniélou, de Lubac, Häring,[72] Küng, Rahner, and Schillebeeckx. All would have a great influence during the years of the council and of the post-conciliar period. Congar himself noted this in his diary on October 21: "I have also been struck, these past few days, by the role played by the theologians. At the First Vatican Council they played almost no role at all."[73]

It is not difficult to understand how the enemy *par excellence* of the progressive theologians would be the Roman curia and in particular the Holy Office, the source of their condemnations. They formed a strategic alliance with the council fathers to demolish the congregation presided over by Cardinal Ottaviani, which was the bastion of orthodoxy. "The collaboration between bishops and theologians meant wresting the council away from the control of Ottaviani."[74]

---

[71] Cf. R. Aubert, "Organizzazione e funzionamento dell'assemblea," *op. cit.*, 179–180.

[72] Bernard Häring (1912–1998), German Redemptorist, ordained in 1933, professor of moral theology at the Alphonsianum (1949–1987), consultor of the Preparatory Theological Commission, conciliar *peritus*.

[73] Congar, *Journal*, 109. Cf. John F. Kobler, C.P., "Were theologians the engineers of Vatican II?" in *Gregorianum* 70/2 (1989): 233–250; E. Fouilloux, "Théologiens romains et Vatican II," *op. cit.*; *idem*, "Comment devient-on expert à Vatican II? Le cas du père Yves Congar," in *Le deuxième Concile du Vatican*, 307–331; Jared Wicks, "I teologi al Vaticano II: Momenti e modalità del loro contributo al Concilio," in *Humanitas* 59 (2004): 1012–1038.

[74] Gerald P. Fogarty, "The Council Gets Underway," in HVT 2:68–106 at 84.

In the "marching flank" of progressivism a patrol of German theologians distinguished themselves,[75] led by Father Karl Rahner,[76] of the Society of Jesus, and by two younger professors, Hans Küng and Joseph Ratzinger.[77] Rahner was the adviser of the cardinal of Vienna, König, Küng—of Bishop Leiprecht[78] of Rottenberg, and Ratzinger—of Cardinal Frings, archbishop of Cologne. They were joined by Father Otto Semmelroth,[79] the theologian of Bishop Hermann Volk of Mainz, who in turn was closely connected with Father Rahner. They criticized the Roman "conceptual theology," which they disparagingly described as "Denzinger theology," and looked

---

[75] Cf. Niklaus Pflüger, "L'influence des théologiens allemands sur le Concile Vatican II," in *Église et Contre-Église au Concile Vatican II: Actes du IIe Congrès théologique de Sì sì no no, janvier 1996* (Versailles: Publications du Courrier de Rome, 1996), 367–402; Franz Schmidberger, "L'apport des théologiens allemands dans le ralliement du Concile à la pensée moderne," in *Penser Vatican II quarante ans après*, Actes du VIème Congrès Théologique de *Sì sì no no*, Rome, janvier 2004 (Versailles: Publications du Courrier de Rome, 2004). Cardinal Siri records that within the council "an ambiguous management of the Church is emerging, represented by the German-language group and its friends and neighbors. It is also organized *aliquatenus* [to some extent].... that there is talk about a *Theologia nova* [new theology] and that the concept thereof, as well as its purpose, seem rather obscure and perhaps dangerous ." (Siri, *Diario*, 383).

[76] Karl Rahner (1904–1984), German theologian of the Society of Jesus, ordained in 1932. Professor of dogmatic theology in Innsbruck (1948–1964). Consultor of the Preparatory Commission for the Discipline of the Sacraments, was appointed an expert at Vatican II in 1962. About him see the critical studies by C. Fabro, *La svolta antropologica di K. Rahner* (Milan: Rusconi, 1974); David Berger, "Abschied von einem gefährlichen Mythos—Neue Studien zu Karl Rahner," in *Divinitas* 156 (2003): 68–89; G. Cavalcoli, *Karl Rahner, op. cit.* and the acts of the scholarly convention organized by Fr. Serafino Lanzetta, entitled *Karl Rahner, un'analisi critica: La figura, l'opera e la recezione teologica di Karl Rahner (1904–1984)* (Siena: Cantagalli, 2008).

[77] Joseph Alois Ratzinger/Benedict XVI, born in 1927, German, ordained in 1951. Adviser to Cardinal Frings, became a *peritus* at the council from the second session on, professor in Bonn, Münster, Tübingen, and Regensburg. Archbishop of Munich and Freising in 1977 and created cardinal that same year. Prefect of the Congregation for the Doctrine of the Faith from 1981 to 2005. Elected pope with the name Benedict XVI on April 19, 2005. See *Milestones, Memoirs: 1927–1977* (San Francisco, Ignatius Press, 1998). In 2008 the publication of the German edition of his *Complete Works* began; the first volume of the English edition appeared in 2012.

[78] Joseph Karl Leiprecht (1903–1981), German, ordained in 1928, bishop of Rottenburg in 1949. Resigned in 1974.

[79] Otto Semmelroth (1912–1979), German Jesuit, professor in Frankfurt, conciliar *peritus*.

forward to a new "theology of existence," in which knowledge and life were supposed to merge in a single act of hope and faith.

Rahner, born in 1904, had entered the Society of Jesus in 1922 and in 1934 had been sent by his superiors to Freiburg to earn a doctorate in philosophy. The professor under whom he was supposed to write his dissertation, Martin Honecker, rejected his study, however, which was published in 1939 with the title *Geist in Welt*[80] (Spirit in World). The student, who read St. Thomas through the lens of his Belgian confrére Joseph Maréchal, became close with Heidegger (who in those same years was teaching in Freiburg) and was profoundly influenced by him.[81]

The German Jesuit had won himself notoriety by calling into question the virginity of Mary.[82] His *Mariologia* had not obtained the *imprimatur* [permission to publish] from the Society to which he belonged, and his position in favor of concelebration in his short work, *Many Masses and One Sacrifice* had been criticized by Pius XII.[83] The "preventive censure" to which Rahner had been subjected by the Holy Office for his heterodox theses had elicited protests, however, from Cardinals Döpfner, Frings, and König. The nunciature of Vienna introduced him to Rome as "the best theologian in Austria,"[84] and Cardinal König, president of the Austrian Episcopal Conference, had asked Rahner to follow him to the council as his theological expert.[85]

Hans Küng, a thirty-four-year-old professor of dogmatic theology at the University of Tübingen, saw Rahner as not just a master but an associate [*sodale*]. With him, he recalls, "we also already considered

---

[80] K. Rahner, *Geist in Welt: Zur Metaphysik der endlichen Erkenntnis bei Thomas von Aquin* (Innsbruck: Rauch, 1939).

[81] Cf. K. Rahner, *I Remember: An autobiographical interview with Meinold Krauss* (New York: Crossroad, 1985), 46.

[82] Cf. Karl Hugo Neufeld, "Mariologie in der Sicht K. Rahners," in *Ephemerides Mariologicae* 50 (2000): 285–297.

[83] Cf. Klaus Wittstadt, "On the Eve of the Second Vatican Council," in HVT 1:405–500, passage on Rahner 454–457, reference to *Die vielen Messen und das eine Opfer* at 456.

[84] ASV, Con. Vat. II, Busta 261, Prot. 362/60.

[85] Cf. H. Vorgrimler, *Understanding Karl Rahner: an introduction to his life and thought* (New York: Crossroad, 1986), 94–101.

plans for thwarting the curial strategy on the council."[86] Whereas Küng took Rahner's theses to their logical conclusions, Joseph Ratzinger,[87] a student of Gottlieb Söhngen,[88] relied rather on the ecclesiology of Father de Lubac and of the Swiss theologian Hans Urs von Balthasar, who had left the Society of Jesus in 1950.[89] "Balthasar," Küng haughtily remarked, "is really more a man of letters, and Karl Rahner is the real theologian."[90]

In the years after the council, the paths of the two young theologians parted: Küng took increasingly heterodox positions, until he left the Church, whereas Ratzinger followed an opposite intellectual course that led him to rediscover the role of tradition and of Roman institutions.[91] Rahner, their common instructor, for his part wanted to prove that he could succeed where modernism had failed, taking on the ambitious task of changing the Church's doctrine while remaining in it. He, as Alberigo emphasizes, "was eventually to become one of the formative and path-breaking theologians of Vatican II."[92]

---

[86] Hans Küng, *My Struggle for Freedom: Memoirs*, (Grand Rapids, MI: William B. Eerdmans, 2003), 249.

[87] Cf. J. Wicks, "Six texts by Prof. Joseph Ratzinger as peritus before and during Vatican Council II," in *Gregorianum* 89 (2008).

[88] Gottlieb Söhngen (1892–1971), ordained in 1917, professor of Fundamental Theology at the University of Munich in Bavaria. Under Söhngen's direction, Fr. Ratzinger defended his habilitation thesis on the idea of the history of salvation in St. Bonaventure. The study displeased the second reader, the theologian Michael Schmaus (1897–1993), who obliged the young Ratzinger to revise it. See Gianni Valente, *Ratzinger professore: Gli anni dello studio e dell'insegnamento nel ricordo dei colleghi e degli allievi (1946–1977)* (Cinisello Balsamo: Edizioni San Paolo, 2008), 50–55.

[89] Cf. Alfred Läpple, *Benedikt XVI. und seine Wurzeln* (Sankt Ulrich Verlag, 2006).

[90] Hans Küng, *My Struggle*, 250.

[91] In 1972, together with Balthasar, de Lubac, and other theologians, Ratzinger created *Communio*, a federation of theologican journals published in various languages and countries (in Italy, from the beginning, by the publishing house Jaca Book), which was opposed to the progressive journal *Concilium*.

[92] K. Wittstadt, "On the Eve of the Second Vatican Council," *op. cit.*, 456. According to Ignazio Sanna, "perhaps no other theologian exercized such a profound and radical influence on Catholic theology of the last quarter-century as Karl Rahner" (*Karl Rahner* [Brescia, Morcelliana, 2000], 21); cf. *Idem*, ed., *L'eredità di Karl Rahner* (Rome: Lateran University Press, 2005).

Just as organized and aggressive as the German group was the French clique, made up of top-flight exponents of the *"nouvelle théologie"* [new theology] condemned by Pius XII, *in primis* [among the first], the Dominicans, Congar and Chenu, and the Jesuits, Daniélou and de Lubac.

Congar and de Lubac were appointed by John XXIII as consultors of the Preparatory Commission. Their names, it seems, were suggested by several conservatives, such as Father Franz Hürth, *"ut pluribus opponentibus os clauderet,"*[93] which surprised many, such as Archbishop Marcel Lefebvre, who wrote to Cardinal Ottaviani: "The names of Fathers de Lubac and Congar are with good reason names that conjure up opposition to the Church's thinking and in particular to *Humani generis*. How can these modernist-minded theologians have been appointed? We wonder."[94]

Daniélou, who was also a conciliar *peritus*, assisted in the work of Bishop Garrone of Toulouse. Chenu, unlike the preceding theologians, had no official duties during the council (he was called as an "expert" by a bishop of Madagascar who had been his student), but exercised a strong influence on it, as the others did and more so.

The French-speaking *periti* were joined by a Flemish-speaking Belgian theologian, the Dominican Edward Schillebeeckx,[95] an instructor of theology first at Louvain, then in Nijmegen. Schillebeeckx, who had studied in Belgium and France and had been a student of Chenu, was, as someone observed, "a perfect illustration of the diffusion of the *nouvelle théologie* from France, via Belgium, to Holland," and of the encounter of the French *"nouvelle théologie"* with German *"Verkündigungstheologie."*[96] Although not officially appointed a *peritus*, he was the adviser of Cardinal Alfrink and had a strong influence above all on the Dutch episcopate.

---

93 "So that he might silence more opponents." Letter of Franz Hürth to Tromp dated June 30, 1960, in Tromp, *Diarium*, 803.

94 Tromp, *Diarium*, 815.

95 Edward Schillebeeckx (1914–2009), a Belgian Dominican, ordained in 1941, professor of theology at the Catholic University of Nijmegen (1957–1982), and theological adviser to Cardinal Alfrink, was one of the founders of the journal *Concilium*. About him see *Nouvelle théologie*, 118–125; John Stephen Bowden, *Edward Schillebeeckx: Portrait of a Theologian* (London: Canterbury Press, 1983); Philippe Kennedy, *E. Schillebeeckx*, with afterword and bibliography by Franco Giulio Brambilla (Cinisello Balsamo: San Paolo, 1997); F. G. Brambilla, *Edward Schillebeeckx* (Brescia: Morcelliana, 2001); Erik Borgman, *Edward Schillebeeckx: A Theologian in his History* (London/New York: Continuum, 2003).

96 Cf. *Nouvelle théologie*, 117–118.

b) The "network of relations"

Progressive bishops and theologians consolidated in the first days of the council session the network of relations that they had already established in the two preceding years. Although among the theologians the most active nucleus was the Franco-German group, among the bishops the pivotal axis was the Belgian-Brazilian group.

On October 29, speaking at the Domus Mariae to the Brazilian bishops, Küng relates that he had asked one of his Lutheran colleagues in Tübingen: "If Luther were alive today, would he feel the need to leave the Catholic Church in order to promote reform or would he attempt reform from within the Church?" Bishop Helder Câmara, who reports the episode, is naturally enthusiastic about the plan for protestantizing the Church that crops up in these words.[97] In the very first week Câmara started an intense collaboration with Cardinal Suenens, whom he mentions in his correspondence by the code name "Padre Miguel."[98] The Brazilian bishop relates how at the beginning of the first session he went to meet Suenens so as to ask him to head the progressive front, which was privately organizing a group that was later called "ecumenical." Suenens asked him, "Everybody knows about your friendship with Montini: why are you thinking about me and not about him for this dialogue and for the council leadership?" Câmara replied without hesitation: "I feel *aux anges* ['enraptured'] with Pope John. But I sense that he will see the end of the council from heaven. We must reserve Montini as the successor to John." Suenens, he adds, was "completely in agreement"[99] with him.

"Our friendship," Cardinal Suenens recalled for his part, referring to then-Bishop Câmara, "goes back to the very early days of the council. Although he never once took the floor in the council assembly, he played a very significant role behind the scenes."[100] From then on the Câmara-Suenens team would be one of the "hidden" driving forces of the conciliar assembly.

---

[97] Cf. Câmara, *Lettres conciliaires*, 1:65–66.

[98] Beozzo, *A Igreja do Brasil no Concílio Vaticano II (1959–1965)* (San Paolo: Paulinas, 2005), 196. It is strange that the existence of this close collaboration is ignored, or dismissed, by one of the leading experts on the work of Cardinal Suenens, Ian Grootaers.

[99] Cf. Câmara, *Lettres conciliaires*, 2:657.

[100] Suenens, *Memories and Hopes*, 216.

Among the Latin American bishops present at the council, other bishops besides Câmara had distinguished themselves by their extreme positions: Cardinal Raul Silva Henríquez,[101] archbishop of Santiago (Chile), and Bishop Manuel Larraín Errazuriz[102] of Talca (Chile), who from 1963 on was president of CELAM,[103] the Latin American Episcopal Council. They were in close contact with the Intercultural Center for Documentation (CIDOC) started by Father Ivan Illich[104] in Cuernavaca in 1961, under the sponsorship of Bishop Sergio Méndez Arceo[105] and with the financial support of Cardinal Francis Spellman,[106] archbishop of New York, the diocese in which Illich was incardinated. The Cuernavaca center became an "ideological laboratory" where a strategy for the upcoming council

---

[101] Raul Silva Henríquez (1907–1999), Chilean Salesian, ordained in 1938. Archbishop of Santiago (Chile) from 1961 to 1983; created cardinal in March 1962.

[102] Manuel Larraín Errazuriz (1900–1966), Chilean, ordained in 1927 and consecrated a bishop in 1938. Bishop of Talca (Chile) from 1939 until his death.

[103] Cf. Marcos G. McGrath, "La creazione della coscienza di un popolo latinoamericano: Il CELAM e il Concilio Vaticano II," in *L'evento e le decisioni*, 135–142; Silvia Scatena, *In populo pauperum: La Chiesa latinoamericana dal Concilio a Medellín (1962–1968)*, with a preface by Gustavo Gutiérrez (Bologna: Il Mulino, 2007), 25–43 and *passim.*

[104] Ivan Illich (1926–2002), Austrian, son of a Croatian father and a Sephardic mother, ordained in 1956, nominated vice-rector of the Catholic University of Puerto Rico in 1956; in 1961 founded the Intercultural Center for Documentation (CIDOC) in Cuernavaca, Mexico (cf. J. García, "La Iglesia mexicana desde 1962," in *Historia general de la Iglesia en América Latina, V, México* [Salamanca: Ediciones Sígueme, 1984], 361–493). In 1967–1968 the *"caso Illich"* was founded when the priest maintained that the personnel and the money sent to the third world for missionary purposes contributed to the perpetuation of injustices. After ecclesiastical censures and the dissolution of the Center, Illich renounced his priestly ministry. See Giancarlo Zizola and Alberto Barbero, *La riforma del Sant'Uffizio e il caso Illich* (Turin: Gribaudi, 1969); Maurizio Di Giacomo, *Ivan Illich: Una voce fuori dal coro* (Milan: Ancora, 2006). About him, see also David Cayley, *Ivan Illich in Conversation* (House of Anansi Press, Inc., 2011).

[105] Sergio Méndez Arceo (1907–1992), Mexican, ordained in 1934, bishop of Cuernavaca from 1952 until the end of 1982. About him see the bombastic *Don Sergio Méndez Arceo, patriarca de la solidaridad liberadora*, ed. Leticia Rentería Chávez and Giulio Girardi (Mexico City, Ediciones Dabar, 2000).

[106] Francis Spellman (1889–1967), American, ordained in 1916. Archbishop of New York from 1939 until his death. Created cardinal in 1946.

was studied, and Illich was a promoter of intense contacts between the European bishops and those from South America.[107]

In 1959 Father Illich had outlined an article, which was then published in 1967 in the Chicago journal *The Critic*, on the topic "The Vanishing Clergyman,"[108] in which he suggested "that we welcome the disappearance of institutional bureaucracy [in the Church] in a spirit of deep joy,"[109] and looked forward to a reduction of the clergy and its radical secularization. Starting in 1961, Câmara and Larraín had organized, with the Austro-American theologian participating, a private meeting in Rio de Janeiro to discuss a joint plan of action.[110] The Belgian priest François Houtart,[111] professor at the University of Louvain, in a letter to Father José Oscar Beozzo, reconstructed in detail the network of contacts between European and Latin American bishops and theologians created by Bishop Câmara.

> The *réseau* had been established by Dom Helder, and among those who had contributed to its formation were bishops not only from Latin American but also from almost all the countries in Europe, in any case Belgium, the Netherlands, France, and Germany, as well as from certain countries of Eastern Europe, especially Poland, with Bishop Karol Wojtyla,[112] and Asia, with Archbishop Binh[113] of Saigon

---

[107] Cf. G. Alberigo, *A Brief History of Vatican II* (Maryknoll: Orbis Books, 2006), 49.

[108] Monsignor Ivan Illich, "The Vanishing Clergyman," in *The Critic* 25/6 (June-July 1967): 18–27.

[109] *Ibid.*, 18.

[110] S. Scatena, *In populo pauperum, op. cit.*, 31.

[111] François Houtart (1925), Belgian, ordained in 1949. Director of the Center for Social and Religious Research in Brussels and instructor at the Catholic University of Louvain from 1958 on. In the early 1960s he organized a revolutionary network, the *Federación Internacional de Investigación Social* (FERES), with one branch in Bogotá and another in Rio de Janeiro.

[112] Karol Józef Wojtyła / John Paul II (1920–2005), Polish, ordained in 1946, auxiliary bishop of Krakow and titular bishop of Ombi in 1958, then archbishop of Krakow in 1964. Created cardinal in 1967, elected pope on October 16, 1978. Beatified May 1, 2011.

[113] Paul Nguyen van Binh (1910–1995), Vietnamese, ordained in 1937, bishop of Can Tho (1954–1960), archbishop of Saigon (later called Ho Chi Minh City) from 1955 to 1995.

> and Archbishop Fernándes[114] of New Delhi. It included also a certain number of theologians, such as Schillebeeckx, Congar, de Lubac and Daniélou.[115]

Beozzo devoted a large chapter to the "council's networks of relations: national conferences, religious families, national and linguistic groups,"[116] but especially to ideological networks: some of them preexisted the council, such as the *Jeunesse Ouvrière Chrétienne* [Christian Working Youth], headquartered in Brussels, and the JEC (*Jeunesse Étudiante Chrétienne* [Christian Student Youth]), based in Paris.

The driving force of the progressive alliance was a group of central European and American bishops known as the Domus Mariae Group,[117] but also by other names: the Conference of Delegates or Conference of the Twenty-two, because delegates from twenty-two episcopal conferences participated in it, or even the "ecumenical" group, to use Bishop Câmara's jargon. Characteristic of the Domus Mariae Group was its twofold composition: representatives from the bishops' conferences and members of the conciliar commission. This duality, Pierre Noël observes, gave the group the appearance of being especially authoritative and representative.[118]

The role of the Domus Mariae was decisive for the beginning of the debate on the schema *De fontibus*, against which an effective opposition was organized.[119]

Jan Grootaers, based on the archives of Cardinal Etchegaray, has drawn a portrait of the Domus Mariae Group. It was made up of the Latin American Episcopal Council (CELAM); the Canadian Catholic Conference (CCC),

---

114 Angelo Fernándes (1913–2000), Indian, ordained in 1937, coadjutor archbishop of Delhi from 1959 to 1967. Member of the Commission for Bishops.

115 J. O. Beozzo, *op. cit.*, 300.

116 *Ibid.*, 178–194.

117 *Ibid.*, 185–186; J. Grootaers, "Une forme de concertation épiscopale au concile Vatican II: La Conférence des vingt-deux (1962–1963)," in *Revue d'histoire ecclésiastique* 91/1 (1996): 66–112; reprinted in *Actes et Acteurs*, 133–165. The group was also called "the Tuesday group" after the day on which it met, but from October 1963 on the meeting day was postponed to Friday.

118 Pierre Noël, "Gli incontri delle conferenze episcopali durante il Concilio: Il 'gruppo della Domus Mariae,'" in *L'evento e le decisioni*, 95–134 at 99.

119 John W. O'Malley, *What Happened at Vatican II, op. cit.*, 124.

and young French prelates who played a fundamental organizational role: Archbishop Pierre Veuillot,[120] coadjutor archbishop of Paris, and Cardinal Roger Etchegaray,[121] Adjunct secretary for the assembly of French cardinals and archbishops. Etchegaray, who was living in Rome as a collaborator of the French episcopate, quickly became *l'homme pivot* ["the pivotal man"] of Domus Mariae, and conciliar opinion, according to Grootaers, was inclined to identify the man with the group that he organized.[122]

No lesser role was played, however, by Bishop Câmara, to whom other semi-secret groups, such as the Opus Angeli[123] and the Church of the Poor, looked to for leadership. Again Beozzo recalls:

> Câmara, with his friend Manuel Larraín, who at the beginning of the council was vice-president of CELAM with six hundred Latin American bishops behind him, were in turn at the heart of [1] the "ecumenical" group, a vantage point [*articolazione*] from which episcopal conferences on five continents could influence the course of the council; they were also at the root of [2] the group Church of the Poor, complemented by a small but seasoned outfit from Brazil; and of [3] the organization of the *periti* in Opus Angeli—three of the most important and effective pressure groups of the council. The Domus Mariae, where the Brazilian bishops resided, ended up functioning as a meeting place and general headquarters for these critical junctures.[124]

---

[120] Pierre Veuillot (1913–1968), ordained in 1939, worked at the Secretariat of State until 1959, when he became bishop of Angers, and, in 1963, archbishop of Paris. Was created cardinal in 1968.

[121] Roger Etchegaray (1922–), French, ordained in 1947, director of the pastoral secretariat of the French episcopate from 1961 to 1966, conciliar *peritus*, then auxiliary bishop of Paris (1969) and archbishop of Marseilles (1970), president of the Bishops' Conference of France (1975). Created cardinal in 1979 by John Paul II.

[122] J. Grootaers, "Une forme de concertation épiscopale," *op. cit.*, 136–137.

[123] The *Opus Angeli* of Bishop Câmara should not be confused with the *Opus Angelorum*, a Catholic movement that promotes devotion to the angels, founded by the Austrian Gabrielle Bitterlich (1896–1978) and connected with the Order of Canons Regular of the Holy Cross.

[124] J. O. Beozzo, *op. cit.*, 531.

c) The "Bologna workshop"

The group of conciliar fathers and *periti* from the "Church of the Poor" began to meet regularly at the Belgian College in Rome at the initiative of Father Paul Gauthier,[125] who was known for his experience as a "worker priest." The first meeting was held on October 26 at the invitation of the Bishop Himmer[126] of Tournai. Pierre-Marie Gerlier, archbishop of Lyons, and twelve bishops in attendance discussed the text prepared by Gauthier. Participating in the group were the cardinal-archbishop of Bologna Giacomo Lercaro and his "private theologian," Don Giuseppe ("Pippo") Dossetti,[127] with whom Giuseppe ("Pino") Alberigo closely collaborated, in conjunction with the Roman curia through Cardinal Montini. "Both of them, Alberigo and Dossetti," de Lubac comments in his *Diary*, "when they studied in Rome, knew Archbishop Montini well, and they have remained connected with him."[128]

During the council the "den" frequented by Dossetti and the others from Bologna was the residence of the Portoghesi sisters at Via della Chiesa Nuova 14, which became a bustling rendezvous for the most progressive fathers and theologians of the council.[129] Dossetti's role in the conciliar proceedings was just as decisive as Rahner's, even though his influence on the post-conciliar period was less relevant. Whereas Rahner dictated the theological lines, Dossetti, based on his legal training and parliamentary

---

[125] Paul Gauthier (1914–2002), French, ordained in Dijon, left the priesthood after the council, married, and espoused liberation theology. Books by him: *Christ, the Church, and the Poor* (Westminster, MD: Newman Press, 1965); *Jésus de Nazareth le charpentier* (Éditions du Seuil, 1969). Cf. Denis Pelletier, "Une marginalité engagée: le groupe 'Jésus, l'Église et les pauvres,'" in *Les Commissions conciliaires*, 63–90.

[126] Charles-Marie Himmer (1902–1994), Belgian, ordained in 1926, bishop of Tournai from 1948 to 1977.

[127] Giuseppe Dossetti (1919–1996), university instructor of Canon Law, leader of the *Democrazia cristiana* party from 1945, deputy of the Italian Constituent Assembly, ordained in 1959. At the council he was the theological adviser to Cardinal Lercaro and a *peritus* from the third session on. Cf. *Giuseppe Dossetti: Prime prospettive e ipotesi di ricerca*, ed. G. Alberigo (Bologna: Il Mulino, 1968); *Giuseppe Dossetti: la fede e la storia: Studi nel decennale della morte*, ed. A. Melloni (Bologna: Il Mulino, 2007).

[128] De Lubac, *Quaderni*, 1:320.

[129] Cf. G. Alberigo, *A Brief History*, 27.

experience, suggested the procedural strategy. Other writers have emphasized the many analogies between Dossetti's work at the Italian constitutional assembly in 1946 and his activity as a conciliar *peritus*.[130] On November 10, 1962, Father Chenu noted this remark by Dossetti: "Effective battle stakes everything on procedure. I have always won in this way."[131]

On November 10, 1962, Chenu had with Dossetti "an impassioned conversation on the state of the Italian episcopate."[132] The Bolognese priest confided that, apart from four or five bishops (Lercaro, Montini, Guano,[133] Bartoletti[134]), it was completely dominated by Cardinal Siri, president of the Episcopal Conference.[135] On the other hand, Bishop Ronca confided to Bishop de Castro Mayer that the ones in charge of the Episcopal Conference were Montini, Urbani, and Lercaro; not Siri.[136]

Dossetti and Alberigo asked Chenu and Congar for some help in "converting" to progressivism the recalcitrant Italian bishops,[137] who underestimated the strength and the organization of the Franco-German group. Dossetti informed Chenu that the Italians had met on November 13, ridiculing the central European "modernists," as though their ideas were a sort of "romantic fantasy."[138]

On December 9, 1962, Congar wrote in his diary: "In my opinion everything that is done with a view to converting Italy to the gospel from political, ecclesiological, or devotional ultramontanism, is that much gained

---

130 Cf. Paolo Pombeni, "La dialettica evento. Decisioni nella ricostruzione delle grandi assemblee: I parlamenti e le assemblee costituenti," in *L'evento e le decisioni*, 17–49 at 46.

131 Chenu, *Diario*, 101. On the role played by Dossetti in the redrafting of the Rules of Vatican II, cf. G. Alberigo, "Dinamiche e procedure nel Vaticano II: Verso la revisione del Regolamento del Concilio (1962–63)," in *Cristianesimo nella storia* 13 (1992): 115–164.

132 Chenu, *Diario*, 98–99.

133 Emilio Guano (1900–1970), ordained in 1922. bishop of Livorno from 1962 until his death.

134 Enrico Bartoletti (1916–1976), ordained in 1939, appointed auxiliary bishop (1958), then archbishop of Lucca (1973), secretary general of the Italian Episcopal Conference from 1972.

135 Chenu, *Diario*, 99–100.

136 Cf. Maranhão Galliez, *Diario* (October 16, 1962).

137 *L'"officina bolognese" 1953–2003*, ed. G. Alberigo (Bologna: EDB, 2004), but also *idem,* "P. Congar, Dossetti e l'officina bolognese," *op. cit.*

138 Chenu, *Diario*, 112.

for the universal Church as well. That is why, in the coming months, I am going to accept a number of engagements with this end in view."[139] On January 19 and 20, 1963, upon meeting the mayor of Florence, Giorgio La Pira,[140] and his young collaborators at the magazine *Testimonianze*, Congar observed: "He is preparing a generation of lay people who will transform Italian Catholicism."[141] On May 14 the French Dominican traveled to Bologna to visit Alberigo's Documentation Center. During dinner and afterward he had a long conversation with Dossetti, who insisted on the notion of a "universal jurisdiction" of bishops, suggesting that this be proposed in the council as a "traditional thesis."[142]

The party of the theologians quickly identified, one by one, their enemies. Father Congar noted them by name in his *Diary*: Archbishop Pietro Parente, assessor at the Holy Office, "the man who condemned [Father] Chenu, the fascist, the monophysite";[143] Father Sebastian Tromp, secretary of the Theological Commission who, although he knew how to reduce a problem to its essential elements, "has a fascist temperament";[144] his confrère Luigi Ciappi (a future cardinal), "a poor and petty soul,"[145] who was "ultra-prudent, ultra-curial, super-papalist";[146] Cardinal Pizzardo, "this wretched freak, this sub-mediocrity with no culture, no horizon [*i.e.* vision], no humanity,"[147] who was guilty of having been "one of the opponents of

---

139 Congar, *Journal*, 247.

140 Giorgio La Pira (1904–1977), professor of Roman Law, deputy in 1946 to the Constituent Assembly, was mayor of Florence for two terms: 1951–1958 and 1961–1965. Cf. *Il laboratorio di Firenze: La Pira, don Milani padre Balducci: Il laboratorio di Firenze nelle scelte pubbliche dei cattolici dal fascismo a fine Novecento*, ed. Pietro De Marco (Rome: Magna Carta, 2009).

141 Congar, *Journal*, 252.

142 *Ibid.*, 288.

143 *Ibid.*, 6. [The Eng. translation does not make perfectly clear the fact that Congar was calling *Parente* names.]

144 *Ibid.*, 56.

145 *Ibid.*, 695.

146 *Ibid.*, 284.

147 *Ibid.*, 299.

Montini, one of those who brought about his departure from Rome."[148] "The Congregation for Studies, with the imbecile Pizzardo, Staffa,[149] and Romeo, is the archetypal concentration of cretins."[150]

"*Ultra*montanism really does exist.... The colleges, the universities and scholasticates of Rome distill all that to varying degrees, the maximum, indeed well-nigh fatal, dose being currently administered at the Lateran [University]";[151] "wretched ultramontane ecclesiology," Congar notes again on February 5.[152] He considered his struggle against the theologians of the "Roman school" as a "mission."

> "My work displeases them because they realize very well that its whole aim is to bring back into circulation certain ideas, certain things that they have been endeavoring to shut out for four hundred years, and above all for the past hundred. But that is my vocation and my service in the name of the gospel and of tradition."[153]

The council unfolded outside the auditoriums also, in the debates in the newspapers and in the conferences given by the *"periti"* and the "experts'; nor should we forget the role of the protestant observers at the council who, as the sociologist John Coleman observes, did not limit themselves simply to "observing."[154] "These were informal meetings," König recalls, "but they

---

148 *Ibid.*, 490.

149 Dino Staffa (1906–1977), ordained in 1929, titular archbishop of Cesarea, secretary of the Congregation of Seminaries and Universities, cardinal in 1967. Member of the Ante-preparatory Commission; during the first session he was nominated a member (and then vice president) of the Commission for Seminaries, Studies, and Catholic Education. See the profile by Luigi de Magistris in PUL, 226–227.

150 Congar, *Journal*, 529. He repeated the same judgment in 1966, after the conclusion of the council, recalling "this congregation that is so important, where some imbeciles are in charge: Pizzardo, Staffa, Romeo...," 876.

151 *Ibid.*, 143.

152 *Ibid.*, 485.

153 *Ibid.*, 222.

154 Cf. John A. Coleman, "Vatican II as a social movement," in *The Belgian Contribution*, 5–28 at 24. See also Robert McAfee Brown, *Observer in Rome: A Protestant Report on the Vatican Council* (New York: Doubleday, 1964).

constituted the true framework [*ossatura*] of the council."[155] Among the protestant observers were the two brothers from Taizé, Roger Schutz and Max Thurian. Once during a dinner, when they asked Hans Küng what they should do at that historical moment, the theologian from Tübingen replied, "It is best for you to remain protestants," an answer, he recalls, that did not please them at all.[156]

Behind the scenes at the council, meanwhile, mimeographed documents began to circulate that dealt with the most varied topics. Fesquet deemed "by far the most interesting" the one on "The Church and Psychoanalysis," which said that psychoanalysis should be introduced into the Church "by theologians and psychologists who have been psychoanalyzed."[157]

The media, for their part, contributed toward the creation of a "parallel magisterium," expressed by means of articles, books, conferences, and meetings.[158] The leading conference speakers were Fathers Rahner or Küng for the German-speaking regions, Chenu, Congar, de Lubac, Daniélou for the Francophone countries, Schillebeeckx for the English-speaking world. Nevertheless the existence of an actual battle was still apparent only to a few. Among them was one of the best collaborators of Cardinal Ottaviani, Joseph Clifford Fenton, who on October 20, 1962, noted in his diary: "In my opinion, the council will deal a painful blow to the Church. The opposition between the liberals and the faithful Catholics will come to light."[159]

6. The "Little Committee" of the conservative fathers

In the first session of the council, while the anti-Roman party was moving in closed ranks along carefully defined strategic lines, the conservatives had no cohesiveness or strategy, except for a group that described itself as the *"Piccolo Comitato."* From this group the *Coetus Internationalis Patrum* [International Group of Fathers] was born between the second and the third session.

---

155 F. König, *Chiesa dove vai?, op. cit.*, 25.

156 Küng, *My Struggle*, 276.

157 Fesquet, *Drama*, 50–51.

158 Yves Chiron has spoken about a "para-council." Cf. "Paul VI et le péri-concile," in *La Papauté contemporaine* (Louvain-la-Neuve: Collège Erasme, 2009), 585–603.

159 Fenton, *Diario*, 16.

As of October, the Brazilian leader Plinio Corrêa de Oliveira had set up in Rome a secretariat made up of fourteen persons;[160] by actively following the proceedings of the assembly, it offered an effective service to the two bishops closest to it: Archbishop Geraldo de Proença Sigaud of Diamantina, who lived at the Casa del Verbo Divino, and Bishop Antonio de Castro Mayer of Campos, who was staying in the Domus Mariae. These two Brazilian bishops, with the organizational support and strategic suggestions of Prof. de Oliveira, had regular contacts with Roman conservative circles. The first meeting was on October 15, with Cardinal Aloisi Masella, formerly nuncio in Brazil, who in conversation confided to them that the main point of the council was the attempt to diminish the power of Rome. "The movement in favor of the curia is only now taking shape, whereas the other had been structured for quite some time already."[161]

Equally significant were their meetings with the two principal representatives of the "Roman party": Bishop Roberto Ronca[162] and Monsignor Antonio Piolanti.[163] The latter advised them to contact Monsignor Antonino Romeo to establish relations with the professors of the Lateran University, among them Monsignor Francesco Spadafora. Besides Romeo,[164]

---

160 Plinio Corrêa de Oliveira decided to invest enormous human and financial resources for the awareness that he had, on the eve of the council, of the importance of what was at stake. His concerns are expressed in a letter that he wrote in those days to his mother: "This journey is the result of long reflection.... In my present state of fatigue, I would gladly prefer to remain here, without overburdening myself with all the occupations and preoccupations that I will have in Rome. But if I did not go to Rome now, I would have a more troubled conscience than if I had been a soldier who deserted. And, placing duty above everything else—especially my duty with regard to the Church—I decided to depart.... On the one hand, the siege by the external enemies of the Church has never been so strong, and never has the activity of her internal enemies been so general, so articulate, and so daring. On the other hand, I know well that I can offer very useful services to help support the edifice of Christianity. You understand, dearest Mother, that I will never, in any way, be able to stop offering to the Church, to which I have devoted my whole life, this service in an historic hour that is almost as sad as the hour of Our Lord's Death" (cf. João Scognamiglio Clá Dias, *Dona Lucilia* [San Paolo: Artpress, 1995], 3:117). [Translated from Italian with reference to the Portuguese.]

161 Maranhão Galliez, *Diario* (October 15, 1962).

162 *Ibid.* (October 16, October 19, 1962).

163 *Ibid.* (October 18, 1962).

164 *Ibid.* (October 18, 1962).

the Brazilians met other prominent theologians from the "ultramontane" or "integralist" world, among them Monsignor Joseph Clifford Fenton[165] and Abbé Raymond Dulac.

One of the most important encounters that the two Brazilian bishops had was with Archbishop Marcel Lefebvre,[166] who participated in the council in his twofold capacity as titular archbishop of Synada in Phrygia and superior general of the Congregation of the Holy Spirit (the Holy Ghost Fathers). Lefebvre was sixty-three years old and could be considered an "exemplary prelate" at the sunset of his ecclesiastical career,[167] and yet, like many other personages at Vatican II, he too would play a leading role in the Church of the twentieth century. He was accompanied by Abbé Victor Alain Berto,[168] his personal theologian, chosen because of the profoundly "Roman" spirit that distinguished him.

Among the most active theologians of the "Little Committee," Abbé Raymond Dulac[169] stood out; he had come to Rome, as he explained to

---

[165] *Ibid.* (October 16, 1962).

[166] *Ibid.* (October 19, December 7, 1962).

[167] Cf. Luc Perrin, *L'affaire Lefebvre* (Paris: Cerf, 1989).

[168] Victor-Alain Berto (1900–1968) studied at the French Seminary (1904–1927), was ordained in 1926, performed pastoral ministry in Brittany and in 1946 was one of the founders of the journal *La Pensée Catholique*, in which he published many essays. A summary biography is contained in *Notre Dame de Joie: Correspondance de l'Abbé V. A. Berto prêtre: 1900–1968* (Paris: Éditions du Cèdre, 1989), 11–48; a fuller treatment in N. Buonasorte, "Per la 'pura, piena, integra fede cattolica': il p. Victor Alain Berto al Concilio Vaticano II," in *Cristianesimo nella storia* 22 (2001): 111–151. Briefly mentioned in L. Perrin, "Il Coetus Internationalis Patrum e la minoranza conciliare," in *L'evento e le decisioni*, 173–187. His contributions to *La Pensée Catholique* and to the conciliar proceedings are collected in *Pour la Sainte Église Romaine: Textes et documents de V. A. Berto prêtre: 1900–1968* (Paris: Éditions du Cèdre, 1976); see also a collection of his writings on the priesthood, V. A. Berto, *Le cénacle et le jardin* (Bouère: DMM, 2000).

[169] Raymond Dulac (1903–1987), trained at the French Seminary in Rome (1920–1926) and ordained in 1926, collaborated from 1928 to 1933 in the *Revue internationale des sociétés secrètes* of Monsignor Ernest Jouin (1844–1932). Then he collaborated with *La Pensée Catholique*, especially in the years 1950–1953, and during the council with *Le Courrier de Rome* and *Itinéraires*. For *La Pensée Catholique* he wrote a series of studies dedicated to the *Sodalitium Pianum* of Monsignor Benigni, of whom he could be considered a disciple during the 1950s (cf. "Simple note sure le Sodalitium Pianum," in *La Pensée Catholique* 23 [1952]: 68–93; "Éloge de l'intégrisme," *ibid.* 21 [1952]: 7–25). He spent the last years of his life near the Carmel in Draguignan, trying to defend its autonomy. Among his publications, see *La collegialité épiscopale au*

them, "to coordinate the integrist bishops, who are naïve and ill prepared."[170] Dulac was a man of great theological, canonical, and historical erudition, who is credited with, among other things, a series of important articles on papal authority and episcopal collegiality that appeared during the years of the council. Like Abbé Berto and *Monseigneur* Lefebvre himself, he belonged to the group of priests who had been formed in the 1920s at the French Seminary in Rome,[171] which until 1927 had been directed by Father Henri Le Floch.[172]

Archbishop Lefebvre would always remember his six-year stay at the Seminary of Santa Chiara in Rome, and above all the three years from 1923 to 1926 that he spent there with Father Le Floch:

> I will never thank God enough for allowing me to know that truly extraordinary man. He was the one who taught us what the popes were to the world and the Church, what they had taught for a century and a half—against liberalism, modernism, and communism, and the whole doctrine of the Church on these topics.... Father Le Floch made us enter into and experience Church history, the struggle that the wayward powers were leading against Our Lord. This incited us against deadly liberalism, against the [French] Revolution and the powers of evil arrayed to destroy the Church, the kingdom of Our Lord, Catholic states, and all Christendom. We had to choose: either leave the seminary if we were not in agreement or else enter into the combat and advance.[173]

---

deuxième Concile du Vatican (Paris: Éditions du Cèdre, 1979), an anthology of nine articles that appeared in *La Pensée Catholique* between 1959 and 1965. About him see M. A. Le Cerf, "In memoriam: L'Abbé Raymond Dulac," in *La Pensée Catholique* 228 (1987): 38–41.

170 Maranhão Galliez, *Diario* (October 16, 1962). There were quite a few meetings with Abbé Dulac (cf. *Idem, Diario*, October 16, 18, 19, and 24, 1962).

171 On the French Seminary in Rome, cf. Philippe Levillain, Philippe Boutry, and Yves Marie Fradet, *150 ans au coeur de Rome: le Séminaire français 1853–2003* (Paris: Karthala, 2004).

172 Henri Le Floch (1862–1950), ordained in 1886, member of the Congregation of the Holy Spirit, of which he was superior general (1923–1927); a consultor of the Holy Office, he was rector of the French Seminary in Rome for more than twenty years, until 1927, when, following the condemnation of the *Action Française*, toward which he was sympathetic, he was ordered by Pius XI to leave Rome. A profile of him can be found in V. A. Berto, *Pour la Sainte Église Romaine, op. cit.*, 113–144. See also D. Menozzi, *La Chiesa cattolica e la secolarizzazione* (Turin: Einaudi, 1993), 211–215.

173 M. Lefebvre "Le Concile ou le triomphe du libéralisme," in *Fideliter* 59 (1987): 32–42 at 32

Among the most important meetings of the two Brazilian bishops was also the one with Cardinal Ruffini,[174] who spoke very frankly to them, confirming that he had suggested the idea of the council so as to arrive at a condemnation of modernism. The archbishop of Palermo described as "very serious" the situation of the Church, which was "demolishing" itself, also by the excessive openness to innovations shown by Pius XII, whose encylical *Divino afflante Spiritu* had caused some confusion in the field of exegesis. Ruffini added that whereas Pius X had been very careful in selecting instructors for the ecclesiastical faculties, Pius XI, in his choice of professors, had imbued Rome with the modernist spirit. Pius XII had been influenced by bad advisers and now, in Roman ecclesiastical circles, the Lateran University was an exception thanks to Monsignor Piolanti, who for this reason was being attacked so much.[175]

Piolanti met Prof. Corrêa de Oliveira on November 9 and confirmed the attacks that he was enduring, also because of some imprudence of friends like Monsignor Romeo and Monsignor Spadafora. The rector of the Lateran University repeated to the Brazilian professor what Bishop Ronca had already told him: preparations were being made for the candidacy of Cardinal Montini for the conclave: if he were to be elected, "it would be the end of everything."[176]

On November 14 Archbishop Lefebvre agreed to be part of the Little Committee[177] that began to meet on the Corso Italia, at the *Procura* of the Holy Ghost Fathers. On November 17 there was another meeting of the group: present, besides Archbishop Sigaud and Bishop Mayer, were

---

[translated from Italian; cf. Tissier de Mallerais, 35–36]. The group of Archbishop Lefebvre's fellow students at the French Seminary in Rome included, besides Fathers Berto and Dulac, also the theologians Lucien (Luc) Lefevre (1895–1987), Henri Lusseau (1896–1973), and Alphonse Roul (1901–1969), who also made the "team" of *La Pensée Catholique*. Cf. Paul Airiau, "Les hommes de la Pensée Catholique," in *Catholica* 60 (1998): 59–74 and, at greater length, *La pensée catholique 1946–1956: Romanité à la française ou intégrisme*, thesis of D.E.A. (Paris: Institut d'Études Politiques, 1995).

[174] Maranhão Galliez, *Diario* (November 6, 1962).

[175] *Ibid.*

[176] *Ibid.* (November 9, 1962).

[177] *Ibid.* (November 14, 1962).

Archbishop Lefebvre and Bishop Ronca, Bishops Marcelino Olaechea[178] of Valencia, Giuseppe Carraro[179] of Verona, and the nuncio Egidio Vagnozzi.[180] Toward the end of the meeting Cardinal Ruffini[181] spoke, calling attention to the biblical question that was being discussed those days in the council hall. On December 1, at the next meeting, Bishops Ngô-Dinh-Thuc, Tortolo,[182] Rupp,[183] and Ronca[184] appeared. On November 22, the Little Committee organized a conference given by Monsignor Garofalo in the *Casa del Verbo Divino*, in the presence of a number of bishops. The success of the initiative encouraged them to organize a more important conference given by Cardinal Ruffini on November 30 at the Domus Mariae. On that occasion the archbishop of Palermo stressed that the sources of revelation were not one, but two, scripture and tradition, and of these tradition had a preeminent role that was denied by the modernists.[185]

On November 28 in a meeting with Ronca, Archbishop Sigaud and Bishop de Castro Mayer decided to form a secretariat to study and circulate explanations of the next schemas during the intersession period. The committee would be presided over by Sigaud and Mayer and would function in Rome with the support of the *periti* of the council. Archbishop

178 Marcellino Olaechea Loizaga (1889–1972), Spanish Benedictine, ordained in 1915. Archbishop of Valencia from 1946 to 1966. Member of the Commission for Seminaries, Studies, and Catholic Education.

179 Giuseppe Carraro (1899–1980), ordained in 1923, bishop of Verona from 1958 to 1978. Member of the Commission for Seminaries.

180 Egidio Vagnozzi (1906–1980), ordained in 1928, titular archbishop, apostolic delegate in the United States from 1958 to 1967, created cardinal in 1967. Prefect of Economic Affairs of the Holy See from 1968 until his death.

181 Maranhão Galliez, *Diario* (November 17, 1962).

182 Adolfo Servando Tortolo (1911–1986), Argentine, ordained in 1934, auxiliary bishop of Paranà (1956), then bishop of Catamarca (1960) and archbishop of Paranà (1963). In 1970 he succeeded Cardinal Antonio Caggiano as president of the Argentine Episcopal Conference. In 1975 Paul VI appointed him Military vicar for the Armed Forces.

183 Jean Rupp (1905–1983), French, ordained in 1953. bishop of the Principality of Monaco from June 1962 to 1974.

184 Maranhão Galliez, *Diario* (December 1, 1962).

185 *Ibid.* (November 30, 1962).

Vagnozzi participated in the last part of the meeting; he approved of the idea and guaranteed help for translations into English.[186] Ronca, who had first suggested to the two Brazilian bishops the creation of a meeting place for the "integrist" bishops, took on the organizational task, assuring the group that his "team" would collaborate.[187]

The Little Committee had resolved to organize the anti-progressive resistance, combining all the forces then on the field and seeking to weld the "ultramontane" bishops, such as de Castro Mayer, Sigaud, and Lefebvre, together with the most conservative wing of the fathers of the curia, represented on the one hand by the cardinals of the curia, such as Ottaviani and Ruffini, and on the other hand by the Italian bishops led by Giuseppe Siri. The only one of the three cardinals who aligned himself, albeit discreetly, with the Little Committee was the archbishop of Palermo, Ruffini. On the other hand it had no support from Ottaviani and especially from Siri. Although Ottaviani's lack of involvement can be explained by the institutional role that he played as head of the Theological Commission, it is more difficult to understand the absence of Siri, who in the later sessions would not participate in the *Coetus Internationalis Patrum*[188] either.

Siri was the youngest cardinal in the whole Sacred College, and one of the best qualified by his theological preparation and episcopal experience. The Gregorian University, where he had studied, considered him as a "star" of the institution, and in 1957 as it was celebrating its fourth centenary it had entrusted to him the task of making the celebratory speech. He would be able to make a decisive contribution to the conservatives, not only by his theological authority, but also because he would be able to bring along with him a large number of Italian council fathers, thus giving the Little Committee greater numerical stability. In fact the Italian Episcopal Conference, over which he presided, had closer ties to the Roman theological school and included valiant prelates such as Archbishop

---

[186] *Ibid.* (November 28, 1962).

[187] *Ibid.* (October 19, 1962).

[188] On Siri's participation at Vatican II, see his *Diario* from October 10, 1962, to November 20, 1964, published in 1993 as an appendix in B. Lai, *Il Papa non eletto, op. cit.*, and Paolo Gheda, "Il Card. Siri e la Conferenza episcopale italiana durante il Concilio Vaticano II," in *Synaxis* 3 (2005): 109–144.

Raffaele Calabria[189] of Benevento, Bishop Luigi Maria Carli[190] of Segni, Bishop Giovanni Battista Peruzzo[191] of Agrigento, and Bishop Luigi Carlo Borromeo of Pesaro.

The cardinal of Genoa guided the Italian Bishops' Conference (CEI) forcefully and authoritatively, and he was convinced that the unity of the bishops around the pope was as important as the political unity of the Catholics in the Christian Democratic Party around the CEI. He thought that the Church's authority should not be impaired by any internal controversy. In the early sixties, however, the visible body of the Church, like the Catholic political community, was already objectively fragmented, riddled with centrifugal forces, and the real priority was to preserve doctrinal unity, even before institutional unity. In late December of 1962, Siri sought to organize a structure that would maintain relations with the other groups during the intersession period, promote an internal "study group," and serve as a center for oversight, but the initiative always remained within the CEI.[192] The lack of cohesiveness between Italian and "ultramontane" bishops was one reason for the weakness of the conservative front what was taking shape.

The largest groups of bishops among the progressives were the French (122) and the Germans (58), for a total of 180, a much smaller number than the total Italian episcopate, which included 271 local bishops, but the Franco-German bloc played a much more incisive role. Roger Aubert points out that the French intervened 210 times in public sessions, in other words, twice as many times proportionately than the Italians, even though in reality only around twenty French prelates were very active, particularly Ancel, Elchinger, Garrone, Veuillot, Gerlier and Feltin, who generally stayed at the *procura* of San Sulpizio, whereas the more conservative

---

189 Raffaele Calabria (1906–1962), ordained in 1929, archbishop of Benevento from 1962 until his death.

190 Luigi Maria Carli (1914–1986), ordained in 1937, bishop of Segni (1957–1973), then archbishop of Gaeta until his death. Cf. A. D'Angelo "Luigi Maria Carli," in DSMCI, *Aggiornamento*, 1980–1995, pp. 264–265.

191 Giovanni Battista Peruzzo (1878–1963), Passionist, ordained in 1901, was superior of the Shrine in Basella di Urgnano, assistant in Mantova in 1924, bishop in Oppido Mamertino from 1928 on and of Agrigento starting in 1932, then archbishop from 1952 until his death.

192 Cf. N. Buonasorte, *Siri: Tradizione e Novecento, op. cit.* 291–292.

fathers resided at the French Seminary.[193] The central European bloc was symbolized by the Rhine, which in this case united and did not divide the French and German banks, but ideological trends were the real glue, more than geographical or national affinities.

7. The overturning of the "schemata"

Once they had occupied their positions with the appointment of their own candidates in the commission, the central European alliance could proceed to the second step: the sinking of the *schemata* approved by the commission and by the pope himself. The document containing the first seven schemas had been sent on July 10, 1962, to John XXIII, who studied it attentively, annotating it, as Monsignor Fagiolo mentions, with handwritten comments: "In the margin of all the schemas there are these oft-repeated [Latin] expressions: *Bene, Optime* [Good, Very good]. Only in one, the schema on the liturgy, which was in fifth place in the volume on pages 157-199, do we find here and there, still written in the pope's own hand, some question marks expressing surprise and not approval."[194]

Now some people wanted to toss back into the sea the monumental work carried out during the three preceding years and collected in the sixteen volumes of the *"antipreparatoria"*: more than two thousand pages containing the initial drafts of fifty-four decrees and fifteen dogmatic constitutions.

On September 4, 1962, before the opening of the council, Chenu wrote to Rahner that he had scarcely become acquainted with the preparatory *schemata* when he experienced "distress and grief" on account of their "strictly intellectualist" perspective. He accused in particular the first two "constitutions" issued by the Theological Commission of restricting themselves to denouncing some "intra-theological errors," "without looking at the dramatic questions that men are asking themselves, whether or not they are Christians, because of a change of the exterior and interior human condition, such as history has never recorded.... The council is becoming an intellectual housecleaning project within the walls of scholasticism."[195]

---

193 Cf. R. Aubert, "Organizzazione e funzionamento dell'assemblea," *op. cit.*, 164–165.

194 Vincenzo Fagiolo (1918–2000), "Il cardinale Amleto Cicognani e mons. Pericle Felici," in *Le deuxième Concile du Vatican*, 229–242 at 234–235.

195 Chenu, *Diario*, 57. The same judgments on the doctrinal schemas were expressed by Cardinal

Rahner, whom Henri Fesquet introduced in the pages of *Le Monde* as "one of the best theologians of the council,"[196] on October 12 explained to Bishop Volk and to his theologian Semmelroth the general lines of his strategy, which was to "substitute a new schema for the present schemas of the Theological Commission."[197]

On October 19, on the eve of the meeting of the Third General Congregation, several German and French bishops and theologians, selected by Bishop Volk of Mainz, met at *Mater Dei*, on the *viale delle Mura Aurelie*. "Purpose of the meeting:" Congar noted in his diary, "to discuss and decide on a tactic in relation to the theological schemas."[198] Twenty-five were present, among them (besides Volk and his auxiliary Joseph Reuss[199]), the archbishop of Berlin, Alfred Bengsch,[200] and bishops Ancel (auxiliary of Lyons), Gabriel-Marie Garrone (Toulouse), Émile Guerry[201] (Cambrai), Paul Schmitt[202] (Metz), Jean Julien Weber[203] (Strasbourg), with his co-adjutor Léon-Arthur Elchinger, and the theologians Congar, Chenu, Daniélou, de Lubac, Küng, Philips, Rahner, Ratzinger, Schillebeeckx, and Semmelroth.

Léger, who, upon meeting Chenu on October 9, described them as "speculative theses that confine themselves to repeating Vatican I and do not respond to the needs and demands of this time" (*ibid.*, 69).

196 Fesquet, *Diario* [Italian edition of *Le Journal du Concile*], 71. Cf. the somewhat abridged English edition, *The Drama of Vatican II*, 53.

197 So Semmelroth noted in his diary on October 12, 1962. Cf. G. Fogarty, "The Council Gets Underway," *op. cit.*, 79.

198 Congar, *Journal*, 99.

199 Joseph Reuss (1906–1985), German, ordained in 1930, auxiliary bishop of Mainz from 1954 to 1978.

200 Alfred Bengsch (1921–1979), German, ordained in 1950, bishop of Berlin in 1961, created cardinal in 1962.

201 Emile Guerry (1891–1969), French, ordained in 1923, archbishop of Cambrai from 1952 to 1966.

202 Paul Schmitt (1911–1987), French, ordained in 1935, bishop of Metz from 1958 to 1987.

203 Jean Julien Weber (1888–1981), French Sulpician, ordained in 1912, bishop of Strasbourg from 1945 on, archbishop of the same diocese from 1962 to 1966.

The importance of the gathering is emphasized by the diaries of Chenu, Congar, and de Lubac.[204] The aim was to discuss a tactic for dismantling the theological schemas. The discussion was lively and lasted for more than three hours. Rahner insisted on a new supplementary draft of the document. The more prudent Frenchmen suggested "not proceeding by way of opposition because that would provoke a contrary reaction." Finally the preliminary task of studying the project was entrusted to a restricted group of theologians, among them Rahner, Daniélou, and Congar.

As of that meeting two movements were delineated: one "Jacobin" group, headed by Rahner and Küng, which intended to reject the schemas of the Theological Commission entirely; the other "Girondist," supported by the French bishops and theologians, which intended in contrast to reshape the schemas through the interventions in the council hall.

Küng proposed calling together in Rome an international meeting of theologians so as to influence the council fathers. Congar advised against the initiative, so as not to give the impression that a conspiracy was being formed. "One must always think about the reaction one risks arousing when planning to do something."[205] A "Jacobin" on the pages of his diary, but a "Girondist" in his relations with the council fathers, to whom he privately handed over documents and outlines, Congar warned about "the danger, and the undesirability, of creating the impression of a para-council of theologians, seeking to influence the true council of bishops."[206] It was advisable to avoid the impression "that some theologians wanted to dictate to the council the line it should take. Such a move would bring back awkward memories of Döllinger;[207] that we were scheming."[208] The Dominican theologian observes that Küng "demands insistently, like a revolutionary"[209] who was too impatient in his claims: "As for me, I believe profoundly in time-lags [*i.e.* in waiting], in the necessary stages."[210]

---

[204] Cf. Chenu, *Diario*, 76–79; Congar, *Journal*, 98–100; de Lubac, *Quaderni*, 120–121.

[205] Congar, *Journal*, 82.

[206] *Ibid.*

[207] Johann Joseph Ignaz von Döllinger (1799–1890), German theologian and historian, ordained in 1822, professor of Church History and Canon Law at the lyceum of Aschaffenburg in 1823 and professor of theology in Munich in 1826.

[208] *Ibid.*

[209] *Ibid.*, 369.

[210] *Ibid.*, 370

On November 18, Bishop Volk called another meeting at *Mater Dei*. De Lubac gives a thorough account of the encounter,[211] in which six German bishops, four French prelates, and theologians from central Europe participated.

The biggest change introduced was in the language of the schemas, rather than in the content. Cardinal Siri mentions in fact that the discursive style was adopted, "and the method of simple propositions, woven together tightly so as to affirm truths or condemn errors clearly, was ruled out."[212] The choice of the discursive method had as its chief consequence a lack of clarity, which in turn was the cause of the ambiguity that was the dominant feature of the conciliar documents.

8. The debate on the liturgy

a) The one "progressive" schema

The balance sheet of the central European alliance was more than satisfactory: the reorganization of the ten conciliar commissions and the elimination of all the preparatory work, whereby of all the schemas prepared in advance only *De liturgia* survived,[213] the one that Pope John liked less, but the only one that satisfied the progressives. The Dominican Edward Schillebeeckx described it as "an admirable piece of work."[214] The Dutch fathers insisted that the schema, which was the fifth on the order of business, should be the first to be discussed.[215] This was, as Wiltgen underscored, another victory for the central European front.[216] The schema was in fact the product of the work of the one commission that was dominated by progressives, the

[211] Cf. de Lubac, *Quaderni*, 1:279–286.

[212] G. Siri, "Il post-concilium," *op. cit.*, 178.

[213] AS I/1:262–303.

[214] Wiltgen, 23.

[215] "The schemas, which the pope had personally deemed well done, with the exception of the one on the liturgy, which he did not consider well done, were rejected, and only the one on the liturgy was considered worthy to be submitted for discussion by the *Patres conciliari*" (V. Fagiolo, *op. cit.*, 235).

[216] Wiltgen, 24.

Liturgical Commission, made up primarily of exponents of the central European liturgical movement.[217]

Cardinal Ottaviani expressed in writing to Cardinal Tisserant his disappointment over "the unexpectedly announced decision to begin the discussion in the council about the liturgy and not about the doctrine of the faith, thus inverting the order already established in the volume of schemas that is in the fathers' possession,"[218] although probably without realizing the full significance of the decision. The progressive troops took the field, displaying their strength not by mowing down a document, but by approving one. Its first victory would make the following ones easier.

The debate started on Monday, October 22, the Fourth General Congregation, and extended until December 7, 1962, over the course of twenty-one congregations, in the course of which the introduction and the first chapter of the schema *De liturgia* were reworked.[219]

The topics that concerned the fathers most were the language (Latin or the vernacular), concelebration, communion under both species, and the revision of the Breviary, the Missal, and the Ritual.

The schema, subdivided into an introduction and eight chapters, was presented by Cardinal Larraona, president of the commission, and by Father Ferdinando Antonelli, who had replaced Father Bugnini as secretary.[220]

On the eve of the discussion a document composed by the Bishop of Linz was circulated; Bishop Zauner[221] was a representative of the "European alliance" within the Liturgical Commission. While approving the text as a whole, the Austrian prelate emphasized the need to "improve" some passages concerning the liturgical language and concelebration. On the first point, Bishop Zauner asked that the episcopal conferences be authorized to set the conditions for the introduction of the vernacular; on the second point he proposed wider permission for concelebration, which the conciliar

---

[217] Members of the Preparatory Liturgical Commission included Bernard Capelle, abbot of Mont-César, and Bernard Botte, director of the Higher Institute of Liturgy in Paris, both Belgians.

[218] ASV, Con. Vat. II, Busta 757, n. 8, Epistolae *Em.mi Praesidis ad varios Patres conciliares*, photocopy (October 18, 1962), ff. 2.

[219] Mathus Lamberigts, "The Liturgy Debate," in HVT 2:107–168 at 108 ff.; Herman Schmidt, *La costituzione sulla Sacra liturgia: Testo, Genesi, Commento, Documentazione* (Rome: Herder, 1966); A. Bugnini, *The Reform of the Liturgy, op. cit.*, 31–37.

[220] AS I/1:304–309.

[221] Franz Zauner (1904–1994), Austrian, ordained in 1931, bishop of Linz from 1956 to 1980.

schema limited to two specific cases: the consecration of the sacred oils on Holy Thursday and the occasion of a very large meeting of priests. These suggestions were promptly developed in the hall by the first orators who spoke, all of them resolved to put themselves in the spotlight, from the outset, as leaders of the progressive forces.

Cardinal Frings opened the debate by praising the schema "for its modern literary and truly pastoral style, full of the spirit of sacred scripture and of the fathers of the Church."[222] Cardinal Lercaro and Cardinal Döpfner,[223] too, underscored the "pastoral" aspect of the document. Lercaro, in his first intervention in the hall,[224] urged the bishops of the "socialist" countries and those of the third world churches to intervene actively in the debate, so as to manifest the need for a renewal of the liturgy. On October 31 he took the floor once again, maintaining the indispensability of participation in the liturgy of the Word.[225]

Equally significant, on October 22, was the intervention of the Cardinal of Milan, Giovanni Battista Montini, who offered an intervention "mediating"[226] between the two camps, even though it was clearly apparent, and he would subsequently demonstrate, where his heart lay.[227] If Latin, he asserted, was preserved in the sacramental and specifically priestly parts [of the liturgy], in the instructional parts it was necessary to eliminate any barrier that could prevent the people from understanding the readings and from expressing their prayers in intelligible words. Therefore it was necessary to abandon, prudently but without delay, a language that was understood by few and was an obstacle to true participation in worship. In this intervention Montini revealed how much importance he assigned to the theme of liturgical renewal, which had been, since his youth, a constant in his concept of the Church.

---

222 AS I/1:309–310.

223 *Ibid.*, 319–322.

224 *Ibid.*, 311–313. Italian text in G. Lercaro, *Per la forza dello spirito: Discorsi conciliari del card. Giacomo Lercaro* (Bologna: Edizioni Dehoniane, 1984), 73–78. On Lercaro's participation in the council, see also Matteo Donati, *Il sogno di una Chiesa: Gli interventi al Concilio Vaticano II del cardinale Giacomo Lercaro* (Assisi: Cittadella Editrice, 2010).

225 AS I/2:56–58.

226 AS I/1:313–316.

227 Cf. A. G. Martimort, "Le rôle de Paul VI dans la réforme liturgique," in Various Authors, *Le rôle de G. B. Montini – Paul VI dans la réforme liturgique* (Brescia: Studium, 1987), 59 ff.

The Melkite patriarch of Antioch, Maximos IV Saigh, "the heavy artillery of the council," as he was described,[228] speaking in French, on October 23 vindicated the role of the episcopal conferences in determining whether and in what ways the vernacular languages should be introduced into the liturgy.[229] "Dozens of prelates walked over to shake the patriarch's hand and to congratulate him for having dared to say what many liturgists were thinking,"[230] Bishop Edelby noted.

The chief objective of the progressives was to deprive the Congregation of Rites [officially called the Congregation for the Discipline of the Sacraments] of its competencies by the establishment in every country of national liturgical commissions connected with the episcopal conferences, and the creation in Rome of an "international commission" of experts.[231] In the press, meanwhile, a debate began to unfold in parallel to the one taking place in the hall and heavily influencing it.

The only Asian member of the Liturgical Commission was the bishop of Ruteng (Indonesia), Bishop Willem van Bekkum,[232] born in Holland, whose candidacy had been strongly supported by the central European group, also because he had been trained in Germany and Austria, at the school of the liturgical movement.[233] On October 23, the day after the discussion on the liturgy began, Bishop van Bekkum held a crowded press conference on the adaptation of the liturgy to the Indonesian culture. The Dutch bishop defended the spontaneity of the national and tribal languages and expressed his hope that Asian and African languages could replace Latin as "ritual languages" in the Mass, thus contributing to the enrichment and revitalization of the liturgy. One hour later Italian radio and the international press agencies broadcast throughout the world the

---

228 Edelby, *Diario*, 269.

229 AS I/1:377–380. On October 13, 1963, simultaneous translation in five languages was installed in Saint Peter's Basilica. Bishop Helder Câmara mentions the episode as a "defeat of Latin as a living language and as the official language of the Church" (Circular letter of October 13, 1963, in *Lettres Conciliaires*, 1:217).

230 Edelby, *Diario*, 76.

231 Fesquet, *Drama*, 34.

232 Willem Van Bekkum (1910–1998), Dutch Divine Word Father, ordained in 1935. Bishop of Ruteng (Indonesia) from 1961 to 1972.

233 Wiltgen, 35.

"revolutionary" ideas of Bishop van Bekkum.[234] The same theses were presented to journalists in the following days by Archbishop Eugenio D'Souza[235] of Nagpur, India, and Bishop Lorenzo Nagae[236] of Urawa, Japan.

b) The question about Latin

In the course of the discussion on the first four chapters, the question of Latin was at the center of the debate. De Lubac mentions[237] two particularly critical opponents of the schema: Archbishop Vagnozzi,[238] apostolic delegate to the United States, and Archbishop Dante,[239] titular archbishop of Carpasia, secretary of the Congregation of Rites, who "demolished" the schema with an intervention subdivided into twelve points.[240] Archbishop Vagnozzi emphasized, for his part, the following aspects:

> 1. One must not indulge excessively in the spirit of innovation, because the liturgy, as it is today, is a sacred and venerable witness of the faith of the Catholic Church, both in the Western and in the Eastern rites.
>
> 2. The drafts of this liturgical section often appear to be wordy, composed in a language that is poetic and ascetical rather than strictly theological, and it seems more like a treatise on liturgy than a conciliar schema.
>
> 3. The theological language often appears vague and sometimes inexact; I humbly maintain that the doctrinal principles of the liturgy, enunciated better and in a more cogent formulation by the supreme

---

234 *Ibid.*

235 Eugenio D'Souza (1917–2003), Indian, Salesian missionary, ordained in 1944. bishop then archbishop of Nagpur (India) from 1951 to 1963, then archbishop of Bhopal from 1963 to 1994.

236 Laurent Satoshi Nagae (1913–1998), Japanese, ordained in 1938, bishop of Urawa (Japan) from 1957 to 1979.

237 De Lubac, *Quaderni*, 1:129.

238 AS I/1:325–326.

239 *Ibid.*, 330–331. Enrico Dante (1884–1967), ordained in 1910. Secretary of the Congregation of Rites as of 1960, titular archbishop, created cardinal in 1965.

240 De Lubac, *Quaderni*, 1:129.

> pontiff Pius XII in the encylical *Mediator Dei* can be repeated word for word by the fathers of the council, rather than the drafts that have been proposed to us....
>
> In my judgment it would be necessary to first of all and in one stroke to articulate and establish these principles:
>
> 1. In the first place, the sacred liturgy is based on the work of redemption accomplished by Christ, as its foundation.
>
> 2. Secondly, the sacred liturgy is the public worship manifested by the body of Christ.
>
> 3. Thirdly, the sacred liturgy brings about the sanctification of man, which is obtained through the work and the exercise of the priesthood of Christ.[241]

Others who intervened in defense of the Latin liturgy on October 24 were Cardinal Antonio Bacci,[242] considered the most eminent Latinist of the Church, Bishop Pietro Parente,[243] consultor to the Congregation of Rites, and Archbishop Dino Staffa,[244] secretary of the Congregation of Seminaries and Universities. Latin—they stressed—should continue to be the only liturgical language, and vernacular languages should be used only for instructions and some prayers.

The American Cardinal McIntyre,[245] supported by Cardinal Spellman, recalled that changing the liturgy means changing dogmas:

> The attack on the Latin language of the sacred liturgy is an indirect but real attack on the stability of the sacred dogmas, because the sacred liturgy necessarily conveys dogmas with it.... All of us in this sacred council can recall fundamental changes in the meaning of the words in the vernacular that is commonly used today. It follows that if the

---

[241] AS I/1:325–326.

[242] *Ibid.*, 408–411. Antonio Bacci (1885–1971), ordained in 1909. Secretary of Briefs to Princes from 1931 to 1960. Created cardinal in 1960. Titular archbishop of Colonia in Cappadocia in 1962.

[243] AS I/1:423–427.

[244] *Ibid.*, 429–430.

[245] James Louis McIntyre (1886–1979), American, ordained in 1921, archbishop of Los Angeles from 1948 to 1970. Created cardinal in 1953.

> sacred liturgy were in the vernacular, the unchangeable character of the doctrine would be in danger. If the vernacular languages are introduced, we foresee countless interpretations of the sacred dogmas. In order that the eternal truth of doctrine may be expressed, let the sacred dogmas keep their meaning and original form unchangeably! The introduction of the vernacular must be separate from the action of the Holy Mass. The Holy Mass must remain as it is. Profound changes in the liturgy provoke profound changes in the dogmas.[246]

Father Benedikt Reetz,[247] superior general of the Benedictine Congregation of Beuron, refuted the thesis of those who maintained that vernacular languages must be used because in the liturgy everyone must understand everything:

> I reply: one should say that the faithful do not have to understand everything—we priests ourselves do not understand everything!—but it is enough for them to understand generally and not all the particulars. The active participation of the faithful does not just consist in song and prayer, but also in watching the things that are done at the altar. Saint Thomas already speaks about those in the Church who do not understand the meaning of the chants, and says in II-II, q. 91, art. 2, ad 5 the very beautiful words: "Even if some of them understand not what is sung, yet they understand why it is sung, namely, for God's glory: and this is enough to arouse their devotion."[248]

On October 30, Cardinal Ottaviani asked to speak and in an impassioned intervention criticized the proposals that had been made to modify the rite of the Mass, seeing in them a veritable liturgical revolution:

> The *Ordo Missae* has been fixed for many centuries; the Mass is the center of all liturgical worship; it is a supremely sacred matter, well known by individual believers, who especially through liturgical pastoral work are well acquainted with the individual parts of it, and

---

[246] AS I/1:369–371 at 370–371.

[247] Benedikt Reetz, O.S.B. (1897–1964), abbot of the Order of Saint Benedict, superior general of the Benedictine Congregation of Beuron.

[248] AS I/1:469–470 at 470.

> there is a danger that excessive changes would cause some reaction of amazement, if not of scandal. We are dealing here with an extremely holy matter, which cannot be changed for each generation as it pleases; a matter that is supremely sacred and must be approached with a holy respect and veneration, and should not be touched except in a limited way. Now the words come to mind that God spoke to Moses when he approached the burning bush: "Put off your shoes from your feet, for the place on which you are standing is holy ground." Let us be cautious therefore about proposals to reform the rite of the Mass.[249]

When Cardinal Ottaviani exceeded his ten minutes, Cardinal Alfrink, who was presiding over the session, rang the bell, but the speaker continued to talk. Alfrink then gave the order to shut off the microphone and the floor was taken away from Ottaviani.[250] For the prefect of the *"Suprema"* this was an unexpected humiliation in front of the whole conciliar assembly. Part of the assembly applauded. Bishop Helder Câmara saw in that applause the emergence of "the spirit of the council."[251] Bishop Borromeo, who in his *Diary* described the episode as "disgusting," pointed out that "the applause originated from well-defined sectors of the left-hand side, the one marked with the letter S, which is then the right wing for someone entering from the main part of the basilica."[252]

The irregularity of the episode was emphasized in the pages of the *Corriere della Sera* by Indro Montanelli, who contrasted the hieratic figure of Cardinal Ottaviani with the "modern" impression made by Cardinal Alfrink: "Tall, athletic, a sportsman, younger than sixty, he does not even make an effort to conceal his anti-Roman sentiments behind theological screens."[253]

---

249 AS I/2:18–20 at 18.

250 Alfrink's version of the episode is recounted in Ton Oostveen, *Bernard Alfrink vescovo cattolico* (Assisi: Cittadella editrice, 1973), 76–77.

251 Câmara, *Lettres conciliaires*, 1:69.

252 Borromeo, *Diario* (October 30, 1962).

253 I. Montanelli, "Sottile ma anche concitato il dialogo tra curia romana e vescovi stranieri," in *Corriere della Sera*, November 26, 1962.

c) Bishop Peruzzo's intervention

The topics of communion under both species and concelebration were also quite prominent. Archbishop Dante emphasized that

> 1. Communion under both species must be absolutely rejected. This is required by reasons which for many centuries have caused the Church to abandon this custom: the dangers inherent in this form of administering the sacrament, and hygienic reasons.
>
> 2. Nor does concelebration seem acceptable, especially in the case of private Masses. If it is a question of concelebration that is to take place with the bishop, in special cases, the opportunity and the permission for this concelebration, and also the number of concelebrants, should be reserved solely to the judgment of the Holy See.[254]

According to Cardinal Alfrink, seconded by Cardinal Bea,[255] communion under both species was a biblical practice, observed by the early Church, given that eating and drinking are part of the true essence of the supper.[256] Cardinal Ruffini warned, however, that if the council were to consent to the request for communion under both species, it would go against the decrees of the Council of Constantinople and the Council of Trent.[257]

The theme of concelebration was addressed by Cardinal Léger at the beginning of the session on October 29; among those in favor was the Belgian bishop of Inongo (Zaire), Bishop Jan van Cauwelaert,[258] who in the name of 262 bishops asserted that in cultures where community was an important factor, concelebration was esteemed as a concrete expression of unity.[259]

On that same day, October 29, the bishop of Agrigento, Bishop Giovanni Battista Peruzzo, recalled how the anti-liturgical movement had arisen between the late fifteenth and the early sixteenth century in pagan

---

254 AS I/1:331.

255 *Ibid.*, 22–26.

256 AS I/2:16–17.

257 AS I/1:600–601.

258 Francis van Cauwelaert (1906–1986), Belgian Benedictine, ordained in 1931.

259 AS I/2:94–95.

humanist circles.[260] Bishop Peruzzo's intervention, which was ridiculed by the progressives, deserves to be reprinted in its entirety because of the wisdom and the foresight that characterize it.

His remarks echo the warnings of Dom Guéranger, who in chapter 14 of his *Liturgical Institutions* vigorously denounced the principles that stand behind the anti-liturgical heresy, the principal feature of which, he wrote, "is the hatred of tradition, of formulas, of divine worship."[261]

> I am the last (to speak) but I am old, the oldest one among you, and perhaps I have learned a few things; therefore pardon me if some clarification of mine does not please you. I have listened to many observations and proposals against the sacred tradition that should be kept regarding the use of the Latin language in the sacred liturgy, and many of these words have caused me anxiety and fear, which I will explain to you briefly, speaking not in theological but in historical terms. I do not like the anti-liturgical movement because of its origins. It is always very important to pay attention to the origin of families, of institutions, of realities, of doctrines: who is the father, who is the mother, who is the guide. If the source (the origin) at the beginning was sound, it will easily be sound over the course of time. If the source is polluted, it will become pure only with difficulty. On the basis of these principles, I have in mind the origin of the anti-liturgical movement: what sort of fathers, what sort of guides.
>
> This movement had its beginning in the late fifteenth century and in the early sixteenth century. The first to be anti-liturgical were the humanists, veritable pagans in Italy, better in France and in the northern countries, under the guidance of Erasmus, but all of them wavering in their faith. Many of our brethren vied in following them and then separated from the Catholic Church. From them came the Jansenists, and in Italy the followers of the Synod of Pistoia, and finally the modernists: this is the company with which many conform their way of speaking.
>
> On the contrary, I find no holy bishop who promoted this movement. They, from St. Charles Borromeo to St. (Anthony Mary)

---

[260] AS I/1:594–595.

[261] P. Guéranger, *De l'hérésie antiliturgique et de la réforme protestante du XVIe siècle, considérée dans ses rapports avec la liturgie*; cited in Italian translation, *L'eresia liturgica e la riforma protestante* (Chieti: Amicizia cristiana, 2008), 27.

Claret, from St. Francis de Sales to St. Alphonsus, ancients and moderns, all of them clung to the Latin tradition. This fact should make us cautious about introducing innovations. It is easy to leave the "old way" that is safe; but the new paths—what a whirlpool they could prepare and stir up for us!

Erasmus, in his preface to the Gospel of Saint Matthew, wrote as follows: "It seems indecorous and ridiculous that the simple folk and the little old ladies, like parrots, should repeat the psalms and murmur their Sunday prayers, whereas they themselves do not understand the meaning." The University of Paris condemned this judgment, which seems simple and right, as impious, erroneous and conducive to new errors; read Duplessy.

The verdict seems excessive to us, but it was prophetic. All those who have asked for at least a reduction of the Latin language in the liturgy, in the past as today, present the same reasons: so as to instruct the people better and to urge them to a greater faith and love of God.

The *Augsburg Confession* asked for nothing but a popular hymn in the vernacular during the celebration of Mass. But what happened? The substitution of the vernacular in Mass, generally, was the first act of separation from Holy Mother Church. This weighty assertion is not mine, but that of the abbot Dom Guéranger, who is truly the father of the liturgical renewal. Here are his words: "For some inexplicable reason, which we do not know, separation from the liturgical language, even if a dispensation has been obtained from the supreme pontiff, almost always has led to schism and to full separation from the Catholic Church." He proves this statement, as you can read in volume III of his *Institutions Liturgiques*. These words and these facts should make us extremely cautious in such an important matter as this.

I will mention briefly the third reason: the fidelity that bishops must always have, more than all the rest, to the supreme pontiff. This is obvious. For almost five centuries the supreme pontiffs have steadfastly resisted prayers, entreaties and threats so as to defend the Latin language in the sacred liturgy. In more recent times, from Leo XIII to the reigning pontiff, they have unanimously recommended the necessity of Latin in the sacred liturgy with various apostolic letters.

Dear brothers, are these regulations merely advice or do their words give an order? Contrary discussions are outspoken, but to me it seems right that they should be conducted quietly and subordinated to obedience to the supreme pontiff. Everyone is asking Christians today to become better. Let us all strive to attain that end; history, indeed,

> teaches us that the sanctification of souls can be united to the liturgy, but that it requires above all our holiness, the strength of our faith, the heroism of the apostolate, the spirit of prayer, of penance, and also that great exterior devotion [*i.e.* reverence] that leads the people of God. Pardon my boldness and pray also for me![262]

d) An ecumenical Mass?

When the conciliar debate resumed on November 5, one of the twenty-four speakers who took the floor, Bishop Duschak,[263] titular bishop of Abbida and apostolic vicar of Calapan in the Philippines, but a German by birth, asserted the need for an "ecumenical Mass," modeled on the Last Supper.[264]

> Christ celebrated the first Mass in the presence of the apostles—turned toward the people, according to the then prevailing custom for suppers. Christ spoke aloud, so that all of them, so to say, heard the Canon of that first Mass. Christ made use of the common language, so that all could understand him and his words without any difficulty. Contained in the words "Do this," according to their full meaning, there seems to be the precept to celebrate Mass as a supper, facing forward, or at least aloud, and in a language that the companions at table understand.

Bishop Duschak therefore urged his listeners

> to collaborate, with the help of experts in all the rites and of the Churches that preserve the Eucharistic faith, so as to compose a Mass that could truly be called ecumenical or "Mass of the world," and to bring about with it the unity that is so much desired, at least in the Eucharistic memorial of the Lord. The people of God would then have the perfect and intimate participation that the apostles possessed at the Last Supper.[265]

---

262 AS I/1:594–595.

263 Wilhelm Josef Duschak (1903–1997), German, Divine Word Missionary, ordained in 1930, bishop of Abidda (1951) and apostolic vicar of Calapan (Philippines) from 1951 to 1973.

264 AS I/1:109–112.

265 *Ibid.*, 111–112.

That afternoon Bishop Duschak elucidated his intervention to the journalists, explaining that his idea was "to introduce an ecumenical Mass, stripped wherever possible of historical accretions, one that is based on the essence of the Holy Sacrifice, one that is deeply rooted in holy scripture."[266] The prelate went so far as to call for a change in the traditional words of the Canon. "If men in centuries gone by were able to choose and create Mass rites, why should not the greatest of all ecumenical councils be able to do so? Why should it not be possible to ordain that a new Mass formula be drawn up with all due reverence, one that is suited to, desired and understood by modern man?"[267] The whole Mass, Bishop Duschak insisted, would have to be celebrated aloud, in the vernacular and facing the people. These proposals seemed radical then but would be put into practice even before the conclusion of the council.

There was no lack of replies, however. To Cardinal Döpfner, who had stated that there was a need to introduce the vernacular also because candidates to the priesthood, educated in the public schools, no longer knew Latin,[268] Bishop Carli, addressing that situation, retorted that those same candidates did not even know Christian philosophy and theology and no one thought of ordaining them before they had completed their studies in those subjects.[269]

The actual conflict proved to be the one between the Roman curia and some episcopal conferences, especially the French and the German, supported by some bishops from third world countries, such as [1] Archbishop D'Souza, who in his interventions on October 27 and November 7, 1962,[270] asked that the episcopal conferences should have not only the right to choose the language in which the rite was celebrated, but also the right "to adapt the liturgy of the sacraments,"[271] and [2] Bishop Bekkers,[272] who said that only

---

266 Wiltgen, 38.

267 *Ibid.*

268 AS I/2:398–399.

269 *Ibid.*, 463–464.

270 AS I/1:497–499 and AS I/2:317–319.

271 AS I/2:318. "If the authority extended to the entire rite and to the use of the vernacular language, it would be excellent. This is what we expect from the council, because it is really necessary for its implementation" (*ibid.*).

272 Wilhelm Marinus Bekkers (1908–1966), Dutch, ordained in 1933, coadjutor bishop in 1956

"the fundamental sacramental nucleus of all the sacraments" would have to be "universal," "but for a more developed and fuller celebration of that sacramental nucleus a broader freedom should be granted, the limits of which can be judged expertly only by the conference of bishops of those peoples, provided that their decisions are approved by the Holy See."[273]

Latin was considered by the anti-Roman party as the instrument that the curia used to exercise its authority. As long as Latin remained the one language of the Church, Rome would have the competence to supervise and approve the rites. But if hundreds of local languages and customs were introduced into the liturgy, the curia would automatically lose its prerogatives and the episcopal conferences would become judges in the matter. "And this was precisely what the evolving majority was insisting upon," Wiltgen emphasizes. "It wanted episcopal conferences to be authorized to make certain important decisions in regard to liturgical practices."[274]

In the hall, the progressive alliance received the support of a strong group of bishops from Latin America, headed by Cardinal Silva Henríquez, archbishop of Santiago, Chile. These fathers, as Wiltgen notes, showed their gratitude for the major financial assistance that they had received, over the last few years, from Cardinal Frings of Cologne, through the associations *Misereor* and *Adveniat*. "Many of those who used the occasion of the council to visit Cardinal Frings and thank him personally found themselves joining the alliance."[275]

e) The liquidation of the Breviary

On November 7, Cardinal Léger proposed liquidating the Breviary, recommending that priests' prayers be limited to the essential parts of the Divine Office: Lauds, to be recited in the morning, Vespers in the evening, and the Office of Readings whenever was most convenient during

---

and then bishop of Bois-le-Duc until his death. His funeral was a sort of public demonstration by the Dutch ultra-progressive movement (*Actes et Acteurs*, 372).

273 AS I/1:313–314.

274 Wiltgen, 42.

275 *Ibid.*, 54.

the day.[276] Cardinal Urbani,[277] in his *Diary*, describes the intervention as "troublesome": "Frankly, I do not understand these bishops," he writes. "They talk about asceticism and then redesign the whole thing in the vernacular reading of the breviary. 'For private recitation,' they add. Yes, of course. When someone is about to be made a canon [who prays in choir] will he have to take a Latin exam? It seems to me that beneath this there is a whole underhanded struggle against the *Veterum Sapientia* [Wisdom of the Ancients]."[278] "The Franco-American *claque* applauded," Bishop Borromeo noted, observing that Cardinal Léger "decidedly wants to be a point man" and "has a good-sized *claque* in the council."[279]

Two days later the intervention of Cardinal Döpfner struck the same notes, claiming that "priests today have too much to do and cannot recite a Divine Office contrived in bygone times by religious who had no other concern but to fill their day with prayers."[280]

"Those bishops and cardinals in their trousers who cannot stand for five minutes without a cigar or cigarette in their mouth, who make light of all the prohibitions (*"on est prié de ne pas fumer!"* [French for "No smoking, please!"]) and couldn't care less about all the misgivings of the Latins (they go to the bar or to the hotel with so many [clerical] insignia with such fine manners [*con tante di insegne*], accompanied by the Gentleman!), it seems that they have lots to do besides pray," the bishop of Pesaro observed bitterly.[281]

The replies in defense of the Breviary extended also to the defense of the Latin language. Thus Cardinal Wyszyński[282] responded to Léger:

---

276 AS I/2:334–336.

277 Giovanni Urbani (1900–1969), ordained in 1922, titular bishop of Axomis, national assistant of Catholic Action in 1946; bishop of Verona in 1955, succeeded Roncalli in 1958 as patriarch of Venice and remained in that post until his death. Created cardinal by John XXIII in 1958.

278 Urbani, *Diario*, 135.

279 Borromeo, *Diario* (November 7, 1962).

280 AS I/2:398–403.

281 Borromeo, *Diario* (November 9, 1962).

282 Stefan Wyszyński (1901–1981), Cardinal archbishop of Warsaw and Gniezno, primate of Poland. Member of the Central Preparatory Commission. About him see, among other accounts, *Actes et Acteurs*, 326–336; Grootaers, *I protagonisti*, 245–260.

> The Roman Breviary … is a very strong bond of the praying Church, of the whole Mystical Body of Christ, of the Chief Shepherd, of the bishops, the priests, and the faithful. It was the source of consolation for all those who endured persecution in prisons and in what are commonly called "concentration camps." What these men are able to relate about the sweet prayer of the Roman Breviary is expressed, at least partially, by the heroic act of that holy martyr and apostle of Moravia, Bohemia, and Hungary who was put in chains and, since he could no longer turn the pages of the Breviary with his blood-stained hands, did so with the help of his tongue. I would like to skip, so to speak, the objections of those who say that they do not have enough time to recite the Divine Office. It seems to me to be a weak argument that is extremely harmful for some pious, good priests. With what strength and piety, and in what an exceptional way, the apostles rejected this idea, understanding that prayer is a magnificent gift! Since we are at the head of the Church of our days, our way of thinking must not be any different. We maintain, rather, that there is need for prayer that is as assiduous, constant, and profound as possible. There are many texts in the Roman Breviary that come from the most ancient times, such as the prayers, which by no means can be translated into contemporary language without the danger of losing their theological meaning, which is expressed in a time-tested, concise manner. It is enough to cite for example many versions of the Roman Missal in modern languages, which are full of defects and errors. The Roman Breviary, if it were ever translated into a modern language, would no longer spur seminary students to learn Latin, the study of which is so dear to the supreme pontiff. All these changes would distance their mind and their sentiments too much from the Roman Missal, the Vulgate, and the writings of the fathers of the Church. Latin-rite priests, finally, would lose the ability to use Latin, which is a very powerful bond of unity. This language is of very great service to us, gathered in this council.[283]

The archbishop of Westminster, William Godfrey,[284] expressed himself in terms that were equally clear:

---

283 AS I/2:393–394.

284 William Godfrey (1889–1963), English, ordained in 1916, archbishop of Westminster from 1956 until his death, created cardinal in 1958.

> I was trained in a very large parish for two years, and for many years I served the parishes in two large dioceses. I never ever heard priests who said that there was not enough time to recite the Divine Office. Certainly I recognize that there can be a difficulty in some regions, but it would not be very wise, if I am not mistaken, to establish universal rules for all the clergy in this Vatican Council. Sometimes it is said that there is a danger of falling into what is called "the heresy of good works," that is, praising pastoral work more than prayer, as though prayer were something subordinate to pastoral work. In my humble opinion, this is a real danger. The Divine Office has already been abbreviated enough. We can find the time for various business of lesser importance. Should we not perhaps preserve the Divine Office as sustenance and an essential support in fatigue, a pastoral staff [walking-stick] both for our youth and for our old age? I ask the venerable fathers not to abandon precious traditions lightly. Let it not seem, O venerable brothers, that we are laboring under a "novelty complex," as though nothing were being done in this council unless everything was being renovated.[285]

On the first ballot, held on November 14, the schema on the liturgy was approved in principle with 2,162 *placet* votes, 46 *non placet* and seven invalid ballots. "This action," Father O'Malley observes, "effectively nullified anon 1257 of the Code, which placed all decisions about liturgy exclusively in the Holy See."[286] The revised text of *Sacrosanctum concilium* would be promulgated the following year.

The day before the vote, Cardinal Cicognani announced that the pope, at the request of many fathers, had decided to introduce the name of St. Joseph in the Eucharistic Prayer immediately after the name of Mary. The decision did not please the liturgists and the promoters of ecumenical dialogue.[287]

---

285 AS I/1:472–473.

286 John W. O'Malley, *What Happened at Vatican II*, *op. cit.*, 139.

287 Cf. M. Lamberigts, "The Liturgy Debate," *op. cit.*, 147–148.

9. The attack on the schema on the sources of revelation

a) Scripture and Tradition

The debate in the council hall had become increasingly animated, clearly showing the existence of two opposing minorities, one progressive and one conservative, which were competing for the consensus of the "inert majority." In that climate, on November 14, after the voting on the schema on the liturgy, discussion began on the crucial topic of the relations between scripture and tradition in Christian revelation.[288] This debate, Riccardo Burigana observes, was "the door through which entered into Vatican II a new practice in the formulation of the doctrine of the Church of Rome,"[289] in other words, "the transition from a theology founded essentially on the papal magisterium to a reflection in which the central thing was a meditation on the word of God."[290]

The magisterium had always taught that there are two sources of revelation, sacred scripture and tradition: the first is inspired, the second—divinely assisted.[291] Tradition is the infallible rule of the Catholic faith, which in the Church precedes scripture: indeed, there was a time when nothing was known about New Testament scriptures, but there was never a time without an oral tradition going back to Jesus himself and the first apostles. This unique deposit of divine revelation is

[288] For a complete reconstruction of the debate, see R. Burigana, *La Bibbia nel Concilio: La redazione della costituzione "Dei Verbum" del Vaticano II* (Bologna: Il Mulino, 1998); Giuseppi Ruggieri, "The First Doctrinal Clash," in HVT 2:233–267. See also Umberto Betti, "Storia della costituzione dogmatica 'Dei Verbum,'" in Various Authors, *La costituzione dogmatica sulla divina Rivelazione* (Turin: LDC, 1967), 11–68; G. Ruiz, *Historia de la constitución "Dei Verbum" sobre la divina revelación* (Madrid: La Editorial Católica, 1969), 33–99. A dense critical analysis in Emmanuel-Marie, O.P., "Les quarante ans de la constitution conciliaire *Dei Verbum*," in *Le Sel de la Terre* 55 (2005–2006): 16–38.

[289] R. Burigana, *La Bibbia nel Concilio, op. cit.*, 15.

[290] *Ibid.*, 17.

[291] Cf. B. Gherardini, *Quod et tradidi vobis, op. cit.*, 300. With regard to the continuity of Catholic teaching, from the fathers of the Church until Vatican I, see the exhaustive essay by Monsignor (now Cardinal) W. Brandmüller, "L'insegnamento dei Concili sulla corretta interpretazione della Sacra Scrittura fino al Concilio Vaticano I," in *Walter Brandmüller: Scripta manent, op. cit.* 89–135.

entrusted to the authority of the Church, which preserves the second (or proximate) rule of faith for all believers. As Cardinal Billot neatly puts it, "Tradition is the rule of faith that precedes scripture with respect to time, knowledge, and extension. It is distinct from scripture... because it is not only a remote rule, but also proximate and immediate."[292] The deposit of revelation in its entirety is contained not in scripture, but in tradition, established by Christ himself as the fundamental instrument by which to transmit his teaching through the centuries.[293]

Biblicism has been, over the centuries, the banner of all movements that have tried to deny the authority of the Church in the name of sacred scripture. In opposition to the magisterium, the Catholic rule of faith, protestantism sets up the "word of God" alone as the one *regula fidei*, the absolute norm by which every doctrine and every action must be measured. John Wycliffe and Jan Hus, even before Luther, developed theories of an all-encompassing biblicism.[294]

The innovators of the Second Vatican Council, while not denying tradition, diminished its role or distorted its meaning. They viewed tradition not as something that constitutes, but as something that only "interprets" revelation, which according to them is contained solely in scripture. In this view, the interpreter of scripture, and hence of tradition, would not be the magisterium of the Church, but rather the teaching authority of the exegetes and theologians who proposed combining the two-fold sources (scripture and tradition) into the oneness of revelation.[295] Their questions were summarized in several documents that were offered as alternatives to the one by the Theological Commission: a *Disquisitio brevis de schemata de fontibus Revelationis*, composed by Father Rahner;[296] a document penned by the Belgian Dominican Schillebeeckx containing his *Animadversiones in primam seriem schematum* [Observations on the first series of schemas], in which the schema *De fontibus* was severely criticized for having a "closed

[292] L. Billot, S.J., *Tradition et modernisme*, ed. Fr. Jean-Michel Gleize (Versailles: Courrier de Rome, 2007), 32.

[293] *Ibid.*, 37.

[294] Cf. Ricardo García Villoslada, S.J., *Radici storiche del Luteranesimo*, Ital. transl. (Brescia: Morcelliana, 1979), 100–118.

[295] Cf. for example K. Rahner, "Scripture and Tradition," in *Theological Investigations*, vol. 6 (Baltimore: Helicon Press, 1969), 98–112.

[296] Cf. Wenger, *Vatican II, op. cit. Première session*, 103–104.

mind" with regard to the method of "historical form criticism" and for its excessive emphasis on the Vulgate;[297] and a schema by Father Congar, *De Traditione et Scriptura*, which circulated among the council fathers alongside the ones previously mentioned.

In the afternoon of October 26, 1962, Congar presented the progressive position on tradition in a conference at the French Seminary that Bishop Charue described as "incomparable," summarizing it in one line: "There are not two sources, but only one, the gospel coming from two ways."[298] Nevertheless, as Giuseppe Ruggieri observes, the main argument during the debate on *De fontibus* was not so much the one about the relations between scripture and tradition as the problem of the "pastoral character" of the Church.[299]

b) The progressive critiques of the schema

The schema on the sources of revelation was presented by Cardinal Ottaviani. It was the first time the red-robed prelate appeared again in the council hall after having been brutally reduced to silence two weeks earlier by Cardinal Alfrink. Ottaviani praised the pastoral value of the schema and ceded the floor to Monsignor Garofalo to elucidate it.[300] Garofalo spoke briefly, affirming that the schema was dogmatic, but also had pastoral value, on account of its clear exposition of the doctrine. Immediately the reaction broke loose, carefully organized by the progressive council fathers. The first to open fire was Cardinal Liénart,[301] the oldest of the cardinals, who started his intervention with the sentence, *"Hoc schema mihi non placet,"* ["This schema does not please me,"] describing the draft as incomplete, seriously deficient and too scholastic. "It was like a bomb in the nave of Saint Peter's: everyone had expected a council without incident, and now history

---

297 R. Burigana, *La Bibbia nel Concilio, op. cit.,* 92–93; G. Ruggieri, "The First Doctrinal Clash," *op. cit.*

298 Charue, *Carnets conciliaires*, 40.

299 Cf. G. Ruggieri, "La discussione sullo schema constitutionis dogmaticae *De Fontibus Revelationis* durante la I sessione del Concilio Vaticano II," in *Vatican II commence… Approches Francophones*, ed. E. Fouilloux (Louvain: Peeters, 1993), 314–328.

300 AS I/3:27–32.

301 *Ibid.*, 31–32.

had begun!"[302] He was followed by Frings,[303] Léger,[304] König,[305] Alfrink,[306] Suenens,[307] Ritter,[308] Bea,[309] and Patriarch Maximos IV Saigh,[310] all of whom said that they were categorically against the schema of the Theological Commission, describing it as "too scholastic" (Liénart), "offensive to our separated brethren" (Frings), "contrary to John XXIII's spirit of renewal" (Léger), "suffering from negativism and pessimism" (Ritter), and "lacking a pastoral character" (Bea). Cardinals Ruffini[311] and Siri,[312] on the other hand, decisively defended the document presented by Ottaviani, recalling the constitutive importance of tradition in the Catholic faith. Siri maintained that it was necessary to confirm solemnly the subject matter as it had been systematized by St. Pius X, given that the errors of modernism were still creeping through the Church.[313]

Archbishop Soegijapranata[314] of Semarang, president of the episcopal conference of Indonesia, speaking in the name of the bishops of his country, attacked not only the schema on the sources of revelation, but also the three other dogmatic constitutions. Wiltgen mentions that the large majority of the Indonesian bishops were Dutch by birth and that

---

302 Marcel Grelot, *Il rinnovamento biblico nel ventesimo secolo: Memorie di un protagonista*, with a preface by Gianfranco Ravasi, Ital. transl. (Cinisello Balsamo: San Paolo, 1996), 172.

303 AS I/3:34–36.

304 *Ibid.*, 41–42.

305 *Ibid.*, 42–43.

306 *Ibid.*, 43–45.

307 *Ibid.*, 45–47.

308 *Ibid.*, 47–48.

309 *Ibid.*, 48–51.

310 *Ibid.*, 53–55.

311 *Ibid.*, 37–38.

312 *Ibid.*, 38–39.

313 *Ibid.*

314 *Ibid.*, 58–59. Albert Soegijapranata (1895–1963), Indonesian Jesuit, ordained in 1931, archbishop of Semarang (Indonesia) from 1961 until his death.

their theological advisor was the Dutch Jesuit Pieter Smulders,[315] known for his vehement opposition to the four dogmatic constitutions.[316] The council fathers from the Netherlands maintained that the document was too negative and intolerant, and especially that it recognized not one source of revelation, but two. Father Schillebeeckx exerted on them an influence as strong as that of Father Rahner on the German bishops. The critical observations of Schillebeeckx and Smulders were utilized extensively from the very first debates.[317] The criticisms of the two theologians were in line with those of the Secretariat for Promoting Christian Unity, which, in its meetings on November 9 and 16, 1962, held at the Hotel Columbus, had devised its own plan of action, convinced, as Father Feiner[318] said, "to provide a point of doctrinal balance which the theology of Vatican II could and should take form."[319]

The debate developed in the next several General Congregations with interventions in defense of the commission's document by Cardinals Ottaviani,[320] Bacci,[321] Santos,[322] Florit,[323] Ruffini,[324] Browne,[325] and, on the

---

315 Pieter Smulders (1911–2000), Dutch Jesuit, ordained in 1939, professor at the Jesuit College in Maastricht (1943–1967), adviser to the Indonesian episcopate at Vatican II, conciliar *peritus.*

316 Wiltgen, 47.

317 G. Ruggieri, "The First Doctrinal Clash," *op. cit.*, 240

318 Joseph Feiner (1909–1985), Swiss, professor of theology at the Diocesan Seminary of Coira (1938–1962), Consultor of the Secretariat for Promoting Christian Unity.

319 G. Ruggieri, "The First Doctrinal Clash," *op. cit.*, 241–242, citation at 242.

320 AS I/3:131–132.

321 *Ibid.*, 127–128.

322 *Ibid.*, 76–79.

323 *Ibid.*, 101–104. Ermenegildo Florit (1901–1985), ordained in 1925, vice-rector and dean of the theological faculty of the Lateran University from 1951 to 1954. coadjutor bishop in 1954 and archbishop of Florence from 1962 to 1977. Created cardinal in 1965. About him, see Nicola Ciola, "Il padre Umberto Betti e il card. Ermenegildo Florit: due servitori della Chiesa al Concilio Vaticano II," in *Lateranum* 70 (2004): 181–194. Cf. R. Burigana, "Sul magistero episcopale tra Roma e Firenze: La partecipazione di Ermenegildo Florit al Vaticano II," in *Vivens Homo* 11/1 (2000): 263–300.

324 AS I/3:249–251.

325 *Ibid.*, 82–84.

opposing side, by Tisserant,[326] Döpfner,[327] Frings,[328] Silva Henríquez,[329] and by the bishop of Bruges, Bishop Emile De Smedt,[330] whom Bishop Borromeo describes as "solemnly stammering and emotionally stuttering,"[331] but with the help of "a good strong voice" and "a longing to appear to be a great orator." De Smedt, taking the floor in the name of the Secretariat for Promoting Christian Unity on November 19, stressed that the schema was particularly lacking in "ecumenical spirit" and was an obstacle to dialogue, also because it was too interwoven with scholastic formulas that are incomprehensible to the "Orthodox" brethren and to many other non-Catholics. His intervention, which resumed the one given by Bea on November 14,[332] had been agreed on at the meeting conducted three days earlier at the Hotel Columbus and was applauded by the "usual French *claque*."[333] Father Schauf reported on a meeting of German theologians that had been held on the afternoon of November 14 in these terms: "It was a conspiracy and a political gathering rather than a theological conversation."[334]

At that moment Bea was the "look-out man" for the innovators.[335] In his intervention on *De fontibus revelationis*, he, like his colleague Frings, accused the schema of not complying with the entire tradition of the

---

326 *Ibid.*, 66; 248–249.

327 *Ibid.*, 124–126.

328 *Ibid.*, 137.

329 *Ibid.*, 81–82.

330 AS I/3:184–186. Emile-Joseph De Smedt (1909–1995), ordained in 1933, bishop of Bruges from 1952 to 1984, member of the Secretariat for Promoting Christian Unity starting in October 1960.

331 Borromeo, *Diario* (November 19, 1962).

332 AS I/3:48–51.

333 Cf. Borromeo, *Diario* (November 19, 1962).

334 Cited in G. Ruggieri, "The First Doctrinal Clash," *op. cit.*, 253.

335 Congar, *Journal*, 204: "The council... is being described as turning into Cardinal Bea's council." On November 22 the Pontifical Biblical Institute, on the occasion of the doctoral thesis of N. Lohfink, organized a demonstration of support in his honor, that Congar interpreted in his journal as "a new victory for Cardinal Bea" (*ibid.*, 201).

Church, and above all of being contrary to the spirit that dominated the papal address at the opening of the council.[336]

The most articulate response from the conservatives came from Archbishop Geraldo de Proença Sigaud, who affirmed that the very serious errors condemned by Pius XII in the encylical *Humani generis* were still alive and were contaminating the Church with their poison.[337] His speech was delivered, though, in an atmosphere of murmuring and confusion, so that he lost the attention of many fathers.[338] His remarks should be recorded:

> It is not permissible, fathers of the council, to ignore or to deny this, without seriously shirking our duty.... We are dealing with a question of life or death for the Catholic Church, and also for Christianity itself. These errors are still creeping about in the Church; in particular, besides the errors in social and moral matters, there are hidden errors concerning sacred scripture and tradition, in other words, the twofold source of revelation.
>
> In the field of biblical studies, we are actually dealing, in the works of many Catholics, with the practical denial of the historical value of almost all of sacred scripture. The historical value of the whole Pentateuch is denied, and they say that Moses is in no way the author of it. The creation of man, his sin in the earthly paradise, the call of Abram, and the flood are reduced to the level of fables and legends. The vicissitudes of the Hebrew people in the desert, of the patriarchs, of Moses, and of the judges are considered simple epics, belonging to the literary genre that is called *"chansons de gestes,"* and are compared to other sagas, such as the *Niebelungenlied*, the *Chanson de Roland*, or *El Cid el Campeador*. David is a figure of the same type as Siegfried.... The stories of Judith, Esther, Ruth, and Tobias are reduced, with a sense of pity, to the genre of pious and fantastic novels, without taking into account at all the magisterium of the Church, of the holy fathers, and of tradition. The story of the prophet Jonah is relegated to the realm of fables. Nor is anything historical acknowledged in the prophets. In this immense shipwreck perhaps the only historical narratives to be rescued are the chronicle of Solomon and Nehemiah.

---

336 AS I/3:48–51.

337 *Ibid.*, 224–227.

338 Maranhão Galliez, *Diario* (November 20, 1962).

> If we look to the New Testament, here, too, almost nothing historical remains. The chapters in St. Luke about Zachariah's vision, about the Annunciation, the Visitation, and the Nativity of Christ are called poetic passages inspired by piety and imagination. The angel Gabriel supposedly was never physically present in Mary's house in the town of Nazareth. They say that these are pious narratives. What St. Matthew recounts about the conception of Christ and about the Magi meets with a fate that is no better. The Magi never came to Bethlehem from the East and did not find the Child with Mary, his Mother. Allegedly the famous scene of St. Peter's profession of faith in Caesarea, which is absolutely fundamental for the Catholic faith, was thoroughly fabricated to justify the primacy of Peter. It is said that the resurrection of Christ must be considered as a Hellenistic apotheosis.
>
> These principles are not taught only by non-Catholic scholars. They are preached to our nuns in conferences and at conventions. They are handed on to our seminarians as true exegesis. They are faithfully introduced in Catholic periodicals. Even in this august city of Rome, they are presented authoritatively to us bishops as the most recent results of true hermeneutics.
>
> This is a reality that it is not permissible to ignore. All this demonstrates the urgent need for some magisterial act of the council that would put an end to such a vast and inauspicious confusion of doctrine and of souls.[339]

That evening Father Congar was invited to speak at the *Collegio Capranica*, where Archbishop Calabria of Benevento was also residing; the latter took part in the lively debate, accusing the speaker of modernism. The young seminarians frantically applauded Congar, but the superiors of the College prudently cancelled the next conference, for which they had invited Rahner.[340]

c) "The crime" of November 20

When it came up for a vote on November 20, something happened that Bishop Borromeo calls "the crime" [*"il fattaccio"*].[341] The Board of Presidency decided to put to a vote this question: "Should the discussion

---

339 AS I/3:225–226.

340 Cf. M. Guasco, *Una giornata di Vaticano II, op. cit.*, 455–460.

341 Borromeo, *Diario* (November 20, 1962).

of the dogmatic schema *De fontibus revelationis* be interrupted?"[342] The confusion resulted from the fact that someone who was in favor of the schema would have to vote *"non placet"* in order to continue the discussion; anyone against it would have to vote *"placet"* to have the document withdrawn and shelved. Many of those who were in favor of the schema, but had not understood the mechanism, voted *"placet,"* not realizing that they had thereby said the opposite. "I think that anyone who reads these notes in a few years," Bishop Borromeo wrote in his *Diary*, "will have difficulty believing that in an ecumenical council a stubborn faction was so intent on imposing its point of view by all means that it would resort to these subterfuges."[343] In the assembly there was a great commotion. Even the cardinals left their position and could be seen debating rancorously.[344] Despite the attempt to force the situation, the result was that out of a total of 2,209 fathers, 1,368 of them voted in favor of suspension, 822 (or 868) were against, and there were nineteen invalid ballots. Since the vote was on an adjournment so as to skip the schema, a two-thirds majority was needed, and the progressives were 105 votes short of reaching it. In the absence of such a majority according to the rule, the schema should be considered approved. Once again, however, the procedure was forced so as to keep to the predetermined course.

This time the decisive intervention was by John XXIII. On November 21 Bishop Felici asked to take the floor and announced to the council fathers that the pope had decided to have the schema *De fontibus Revelationis* withdrawn and to have it reworked by an *ad hoc* commission made up of members of different opinions, before resuming the debate. Cardinal Bea's secretary, Father Stjepan Schmidt, testifies that the pope had charged Bea with "sounding out" several cardinals, and after speaking with Liénart and Frings, Bea had advised the pope to postpone the schema.[345] Despite the perplexity of Cardinal Cicognani, John XXIII wanted to manifest with this decision the trust that he placed in Cardinal Bea and in the secretariat.[346] The pope, Father Martina comments, "took note of the unexpected situation that had been created, gave up the naïve hope of concluding the

---

342 AS I/3:220–222.

343 Borromeo, *Diario* (November 20, 1962).

344 Cf. Edelby, *Diario*, 114.

345 Cf. Schmidt, *Bea*, 458–459.

346 Cf. S. Schmidt, "Giovanni XXIII e il Segretario per l'Unione dei cristiani," *op. cit.* 109–113.

assembly by Christmas, played along, and allowed the innovating forces to have free rein."[347] This however was a procedural decision that plainly violated the council rules and imposed an "obligatory" direction on the workers. It had one important psychological consequence: the pope himself was sanctioning the possibility of the council fathers rejecting a schema proposed by the Roman commissions.[348] "The importance of the vote of November 20 and of the papal intervention on November 21," Father O'Malley observes, "can hardly be exaggerated."[349] According to Robert Roquette, "It can be said that with this vote on November 20, the counter-reformation era was concluded and a new era began for Christianity that would have unforeseeable consequences."[350] "At the *Salvator Mundi*," the institute where a good-sized number of council fathers resided, "all are joyful," Bishop Edelby noted, "because I must say that in this boarding-house we are all avant-garde progressives: Americans, Germans, Africans, and Orientals."[351]

The psychological effect of the "turn of events" on November 21 was enormous. The progressives, strengthened by the pope's support, although constituting a minority, felt for the first time that they were a "majority."[352] That evening, the Dutch editor Paul Brand went to visit Karl Rahner at the Gregorianum to propose to him the creation of a progressive international journal. The next day, Brand obtained the support of Küng and Schillebeeckx. The "theological trio" Rahner-Küng-Schillebeeckx would constitute the nucleus of the journal *Concilium*, which started publication in 1965.[353]

---

[347] G. Martina, *La Chiesa in Italia negli ultimi trent'anni* (Rome: Edizioni Studium, 1977), 90.

[348] Wilde, 22.

[349] John W. O'Malley, *What Happened at Vatican II, op. cit.*, 151. According to the French historian Étienne Fouilloux, this signaled that "the phase of antimodernist reaction is truly coming to an end" (*Une Église en quête de liberté, op. cit.* 310). "The victory won by the majority thanks to the papal intervention decided the orientation of the council and of its future" (P. Levillain, *La mécanique politique, op. cit.*, 260).

[350] Robert Roquette, *La fin d'une chrétienté: Chroniques I* (Paris: Cerf, 1968), 259.

[351] Edelby, *Diario*, 117.

[352] "[T]he outcome of the schema on the sources of revelation heartened progressives and solidified the newfound sense among council participants that change was possible." Wilde, 22.

[353] Küng, *My Struggle*, 299.

Four days later, *L'Osservatore Romano* announced "a Joint Commission" to revise the schema (no longer entitled 'On the Sources of Revelation" but rather "On Divine Revelation") that would be composed of members of the Theological Commission, the Secretariat for Promoting Christian Unity, and other fathers and cardinals.[354] The council thereby recognized and institutionalized the need to take ecumenical requests into account, even in the absence of a majority of votes. The commission had two presidents with opposing views: Ottaviani and Bea; four progressive members, Cardinals Liénart, Frings, Meyer, and Lefebvre, and two conservatives, Ruffini and Browne. The solution by way of a mixed commission bore "Bea's imprint."[355]

On November 24, nineteen cardinals, among them Antoniutti, Bacci, Marella, Ottaviani, Ruffini, Siri, and Traglia, expressed to the pope their concern in a letter asking him to "safeguard the Catholic faith against the errors and deviations that have spread almost everywhere."[356]

On the evening of November 27, in the course of the usual meeting of the Italian Episcopate at the Domus Mariae, Cardinal Siri confided to Bishop Borromeo. "There are three," he said, raising his hand with the first three fingers spread out and the others folded, like the pope when he gives a blessing, "there are three, at most four persons who are waging war and causing nasty weather at the council, with the help of a clientele and an organization that unfortunately we do not have. But I am on the look-out: I speak little in the hall, but in other settings I speak a lot and make them listen, you can be sure of that!"[357] Cardinal Siri's voice, unfortunately would be drowned out by the voice of the theologians and the progressive council fathers, amplified by the mass media.

The *International Press Review* of the Press Office of the Holy See (n. 561, 23 November 1962) reported the repercussions of the conciliar debates in newspapers all over the world, highlighting some headlines such as those in the *Times* ("Modernists in action at the Vatican Council") and the November 15 issue of the *New York Herald Tribune* ("Vatican II divided on theology"). The November 16 issue of the *Frankfurter Allgemeine Zeitung* went so far as to speak of the "birth pangs" in which the council was finding

[354] G. Ruggieri, "The First Doctrinal Clash," *op. cit.,* 264–265.

[355] John W. O'Malley, *What Happened at Vatican II, op. cit.*, 150.

[356] F. Stabile, "Il cardinal Ruffini e il Vaticano II," *op. cit.*, 124–126.

[357] Borromeo, *Diario* (November 27, 1962).

its format, whereas according to the *Süddeutsche Zeitung* that same day, the predictions that the council would mean decisive progress for the Church were coming true.

10. Discussion on the constitution of the Church

a) The various schemas brought to the hall

November 23, the day when the 25th General Congregation opened, was a decisive date. Indeed, on that day three different schemas treating similar subjects were distributed to the council fathers: a bulky schema on the Church prepared by the Theological Commission, with an outline for a constitution on the Blessed Virgin Mary as an appendix, a schema containing a chapter entitled *De oecumenismo*, and a schema on Catholic ecumenism prepared by the Secretariat for Promoting Christian Unity.

The Theological Commission's schema, extolled by Archbishop Primo Principi,[358] was attacked by most of the speakers who intervened, who proposed that the three documents should be combined into only one schema. The promoters of ecumenical dialogue were in complete disagreement with the chapter on ecumenism prepared by the Theological Commission, and in order to get it changed they asked that it be integrated into the other two schemas. The maneuver succeeded. In the twenty-seventh General Congregation, held on November 26, the secretary general announced that there would not be debate on the schema *De unitate ecclesiae*, the one *De ecclesia,* and the one *De Beata Maria Virgine*,[359] with a view to merging the three documents into one schema. The formation of a group including Cardinal Ottaviani, Cardinal Bea, president of the Secretariat for Promoting Christian Unity, and Cardinal Cicognani to formulate a new combined text, would inevitably lead to a compromise, as it then happened, considerably reducing the influence of the text composed by the Theological Commission.[360]

With Cardinal Tisserant presiding, a discussion began on the schema *De unitate ecclesiae*, about which there were differences of opinion. The

358 AS I/3:621–622. Primo Principi (1894–1975), ordained in 1918, titular archbishop of Tyana, bursar and secretary of the Fabric of Saint Peter's from 1952 to 1969.

359 AS I/3:501–502.

360 Wiltgen, 53.

last six sessions, starting on December 1, 1962, were dedicated to the discussion of the draft document on the Church, drawn up by a sub-commission in 1961 and forwarded to the central Theological Commission in 1962.[361] The schema was made up of eleven dense chapters: the nature of the Church Militant; its members and the necessity of the Church for salvation; the episcopate as the highest degree of the sacrament of Holy Orders; residential bishops; the states of evangelical perfection; the laity; the ecclesiastical magisterium; authority and obedience in the Church; relations between Church and state; the need to proclaim the gospel throughout the world; ecumenism.

As early as October 15, Cardinal Suenens had asked the theologian Gérard Philips[362] to compose a new text of the schema *De Ecclesia*. Philips had worked on it secretly with the collaboration of several theologians that he trusted, such as Congar, Colombo,[363] Rahner, Ratzinger, Semmelroth, McGrath,[364] unbeknownst to the Preparatory Theological Commission,[365] but the document had fallen into the hands of the secretary of the

---

[361] Cf. A. Acerbi, *Due ecclesiologie, op. cit.*

[362] Gérard Philips (1899–1972), Belgian priest, professor of Dogmatic Theology on the Faculty of Theology in Louvain, consultor of the Preparatory Theological Commission, appointed conciliar *peritus* in 1962, became adjunct secretary of the Doctrinal Commission of the Council in 1963. About him, see *Actes et Acteurs*, 382–419; J. Grootaers, "Le rôle de Mgr Philips à Vatican II: Quelques réflexions pour contribuer à l'étude du dernier Concile," in *Ecclesia a Spiritu Sancto edocta: Mélanges théologiques: Hommage à Gérard Philips*, ed. Albert Descamps (Gembloux: Duculot, 1970), 343–380; Cesare Antonelli, "Le rôle de Mgr Gérard Philips dans la rédaction du chapitre VIII de 'Lumen gentium,'" in *Marianum* 55 (1993): 17–97.

[363] Carlo Colombo (1909–1991), ordained in 1931, member of the Preparatory Theological Commission, *peritus* of Cardinal Montini (1962–1963) as of March 7, 1964, participated in the last two sessions (1964–1965) as a council father. In 1962 became president of the Pontifical Theological Faculty in Milan. From 1964 to 1985 was auxiliary bishop of Milan. About him, see Grootaers, *I protagonisti*, 83–102; *Actes et Acteurs*, 287–300; F. G. Brambilla, "Carlo Colombo e G. B. Montini alle sorgenti del concilio," in *La Scuola Cattolica* 130 (2002): 221–260. See also Antonio Rimoldi, "Mons. Carlo Colombo (1909–1991): Bibliografia," in *La Scuola Cattolica* 119 (1991): 283–300.

[364] Marcos Gregorio McGrath (1924–2000), American ordained in 1949, auxiliary bishop of Panama (1961), bishop of Santiago de Veraguas (1964), archbishop of Panama from 1969 to 1994. Member of the Doctrinal Commission. Cf. Grootaers, *I protagonisti*, 185–194.

[365] Philips, *Carnets conciliaires*, 82–86.

Theological Commission, Tromp, causing him to become irritated. It was decidedly disloyal for a theologian to work secretly on an alternative to the text by the same commission of which he was a member and consultant.[366] Philips was aware of the incorrectness of the initiative. "The work," he noted, "is so to speak secret.... I foresee that at some point the matter will become known and that I will be in a very inconvenient situation. But I cannot refuse this service requested by the Belgian episcopate."[367]

b) The full-scale attack on the Theological Commission's schema

On December 1, when Cardinal Ottaviani in his capacity as president of the Theological Commission extolled the document in the hall, he explained that it had been composed by thirty-six experts, with an additional thirty-six consultants from fifteen different nations, most of them university professors or instructors in major international ecclesiastical institutions. To forestall criticism, Ottaviani declared in his intervention: "The concern of the authors of the schema was to prepare a document that would be as pastoral and biblical as possible, not academic, and written in a form comprehensible to all. I say this because I expect to hear the usual litanies of the council fathers: it is scholastic, it is not ecumenical, it is not pastoral, it is negative, and so forth. Well, I must tell you a secret: before this schema was distributed—listen, listen!—before it was made public, a substitute schema was already being circulated! Hence it had already been judged *ante praevisa merita* [independently of its merits]. There is nothing left to do but to remain silent, because scripture teaches us, *'Ubi non est auditus, noli effundere sermonem'* ['Where there is no hearing, pour not out words,' Ecclesiasticus 32:6 Douay Rheims]."[368]

That is what happened promptly. Edelby mentions that "Cardinal Lienart[369] fired the first cannon shot. The schema—he says—conceives of the Church merely as a human institution, whereas she is a mystery and the sacrament of all the nations. In particular he asked that the Roman Church

366 *Ibid.*, 82.

367 *Ibid.*, 82.

368 AS I/4:121.

369 *Ibid.*, 126–127.

and the Mystical Body of Christ not be identified. At least in heaven—he says—the Mystical Body and the Roman Church fortunately will not be identified."[370] Other speakers reproached the commission's document for being one-sided, apologetic, legalistic, scholastic, not ecumenical, and not sufficiently "pastoral."[371] The most vehement was Bishop De Smedt, who "with a prosecutorial tone and bearing,"[372] accused the schema of three serious faults: Roman triumphalism, clericalism, and legalism.[373] "Of triumphalism because the Church, at one point, is called *agmen*, an army on the march; of clericalism because first it speaks about bishops, then about priests and then about the laity; of legalism—I no longer know why," Bishop Borromeo reports. "I know that it was a wretched reason and that not even the French had the courage this time to applaud the fiery speaker, who in vain dawdled over collecting his papers, expecting an expulsion that did not occur."[374] "One would not have expected to see clericalism attacked in a council of bishops!" Edelby noted for his part.[375]

Bishop De Smedt's accusations summed up the usual remarks against the Roman curia, which were destined to re-echo countless times within the council hall and beyond. The Belgian bishop was backed up by Cardinals Döpfner[376] and Léger,[377] who used seemingly more moderate tones but were no less decisive in their substance; they in turn were supported by Cardinals Suenens,[378] Frings,[379] Bea,[380] and Montini.[381] Frings went so far as to maintain that the document was not "Catholic," because

---

370 Edelby, *Diario*, 131.

371 A. Acerbi, *Due ecclesiologie, op. cit.*, 154–166.

372 Borromeo, *Diario* (December 1, 1962).

373 AS I/4:142–144.

374 Borromeo, *Diario* (December 1, 1962).

375 Edelby, *Diario*, 132.

376 AS I/4:183–186.

377 *Ibid.*, 182–183.

378 *Ibid.*, 222–225.

379 *Ibid.*, 218–220.

380 *Ibid.*, 227–230.

381 *Ibid.*, 291–294.

it did not cite the fathers of the Church and the medieval theologians, but only post-Tridentine theology. Even though Father Tromp reckoned that the number of interventions in the hall against the schema was smaller than the number of interventions in favor (40 against 55), the fate of the schema was already sealed.[382]

On December 4 Cardinal Suenens presented the main themes of an alternative draft, which had been formulated in the circles of the University of Louvain and discussed in a private meeting at the Belgian College in Rome. The document was subdivided into two parts: the first, *Ecclesia ad intra*, was to speak about the internal reality of the Church; the second, *Ecclesia ad extra*, about the dialogue between the Church and the modern world. Father John F. Kobler mentions that the University of Louvain had been imbued, since the 1930s, with the phenomenological ideas of Husserl and Heidegger, and the outline by Suenens, rector of that university from 1940 to 1945, echoed those ideas in the distinction *ad intra/ad extra*, "which refers not so much to the internal things of the mind in their relations with the things of the external world, as to the way in which ideas settle down in our consciousness."[383] Suenens' suggestion was destined to become the basis for the constitution *Lumen gentium*.

On December 5, Cardinal Montini made his second intervention at the council to express his full support of Suenens' project.[384] The most important point of this speech is the passage in which the Cardinal of Milan asked for the development of a new theology of the episcopal body, echoing themes dear to Cardinal Alfrink,[385] and signaling to the progressive alignment that he was in fact *"papabile."*[386] Cardinal König recalls: "I, with my whole group, Suenens, Döpfner, Liénart, Frings, met the archbishop of Milan often, for an exchange and in-depth discussion of ideas: he was entirely on our side."[387]

---

382 A. Acerbi, *Due ecclesiologie, op. cit.*, 159.

383 J. F. Kobler, "Were theologians the Engineers of Vatican II?" *op. cit.*, 238.

384 AS I/4:291–294. On this intervention, cf. *Actes et Acteurs*, 46–50.

385 *Actes et Acteurs*, 48–49.

386 Küng, *My Struggle*, 300

387 F. König, *Chiesa dove vai?, op. cit.* 24–25.

11. Toward a new leadership

Meanwhile Father Jedin and Father Dossetti continued working to change the rules of the council so as to weaken the power of the Roman curia. On November 25 Giuseppe Alberigo, a close collaborator with Dossetti, brought to de Lubac the document "Provisions with a view to participation between the first and second session of the council." The draft, which provided for the limitation of the powers of the presidents of commissions and the institution of a coordinating body during the period between one session and the next, was presented by Cardinal Döpfner to the pope in early December. Starting in those days the new leadership of the council emerged, which Grootaers called "the Decembrists," because they had taken the floor and spoken along the same lines during the first days of December: Montini, Suenens, Léger, Lercaro, Döpfner.[388] On December 6, John XXIII ordered the institution of a commission responsible for coordinating and directing the business of the council. Members included Cardinals Confalonieri,[389] Döpfner, Liénart, Spellman, Suenens, and Urbani; the Cardinal Secretary of State Cicognani became the president and Bishop Felici was secretary. The "European alliance," Wiltgen emphasizes, was represented on the commission by three authoritative members (Liénart, Döpfner, Suenens) who therefore held fifty percent of the votes. Only one conservative, Spellman, was included, but he was moderate. Urbani and Confalonieri belonged to the "Third Party." Cicognani and Felici, who were also moderate conservatives, faithfully followed papal instructions. Döpfner and Suenens were the only ones to participate in this strategic planning body from the start of the council to the finish.

Besides creating the commission, John XXIII approved several norms that were to regulate the council between the first two sessions. The first of these norms determined that in such periods all the schemas would be "examined once again and improved" by the conciliar commissions.

The new rule went into effect only with Paul VI, on September 13, 1963. In this way the role of the Preparatory Commissions was

---

388 *Actes et Acteurs*, 304.

389 Carlo Confalonieri (1893–1986), ordained in 1916, bishop of Aquila in 1941, had arrived in Rome as personal secretary of Pius XI. Created cardinal in 1958, then as of March 1961 served as secretary of the Sacred Consistorial Congregation. About him see S. Garofalo, *Il cardinale Carlo Confalonieri (1893–1986)* (Rome: Studium, 1993).

reorganized and a body was created that interpreted more directly the guidelines that Pope John intended to impose on the council. This was a new defeat of the curia.[390]

On that same day, December 6, Cardinal Lercaro, in a "programmatic" speech, asserted that Vatican II would have to be above all the council of the "Church of the poor." "This is the hour of the poor," the archbishop of Bologna declared, "of the millions of poor people all over the world; this is the hour of the mystery of the Church, mother of the poor; this is the hour of the mystery of Christ especially in the poor…. This is not just any theme, but in a certain sense the only theme of the whole Vatican Council."[391] The theme of the "Church of the poor," which was destined to turn into the "preferential option" for the poor, was officially launched.

12. The role of the means of social communication

From the very first day, the Second Vatican Council was a "media event."[392] Italian state television transmitted images of it, which were then rebroadcast by the major television stations of Europe and the world. The impact of these images on public opinion was very strong. One contemporary historian observes:

> Public opinion, etymologically speaking, is the opinion of philosophers and learned people who think in public. Can anyone deny, then, that it played a supporting role in a council that was, as we can deduce with irrefutable proofs from these volumes, to a great extent a council of theologians, *periti*, and commissions that worked by not infrequently getting the upper hand over an absent, distracted assembly that ultimately was also rather tired in the most trivial sense of the word? Besides the innovations in the documents, the revolution of the council occurred on this level and, as was inevitable, both those who looked forward to it and those who fought against it contributed to it. With the event itself, which is ineradicable, they had entered into this new phase, and with

[390] Wiltgen, 57–58.

[391] AS I/4:327–330; Italian text in G. Lercaro, *Per la forza dello spirito, op. cit.*, 114–115.

[392] Thus for example, E. Poulat, "La modernité à l'heure du Vatican II," in *Le deuxième Concile du Vatican*, 809–826 at 821.

> respect to this revolutionary event the documents that were produced have the importance of all the laws, which are the most malleable, adaptable, and transformable ordinances that exist.[393]

Something historical was happening in Rome, and it was necessary to be informed. News organizations from all over the world sent their correspondents to the Eternal City. Archbishop Lefebvre relates that one day when he asked Cardinal Garrone how a "good" council could have produced such bad fruits, the latter replied: "It is not the council, it is the means of social communication."[394]

The information problem had been addressed by the Holy See during the preparatory phase of the council. On October 30, 1959, during a press conference attended by more than one hundred journalists, Cardinal Tardini announced that a press office would be created to provide journalists with "precise, up-to-date information on the various phases of the council." The office was inaugurated on April 18, 1961, and began to act as mouthpiece for the preconciliar Central Commission. On October 5 of the following year, six days before the start of the proceedings, Cardinal Cicognani, Secretary of State, blessed the new *Sala Stampa* [Press Office] of the council. On October 12 it was announced that an Italian prelate, Bishop Fausto Vallainc,[395] had been appointed to head the office. Over the course of the four sessions, 176 news bulletins and 141 monographs [special studies] in ten languages were issued.[396]

The first problem on the agenda was confidentiality. Pius IX, in 1869, had ordered the participants in the First Vatican Council to observe complete and absolute secrecy about the assembly's business. In the Second Vatican Council the question of confidentiality was discussed in three articles of the internal rules of the council, approved by the pope two months before it opened. Art. 26 imposed secrecy on the council fathers, art. 27 extended it to the experts, the staff, and everyone who worked at the council,

---

393 P. Pombeni, "Sulla 'rivoluzione' del Vaticano II," in *Cristianesimo nella storia* 23 (2003): 813–822 at 821.

394 Conversation on February 13, 1975, cited in M. Lefebvre, *They Have Uncrowned Him: From Liberalism to Apostasy: The Conciliar Tragedy* (Dickinson, TX: Angelus Press, 1988), xv-xvi.

395 Angelo Fausto Vallainc (1916–1986), ordained in 1940, bishop of Frigento in 1970 and of Alba in 1975.

396 Wiltgen, 30.

while art. 18 applied it to the non-Catholic observers from the Christian churches. The confidentiality to which the participants in the council were bound was not kept however by the Vatican Press Office, which in its press releases, and especially in its informal meetings with journalists, allowed plenty of information about the proceedings to filter out.

The ecclesiastical hierarchies of the various countries soon organized news and documentation centers for their own bishops. Jan Grootaers has documented the role of the *"Rencontres Internationales d'Informations Religieuses"* (RIIR),[397] an informal *"réseau"* ["network"] of journalists that originated in 1961 in Paris. The RIIR played a role not only as a "news source" but also as a "drive belt" to transmit to the top ecclesiastics the *"desiderata"* of the base structures and to "reassure" the periphery about what was happening at the "center."[398]

This attention to the means of social communication was fostered by the young secretary of John XXIII, Don Loris Capovilla. Editor of the diocesan newspaper of Vicenza and correspondent for Catholic newspapers, Capovilla contributed to the creation of the media image of "good Pope John." He persuaded the pope and the Secretary of State to introduce television cameras into the papal apartments so as to tell in pictures the story of how John XXIII spent his days. This novelty aroused strong misgivings in the curia, but it also revealed the role played by Capovilla, who had assumed the unheard-of title of "personal secretary" to the pope.[399]

The newspapers offered some correspondents a tool with which to influence, by their reports, the progress of the council business and then to shape the historical interpretation of the event with the volumes that collected their reportage: Father Antoine Wenger in *La Croix*, Raniero La Valle[400] in *Avvenire d'Italia*, Henri Fesquet[401] in *Le Monde*, Reverend

---

397 Cf. *Actes et Acteurs*, 116–182.

398 *Ibid.*, 179–180.

399 Cf. B. Lai, *I segreti del Vaticano da Pio XII a papa Wojtyla* (Bari: Laterza, 1984), 50–51.

400 Raniero La Valle (1931–) was editor of *Il Popolo* until he was recruited to edit the daily Catholic newspaper in Bologna, *L'Avvenire d'Italia* (1961–1967). After pledging to promote the introduction of divorce in Italy, he became in 1967 senator of the independent left. About him see *Il coraggio del Concilio* (Brescia: Morcelliana, 1964) on the 2nd session; *Fedeltà al Concilio* (Brescia: Morcelliana, 1965) on the 3rd session; *Il Concilio nelle nostre mani* (Brescia: Morcelliana, 1966) on the 4th session.

401 Henri Fesquet (1916–1982), French journalist, correspondent of the daily newspaper *Le Monde.*

René Laurentin[402] in *Le Figaro*, and the American Redemptorist Francis X. Murphy, under the pseudonym Xavier Rynne,[403] in *The New Yorker Magazine*. Giancarlo Zizola tells of how during the council "some people perhaps in the Secretariat of State itself—Archbishop Dell'Acqua, for example, who acted in concert with Monsignor Capovilla—worked discreetly to promote the flow of information."[404] Thanks to this discreet help, Zizola managed to become an unofficial, alternative news source for the network of Italian Catholic newspapers and for *Il Messaggero* of Rome. Every day he had an appointment, in the early hours of the afternoon, with the bishop of Verona, Giuseppe Carraro, who, thanks to his personal relations with Cardinal Montini and Archbishop Dell'Acqua, conveyed to him all the information needed to reconstruct the sessions. Using the same method followed by Bishop Carraro with Zizola, Archbishop Jean Villot,[405] future Secretary of State of Paul VI, held a meeting every afternoon with the editors of the newspaper *La Croix*, Antoine Wenger and Jean Pélissier, to whom he transmitted first-hand information about what happened in the most private commissions also.[406] At the start of the second session, Paul VI authorized Wenger to attend the sessions of the council, without binding him to secrecy.[407]

---

[402] René Laurentin (1917–), French theologian, ordained in 1946, professor at the Catholic University of Angers and vice president of the Society of French Studies on Mary (1962). Editorialist and Rome correspondent for *Le Figaro* during the council. See his five-volume work, *L'enjeu du Concile* (Paris: Seuil, 1962–1966), and *Mémoires: Chemin vers la Lumière* (Paris: Fayard, 2005), in which pages 377–452 are dedicated to the council, and pages 453–556 to the post-conciliar period.

[403] Xavier Rynne was the pseudonym of the Redemptorist Francis X. Murphy (1915–2002), journalist and instructor at the *Accademia alfonsiana*, where he taught patristics and missiology. See Xavier Rynne, *Letters from Vatican City*, 5 vols. (New York: Farrar-Straus and Company, 1963–1965).

[404] G. Zizola, *La Chiesa nei media* (Turin: SEI, 1996), 675.

[405] Jean Villot (1905–1979), ordained in 1930, general secretary of the French episcopate (1950) and auxiliary bishop of Paris (1954), coadjutor archbishop with the right of succession in Lyons (1959). Participated in Vatican Council II as an undersecretary. Then was promoted as archbishop of Lyons and created cardinal by Paul VI in 1965. In 1969 he became Secretary of State, and the following year *camerlengo* of the Holy Roman Church.

[406] Cf. A. Wenger, *Le cardinal Villot (1905–1979)* (Paris: Desclée de Brouwer, 1989), 37–38, 41–42; G. Zizola, *La Chiesa nei media, op. cit.*, 676.

[407] Cf. R. Aubert, "Organizzazione e funzionamento dell'assemblea," *op. cit.*, 226.

Among those who exerted a major influence on the council we should mention Henri Fesquet, correspondent for *Le Monde*, who provided an almost daily news report. "Many people," Father Beozzo recalls, "preferred the platform of *Le Monde* to the platform of the council hall to transmit their ideas, concerns or dreams."[408] Bishop Câmara, who considered him a close friend, made use of him to propagate his ideas. "I tell him what I want him to say in *Le Monde*," he declared. "There are indiscretions that help the council. Sometimes a headline in the press is enough to open up certain breaches…."[409]

The major newspapers and the television networks informed in a timely fashion not only the general public, but also many members of the council, frequently offering, as Alberigo observes, "an interpretive key to the significance of the individual sessions, which often escaped many of the fathers themselves."[410] "Nor was it by chance," Melloni notes, "that one of the first actions of Lercaro as 'moderator' was to ask and obtain from the Secretary of State that *L'Avvenire d'Italia*, the Bologna daily edited by Raniero La Valle, be sent to all the fathers, subscriptions being paid by the Vatican for the entire period."[411]

The council entered into the news cycle, institutionally as well, after the appointment of a "Press Committee" by Paul VI.[412] "Vatican II," Laurentin writes, "had roused religion news to a new style, while it opened the Church to a new relation with the world."[413]

13. "Some fresh air in the Church"

John XXIII celebrated his 81st birthday on Saturday, November 25, 1962, at the Collegio Urbano of the Propaganda Fide, celebrating Mass for the 320 students who had gathered there from all parts of the world.

---

[408] J. O. Beozzo, *op. cit.*, 135.

[409] Câmara, *Lettres Conciliaires*, 2:877.

[410] G. Alberigo, "Transizione epocale," *op. cit.* 799.

[411] Alberto Melloni, "The Beginning of the Second Period: The Great Debate on the Church," in HVT 3:1–116 at 32; Norman Tanner, "The Church in the World (*Ecclesia ad extra*)," *Ibid.*, 270–387 at 330.

[412] Cf. Annibale Zambarbieri, *I Concili del Vaticano* (Cinisello Balsamo: San Paolo, 1995), 260.

[413] R. Laurentin, "L'information au Concile," in *Le deuxième Concile du Vatican*, 359–378 at 363.

In his speech, Papa Roncalli stressed that he was convinced that God was guiding the council.

The month of November had been particularly tiresome for him. Besides his ordinary duties, he had had to receive in audience thirty-six episcopal conferences, in other words two per day, except Sundays. Few people knew that he was under strict medical supervision at the time, because of frequent hemorrhages. The night after his birthday he experienced loss of blood once again, which forced him to cancel his audiences. He remained in bed for eight days, but rallied to preside at the closing ceremonies of the first session on December 8.

In late October of 1962 a top-secret meeting had been held at the Vatican: a collegial consultation with four leading Italian surgeons, Pietro Valdoni, Achille Dogliotti, Ettore Ruggieri, and Paride Stefanini, who, after examining the pope, had diagnosed cancer of the stomach and recommended an operation.[414] But the pope postponed the surgical procedure, continuing to attend ceremonies and to follow the business of the commissions.

On December 5, at midday, John XXIII appeared at his window to recite the Angelus, and many council fathers left the hall so as to be able to see him. The pope, weary, spoke briefly and gave his blessing.

Chenu relates that the non-Catholic observers, including those from Moscow, during a private conversation, had asked John XXIII what he expected from the council. The pope had then opened the window, saying, "This: some fresh air in the Church."[415] The episode, which went back to the month of October, was reported also by Hans Küng when, in early December, he was invited to speak to the U.S. bishops' press panel. During the meeting, without revealing the names of the pope's guests, he related that, turning to the person who asked him why he had convened the council, John XXIII had gone to the window of his apartment, had opened it and said, "Let's let a bit of fresh air into the Church." The theologian Küng, not concealing his joy, declared that what until then had been the dream of a small, avant-garde group "had spread and permeated the entire atmosphere of the Church, due to the council." "Perhaps," he added, "the most decisive outcome of the first session is the realization on the part of the bishops that they, and not merely the Roman curia, make up the Church."[416]

---

[414] Cf. B. Lai, *I segreti del Vaticano, op. cit.*, 68–74.

[415] Chenu, *Diario*, 73.

[416] Wiltgen, 59–60.

The slogan about the "breath of fresh air" from then on entered into circulation as a symbol of the necessary *"aggiornamento"* and "rejuvenation" of the Church. For John XXIII, evidently, Monsignor Gherardini comments, the air that circulated within the Church until the eve of the council was not fresh air. "One could even think that for him—and certainly not for him alone—it was heavy and stifling."[417]

14. Assessment of the first session

The first session was by far the most important one of the council, because it imprinted upon it the direction that it would maintain until the conclusion of its business. "In a tumultuous first few weeks," Melissa Wilde observes, "through a combination of protest events and hard-won votes, progressives succeeded in changing the course of the council and building an organizational structure which would serve them well in the years ahead."[418]

Cardinal Siri's assessment of the proceedings during the first period was disturbing.

> The council revealed: that an ambiguous management of the Church is emerging, represented by the German-language group and its friends and neighbors. It is also organized *aliquatenus* [to some extent]. This is an extremely biased attempt, about which one cannot say with certainty that someone has it in mind as a clear, deliberate plan, yet it exists in fact;
>
> a) that there are furious attacks against reason, theology and law. One can see the purpose of kerygmalism, which is often to eliminate tradition, the Church, etc. This is more unconscious than conscious, but it is abetted by the lack of insight of those who absolutely want to adapt everything as much as possible to the protestants, to the Orthodox, etc.
>
> b) that in the great majority of cases literature prevails over theology. Many beautiful and even true dissertations belong to the genre of literary reflections on dogma, but not *per se* to dogma itself;
>
> c) that there is talk about a *theologia nova* [new theology] and that the concept thereof, as well as its purpose, seem rather obscure and

417 B. Gherardini, *The Ecumenical Vatican Council II*, op. cit., 37.

418 Wilde, 17.

> perhaps dangerous. The term *Theologia nova* was coined by a Belgian bishop at the council.[419]

The climate typical of this first phase of the debate has been described by Melissa Wilde as "collective effervescence."[420] With this expression the sociologist Durkheim describes "the state in which men find themselves when … they believe they have been swept up into a world entirely different from the one they have before their eyes."[421] This state of mind, from a sociological perspective, is the result of the interpersonal relations of a vast group of people who find themselves together for the first time and, in a climate of euphoria, attribute a meaning to their "being together." "It is a euphoric state," Wilde explains, "a result of individuals gathering together, in this case, to worship, to discuss, and to engage in changing an ancient institution in which they all fervently believed."[422]

The phenomenon is well known to historians. Ronald A. Knox outlined a penetrating history of "religious enthusiasm,"[423] demonstrating that the model of "charismatic enthusiasm" has been a recurring model from the

---

[419] Siri, *Diario*, 383. The items of concern singled out by Cardinal Siri in a letter to Bishop Alberto Castelli, secretary of the Italian Episcopal Conference, were as follows: "1. Antipathy if not outright hatred toward theology. 2. Proposal of a new theology. 3. Proposal of a new method for theology. 4. Predominance of oratorical and literary discourse, comparable to musical variations on a theme, over serious, rational statement and theological deduction. 5. An ecstatic infatuation with new words and new paradigms for very common, ancient 'words,' which are assumed, however, to reveal something that is also considered 'new' and 'better.' 6. 'Collegiality' in the Church: I suspect that it aims to reduce the primacy and to slip a democratic principle into the constitution of the hierarchical Church. 7. The *congubernium* [joint governance] of the Church. 8. The solemn magisterium alone. 9. The charismatic action of the Holy Spirit. 10. The divine tradition evaporates. 11. The subordination of biblical exegesis to the data or postulates of rationalistic criticism. 12. Everything must be subordinate to 'pastoral care.' 13. Everything must be subordinate to the 'ecumenical' goal. 14. One must respond to the expectations of the world" (Siri to Castelli, January 1, 196[3], cited in N. Buonasorte, *Siri: Tradizione e Novecento, op. cit.*, 291).

[420] Wilde, 22–26; J. A. Coleman, "Vatican II as a Social Movement," *op. cit.*, 12–19.

[421] Wilde, 24.

[422] *Ibid.*

[423] Ronald A. Knox, *Enthusiasm: a chapter in the history of religion, with special reference to the XVII and XVIII centuries* (New York: Oxford University Press, 1950).

times of the Montanist heresy. The letters of Bishop Helder Câmara seem to present a typical example of this climate of self-exaltation which, with not much spiritual discernment, was attributed to the intervention of the "Holy Spirit."[424] It is not surprising that many bishops, interviewed by Father Rocco Caporale during the council, traced back to the "Holy Spirit" their personal experience of the first session.[425] That was the session in which the "spirit of the council" began to become a "theological commonplace."

15. Majority and minority at the council

If we were to limit ourselves to an "official" history, based on the results of the voting, we would have to deny the existence of an internal struggle at the council between antagonistic alignments, given that the conciliar documents were all approved by an overwhelming majority. In reality, no council experienced tensions and conflicts between opposed groups more than Vatican II did. While not denying this obvious fact, historians trace it back to the contrast between a progressive "majority" and a conservative "minority" that was doomed to be defeated.

In reality the clash occurred between two minorities that a theologian from Louvain, Gérard Philips, described in 1963 as two opposing "trends" in twentieth-century philosophy and theology:[426] one more preoccupied with being faithful to traditional formulations, the other more concerned about spreading the message among modern men and women.[427]

The first "trend" was, however, the official position of the Church's magisterium, which had always been stressed until the pontificate of Pius XII;

---

[424] See also Matthew P. Lawson, "The Holy Spirit as Conscience Collective," in *Sociology of Religion* 4 (1999): 341–361.

[425] Bishop Miguel Miranda y Gomez, representative of Bishop Câmara's group for Mexico, confided for example to Father Caporale that he was convinced that he was not the only one to feel the profound presence of the Holy Spirit. Cited in Wilde, 25.

[426] Cf. G. Philips, "Deux tendances de la philosophie contemporaine: En marge du II Concile du Vatican," in *Nouvelle Revue Théologique* 85/3 (1963): 225–238. Father Tromp wrote to Philips in May 1963: "To be honest, I find that that (the article published in March 1963) is just a cheap caricature, which made a painful impression on me" (Letter from Tromp, in the Archives of Monsignor Philips, translated from Dutch by J. Grootaers, in *Actes et Acteurs*, 387).

[427] G. Philips, *Deux tendances, op. cit.*, 9.

the second, heterodox "trend" was repeatedly censured and condemned by that same ecclesiastical magisterium. In Philips' article—the importance of which would be difficult to overestimate, as Melloni observes[428]—the author puts the two positions on the same level and clearly prefers the second.

Moreover there was a balance between essentially equal forces, as seen in several votes, such as the first one on *De fontibus Revelationis*. From then on, however, counting on a slight numerical superiority, the progressives began to refer to their adversaries as a "minority," until they convinced them of being one. As soon as the "moderate" council fathers, who made up the majority, accepted this view of the actual contrast, they signaled their own defeat.

Before the last session of the council, in a letter to Bishop Carli, Father Berto wrote:

> The more I study what happened in the first three sessions, the more I think that there is not a convinced "majority" in the council, but rather a "majority" that has been carried away. There are two "minorities," one Roman and Thomist in which Your Excellence holds an eminent position, the other anti-Roman and anti-Thomist, not much more numerous than the first, and very inferior in quality, but by a sorrowful divine concession (*quam incomprensibilia sunt iudicia Eius!* [how inscrutable are his judgments!]), the latter is the one that is dragging with it the "majority" through powerful human means, the mainstream press, radio, political and diplomatic influences, and money.[429]

According to Melissa Wilde, the success of the progressives can be explained by a simple sociological fact: "Because progressives built a far more extensive and flexible organization than their conservative counterparts, they were more successful at developing compromise positions that the vast majority of bishops could support."[430] The progressive minority prevailed certainly thanks to the greater strength of their own organization, but this in turn resulted from the greater force of their own convictions.

---

[428] Cf. A. Melloni, "The Beginning of the Second Period," *op. cit.*, 63.

[429] Letter from Father Berto to Bishop Carli dated June 29, 1965, in N. Buonasorte, "Per la 'pura, piena, integra fede cattolica,'" *op. cit.*, 141.

[430] Wilde, 57.

One scholar of the laws of revolutions writes:

> The success of a minority results from a combination of forces by virtue of which the shrewdest and most decisive ones succeed in gaining the approval of the less active and of the majority. In a case like this, the more impassioned have the advantage over the less impassioned, the more decisive over the less ardent, the daring over the timid, the energetic over the weak, the more persevering and more tenacious over those who digress or equivocate, and in general those who know what they want and desire it strongly over those who doubt, change their minds, hesitate and start over.[431]

History is always made by minorities, and what prevails in a conflict is not numerical strength but the determination and the intensity with which these minorities fight their battles. The tendency of moderates is always to yield when faced with the extreme currents of revolution, as it happened with Kerensky's supporters in the Russian Revolution and with the Girondists in the French Revolution. "Confronted with revolution and counter-revolution, moderate revolutionaries generally waver, seeking to win absurd reconciliations. But in the end they systematically favor the former against the latter."[432]

Minorities, when they organize, always do so discreetly, and sometimes secretly. It is not inappropriate to speak, in this sense, about conventicles and conspiracies. Today, in order to belittle a historical study, critics accuse it of leaning toward a "conspiracy theory." To admit the existence of conspiracies is simply to admit that history is shaped by men's freedom and is not the result of a World Spirit or Reason that is immanent in history, of which men are only the instruments. Actually there is no major historical event, starting from the two major revolutions of the modern era, the French and the Russian, that was not started by more or less successful "conspiracies." James H. Billington,[433] who has studied the origins of revolutionary "faith," has documents the conspiratorial and secret origins of the principal political

---

[431] André Joussain, *La loi des révolutions* (Paris: Flammarion, 1950), 173.

[432] P. Corrêa de Oliveira, "Una osservazione di San Giovanni Bosco illumina la causa della Rivoluzione," in *Rivoluzione e Contro-Rivoluzione, op. cit.*, 285–292 at 289.

[433] Cf. James H. Billington, *Fire in the Minds of Men: Origins of the Revolutionary Faith* (London: Temple Smith, 1980).

movements of the nineteenth and twentieth centuries. The Second Vatican Council does not escape from this historical law, which in a subterranean way linked the progressivism of the innovators with the modernism of the early years of the century.

On December 3, Bishop Borromeo noted in his *Diary*:

> We are in the full flowering of modernism. Not the naïve, frank, aggressive and combative modernism of the days of Pius X, no. Today's modernism is subtler, more disguised, more penetrating, and more hypocritical. It does not want to stir up another storm; it wants the whole Church to find that it has become modernist without noticing it.... Tradition is admitted too by the new modernism, but as a consequence of scripture, having originated from scripture and from the magisterium, which originally had only scripture as its object. Christ is salvaged in modernism but He is not the historical Christ; he is a Christ devised by religious consciousness so that a well-delineated, concrete human figure might support religious experiences that could not be expressed in their richness and intensity by way of merely rational and abstract concepts.... Thus today's *modernism* salvages all of Christianity, its dogmas and its organization, but empties it all out and turns it on its head. It is no longer a religion that comes from God, but a religion that comes directly from man and indirectly from the divine element that is in man.[434]

[434] Borromeo, *Diario* (December 3, 1962).

IV

1963: The Second Session

1. From John XXIII to Paul VI

a) Assessment of the council according to Father Tucci

On January 6, 1963, the feast of the Epiphany, John XXIII wrote a long letter to all the council fathers, reminding them that the period between January 6 and September 8, the date when the session was to resume, should be considered as a true and proper continuation of the work that the council would have to carry out. The fathers therefore had a sacred duty not only to be present at the next meetings in the Vatican Basilica, but to remain, during those eight months, closely united in spirit with their brothers in the episcopate.

The activity of the commissions and the sub-commissions was intense during the first months of 1963. The Coordinating Commission, which supervised and coordinated the activity of all the commissions, met in the Vatican from January 21 to 27, with the Secretary of State presiding, to discuss the plan to rework the schema *De Ecclesia* by Cardinal Suenens.[1] The ecclesiastical question, as articulated by Cardinal Döpfner, was "the first and most essential question of the entire council."[2] On January 28, the

---

[1] Cf. AS V/1:90–96.

[2] Ibid., 100.

pope received in audience the members of the commission and expressed to them his conviction that the council, having got off to such a good start, would soon be in a position to attain all of its objectives.

On February 9, 1963, John XXIII received in an audience lasting more than an hour and a half Father Roberto Tucci,[3] a Neapolitan Jesuit in his forties, who since 1959 had been editor of the *Civiltà Cattolica*. This conversation, recorded by Father Tucci in his diary, is revealing: the pope appears to be decisively aligned against the curial culture, and when he remarks that curia members "have a petty, restricted mentality, because they have never been outside of Rome, outside of their 'village,'" the allusion to Cardinal Ottaviani is evident. It is worth reproducing a long passage from Father Tucci's diary, because it offers an assessment of the council made by John XXIII just a few months before his death:

> He told me that the *Civiltà Cattolica* now seems to him to be on the right track, more so than in the past, although he did not specify what his criticisms were with regard to the past.
>
> He spoke to me about his relations with the separated brethren, which he characterized as based on good will united with prudence and without illusions: nothing is gained by pressing them with talk of return, even though it is true that that is the only way; in the case of Fisher, who insists on speaking to him about reunion and unity, he gives him to understand that he does not quite follow, and then he changes the subject to the imitation of Christ and similar topics, and the Anglican prelate goes away contented; it was the same yesterday with the Methodist prelate; with regard to the latter, he told me: "Yesterday they once again declared me a saint!"
>
> As an example of the good fruits produced by his attitude of simplicity and kindness, he told me confidentially the news about the release from prison of the Metropolitan of the Ukrainians: Bishop Willebrands has gone to Russia to pick him up; he is expected in Rome by evening and he will reside for now in the monastery at Grottaferrata. He kept emphasizing that certain nationalistic attitudes, the type found among the Ukrainian bishops at the council, especially Bishop Bucko, can only cause annoyance; on the contrary, good relations with Khrushchev have brought about a more relaxed situation; he does

[3] Roberto Tucci, (1921–), Jesuit, ordained in 1950, editor (1959) then editor-in-chief (1959–1973) of the *Civiltà Cattolica*, conciliar *peritus*, created cardinal by John Paul II in 2001. Although he received the purple hat, he was never consecrated a bishop.

not think that Khrushchev is as cynical as some say; he has his own serious internal difficulties and is animated by good intentions, even though he remains firmly committed to principles altogether opposed to ours. He told me that after the exchange of messages and other courtesies, an American journalist, who had had an occasion to speak with Khrushchev at length, had brought him personal Christmas greetings from him and that he, by the same channel, had sent his own greetings back, adding to them a request to free the Metropolitan. The journalist had told about hearing from Khrushchev how he had been raised in a religious family, but later had become quite alienated from religion because he wanted to work for renewal in society, and he had seen that the "popes" [slang for "clergy"] in Russia were all slaves of the tsarist regime and of the rich. With regard to improving official relations with the Holy See, the Holy Father had sent a response that there were no difficulties with that provided that the fundamental rights of the human person were recognized and hence also the right to religious liberty. From what I understood of the matter, Kennedy was not uninvolved; the Holy Father said that he understood his caution about not appearing to be too favorable to the Catholic Church, so as not to lose the support of the protestants; nevertheless members of his family had come to see the pope, etc.

As far as the council was concerned, he said that he was completely satisfied: the council had really got into its work only in recent weeks when it began to understand the implications of the September message and of his inaugural address on October 11. He complained, however, about the fact that the Holy Office thought that it was in charge; he said that he had had to set them straight; while praising the good dispositions of Cardinal Ottaviani and Archbishop Parente and others, he said that they still had not understood that certain ways of acting could by no means meet with his approval. He strongly criticized Father Tromp, who thinks that he needs to teach the bishops and who expresses himself in a way that shows little respect for them; he also observed that unfortunately some eminent council fathers, because they once taught theology, think that they have to turn the council documents into manuals of theology; he reaffirmed that it is not a matter of settling doctrinal questions, since it does not seem to him that there are any disputed questions today that must solved in order to avoid grave harm to the faith of the Church. He forcefully critiqued also the intervention of Archbishop Vagnozzi, a fine young man, but one whose impertinence he had already noticed, since the former was out of place both because of the substance of what he said and above all because of his manner of saying it; he knew, moreover, that in this case it was not the archbishop's own work [*literally:* it was not flour from his own sack], since it had been prepared for him.

During the first session he had preferred not to intervene in the debates, so as to allow the fathers freedom to discuss and the opportunity to find the right path on their own; on the other hand, he, not having the necessary competence in the various matters, might be more of a disturbance than a help with any intervention of his own. The bishops needed to learn on their own—and they had done so.

As for his recent letter to the bishops,[4] he appeared to be proud of having written the whole thing by himself; when asked whether he had meant to fault the liturgical movement when he talked about *novae praedicationes* [new sermons], etc., he said that that was entirely absent from his mind; he was thinking about the good sisters who want to spread new forms of prayer, and about devotions to Our Lady of this place or that, which people were trying to extend to the whole Church, and the like. With regard to the curial culture, he noted that they have a petty, restricted mentality, because they have never been outside of Rome, outside of their 'village': they cannot manage to see Church matters in a truly universal perspective.

He then asked me whether I had any remarks or observations about the pope's attitude, about the things people are saying. (He realizes that, even in my community, there will be some who do not agree with his approach!) I spoke then on the need for more abundant information on the council so as to help journalists, and so as not to reinforce the inferiority complex of Catholic publications, etc. He asked me whether Vallainc was doing well or not. I replied that it did not depend on him, but on Archbishop Felici. At that point he observed that Archbishop Felici is a really fine man, though he is somewhat limited in his thinking; he knows Latin very well and also Italian, but that is more or less all; it is true that he did not put himself in that position, since he had been proposed by Tardini without him knowing anything about it; he is obedient and a good worker. But the pope rescued him (by adding the five undersecretaries), and Archbishop Felici knows this and is grateful. Understands the problem but doesn't

[4] Cf. *Docum. Intersessione* 1963, n. 2: copy delivered to Monsignor Dell'Acqua several days before its publication in *L'Osservatore Romano*.

> get into the details. Just says that in order to contain the bad press it would be necessary for Manzini[5] at *L'Osservatore Romano* to expose and give the lie to malicious interpretations and the like as soon as they occur; in that way everyone who is in error will fall into that category. The pope has not spoken to Manzini.[6]

John XXIII, who for several weeks had been obliged to "practice patience with 'Brother Body' [a droll Franciscan personification]," on January 24 received Cardinals Suenens and Döpfner, "two strong and beautiful columns of Holy Church"[7]—as he recorded in his diary.

b) The last months of John XXIII's life

On March 1, 1963, the international Balzan Foundation, thanks also to the support of its Soviet members, decided to award John XXIII the Balzan "Peace Prize." A few days later, on March 7, the pope granted a personal audience to Alexei Adzhubei, the editor of *Izvestia* but, more importantly, the son-in-law of Khrushchev and his private ambassador. This meeting did not lead to any substantial conclusions, but it had an impact in the Italian and world media. A few days after this audience, the secretary of the Italian Communist Party, Palmiro Togliatti, in the midst of an election campaign, gave a speech in Bergamo in which he officially proposed that there be collaboration between Catholics and communists, and he attacked Cardinal Ottaviani as a "defeated man" at the council. In the same speech, Togliatti spoke of his "certainty that the socialist transformation of society for which we are fighting is not only a necessity but an obligation that engages the better part of humanity, with the certainty of success." He went so far as to call for "the dictatorship of the proletariat" as "a coalition of all the working classes, whether manual or intellectual laborers," saying that "it was up to them to direct social life as a whole."[8]

---

[5] Raimondo Manzini (1901–1988), Italian journalist, member of the national council of the Christian Democratic Party; edited *L'Avvenire d'Italia* (1927–1959) and *L'Osservatore Romano* (1960–1978). Among his books: *Fedeli infedeli* (1979); *L'unità dei cattolici* (1982); *I sentiere dell'assoluto* (1986).

[6] Tucci, *Diario* (February 9, 1963), 44–47.

[7] John XXIII, *Pater Amabilis*, in *Agende del Pontefice*, 490.

[8] Cf. *Rinascita* 13 (1963), reprinted in Palmiro Togliatti, *Opere (1956–1964)*, vol. VI, ed. by

On April 9, 1963, John XXIII signed his eighth and final encyclical, *Pacem in terris.*[9] Its basic themes were the rise of the working classes, recognition of women's role in contemporary society, and the centrality of peace in the Church's magisterium.

In paragraphs 83-85 of the encyclical, three fundamental principles were enunciated: 1) One should never confuse error with the erring person, even when it is a question of error or of inadequate knowledge of the truth in the moral-religious sphere; 2) one cannot simply identify false philosophical doctrines on the nature, origin, and destiny of man and of the universe with historical movements having economic, social, cultural, and political aims, even if these movements originated with the doctrines in question, and have drawn and continue to draw inspiration from them; 3) it can happen that a *rapprochement* or a meeting in the practical order that was thought to be neither opportune nor useful yesterday, could very well be so today or could become so tomorrow.

These three principles would constitute the interpretive key to the whole political-diplomatic phenomenon known as the *Ostpolitik* of the Holy See,[10] and, more generally, to its "overture" to communism.

The encyclical appeared on April 11, 1963, and was presented to public opinion as the basis for a future collaboration between movements with a Christian inspiration and those with a socialist inspiration. It would be cited by many theoreticians of a convergence between Catholics and communists, ranging from the French philosopher, Roger Garaudy, to the inspirer of the Italian "historical compromise," Franco Rodano.[11]

In Italy, the elections held on April 28, 1963, saw consistent gains for the Communist Party and an equally significant loss for the Christian Democrats. On the morning of May 1, several hundred communists,

---

Luciano Gruppi (Rome: Editori Riuniti, 1984), 697–707 at 698.

[9] Teste in AAS 55 (1963): 257–304. For a reconstruction of its redaction, see A. Melloni, *Pacem in terris: Storia dell'ultima enciclica di Papa Giovanni* (Rome-Bari: Laterza, 2010), particularly concerning the role of Monsignor Pietro Pavan in its composition, 41–52.

[10] Giovanni Barberini, *L'Ostpolitik della Santa Sede: Un dialogo lungo e faticoso* (Bologna: Il Mulino, 2007), 73.

[11] On Roger Garaudy (1913–2012) see P. Corrêa de Oliveira, "Garaudy esboça nova aproximação" and "A manobra Garaudy," in *Folha de S. Paulo* (March 8 and 15, 1970); on Franco Rodano (1920–1983), see A. Del Noce, *Il cattolico comunista* (Milan: Rusconi, 1981).

returning from a fiery meeting on the Piazza San Giovanni, where they had celebrated their electoral victory along with their May Day demonstrations, made their way to St. Peter's Square, waving red banners and raising their arms with fists clenched. Turning towards the windows of the Apostolic Palace, they shouted at the top of their lungs: "*Viva Giovanni XXIII!* Long live the pope of peace!"

For the communists Pope John was "the good pope" and Vatican II was considered to be the "council of peace."[12] As of 1960, the Kremlin had launched the doctrine of "peaceful co-existence" as a strategic plan on a worldwide scale for the whole period of transition from capitalism to socialism.[13] In reality, as Khrushchev had made clear in a famous speech on January 1, 1961, as far as its social contents were concerned, it meant an intensely fought economic, political, and ideological battle of the proletariat against the aggressive forces of international imperialism. Communism ran on the two rails of fear and sympathy, while invoking the universal aspiration for peace. Without abandoning its policy of intimidation and its explicit proselytism, it employed new techniques of implicit persuasion, through the use of expressions such as "peace," "peaceful co-existence," and "dialogue."[14]

The pope's health, meanwhile, was deteriorating rapidly. On May 10 and 11, the Balzan Peace Prize was solemnly conferred on the pope at the Vatican and at the Quirinal. John XXIII recorded these events in his diary as "two historic and beneficent days in the course of my life and of my service to the Holy See and to Italy."[15] Two days later, in New York, Cardinal Suenens delivered to the secretary general of the United Nations Organization, U Thant, a copy of *Pacem in terris* autographed personally by the pontiff. In an unprecedented initiative, the Kremlin had a translation of the encylical published in Russian translation, with the

---

[12] R. Burigana, "Il Partito Comunista italiano e la Chiesa negli anni del Concilio Vaticano II," in *Vatican II in Moscow*, 189–226 at 202–212.

[13] Richard V. Allen, *Peace or Peaceful Coexistence* (American Bar Association, 1966), 119 ff. See also Giorgio Caredda, *Le politiche della distensione, 1959–1972* (Rome: Carocci, 2008).

[14] Cf. P. Corrêa de Oliveira, "Baldeção ideológica inarvertida e diálogo," in *Catolicismo* 178–179 (1965): 2–12.

[15] John XXIII, *Pater Amabilis*, in *Agende del Pontefice*, 519.

pope's signature in Cyrillic script.[16] On May 20, John XXIII wrote another long letter to all the bishops of the world, announcing to them that he was going to make the spiritual exercises from May 25 to June 2, during the Novena of Pentecost. But during those days the end came instead. The front page of the May 28 issue of *L'Osservatore Romano* had a full-page headline : "The pope invites you to pray that the will of God might be accomplished, even if this means a sacrifice such as the prolonging of his life, for the successful outcome of the council, for the Holy Church, and for peace." In the night between Thursday, May 30, and Friday, May 31, the pope's conditions worsened. On Friday, Monsignor Capovilla told the pope: "Holy Father, I am keeping my word. I must do for you what you did for Bishop Radini-Tedeschi at the end of his life. The hour has come. The Lord is calling you."[17]

On the evening of Monday, June 3, 1963, at 7:45, John XXIII died, after a pontificate of four years and seven months.

The last hours of the pope were followed closely in radio reports, and his funeral, on June 6, was broadcast by television throughout the world. On June 7, John XXIII was entombed in a nocturnal ceremony in the Vatican Grotto. Afterward it was decided that the *Novendiale*, the solemn nine-day funeral ceremony, should end on June 17, so as to allow the convocation of the eighty cardinals who would elect the new pontiff. The mass media contributed to the creation of the image of "the good pope," "the unarmed prophet" of the "new Pentecost"[18]— which the publication of the pope's diary discredited to some extent. John XXIII was not the "simple" man described by some hagiographers, but was rather a complex person—and sometimes a "disconcerting" one, as Father Robert Roquette

---

16 A. Melloni, *Pacem in terris: Storia dell'ultima enciclica di Papa Giovanni, op. cit.*, 85.

17 L. F. Capovilla, *Ite Missa est* (Padua: Edizioni Messaggero, 1983), 218.

18 Cf. *Idem,* "Giovanni XXIII: profeta della nuova Pentecoste," in *Il Vaticano II nella Chiesa italiana* (Assisi: Memoria e Profezia, 1985); Jules Gritti, in *Jean XXIII dans l'opinion publique* (Paris: Éditions du Centurion, 1967), reports the exaggerated titles reserved by the French press for John XXIII in the days after his death: "The pope of the century" (*France soir*, June 5), "Perhaps the most humane pope in history" (*Le Figaro*, June 4), "The greatest transformation accomplished in Catholicism since the Council of Trent" (*Express*, May 30). On the theme of "Good Pope John," see the article by I. Colosio, O.P., "Discussioni sulla 'bontà' del Papa Giovanni XXIII," in *Rassegna di Ascetica e Mistica* 3 (1975): 235–248.

has observed.[19] Father Roquette, who was the first to speak of a "Roncalli mystery," maintains that in his "peasant wisdom" the pope conducted a policy of "balance of power." One day in Paris, while smoking a cigar after a meal, he explained his policy to Father Roquette in these terms: "Huh! As you say in French, a half turn to the right, and a half turn to the left."[20]

The figure of Pope John XXIII, however, has gone down in history as indissolubly linked to Vatican Council II, which had been his idea and which he had opened and guided in its first session—the one that would prove to be decisive.

2. Giovanni Battista Montini on the papal throne

a) The conclave of 1963

The maneuvering began immediately in the corridors of the Vatican and in the European chanceries. In the days immediately preceding the conclave, as Giulio Andreotti recalls, a meeting was held in a Grottaferrata villa at the invitation of Cardinal Frings, in which a good number of cardinals participated.[21] The villa belonged to an attorney, Umberto Ortolani, a close collaborator of Cardinal Giacomo Lercaro; Ortolani was later involved in the Masonic Lodge P2 affair as well as in the failure of the Ambrosian Bank. Ortolani himself, in a later interview with Andrea Tornielli, confirmed that the meeting had taken place on June 18, 1963, and among the numerous and illustrious cardinals who attended were Cardinals Frings, Suenens, König, Alfrink, Léger, and Liénart. There was no doubt, according to Ortolani, about who the emerging candidate was: "The archbishop of Milan, Giovanni Battista Montini, even though some would have preferred that the organizer of the meeting be elected, that is, Cardinal Lercaro…"[22]

The Grottaferrata meeting had been organized by Cardinal Lercaro, who considered himself the heir of the "Johannine" spirit. On that same

---

[19] Robert Roquette, "Le mystère Roncalli," in *Études* 318 (1963): 4–18.

[20] *"Eh! Comme vous dites en français: demi-tour à droite, demi-tour à gauche."* Ibid., 12–13.

[21] Giulio Andreotti, *A ogni morte di Papa: I Papi che ho conosciuto* (Milan: Rizzoli, 1980), 106.

[22] "Colazioni a casa Ortolani," interview by A. Tornielli with Umberto Ortolani, in *30 Giorni* no. 3 (1993): 41–42.

June 18, he wrote to his "family," the house of needy boys whom he aided: "I ardently hope and think it probable that I will return to you; but it is somewhat less likely than I thought when I left Bologna. I see that you too have noticed the rounds that the rumors are making."[23] In reality, the meeting allowed Montini to secure the support of the central European bloc,[24] and that of Lercaro himself, who met with him privately at the convent of Santa Priscilla, where the two had a meeting of minds about their aims.[25] On June 19, the opening day of the conclave, the *Corriere della Sera* credited Indro Montanelli with a portrait of the Cardinal of Milan under the significant headline: "Montini a Central Figure of the Conclave."

On the evening of June 19, 1963, eighty cardinals entered into the conclave. Missing at the roll call were the Hungarian Cardinal Mindszenty, who was still confined to the American Embassy in Budapest, and the ninety-year-old Cardinal Carlos María de la Torre.[26] Fifty-four votes were required to be elected. The Conclave lasted from the evening of June 19 to the late morning of June 21. König recorded the reassuring words that Montini said to him during those days: "Whoever becomes pope cannot but continue on the path of John."[27]

The clashes within the conclave, according to Cardinal Testa,[28] were intense.[29] Cardinal Ottaviani fought to the end against Montini, pressing for the election of Cardinal Ildebrando Antoniutti,[30] a sixty-four-year-old

---

[23] Cited in A. Tornielli, *Paolo VI, op. cit.*, 326–327.

[24] Cf. G. Zizola, *Il Conclave, op. cit.*, 235; B. Lai, *Il Papa non eletto, op. cit.*, 201.

[25] Cf. A. Tornielli, *Paolo VI, op. cit.*, 327.

[26] Carlos María Javier de la Torre (1873–1968), Ecuadorian, ordained in 1896, bishop of Loja in 1912, of Bolivar in 1919 and of Guayaquil in 1926, archbishop of Quito from 1933 to 1967, created cardinal in 1953.

[27] F. König, *Chieesa dove vai?, op. cit.*, 27–81.

[28] Gustavo Testa (1886–1969), ordained in 1910, titular archbishop of Amasea in 1934, created cardinal in 1959, prefect of the Congregation for the Eastern Churches in 1967.

[29] Cf. A. Riccardi, *Il "partito romano": Politica italiana, Chiesa cattolica e curia romana da Pio XII a Paolo VI* (Brescia: Morcelliana, 2007), 297; G. Zizola, *Il Conclave, op. cit.*, 240, who attributes to Cardinal Testa the remark: "There was a fight. Horrendous things happened. I feel the need to ask the pope's permission to relieve me of the duty" (ibid.).

[30] Ildebrando Antoniutti (1898–1974), ordained in 1920, Titula archbishop of Sinnada (1937),

prelate from Friuli, who had considerable diplomatic experience, and who would have represented an interruption of the "Johannine" course. The stories that leaked out of the conclave tell also of Cardinal Siri's refusal to make himself available for possible election, thus shifting the votes in his own favor toward the archbishop of Milan: "For the good of the Church, I did not want to oppose Montini," the archbishop of Genoa confided to Benny Lai.[31] The progressive cardinals, for their part, sought to concentrate their votes on a single candidate, and when the Lercaro votes began to go over to Montini, it was the conservatives themselves who gave way, in the hope of influencing the new pope. According to a reconstruction of the conclave published in the *Corriere della Sera*, the cardinal-vicar of Rome, Clemente Micara, was the one who calmed down some of the electors from the conservative party by putting himself at the head of the Montini supporters.[32] With the sixth ballot on the morning of June 21, the cardinals greeted with loud applause the reading out of the name of Giovanni Battista Montini on the fifty-fourth of the ballot papers. It seems that the election results were more precisely fifty-seven votes against twenty-two that remained in tenacious opposition.[33] It was the duty of Cardinal-Protodeacon Alfredo Ottaviani, to proclaim from the outer balcony of St. Peter's the name of the newly elected pope.

The archbishop of Milan took the name of Paul VI. This name, as he noted in his first message and repeated on the day of his coronation on June 30, 1963, announced the program for his pontificate.[34] On the day of his election the new pope confirmed Cardinal Amleto Cicognani in the office of Secretary of State.

---

was *Chargé d'affaires* to the National Government headed by General Franco, and then nuncio to Spain from 1953 to 1962. Created cardinal in March 1962, prefect of the Congregation for Religious in 1963.

[31] B. Lai, "Siri, il culto della verità," in *Il Giornale* (May 3, 1989). Benny Lai also records a conversation of Siri with his confessor, Father Damaso da Celle, in which the Cardinal of Genoa is said to have admitted that he had given up competing for the throne of Peter with an enlightening comment: "Now, though, I will behave differently" (B. Lai, *Dal diario di Padre Damaso, "Mneme Ammentos,"* I/1(2005): 126 ff., cited in P. Gheda, *Siri e Montini, op. cit.*, 76–77.

[32] Cf. Fabrizio De Santis, "Come elessero Montini," in *Corriere della Sera* (June 18, 1978).

[33] Cf. G. Zizola, *Il Conclave, op. cit.*, 241.

[34] Paul VI, "Message to the human family" (June 22, 1963), in *Insegnamenti* 1:11–12; Address "In die coronationis Papae" ["On the day of the pope's coronation"] (June 30, 1963), ibid., 24–25.

Although the West German Chancellor, Konrad Adenauer, in conversation with a French diplomat, had expressed fear that the election of Montini meant "a real danger to Europe,"[35] the latter's ascent to the papacy was welcomed with satisfaction by Italian and European communists,[36] who interpreted it as a sign of the cardinals' intention to continue the activity of Pope John. The secretary of the Italian Communist Party himself, Palmiro Togliatti, wrote a piece for the communist publication *Rinascita* to demonstrate the elements of continuity between Paul VI and John XXIII.[37] Even the Kremlin, according to the Russian historian Victor Gaiduk, who consulted documents in the Soviet archives, was concerned about the choice of a successor to John XXIII and hoped for the election of "a man of the dialogue" like Montini.[38]

In the election of Paul VI a decisive role was played by Archbishop Angelo Dell'Acqua, the *Sostituto* (deputy Secretary of State). Archbishop Loris Capovilla, who often spoke about this, confirmed this in an interview with Andrea Tornielli: "The substitute was in a privileged position; he could approach all of the cardinals. He convinced the Spaniards by assuring them that Cardinal Montini was a friend of Spain, contrary to the way others had described him. He allayed the concerns of those who thought that the archbishop of Milan was a 'Frenchman,' exclusively imbued with the culture of that great nation. He did his part to eliminate several prejudices that had been built up over the years with regard to the figure of Montini, and who during his years in Milan had been constantly and severely attacked by a certain element in the press, which presented him as a prelate of the left."[39]

---

[35] Cited in A. Melloni, "Chiese sorelle, diplomazie nemiche: Il Vaticano II a Mosca fra propaganda, Ostpolitik ed ecumenismo," in *Vatican II in Moscow*, 12. General de Gaulle, however, had expressed his hopes and given assurances of his support for the election of Montini (cf. A. Wenger, *Les trois Rome: L'Église des années Soixante* [Paris: Desclée de Brouwer, 1991], 125–127).

[36] R. Burigana, "Il Partito Comunista italiano e la Chiesa negli anni del Concilio Vaticano II," in *Vatican II in Moscow*, 213–214.

[37] Cf. P. Togliatti, "Da Giovanni a Paolo," in *Rinascita* 26 (1963): 1–2; reprinted in P. Togliatti, *Opere (1956–1964), op. cit.*, 6:715–718.

[38] Cf. V. Gaiduk, *op. cit.*, 28–29.

[39] Cited in A. Tornielli, *Paolo VI, op. cit.*, 333.

b) The election of Paul VI

Giovanni Battista Montini came from a middle-class family in Brescia. His father, Giorgio, had been the editor of the local Catholic daily newspaper and also a deputy representing the Popular Party.[40] Battista had received his formation during his high-school years in a school run by the Oratorians of *Santa Maria della Pace*, where two figures in particular made a great impression on his life, fathers Giulio Bevilacqua and Paolo Caresana. The latter was, from 1913 on, his spiritual director and confessor. On May 19, 1920, young Montini received priestly ordination at the age of only twenty-two, without ever having studied theology in a seminary; he had been an extern student on account of his fragile health. When he went to Rome, he was taken on at the Secretariat of State and appointed an "ecclesiastical assistant," or chaplain, to the University Federation of Italian Catholics (*Federazione Universitaria Cattolici Italiani*). He was intensely active in the latter position, but he was eventually removed from it because of the kind of formation he was giving to the students, particularly because of his "innovative" concept of the liturgy and because of a pronounced tendency to "politicize" the youth.[41] Politics always remained Montini's great passion until the day of his death; from his youth he had been a strong supporter of the Popular Party and later of the Christian Democrats; he followed the political developments of these parties attentively. In those days he lived in an apartment on the Aventine Hill, where he also provided lodging for his mentor, Father Giulio Bevilacqua, who had been "exiled" from Brescia on account of his ongoing conflicts with the local Fascists.[42] This was probably a particularly important time in the biography of Montini because of his direct contact with the strong personality of that Oratorian religious.[43]

Thanks to the support of Secretary of State Pacelli, in December 1937, Montini was promoted to be substitute in the Secretariat of State, succeeding Archbishop Tardini, who that same day was appointed secretary

---

[40] Cf. N. Vian, "Le radici bresciane di G. B. Montini," in *Paul VI et la modernité, op. cit.*, 16–31.

[41] See the private letter sent on March 19, 1933, to Bishop Gaggia of Brescia, in which Monsignor Montini defends himself against the accusations leveled against him, in A. Fappani and Franco Molinari, *Giovanni Battista Montini giovane* (Casale Monferrato: Marietti, 1979), 285–291.

[42] Cf. A. Fappani, *Padre Giulio Bevilacqua, op. cit.*, 171–193.

[43] Renato Moro, "Giovanni Battista Montini e il fascismo," in *Paul VI et la modernité, op. cit.*, 41–65 at 51.

of the Congregation for Ecclesiastical Affairs. Montini had not really had diplomatic experience, except for a brief period of six months spent at the papal nunciature in Warsaw; instead he worked almost uninterruptedly in the Secretariat of State until 1954, when Pius XII appointed him archbishop of Milan, though without a cardinal's hat.

This promotion was in fact a "removal," the reasons for which are still unclear.[44] Some think that Archbishop Montini was involved in the betrayal of Father Alighiero Tondi.[45] According to Cardinal Siri, he was sent off to Milan following a negative judgment issued about him by a secret commission established by Pius XII, who had lost confidence in the substitute because he had been protecting the president of the Catholic Action Youth group, Mario Rossi, who was fighting for a Church engaged on the left.[46] Cardinal Casaroli, at a much later date, told Andrea Tornielli that the pope's relations with his principal collaborator "deteriorated substantially because of contacts made by Montini with elements of the Italian political left without the knowledge of Pius XII."[47] From Archbishop Montini's correspondence with Father Giuseppe De Luca, on the other hand, it can be deduced that the substitute, through the Roman clergy, was maintaining relations with communist Catholics and some sectors of the Italian Communist Party.[48] Andrea Riccardi recalls, on the other hand, that several appointments of bishops in Lithuania, which had been made "in a way that was obscure if not mysterious," had given rise to rumors about Montini's possible disloyalty on Soviet matters.[49] These rumors went back to a "secret report" made by a French Colonel, Claude Arnould, a

---

[44] Cf. A. Riccardi, *Il potere del Papa da Pio XII a Paolo VI* (Bari: Laterza, 1988), 68–75; Y. Chiron, *Paul VI: Le Pape écartelé* (Paris: Perrin, 2008), 142 ff.; A. Tornielli, *Paolo VI, op. cit.*, 169–183.

[45] Alighiero Tondi (1908–1984), Jesuit, left the Society of Jesus in 1952 to join the Communist Party. Legally married the communist leader Carmen Zanti and worked in Communist Germany but, after another crisis of conscience, at the death of his wife in 1978, was reinstated in the priesthood.

[46] B. Lai, *Il Papa non eletto, op. cit.*, 100.

[47] A. Tornielli, *Paolo VI, op. cit.*, 172.

[48] Cf. Giuseppe De Luca and G. B. Montini, *Carteggio (1930–1962)*, ed. Paolo Vian (Rome: Edizioni di Storia e Letteratura, 1992), 183–184.

[49] Cf. A. Riccardi, *Il Vaticano e Mosca, op. cit.*, 195; *Idem, Il "partito romano," op. cit.*, 287–288. On Montini's dismissal, see ibid., 282–293.

Catholic and an anti-communist, who had been asked to investigate the passing of confidential information from the Secretariat of State to communist governments in the East. Arnould had traced the responsibility for the leaked information to Montini and his *entourage*, causing alarm at the Vatican. Andrea Tornielli himself brought to light several documents that appear to demonstrate the reliability of Arnould, who enjoyed the full confidence and friendship of Cardinal Tisserant and was introduced into the highest levels of the state and the Church in France.[50]

Certainly the new pope *was* imbued with French culture[51] and did in fact harbor great sympathy for the new progressive causes in France, in particular for the work of Jacques Maritain.[52] Riccardi observed that it "appears likely" that Montini "sought new openings on the frontiers of the East, perhaps only as working hypotheses," because "Maritain's reading of communism and the conditions Catholics lived under in the East strongly motivated him to try."[53] During the preparatory phase of the council, Archbishop Montini participated in the work of the Central Preparatory Commission, always siding with the progressives, although in a moderate fashion.

In the preface that he wrote in 1954 to a book compiled by Archbishop Pierre Veuillot, *Notre Sacerdoce* [Our Priesthood], the Archbishop of Milan, as has been noted, depicted himself.[54]

---

[50] The reliability of Arnould has been denied by many, including Father Robert Graham ("G. B. Montini Substitute Secretary of State," *op. cit.*, 81–82), but Tornielli cites several passages from correspondence between Cardinal Tisserant and the colonel, contained in the archives of the Association of Friends of Cardinal Tisserant, from which "it appears quite evident that Arnould had access to the highest levels of the French state (he accompanies Tisserant to a luncheon at the Élysée Palace hosted by President Auriol) and of the Church" (A. Tornielli, *Paolo VI, op. cit.*, 174–177 and 643). The first to speak about the "Arnould report" were George Roche and Philippe de Saint-Germain (*Pie XII devant l'histoire* [Paris: Laffont, 1992], 440). Monsignor Roche, like Colonel Arnould, was closely connected with Cardinal Tisserant.

[51] Cf. Jacques Prévotat, "Les sources françaises dans la formation intellectuelle de Gl B. Montini (1919–1963)," in *Paul VI et la modernité, op. cit.*, 101–127. Prévotat, who was able to examine the private library of the future pope in Brescia, confirms that the overwhelming majority of works consulted by Montini were French books.

[52] Cf. P. Chenaux, *Paul VI et Maritain, op. cit.*; Various Authors, *Montini e Maritain tra religione e cultura* (Vatican City: Libreria Editrice Vaticana, 2000).

[53] A. Riccardi, *Il Vaticano e Mosca, op. cit.*, 160.

[54] Y. Chiron, *Paul VI, op. cit.*, 150–151.

"The priest," Archbishop Montini wrote, "must be highly skilled: an artist, a specialized worker, an indispensable physician, one who has been initiated into the subtle and profound mysteries of the soul: he must be a student, a speaker, a man of taste, tact, sensibility, finesse, and strength. To equip himself to work on others, what labours must not the priest spend upon himself! … [He must] listen to the sirens which sound from the factories, those temples of industrial technique [*i.e.* technology] where the modern world lives and breathes; the priest must once again become a missionary if he wants Christianity to remain and to become once more the vital leaven of civilization."[55]

Roncalli was a shrewd man, but although he had spent the greater part of his life in diplomacy, he had never acquired the refinement of the diplomat. Montini, on the other hand, although he had traveled very little, was a natural diplomat, or, even more so, a natural politician. Even before he worked in the Secretariat of State, politics had been part of the atmosphere in his family, and it remained the great passion of his life. Carlo Falconi popularized the idea of Montini's "Hamlet complex," but the complex was not a lack of resolution; it was rather an ambivalence that would allow the Cardinal of Milan to attain better the objectives that he set for himself once he had ascended to the papacy.

On June 22, Paul VI addressed his first radio message to "the entire human family"[56] and announced that the pre-eminent part of his pontificate would be dedicated to the continuation of the Second Vatican Ecumenical Council. The following day, a Sunday, the pope recited the Angelus with the crowd on St. Peter's Square and, as soon as the prayer was completed, called to his side at the window of the Apostolic Palace, Cardinal Suenens and presented him to the crowd.[57] This was an unprecedented privilege that confirmed the close relationship that for some time had existed between the newly elected pontiff and the primate of Belgium.[58]

---

55 G. B. Montini, Letter-Preface to P. Veuillot, *Notre sacerdoce: Documents pontificaux de Pie X à nos jours* (Paris: Fleurus, 1954), xiv, viii; Eng. transl. *The Catholic Priesthood according to the teaching of the Church* (Dublin: Gill and Son, 1957), vol. 1, xiii-xx at xviii, xv.

56 Message (June 22, 1963), in Paul VI, *Insegnamenti* 1 (1963): 3–12.

57 Cf. *L'Osservatore Romano* (June 24–25 and June 29, 1963). The pope was assisted by two private secretaries, Don Pasquale Macchi, who had followed him from the Archdiocese of Milan, and the Irishman John Magee, who revised the pope's speeches in English.

58 Cf. L. Declerck and T. Osaer, "Les relations entre le cardinal Montini-Paul VI et le cardinal Suenens," *op. cit.*

During that same week Paul VI wanted to take a look at the text of the secret of Fatima, which was preserved in the Vatican. When he could not find it, he had Archbishop Capovilla, formerly the secretary of John XXIII, explain to him where it was kept. The envelope contained a note stating that John XXIII had seen the document, but had left to others the task of making it public. "On June 28," Archbishop Capovilla recalls, "Pope Paul called me and asked who had written the lines on the envelope. I explained that it had been the pope himself who wanted to indicate the persons who had read the document. Paul VI then asked me: 'Did Pope John tell you anything else?' 'No, Holy Father, he left the decision to others.' 'And I will do the same,' Pope Montini responded. The envelope was then closed and nothing more was said about it."[59]

Paul VI's coronation ceremony took place in St. Peter's Square on June 30, 1963. When the pope removed his miter after the pontifical Mass and put on the tiara, or triple crown, there resounded for the last time the solemn, centuries-old coronation formula: "Receive the tiara adorned with three crowns and know that you are the father of princes and of kings, the ruler of the world, and the vicar on earth of our Savior Jesus Christ, to whom be honor and glory forever and ever." Among the first official acts of Paul VI was his decision to abolish, along with the tiara, the papal coronation ceremony itself, which dated back to before the ninth century, as is evident from the *Ordo Romanus IX* from the time of Pope Leo III (795-816). The ceremony began with a solemn procession that accompanied the newly elected pope seated on his *sedia gestatoria*, or gestatorial chair, from the Apostolic Palace to the Altar of the Confession of St. Peter. While passing through the basilica on the way, a master of ceremonies knelt down before the pope three separate times; carrying a silver baton with a wad of tow burning on one end, he recited each time the words: *"Sancte Pater, sic transit gloria mundi"* ("Holy Father, so fleeting is worldly glory"), pronouncing them the first time softly, then more forcefully, and finally in a loud voice. And while the choir chanted the ancient hymn *Corona aurea super caput eius* ("The golden crown on his head"), the Cardinal-Protodeacon placed the triple tiara on the pope's head while reciting in Latin the coronation formula.

In 1978 the flabellum, or feather fan, the baldachin, or canopy, and the *sedia gestatoria* had all disappeared, along with the tiara. Instead, the Cardinal-Protodeacon would henceforth impose on the newly-elected pope the sacred pallium.

---

[59] Filmed interview of G. De Carli with Monsignor L. Capovilla, cited in A. Tornielli, *Paolo VI, op. cit.*, 343.

c) The turn to the left in Italian politics

A few weeks before he died, Pope Roncalli had sent Archbishop Casaroli on an exploratory mission to Budapest and Prague. On July 16, 1963, Pope Paul VI convoked a meeting of the Congregation for Extraordinary Ecclesiastical Affairs in order to discuss whether, "in spite of the many very serious difficulties, confirmed by our initial contacts, it is in the interest of the Church and of souls to continue with the negotiations that had been started confidentially."[60] The unanimous favorable opinion of the cardinal-members of the congregation confirmed the course of action favored by Paul VI himself, and Casaroli met in the most absolute secrecy with the Czechoslovak and Hungarian ambassadors, accrediting them to the Italian government on September 6 and 12 and on October 1 and 5.

With regard to Italian politics, despite the fact that he was personally acquainted with its protagonists from the years of their youth, Pope Montini nevertheless wanted the Vatican's command post on politics to remain in the hands of the secretariat of state.[61] The American President Kennedy, who during a visit to Rome had been received in audience by the pope on July 2, 1963, encouraged a political "opening to the left." A CIA document from that same month of July asserted that there "were no alternatives" to the alliance between the Christian Democrats and the Italian Socialist Party brought about by Aldo Moro, who after all enjoyed the pontifical blessing: "The new pope, Montini, is a liberal who would have to back Moro."[62]

On November 23, 1963, Moro formed the first center-left government. A few hours prior to that, in Dallas, President Kennedy had been assassinated. On two occasions in the years 1963-1964, during the council, the unity of the Christian Democrats would be rescued, *in extremis,* by specific actions of Pope Montini. He accomplished this by means of two well-aimed interventions published in *L'Osservatore Romano* allowing Moro to proceed with the development of his political strategy.[63]

---

[60] G. Barberini, *L'Ostpolitik della Santa Sede, op. cit.*, 96.

[61] Cf. A. Tornielli, *Paolo VI, op. cit.*, 350.

[62] Ennio Carretto, "La Cia: anche il papa per il centrosinistra," in *Corriere della Sera*, September 19, 2003.

[63] Cf. Pier Paolo Saleri, "Moro e la trasfigurazione del dossettismo," in G. Baget Bozzo and P. P. Saleri, *Giuseppe Dossetti: La costituzione come ideologia politica* (Milan: Edizioni Ares, 2009), 155.

The "turn to the left" by the Christian Democrats concluded, and in a certain sense overturned, the epoch that had started with the elections of April 18, 1948. Whereas those elections had represented the clear rejection of communism on the part of Catholic Italy, the opening to the left set in motion a process of "cooperation" with the communists which would progressively lead to the plan for an "historic compromise"—which then failed. Yet the end of Christian Democratic anti-communism and the onset of center-left governments was not a merely political fact; it was also a cultural fact, because it marked a new way of viewing the relations between Christianity and the modern world, under pressure from the secularizing ideologies that were spreading during those years.[64] Paul VI wanted to encourage that "turn," from the beginning of his pontificate.

3. The intersession of 1963

a) The Fulda Conference and Father Rahner

The national episcopal conferences acted as organized places where preparations were made for the debate on the conciliar schemas.

In the United States, around 125 bishops met in Chicago in early August of 1963. During the same period, the Argentine bishops met in Buenos Aires. The Italian Episcopal Conference met in Rome on August 27-28, and the Spanish Conference in Madrid in mid-September.

For their part, the German-speaking bishops and their theologians met in Munich on February 5 and 6 to examine in particular the schema *De Ecclesia*. The meeting that attracted the most attention, however, was the one that was held in Fulda, Germany, from August 26 to 29,[65] through the initiative of the three German-speaking Cardinals, Döpfner, Frings, and König. On July 9, Döpfner sent to all the bishops of Germany and Austria a letter inviting them to the gathering; enclosed was a program for discussion on the twelve schemas that had been approved by John XXIII

[64] Cf. R. de Mattei, *Il centro che ci portò a sinistra* (Rome: Edizioni Fiducia, 1994); Marco Invernizzi, "Il 18 aprile 1948: un voto dimenticato: Le conseguenze di un'anomalia," in *Dal "centrismo al Sessantotto,"* ed. M. Invernizzi and Paolo Martinucci (Milan: Ares, 2007), 13–33; A. D'Angelo, *Moro, i vescovi e l'apertura a sinistra, op. cit.*

[65] Cf. Wiltgen, 78–84.

on April 22. The same invitation was extended to the council fathers of Switzerland and the Scandinavian countries.

The Fulda meeting, with Cardinal Frings, presiding, began on August 26 with four cardinals in attendance, along with seventy archbishops and bishops representing ten countries. In addition to Austria, Germany, Switzerland, and the Scandinavian countries, France, Belgium, and Holland had also sent representatives. Cardinal Alfrink had come in person representing Holland.

Ralph Wiltgen observes: "Since the position of the German-language bishops was regularly adopted by the European alliance, and since the alliance position was regularly adopted by the council, a single theologian might have his views accepted by the whole council if they had been accepted by the German-speaking bishops. There was such a theologian: Father Karl Rahner, S.J."[66]

It would be impossible to summarize more efficaciously the decisive influence of Rahner on the council fathers; in a private conversation Cardinal Frings described him as "the greatest theologian of the century."[67] The other "experts" were also counting on Rahner's reputation; Chenu wrote to him: "may your influence contribute toward giving this council its countenance and its aims."[68] On December 14, 1962, *Time* magazine, in its religion section, had dedicated an article to the Jesuit theologian, with a photo and the headline: "A Holy Boldness." For many people, as the article averred, the most vitally important place of the council was not St. Peter's, but rather a third-floor room at the German College that was occupied by Father Rahner, who was considered as "the most profound of contemporary theologians."[69]

Theoretically, Rahner was only the theologian of Cardinal König. In fact, as Wiltgen points out, his was "the most influential mind at the Fulda conference."[70] Rahner, with the help of Father Joseph Ratzinger

---

[66] Ibid. 80.

[67] Ibid.

[68] Chenu, *Diario*, 58. [corrected from "Wiltgen"]

[69] Father de Lubac reports this in his Diary, commenting, "The fact is sufficiently well documented" (De Lubac, *Quaderni*, 439).

[70] Wiltgen, 80.

and German Jesuit Fathers Grillmeier[71] and Semmelroth, had been the one who examined the three schemas under discussion by the Theological Commission: the texts on revelation, the Blessed Virgin Mary, and the Church. On August 26 and 27, the Fulda conference examined these documents, adopting the amendments proposed by Rahner. Cardinal Döpfner then took the new revised texts to Rome, delivering them to the general secretariat on behalf of the German-speaking council fathers and the Episcopal Conference of the Scandinavian countries. The conference did not escape notice by the press, which had spoken about "a conspiracy against the Roman curia."

On September 2, Cardinal Döpfner went to visit Paul VI in Castel Gandolfo to reassure him. "It was a great relief to me," he later said, "when I saw that His Holiness had not taken seriously the reports which had appeared in the Italian press about Fulda."[72] An article clarifying the issue, published in agreement with the secretary of the council, Archbishop Felici, appeared in *L'Osservatore Romano* on September 4, 1963. On September 7, Döpfner wrote to the bishops who had participated in the Fulda conference, informing them about his audience with the pope, the article in *L'Osservatore Romano*, and the order in which the schemas would be treated in the up-coming session of the council: 1) the Church; 2) the Blessed Virgin Mary; 3) the bishops; 4) the laity; and 5) ecumenism.

On September 12, 1963, Paul VI announced the creation of a Secretariat for Non-Christian Religions. This initiative had been started eight months earlier by Cardinal Tien,[73] the archbishop of Taipei, and by Dutch Bishop Thijssen,[74] ordinary of the Diocese of Larantuka in Indonesia. At a press conference on April 8, Cardinal Tien had declared

---

[71] Aloys Grillmeier (1910–1998), German Jesuit, ordained in 1937. Professor of fundamental theology and of dogmatic theology at the Jesuit scholasticate in Sankt-Georgen (Frankfurt) from 1950 to 1978. Created cardinal in 1994. At the council he was the expert of Wilhelm Kempf, bishop of Limburg, and *peritus* in the second session.

[72] Wiltgen, 81.

[73] Joseph Cheng Tien-Siang, O.P. (1922–1990), ordained in 1952, bishop of Kaohsiung (Taiwan) in 1961, archbishop of Kaohsiung in 1979.

[74] Antoine Hubert Thijssen, S.V.D. (1906–1982), ordained in 1932, apostolic vicar of Endeh (Indonesia) and titular bishop of Nilopolis in 1951, bishop of Larantuka in 1961, titular bishop of Eguga in 1973.

that "it is most important that the Catholic Church come to understand better the major non-Christian religions of the world, and that the non-Christian religions come to understand the Church better."[75] The proposal had had the support of Cardinals Bea, Frings, Liénart, and König. The last-mentioned prelate had been proposed as the president of the new organization.

b) The "moderators" of the council

On the day after the election of Paul VI, Cardinal Suenens suggested that he create a "brain trust" to give direction the council and provide it with the necessary impetus.[76] In the summer of 1963, Suenens, Döpfner, and Lercaro developed a plan to rewrite the conciliar rules, based on the creation of a single organ to guide the assembly.[77] The pope adopted the plan and on September 13, 1963, announced the appointment of four cardinal "moderators" of the council with the task of directing the conciliar assemblies with an executive mandate. The cardinals named were, conveniently, Döpfner, Suenens, and Lercaro, to whom the pope wanted to add Agagianian,[78] a curia cardinal who had been a candidate favored by the conservatives in the last two conclaves, but was also noted for his silence in the assembly hall.

Moreover, Cardinal Lercaro had designated his own personal counselor (and inspirer), Father Giuseppe Dossetti, as secretary of the college (of moderators). Dossetti's work was not limited simply to being the personal theologian of Cardinal Lercaro; he was rather heavily involved in preparing a new draft of the rules, in close collaboration with the historian Hubert Jedin.[79] With this decision Paul VI seemed to be trying to give Vatican II a collegial management. Monsignor Michele

---

[75] Wiltgen, 75–76.

[76] Cf. Poswick, *Journal*, 363–364.

[77] Alberto Melloni, "The Beginning of the Second Period: The Great Debate on the Church," in HVT 3:1–116 at 9–10.

[78] AS II/1:9–13.

[79] M. Maccarrone, "Paolo VI e il Concilio," *op. cit.*, 105.

Maccarrone[80] recalls that the one who steered the college of moderators (and through the college—the council) was Fr. Dosetti, who prepared the texts to be submitted to the council fathers in the assembly.[81] Dossetti made use of the newspaper *L'Avvenire d'Italia*, edited by a faithful friend of his, Raniero La Valle, who published confidential material as well. The most sensational case was the publication on the front page of the issue dated October 16, 1963, of the text of four queries from the moderators concerning collegiality and the diaconate. "The text had not yet been distributed to the fathers, and already it was ostentatiously made public!" Monsignor Maccarrone comments.[82] He recalls how Paul VI, who was thoroughly annoyed by the publication, promptly ordered the secretary general to burn the three thousand copies that had been printed at the request of Cardinal Lercaro. Dossetti was then removed on account of the casual and uncalled-for manner in which he claimed to perform his duties as "secretary" of the moderators.

As Cardinal Ruffini quickly pointed out, a kind of authority had been granted to the moderators that until then the council presidency had never possessed.[83] The choices made by Paul VI, however, showed that he intended to continue along the same line as his predecessor. The papal appointments gave the "European alliance" new power and influence. As Ralph Wiltgen emphasizes: It already had advanced "from control of thirty percent of the council presidency and control of fifty percent of the Coordinating Commission to control of seventy-five percent of the board of cardinal moderators."[84]

---

80 Michele Maccarrone (1913–1993), professor of Church History at the Lateran University, secretary from 1954 and president from 1963 of the Pontifical Committee for Historical Sciences, member of the Secretariat for Promoting Christian Unity, conciliar *peritus*. Cf. Fermina Álvarez Alonso, "Primato e collegialità alla luce del 'Fondo Maccarrone,'" in *CVII: Centro Vaticano II: Ricerche e documenti* III/1 (2003): 11–59; Mario Sensi, "Monsignor Maccarrone e l'apporto della scuola Lateranense al Vaticano II," in *CVII: Centro Vaticano II: Ricerche e documenti* V/2 (2005): 51–69.

81 Cf. M. Maccarrone, "Paolo VI e il Concilio," *op. cit.*, 108.

82 Ibid.

83 On the profile of the moderators, see R. La Valle, *Il coraggio del Concilio, op. cit.*, 5–95; on the role of Lercaro and Dossetti see Lercaro, *Lettere*, 157–167.

84 Wiltgen, 83.

c) The reform of the Roman curia

The address by Paul VI to the Roman curia on September 21, 1963,[85] was mellifluous in its tone but tough in its substance, and it had programmatic significance. Paul VI urged the curia not to offer resistance to papal decisions: "We are certain," he declared, "that there will never be any trace of hesitation from the curia with respect to the most important wishes of the pope; that it will never be suspected of any differences of judgment or opinion with regard to the judgment or opinion of the pope."[86] He called for both "an identity of views" and "a uniformity of intent." with the wishes of the pontiff himself. He announced "various reforms," among which were "a more far-sighted supernatural vision" and "a more attentive ecumenical preparation." Such reforms, he explained, "will certainly be pondered, and will be drawn up according to venerable and reasonable traditions on the one hand, and according to the needs of the present time on the other. And they will certainly be practical and beneficial, because they will have no other purpose than to eliminate what is weak or superfluous in the formalities and norms that regulate the Roman curia; and to bring into being what is vital and beneficial for its most efficient and appropriate functioning." These reforms "will be formulated and promulgated by the curia itself! Therefore the Roman curia will not be afraid, for example, of being enlisted for a broader international vision, or of being educated by a more attentive ecumenical preparation."[87]

The young theologian Joseph Ratzinger understood very well what these words of the pope meant in that historical predicament: "It may be said without exaggeration," Ratzinger recalls, "that this speech constituted not merely an episode in the history of curia and papacy but that it was also part of conciliar history."[88] He added: "What was happening was that the traditional solidarity between pope and curia was now giving way to an unprecedented new solidarity between pope and council."[89]

---

[85] AS II/1:49–56; Caprile, 3:7–12.

[86] Ibid., 51.

[87] Ibid., 54.

[88] J. Ratzinger, *Theological Highlights of Vatican II* (New York: Paulist Press, 1966), 34.

[89] Ibid., 35.

4. The opening of the second session

The second session of the council started on September 29, 1963. During the Mass the gospel was solemnly enthroned—the homage that Paul VI wished to render to sacred scripture. In his inaugural address,[90] which was the prelude not only to that session of the council but to the new pontificate as well, the basic theme was the need for a structural reform of the Church, so as to determine the nature and the role of the episcopacy. Paul VI listed four objectives of the council: "a more thorough definition"[91] concerning the essence and the constitution of the Church; the renewal of the Church understood as "a springtime reawakening of the immense spiritual and moral energies that are, so to speak, dormant within the Church;"[92] the promotion of unity among Christians; and dialogue with contemporary man "beyond the confines of the Christian horizon."[93]

"It seems that the time has now come," the pope added, "when the truth about the Church of Christ should be more profoundly examined, reworked, and expressed, perhaps not in those solemn pronouncements that are called dogmatic definitions, but rather by making use of declarations in which, with a clearer and more authoritative teaching, the Church declares what she thinks about herself."[94]

His words on the dialogue with the world were striking: "Let the world know with certainty that it is viewed lovingly by the Church, which nourishes a sincere admiration for it, and is moved by the frank intention not to dominate it but to serve it, not to despise it but to augment its dignity, not to condemn it but to offer it comfort and salvation."[95]

On the subject of ecumenism, the pope seemed to go farther than John XXIII by admitting past errors committed by the Church. Addressing himself to the representatives of the Christian confessions separated from the Catholic Church, he declared: "If there is any blame that can be imputed to us for that separation, we humbly ask God's pardon for it, and

90 AS II/1:183–199.

91 Ibid., 189.

92 Ibid., 191.

93 Ibid., 198.

94 Ibid., 190.

95 Ibid., 197.

we also ask for forgiveness from those brethren who feel that they have been offended by us."[96]

Twenty days later, on October 17, while receiving in his private library the non-Catholic observers at the council, Paul VI described "reciprocal pardon" as "the best method" of turning "towards something new that is to be brought to birth, a dream to be realized."[97] This was perhaps the first in a disconcerting series of unusual acts of "repentance" and requests for pardon in the history of the Church.[98] The Mystical Body of Christ is, in fact, indefectible it itself, through the divine promise of its founder. Faults and errors may be committed by its members, but the responsibility for them is personal and never falls on the Church, which cannot "repent" retroactively on their behalf. The distinction between the Church and her members was, however, not clear in the pronoun "we" utilized by Paul VI with reference to the admission of faults and the request for pardon. The style and the language of Paul VI appeared to be quite far-removed from those of Pius XII and of John XXIII himself. Father Kobler underscores in particular the use by Pope Montini of concepts and terms borrowed from phenomenology and "transcendental Thomism," such as "conscience" and "experience,"[99] which were destined to reemerge forcefully in the encylical *Ecclesiam suam* dated August 6, 1964.

5. Pilgrim church and church militant

The first General Congregation, or plenary meeting, of the second session—the 37th of the council—opened on September 30, 1963. The first schema on the day's agenda was the new draft on the Church,[100] which had been revised by the Belgian theologian Gerard Philips, at the

---

[96] Ibid., 194.

[97] Caprile, 3:149.

[98] Cf. Luigi Accattoli, *Quando il Papa chiede perdono: Tutti i mea culpa di Giovanni Paolo II* (Milan: Mondadori, 1997).

[99] J. F. Kobler, "Were theologians the Engineers of Vatican II?" *op. cit.*, 239–242.

[100] On *Lumen gentium*, see *La Chiese del Vaticano II: Studi e commenti intorno alla costituzione dommatica "Lumen gentium,"* ed. Guilherme Baraúna, O.F.M. (Florence, Vallecchi, 1965). For the various rewritings of the document, see G. Alberigo and Franca Magistretti, *Synopsis historica constitutionis dogmaticae, Lumen gentium* (Bologna: Istituto per le Scienze Religiose, 1975).

behest of Cardinal Suenens. The schema began with the words, *Lumen gentium* ("Light of nations"), referring not to the Church, however, but to Christ: *Lumen gentium cum sit Christus* ("Since Christ is the light of nations"). For more than two years, Philips had dedicated himself, body and soul, to the success of this schema, with the collaboration of an international team of "experts." In February of 1963, the Coordinating Commission had told the Doctrinal Commission to prepare a new text *De Ecclesia* for the beginning of the second session. A sub-commission was then formed, headed by Cardinal Michael Browne,[101] which was made up of seven bishops, each one of whom designated a theologian to work on it. Of the "seven" *periti* named, only two (Gagnebet by Browne and Balić by Parente) belonged to the conservatives; five were progressives (Lafortune[102] named by Léger; Rahner by König; Philips by Charue; Congar by Garrone; and Thils[103] by Schröffer[104]).

Cardinals Ottaviani and Browne, president and vice-president, respectively, of the Doctrinal Commission, wrote a concise introduction to the text, with which they were obviously dissatisfied.[105] When the debate began, the first two interventions, those of Cardinals Frings[106] and Siri,[107] confirmed that a profound divergence of views existed within the assembly. On one side, there was the concept of the *Nouvelle Théologie*, or "New Theology," in particular Congar's, which pitted the "Church of rights"

---

[101] Michael Browne (1887–1971), Irish Dominican, ordained in 1910, professor and then rector of the Angelicum from 1923 to 1941, master of the Sacred Palace (1951), master general of the Dominican order from 1955 to 1962, member of the Preparatory Commission for Bishops. Created cardinal in 1962.

[102] Pierre Lafortune (1926–1984), Canadian, ordained in 1951, private theologian of Cardinal Léger, expert at the council.

[103] Gustave Thils (1909–2000), Belgian, ordained in 1931, professor of theology at the Catholic University of Louvain (1947–1979), member of the Secretariat for Promoting Christian Unity.

[104] Joseph Schröffer (1903–1983), ordained in 1928, bishop of Eichstätt from 1948 to 1967, secretary of the Congregation for Catholic Education from 1967 to 1976. Created cardinal in 1976.

[105] AS II/1:337–342.

[106] Ibid., 343–346.

[107] Ibid., 366–368.

against the pneumatic "Church of love."[108] On the other side, there was the traditional view based on the doctrine of St. Robert Bellarmine, interpreted in the light of *Mystici Corporis*.[109] The contrast was confirmed the following day by the opposing speeches by Cardinal Raul Silva Henríquez of Santiago, Chile, and Cardinal Ernesto Ruffini, of Palermo, Sicily. Silva Henríquez maintained that the Church must be considered as a communion of local churches in the same sense in which St. Paul addressed "the church of Corinth" and "the church of Ephesus."[110] Ruffini, in a polemic aimed also at Frings, criticized the concept of church-as-sacrament, a term already used by the heretic Tyrell, and disputed the scriptural basis for collegiality, recalling that Christ said to Peter alone: "You are Peter and upon this rock I will build my Church."[111]

The discussion on ecclesiology, which was at the center of the debate during the second session, focused on the four chapters of the schema: 1) the mystery of the Church in the economy of salvation; 2) the hierarchical constitution of the Church; 3) the people of God and the laity; and 4) the universal call to holiness.

Inside the hall two tendencies collided: the first reiterated the classic concept of the Church as a society both visible and invisible at the same time; the second tended to emphasize the invisible, charismatic dimension of the Church at the expense of the juridical, visible dimension.

On October 12, 1963, Bishop Franić[112] of Split, Yugoslavia, proposed that in article 7 the traditional title "Church Militant" should be added to the title "Pilgrim Church" already found in the schema.[113] Bishop Franić explained:

---

[108] Cf. A. Acerbi, *Due ecclesiologie, op. cit.*, 30–105.

[109] "The hundreds of attempts to find an adequate definition of the Church, a broader formula than the one offered by St. Robert Bellarmine, find a solution in *Mystici Corporis*," Monsignor Fenton had written, concluding his extensive treatise on traditional ecclesiology ("Scholastic Definitions of the Catholic Church," *op. cit.*, 227).

[110] AS II/1:366–367.

[111] Ibid., 391–394. Frings adopted the theses of K. Rahner, *Kirche und Sakramente* (Freiburg im Breisgau: Herder, 1960) and E. Schillebeecks, *Christ, the Sacrament of the Encounter with God* (New York, Sheed & Ward, 1963) (original ed. 1957).

[112] Frane Franić, auxiliary bishop (1950) then archbishop of Split-Makaraska (1969–1988), member of the Preparatory Theological Commission and of the Doctrinal Commission.

[113] AS II/1:442–444.

> The reason for this proposal is certainly not an appetite for provocation; far be it from us especially who desire the precious treasure of religious peace. But it does seem to me, venerable fathers, that this observation is somehow fundamental for the council as a whole. In fact, peace is the highest good: Christ himself is called our peace, but, alas, we cannot achieve and preserve peace, either in our souls or in the Church, without a difficult and continuous daily battle, of course not a battle with atomic bombs or any kind of classical weapons, but with spiritual weapons. Unless we clearly present the Church with such an image and in such a situation, then she really could find herself in the condition that is commonly called psychological disarmament. In that case, we would be presenting the Church to the faithful and to the world as being essentially defective. And that would not only be harmful to our faithful; it would represent spiritual harm for the whole world.... How can we fight as good soldiers of Christ, as St. Paul teaches, unless in addition to charity and the other virtues we cultivate also in ourselves and in our priests and in our faithful the virtue of fortitude in confronting the malicious and atheistic world?! For the love of the world, then, and also for the atheistic world, we must not only *call* the Church militant, make sure that she is militant. I firmly believe that no reasonable man, not even the Marxists themselves, could be offended by the use of this term: Church Militant. Otherwise, the atheists would have to start despising themselves, since they too describe themselves as militant."[114]

The bishop of Split was recalling an elementary truth: the Church will never cease to be confronted by enemies, who are not abstract ideas but men and groups organized to fight and, if possible, to destroy the Church. The militant nature of the Church had often been mentioned by Pius XII; according to him, "what is going on is a battle that is increasing almost every day in scale and violence, and it is therefore necessary for all Christians, but especially all militant Catholics, 'to stand up and fight, if necessary even to the death, for their mother the Church, with the weapons that are allowed' (St. Bernard, *Ep.* 221, n. 3)."[115] Bishop Franić, however, was not an intransigent hard-liner like his predecessor, Archbishop Stepinac.

---

[114] Ibid., 443.

[115] Pius XII, Address to Catholic Action of Italy (December 8, 1953), in DRM 15:501–509 at 506.

Yet his request seemed too strong to Cardinal Wyszyński,[116] who the next day rejected the concept of a Church Militant, inasmuch as "the men of our time oppose all armed strife, because, for the most part, if not usually, they are defeated in that battle."

The archbishop of Warsaw expressed himself as follows:

> The notion of a Church Militant is certainly a theological concept, and no doubt it points to the very great merits of the Church in the universal human family. We do not want to disregard what is taught by fundamental dogmatic theology or the public law of the Church; but we cannot ignore the real situation in which many hundreds of thousands of the children of God's Church find themselves.... We fear that the notion of the Church Militant, still keeping the traditional definition, at this particular psychological moment, will end up replacing the more essential notion of the Church, namely, a life-giving Church (the life and light of men) and a sanctifying Church ("be holy..."). The men of our time who possess the gift of faith are opposed to all strife, because for the most part, if not usually, they are defeated in these battles [pl. sic]. Nevertheless they prefer to trust in the Church, which gives life and holiness, which defends the natural rights of man, which forms souls and urges them to sustain and defend the natural, moral, and social order, and above all the supernatural order in the world."[117]

With these words, the Polish Cardinal, although staunch in his defense of the liturgy and of moral principles, confirmed that he advocated an "accommodating" line with regard to communism, an approach that was quite different from the one personified in those same years by Cardinal Mindszenty. Bishop Franić himself recorded this in his memoirs: "A new line had to be followed at the council: avoid provocations or condemnations of any kind, and to make only conciliatory speeches...."[118]

---

[116] AS II/2:574–577.

[117] Ibid., 575–576.

[118] F. Franić, *L'Église, colonne de la vérité: Mémoires de mes activités doctrinales au Concile Oecuménique Vatican II* (Split: Knjizevni Krug, 1998), 138–139.

6. The Marian question

a) "Maximalists" and "minimalists" at the council

Early in October a new conflict broke out when it came time to decide whether the schema on the Blessed Virgin should be discussed by itself or included in the schema on the Church.[119] The debate revealed the existence of two opposing tendencies, "maximalist" and "minimalist." The "maximalists" were the supporters of the great Marian movement of the twentieth century,[120] which, after the definition of the dogma of the Assumption, looked forward to the proclamation of a new dogma by the pope and the bishops assembled in council: the dogma of Mary, Mediatrix of all graces.[121]

No Catholic theologian at that time doubted that Mary exercised an influence that was in a certain way immediate and actual in the application of the fruits of the redemption, or rather in the distribution of all graces to each and every human being. At the Marian Congress held at Lourdes in 1958,[122] two tendencies among Mariologists had emerged, however: a

[119] Cf. R. Laurentin, *la Vierge au Concile: présentation, texte et traduction du chapitre VIIIe de la constitution dogmatique Lumen gentium consacré à la Vierge Marie dans le mystère de l'Église* (Paris: Lethielleux, 1965); G. M. Besutti, O.S.M., "Note di cronaca sul Concilio Vaticano II e lo Schema 'De Beata Maria Virgine,'" in *Marianum* 26 (1964): 1–42; *Idem,* "Lo schema mariano al Concilio Vaticano II: Documentazione e note di cronaca," in *Marianum* 28 (1966): 1–203; Candido Pozo, "La doctrina mariológica del Concilio Vaticano II," in *María en la obra de la salvación* (Madrid: BAC, 1974), 19–56; Ermanno M. Toniolo, *La Beata Vergine Maria nel Concilio Vaticano II: Cronistoria del capitolo VIII della costituzione dogmatica "Lumen gentium" e sinossi di tutte le relazioni* (Rome: Centro di Cultural Mariana Madre della Chiesa, 2004); C. Antonelli, *Il dibattito su Maria nel Concilio Vaticano II* (Padua: Edizioni Messaggero, 2009).

[120] The seeds of the "Marian movement," in its modern phase, go back to the apostolate of St. Louis-Marie Grignion de Montfort (1673–1716), with his treatise on *True Devotion to the Blessed Virgin* (published for the first time in 1942) and of St. Alphonsus Maria de Liguori (1696–1787) with his *Glories of Mary* (1750).

[121] On Mary's mediation, see the study by Father Alessandro M. Appollonio, F.I., "Maria Santissima Mediatrice di tutte le grazie: La natura dell'influsso della Beata Vergine nell'applicazione della Redenzione," in *Immaculata Mediatrix* VII/2 (2007): 157–181.

[122] The acts were published by Academia Mariana Internationalis under the title *Maria et Ecclesia:*

maximalist tendency, which held that all of Mary's privileges stemmed from her divine maternity within the hypostatic order;[123] and a minimalist tendency, according to which Mariology had its foundation in the parallel between Mary and the Church.[124] The first tendency was defined as "Christotypical" because it emphasized the intimate connection between Christ and his Mother in the one act of salvation. The co-redemption and the mediation of Mary derived from this union. The second tendency asserted instead that Mary's role was subordinate to that of the Church, which held the first place after Christ and of which Mary was only a member. Her privileges were to be understood within the Christian community, of which she remained the "type" and model. For this reason the second tendency was called "ecclesiotypical."

The "maximalists" were represented among the council *periti* by two strong personalities: Father Carlo Balić,[125] president since 1960 of the Pontifical International Marian Academy, and Father Gabriele Maria Roschini, head of the Marianum in Rome.

Carlo Balić, born in Croatia in 1899, brought to the debate the rugged character of his birthplace. He had been living in Rome since 1933, when he had been called to teach at the Antonianum, where he was engaged in various activities as a scholar, editor, and, especially, organizer of

Acta Congressus Mariologici—mariani civitate Lourdes, anno 1958 celebrati, in 16 vols. (Rome, 1959–1962). On that occasion, Father Gabriele Maria Roschini, O.S.M., had presented a foundational study on Mary's mediation: *De natura influxus B. M. Virginis in applicatione redemptionis, ibid.*, vol. II, *De munere et loco quem tenet Beata Virgo in corpore Christi mystico* (1959), 223–295.

123 Cf. M. J. Nicolas, "L'appartenance de la Mère de Dieu à l'ordre hypostatique," in *Études Mariales* 3 (1937): 145–181.

124 Cf. F. Courth, "Heinrich Maria Köster (1911–1993): Forscher und Künder Mariens," in *Marianum* 55 (1993): 429–459; Manfred Hauke, *Introduzione alla mariologia* (Lugano: Eupress FTL, 2008), 92–93; C. Pozo, "La doctrina mariológica", *op. cit.*

125 Carlo Balić (1899–1977), Croatian member of the Order of Friars Minor. Ordained in 1927, was professor and rector of the Pontifical Athenaeum Antonianum, president of the commission for the critical edition of the works of Duns Scotus, founder and president of the Pontifical International Marian Academy, consultor of the Holy Office, conciliar *peritus*. About him see J. A. de Aldama, S.J., "Semblanza del P. Carlos Balić ofm (1899–1977)," in *Antonianum* 52 (1977): 702–707; *P. Carlo Balić o.f.m., Profilo, impressioni, ricordi*, ed. Paolo Melada, O.F.M., and Dinko Aračič (Rome: Pontificia Accademia Mariana Internazionale, 1978); D. Aračič, *La dottrina mariologica negli scritti di Carlo Balić* (Rome: Pontificia Accademia Mariana Internazionale, 1980).

Mariological Congresses, including the one held on the occasion of the Lourdes Centenary (1958), which was a kind of "dress rehearsal" for the conciliar conflict between "maximalists" and "minimalists." Father Congar, who did not share Balić's passionate Mariology, described him disdainfully in his diary as making a "voluble sales-pitch"[126] and being "a Dalmatian street vendor,"[127] a "clown,"[128] and a "fairground tumbler."[129]

Monsignor Antonio Piolanti, on the other hand, wrote of Balić as "a titan, as it were, built overlooking the abyss of the contrasts of a great soul with unlimited horizons and immense desires. It was easy to detect in the vigorous physiognomy of this worthy son of strong, noble Croatia a kind of *coincidentia oppositorum* (combination of opposites): the heart of a child and the driving force of St. Jerome; the tenderness of a mother and the imperiousness of a captain; an acute and penetrating intelligence and a fiery, decisive will; a broad-minded generosity and Dantean indignation."[130]

Father Roschini, a Servite priest from Viterbo, was a man of faith and scholarship and had to his credit, like Balić, a very extensive bibliography, including ponderous treatises and an entire *Dictionary of Mariology*,[131] published in 1960, in which he explored the mystery of Mary in all of its aspects. It was owing to his diligence that the Pontifical Theological Faculty Marianum was established on December 8, 1950. His extraordinary scholarly, organizational, and popularizing work has yet to be studied in its entirety.[132]

The dream of both Balić and Roschini to have Mary proclaimed as Mediatrix was shattered in the council hall. Recalling the strenuous battle that he had waged at the council in defense of the Marian privileges, Father Balić, still clear-eyed though exhausted, declared to Piolanti: "There, of all places, all my work was ruined!"[133]

---

126 Congar, *Journal*, 52.

127 Ibid., 54.

128 Ibid., 538.

129 Ibid. 605.

130 A. Piolanti, "Abisso dei contrasti," in *P. Carlo Balić o.f.m., Profilo, impressioni, ricordi, op. cit.*, 192.

131 Cf. G. M. Roschini, O.S.M., *Dizionario di Mariologia* (Rome: Studium, 1960).

132 On his role in the council, cf. P. Parrotta, *op. cit.*, 54–62.

133 A. Piolanti, "Abisso dei contrasti," in *P. Carlo Balić o.f.m., Profilo, impressioni, ricordi, op. cit.*,

The majority of the council fathers, as the various votes had highlighted, cultivated a lively devotion to Mary and leaned toward the positions of the "maximalists." The central European minority, in contrast, was characterized by its aversion to what Father Yves Congar described as "Mariano-Christianity."[134] Congar's diary entry for the evening of September 22, 1961, reads: "I [realized] the drama which I have experienced all my life. The need to fight, in the name of the gospel and of apostolic faith, against a development, a Mediterranean and Irish proliferation, of a Mariology which does not come from revelation, but is backed up by pontifical texts."[135]

Congar had the support of Rahner, but also that of the young Mariologist René Laurentin, the best-grounded of the "minimalists," whom Congar credited with launching "the anti-maximalist battle" at the council.[136] "We tell each other that we must not be TOO antagonistic, for fear of bringing about something worse than what we are anxious to avoid."[137]

b) The anti-maximalist offensive gets underway

The signal for the anti-maximalist offensive was the publication, immediately before the second session, of Laurentin's book, *The Question of Mary*,[138] in which the Marian movement was presented as "a problem." "There is no doubt that the Marian movement is fruitful, fervent, and prosperous," Laurentin wrote. "But would it not be true to say that its abundance is excessive, its intensity unhealthy, its development specialized and partly pathological?"[139] Contemporary Mariology, characterized by an

191–192.

[134] Letter to the Marist Father Maurice Villain dated November 23, 1950, in E. Fouilloux, "The Antepreparatory Phase: The Slow Emergence from Inertia," in HVT 1:55–166 at 83.

[135] Congar, *Journal*, 54.

[136] Ibid.

[137] Ibid.

[138] Cf. R. Laurentin, *La question mariale* (Paris: Éd. du Seuil, 1963); Eng. transl. *Mary's Place in the Church* (London: Burns & Oates, 1965); American edition: *The Question of Mary* (New York, Chicago, San Francisco: Holt, Rinehard and Winston, 1965).

[139] *The Question of Mary*, 27–28.

excessive abundance of writings,[140] had exhibited, according to Laurentin, an *a-priori* tendency that was committed to the unconditional exaltation of Our Lady.[141] It was necessary to "purify" this tendency in order to make it compatible with the requirements of ecumenism and of the new theology.

The minimalist line that the French Mariologist suggested following was the typically hypocritical line of the "Third Way": neither "a Christianity of the Virgin that St. Paul would not recognize," nor "a Christianity without the Virgin that would no longer be Catholic."[142] This framing of the issue won the sympathy of the moderates, and above all the support of the media, whose mechanisms Laurentin, a theologian-journalist, was well acquainted with.

Laurentin's book was refuted in great detail by a great Mariologist, Father Aldama,[143] at the request of Father Balić and Father Roschini; the latter in turn joined in the debate with a little volume on *The So-called "Marian Question."*[144]

Father Aldama recalled, as characteristic of the great Marian revival of the twentieth century, the numerous religious congregations, of both men and women, that had arisen with the name of Mary; the repeated Marian apparitions in Paris (in 1830 to St. Catherine Labouré), LaSalette (1846), Lourdes (1858), Philippsdorf (1858), Pontmain (1871), Fatima (1917), Beauraing (1932), and a Banneux (1933), with their respective shrines, pilgrimages, and devotions; the congresses, societies, publications, and cathedrals dedicated to Mary; the countless pronouncements by the Roman pontiffs, true promoters of the Marian movement.[145] Pius XII, in particular, saw in the ever growing devotion of the faithful to the Blessed Virgin "the

---

140 Ibid., 12–16.

141 Ibid., 17–18.

142 "It is to allow oneself to slip down these two slopes that would lead on the one hand to a Christianity of the Virgin that St. Paul would not recognize, and on the other to a Christianity without the Virgin that would no longer be Catholic." [The passage does not appear in the American edition. The author gives an Italian translation of the French text at page 81.]

143 J. A. de Aldama, S.J., *De quaestione mariali in hodierna vita Ecclesiae* (Rome: Pontificia Accademia Mariana Internazionale, 1964).

144 G. M. Roschini, O.S.M., *La cosidetta "questione mariana"* (Vicenza: Tip. S. Giuseppe, 1963).

145 J. A. de Aldama, S.J., *De quaestione mariali, op. cit.*, 2–35.

most encouraging sign of the times"[146] and "an infallible touchstone to distinguish true from false Christians."[147] It was thus a matter of continuing down a path already marked out.

Roschini, in his study, compared the attempts to "diminish" the impetus of the Marian movement to the *Monita salutaria* [*Salutary Warnings*] (1673) of the German jurist, Adam Widenfeld (1618-1680) who, three centuries earlier, had attacked the Marian devotion of his day. "History repeats itself," Roschini declared. "Around three centuries later, here we see a new, undoubtedly exaggerated reaction against the Marian movement, against today's Mariology, and against devotion to Mary." It was not possible, in his opinion, to speak about a maximalist tendency; "one can, however, with real grounds, speak about a *minimalist* tendency, which, prescinding completely from the teachings of the ordinary magisterium of the Church, not only denies absolute truths or calls them into question, but has gone so far as to privilege faith in the divine maternity, so as to identify the most Holy Mary with the Church, thus lowering her to the level of all the other members of the Mystical Body of Christ, as a *prima inter pares* (first woman among equals)."[148]

The "minimalists" enjoyed the support of John XXIII who, in 1954, six months before the encyclical by Pius XII, *Ad Coeli Reginam*, which instituted the feast of the Queenship of Mary, had experienced "considerable hesitation" in his mind with regard to a new feast of the Queenship of Mary, "fearing some serious harm to the apostolic efforts being undertaken to restore the unity of the Holy Catholic Church in the world."[149] This explains why Pope Roncalli was disposed to accept the requests of the "minimalists," who accused the "maximalists" of prejudicing ecumenism. (Paul VI would later subscribe to the same minimalist line.) His final

---

[146] Pius XII, Address *Una ben intima gioia* (March 10, 1948), in AAS 40 (1948): 120.

[147] Pius XII, Address *La Pentecôte* (May 29, 1950), in AAS 42 (1950): 483.

[148] G. M. Roschini, O.S.M., *La cosidetta "questione mariana," op. cit.*, 63.

[149] A. Roncalli, letter dated April 22, 1954, to the Secretariat of the Movement *Pro Regalitate Mariae*, in Angelina and G. Alberigo, *Giovanni XXIII: Profezia nella fedeltà* (Brescia: Queriniana, 1978), 489. The patriarch of Venice continued: "While dying, Jesus said to John: Behold your mother—this is enough for faith and the liturgy. The rest can be and is, to a great extent, edifying, and moving for a great many devout and pious souls: but for many, many others, although they are well disposed toward the Catholic Church, it can be irritating and—as is said nowadays—counterproductive" (ibid.).

intervention, during the work of the Preparatory Commission, had been on June 20, 1962, when he had sided with Cardinal Liénart against a proposal to confer on the Virgin the title of "Mediatrix,"[150] which he had described as "inopportune and even harmful." Father Bevilacqua confided in then-Bishop Helder Câmara: "I call the pope's attention to it every time I see a good book like *The Marian Question* by René Laurentin, or the books on the council written by Hans Küng. He likes Rahner and Häring very much. I do too."[151] Bishop Helder Câmara, for his part, commented: "Little by little the citadel of reaction is being transformed."[152]

In January, 1963, after the closing of the first session, the Coordinating Commission of the council decided that the schema on the Blessed Virgin Mary, Mother of the Church, would be treated independently from the schema *De Ecclesia.* "There is no doubt," Komonchak admits, that the schema *De Beata Maria Virgine*, even in its section on her mediatorial role, met the expectations and desires of a very large number of the bishops, as expressed in their antepreparatory *vota.*"[153]

The revised *Schema constitutionis dogmaticae de Maria Matre Ecclesiae* was sent to the fathers during the month of May. Neither the decision nor the text approved by the commission pleased Father Rahner. In a paper addressed to all the participants in the Fulda conference in August 1963, he expressed his lively concerns with regard to the document, assuring his readers that these concerns were shared by Fathers Grillmeier and Semmelroth. If the text were to be adopted, he said, "unimaginable harm would result from an ecumenical point of view, in relation to both Orientals and protestants."[154] Of course, Rahner added, it was not possible to try to scrap the schema, as had been done with the schema on the sources of revelation. In order to diminish its importance, therefore, it was a question of pressuring the fathers, as insistently as possible, to make the schema into a chapter or the epilogue of the schema on the Church. This, in his opinion, "would be the easiest way to delete from the schema statements which, theologically, are

---

150 AD II-II/4:77.

151 Câmara, *Lettres Conciliaires*, 2:583.

152 Ibid., 1:342.

153 J. A. Komonchak, "The Struggle for the Council during the Preparation," *op. cit.*, 260. See also Salvatore Perrella, *I "vota" e i "consilia" dei vescovi italiani sulla mariologia e sulla corredenzione nella fase antipreparatoria del Concilio Vaticano II* (Rome: Ed. Marianum, 1994).

154 Wiltgen, 91.

not sufficiently developed and which could only do incalculable harm from an ecumenical point of view. It would also prevent bitter discussion."[155]

The point that Rahner attacked more forcefully was the schema's teaching on the mediation of the Blessed Virgin Mary, and, more precisely, the title accorded to her of "Mediatrix of all graces." This teaching, proposed in the schema not as a dogma of faith but rather as a common doctrine of the Church, was rejected by Rahner, on account of the negative consequences which, in his opinion, it could have on Mariology and on the devotion of the faithful to Mary. Protestants flatly denied any cooperation whatsoever by Mary in redemption and abhorred the terms "Mediatrix" and, even more so, "co-redemptrix." He concluded by asserting that the bishops of Austria, Germany, and Switzerland should consider themselves obliged to commit themselves to an outright rejection of the schema in its current form.[156]

The Fulda conference adopted Rahner's suggestions, but on the question of Mary's mediation the participants limited themselves to criticizing the expression, "Mediatrix of all graces." Their proposal, officially submitted by the fathers of Fulda to the secretary general of the council, cited protestant sources too, recalling that the German Lutheran Bishop Debelius had declared in 1962 that the teaching of the Catholic Church on Mary was one of the major obstacles to ecumenical union. According to other German protestant authors, the council fathers had to remember that by approving a schema on Mary, they would set up another wall of division; they should therefore remain silent on the whole matter or else call back to order those who were guilty of excesses.

c) The success of the "minimalists"

On the day of the opening of the debate, September 30, 1963, the "minimalists" suddenly requested, through a speech by Cardinal Frings,[157] that everything related to the Blessed Virgin Mary be included in the schema on the Church, in order to facilitate ecumenical dialogue with

---

[155] Ibid.

[156] Wiltgen, 91–92. See also Antonio Escudero Cabello, *La cuestión de la mediación mariana en la preparación del Vaticano II: Elementor para una evaluación de los trabajos preconciliares* (Rome: LAS, 1997).

[157] AS II/1:343–346.

the separated brethren. The next day, Cardinal Silva Henríquez,[158] too, maintained that in Latin America devotion to the Virgin Mary went beyond the limits of Christian devotion and that the approval of a schema on Our Lady would aggravate the situation. Consequently, speaking on behalf of forty-four bishops from Latin American countries, he supported the proposal of Cardinal Frings. A similar declaration was made that same morning by Archbishop Garrone[159] of Toulouse, on behalf of "numerous French bishops," and others were made by Bishop Elchinger[160] and Bishop Méndez Arceo.[161]

On October 4, the hierarchy of England and Wales also came out in favor of Frings's proposal. Meanwhile, that same day, a document composed by the Servite Fathers was distributed to the council fathers which suggested that, besides the title of "Mediatrix," the title of "Co-Redemptrix" should also be applied to Mary. Father Balić, an expert on the Theological Commission, circulated in his turn a document in which he expounded the reasons why the schema on the Blessed Virgin Mary should be kept separate from the schema on the Church. Cardinal Arriba y Castro,[162] archbishop of Tarragona, taking the floor in the name of sixty Spanish bishops, declared that, given the importance of the Mother of God in the economy of redemption, and contrary to what had been said in the hall until then, it would be preferable to adopt a separate schema on the Blessed Virgin Mary.[163]

The discussion continued with interventions from the opposing sides. On October 24, the cardinal moderators announced that, in view of the large number of fathers who had called for the inclusion of the schema on the Blessed Virgin Mary in the schema on the Church, the Holy Father had charged the Doctrinal Commission with choosing two of its members to set forth the different positions. The commission designated Cardinal Rufino

158 Ibid., 366–368.

159 Ibid., 374–375.

160 Ibid., 378–380.

161 Ibid., 385–386.

162 Benjamín de Arriba y Castro (1886–1973), Spanish, ordained in 1912. Archbishop of Tarragona from 1949 to 1970, created cardinal in 1953.

163 AS II/2:14–16.

Santos[164] of Manila as the advocate of the separate schema and Cardinal Franz König of Vienna as the advocate for its incorporation. The two council fathers presented their contrasting theses in the hall on October 24.[165]

The archbishop of Manila articulated ten arguments in favor of a separate schema, affirming that Our Lady is the first and principal member of the Church, but at the same time is above the Church and, in the words of St. Bernard, *"stat intra Christum et Ecclesiam"* ["stands between Christ and the Church"]. He added that the faithful would interpret the incorporation of *De Beata* into *De Ecclesia* as the sign of a downgrading of Marian devotion. König affirmed, on the contrary, that the faithful needed to "purify" their Marian devotion in order to avoid an attachment to what is secondary and accidental and, above all, so as not to damage to the cause of ecumenism. The texts of the two cardinals' reports were distributed on October 25. The "ecclesiotypical" conception of the "minimalists" aimed at relativizing the role of the Blessed Virgin, considering her not in relation to her divine son, but with the common faithful of the Church.[166] They turned upside down the traditional understanding, which had always considered Mary not the image, but as the model and exemplar of the Church. In fact, "the image is inferior to that which is imaged, of which it is the effect, while the model or exemplar is superior to its image, of which it is the cause. Therefore the Church is sooner the image and figure of the Virgin."[167]

On October 29, the following question was put to a vote: "Does it please the council fathers that the schema on the Most Blessed Virgin Mary, Mother of the Church, should be revised so as to become chapter 6 of the schema on the Church?"[168] The results of this vote were 1,114 in favor, 1,074 opposed. The assembly proved, for the first time, to be split down the middle, with a difference of only forty votes between the two sides; this

---

164 Rufino J. Santos (1908–1973), Filipino, ordained in 1973, auxiliary bishop (1947), then archbishop of Manila from 1953 until his death. Created cardinal in 1960. Member of the Central Preparatory Commission and the Doctrinal Commission.

165 AS II/3:338–342 and 342–345.

166 Cf. François-Marie, O.F.M., "La nouvelle mariologie dans le chapitre 8 de Lumen gentium," in *L'unité spirituelle du genre humain*, 269–288 at 272–273.

167 Ibid., 282.

168 AS II/3:627; Caprile, 3:160–163.

division corresponded to the one between two opposing theological views and marked the victory of the "minimalists," if only by a narrow margin.[169]

The success of the progressives was due, according to Melissa Wilde, not so much to their strength as to the weakness of the conservatives, who had not yet found an organizational structure. In spite of the individual efforts of some of them, such as Father Balić, who on his own initiative had passed out one of his leaflets to the council fathers, there was no systematic or coordinated action. "As the council was voting on Mary, CIP [*Coetus Internationalis Patrum*] leaders were just beginning to correspond and had not yet formed their organization in earnest. In fact, their defeat on the Marian schema, combined with the 'disastrous' votes on collegiality the following day, is what probably spurred conservatives to organize.... Evidence suggests that they could have done much better in regard to the Marian schema had they organized a bit more effectively earlier in the council."[170]

7. The anti-Roman party in the second session

a) Jacobins and Girondists

The rapidity of the success of the progressive European alliance, which by now had become "worldwide," led also to a divergence of strategic visions within its ranks. Within the progressive alignment, therefore, a split opened up between Jacobins and Girondists or, as Grootaers puts it, between "possibilists" and "maximalists." "The latter defended positions on principle, denouncing as a betrayal any concession on the doctrinal level; the former, in contrast, cited the concrete situation of the moment and the need to win a solid majority."[171] The German theologians and an Italian group headed by Cardinal Lercaro signed on to the Jacobin approach, while Cardinal Suenens became the leader of the "Girondist" council fathers.

At the beginning of the second session, Helder Câmara described Suenens as "the key man at the council, sure to have the direct and personal

---

[169] For an overall description of the two concepts, see Laurentin, *La Vierge au Concile, op. cit.*, 138.

[170] Wilde, 108.

[171] Cf. J. Grootaers, "Protagonisti del Concilio," in *SC, La Chiesa del Vaticano II*, 26/1:392; *Idem*, "Diversité des tendances à l'intérieur de la majorité conciliaire," in *The Belgian Contribution*, 529–562.

confidence of the Holy Father,"[172] and on October 27, emphasizing the progress made since the first session, he wrote that the Belgian cardinal was not incorrectly being referred to as "the head of progressivism worldwide."[173]

The two met every day, dividing up the parts to be played, Suenens in the council hall, and Câmara in the extra-conciliar corridors, granting interviews in Italian, English, and French, always to large crowds. His biographers recall that "during the four sessions of the council, Dom Helder would not make any intervention in the plenary assemblies, but would accomplish a real piece of work as an '*éminence grise*' in designing what he himself called a 'sacred conspiracy' to put on the agenda of council business the problem of poverty in the world and the issue of the underdeveloped countries, and to promote a process of internal reform within the Catholic Church."[174]

From the second session of the council on, Suenens and Câmara, as the latter divulged, set several goals:

1) To replace the presidents of the conciliar commissions who were connected with the curia.

2) To prepare the reform of the Roman curia.

3) To promote episcopal collegiality on the national and international level.[175]

b) The Belgian "middle way"

Cardinal Suenens was assisted by his theologian Gérard Philips, a professor at the University of Louvain, chosen by the Belgian primate because "he personified a kind of *via media* that neither Cardinal Ottaviani nor the

---

172 Circular letter dated October 4, 1963, in Câmara, *Lettres conciliaires*, 1:198.

173 Ibid., 273. On January 28, 1963, Bishop Câmara had sent to Cardinal Suenens from Rio de Janeiro a letter in which he enclosed the statutes of the Brazilian Episcopal Conference and that of CELAM, suggesting that he compose "a) a statute for episcopal conferences considered as organs of episcopal collegiality on a national scale; b) a statute for CELAM-type councils considered as organs of episcopal collegiality on a continental scale" (Prignon, "Card. Suenens: correspondance," in CLG no. 281).

174 Nelson Piletti and Walter Praxedes, *Dom Helder Câmara: Tra potere e profezia*, Ital. transl. (Brescia: Queriniana, 1999), 436–437.

175 Circular letter dated October 5, 1963, in Câmara, *Lettres conciliaires*, 1:200–201.

Dutch secretary, Fr. Tromp, could find threatening."[176] This "middle way" turned out to be the most effective way to assure the success of the anti-Roman party. Philips, who had had parliamentary experience as a member of the Belgian Senate from 1953 to 1968, was accustomed to political maneuvering. In his *"carnets"* [notebooks] he used the terms "left" and "right" to designate the two movements, traditional and progressive, that fought each other at the council. These terms were not at all inappropriate. The historian of the councils, Hefele, writes that at Nicaea the orthodox bishops along with Athanasius and his followers formed the right, whereas Arius and his partisans made up the left, while the center-left was occupied by Eusebius of Nicomedia and the center-right by Eusebius of Caesarea.[177] Philips himself was a man of the "left" who sought to gain a reputation as a "centrist" in order to achieve his objectives and therefore disagreed with the maximalist attitude of some of his fellow travelers. He wrote: "I always strove to reach an agreement. People prefer a battle: it is a pity."[178]

"From the very outset," according to Giuseppe Ruggieri, Philips' tactic in the debate on the Church "was very skillful."[179] The theologian from Louvain would propose, as a "working hypothesis," a new text with slight modifications of wording and a few changes, but substantial ones, such as abandoning the concept that in order to be saved it was necessary to belong to the Church.[180] Schillebeeckx and Rahner, on the contrary, rejected every attempt at "mediation" so as to attack the schema head-on, especially on the issue of collegiality.

"This council has been called: *Primum Concilium Lovaniense, Romae habitum* [The First Council of Louvain, held in Rome]. That is true enough, at least as regards theology," Congar observed on March 13, 1964,[181] explaining that the Belgians, although there were not many of them (five or six), "are everywhere." Charles Moeller,[182] for example, "was present at

---

176 Suenens, *Memories and Hopes*, 132.

177 Cf. J. Hefele, *op. cit.*, 1:285–292.

178 Cf. Philips, *Carnets conciliaires* (December 2, 1963), 116.

179 Giuseppe Ruggieri, "Beyond an Ecclesiology of Polemics: The Debate on the Church," in HVT 2:281–358 at 298.

180 Ibid., 303–305.

181 Cf. Congar, *Journal*, 508 and 508–511.

182 Charles Moeller (1912–1986), Belgian, ordained in 1937. Professor of theology at Louvain

all the decisive moments and places!"[183] They all came from Louvain or referred to Louvain. "When a question is about to be raised, a new focus of work opened up, they alert one another, they get themselves involved, or have themselves called in, they share amongst themselves opinions on the sensitive issues. And what one of them passes on to another, or prepares for another, is made use of. They organise themselves, meet each other again and again. The result is that, where one of them is, they all are."[184]

The Belgian College, on the *via del Quirinale*, was the strategic outpost for a large-scale maneuver that had as its protagonists: Cardinal Suenens, a member of the Coordinating Commission and then a "moderator" of the council; Monsignor Philips, adjunct secretary of the same commission and "the mainspring of the important texts";[185] and Bishop Charue, a member and later vice-president of the Doctrinal Commission.

Congar emphasizes the effectiveness of the system, admitting that one was forced to turn to them when one wanted to get something or other done. "During the second session, the Belgian College was the place where Tucci, Dossetti, Medina,[186] and Rahner came."[187] "The theological centre is

---

(1949), literary critic (author of a *Littérature du XX siècles et christianisme* in 6 volumes). Conciliar *peritus* from 1963 to 1965, undersecretary of the Congregation for the Doctrine of the Faith. Cf. Claude Soetens, "La contribution de Charles Moeller au Concile Vatican II d'après ses papiers conciliaires," in *The Belgian Contribution*, 495–528.

[183] Congar, *Journal*, 508. See also C. Soetens, "La 'squadra belga' au Concile Vatican II," in *Foi, gestes et institutions religieuses au XIXe et XXe siècle*, ed. Luc Courtois and Jean Pirotte (Louvain-la-Neuve: Centre d'Histoire des Religions, 1991), 159–169 (reprinted in *L'evento e le decisioni*, 143–172); L. Declerck, "Le rôle joué par les évêques et periti belges au Concile Vatican II: Deux exemples," in *Ephemerides Theologicae Lovanienses* 76 (2000): 445–464 and, in greater detail, the many contributions to the 2005 Louvain Convention reprinted in *The Belgian Contribution, passim.*

[184] Congar, *Journal*, 509.

[185] *Actes et Acteurs*, 391. Among the Belgian experts who played an important role the following should be mentioned also: Lucien Cerfaux (1883–1968), Philippe Delhaye (1912–1990), Albert Dondeyne (1901–1985), Pierre Durmont (1901–1970), Victor Heylen (1906–1981), Guillaume Onclin (1905–1989), about whom see *The Belgian Contribution, passim.*

[186] Jorge Arturo Augustin Medina Estévez (1926–), ordained in 1954, auxiliary bishop of Rancagua and titular bishop of Thibilis in 1984, bishop of Valparaíso in 1993, pro-prefect of the Congregation for Divine Worship and the Discipline of the Sacraments in 1996, created cardinal in 1998. Followed the line of Cardinal Ratzinger (Benedict XVI).

[187] Congar, *Journal*, 509.

Mgr Philips. He combines an extraordinary gift with average qualities."[188] "With consummate art," Philips "knows how to propose a question in such a way that, disarming preconceptions, neutralizing objections in advance, he points the others toward the solution he wants WITHOUT THEIR REALISING IT."[189] The coordinating center, in contrast, was Monsignor Albert Prignon,[190] rector of the Belgian College in Rome, who according to Ambassador Poswick was the real behind-the-scenes coordinator and the most active collaborator of Cardinal Suenens.[191]

In a letter to Suenens dated March 8, 1963, Monsignor Prignon gave a detailed report on the ongoing maneuvers in the debate "On the Church" in the commission,[192] emphasizing the role of the Belgian bishops and experts at the council. "It can be said without exaggeration," he wrote, "that as far as *De revelatione* and *De Ecclesia* are concerned, the church of Belgium is the one directing the council as its driving force."[193]

---

[188] Ibid.

[189] Ibid. 509–510.

[190] Albert Prignon (1919–2000), priest of the Diocese of Liege, ordained in 1942. Rector of the Pontifical Belgian College in Rome from 1962 to 1972, conciliar *peritus*.

[191] Poswick, *Journal*, 390. Baron Prosper Poswick (1906–1992), ambassador from Belgium to the Holy See (1957–1968), almost literally had access to Prignon's confidential documents, which enabled him to compose the reports that he then transmitted to his government.

[192] At the request of all, I invited to lunch tomorrow at the college Cardinal Léger, Archbishop Garrone, Bishop McGrath (who at the same time will give me the information for schema XVII), Bishop Schröffer and the usual *periti*, so that they can come to an agreement on the tactic to follow. They all accepted enthusiastically. Cardinal Léger had telephoned again this morning to ask whether you might not come. Sincerely, Your Eminence, having heard the opinion of the bishops, I think that, from a tactical point of view, your arrival would be premature at the moment. None of the other members of the Coordinating Commission has arrived and the other side would accuse you of trying to exert pressure" (Letter from Prignon to Suenens dated March 8, 1963, in Fonds Prignon, "Card. Suenens: correspondance," in CLG, no. 288).

[193] "After the departure of the bishops, Canon Moeller and, at his request, Father Congar are residing at the college. They are working continually with Monsignor Philips. Their presence on site saves a lot of time. On the other hand, the fact that Father Congar is asking to leave the French Seminary for the Belgian College is a fact that evidently shows the extraordinary role played by our bishops and by our *periti* within this commission. Cardinal Léger no longer does anything without coming to speak to one of us. One may say, without exaggeration, that with regard to *De Revelatione*

The diplomatic ability of the Belgians compensated for the impetuousness of the Germans and for the excessively "Cartesian" logic of the French. Congar notes with admiration that whereas the French are content to propose timid corrections of details, while accepting the text as is, the Belgians "alter the text."[194] "The whole movement of the council, in its Theological Commission," he concludes, "has been to pass from the Roman colleges to theological centers outside Rome. But, among such universities, Louvain is the only one that has been effective."[195]

No less important than Philips' role, however, was the part played by Bishop Carlo Colombo, the theological *"trait d'union"* ["connecting link"] between Cardinal Suenens and Paul VI.[196] "I want to bring him to Brazil in the period between the second and the third session," Helder Câmara noted. "Our dear Fr. Dossetti and Bishop Guano will help us to conquer Bishop Colombo."[197]

Every Friday, moreover, the "conciliar strategy group" organized by Bishop Elchinger met at the House of the Redemptorists. Participants included Bishop Volk (and his auxiliary Reuss), Guano, Garrone, Philips, Rahner, Häring, Laurentin, Ratzinger, Semmelroth, Daniélou, and Congar.[198]

The Jacobin Küng was among those who preferred to move outside of the council hall and corridors. "There must be those who remain outside and those who work within," he told his Belgian friend Moeller. "We must both attempt to achieve what we can for the council."[199] At the invitation of Helder Câmara, the Jacobin positions were expounded on the evening of November 5 at the Domus Mariae by the Dominican,

---

and *De Ecclesia*, the church of Belgium is the one that is directing the council and pulls all the weight" (ibid.).

194 Congar, *Journal*, 510.

195 Ibid. 511.

196 Circular letter dated October 24, 1963, in Câmara, *Lettres conciliaires*, 1:259.

197 Ibid.

198 Cf. Alberto Melloni, "The Beginning of the Second Period: The Great Debate on the Church," in HVT 3:1–116 at 62.

199 Küng, *My Struggle*, 356.

Christophe-Jean Dumont,[200] the director of an ecumenical center in France. The friar asserted that the great sin of the Church of Rome was that it had remained a prisoner of scholasticism, legalism, and Latin, and had not understood the theological and spiritual richness of Eastern Orthodoxy. The creation of the Holy Roman Empire and the Crusades had been terrible mistakes. Now, however, with the council, the possibility of a miracle was emerging.[201]

8. The birth of the *Coetus Internationalis Patrum*

Although the progressive, anti-Roman party constituted an organized bloc, the bishops faithful to the conservative "Roman" line gave the impression from the start of being a broad but disorganized front made up of the chief representatives of the Roman curia and a considerable group of foreign cardinals. They began to organize only in the second session.

The natural leader of this alignment was Cardinal Alfredo Ottaviani, who in an interview on Bavarian radio broadcast on December 16, 1962, did not decline to be considered as "a representative of a frankly conservative group of council fathers."[202] Besides him, Cardinal Ernesto Ruffini, archbishop of Palermo, and Cardinal Giuseppe Siri, archbishop of Genoa, stood out. Ruffini gave no less than thirty-six speeches in the council hall, making an impression by the strength and coherence of his interventions. His voice was raised at the beginning of every debate, and he became the one who "opened fire."[203] The Cardinal of Palermo turned his apartment in the Domus Mariae into an office where he carefully prepared his interventions. He spent long evenings, sometimes until midnight, in the libraries of the Pontifical Biblical Institute and the Gregorian University, collecting documentary proof, and then he scrupulously and diligently annotated the conciliar schemas, adding his own observations, which were always lucid and to the point. His public interventions were remarkable for

---

[200] Christophe Jean Dumont (1898–1991), French Dominican, directed the Istina center for ecumenical study from 1927 to 1967. Cf. Hyacinthe Destivelle, "Souvenirs d'un pionnier: Les Mémoires inédites du Père Christophe-Jean Dumont," in *Istina* 3 (2009): 279–297.

[201] Câmara, *Lettres conciliaires*, 1:307–309.

[202] Caprile, 2:291.

[203] Grootaers, *I protagonisti*, 221.

their extraordinary clarity and ability to synthesize, and for their exemplary form in fluent, correct Latin.[204]

Besides Ruffini and Ottaviani we should mention the Spanish Claretian, Arcadio Larraona, and the Irish Dominican, Michael Browne, who had spent their whole life in Rome holding important posts and were profoundly imbued with the Roman spirit. John XXIII had elevated them to the cardinalate, the former in 1959 and the latter in 1962. Similar positions were publicly taken by other less brilliant cardinals, such as the Italians Pizzardo, Marella, and Alois Masella, the Filipino Santos, the Americans Spellman (New York) and McIntyre (Los Angeles), many Spanish prelates, and a group of Dalmatian [Yugoslav] bishops guided by the archbishop of Split, Frane Franić.

Cardinal Siri confided to Benny Lai that the reality of the council had been "the battle between the Horatii and the Curatii. They were three against three; in the council we were four against four. On their side were Frings, Liénart, Suenens, and Lercaro. On our side were Ottaviani, Ruffini, Browne, and I. Behind us were about a dozen bishops, and behind them were twenty or thirty council fathers."[205] Siri, in reality, never played a leading role. He realized, with consternation, that the theologians of central Europe had the support of Paul VI, whose *longa manus* [long arm] was Bishop Carlo Colombo.[206]

Pope Montini's support for the progressive wing produced deep despondency in the archbishop of Genoa, who had been trained in the spirit of unconditional obedience to the Roman pontiff. On April 24, 1964, Congar wrote in his diary: "Cardinal Siri is ill. According to Cardinal Lercaro, it is not just physical illness, but he sees his 'ideas' as good as rejected, even by the pope, and he is completely at a loss."[207] In those days

---

[204] Cf. Giuseppe Petralia, "Il padre conciliare," in *Il pastore sulla breccia: Ernesto card. Ruffini*, ed. Emanuele Gambino (Rome: Editrice Ancora, 1967), 115–121; A. Romano, *Ernesto Ruffini, op. cit.*, 489–590.

[205] Conversation on November 28, 1985, in B. Lai, *Il Papa non eletto, op. cit.*, 233.

[206] "The pre-eminent position in the doctrinal field held by Monsignore Carlo Colombo in the pope's opinion seems obvious. The prelate is entirely with the Transalpine fathers and has never shown interest in having contacts with us" (Siri, *Diario*, 385).

[207] Congar, *Journal*, 514. "The symptoms pointed out by Siri, among them labyrinthine attacks, were obviously connected with the strong preoccupation with the evolution of the council" (N. Buonasorte, *Siri: Tradizione e Novecento, op. cit.*, 306).

Congar wrote that Paul VI "expressed himself in an astonishingly bold and forthright manner about the need to overcome a fossilised tradition; everything must be started again, as though we were in the first centuries of the Church."[208]

Shortly before that, from April 14 to 16, the Italian Episcopal Conference (CEI) had held its general assembly, at which instead of Siri, who was officially absent for health reasons, Paul VI had spoken, delivering a speech that laid down the new line for the episcopal body. On August 12 of that year, the pope replaced Siri with Cardinal Luigi Traglia,[209] pro-vicar general of Rome, as pro-president *ad interim* of the CEI.

Cardinal Siri never openly took sides at the council, with rare exceptions, since he believed that the Italian Episcopal Conference which he represented should play a moderating role between the opposing conciliar groups. Even after his removal from the CEI, the strategic line of the "Roman party" to the very end was to try to resist the mindset of the opposing blocs, in the conviction that its own function was to be not just a "group," but rather the central guide at the council.[210] This position was the chief cause of the defeat of the conservative bishops. Indeed, they overrated their own positions and did not realize that, since they had the support of neither John XXIII nor Paul VI, they would be able to prevail only if they joined forces with the "ultramontane bishops" throughout the world.

During the first session of the council, the "ultramontane" fathers, gathered around two Brazilian prelates, de Castro Mayer and de Proença Sigaud, had organized a "Little Committee" to coordinate their actions. In the second session, they sought to organize their forces better, establishing a veritable group of conservative council fathers. Archbishop Geraldo de Proença Sigaud, who had become the archbishop of Diamantina, wrote from Brazil on April 18, 1963, to Archbishop Lefebvre to invite him to be part of a group that was forming, of which Archbishop Sigaud himself

---

[208] Congar, *Journal*, 526.

[209] Luigi Traglia (1895–1977), ordained in 1917, consecrated bishop in 1937 and created cardinal in 1960, pro-vicar general of Rome from 1960 to March 1965, then vicar general of Rome until 1968, appointed acting president *ad interim* of the Italian Episcopal Conference in 1964.

[210] Cf. A. Riccardi, "The Tumultuous Opening Days of the Council," *op. cit.,* 60–61. "The more important leaders of the curia or those connected with them, in short 'the Romans,' did not feel that they should descend to the level of a fight among 'factions'; they possessed a confidence in their own authority and in the appeal to the power of tradition. Would not the authority of the Holy Office suffice to guide the fathers in their choices, especially those of a theological kind?" (ibid., 61).

would be the secretary.[211] The French archbishop agreed with prudent reserve on May 4, promising the collaboration of the Fathers of the Abbey of Solesmes and the help of his fellow student at Santa Chiara, Father Victor-Alain Berto, as a theologian.[212]

On October 22, 1963, at the general curia of the Augustinians on the *via del Sant'Uffizio*, the first meeting of the group was held; only later would it take the name of *Coetus Internationalis Patrum*.[213] Archbishop Geraldo de Proença Sigaud was named secretary, assisted in turn by an efficient secretariat placed at his disposal by members of the association Tradition, Family, and Property (TFP) who were present in Rome.[214] Archbishop Sigaud, still working in close collaboration with Bishop de Castro Mayer, was the true driving force of the *Coetus*, while Archbishop Lefebvre was its most visible face.[215] They assumed the role of guide that the Italian council fathers, with a few exceptions, failed to play.

In October of 1963, Bishop Luigi Carli of the Diocese of Segni (Italy) joined the group. Carli was one of the best theologians at the council and was particularly feared by the anti-Roman party. Invited by the group of conservative fathers who used to meet at the house of the Divine Word Fathers, he agreed to unite with them, while maintaining his independence

---

[211] Letter from Archbishop de Proença Sigaud to Archbishop Lefebvre dated April 18, 1963, in A-Ecône, 02–09 A.

[212] Cf. B. Tissier de Mallerais, *op. cit.*, 291.

[213] On the *Coetus Internationalis Patrum idem in re theologica ac pastorali sententium*: Wiltgen, 148–149; R. Laurentin, "Bilan de la troisième session," in *L'enjeu du Concile, op. cit.*, 3:291; R. Aubert, "Organizzazione e funzionamento dell'assemblea," *op. cit.*, 177–179; V. A. Berto, *Notre Dame de joie, op. cit.*, 290–295; L. Perrin, "Il Coetus internationalis," *op. cit.*, 173–187. S. Gómez de Arteche y Catalina, *op. cit.*, vol. II, lib. II, 240–265; vol. III, lib. III, 290–295, 326–333. See also N. Buonasorte, *Tra Roma e Lefebvre: Il tradizionalismo cattolico italizno e il concilio Vaticano II* (Rome: Studium, 2003), 73–86.

[214] Archbishop Lefebvre recalls that "Some Brazilians, members of the T.F.P., helped us with an unheard-of devotion, working at night to copy the studies that had been written up by five or six bishops, that is to say, the directing committee of the *Coetus Internationalis Patrum*, which I had founded with Bishop Carli, bishop of Segni, and Bishop de Proença Sigaud, archbishop of Diamantina in Brazil" (M. Lefebvre, *They Have Uncrowned Him*, 166–167). "We must recognize that the TFP saved Brazil from communism" (cited in B. Tissier de Mallerais, *op. cit.*, 290).

[215] J. O. Beozzo, *A Igreja*, 531; H. Raguer, "An Initial Profile of the Assembly," in HVT 2:169–232 at 195–197.

in certain cases. Thus, as Archbishop Lefebvre later explained: "The soul of the *Coetus* was Archbishop de Proença Sigaud as secretary. I myself, as a former apostolic delegate and superior general of a [religious] congregation, was the 'public face' in my role as chairman. Bishop de Castro Mayer was vice-chairman and 'the thinker,' while Bishop Carli was 'the pen,' with his talents, his lively mind, and his Italian know-how."[216]

Fr. Berto explained in a letter how the main work carried out by the *Coetus* was "the preparation of *Modi* [Amendments] for the *Placet iuxta modum* votes."

> When one votes *iuxta modum*, it is necessary to provide on the spot the *modus* that is desired and the reason why it is being proposed. Out of two thousand fathers, there are not two hundred capable of doing this, for lack of inclination and time, but if the *modus* and the *Ratio modi* [rationale for it] are provided for them in advance, many of them ask for nothing more than to utilize them, since basically they are not content with the documents that are presented to them in the council hall. Our work (in our little college of theologians) consists therefore of sifting through the document to determine which passages are unacceptable, preparing the *modus* and the *Ratio modi*, and composing both with the maximum density and brevity—no small task! But since there are still fewer secretaries than theologians, it is necessary also to do their clerical work: mimeographing, filing papers, stapling, distributing to the fathers.... Is all this work effective? It could be more so, but it is already very much so. Until now, on the most important vote of the session, there have been 574 *Placet iuxta modum* votes. Of those 574, there were at least 540 that used *modi* that we had proposed. We had distributed six hundred of them, for lack of time to distribute more. As you can see, it was not useless labor.
>
> All of this does not impede action in other ways, during meetings and conversations. There is only one method that none of us considers, namely intrigue and maneuvering. The distribution of the *modi*, however, is accessible to the various episcopal conferences, and our Tuesday working meetings are public. *Filii lucis sumus.* (We are sons of light).[217]

216 "Le *Coetus Internationalis Patrum*, un combat qui aurait pû être victorieux," in *Fideliter* 59 (1987): 43–44. Eng. transl. in B. Tissier de Mallerais, 291.

217 Letter dated October 12, 1964, in *Notre Dame de joie, op. cit.*, 290–291. "You can see from the

One cannot help making a connection between concerns about the founding of the *Coetus* and the visit of Paul VI to the Lateran University, the bastion of anti-progressive resistance, on October 31, 1963, for the beginning of the academic year. The pope concluded his address by stating that the university had the duty to work in a positive way, forever abandoning all that was negative and critical. "The students," Congar wrote, "received these words with a thunder of applause. It was understood that this indicated a disavowal of the spirit of Monsignor Piolanti and an end to the attacks on the Biblicum."[218]

9. Between the primacy of Peter and collegiality

a) The roots of the debate

The discussion on the chapter concerning the collegiality of bishops was the heart of the conciliar debate to which the fathers would devote nine General Congregations.[219] In the final analysis, the council was asking the bishops to define their authority with regard to the Roman pontiff. They were both judges and parties to the dispute over the doctrinal problem being proposed to them.

newspapers," wrote Father Berto on November 12, 1963, to the Dominican Sisters of the Holy Spirit, "that the whole enormous machine that revolves around the council (since I do not want to say anything about the council as such) runs contrary to theological *romanità*.... We (I mean the Roman theologians) have no access on any side; we are outlaws in our own homeland. We are resisting the current, but are far from being able to reverse its course" (Letter dated November 12, 1963, ibid., 277).

[218] Congar, *Journal*, 409. De Lubac too notes: "At the Gregorianum (and I suppose at the Biblicum) there is [sic] exultations" (De Lubac, *Quaderni*, 469).

[219] Cf. AS II/2:82–124 and 222–914. See also A. Acerbi, *Due ecclesiologie, op. cit.,* 271 ff.; Piero Coda, "La Chiesa Corpo di Cristo e l'ordinazione universale al popolo di Dio: Rileggendo la 'Lumen gentium,'" in *Lateranum* 68 (2002): 267–278; Claudio Delpero, *La Chiesa del Concilio: L'ecclesiologia nei documenti del Vaticano II*, Ricerca e teologia, 2 (Florence, Libreria Editrice Fiorentina, 2005); Laurent Villemin, *Pouvoir d'ordre et pouvoir de juridiction: Histoire théologique de leur distinction* (Paris: Cerf, 2003). See also M. Wilde, "How Culture Mattered at Vatican II: Collegiality Trumps Authority in the Council's Social Movement Organizations," in *American Sociological Review* 69 (2004): 576–602.

In the Church, the power of jurisdiction belongs, *iure divino*, to the pope and to the bishops. The fullness of the power of jurisdiction, however, resides in the pope alone, on whom the entire ecclesiastical edifice is founded. The Roman pontiff is the sovereign authority over the whole Church, and by virtue of his primacy of universal governance, he is the supreme legislator in the Church.[220]

The Catholic doctrine on the primacy of Peter and the universal jurisdiction of the Roman pontiff, expounded in the Second Council of Lyons in 1274,[221] in the Council of Florence in 1439,[222] and in the Tridentine *Professio Fidei*,[223] was solemnly defined by the First Vatican Council in its dogmatic constitution *Pastor aeturnus* (July 18, 1870),[224] which reaffirmed that the Roman pontiff's primacy is not just a primacy of honor but also entails a true and proper jurisdiction over the universal Church. According to this definition, the Roman pontiff can do anything in the Church, can exercise this authority over anyone, and can do so without being limited by anyone. This rules out the possibility of a "collegial" or "democratic" concept, whereby the college of bishops, with or without the pope as a member, could have any authority whatsoever independent of his. The Vatican I definition had erected an insurmountable bastion against the anti-papal tendencies lurking even within the Catholic Church. The slogan of the "innovators" was to "balance" the dogma of Vatican I by setting up alongside it the principle of "collegiality" in governance.

The progressives maintained that Jesus Christ had not entrusted the government of the Church to Peter alone, but to the "Twelve," in other words, to an apostolic college to which Peter belonged as its head. They maintained that although the First Vatican Council had reaffirmed the primacy of the Roman pontiff, Vatican II would have to recognize the existence of an episcopal college, the heir of the apostolic college.[225]

---

220 Cf. Joël-Benoît D'Onorio, *Le Pape et le gouvernement de l'Église* (Paris: Fleurus-Tardy, 1992), 100.

221 Denz-H, n. 861.

222 Ibid., n. 1307.

223 Ibid., nn. 1868–1869.

224 Ibid. nn. 3050–3075.

225 Cf. Liénart, *Vatican II*, 98.

The first reason for this claim was "ecumenical." The dogma of the primacy was the principal stumbling block in the ecumenical dialogue, and so, in order to foster this dialogue, it was necessary to minimize its importance, while highlighting the "collegial" dimension of Church governance. The "rediscovery" of the role of the episcopate alongside that of the papacy (and implicitly opposed to it) came about at the initiative of Dom Beaudin,[226] in the circles associated with the monastery of Chevetogne, the gravitational center that produced the journal *Irénikon*. The term "collegiality" had been coined by Father Congar in 1951 in the pages of *Irénikon* as a translation of the Russian word *"sobornost"*.[227] It was supposed to indicate that the bishops who govern the various dioceses around the world have a power to govern collectively, as a "college" that is the heir to the apostolic college of the twelve.

In 1960, four professors from the Orthodox St. Sergius Institute in Paris had published a book entitled *The Primacy of Peter*,[228] in which they contrasted Catholic ecclesiology, which is based on the juridical notion of "power," and a "collegial" ecclesiology based on the primacy of love. Dom Olivier Rousseau, a monk at Chevetogne connected with the St. Sergius Institute, but also very close to Bishop Charue of Namur, vice-president of the council's Theological Commission, had helped to bring these ideas into circulation.[229]

A second reason for the episcopal claims was theological in nature: within the Church there were revivals of fifteenth-century "conciliarist" tendencies, of eighteenth-century Febronianism, and of nineteenth-century anti-infallibilism, which had sought in various ways and at various times to limit the authority and influence of the papacy. At Constance, in

---

226 Cf. C. Moeller, "Il fermento delle idee nella elaborazione della costituzione," in *La Chiesa del Vaticano II, op. cit.*, 155–159.

227 Cf. Y. Congar, "Le peuple fidèle et la fonction prophétique de l'Église," in *Irénikon* 24 (1951): 440–466 at 446. Cf. Nicolas Afanasieff, "Le Concile dans la théologie orthodoxe russe," in *Irénikon* 335 (1962): 316–317; O. Rousseau, O.S.B., "I movimenti rinnovatori degli ultimi decenni," in *La Chiesa del Vaticano II, op. cit.*, 119–120; A. Cavazza, "L'idea di Sobornost," *op. cit.*, 129–144.

228 N. Afanasieff, Nicolas Koulomzine, Jean Meyendorff, and Alexandre Schmemann, *La primauté de Pierre* (Neuchâtel: Delacroix et Niestlée, 1960). The volume appeared also in German (1961) and in English (1963).

229 Cf. E. Lanne, "La perception en Occident," *op. cit.*, 122–123.

particular, during the fifth session on April 6, 1418, the council, voting by nations, had approved the decree *Haec sancta*,[230] which stated that "the Council of Constance, legitimately assembled in the Holy Spirit, forming an ecumenical council, and representing the Church Militant, derived its power immediately from God, and all, including the pope, were obliged to obey it in matters concerning the faith and the extinction of the schism."[231]

This formulation had been condemned repeatedly,[232] but in 1959 a series of essays by the Benedictine, Paul de Vooght were published, proposing a revision of the traditional theological judgment on the decree of Constance, on the basis of a distinction between moderate conciliarism, from the medieval writers until the Council of Constance, and radical conciliarism, from Marsilius of Padua to the (heterodox) Council of Basel.[233]

Finally, there was a third reason of a more political character. In progressive circles, particularly in France, the model of the Church as an "absolute monarchy" seemed to clash with the "democratic" models of modern society. The progressives saw the council as a representative assembly analogous to modern parliaments, and the bishops as the agents of "the will of the people of God."

In some theologians, such as Congar and Küng, the three motives combined and expressed themselves in a clear rejection of papal supremacy. "For a thousand years everything among us has been seen and constructed from the papal angle, not from that of the episcopate and its collegiality.

---

[230] Cf. Mansi, vol. 29, cols. 21–22.

[231] On the Council of Constance, see the article by Léon Cristiani, "Constance," in DDC IV (1949): 390–424.

[232] In Florence, on September 4, 1439, Eugenius IV solemnly defined, *Haec Sancta* notwithstanding, the primacy of the Roman pontiff (Denz-H, n. 1307). Pius II did the same with the Bull *Execrabilis* dated January 18, 1460 (Denz-H, n. 1376).

[233] Cf. Paul de Vooght, "Les controverses sur les pouvoirs du Concile et l'autorité du Pape au Concile de Constance," in *Revue théologique de Louvain* 1 (1970): 47–75; "Le conciliarisme aux conciles de Constance et de Bâle," in *Le concile et les conciles* (Paris: Cerf, 1960). 143–181; "Le concile oecuménique de Constance et le conciliarisme," in *Istina* 9 (1963): 57–86; "Le conciliarisme aux conciles de Constance et de Bâle: Compléments et précisions," in *Irénikon* 36 (1963): 61–75 and, finally, *Les pouvoirs du concile et l'autorité du Pape au Concile de Constance* (Paris: Cerf, 1965). Situated along the same line was the study by Brian Tierney, *Foundations of the conciliar theory* (Cambridge: Cambridge University Press, 1955).

Now THIS history, THIS theology, THIS canon law needs to be done," the Dominican theologian wrote in his diary on September 25, 1964.[234]

In order to expand the role of the episcopacy, the anti-Roman party emphasized the bishops' power of orders, conferred by means of episcopal consecration, over and above the power of jurisdiction, which is conferred by mandate. This one-sided emphasis on the sacramental nature of the episcopate was accompanied by an emphasis on the eminently episcopal role of the pope, who was reduced to the *primus inter pares* [first among equals] within the college of bishops. The traditional doctrine, conveniently dismissed as "legalistic,"[235] was pitted against the thesis that the Church is ruled by an apostolic authority with a sacramental and collegial structure. The slogan was to liberate the Church from the legalistic trappings that were suffocating her, and to transform her from a top-down structure into a democratic and egalitarian structure.

b) The discussion in the council hall

When the debate commenced, on October 4, the speakers in favor of collegiality included Cardinals Meyer,[236] Léger,[237] König,[238] Alfrink,[239] and Bishop De Smedt of Bruges.[240] On the other side, there were interventions in favor of Petrine primacy by Cardinals Siri[241] and Ruffini,[242] Archbishop Dino Staffa,[243] and Archbishop Proença Sigaud.[244] The last-mentioned, on

---

234 Congar, *Journal*, 593.

235 A. Acerbi, *Due ecclesiologie, op. cit.*, 94 ff.

236 AS II/2:230–232.

237 Ibid., 223–225.

238 Ibid., 225–227.

239 Ibid., 232–233.

240 Ibid., 263–266.

241 Ibid., 222–223.

242 Ibid., 84–87.

243 Ibid., 323–324.

244 Ibid., 366–369.

October 9, declared in the hall that a comparative study of articles 12, 13, and 16 of the schema gave the impression that a new doctrine was being taught. Upon returning to his seat, he received a note from Bishop Luigi Carli congratulating him. It was the beginning of a close collaboration.

On October 10, in an interview with the Divine Word Service, Archbishop Sigaud said that he was convinced that strengthening the national episcopal conferences would restrict both the powers of the local bishops and those of the pope.[245] He added that the power to rule the universal Church "was given to Peter alone as a personal power and was transmitted by Peter to his successors in the papacy. Not even the pope himself," the prelate concluded, "could modify this structure established by Christ and begin to rule the Church by means of a sort of permanent council."[246]

On October 11, the new auxiliary bishop of Bologna, Bishop Luigi Bettazzi,[247] took the floor; the youngest council father, he was destined to become famous for supporting the "historical compromise" between Catholics and communists.[248] His intervention in the hall, based on a memorandum prepared by Alberigo and Dossetti, described the opponents of collegiality as "innovators"; he maintained that the ecclesiastical jurisdiction of the college of bishops was in continuity with the theological tradition of the eighteenth and nineteenth centuries.[249] "He rejected the positions of Ruffini and Siri, whom he described as *novatores*—

---

[245] Divine Word Service, October 10, 1963.

[246] Ibid.

[247] Luigi Bettazzi (1923–), ordained in 1946. Auxiliary bishop of Bologna from August 1963 to 1966, then bishop of Ivrea. See his books, *Non spegnere lo spirito: Continuità e discontinuità del Concilio Vaticano II* (Brescia: Queriniana, 2006); *In dialogo con I luterani: memorie e riflessioni di un vescovo un po' laico* (Reggio Emilia: Aliberti, 2008).

[248] See the open letter sent by the secretary general of the Italian Communist Party to Enrico Berlinguer ("Comunisti e cattolici: chiarezza di principi e basi di un'intesa," in *Rinascita* 40 (1977): 3–5), in response to a similar letter from Bishop Bettazzi ("Lettera aperta all'on. Berlinguer," in *Il Risveglio popolare*, July 8, 1976). About this "case" see G. Cantoni, *La "Lezione italiana": Premesse, manovre e riflessi della politica di "compromesso storico" sulla soglia dell'Italia rossa* (Piacenza: Cristianità, 1980), 167–176.

[249] AS II/2:484–487.

what a joke!"[250] a delighted Chenu commented in his diary, while *L'Avvenire d'Italia* ran the triumphant headline: "Round of Applause at the Council for Youngest Italian Bishop."[251] On October 15, Siri, Wyszyński, Jubany,[252] and Browne[253] replied. Archbishop Marcel Lefebvre, corroborating Sigaud's thesis with his own missionary experience (he had founded four episcopal conferences in Madagascar, in the French Congo, in Cameroon, and in Dakar in French West Africa), declared that the excessive power of the bishops' conferences would threaten not only the papacy, but also the teaching and pastoral authority of the individual bishops.[254]

During those same days the topics of the diaconate and the laity were addressed. Opposed to the idea of a diaconate as a permanent structure in the Church were Cardinals Bacci[255] and Spellman,[256] to whom Döpfner[257] and Suenens[258] responded. Archbishop Alvim Pereira[259] of Lourenço Marques (Mozambique), spoke in the name of thirty-eight Portuguese bishops, saying that if a candidate did not have the knowledge expected of a priest and was not celibate, he was not qualified for the diaconate; if on the contrary he did possess that knowledge and was celibate, then he should be ordained a priest.[260]

On October 22, Cardinal Suenens proposed that chapter 3, which dealt with the "People of God," should come before chapter 2, which spoke about

---

250 Chenu, *Diario*, 146.

251 *L'Avvenire d'Italia*, October 12, 1963.

252 Narciso Jubany Arnau (1913–1996), Spanish, ordained in 1939, auxiliary bishop of Barcelona in 1955, consecrated bishop of Ortosia in Phoenicia in 1956, bishop of Gerona in 1964, archbishop of Barcelona in 1971, created cardinal in 1973.

253 AS II/2:572–573; 574–577; 580–586; 600–601.

254 Ibid., 471–472.

255 Ibid., 87–89.

256 Ibid., 82–83.

257 Ibid., 227–230.

258 Ibid., 317–320.

259 Custodio Alvim Pereira (1915–2006), Portuguese, ordained in 1937, archbishop of Lourenço Marques (Mozambique) from 1962 to 1974.

260 AS II/2:500–501.

the hierarchy of the Church. This was not simply a matter of arranging chapters, but the transition from the traditional theology of the Mystical Body to the new ecclesiology of the "People of God."[261] Suenens had asked Hans Küng to prepare a speech for him, which was framed entirely in terms of the "charismatic" and "prophetic" aspect of the Church.[262] Charisms, the primate of Belgium said, are a central and not just peripheral aspect of the Church's constitution; the Holy Spirit is always present in the Church with all his gifts, which are poured out on all Christians without exception. The Church is not "juridical" but is essentially "pneumatic," built not only on the apostles but also on the prophets.

The debate was prolonged throughout the month of October without reaching an agreement, but with a strong tendency to develop a new concept of the Church as *communio*.

Within the Theological Commission, then, a sub-commission styled *De Collegialitate* was formed to discuss the problem of episcopal collegiality contained in the schema *De Ecclesia*. Among the members were the theologians Maccarrone, Rahner, Ratzinger, and Salaverri.[263] Maccarrone and Salaverri would have liked to introduce into the third chapter of the schema *De Ecclesia* an explicit citation from Vatican I on papal authority, but the proposal was blocked by their expert colleagues, Rahner and Ratzinger.[264]

---

[261] See the editorial "Dalla teologia del 'Corpo Mistico' all'ecclesiologia del 'popolo di Dio," in *Civiltà Cattolica*, q. 3231 (1985): 209–221. Father Congar, the main author of what would become paragraph 9 of *Lumen gentium*, would propose the expression "messianic people" (cf. Y. Congar, *Un Peuple messianique* [Paris: Cerf, 1975]).

[262] Küng, *My Struggle*, 360–361; J. Grootaers, "Diversité des tendances ", in *The Belgian Contribution*, 560. "It is obvious," Grootaers commented, "that Suenens with this intervention at Vatican II was in the avant-garde of the charismatic movements which, twenty years later, would invade the stage of John Paul II and become a defining characteristic of the Wojtylian pontificate" (*ibid.*, 561, translated from French).

[263] Joaquín Salaverri de la Torre (1892–1979), Spanish theologian of the Society of Jesus, ordained in 1925, professor of Ecclesiology at the Pontifical University Comillas until 1972. Consultor of the Preparatory Commission of the Council (1960–1962) and theological *peritus* (1962–1965). See the article by J. Escalera, in DHCJ, 3648.

[264] M. Sensi, "Monsignor Michele Maccarrone," *op. cit.*, 18–19; F. Álvarez Alonso, "Primato e collegialità," *op. cit.*

c) The battle of The Twelve is won

The voting on collegiality on October 29 and 30, at the end of the 48th General Congregation, marked the culminating point of the second session. On October 29, after the voting on the schema *De Beata Maria Virgine*, a series of questions was proposed to the fathers, gradated as follows:

> Does it please the fathers that the council should affirm: 1. That episcopal consecration is the highest degree of the sacrament of Holy Orders. 2. That each bishop who is legitimately consecrated in communion with the bishops and with the pope, their head and principle of unity, becomes a member of the Episcopal College. 3. That this Body or College of Bishops succeeds the College of the Apostles in the mission of evangelizing, sanctifying, and governing, and that this College of Bishops, united with its head, the Roman pontiff, and never without this head—it being understood that the primatial right of this head remains whole and entire—possesses a supreme and plenary power in the universal Church. 4. That this power belongs, by divine right, to the Episcopal College united with its head. 5. That the revival of the diaconate as a distinct and permanent grade of the sacred ministry is opportune.

The supporters of collegiality could only have been satisfied by the way in which these questions were enunciated and by the subsequent results of the vote. For the first question there were 2,123 yeas and thirty-four nays; for the second, 2,049 yeas, 104 nays, and one invalid ballot; for the third, 1,808 yeas, 336 nays, and four invalid ballots; for the fourth, 1,717 yeas, 408 nays, and thirteen invalid ballots; and for the fifth, 1,588 yeas and 525 nays. The third question was the key because it instituted a legal subject unknown to the tradition of the Church: the episcopal college as a whole, to which was attributed the supreme power in the Church. The first two questions were the presupposition for the third: the whole college of bishops could assume its supreme power only on condition that they assumed the highest degree of Holy Orders in their episcopal consecration (which the Council of Trent had implicitly denied), and that a bishop became a member of the episcopal college through his consecration, and not by papal appointment. The fourth question sanctioned what had been established previously. More than four hundred bishops therefore rejected the statement that the supreme and plenary power over the universal Church belonged by divine right to the Episcopal College. The two-thirds majority had been achieved, however, and newspapers all over the world announced that a page was turning in the governance of the Church. The voting, Küng notes, was described as "the peaceful 'October Revolution' of the Catholic Church."[265] The Church seemed to be trying to replace its monarchical juridical structure with a democratic juridical structure guided not by the pope but by the bishops as a whole. In Brussels, Cardinal Suenens triumphantly declared that "October 30 is a decisive date in the history of the Church. The battle of the Twelve has been won!"[266] With similar words Paul VI had received the three "progressive" moderators of the council (Döpfner, Lercaro, Suenens) the day after the "historic" October 30 vote with similar words: "So we have won!"[267]

The document on which they had voted, however, was indicative and not definitive. It was obviously absurd to imagine that the October 30 vote, which had not been ratified by the pope, could be a decisive vote. The opponents of collegiality turned directly to Paul VI, with the help of secretary Felici who, according to König, "in his daily visits to the pope certainly did not fail to point out the dangerous features of the new statute that the council was intending to introduce."[268]

On October 31 assistants distributed the report of the commission that had developed the schema concerning the bishops and the governance of dioceses. This time the target of the progressives was the Roman curia. On November 5, Cardinal Marella[269] presented the draft of the decree *De Episcopis ac de diocesium regimine*, produced by the commission that he headed.[270] After Bishop Carli explained the

---

[265] Küng, *My Struggle*, 364.

[266] *Informations catholiques internationales* (November 1, 1963): 3.

[267] Chenu, *Diario*, 148.

[268] König, *Chiesa dove vai?, op. cit.*, 29.

[269] Paolo Marella (1895–1984), ordained in 1918, archbishop of Doclea in 1933, created cardinal in 1959, president of the Secretariat for non-Christians from 1964 to 1973.

[270] AS II/4:435–438. The debate in AS II/4:393–748; AS II/5:9–411.

origin, development, and contents of the schema,[271] Cardinals Ruffini,[272] Browne,[273] and Ottaviani[274] came to its defense, warning of the danger that national episcopal conferences might usurp the authority of the Holy See. The first attack against the curia was launched by Cardinal Richaud,[275] archbishop of Bordeaux, who was followed by Monseigneur Gargitter,[276] bishop of Bressanone. Both called for a reorganization and a greater "internationalization" of the curia. The next day, Cardinal Alfrink, speaking on behalf of the Dutch bishops, stressed that if collegiality was of divine right, it followed that the College of Bishops had pre-eminence over the curia and that the latter did not have the right to interpose itself between the pope and the bishops. Alfrink called for the institution of a central organ of the Church comprised of bishops from every part of the world, which would serve "as a sign of the collegial governance… and at the same time an instrument with which such collegial governance of the Church could, in a certain way, be put into practice."[277]

On November 6, Maximos IV Saigh, speaking in French as always, gave a speech that was, as Jedin put it, "incendiary"[278] against the Roman curia and College of Cardinals, which in his opinion needed to be replaced by a "sacred college of the universal Church" made up of apostolic patriarchs, cardinal-archbishops or residential bishops, and of bishops selected from the episcopal conferences of every country.[279] Cardinal König had just made a similar proposal, suggesting that once or twice a year the pontiff could call a meeting with the presidents of the episcopal conferences and other bishops to hear their opinions on matters concerning the universal

---

271 Ibid., 439–445.

272 Ibid., 476–478.

273 Ibid., 486 and 626–627.

274 Ibid., 624–625.

275 AS II/4:450–452. Paul-Marie Richaud (1887–1968), French, ordained in 1913, , archbishop of Bordeaux from 1950 until his death. Created cardinal in 1958.

276 AS II/4:453–455. Joseph Gargitter (1917–1991), ordained in 1942, bishop of Bressanone from 1952 to 1986.

277 AS II/4:479–481 at 480.

278 H. Jedin, *op. cit.*, 313.

279 AS II/4:516–519.

Church.[280] König invoked the principle of subsidiarity in connection with the government of the Church and, in a statement to the Divine Word Service, said that he was in favor of expanding the role of the episcopal conferences.[281] That same day Fr. Berto wrote a worried letter to Bishop Carli, showing that the love owed to the pope is by nature filial, directed towards a specific person *"in carne et ossibus"* ["of flesh and bones"] occupying the papacy. Collegiality, Berto explained, "is fatal to 'love for the pope' because it destroys his fatherhood."[282] "The father-son relation is a relation between two physical persons who are directly conjoined. If the pope is the head of the Church only because he is the head of the *Collegio Episcoporum*, then the true sovereign of the Church is that college, *i.e.*, a moral person.... Now let the 'collegialists' tell me: who would ever love a moral person? Who would ever love a college with a filial love while thinking in his heart: This college is my father and I am its son? ... And who could ever believe that the fatherhood of God *'ex quo omnis paternitas in coelo et in terra nominatur'* ['from whom all paternity in heaven and earth is named'] should be represented, symbolized, or shared by a collegial entity, precisely in the highest order of created things, namely, in his Church?"[283]

Speaking in defense of the curia on November 7 were Bishop Mason,[284] apostolic vicar of El Obeid in the Sudan, the Armenian patriarch of Cilicia, Ignace Pierre XVI Batanian,[285] and Bishop Aurelio Del Pino Gómez[286] of Lerida (Spain). The last speaker affirmed that the Roman curia has had men who excelled in holiness, wisdom, prudence, and charity, many of whom were subsequently elevated to the office of supreme pontiff. The Roman curia is made up of men "chosen from all nations," the Spanish bishop added, emphasizing that "since the Sacred Congregations are the

---

280 Ibid., 478–479.

281 Divine Word Service, November 7, 1963.

282 V. A. Berto "Lettera a mons. Carli del 6 novembre 1963," in N. Buonasorte, *Per la "pura, piena, integra fede cattolica," op. cit.,* 124.

283 Ibid.

284 AS II/4:606–607.

285 AS II/4:558–559. Ignace Pierre XVI Batanian (1899–1979), born in Turkey, ordained a priest in 1921. Armenian patriarch of Cilicia (Lebanon) from September 1962 to 1976. Member of the Commission for the Oriental Churches.

286 AS II/4:596–599.

instrument that the pope uses to govern the Church, we must realize that whatever is said against the sacred Roman curia is, in some way, said also against the pope of Rome himself."[287]

d) The attack on the Holy Office

The thoroughgoing attack on the curia was set for November 8. Cardinal Frings of Cologne launched it. In his intervention he directly attacked the Holy Office, which was headed by Ottaviani, declaring that its procedures were "no longer suitable for our era, harmful to the Church, and an object of scandal for many." The defense of the faith is an extremely difficult task, he added, "but nobody should be judged or condemned without being heard and without having had the opportunity to correct his work and his actions."[288] From the back of the basilica, a group of young progressive bishops applauded frenetically.[289]

Cardinal Ottaviani, who was scheduled to speak that day, went to the microphone and replied immediately with a resounding intervention:

> I must protest most strongly concerning what has just been said against the Holy Office, whose president is the supreme pontiff. Such words were spoken out of lack of knowledge—I do not use another word lest I offend—of Holy Office procedure.[290]

The atmosphere became very tense. Cardinal Lercaro tried to calm the assembly with a skillful intervention; feigning moderation, he pushed the attack against Ottaviani to the limit.[291] In the following days an anonymous "Memorandum on conciliar commissions" circulated among the council fathers, in which the president of the Doctrinal Commission, Ottaviani, was denounced for his incompetence (in matters of exegesis, history, and contemporary theology), for his physical inability to direct

---

287 Ibid., 597.

288 Ibid., 616–618.

289 Câmara, *Lettres conciliaires*, 1:314.

290 AS, II/4:624–626 at 624. See also Wiltgen, 116. On the clash between the two cardinals, see Joseph Famerée, "Bishops and Dioceses …," in HVT 3:117–191 at 126–132.

291 AS II/4:618–621.

the commission's work, and for his authoritarian concept of his official duties.[292] The document asked the pope to remove Ottaviani and to proceed to new elections for the conciliar commissions before the end of the second session.

The clash between Frings and Ottaviani was, according to Jedin, "one of the most emotional scenes of the whole council,"[293] and was covered widely in the press. Ten days later Bishop Dino Luigi Romoli,[294] the Dominican bishop of Pescia, who had spent eight years at the Holy Office, granted to Fr. Wiltgen's Divine Word Service an interview, authorized by Cardinal Ottaviani, in which he explained in detail the procedures of the Holy Office.[295]

"If one member of the Church accuses another of a crime for which the Holy Office is the competent tribunal, then the accused is always given a full hearing and has every opportunity of defending himself. He receives the assistance of a lawyer and may himself present the lawyer of his choice to the tribunal. The precautions taken to safeguard the accused in such a case are so extensive and elaborate as to appear at times even excessive." The condemnation of published writings is a different case, "since here it is a question of a theory which, considered in itself, might be injurious to the integrity of Catholic doctrine and to souls." In this kind of judgment the Holy Office gives no hearing to the interested party before pronouncing its verdict, because the intentions of the author are not being called into question or condemned but rather the doctrines considered in themselves. Nevertheless, "Before the Holy Office condemns a published work or issues a solemn warning [*Monitum*] to an author, it makes a vast, accurate, and intensive investigation by consulting with highly qualified experts from various linguistic and national groups in order to be incontestably

---

292 Cf. J. Grootaers, "Sinergia e conflitti nel Vaticano II: Due versanti d'azione degli 'avversari' del rinnovamento (ottobre 1962–ottobre 1964)," in *L'evento e le decisioni*, 376–377; Soetens, "The Ecumenical Commitment of the Catholic Church" HTV 3:257–346 at 304–305. A copy of this memorandum is found in the papers of Monsignor Philips, who added to it a handwritten note, "Chile." Soetens says that it apparently originated with the Chilean Cardinal Silva Henríquez (ibid., 304).

293 H. Jedin, *op. cit.*, 314.

294 Dino Luigi Romoli, O.P. (1900–1985), ordained in 1924, consecrated bishop of Pescia in 1951.

295 Divine World Service, November 22, 1963.

objective and secure in its judgment."[296] It must be recalled moreover that the Congregation of the Holy Office was an administrative body which, unlike other Roman congregations, could not make any decision because the head of the dicastery, the "prefect," was not a cardinal but the pope himself, while the senior cardinal-member merely had the title of "secretary." Cardinal Bea himself, who had been a consultor to it, recalled not only the seriousness of the methods, but also the freedom that reigned at the Holy Office, where the cardinals and the counselors used to say: "Here we are at the Holy Office and can say anything we want, without fear of taking sides [*difendere persone*] or of running into condemnations."[297]

The progressives denounced the repressive power of the Holy Office, heir to the Holy Roman Inquisition, but the power of censure that they exercised through the new tribunal of the media was even more invasive. The custodians of orthodoxy were depicted in the press as sullen, outmoded, and intolerant, while anything heterodox was presented as "open," "stimulating," and "constructive." The clash henceforth took place in the newspapers even more than in the council hall.

Equilibrium was restored by a strong intervention by Bishop Luigi Carli who, on November 13,[298] thoroughly critiqued the principle of so-called "episcopal collegiality of divine right" which some orators claimed as justification for the creation of national episcopal conferences. The central part of his intervention deserves to be quoted on account of the impression that it made:

> Even assuming that the alleged episcopal collegiality of divine right will be defined by the supreme pontiff with the approval of the sacred council, the institution of episcopal conferences still could not be legitimately founded on it, in my opinion at least, for the following reasons:
>
> a) Theological reason. Even if one says that the conferences are forms of that collegiality, they nevertheless lack the three elements that seem to be essential to that collegiality, namely, the union of all the bishops, the authoritative and also formal participation of the head of the college, *i.e.*, the Roman pontiff, and issues that pertain to the whole Church. Hence if, as is evident, these three elements are missing in

---

[296] Wiltgen, 118–119. See also A. Wenger, *Vatican II, op. cit. II session*, 149–153.

[297] Schmidt, *Bea*, 143.

[298] AS II/5:72–75.

> national conferences, there is no point in saying that these conferences proceed from episcopal collegiality of divine right, as do species from their proper genus.
>
> b) Juridical reason. On the hypothesis that we have stated, the proper, ordinary, and immediate power of each bishop in his diocese—an authority which since ancient times has been regarded as "monarchical"—in reality would be limited, not only by divine right, and by the supreme pontiff (which is certainly correct), but also by the other bishops of the same nation. This is something that certainly no bishop is ready to allow in his own See, not even those whom we have heard speak so eloquently about collegiality in the Sees of others.... Even those who have not hesitated to allow, as it were, two heads having full and supreme power in the governance of the universal Church—they themselves declare that even the slightest shadow of "diarchy" must be kept away from their dioceses.
>
> c) Historical reason. In drawing up the schema on [episcopal] conferences, the thought never occurred to anyone on the Preparatory Commission that they were founded on a collegiality of divine right. But even more importantly, not even the Roman pontiffs, when they recommended and urged national conferences and granted them official status, ever spoke about them being founded on divine-right collegiality, but rather always and only about reasons of a pastoral nature.[299]

As he returned from the hall, Archbishop Lefebvre described Bishop Carli's intervention as "the turning point of the council."[300] Writing several weeks after Carli, Father Berto added that historians would have to record that his intervention "changed the atmosphere" of the session.[301] In a subsequent letter to the bishop of Segni, Father Berto wrote: "I truly believe that many fathers who had voted *placet* on points 3 and 4 on October 30 without realizing where this was trying to take them, understood it only because of your memorable intervention."[302]

---

299 Ibid., 73–74.

300 Letter from Fr. Berto to Bishop Carli dated November 13, 1963, in N. Buonasorte, *Per la "pura, piena, integra fede cattolica," op. cit.*, 126.

301 Ibid., 128.

302 Letter dated March 13, 1964, ibid., 133.

10. From the European alliance to the progressive world alliance

On November 15, in the presence of the other three moderators, the commission, and the council presidency, Cardinal Lercaro read to the pope an initial report on the activity of the second session. He said that the council could have advanced more rapidly "if we moderators can use the method that we used at the conclusion of the debate on chapter 2 of the schema on the Church."[303] The request was aimed at giving the moderators the power to decide what questions were most important based on the orientation of the majority in the assembly, giving them a role very different from the one originally assigned to them. Papal authorization was not granted: Paul VI realized that in that case he would lose control of the assembly, which he intended to guide resolutely. The anti-Roman party did not surrender, however, and claimed greater power within the commissions that were "dominated by the curia." On November 21, the secretary general announced that the pope had authorized an increase in the number of members on the commissions from twenty-five to thirty, "so as to accelerate and make more efficient the development of their work".[304] He added that four of the five new members would be appointed by the council fathers, and the fifth directly by the pope, who authorized each commission to choose internally an additional vice-president and an additional secretary from among the experts. It was further suggested that the episcopal conferences should "unite and present a combined list." Wiltgen observes that this was actually a gift to the progressive alliance, the only organized group capable of drawing up an unbeatable international list on short notice.[305]

On this occasion, the anti-Roman party consolidated its transformation from a European alliance to a "world alliance." Wiltgen recorded that "the world alliance during the first session was an undercover group of five or six bishops and archbishops, representing national, regional, or continental episcopal conferences, who met periodically. From the beginning of the second session, when they considered themselves strong enough to act more openly, they held meetings at Domus Mariae each Friday evening and saw their membership grow to twenty-four bishops and archbishops, who represented approximately sixty-five episcopal conferences. The one

[303] Wiltgen, 128.

[304] AS II/5:635–636.

[305] Wiltgen, 129–130.

who presided over the meetings was coadjutor Archbishop Pierre Veuillot of Paris, whenever he was in Rome."[306]

After intensive meetings the secretaries of the episcopal conferences belonging to the alliance agreed upon a common list. The mechanism was perfectly organized. The elections held on November 28 confirmed the absolute preponderance of the new anti-Roman bloc on a worldwide scale.[307] All forty-three fathers elected were on the international list. The pope completed the list with eight more nominations on January 8, 1964. This thoroughgoing attack was aimed especially at the Doctrinal Commission, where two Belgian "innovators," Bishop Charue and the *peritus* Philips, became vice-president and adjunct secretary, respectively.

However on November 28, of all days, the progressives suffered their first defeat when the Roman Union of Superiors General[308] and the Secretariat for Bishops garnered 679 favorable ballots from the council fathers in the vote on religious life. Paul VI informed Bishop Perantoni[309] that during the third session a new chapter entitled *Dei religiosi* would be added to the schema on the Church, as requested by the Roman Union, contrary to the updating of religious life desired by the central European theologians. The anti-progressive reaction was beginning, albeit tardily, to achieve its first successes.

11. The debate on ecumenism

The debate, which began in the council hall on November 18, 1963, was described by Father Wenger in *La Croix* as "the moment of truth."[310] From the second half of November until the beginning of December the

---

306 Ibid., 129–130.

307 The official list of the results was published on January 11, 1964, in *L'Osservatore Romano.*

308 The organization was officially recognized by the Congregation for Religious in March 1955, with the title of Roman Union of General Superiors. Both before and during the council there were various meetings of the general superiors to study the various proposed documents and to help in the preparation of the emendations to the texts, as well as in the preparation of the interventions of those general superiors who were participating in the council. This activity was particularly intense with reference to the two documents *Perfectae caritatis* and *Ad gentes.*

309 Luigi Perantoni (1895–1982), ordained in 1920, Bishiop of Gerace in 1952, archbishop of Lanciano and Ortona in 1962, then archbishop emeritus in 1982.

310 *La Croix,* November 20, 1963.

fathers discussed the schema on ecumenism composed by the Secretariat for Promoting Christian Unity, in collaboration with the Commission for Oriental Churches.[311] The document, which arrived in the hall on November 18, consisted of five chapters that elucidated: the Catholic principles pertaining to the problem; the way of applying them in ecclesial life; the Church and the separated communities; the relations of Catholics with non-Christians and in particular with the Jews; and religious liberty. Cardinal Cicognani, president of the Coordinating Commission, presented the general report, whereas the first three chapters were explained by Archbishop Joseph-Marie Martin[312] of Rouen, the fourth by Cardinal Bea,[313] and the fifth by Bishop De Smedt.[314]

When Cardinal Ruffini[315] took the floor complete silence fell over the assembly. The Cardinal of Palermo expounded, with his customary logical rigor, the reasons for his concern:

1) The term "ecumenism," which had introduced into theology by protestants, is ambiguous, because it is understood differently by protestants and by Catholics. If it is kept in the document, its meaning must be clearly defined.

2) The schema would have to show more clearly that Catholics are much closer to the Eastern Orthodox than to the protestants, who recognized very little of the ancient Catholic faith besides scripture and baptism.

3) If a special chapter on the Jews is added, why not discuss in it those who belong to other religions? And why should ecumenism neglect the countless Catholics who are interested in Marxism, which is spreading atheism around the world?

Two Spanish cardinals spoke along the same lines as Ruffini: the archbishop of Tarragona, Benjamin Arriba y Castro,[316] and the archbishop

---

311 For the entire debate: AS II/5:405–495, 527–574, 597–637, 661–700, 744–833; AS II/6:9–91, 97–367, 375–401. See also Caprile, vol. III, *passim.*

312 AS II/5:472–479. Joseph-Marie Martin (1891–1976), French, ordained in 1920. Archbishop of Rouen from 1948 to 1968. Created cardinal in February 1965. Member of the Secretariat for Promoting Christian Unity.

313 AS II/5:481–485.

314 Ibid., 485–495.

315 Ibid., 528–530.

316 Ibid., 530–531.

of Seville, José Maria Bueno y Monreal.[317] "It should not be forgotten," the former declared, "that the teaching of Christ was entrusted to the one Catholic Church which has the right and the duty to preach the gospel to the whole world."[318] The "ecumenist" position was opposed that same day by the American Cardinal Ritter, the spokesman for ninety-one of the 120 American bishops.[319] Ritter praised the schema on ecumenism which, in his opinion, signaled the end of the Counter-reformation era, and asserted that it was not possible to arrive at the practice of ecumenism without first establishing the principle of religious liberty. Cardinal Léger also delivered a ringing panegyric on ecumenism.[320] Archbishop Garrone described it in the following words as a general spirit within Christianity as a whole, a characteristic mark of the mystery of God and the Church: "Ecumenism is a providential event, an opportunity to overturn centuries-old barriers and to dispel the darkness covering the world. Since night has come, God is revealing to us some stars that we had not seen until now, to guide our steps until the dawn of the day, when he will reveal himself to the world through the union of all Christians."[321]

While in the hall some were calling for a fundamental reform of the Catholic attitude towards revealed truth, on November 22, Archbishop Corrado Mingo of Monreale[322] spoke about the need to preserve the faith intact, without mutilation, because rejection of the truth results in evil.

> Certainly our work is required in order to bring about the unity of the Church; human means are necessary, but with negotiations, meetings, discussions, and other methods little progress is made. Rather, we must place our hope in divine grace: unity is a gift of God that we can obtain especially through prayer and fasting. Like John the Baptist, we can prepare the paths of unity and remove obstacles. To speak frankly, many great difficulties remain before unity can be attained; for

---

[317] AS II/5:532–534. José Maria Bueno y Monreal (1904–1987), Spanish, ordained in 1927, archbishop of Siviglia from 1957 to 1982. Created cardinal in 1958.

[318] AS II/5:531.

[319] Ibid., 536–538.

[320] Ibid., 550–552.

[321] Ibid., 561–562 at 562. See also A. Wenger, *Vatican II, op. cit., II Session*, 189.

[322] Corrado Mingo (1901–1980), ordained in 1925, archbishop of Monreale from 1961 to 1978.

> example, among our protestant brethren some ministers not only deny the primacy and infallibility of the Roman pontiff and the real presence in the most holy Eucharist, but also other natural precepts with regard to marriage; some do not admit the divinity of our Lord Jesus Christ; some even declare themselves indifferent to the existence of a personal God. A great distance remains between us and those brethren.
>
> I regret however that nothing is said in the schema about the Virgin Mary and her maternal intercession. The mother is always the one who calls her children back to their father's house. Mary is the Mediatrix of all graces. I know that many council fathers have the same conviction in regard to this matter. Venerable fathers, we who are members of the Mystical Body of Christ have two mothers: the Church and the Blessed Virgin Mary. St. Cyprian, strong champion of Church unity, used to say: no one can have God as Father who does not have the Church as Mother; but we, with the patristic and theological tradition before our eyes, together with the *sensus fidei* of the Christian people—all of which has its foundation in sacred scripture—can say that no one can have God as Father who does not have Mary and the Church as Mothers. I note that the venerable Eastern communities, even though separated, have preserved their own religious heritage of devotion to the Virgin Mary, while our protestant brethren have lost much because they have forgotten the Blessed Virgin Mary—even though in our times some of them have turned back to devotion to the Virgin. Venerable brothers, the ardent desire of Christ that "they may all be one" cannot be in vain, because Christ's prayer is always heard by the Father; the time will come in the world, and it will come by means of Mary. Speaking to our separated brethren we can say, again with the words of St. Cyprian, "Return to the Mother whom you left." Then there will be one fold and one shepherd.[323]

Archbishop Zoghby,[324] the vicar of the patriarch of the Melkites, Maximos IV, observed that as far as he was concerned the Eastern schism was somehow a *"felix culpa"* ("happy fault") because it allowed certain traditions and certain values of the Eastern Churches to be preserved which otherwise would have been "Latinized." Actual unity, according to Archbishop Zoghby, would not have been total, but "Latin": full unity

323 AS II/6:159–160.

324 AS II/6:142.

will come about when the East with its authentic tradition unites with the Catholic Church in variety, not in uniformity.

The discussion continued, and on December 2 there was another intervention by Cardinal Ruffini,[325] who reiterated that Jesus Christ founded one Church, which is the infallible and indefectible Catholic Roman Church, with the pope as head; it is not possible to attribute faults to the Church as such, but only to her members; to abandon her because her members are sinners is itself a sin.

In his conclusions, Bea judged that the debate of the two previous weeks had been productive, even though the schema needed further improvements.[326]

On December 1, *L'Avvenire d'Italia* published in its entirety the lecture that Cardinal Suenens, a council moderator, had given on November 29 at the University of Florence on the topic "The Church Facing the Development of the Contemporary World." Suenens proposed the creation of a new organ of Church governance, "a so-called apostolic council, with limited representation of the entire episcopate, and with consultative and deliberative functions in reference to the most important problems of the universal Church."[327]

12. The constitution *Sacrosanctum concilium*

In his speech at the opening of the second session, on September 29, 1965, Paul VI indicated that the liturgy was one of the principal fields of the council's work.[328] In the years 1925-1933 when he had been a "general assistant" (chaplain) for the FUCI (Italian Catholic University Federation), Giovanni Batista Montini had given special attention to the "liturgical education" of the university students, prompting the cardinal vicar of Rome, Francesco Marchetti Selvaggiani, to suspect him of "liturgism."[329] Montini, who had received his liturgical formation from Father Giulio

---

[325] AS II/6:339–340.

[326] Ibid., 364–367.

[327] Text of the conference in R. La Valle, *Il Coraggio del Concilio, op. cit.*, 547–560, cf. 559.

[328] AS II/1:193.

[329] Cf. Virgilio Pontiggia, "L'interesse per la liturgia in G. B. Montini: gli anni giovanili e alla Fuci," in *Liturgia: temi e autori, op. cit.*, 35–81 at 36–40.

Bevilacqua, who in turn had been trained in Belgium at the school of Dom Beauduin,[330] appointed his Oratorian master a member of the council's Liturgical Commission, thus continuing to be influenced by him. The schema of the liturgical constitution also bore the imprint of this religious from Brescia, a future cardinal.

Starting in the autumn of 1963, at the encouragement of Paul VI, a group of liturgists worked to "prepare for the Holy Father a list of the liturgical innovations that could be introduced immediately."[331] Piero Marini, a disciple of Monsignor Bugnini, recalls that "the last three months of 1963 remain one of the least-known periods in the history of the liturgical implementation of the Second Vatican Council. The names of the persons who worked together, and the texts and the outlines that were prepared, remain undisclosed. No trace remains in any official document of the work carried out then."[332] The men who were working in obscurity, under the mandate of Paul VI, were, as Archbishop Marini himself recalls, Cardinal Lercaro and Father Bugnini. The private meetings—in which some of the more "audacious" liturgical reformers participated, such as Father Joseph Jungmann, Canon Aimé-Georges Martimort, who was in charge of revising the Breviary, and Monsignor Johannes Wagner, who was in charge of revising the Roman Missal—took place at the convent of the Benedictine Sisters of Priscilla on the Via Salaria, where Cardinal Lercaro resided. "That was when the understanding between the pope, Lercaro, and Bugnini was established that would carry the reform forward in the midst of so many difficulties."[333]

Some have tried to make Bugnini the "architect" of the liturgical reform against the will of Paul VI. In reality, as Bugnini himself testifies, the liturgical reform was born from a close collaboration between this Vincentian religious and Paul VI. "How many evenings I spent with him," Bugnini wrote, "studying the many and often voluminous files heaped on his table! He read and reflected on them all, line by line, word by word, annotating everything in black, red, and blue pencil and

---

330 S. Marsili, *Storia del movimento liturgico, op. cit.*, 324–325.

331 R. Kaczynski, "Toward the Reform of the Liturgy," *op. cit.*, 239.

332 Piero Marini, "Le premesse della grande riforma liturgica," in *Costituzione liturgica, op. cit.*, 69–101 at 94.

333 Ibid., 88.

criticizing it if need be with that logical mind of his that could formulate ten questions on a single point."[334]

The Introduction and chapter 1 of the liturgical schema were in a draft form that was essentially definitive. At the end of the General Congregation of October 3, Archbishop Felici announced the proposed amendments to chapter 2 on the Mass and scheduled the vote for October 8. That same day Cardinal Lercaro presented his *Relatio Generalis.*[335] On October 10, when chapter 2 was put to a vote, the result of the ballot was only 1,417 *placet* votes, thirty-six *non placet*, 781 *placet iuxta modum*, and eight invalid votes. There was a similar outcome to the voting on chapter 3 on October 18: 1,130 voted *placet*, thirty *non placet*, and a good 1,054 *placet iuxta modum*. Therefore not even chapter 3 could be approved. Chapters that were definitively approved, however, were: chapter 4 on the divine office on October 24, chapter 5 on the liturgical year on October 29, chapter 6 on sacred music on October 30, and chapter 7 on sacred art on October 31. On November 18, 20, and 21 the amended texts of the first three chapters of the schema *De sacra liturgia* were approved. Bishop Zauner of Linz, Austria, a member of the Liturgical Commission, explained in an interview how the conciliar constitution would be applied. "Divine worship," he said, "must be a communal action. The people who attend Mass, for example, like the priest, must take part by prayer, singing, and gestures." "In fact," he added, "the point of the entire constitution is that the priest carries out everything with the active participation of the people and never alone."[336]

In the public session on December 4, 1963, in the presence of Paul VI, the decree *Inter mirifica* on the Means of Social Communication[337] and the constitution on the sacred liturgy, *Sacrosanctum concilium*,[338] were definitively approved and promulgated. For *Inter mirifica*, the result was 1, 960 votes in favor and 164 against, the highest number of negative votes for any of the conciliar documents, whereas *Sacrosanctum concilium*

---

[334] A. Bugnini, *op. cit.*, xxviii. Translation slightly emended. See also *Le rôle de G. B. Montini, Paul VI dans la réforme liturgique*, study day at Louvain-la-Neuve on October 17, 1984 (Brescia: Pubblicazioni dell'Istituto Paolo VI, 1984).

[335] AS II/2:276–279.

[336] Divine Word Service, November 26, 1963.

[337] Text in AS II/6:497–504. See also COD, 843–848.

[338] Text in AS II/6:409–439. See also COD, 820–843.

received an almost unanimous vote, with 2,147 votes in favor and four against. Cardinal Noé mentions that exactly four hundred years earlier, on December 4, 1563, the Council of Trent reached its conclusion, after having asked the pope for the reform of the liturgy. "Now with the liturgical constitution the history of the Tridentine liturgy was finished, in a certain sense, and a new phase of liturgical reform or 'innovation' opened up."[339] Canon Aimé-Georges Martimort interpreted this symbolic coincidence as "the end of the Counter-reformation era."[340] Secretary General Felici explained that since the liturgical constitution, like the decree on the media, *Inter mirifica,* was not a doctrinal text, it dealt *"tantum de re disciplinari"* "solely with disciplinary matters,"[341] but many liturgists such as Martimort saw in it the expression of a "new ecclesiology."[342] What was most characteristic of the document, according to Martimort, was its new language and its pastoral concern.

The constitution *Sacrosanctum concilium* was a "framework law" which nevertheless involved, as Jean Vaquié has noted, a fundamental transformation of the Catholic liturgy.[343] In particular, it announced the revision of the rite of the Mass (n. 50), a new rite of concelebration (n. 58), and the revision of the rites of baptism (n. 66), confirmation (n. 71), penance (n. 72), ordination (n. 75), and matrimony (n. 77).

That evening the pope had dinner with Jean Guitton, who had been invited by John XXIII to sit among the "observers" at the council. With them was Father Giulio Bevilacqua, who during the meal dwelt on Sartre, Simone de Beauvoir, and Camus, all of them "fashionable" authors steeped in anti-Christian sentiments.[344] Guitton, for his part, considered Helder

---

339 Virgilio Noé, "Storia della costituzione liturgica: Punti di riferimento," in *Costituzione liturgica "Sacrosanctum Concilium": Studi*, ed. by the Congregation for Divine Worship (Rome, Edizioni Liturgiche, 1986), 9–24 at 15. See also Emil Joseph Lengeling, "Zum 20. Jahrestag der Liturgie Konstitution," in *Liturgisches Jahrbuch* 34 (1984): 114–124 at 114.

340 A. G. Martimort, "La constitution liturgique et sa place dans l'oeuvre de Vatican II," in *Le Deuxième Concile*, 497–509 at 501–502.

341 C. Soetens, "The Ecumenical Commitment," *op. cit.*, 324–325.

342 A. G. Martimort, "La constitution liturgique et sa place dans l'oeuvre de Vatican II," *op. cit.*, 505–509.

343 Cf. Jean Vaquié, *La Révolution liturgique* (Paris: Diffusion de la Pensée Française, 1971), 39.

344 Cf. J. Guitton, *Paul VI secret, op. cit.*, 57.

Câmara to be a "prophet"—so much so that he asked him to review and correct the speech he was going to deliver in the council hall.[345] Câmara in turn regarded Father de Lubac[346] as a "prophet" and the protestant Brother Roger, the prior of Taizé, as a "saint."[347]

On the morning of January 3, 1964, Father Bugnini was summoned by Cardinal Cicognani, the Secretary of State, who informed him that the Holy Father had appointed him secretary of the *Consilium ad exsequendam Constitutionem de Sacra Liturgia*, the new administrative body responsible for implementing the liturgical constitution under the presidency of Cardinal Lercaro.[348] "In the spring of 1964," Alberigo writes, "the Consilium seemed to be the 'model' for the bodies that were to coordinate post-conciliar activities... the prototype of a shadow alternative to the congregations of the Roman curia."[349]

The *Consilium* functioned from February 29, 1964, the date of its official institution, until 1969, as an organism directly dependent on the pontiff, thus depriving the Sacred Congregation of Rites of its powers.

13. Appeals against communism

Right at the beginning of the second session, the question about communism was posed for the first time in the council hall.

In the year running from the end of the Cuban Crisis in October 1962, until the death of the American president, John F. Kennedy, in November, 1963, a new spirit of détente wafted about the world. It was during this period that a new climate emerged, a "thaw" between realities that had already been defined by the magisterium as antithetical.[350]

---

[345] Cf. Câmara, *Lettres conciliaires*, 1:395.

[346] Ibid., 397.

[347] Ibid., 221.

[348] Caprile, 3:373–376; A. Bugnini, *op. cit.*, 49. The motu proprio *Sacram liturgiam* (January 25, 1964) is published in AAS 56 (1964): 139–169.

[349] Giuseppe Alberigo, "The New Shape of the Council," in HVT 3:493–513 at 508.

[350] "We are right not to fear when confronted with communism. We are right to have nothing to tremble about when faced with the prospects of the year 2000. We are right to help de-Europeanize the Church, disconnecting her from the past and thrusting her forward toward the future" (Câmara, *Lettres conciliaires*, 1:110).

The influence of the encyclicals of John XXIII and Paul VI on the council proved to be decisive.[351] They gave the impression of trying to reverse the Church's position towards communism, since they dispensed with all condemnations, even merely verbal ones. This was the period in which the *Ostpolitk* was born, the Vatican's policy of openness toward the communist countries of the East,[352] which was symbolized by then-Archbishop Agostino Casaroli.[353]

The attitude of the communist governments towards the Church and other religions was evolving from overt persecution to a limited tolerance that allowed restricted freedom of worship and of speech. The Kremlin moreover showed great interest in what was happening in Rome during the years of the council. On November 21, 1963, the weekly *Il Borghese* published an article entitled "A Council Full of Spies," which put forward strong suspicions concerning some Polish bishops present in Rome, who were openly accused of espionage in behalf of the communist regime in their country. On November 22 Cardinal Wyszyński, the primate of Poland, addressed a vehement protest to the Minister of Foreign Affairs, Attilio Piccioni, assuring him that "never has the regime in Poland imposed such

---

[351] P. Chenaux, *L'Église catholique et le communisme, op. cit.*, 260.

[352] On *Ostpolitik*, whose presuppositions go back to the twenties (A. Wenger, *Rome et Moscou 1900–1950* [Paris: Desclée de Brouwer, 1987]), see Alessio Ulisse Floridi, *Mosca e il Vaticano* (Milan: La Casa di Matriona, 1976); Dennis J. Dunn, *Détente and Papal-Communist Relations, 1962–1978* (Boulder, CO: Westview Press, 1979); Mirielle Maqua, *Rome-Moscou: L'Ostpolitik du Vatican* (Louvain-la-Neuve: Cabay, 1984); G. Zizola, *Giovanni XXIII: La fede e la politica* (Rome-Bari: Laterza, 1988), 55–211; A. Riccardi, *Il Vaticano e Mosca, op. cit.*, 217–264; Sergio Grossu, *L'Église persécutée: Entre Goulag et société opulente* (Lausanne: L'Âge d'Homme, 2002); *Il filo sottile: L'Ostpolitik vaticana di Agostino Casaroli*, ed. A. Melloni (Bologna: Il Mulino, 2006); *L'Ostpolitik della Santa Sede: Un dialogo lungo e faticoso*, ed. G. Barberini (Bologna: Il Mulino, 2008); Agostino Giovagnoli, "Ostpolitik: un bilancio storiografico." In *L'Ostpolitik di Agostino Casaroli (1963–1989)* (Bologna: EDB, 2009), 103–131; P. Chenaux, *L'Église catholique et le communisme, op. cit.*, 269–295.

[353] Agostino Casaroli (1914–1998), ordained in 1937, in 1940 entered the service of the Secretariat of State, where he spent his entire ecclesiastical career. In 1979 John Paul II appointed him cardinal, prefect of the Council for Public Affairs and his Secretary of State, a post that he kept until December 1, 1990. See his posthumous memoirs, *Il martirio della pazienza: La Santa Sede e i Paesi comunisti (1963–1989)*, introduction by Cardinal Achille Silvestrini (Turin: Einaudi, 2000), and, besides the previously cited works, Alceste Santini, *Casaroli, l'uomo del dialogo* (Cinisello Balsamo: San Paolo, 1993).

conditions on any of the Polish bishops."[354] The historian Victor Gaiduk, however, recalls that the strategy of "collaboration" with the Catholics had worked in Poland "thanks to Cardinal Wyszyński's policy of national solidarity," but not in Hungary, on account of Mindszenty's opposition.[355]

East and West of the Iron Curtain two lines faced off: many fathers maintained that it was not licit for Catholics to reach an agreement with the communist regime, not even at the price of the concession of a certain freedom of worship; others proved to be "possibilists." Then in August 1963 Plinio Corrêa de Oliveira published a study entitled "The Church's Liberty in a Communist State."[356] In this work, dedicated to the problem of whether "peaceful co-existence" between the Church and a communist regime was licit, the author demonstrated that Catholics cannot accept any *modus vivendi* with communism that would involve giving up the defense of their natural rights, among which was the right of private property sanctioned by the Seventh and Tenth Commandments, but denied by communism. The essay, which was translated into Spanish, French, and Italian, was distributed to the 2,200 council fathers and the 450 journalists from around the world present in Rome, causing a stir that reached beyond the Iron Curtain.[357] On January 4, 1964, the unabridged text appeared in the Roman daily newspaper *Il Tempo*, attracting the attention of public

---

354 Wyszyński to the Hon. Attilio Piccioni, letter dated November 22, 1963, in ASV, Conc. Vat. II, Busta 332, n. 2, 3 ff.

355 Cf. Gaiduk, "Vaticano e Cremlino," *op. cit.*, 22–23.

356 Cf. P. Corrêa de Oliveira, "A liberdade da Igreja no Estado comunista," in *Catolicismo* 152 (1963); ibid., 161 (1964); reprinted with the title *Acordo com o regime comunista: para a Igreja, esperança ou autodemolição?* (San Paolo: Editora Vera Cruz, 1974). The essay was published in 40 newspapers and in 5 different languages.

357 The study was violently attacked in Poland by the Catholic-communist movement "Pax" in its publications *Kierunki* (n. 8 dated January 3, 1964) and *Zycie i Mysl* (n. 1–2, 1964). The magazine *Wiez* in Warsaw also aligned itself with "Pax." In France, *L'Homme Nouveau* (March 5, 1964) defended the work, which on the other hand was attacked by the progressive publication *Témoignage Chrétien* (n. 1035, 1964). Concerning the Polish "anomaly," in other words, concerning that unique historical model of coexistence between the Catholic Church and the communist state in Poland, see G. Barberini, *Stato socialista e Chiesa cattolica in Polonia* (Bologna: CSEO, 1983); Norbert A. Zmijewski, *The Catholic-Marxist ideological dialogue in Poland, 1945–1980* (Aldershot, England: Darmouth Publishing Company, 1991).

opinion in the Eternal City.[358] On January 9, 1964, one council Father, Bishop Cicuttini of Città di Castello,[359] wrote to the pope: "I can state that a conciliar schema on communism is expected and would be providential. The council at this time cannot ignore such a grave danger and such a serious set of denials."[360]

The distribution of "The Church's Liberty in a Communist State" was connected with two other important initiatives suggested by the Brazilian thinker. The first concerned the problem of communism. On the eve of the second session, Archbishop Geraldo de Proença Sigaud and Bishop Antonio de Castro Mayer consulted many fathers by letter to determine whether they considered it opportune for the council to make a clear and solemn pronouncement on communism. Of the 243 responses received, 218 were affirmative. On December 29, 1963, they sent the petitions to Cardinal Amleto Cicognani, the Secretary of State, asking him to present them to the pope. Cardinal Cicognani noted on the text of the letter: "Reported during audience on 12/9/63. *Aliquid* [Something] brief, solemn, clear must be said. In [the schema] *De praesentia Ecclesiae.*"[361]

Faced with the growing efforts at expansion and domination by Marxism and communism, and considering the insidious errors and states of mind that were rife among many Catholics, making them prone to accept the Marxist doctrine and the social structure of communism, the signatories of the petition, who were from various countries (among them a good fifty-four Brazilian, twenty-nine Italian, but only five French fathers), held that the council was an excellent occasion to treat the subject of communism, a problem of such great importance for the good of the Church and the salvation of souls. They therefore asked the

---

[358] The book went through many editions worldwide in various languages and received a letter of approval signed by Cardinal Giuseppe Pizzardo, prefect of the S. Congregation of Seminaries, and by Archbishop Dino Staffa, secretary of the same dicastery. This letter hoped for "the broadest diffusion of this short, compact work, which is a very faithful echo of the documents of the supreme magisterium of the Church."

[359] Luigi Cicuttini (1906–1973), ordained in 1933, auxiliary bishop of Udine and titular bishop of Amizione in 1953, bishop of Città di Castello and Lamfua in 1956.

[360] Cited in V. Carbone, "Ateismo e marxismo," *op. cit.*, 21.

[361] ASV, Conc. Vat. II., Busta 140, *Petitiones.*

Holy Father to arrange for the development and study of a schema for a conciliar constitution that would:

> 1. Expound with great clarity Catholic social doctrine and denounce the errors of Marxism, socialism, and communism from a philosophical, sociological, and economic perspective.
>
> 2. Dispel the errors and the mentality that prepare the minds of Catholics to accept socialism and communism and make them well disposed to those ideologies.[362]

On December 18, 1963, the Secretariat of State sent the petition to Archbishop Felici for him to forward to the mixed commission in charge of drafting the schema on the Church in the modern world. From then on it had a difficult road ahead.

The second initiative was set in motion by Archbishop Geraldo de Proença Sigaud, who on February 3, 1964, personally delivered to Paul VI another petition signed by 510 prelates from 78 countries, which implored the pontiff, in union with all the bishops, to consecrate the world, and explicitly Russia, to the Immaculate Heart of Mary.[363] This was an equally burning issue connected with the previous one.

Father Congar for his part wrote: "I am campaigning, AS MUCH AS I CAN, against a consecration of the World to the Immaculate Heart of Mary, because I can see the danger that a move in this direction would constitute."[364]

The petitions presented by the two Brazilian bishops and the book by Professor Corrêa de Oliveira, as the latter noted in the review *Catolicismo*, constituted a coherent and organic whole. "Taken together, the three documents are, each in its own way, three episodes of unmistakable importance in the contemporary battle against the greatest adversary of the Holy Father, of the Catholic Church, and of Christendom."[365]

---

362 Cf. the text of this petition in *Catolicismo* 157 (1964), Ital. transl. in *Cristianità* 19–20 (1976). Plinio Corrêa de Oliveira was the one to compose the petition against communism signed by the council fathers. Cf. A-IPCO, Meeting of August 26, 1989.

363 The text of the document in *Catolicismo*, 159 (1964).

364 Congar, *Journal*, 578.

365 P. Corrêa de Oliveira, "A margem de três documentos providenciais," in *Catolicismo* 159 (1964): 3.

14. Paul VI's journey to Palestine

The second session officially concluded on December 4, 1963, and the intense work of the commissions and sub-commissions began. Although the bishops had now returned to their dioceses, at dawn on January 4, 1964, on a frosty morning with a northerly wind, Paul VI left the Vatican to travel to Palestine. It was the first time that a pope had voluntarily made a trip outside of Italy, traveling not only to the holy places, but also to a territory that was bitterly contested between Arabs and Israelis. Many supposed that the initiative was intended to distract the attention of public opinion from the disappointing conciliar results; others saw it as arising from the wish to reaffirm papal primacy before public opinion worldwide. The interest of the mass media in Paul VI's visit, however, was extraordinary.[366] The crucial moment of the visit was, on January 6, the meeting with the ecumenical Patriarch Athenagoras I, which inaugurated the dialogue between the Catholic world and the Orthodox world.[367] In the Holy Land, wrote François Mauriac, "we saw the acceleration of history become, before our very eyes, the acceleration of Grace."[368]

---

366 To get an idea of the media impact of the journey of Paul VI, see the Italian weekly *Epoca* which transferred its entire editorial staff to Palestine to perform the greatest service ever performed by the publication until then ("Il Papa pellegrino," in *Epoca* 694 [January 12, 1964], 20–83).

367 B. Lai, "Il lungo abbraccio fra Paolo VI e Atenagora," in *Il Giornale*, January 4, 1985.

368 François Mauriac, "Pietro ha spezzato le catena della Chiesa," in *Epoca* 694, p. 76.

V

1964: The Third Session

1. The opening of the third session

On September 14, 1964, Pope Paul VI, surrounded by twenty-four council fathers, opened the third session of the council with a concelebrated Mass. The ceremony, the first of its kind to take place in the council assembly, seemed like the liturgical expression of the new principle of collegiality.[1] "The solitude of the pope," the correspondent of *Le Monde* commented, "has given way to a chorus of twenty-five prelates—including the bishop of Rome—celebrating the Mass together, with the same voice

[1] On June 26, 1964, Paul VI had authorized the first experiments in six Benedictine monasteries: San Anselmo, Montserrat, En-Calcat, Maredsous, Maria Laach, Collegeville and in the Dominican convent of Le Saulchoir. On Holy Thursday, April 15, 1965, concelebration was to become a normal rite of the Western Church. The teaching of the Church, reiterated until Pius XII, is that in concelebration there is one Sacrifice of the Mass, and that it is not multiplied depending on the number of celebrants (cf. Pius XII, Allocution on November 2, 1954, in AAS 46 [1954]: 669; *Idem*, Audience on September 22, 1956, on the occasion of the Second International Congress of pastoral liturgy, in AAS 48 [1956]: 717). On the topic of concelebration see the excellent study by Joseph de Sainte-Marie, O.C.D., *L'eucharistie, salut du monde: Études sur le Saint Sacrifice de la messe, sa célébration, sa concélébration* (Paris, Éditions du Cèdre, 1982), and the one by Monsignor R. M. Schmitz, "Zur Theologie der Konzelebration," in *Theologisches* 139 (1981): 4323–4334 (expanded as "La concelebrazione eucaristica," at http://www.haerentanimo.net, September 8, 2009).

and the same gestures."[2] The Mass was moreover completely in dialogue and, as Bishop Câmara pointed out, gave the impression of an "enormous distance from the opening Mass, which had been sung from beginning to end by the Choir of the Sistine Chapel."[3] Shortly after the beginning of the third period, the delegates of the episcopal conferences asked to concelebrate in suitable chapels or churches, following the pope's example, and from then on concelebrations began to multiply.[4]

The allocution,[5] too, with which Paul VI opened the work of the council session seemed to be an exaltation of collegiality, but the pope stressed also the importance of a "central leadership" of the Church, as it were to try to calm those who feared the reduction of the papal primacy. Contrary to appearances, Paul VI discreetly but firmly directed the proceedings through the Coordinating Committee and the four moderators (Agagianian, Döpfner, Lercaro, and Suenens) who were closely connected to him. The third session was the one in which greater control of the conciliar proceedings on the part of the pope was manifested.

On September 29 Alberigo met Father de Lubac, invited him to Bologna, and confided to him his concerns, which the Jesuit theologian reports as follows: "The pope, he [Alberigo] tells me, does not wish to break with the curia; he, Dossetti, and their other friends in common hardly see him anymore. He is afraid that Paul VI may not continue for long on the lines of John XXIII. He deplores the power of Felici who is, in his opinion, a pure curialist [legalist]. Tardini's great victory over Montini is Felici."[6]

New groups of participants were added in this period to the already vast assembly: five "observers" from the Orthodox world, eight laymen selected from among the "auditors," eight religious women and seven laywomen in the new category of "female auditors"; finally thirty-eight parish priests who had arrived from fifteen countries of the world. The decision of the patriarch of Constantinople, Athenagoras, to invite some observers to the council was considered a new step forward on the path of ecumenism.

---

2 Fesquet, *Drama*, 298.

3 Câmara, *Lettres Conciliaires*, 2:505.

4 Ibid., 694–695; J. A. Komonchak, "Toward an Ecclesiology of Communion," in HVT 4:1–94 at 7–8.

5 AS III/1:140–151.

6 De Lubac, *Quaderni*, 605.

The volume of questions on the carpet was such that, in January 1964, the Coordinating Committee had decided to restrict debate to the essential themes: the Church, the bishops, ecumenism, revelation, the apostolate of the laity, and the Church in the modern world, in other words, to six of the thirteen schemas foreseen in the calendar. As far as the other seven were concerned, they were reduced to "proposals" and "suggestions" for the assembly, drafted by the different commissions that were engaged in examining them.

In June the commission adopted new measures to speed up the conciliar proceedings. On the very day of his coronation, June 30, 1963, Paul VI had received in audience the archbishop of Munich and had entrusted to him a plan for bringing the council to an end.[7] Döpfner presented a plan at the end of December and gathered together in Innsbruck from May 19 to 22, 1964, the bishops of Germany, Austria, Luxemburg, Switzerland, and the Scandinavian countries, as well as the observers who had taken part in the conferences in Munich and Fulda to study the topics that were to be discussed and put to vote during the third session. According to the "Döpfner plan," whoever wished to speak in the meeting hall would have to give a summary of his intervention to the general secretary at least five days before the discussion. This made it practically impossible for the minority to oppose the schemas, given that the regulation added that, in the case of a refusal of a document, the opposing declaration would have to be presented by as many as seventy signatories. The objective was clearly to discourage the initiative of all of those who did not belong to a well-organized group.

2. The encylical *Ecclesiam suam*

Paul VI's first encyclical, *Ecclesiam suam*, announced on June 26, 1964, was published the following August 6.[8] In the document the pope dealt with

[7] Cf. Wiltgen, 147; Evangelista Vilanova, "The Intersession (1963–1964)," in HVT 3:347–492 at 350–359; R. Aubert, "Lo svolgimento del Concilio," in *SC, La Chiesa del Vaticano II*, vol. XXV/I:271–273; J. Grootaers, "Sinergie e conflitti," *op. cit.*, in *L'evento e le decisioni*, 386–413.

[8] Text in Paul VI, *Insegnamenti*, 10:9–53 at 12. Cf. E. Vilanova, "The Intersession," *op. cit.*, 448–457; G. Colombo, "Genesi, storia e significato dell'Enciclica 'Ecclesiam suam,'" in *"Ecclesiam suam": Première lettre encyclique de Paul VI*, Acts of the International Convention of the Paul VI Institute in Rome, October 24–26, 1980 (Brescia: Studium, 1982), 131–160. The Abbé de Nantes published a theological critique of the encylical in his *"Lettres à mes amis,"* nos. 180 and 181, dated August 20

the topic that was very dear to him, that of ecclesiology, specifying that he did not wish to give a doctrinal and dogmatic treatment of it, but simply to offer a "simple conversational letter" and "a sincere message, as between brothers and members of a common family."[9]

Paul VI developed the points that he had already treated in his allocution of September 29, 1963: the Church's need for "a vivid and lively self-awareness"[10] and the "relations which the Church must establish with the surrounding world in which it lives and works."[11] The pope appeared to think that it was possible for the Church to "adapt itself to the forms of thought and living which a temporal environment induces, one might almost say imposes,"[12] without letting herself be influenced by them, thus adapting to worldly sensibilities and customs. He denounced the dangers of "naturalism," that "attempts to undermine the fundamental conception of Christianity," and of "relativism… [that] seeks to justify everything and treats all things as of equal value,[13] but he confirmed the Joannine concept of *"aggiornamento,"* a word that "We have adopted as expressing the aim and object of our own pontificate."[14]

"Dialogue" was the prescription called for in order to develop relations between the Church and the world. "The Church must enter into dialogue with the world in which it lives. It has something to say, a message to give; a communication to make,"[15] because, "before we [*i.e.* the Church] can convert the world—as the very condition of converting the world—we must approach it and speak to it."[16] Dialogue would have to be developed

---

and 28, 1964. "Paul VI," he wrote, "has personally been won over to the very principle of Congarian reformism. This date will go down in Church history" (*Lettre*, no. 180). A conservative interpretation in its favor, on the other hand, was written by Fr. P. de la Trinité, O.C.D., *Dialogue avec le marxisme? "Ecclesiam suam" et Vatican II* (Paris, Éditions du Cèdre, 1966), in which he forcefully critiqued the book by the Dominican Dominique Dubarle, *Pour un dialogue avec le marxisme* (Paris: Cerf, 1964).

[9] Paul VI, encylical *Ecclesiam suam*, nos. 6 and 7. [English translation at Vatican website].

[10] *Ibid.*, 10.

[11] *Ibid.*, 12.

[12] *Ibid.*, 42.

[13] *Ibid.*, 49.

[14] *Ibid.*, 50.

[15] *Ibid.*, 65.

[16] *Ibid.*, 68.

according to "a series of concentric circles": the first would have to include "the entire human race";[17] the second would have to extend to all who believe in God, including "the followers of the great Afro-Asiatic religions";[18] the third would be concerned with the "separated brethren," a "varied and wide" sector marked by "spiritual fervor" that "would seem to augur well for the future unification of all Christians in the one Church of Christ."[19] Finally, the last dialogue necessary was the one within the Catholic Church, that the pope already saw in progress: "The Church today is more alive than ever before!"[20]

Ecclesiam suam has been described as "the encyclical of dialogue," a term that was "used fifty-seven times!" (The American bishop Fulton Sheen kept count.)[21] Bishop Giuseppe Colombo comments, "Really, the three parts of the encyclical are thought out in a strict, logical succession, in such a way that from the first—the Church's coming to an awareness; the second—the renewal of the Church; is 'derived' or ought to be derived, and both of them come together to produce the third part, dialogue. The end, the last thing in execution, is the first in intention."[22] "Dialogue" is the problem of "the relations which the Church must establish with the surrounding world in which it lives and works." "The Church cannot remain indifferent to or unaffected by the changes which take place in the world around. They influence, modify, and condition its course of action in all sorts of ways. As we know, the Church does not exist in isolation from the world. It lives in the world."[23]

The adoption of dialogue as an instrument of language was not only a strategic choice, but also, as Father O'Malley notes, the outward expression of an inner system of interior values.[24] The pastoral style, which sometimes is taken to be the simple outer clothing of a thought, is in reality the

---

[17] *Ibid.*, 96, 97.

[18] *Ibid.*, 107.

[19] *Ibid.*, 112.

[20] *Ibid.*, 117.

[21] *"Utitur quinquagies septies!"* AS, III/1:773–775 at 773.

[22] G. Colombo, "Genesi, storia e significato dell' 'Ecclesiam suam,'" *op. cit.*, 135–136.

[23] Paul VI, encylical *Ecclesiam suam*, 42.

[24] Cf. John W. O'Malley, *What Happened at Vatican II*, *op. cit.*, 305–306.

ultimate and true expression of its meaning. "Dialogue" was a method that implied a concept of the world and of history.

3. The conservatives to the counter-attack

a) The official birth of the *Coetus Internationalis Patrum*

The make-up of the conciliar assembly was meanwhile changed once again. About 250 fathers (more that 10%) took part for the first time in the work of the third session.

Among the more worrisome corrections introduced to the document on collegiality that arrived in the hall was the one that replaced the expression *"Haec igitur Ecclesia (...) est Ecclesia catholica, a Romano Pontifice et Episcopis in eius communione directa"* ["This Church, therefore, (...) is the Catholic Church, directed by the Roman pontiff and the bishops in communion with him"] with the new verbal formula: *"Haec Ecclesia (...) subsistit in Ecclesia catholica, a successore Petri et Episcopis in eius communione gubernata"* ["This Church (...) subsists in the Catholic Church, which is governed by the successor of Peter and the bishops in communion with him."[25] This seemed to rule out full identification between the Church of Christ and the Catholic Church, while admitting the presence of ecclesiastical elements outside the Church itself as well.

From January 11 to 14, 1964, Archbishop Lefebvre, Bishop de Proença Sigaud and Dom Prou, abbot general of the Congregation of Solesmes, met at Solesmes with a group of theologians for a program of five days of work together.[26] "The guiding thought," Fr. Berto wrote to Bishop Carli on February 10, "has been that of strictly following the intentions of the Holy Father, namely, to think of Vatican II, as *continuantem, non adversantem* [continuing, and not opposing] Vatican I."[27]

On February 8, Archbishop Lefebvre sent to the bishops associated with

---

[25] Schema *constitutionis De Ecclesia,* in AS III/1:158–168 at 167.

[26] The four theologians were Dom Frénaud and Dom Nau of Solesmes, Monsignor Lunaut, dean of the Faculty of Theology in Angers, and Canon Berto; all of them held doctorates in philosophy and theology from the Gregorian University.

[27] Letter from Father Berto to Bishop Carli dated February 10, 1964, in N. Buonasorte, "Per la 'pura, piena, integra fede cattolica,'" *op. cit.*, 129–130.

him the document composed at Solesmes, asking them to sign it. The same document was sent to the general secretary of the council.[28]

The conservative council fathers had entrusted to Archbishop Lefebvre the task of reorganizing their ranks. Bishop Sigaud wrote to Archbishop Lefebvre on July 15:

> "Here in Brazil, we have no information about the progress of the work and, therefore, we cannot organize anything for the third session. I hope that you have more luck than I and that you can prepare the proceedings and make the contacts that will be useful in the future. I see in the press that the approval of rather revolutionary proposals is considered certain. Therefore, we will have much work to do. I am delighted as I think of the joy of seeing you again in Rome."[29]

On September 29, 1964, once the session had started, Cardinal Santos, the archbishop of Manila, agreed to be the spokesman of the conservatives among the members of the Sacred College. On October 6, 1964 Bishop de Proença Sigaud announced, in a letter sent to the council fathers, that the group would organize every Wednesday evening, near the generalate of the Augustinians, a series of meetings that would be open to all the council

---

[28] "Your Excellency, please excuse the delay in delivering this study to you. It may seem to you a bit bold. But we were encouraged in this effort by the thoughts on this subject that the Holy Father himself was so kind as to reveal to me during my audience on December 6, 1963. The allusions by the supreme pontiff in his speech at the close of the second session also suggested that we should propose one general schema, which has been studied by several qualified theologians, four French theologians: Dom Frénaud and Dom Nau of Solesmes, Monseigneur Lunaut, dean of the Faculty of Theology in Angers, and a Doctor of sacred scripture, Canon Berto, all of them doctors in philosophy and theology from the Gregorian University. His Excellency Archbishop Sigaud of Diamantina, the Most Reverend Dom Prou, abbot general of the Congregation of Solesmes, and myself have guided and directed these efforts, which must still be continued, and the results will be transmitted as soon as they are written. Very humbly we submit this study to the Coordinating Commission and to the Theological Commission of the Council, hoping that this clarification of dogmatic concepts will facilitate an understanding of the subjects addressed by the council fathers during the next session. Please be assured, Your Excellency, of my respectful and devoted sentiments in Our Lord" (Letter of Archbishop Lefebvre to Archbishop Felici dated February 8, 1964, in A-Ecône, 02–09 A).

[29] Letter of Archbishop de Proença Sigaud to Archbishop Marcel Lefebvre dated July 15, 1964, in A-Ecône, 02.10.007.

fathers. "The purpose of these meetings is to study together, with the help of theologians, the schemas that have been submitted for the fathers' discussion in the light of the Church's traditional teaching, and according to the teaching of the supreme pontiffs." "These studies," the letter explained, "are undertaken in accordance with the spirit of the interventions made in the conciliar hall by their Eminences, the Most Reverend Lords Cardinals Ruffini, Siri, Santos, Browne, and others."[30] The first conference in the program,[31] on October 13, was given by Cardinal Ernesto Ruffini on the thirteenth schema *De Ecclesia in mundo huius temporis*; the second, on October 27, was given by Father Ermenegildo Lio,[32] on the schema *De matrimonii sacramento*. In November the group chose the definitive name of *Coetus Internationalis Patrum,* "the International Group of Fathers."

b) Cardinal Larraona's "confidential comment"

Over the course of 1964, various documents issued from the meetings of the *Coetus*, among them a confidential "Note addressed to the Holy Father on the Schema *Constitutionis De Ecclesia* (September 11-12, 1964),"[33] that Cardinal Larraona presented to the Holy Father on September 13, on the eve of the third session. It was signed by twenty-five Cardinals and thirteen superiors of religious orders among whom were the superiors of the Dominicans, Aniceto Fernández, and of the Jesuits, Jan B. Janssens.[34] Cardinal Larraona also asked Cardinal Ottaviani to endorse the document,

---

[30] A-Ecône, 02.10.004, f. 63.

[31] A-Ecône, 02.10.004, f. 66.

[32] Ermenegildo Lio (1920–1992), Franciscan Friar Minor, professor of moral theology at the Lateran University. See his book *L'ordine morale cristiano* (Rome: Pontificia Università Lateranense, 1972).

[33] *Quidam Patres Cardinales, Nota personalmente riservata al Santo Padre sullo schema* constitutionis De Ecclesia, in AS, VI/3:322–328; *adnexa*, 330–338. The document is reprinted in G. Caprile, "Contributo alla storia della *'Nota explicativa praevia',*" in *Paolo VI e i problemi ecclesiologici al Concilio*, 596–603; complete text of the note translated into English in M. Lefebvre, *I Accuse the Council!* (Dickinson, TX: Angelus Press, 1982), 42–53. On this incident see also J. A. Komonchak, "Toward an Ecclesiology of Communion," *op. cit.*, 66–72.

[34] Jean-Baptiste Janssens (1889–1964), Belgian Jesuit, ordained in 1919. superior general of the Society of Jesus from 1946 until his death. Member of the Conciliar Commission for Religious.

but the secretary of the Holy Office wrote to Larraona saying that, although he shared many of the same concerns, it was impossible for him to accept the invitation to sign the document because of his position as president of the commission that was presenting the schema in the council.[35]

The importance of Cardinal Larraona's comment cannot be underestimated, and it was confirmed by Father Caprile, who published it in its entirety in a collection of more than fifty documents that testify to the debate that took place on chapter III of *De Ecclesia*, especially in the months of September and November 1964.

The signers of the document passed judgment on the chapter in these terms:

> While fully acknowledging the good it contains, we cannot refrain from expressing *serious reservations* on this chapter as a whole. Since, then, we sincerely believe what we are going to say, we have the right *in Domino*—and not only the right, which we could sacrifice, but the inalienable duty—to make known our fears and our opinions on the subject to the proper authority.
>
> In fact, after careful study, we think it out duty to say in conscience and before God that chapter 3:
>
> 1. *As far as doctrine is concerned* brings us
>
> a) doctrines and opinions that are new;
>
> b) doctrines and opinions that are not only uncertain, but not even more probable or solidly probable;
>
> c) doctrines and opinions that are often vague or insufficiently clear in their terms, in their true meaning, or in their aims.[36]

With regard to the argumentation, the schema was described as being: "a) rather weak and full of errors, both historically and doctrinally; (…); b) curiously heedless of fundamental principles, even those emanating from earlier councils or from solemn definitions; c) such that a dubious and readily proved *partiality* can be clearly seen (…); d) *not very precise*, not very logical, not very coherent and, therefore, encouraging—if it were

---

[35] ASV, Conc. Vat. II, Busta 781, *De Ecclesia: Epistola et alia* (1964). Ottaviani to Larraona, Rome, September 10, 1964, f. 1; Larraona to Ottaviani, September 13, 1964, f. 1, n. 365.

[36] "Nota personalmente riservata," cited in G. Caprile, *Contributo alla storia della "Nota explicativa praevia,"* op. cit., 596. "Note addressed to the Holy Father," cited in M. Lefebvre, *I Accuse the Council!*, 43. [In this and the following citations, the English translation is lightly emended.]

approved—endless discussions and *crises,* painful aberrations and deplorable attacks on the unity, discipline, and the government of the Church."[37]

The teaching on the primacy of the pope and the collegiality of the apostles contained in the schema, according to the document presented by Cardinal Larraona, is as follows:

> 1. ...[It is] a new doctrine which, until 1958 or rather 1962, represented only the opinions of a few theologians; even these opinions were *less common* and *less probable*. It was the contrary doctrine which even recently was *common* and *encouraged* by the Church's magisterium.
>
> 2. The *common* doctrine, accepted in the Church as sound and more probable until 1962, was *at the root of constitutional discipline and also concerned the essential validity of acts*, both in the sphere of the councils, whether ecumenical, plenary, or provincial, and in the sphere of government (at all levels: pontifical, regional, provincial, missionary, etc.).
>
> 3. The *new* doctrine has become neither more certain, nor objectively more probable than before as a result of the disturbing campaign of pressure groups who have deplorably politicized the council and disconcerted some episcopates [*i.e.* groups of bishops from a given country or region]. Nor has it become more certain as a result of the actions of many audacious experts who, unfaithful to their true ministry, made biased propaganda instead of objectively enlightening the bishops by acquainting them with the *status quaestionis.* And, finally, it has not become probable through wide coverage of the press, which, with its characteristic methods—methods utilized by the progressives—has created an atmosphere which makes calm discussion difficult, fettering and hampering true liberty by making those who do not show approval appear ridiculous and unpopular. In such an atmosphere scientific reasoning can no longer exert its legitimate influence in any practical way and does not even get a hearing."

In the opinion of those who signed the document, the teaching of the schema *De Ecclesia* was not "ripe" for discussion, much less for "conciliar approval."[38] "If the doctrine proposed in the schema were true," the document reads, "the Church would have been living in direct opposition to divine law for centuries! Hence it would follow that, during these centuries,

[37] Ibid.

[38] Ibid., 45–46.

its supreme 'infallible' organs would have been teaching and acting in opposition to divine law. The Orthodox, and, in part, the protestants, would thus have been justified in their attacks against the primacy."[39]

The cardinals' "Confidential Note" exploded like a bomb, because of the authority of the signers and the gravity of the problems it raised. On September 20, the authors of the document turned to the pope, in a new letter signed by Cardinal Larraona, which stated: "Approval by the supreme pontiff of a similar schema—even if the majority were to wish it—would seem impossible to us. The teaching found in it—even with all the reservations that some have sought to make—cannot help but be profoundly disconcerting and cause some awful crises in more solid and more faithful circles, both of theologians and of the people, especially in traditionally Catholic countries; there is no hiding the fact that this has already raised terrible doubt in the minds of many; if the Church were to go so far as to accept the proposed teaching, she would deny her past, and the teaching that she has upheld until now would automatically accuse her of having failed and of having acted for centuries against divine law." [40]

Having received the letter through Cardinal Larraona,[41] Paul VI sent to the Spanish cardinal on October 18 an eight-page reply, written in his own hand, in which he expressed "surprise and concern: because of the number and high offices of the signatories, because of the gravity of the objections raised on the subject of the schema's doctrine and of its fundamentally contradictory statements—objections supported in Our personal opinion by arguments that are not beyond dispute; also because of the timing when the 'Note' reached us, namely, on the night immediately prior to the opening of the third session of the Second Vatican Ecumenical Council, when it was no longer possible to submit the schema to fresh examination; and because of the easily foreseeable grave and harmful repercussions on the outcome of the council and hence on the whole Church, particularly on the Roman Church, if the suggestions made to Us in the 'Note' itself were to be put into practice."[42]

---

[39] Ibid., 50.

[40] Cf. G. Caprile, "Contributo alla storia della 'Nota explicativa praevia,'" *op. cit.*, 620.

[41] Cf. the text of the accompanying letter by Cardinal Larraona, in G. Caprile, "Contributo alla storia della 'Nota explicativa praevia,'" *op. cit.*, 619–621. To this letter dated November 20, the Spanish prelate added another, written on September 21, after having heard the reports of the General Congregation on that day (ibid., 622–623).

[42] Text in G. Caprile, *Contributo alla storia della "Nota explicativa praevia,"* cit., 632–635. English

On the October 24, Cardinal Larraona showed Siri the long, handwritten response of the pope, and asked his advice on how to respond: whether to limit himself to a thank-you or to pursue his arguments. Siri, who judged Cardinal Larraona to be "one of the best and most constant servants of the Church and of the pope,"[43] notes: "He was with me for a long time and left the document [the pope's letter] for me to read. I examined it and found that the cardinal had reason to be in doubt: the document, very polite in form, is stern in its substance and does not hide the fact that the contents of the letter from the twenty-two cardinals was upsetting. I found that there was a way of replying without stopping at a mere thank-you and immediately drafted a memorandum for the cardinal."[44] On October 28 Larraona, following Siri's advice, replied to the Holy Father with a polite but firm letter, in which, although expressing "sincere regret" for having caused "anxiety and pain" to the august person of the pope, he confirmed that "unless some formulas are not revised, in many questions disputed among the theologians we will end up taking a position contrary to what has been until now the more common opinion, reinforced by the Church's magisterium and by its practice for entire centuries, and, therefore, still defended today by highly renowned theologians."[45]

The "Confidential Comment" revealed, for the first time, the existence of an organized opposition to the progressive minority that until then had imposed the agenda and the style of the proceedings.

c) Bishop Helder Câmara's maneuvers

At work on the opposing front, with quite a different abundance of financial means and media support, was the DO-C (*Documentatie Centrum Concilie* or Documentation Center of the Church of the Low Countries),

translation in M. Lefebvre, *I Accuse the Council!*, 53–57, excerpt at 53–54 [emended]. Cf. also ASV, Conc. Vat. II, Busta 345, Segreteria generale del Concilio. *Nota explicativa praevia* 1964, photocopy 8 gg.

43 Siri, *Diario*, 394.

44 Ibid.

45 Letter from Cardinal Larraona to Paul VI dated October 28, 1964, in G. Caprile, "Contributo alla storia della 'Nota explicativa praevia,'" *op. cit.*, 648–650 at 649.

with its headquarters in the *via dell'Anima*, behind the Piazza Navona. Set up with financing by the Dutch bishops' conference,[46] the DO-C had published thirty theological documents in six languages between January 1 and September 14, 1964, and had distributed them to the council fathers and to their experts. In one of its letters, dated November 6, the center announced a meeting on the 18th of the same month, in which the theologian Schillebeeckx ("The development of theology during the third session of the council") and Bishop Helder Câmara ("Prospects of new Church structures") would take the floor.[47]

For Câmara[48] the point of reference in the council remained Cardinal Suenens, or, as he casually called him, "Father Miguel." But the one who was directing the orchestra was, according to the Brazilian bishop, Don Ivan Illich, whom he described as "the leader of the band and the ringmaster of the circus."[49] On the evening of September 15, on the occasion of a conference given by Fr. Lauretin at the Domus Mariae, an exclusive dinner was served at the Belgian College with Illich, Câmara, and Suenens to "to get the general outline straight."[50] Suenens revealed to Câmara that the *relator* for the upcoming discussion on collegiality would be the "reactionary" Bishop Parente, who had been won over by the "collegialists": the fact that he had switched sides would have considerable weight with the Italian episcopacy.[51] Câmara ensured that there would be

---

[46] In 1965, at the end of the Second Vatican Council, the Dutch DO-C combined with the Center for Coordinating Conciliar Communication for the Press (CCC-C). From this merger was born the IDO-C, the International Center for Information and Documentation on the Conciliar Church. After the council, the latter was structured as an international organization with headquarters in Rome.

[47] Fond Thils, in CLG, n. 1706.

[48] "Although he never once took the floor in the council assembly," Cardinal Suenens recalls, "he played a very significant role behind the scenes." Suenens, *Memories and Hopes*, 216.

[49] Câmara, *Lettres conciliaires*, 2:488.

[50] Ibid., 508.

[51] Ibid., 509–510. Suenens' advisor, too, Monsignor Prignon, noted that "the assessor of the Holy Office, Archbishop Parente, from the beginning, has been clearly aligned in favor of collegiality and defends it with a sometimes noisy vehemence" (Fonds Prignon, "Rapport sur la première décade de la IIIe session conciliaire (14–24 septembre 1964)," in CLG, n. 1056).

fawning admiration for the interventions of Suenens in the council hall.[52] "At the council, he is my leader," the Brazilian bishop wrote in his 13th circular letter to his faithful.[53] Paul VI, on receiving him in an audience on March 13, 1964, after his appointment as archbishop of Olinda and Recife, had reassured him with these words: "Don't worry. It is evident that God's hand is on your head. Providence has made itself palpable."[54]

4. A compromise on the chapter *De Beata Maria Virgine*

In the second session, the conservative bishops had lost the battle over the schema on the Blessed Virgin Mary, which, instead of being treated independently, was included as the eighth and final chapter of the schema on the Church, and then made an integral part of the constitution *Lumen gentium*. The delicate point of the Marian issue, which opened the third session, was the question about Mary's mediation, a stumbling block and a cause for "scandal" among the council fathers themselves.[55] The debate on the subject was short, but heated and intense.[56]

Within a century, the Popes Pius IX and Pius XII had defined two major Marian dogmas: the Immaculate Conception (1854) and the Assumption of the Blessed Virgin Mary into heaven (1950). A third dogma was ardently awaited by the Catholic world, the dogma of Mary, the Mediatrix of all graces. The Second Vatican Council would have been an extraordinary occasion for the pope, in union with all the bishops of the world, to proclaim it solemnly. Paul VI, however, as Father Congar noted in his *Diary*, definitely did not want the council to make a pronouncement on the subject, while he insisted that the title *"Mater Ecclesiae"* ("Mother of the Church") be attributed to Mary.[57]

---

52 Câmara, *Lettres conciliaires*, 2:510.

53 Ibid., 825.

54 Ibid., 1:476. In that conversation Bishop Colombo confided to Bishop Câmara that the pope "liked Rahner and Häring very much" (ibid., 2:583).

55 See the eloquent title of the work by the philosopher Charles de Koninck, *Le scandale de la Médiation* (Paris: Nouvelles Éditions Latines), 191. On this topic, see François-Marie, O.F.M., "La nouvelle mariologie dans le chapître 8 de Lumen gentium," *op. cit.* 269–288.

56 AS III/1:435–476; 504–544 and III/2:99–188.

57 Congar, *Journal*, 467.

Congar, a member of the sub-committee on Marian mediation, belonged to the group of "anti-Marian" theologians, who were determined to do everything possible to avoid having the council increase devotion to the Blessed Virgin. "How are a few, already overburdened," he writes, "to struggle against the enormous mass of fanatical Mariologues?"[58] The French Dominican describes in his *Diary* the meeting of June 3, 1964, that witnessed the encounter between the two groups: on the one hand, the "Marian" bishops and theologians: Balić, Parente, Tromp; on the other hand the "anti-Marian" theologians: Garrone, Philips, Rahner. René Laurentin, a Mariological minimalist connected with the anti-Roman party, sought for his part to establish an intermediate position. During the revision of the schema, during the months between sessions, Philips himself, it appears, was the one to persuade Paul VI that in order for the schema to succeed in the council, the term of "Mediatrix" would have to be mentioned at least as one of the titles traditionally used within the Church.[59] The pope approved, but insisted that the title "Mother of the Church" should be inserted and should have a privileged place in the schema.

When the schema arrived in the hall, a considerable number of the fathers took the floor. Cardinal Ruffini said that the schema "obscured" Mary's cooperation in the work of redemption and since it limited itself to stating, without further explanation, that "Mediatrix" was a title reserved to Our Lady, it became essential to elucidate the meaning of this title, so that non-Catholics would come to realize that the use of this title implies no lessening of the dignity of Christ, who is the one absolutely necessary Mediator.[60]

Speaking in the name of seventy Polish bishops, Cardinal Wyszyński,[61] archbishop of Warsaw, mentioned that in the encylical *Ecclesiam suam*, that had appeared six weeks before, Paul VI had called attention to the fundamental importance of the Blessed Virgin in the life of the Church. With this statement as their support, the Polish bishops had sent the pope a memorandum in which they requested that Mary be proclaimed

---

[58] Ibid., 555.

[59] Cf. J. A. Komonchak, "Toward an Ecclesiology of Communion," *op. cit.*, 56–58; cf. C. M. Antonelli, "Le rôle de Mgr Gérard Philips dans la rédaction du chapître VIII de 'Lumen gentium,'" in *Marianum* 55 (1993): 17–197.

[60] AS, III/1:438–441 at 440–441; Wiltgen, 154.

[61] Ibid., 441–444.

the "Mother of the Church." In the name of the same bishops, Wyszyński requested that the chapter on the Blessed Virgin be made the second of the schema, so as to give it greater importance and to emphasize the role of Mary in relation to Christ and to his Church. He requested, moreover, that the consecration of the world to the Immaculate Heart of Mary, made by Pius XII on October 31, 1942, be renewed in a collegial manner by all the bishops of the entire world. The archbishop of Monreale, Corrado Mingo, asked more precisely, in keeping with the requests of Fatima, for "the renewal of the consecration of the Church, of the world, and, in particular, of Russia to the Immaculate Heart of Mary at the closing of Vatican II."[62] For his part Congar noted: "I am campaigning AS MUCH AS I CAN, against a consecration of the world to the Immaculate Heart of Mary, because I can see the danger that a move in this direction would constitute."[63]

Then there were interventions in defense of the Marian privileges by Bishop Hervas y Benet,[64] bishop of Ciudad Real in Spain, and by Bishop García y García de Castro, bishop of Grenada, who in the name of eighty Spanish bishops reprimanded the Theological Commission for having "completely recast the document instead of adapting it as the council fathers had wished."[65] Bishop Rendeiro,[66] bishop of Faro in Portugal, in the name of eighty-two bishops, joined in Cardinal Wyszyński's request for the consecration of the world and expressly asked that the title of "Mediatrix" be kept in the document, so as to avoid provoking an inevitable scandal among the faithful by removing it.

Conspicuous among the "anti-Marian" council fathers were Cardinal Döpfner,[67] who became the spokesman for ninety bishops who were German-speaking or from the Scandinavian countries, and Cardinal Alfrink,[68] the spokesman for 124 bishops of the Netherlands, Africa, Latin America, Germany, Italy, and other countries, who demanded the removal

[62] Ibid., 463–466 at 465.

[63] Congar, *Journal*, 578.

[64] AS III/1:472–473.

[65] Ibid., 536–539 at 536.

[66] Ibid., 506–508.

[67] Ibid., 449–452.

[68] AS III/2:12–14.

of the expression "Maria Mediatrix," as "equivocal and dangerous," because Christ is the unique mediator. The bishop of Cuernavaca, Mendez Arceo, declared on September 17 that he opposed the title of "Mother of the Church," as being "alien to the Eastern tradition" and "of such recent use that it cannot be contained in a dogmatic constitution."[69]

Cardinal Léger, a member of the doctrinal commission of the council, stressed the need for a "renewal" or "reform" of Marian devotion and doctrine. This renewal or reform, he said, has already begun among the theologians, but ought to reach also the pastors and the faithful, and this final chapter of the constitution on the Church offers the best opportunity for promoting it. "The desired reform consists in using accurate, precise, and simple words to express Mary's role." He added that it was a custom, in praying to her, "to make exaggerated use of superlatives and to pay no attention to the true meaning of words and of formulas." "It is an illusion," he said, "to think that hyperbole helps the faithful nowadays to pray better to Mary and to understand better her dignity." "Sober language and simple discourse would produce many more fruitful results."[70]

In contrast, the "Marian"-style intervention by Cardinal Suenens caused surprise. According to him, the diminishing of Mary's importance that surfaced in the schema represented a "tendency that constitutes a real danger today."[71] Wiltgen observes that for a brief time Suenens "had the courage to break away from the party line of the European alliance and speak his own mind." On the other hand, he adds, "it would have been strange if the cardinal of Belgium—a land so noted in the Catholic Church for its great devotion to the Virgin Mary—had taken any other public stand."[72] In 1913, as a matter of fact, Cardinal Mercier, along with the

---

[69] AS III/1:541–544 at 541.

[70] Ibid., 445–448.

[71] Ibid., 504–505.

[72] Wiltgen, 156. It should be mentioned that in the late 1940s Suenens had become an ardent proponent of the Legion of Mary founded by Frank Duff (1889–1980) and had defended it at the Vatican against the critiques that Father de Lubac had made in 1946 against that movement, in a message circulated privately among the French bishops. Suenens was moreover the author of *The Theology of the Apostolate of the Legion of Mary* (Cork: Mercier Press, 1960), and *Edel Quinn, envoy of the Legion of Mary* (Dublin: C. J. Fallon, 1954). A strong influence was exerted on him by Veronica O'Brien (1905–1998), an Irishwoman and member of the Legion of Mary, who had met Suenens in Paray-le-Monial in 1947, and subsequently played a decisive role in pushing him toward the charismatic renewal.

Belgian episcopacy, had asked the pope for a dogmatic definition of the mediation of graces by the Blessed Virgin Mary, and in 1922 Pius XI had granted to the church of Belgium the Holy Mass and Divine Office in honor of Mary Mediatrix.[73]

Finally an intermediate solution appeared, supported by Cardinal Frings,[74] with the backing of Cardinal Alfrink. Frings spoke of a "compromise" that could be accepted "either by the right or by the left," using an expression from parliamentary language to situate on the "right" the more "Marian" fathers, and on the left the "minimalists."[75] The author of this "compromise" text was Father Balić, to whom Frings lent support, realizing that the required two-thirds majority would never have carried the progressive theses to victory.[76] Philips and Balić got together to find the point of agreement and worked out together a document that was entitled *The Blessed Virgin Mary, Mother of God, in the Mystery of Christ and of the Church*. The term "Mediatrix" was hallowed even though it was positioned in a completely secondary way. "[The title] *'Mediatrix'* could not be avoided," Congar writes. "The manner in which it is spoken of is still the most discreet."[77]

The text was sent back to the Theological Commission that corrected it on the basis of the proposals, so as then to put it to a vote on October 29, 1964. The result was as follows: 1,559 *placet*, 521 *placet iuxta modum*

[73] Cf. M. Hauke, "The Universal Mediation of Mary according to Cardinal Mercier," in Various Authors, *Mary at the Foot of the Cross* (New Bedford, MA: Academy of the Immaculate, 2003), 4:387–407; *Idem*, "Maria 'Mediatrice di tutte le grazie' nell'Archivio Segreto Vaticano del Pontificato di Pio XI: Rapporto intermedio sulle tracce trovate," in *Immaculata Mediatrix* VII/1 (2007): 118–129; *Idem, "Mediatrice di tutte le grazie": La mediazione universale di Maria nell'opera teologica e pastorale del cardinale Mercier* (Lugano: Eupress, 2005).

[74] AS III/2:10–11.

[75] "Relative to the Marian schema, as was expected, many various and conflicting opinions were presented in the hall. The same schema, it seems to me, contains nothing against Catholic truth or against the rights of our separated brethren. But it does not satisfy all the wishes that have been put forward both from the right and from the left. And yet the schema calls for a middle way, by which all can go forward. In this sense there is a compromise" (AS III/2:10).

[76] Wiltgen, 157.

[77] Congar, *Journal*, 629.

and ten *non placet*.[78] Three weeks later, on November 18, after being reviewed in light of the 521 votes *iuxta modum*, the document was again put to the vote. This time there was almost unanimous consent. The title of "Mediatrix," in keeping with the suggestions by Cardinal Ruffini, Bishop Ancel, and others, had been retained in article 62, according to which, "the Most Blessed Virgin Mary is invoked by the Church under the titles of Advocate, of Helper [*Auxiliatrix*], of Benefactress [*Adjutrix*], and Mediatrix"; titles, the document went on to say, that "neither takes away anything from nor adds anything to the dignity and efficacy of Christ the one Mediator."

The maneuvers to eliminate every reference to Mary's mediation were therefore unsuccessful, but the resulting text seems, nonetheless, reductive: indeed, the words "of all graces," which give meaning to the title "Mediatrix," were left out. Thus there is no reference in the document to the active participation of Our Lady in the redemption of humanity. Mary's mediation was not completely ignored, but neither was it solemnly proclaimed, as the council fathers could have done, and as many of them would have desired.

5. Why doesn't Vatican II speak of hell?

Among the first problems on the agenda for the proceedings was also the problem of final ends of man, the central point of chapter 7 of the schema *De Ecclesia*. Cardinal Ruffini[79] noted that there was no mention of hell, which is reserved for those who die in mortal sin. The failure to mention hell was underscored by Archbishop Nicodemo,[80] archbishop of Bari, by Bishop Biagio d'Agostino,[81] Bishop of Vallo di Lucania, and by Archbishop

---

[78] AS III/6:49.

[79] AS III/1:377–379.

[80] AS III/1:385–386. Enrico Nicodemo (1906–1973), ordained in 1928, bishop of Mileto in 1945, bishop of Bari in 1952. See the anthology of his writings, *Scritti pastorali degli anni del Concilio e dopo il Concilio (1963–1970)* (Bari: Arti Grafiche Favia, 1970).

[81] AS III/1:434–435. Biagio d'Agostino (1896–1984), ordained in 1926, auxiliary bishop of Termoli in 1951, titular Bishiop of Citium in 1951, bishop of Gallipoli in 1954 and of Vallo di Lucania in 1956, bishop emeritus of Vallo di Lucania in 1984.

Gori,[82] Latin patriarch of Jerusalem. The latter's intervention deserves to be remembered on account of the clarity with which it presents the problem.

> While the text, in a rather opportune manner, does mention the judgment that awaits every man, and holds up the prospect of eternal beatitude, it is surprisingly silent about the other alternative, that is, about the eternal unhappiness that revelation and the entire tradition foresees for every impenitent sinner.
>
> The omission of a clear reference to eternal unhappiness seems to me unacceptable on the part of an ecumenical council, the task of which is to recall the integral doctrine, in a matter of such great importance, to all human beings and especially to Catholics.
>
> Just as with the existence of judgment and of happiness, so too must be plainly affirmed the certainty of eternal unhappiness for those who have despised the divine friendship. It seems to me that three reasons require it:
>
> The first is that the existence of hell is an undisputed truth of Christian revelation. The savior himself, who certainly knew more than anyone else the best method for proposing his doctrine, and at the same time was kindness itself in person, nevertheless many times, clearly and passionately, proclaimed the existence and the eternity of hell. In the preliminary exposition of this eschatological chapter, together with the existence of judgment and of eternal happiness, there must be an explicit reference to that revealed truth that complements it, namely the state of eternal unhappiness.
>
> The second reason why it is necessary to recall this truth explicitly is the very great importance of this horrendous possibility for every human being. Men, indeed, who are attracted so strongly by concupiscence to despise the divine friendship, certainly need to be dissuaded from sin with the fear of this eternal unhappiness that threatens every impenitent sinner. As the whole Christian tradition taught by Christ himself and by the apostles has always done, so too our council likewise, in this eschatological exposition, must remind every man explicitly of the grievous possibility of this truth.
>
> The third reason for this express mention is a special need of our time, which must be impressed upon our pastoral ministry. Indeed, in our time, the desire prevalent everywhere for a better

[82] AS III/1:383–385. Alberto Gori (1889–1970), of the Orders of Friars Minor, ordained in 1914, patriarch of Jerusalem in 1949.

> material life and rampant hedonism gravely diminish in the eyes of many people the value of the divine friendship and the sense of sin. A consequence of this is the fact that the existence of hell, of eternal unhappiness, is foreign to their thinking, and is commonly rejected as an inappropriate consideration, and is even increasingly fought against as something contrary to the modern mindset. As many sorrowfully notice, quite a few preachers today no longer dare to mention these terrible truths and remain silent about them. But as a result of these fears of the preachers, it is to be feared that among the faithful a practical conviction will prevail that this punishment is a now-obsolete doctrine, the reality of which they have every right to doubt. And in this way the corruption of minds and morals is promoted. And therefore I strongly urge you, venerable brothers, that the proposed text of article 48 should affirm briefly, according to the words of the bible, but clearly, along with the judgment, the alternative that is presented to every human being, namely of eternal happiness but also of eternal unhappiness.[83]

Hell is everlasting perdition for those who die in a state of mortal sin, without having repented, and having refused God's merciful love.[84] This is a truth of faith that has always been taught by the Church and was confirmed by Our Lady, herself, in the message of Fatima, that begins precisely with the terrifying vision of hell, into which the three shepherd children saw a multitude of souls falling, having the appearance of "transparent and black or bronze embers in human form," like "sparks" in great fires, "amidst screams and moans of sorrow and despair," terrifying them so much that, had the vision lasted one more moment, it would have been enough to make them faint.

Fatima—the same Sister Lucia comments—offered a "further proof" guaranteeing "that hell really exists and that the souls of poor sinners go

---

83 AS III/1:384–385.

84 Cf. M. Schmaus, *Dogmatica cattolica: I Novissimi* (Turin: Marietti, 1969), IV/2:423–479; C. Pozo, S.J., *Teologia dell'aldilà* (Rome: Paoline, 1983), 397–433. See also the special issues of the review *Fides Catholica* on hell: no. 2 (2008): 351–568, with essays by Monsignor Brunero Gherardini, Don Nicola Bux, Christopher J. Malloy, Fr. Giovanni Cavalcoli, Fr. Paolo M. Siano, Monsignor Arthur B. Calkins, Fr. Stefano M. Manelli, and no. 1 (2009): 21–260, with essays by Monsignor Michelangelo Tabet, Fr. Settimio M. Manelli, Fr. Manfred Hauke, Fr. Alessandro Apollonio, Fr. Serafino M. Lanzetta. See also S. M. Lanzetta, F.I., *Inferno e dintorni* (Siena: Cantagalli, 2010).

there," while combining this terrible truth, however, with the salvific truth of devotion to the Immaculate Heart of Mary.[85]

During the council and in the following years there were many theologians, from Hans Küng to Karl Rahner, from Hans Urs von Balthasar to Edward Schillebeeckx, who reduced hell to a mythological description, or admitted its reality but considered it "empty."[86] The denial or reappraisal of hell was, moreover, the result of an at-times obsessive insistence on the divine mercy, that tended to set aside completely the role of divine justice. The consequences were doomed to be disastrous, on the level of men's personal responsibility in regard to the faith and morals of the Church.

6. The clash over religious freedom

a) Two contrasting concepts

No schema underwent as many modifications and revisions as the one on religious freedom; discussions on it began in the third session from September 23 to 28, 1964.[87]

The papal magisterium, as opposed to the theories that sprang up from the French Revolution, holds that in the social life of a nation error can be at most tolerated as a fact, never as a right. Liberal relativism and the false principle of freedom of conscience and of religion were condemned uninterruptedly by the magisterium. In the nineteenth century, this condemnation was affirmed by Gregory XVI in his encylical *Mirari vos*,[88] by Pius IX in his encylical *Quanta cura* and in the *Syllabus*, and by Leo XIII in his encylicals *Immortale Dei* and *Libertas*.[89] Pius XII had confirmed

---

[85] Suor Lucia, *Gli appelli del messaggio di Fatima* (Fatima: Secretariado dos Pastorinhos, 2006), 142. See also S. M. Manelli, F.I., "Fatima, l'inferno e il Cuore Immacolato," in *Fides Catholica* 2 (2008): 529–568.

[86] Cf. G. Cavalcoli, O.P., *L'inferno esiste: La verità negata* (Verona: Fede e Cultura, 2010), 54–92.

[87] AS III/2:317–327. Cf. M. Davies, *The Second Vatican Council and Religious Liberty, op. cit.*; S. Scatena, *La fatica della libertà: L'elaborazione della dichiarazione "Dignitatis Humanae" sulla libertà religiosa del Vaticano II* (Bologna: Il Mulino, 2003).

[88] Gregory XVI, encylical *Mirari vos* (August 15, 1832), in Denz-H, nn. 2730–2732.

[89] Leo XIII, encylical *Libertas* (June 20, 1888), in ASS 20 (1887–1888): 593–613 at 604 and

that "that which does not correspond to truth or to the norm of morality objectively has no right either to exist, to be spread, or to be activated."[90]

The draft of the constitution on the Church that was presented in a session of the Preparatory Commission by Cardinal Ottaviani contained in its second part a chapter, the ninth, dedicated to "Relations between the Church and state and religious tolerance."[91] The Preparatory Commission summarized the Catholic teaching on the relations between ecclesiastical authority and civil authority, making a distinction between states where the majority of the citizens profess the Catholic faith and those where a large part of the citizens does not profess it, or does not even know about revelation. In the first case it is the state's duty to profess the Catholic religion, in the second—to conform itself at least to the precepts of the natural law, while respecting the Church's complete freedom to fulfill her divine mission. The original draft had already been rejected, however, in the first session of the council, in favor of a new draft, composed by the Secretariat for Christian Unity, under the direction of Cardinal Bea, and distributed to the council fathers on November 19, as chapter V of the schema on ecumenism, in the conviction that religious freedom would be a preamble to ecumenical relations with the other Christian communities.

In the second session, there was, first of all, discussion of whether the text on religious freedom should be part of the schema on ecumenism, as Cardinal Meyer[92], for example, asked, or whether it should figure instead as a separate schema, in keeping with the request of Cardinal Léger.[93] The cardinal moderators favored the second solution, but they realized, in the course of the discussion, that the proposal was at any rate premature and that it would be better to postpone the discussion.

On September 16 a group of nine bishops, for the most part Latin-American, had written to Paul VI to make clear to him their own "emotion" and "lively anxiety" with regard to the language of the conciliar documents that were about to be discussed; the texts were interwoven with "new and sometimes entirely unexpected formulations" that "do not seem to

---

Immortale Dei (November 1, 1885), in ASS 18 (1885): 161–180.

[90] Pius XII, Address *"Ci riesce"* to Catholic lawyers (December 6, 1953), in AAS 45 (1953): 799; English translation in *The Pope Speaks* 1 (1954): 64–71 at 68b.

[91] AD II-II/4:657–684.

[92] AS III/2:366–368.

[93] Ibid., 359–360.

preserve the same sense and the same significance as those images used by the Church."[94]

> In some schemas, and in particular the one on "ecumenism," along with its declaration on Religious Liberty, they are used, with satisfaction and support, in terms and with a meaning that, although not always contradicting them, are at least formally opposed both to the teaching of the ordinary magisterium and to the declarations made by the extraordinary magisterium for more than a century. In them we no longer recognize Catholic theology, nor the sound philosophy that should illuminate its path. What seems to us to aggravate the question is the fact that the schemas' lack of precision threatens to allow the intrusion of ideas and theories against which the Apostolic See has not ceased to warn us.
>
> ...Allow us to add that many faithful and priests, to whom very extensive press coverage presents these projects for a risky "updating," say that they are very disturbed.[95]

The first signer of the document, which Archbishop de Proença Sigaud and Bishop de Castro Mayer had supported, was the archbishop of Nueva Pamplona (Colombia), Anibal Muñoz Duque.[96]

By this time it was clear, as Bishop Felici wrote, that they were faced with "two diametrically opposed concepts."[97] The "manifestos" of the two tendencies could be found, in the one case, in the lucid pages of the *Institutiones Juris Publici ecclesiastici* of Cardinal Ottaviani,[98] that

---

[94] AS VI/3:339–340.

[95] Ibid., 340.

[96] Aníbal Muñoz Duque (1908–1987), Colombian, ordained in 1933, bishop of Socorro y San Gil in 1951, bishop of Bucaramanga in 1952, archbishop of Nueva Pamplona in 1959, titular archbishop of Cariana in 1968, archbishop of Bogotá in 1972, created cardinal by Paul VI in 1973.

[97] Cf. the memorandum addressed to the pope by archbishop Felici dated October 14, 1964, in AS V/2:795.

[98] Cf. A. Ottaviani, *Institutiones Juris Publici ecclesiastici* (Vatican City: Typis Polyglottis Vaticanis, 1960), 2 vols, esp. vol. II. Cardinal Ottaviani had summarized the Church's doctrine in the conference "Duties of the Catholic State toward religion" given by him on March 2, 1953 in the Great Hall of the Pontifical Lateran University and published that same year by the Libreria del Pontificio Ateneo.

recapitulated the traditional concept of the Church, and, in the second case, in Father Chenu's pamphlet, *La fin de l'ère constantinienne* [The end of the Constantinian era], that came out in Paris in 1961 and announced the hour of an "anti-Constantinian turning point."

The supporters of the new project, in its decisive phase, did not belong to the Franco-Belgian *noyau* [nucleus], but rather to a group of American bishops who were strongly influenced by the Jesuit John Courtney Murray, supported by Bishop Pietro Pavan,"[99] one of the principal writers of the encylicals of John XXIII, *Mater et magistra* and *Pacem in terris.*

According to Grootaers, one could even say that the most important American contribution to Vatican II is found in the subject of religious freedom,[100] even though, in his opinion, "only two persons were pivotal to the 'Declaration' from day one (1960 in Fribourg) to the last day (December 7, 1965 at Rome), Bishop E. J. De Smedt, bishop of Bruges, and Father Hamer,[101] rector at Saulchoir."[102]

It was no coincidence that Father Murray, in an article published in *America* on November 31, 1963, had spoken about "the question of religious liberty" as the "American problem" of the council. Murray, the long-time adversary of Monsignor Fenton, had been forbidden in 1955 to write on the subject of religious liberty, but enjoyed the sympathy of Bishop Montini, whom he knew from the fifties. Fenton was in Rome, from 1960 on, as a trusted theologian of Cardinal Ottaviani, whereas Murray had been appointed a "conciliar expert" in April of 1963 and only from that moment on was involved, with Pavan, in composing the new schema,[103] with the encouragement of Paul VI, with whom he shared an intellectual debt to Maritain.[104]

---

99 Pietro Pavan (1903–1994), ordained in 1929, professor at the Lateran from 1948 to 1969, became its rector in 1969. Created cardinal in 1985. Cf. Franco Biffi, *Prophet of Our Times: The Social Thought of Cardinal Pietro Pavan*, transl. Rosemary Goldie (Hyde Park, NY: New City Press, 1992).

100 J. Grootaers, "Paul VI et la déclaration conciliaire sur la liberté religieuse 'Dignitatis humanae,'" in *Paolo VI e il rapporto Chiesa mondo*, 85–125 at 87.

101 Jean Jérôme Hamer (1916–1996), French Dominican, ordained in 1941, titular archbishop of Lorium and secretary of the Congregation for the Doctrine of the Faith in 1973, created cardinal in 1985.

102 J. Grootaers, "Paul VI et la déclaration conciliaire," *op. cit.*, 86.

103 Cf. D. E. Pelotte, *John Courtney Murray, op. cit.*, 34–35; P. Granfield, *op. cit.*, 196–197.

104 On the affinity between Paul VI's vision of religious liberty and that of Murray, cf. P. Granfield,

b) The debate in the hall

The debate was restarted on September 23, 1964, nine days after the opening of the third session.[105] The General Congregation began with a ceremony venerating the relic of St. Andrew which, having been taken from the Turks and brought to Rome in 1462, was now about to be returned to Patras in Greece as a sign of ecumenical respect.[106] Bishop De Smedt presented a new report, stating that during the intersession, the council fathers had proposed 380 observations and emendations, which had been examined "very carefully by the secretary for the Unity of Christians."[107] The new schema on religious liberty, however, needed to be further improved on a certain number of points, since "as everyone knows, the question of religious liberty had never been dealt with by any ecumenical council."[108] "This is not the opinion of the commission, because it is a question of an essential freedom founded on the very nature of the human person." "The limitation of freedom on the part of the state poses some very difficult problems," the reporter acknowledged. "The state, as a matter of fact, has a 'lay' character, which is to say that it is necessary to believe firmly that it has no power to judge the truth of religious affairs and that it can in no way make suggestions in that regard."[109]

Cardinals Meyer[110] of Chicago, Ritter[111] of St. Louis, Cushing[112] of Boston, the last- mentioned a personal friend of the Kennedy family, stressed the "political" aspect of the declaration, while asserting that with this declaration the Catholic Church would appear to the world as a

---

American Theologians, op. cit., 201–204. On the influence of Maritain on Paul VI, cf. P. Chenaux, *Paul VI e Maritain: Les rapports du "Montinianisme" et du "Maritainisme"* (Brescia: Istituto Paolo VI; Rome: Studium, 1994).

105 AS III/2:348–381, 468–578 and 611–752.

106 Ibid., 285–287. On the event, cf. A. Bea, *Ecumenismo nel Concilio: Tappe pubbliche di un sorprendente cammino* (Milan: Bompiani, 1968), 163–176.

107 AS III/2:348–353.

108 Ibid., 348.

109 Ibid., 352–353.

110 Ibid., 366–368.

111 Ibid., 368–369.

112 Ibid., 361–362.

protagonist in the struggle for freedom. Cardinal Heenan of Westminster also spoke in support of the declaration, but Cardinal Norman Gilroy[113] of Sydney broke the unanimity of the English-speaking world with a stern, written denunciation: "Is it truly possible," he asks, "that an ecumenical council should say that every heretic has the right to alienate the faithful from Christ, the Chief Shepherd, and to carry them to pasture in his poisonous fields?"[114]

The individuals most critical of the text, however, were the Italians and Spanish bishops. Cardinal Ruffini emphasized the connection between liberty and truth, asserting that the true religion could only be unique and to it alone did freedom belong by right; otherwise, he observed, the council would give the impression of requesting nothing more than article 18 of the U.N. Declaration of Human Rights.[115]

Cardinal Silva Henríquez, who was speaking in the name of fifty-eight bishops of Latin America, replied by saying that the great significance of the declaration lay in the fact that it was presented not as a chapter of a schema, but as an independent declaration, addressed to all mankind.[116]

Then Cardinal Ottaviani took the floor. The declaration, he said, stated a principle that had always been acknowledged, namely, that no one could be compelled in matters of religion. But it was an exaggeration to assert that someone who follows his own conscience "is deserving of honor," without making it clear that the conscience to be followed should be correct and not contrary to divine law. "The principle," he said, "in accordance with which everyone has the right to follow his own conscience must presuppose that his conscience is not contrary to divine law," while adding that the text lacked "an explicit and solemn affirmation of the first and genuine right to religious liberty, which belongs objectively to those who are members of the true revealed religion." Such a religious right is simultaneously subjective and objective, while on the contrary, for those who are in error it is a question of subjective right only.

> At present I note with Cardinal Ruffini a substantial omission; it does not speak about the liberty of the faithful to observe the true religion....

---

113 Norman Thomas Gilroy (1896–1977), Australian, ordained in 1923, bishop of Port Augusta in 1935, archbishop of Sydney from 1940 to 1971, created cardinal by Pius XII in 1946.

114 AS III/2:611–612.

115 Ibid., 354–356.

116 Ibid., 369–373.

> Indeed not only is it necessary to appeal to natural rights, but also to those supernatural rights that surely give man abilities that exceed even the limitations that can be instigated by human societies for reasons of social coexistence. Thus the apostles were able to say: "I must obey God rather than men." (…) Here we are not at some philosophical or purely human convention, but rather we are in a council of the Catholic Church, and we must profess and defend the Catholic truth so that there may be full liberty to act according to Catholic doctrine especially in our times, when we could say, with the first fathers, with the first Christians, in regard to those who are suffering in places of persecution: how many prisons you have made holy! (…) Finally, I too do not like saying that society is not capable of exercising discernment about religion. If that principle were valid, we would have to say farewell to all the concordats, to all the agreements that the Church has always made, and that even in our century she has drawn up with the civil societies that she has permitted to discuss religious problems. And there is no doubt about the fact that concordats bring enormous advantages to the Church. It would suffice to note, for example, how much power the concordat with Italy has to defend Christian marriage and also to defend the religious instruction of children and students, and other things of this sort.[117]

Ottaviani asked that religious liberty not be urged so energetically, recalling St. Paul's admonition to Timothy" "Convince, rebuke, and exhort, be unfailing in patience and in teaching. For the time is coming when people will not endure sound teaching" (2 Tim 4:2-3).

Other authoritative interventions followed this same line. Citing Ruffini's intervention, the archbishop of the Spanish military vicariate, Alonso Munoyerro,[118] stressed the danger that the teaching on religious liberty posed to the concordats. Catholic rulers, according to the council, would be obliged to violate them, and thus sacrifice the national Catholic unity that it enjoyed: for example, Spain, a country that had the great honor of having preserved Catholicism in the modern age, of having made Latin America and the Philippines Catholic, and of having won in our time "the great and unique victory over communism."[119]

---

[117] Ibid., 375–376.

[118] Ibid., 614–615.

[119] Ibid., 64.

> This will be the case for Spain: it has enjoyed Catholic unity since the seventh century, since the time of King Recaredo. It had a tolerant attitude toward the Jews for many centuries. It showed and shows tolerance toward the protestants, for whom it is preparing a law that defends their rights without repudiating Catholic unity. Because of the strength of that unity, the Catholic religion is found today in twenty-two republics in America and on the Philippine Islands. To this religiosity of the Spaniards is owed whatever of the Catholic religion remains in the protestant regions. To it is owed also to a great extent the Council of Trent, the victory over the Mohammedans in Spain and in Lepanto, and in our own times a great victory against communism.
>
> On the other hand, statistics show (with the Jews and the Muslims it is insignificant) that there are only 30,000 protestants (a generally accepted number), counting Spaniards and foreigners, among whom only 15,000 are Spaniards. For the most part they are attracted by the strength of proselytism and belong to the lowest social class.
>
> Most Reverend sirs, I beg you to keep in mind these aspects so as to avoid the evils that are necessarily foreseeable if the Spanish government were to decide to terminate the concordat and to promote freedom in this matter of religion, as is proposed in the schema.[120]

The concordat between the Holy See and the Spanish state had been signed on August 27, 1953, by the Pro-Secretary of State, Bishop Tardini, and by the Spanish head of state, Francisco Franco Bahomonde. It began "In the name of the Most Holy Trinity," and in article 1 defined "the Catholic, apostolic, Roman religion" as "the one religion of the Spanish nation." The Spanish state acknowledged that the Catholic Church had the "character of a perfect society" (art. 2), recognized the international juridical personality of the Holy See, of the state, of Vatican City (art. 3), and then went on to regulate in minute detail in thirty-six articles the agreements between the Holy See and Spain.[121] It would be overturned after the council.

Cardinal Quiroga y Palacios[122] (Santiago di Compostella) also asked that the schema on religious liberty be completely revised on account of

120 Ibid.

121 AAS 45 (1953): 625–656.

122 AS III/2:357–359. Fernando Quiroga y Palacios (1900–1971), Spanish, ordained in 1922, archbishop of Santiago di Compostela from 1949 to 1971. Created cardinal in 1953.

its ambiguity: there was the risk that the council might give its solemn approval to the liberalism that the Church had always condemned. Cardinal Browne[123] stressed, for the same reasons, that the declaration could not be approved in the terms in which it was presented. Furthermore some spokesmen of the great religious families, like Fernández,[124] the general of the Dominicans, and Dom Prou, the superior of the French Benedictine Congregation, took a stand against the schema.[125] Among the other interventions we should mention those of Archbishop Lefebvre,[126] Bishop de Castro Mayer,[127] and Cardinal Wojtyla,[128] archbishop of Cracow. The last-mentioned observed that the document did not clearly state, as Christ did, that "only the truth sets free."

The critical interventions of so many influential bishops had created among the majority of the fathers many doubts and questions about the document that was being proposed for their approval. Still, the larger an assembly, the more easily its moods can change. In this case, the atmosphere in the hall changed when Bishop Carlo Colombo, a bishop for only a few months, who was known as the chief theological adviser of Paul VI, confidently stated that the declaration on religious liberty was "of the utmost importance," not only because of its practical consequences, but also, and perhaps especially, because educated men would see in it a key to dialogue between Catholic teaching and the modern mindset.[129] "For us, in Italy, it is the salient point of a possible dialogue or of an incurable difference of opinion between Catholic doctrine and modern man's way of thinking."[130] He was the last to speak, as if it were up to him, by a tacit commission from the Holy Father, to draw the conclusions of the debate.

Paul VI, who called for the approval of the text, could not, however, ignore the criticisms made against it. On October 9, Cardinal Bea

[123] AS III/2:470–471.

[124] Ibid., 539–542.

[125] Ibid., 734–737.

[126] Ibid., 490–492.

[127] Ibid., 485–486.

[128] Ibid., 530–532.

[129] Ibid., 554–557.

[130] AS III/2:554.

received a letter from Bishop Felici informing him of the Holy Father's wish that the text on religious liberty be rewritten and telling him that for this purpose a Joint Commission would be set up, comprised of members of the Secretariat for Christian Unity and the Theological Commission, along with Cardinal Michael Browne, the master general of the Dominicans Aniceto Fernández, Archbishop Marcel Lefebvre and Bishop Carlo Colombo. Apart from the last-mentioned, a man on whom the pope relied, the other three were staunch opponents of the declaration on religious liberty.[131]

The progressives immediately mobilized, alarmed especially by the name of Archbishop Lefebvre. On Sunday, October 11, there was an afternoon meeting at the residence of Cardinal Frings, attended by Cardinals Léger, Joseph-Charles Lefebvre, Meyer, Ritter, Silva Henríquez, Döpfner, and Alfrink[132] attended. That same evening a dramatically phrased letter, signed by thirteen cardinals, arrived on the pope's desk. It read: "Not without great sorrow have we learned that the declaration on religious liberty (…) is to be sent to a certain Joint Commission, of which, it is said, four members have already been designated, three of whom seem to stand in contradiction to the orientation of the council on this question."[133]

On October 12 a note by the Secretary of State referred to the fact that the French episcopate was not disposed to accept the possible nomination of Archbishop Marcel Lefebvre as a member of the commission for the revision of the schema. The note, passed on by Cardinal Cicognani to the pope, was expressed in these words: "1) His Excellency Bishop Martin relates that in the French episcopacy the possible choice of His Excellency Archbishop Marcello Lefebvre (sic) would be considered as a sort of lack of confidence in the episcopacy, among whom such a nomination would not be favorably received (sic), given the more than 'extremist' positions that Archbishop Lefebvre has taken in various circumstances. I thought it advisable to authorize Bishop Martin to announce that no nomination had been made and that Archbishop Lefebvre will not be among those chosen beforehand."[134]

---

131 AS V/2:773.

132 Cf. Fesquet, *Drama*, 413; G. Miccoli, "Two Sensitive Issues: Religious Freedom and the Jews," in HVT 4:95–195 at 186–187.

133 AS VI/3:440.

134 ASV, Con. Vat. II, Busta 114, *De libertate religiosa*, n. 4, 1 f. A second memorandum on that same day related that the Secretariat of State also "was surprised by the choice of His Grace

Two days later, the notice was made public by the daily *Il Messagero* and caused quite a stir. On October 16, in the new instructions conveyed by the Secretary of State to Bishop Felici,[135] the names of Archbishop Lefebvre and of Father Fernández had disappeared and the role of the commission was reappraised. The two principal "theorists" of religious liberty, John Courtney Murray and Pietro Pavan, would assume the task of working on the revision of the text, favoring an "Anglo-Italian" approach of a political-juridical type rather than the theological and moral one, as the French-speaking theologians[136] were requesting instead. The day after the crisis, Paul VI calmed Bishop De Smedt with these words: "You shall see, our document will be approved."[137] In an interview with Daniel Pézeril, the pope asserted: "Perhaps I am slow. But I know what I want. After all, it is my right to give careful consideration."[138] Bishop Pavan described Paul VI's intervention on the conciliar document as "decisive."[139]

7. The Jewish question in the council

a) From 1959 to 1964

After religious freedom, the council fathers dealt with an equally thorny topic: the document on the Jews and the non-Christians, which had been changed into an appendix to the decree on ecumenism and which, between November 1963 and October 1965, was at the center of impassioned discussion.[140]

Archbishop Lefebvre, saying that it was inopportune" (*ibid.*).

[135] Cf. AS V/2:798 ff.

[136] Cf. D. E. Pelotte, *John Courtney Murray, op. cit.*, 94; J. Grootaers, "Paul VI et la déclaration conciliaire," *op. cit.*, 93.

[137] J. Grootaers, "Paul VI et la déclaration conciliaire," *op. cit.*, 122

[138] Daniel Pezeril, "Paul VI et le Concile," in *Le Monde*, February 27, 1965.

[139] P. Pavan, "Testimonianza," in J. Grootaers, "Paul VI et la déclaration conciliaire," *op. cit.*, 186.

[140] AS III/2:579–607 and AS III/3:11–55, 141–142, and 155–178. On Vatican II and the Jews, see R. Laurentin, *L'Église et les juifs à Vatican II* (Paris: Casterman, 1967); Arthur Gilbert, *The Vatican*

On the occasion of Holy Week in 1959, John XXIII, five months after his election, ordered the deletion of the expression "*pro perfidis Judaeis*" ("for the faithless, treacherous Jews") from the Good Friday liturgy, eliciting the praises of the international Jewish world.[141] On January 18, 1960, a delegation from the international Jewish organization B'nai B'rith had met the pope in the Vatican. But the main inspiration for a document on relations between Christianity and Jews came from a meeting of John XIII with Jules Marx Isaac,[142] a French Jew, an octogenarian like Roncalli, the former Inspector general of Education and author of a *Handbook of History*, used in the thirties in secondary schools in France. After the loss of his wife and daughter in a Nazi concentration camp, Isaac, who had combatted "Christian anti-Semitism" for years, dedicated his last twenty years of life to the critical study of the relationships between Judaism and Christianity, dedicating two important books to this subject: *Jesus and Israel*, published in 1946 and reprinted in 1959, and *The Teaching of Contempt: Christian Roots of Anti-Semitism*, published in 1948 and reprinted in 1956. Their fundamental thesis was that Christian theological anti-Judaism was the most terrible form of anti-Semitism. The Christian "teaching of contempt," summed up in the idea of the "deicide people," had its roots in the gospels, especially the Gospel of Matthew, who according to Isaac was the most Jewish of the Evangelists, but also the most "anti-Semitic." This anti-Jewish teaching had been developed by almost all of the fathers of the Church: St. Hilary of Poitiers, St. Jerome, St. Ephrem, St. Gregory of Nyssa, St. Ambrose, St. Epiphanius, St. Cyril of Jerusalem, but in a particular way by St. John Chrysostom and St. Augustine.[143] Isaac demanded from the Church an act of reparation and correction of her teaching, by exonerating the Jews from the charge of deicide and by making every effort to make amends for the wrong caused them in the ages.

Council and the Jews (Cleveland/New York: World Publishing Co., 1969); Ilaria Pavan, "Roncalli e gli ebrei dalla Shoah alla *Declaratio Nostra aetate*: Tracce di un percorso," in *L'ora che il mondo sta attraversando, op. cit.*, 276–300. For a traditional theological interpretation, cf. E. M. Radaelli, *Il mistero della sinagoga bendata* (Milan: Effedieffe, 2002), with a preface by Monsignor Antonio Livi.

141 M. Paiano, *op. cit.*, 667–710.

142 Jules Marx Isaac (1877–1963), from a Jewish family of Lorena, inspector for history instruction in the schools and a high-ranking official in the government of Léon Blum.

143 J. Isaac, *Genèse de l'Antisémitisme* (Paris: Calmann-Lévy, 1956), 10.

On June 13, 1960, John XXIII received Isaac, who delivered to the pope a memorandum and a dossier on the question that always preoccupied him, requesting "a reformulation of Christian teaching, preaching, and catechesis for the purpose of eradicating the roots of antisemitism."[144] The pope told the Jewish historian to speak to Bea, "whom he trusted and in whom he confided."[145] Bishop Capovilla, recalling the episode, attests that until that day it had not entered into John XXIII's mind that the council should deal also with the Jewish question and anti-Semitism. But from that day, "he was completely taken up with it."[146]

As if it had been ready for some time, in an audience on September 18, Bea presented the working outline for a schema of a *Decretum de Judaeis* to John XXIII, who accepted the proposal.[147] In the first plenary session of the secretariat in November 1960, Cardinal Bea officially claimed the question about the Jews to be within the scope of its competency also.[148] Elio Toaff, the chief Rabbi of Rome, remembers having known Bea from the early fifties, when he began to frequent the library of the Biblical Institute that Bea directed. "Our acquaintance very quickly turned into friendship, and one day Monsignor Bea confided in me that, since he was German by birth, he felt the whole weight of the evil that his people had done to the Jews, and he wished to do something to make up for it, even if only in a small way. Thus the idea occurred to him of an ecumenical council in which a document on the Jews would have to be approved. He himself wanted to be its promoter and author."[149] Bea's dream was able to come true at the council with the Declaration *Nostra aetate*."[150]

The only mention made of the Jews in the council during the first session is attributed to Bishop Méndez Arceo who on December 6, 1962,

---

144 Cf. the document "La réception de Jules Isaac par Jean XXIII," in *Documentation catholique* 65 (1968): 2015–2016. See also José Oscar Beozzo, "The External Climate," *op. cit.*, 395–397 at 396.

145 Schmidt, *Bea*, 354.

146 Ibid.

147 Cf. A. Melloni, *L'altra Roma, op. cit.*, 87–89. On the thought of the cardinal in reference to the Jewish question, cf. A. Bea, *La Chiesa e il popolo ebraico* (Brescia: Morcelliana, 1966).

148 Cf. J. A. Komonchak, "The Struggle for the Council during the Preparation," *op. cit.*, 265–266.

149 Emilio Toaff, *Perfidi giudei-fratelli maggiori* (Milan: Mondadori, 1987), 215.

150 Cf. Jean-Marie Delmaire, "Vatican II et les juifs," in *Le Deuxième Concile du Vatican*, 577–606.

two days before the close of the session, suggested that the council explain the relations between the Catholic Church and the Jews.[151] Subsequently, in the same month of December, Cardinal Bea sent the pope a long report on the question, maintaining that there was no danger that the council would find itself involved in the current polemics between the Arab nations and the State of Israel.[152] On December 13, John XXIII replied to Bea with a handwritten letter in which he expressed his agreement with him on the importance of the subject and on the responsibility that the Church has to take it into consideration: "The phrase '*Sanguis eius super nos and super filios nostros*' ('His blood be upon us and upon our children') does not give any believer an excuse not to be interested in the problem and in the apostolate for the salvation of all the children of Abraham and likewise of everyone alive on earth."[153] The Secretariat for Christian Unity felt encouraged by the reply to prepare a plan, but no initiative was taken before the death of Pope Roncalli.

On the evening of February 20, 1963, two months after the close of the first period of the council, performances began in Berlin of a work by the German writer, Rolf Hochhuth, *Der Stellvertreter (The Deputy)*,[154] which depicted the alleged silence of Pius XII during the persecution of the Jews at the time of the Second World War. The former general of the Romanian secret service, Ion Mihai Pacepa, revealed that the work was based on material that had been manipulated by the KGB within the framework of disinformation on a vast scale that was aimed at destroying the moral authority of the Vatican in Western Europe. Although the play caused no permanent damage, it immediately had a strong psychological effect. On March 31, 1963, Bea met in New York at the headquarters of the American Jewish Committee about ten representatives of Jewish organizations of various sorts.[155] Later, in June 1963, when Paul VI

---

[151] Cf. AS I/4:338–341.

[152] Cf. AS II/5:481–485 at 485.

[153] Schmidt, *Bea*, 568.

[154] Cf. Rolf Hochhuth, *Der Stellvertreter: Schauspiel* (Reinbek bei Hamburg, 1963); *The Deputy: A Play*, Eng. transl. by Richard and Clara Winston (Grove Press, 1964). On Hochhuth's writings, see G. M. Vian, "Il silenzio di Pio XII: alle origini della leggenda nera," in *Archivum Historiae Pontificiae* 42 (2004): 223–229; Emanuele Gagliardi, "L'attaco di Mosca a Pio XII," in *Lepanto* 175 (2008): 17–20.

[155] Cf. Schmidt, *Bea*, 466–467.

announced the continuation of the conciliar proceedings, Cardinal Bea submitted to the Coordinating Committee a document "on the relations of a strictly religious nature between Catholics and Jews." On November 8, the Secretariat for Christian Unity distributed to the council fathers a plan concerning "the attitude of Catholics with regard to non-Christians and especially Jews," specifying that it ought to make up chapter 4 of the schema on ecumenism.

b) The 1964 discussion

Before tackling the debate on the schema on ecumenism, the council began to discuss the document on the Jews on November 18, 1963.

The heads of the Oriental Churches at once found fault with the timeliness of Cardinal Bea's document. Among others, the Patriarchs Tappouni,[156] of Antioch of the Syrians, Stephanos I Sidarouss,[157] of Alexandria, Maximos IV Saigh [Sayegh],[158] of Antioch of the Melkites, intervened and maintained that to speak about the Jews at the council could prejudice the situation of the Christians in many Arab countries.

The Secretariat for Christian Unity and the moderators realized that the chapter on the Jews was in danger of being rejected. The only chance of saving it was to publish a document, distinct from the one on ecumenism, in which not only Judaism but also other non-Christian religions would be mentioned, and in particular Islam. The unexpected announcement of Paul VI's trip to the Holy Land at the end of the second session seemed to be a good occasion to help the council fathers resolve the thorny problem.[159] Thus we come to the third session.

In the General Congregation of September 25, 1964, Cardinal Bea presented the new document that no longer cleared the Jews of the charge

---

[156] AS II/5:527–528. Ignazio Gabriel Tappouni (1879–1968), ordained in 1902, bishop of Batnae for the Syrians (1913), then archbishop of Aleppo (1921) and patriarch of Antioch for the Syrians from 1929 until his death.

[157] AS II/5:541–542. Stephano I Sidarouss, C.M. (1904–1987), ordained in 1939 in the Congregation of the Mission, consecrated bishop of Sais (1948), patriarch of Alexandria of the Copts (1958). Created cardinal in 1965.

[158] AS II/5:542–544.

[159] Wiltgen, 170.

of "deicide," as the previous one had done, even though Bea himself hoped for an intervention recommending a modification on this point.[160]

On the second day of debate, September 29, Cardinal Tappouni, a member of the Board of Presidency, mounted the rostrum, and speaking in the names of six Oriental patriarchs and of their vicars, requested that the declaration be abandoned in order to avoid "very serious pastoral difficulties." "In our countries they will say that the council is pro-Zionist, which will do us great harm."[161]

Confronting the objections of Tappouni and the other Oriental patriarchs, the greatest spokesmen for the progressive alliance intervened in defense of the document: Cardinal Liénart[162] maintained that the patriarchs were worried about eminently political questions, while the subject under consideration was of a purely religious nature and should be approached from an ecumenical and pastoral viewpoint. Cardinals Frings,[163] Lercaro,[164] Léger,[165] and Ritter[166] spoke along the same lines, and then Bishop Jaeger[167] of Paderborn, Bishop Nierman[168] of Groningen, and Bishop Daem[169] of Anversa. Cardinal Ruffini[170] replied by stating that one cannot attribute deicide to the Jews because the word itself is meaningless: no one can kill God. Nonetheless, one has the right to expect the Jews to admit that they unjustly condemned Christ to death, and one must pray that God "will remove from their eyes the veil" that prevents them from seeing in Christ the Messiah. The cardinal of Palermo added that, if the Jews and Muslims had to be mentioned in the document,

160 AS III/2:558–564.

161 Ibid., 582.

162 Ibid., 579–581.

163 Ibid., 582–583.

164 Ibid., 587–589.

165 Ibid., 590–591.

166 Ibid., 599–600.

167 Ibid., 600–601.

168 Ibid., 603–604.

169 Ibid., 604–606.

170 Ibid., 585–587.

then why not mention Hindus and Buddhists as well? He hoped, moreover, that in the declaration "the Jews would be earnestly encouraged to respond lovingly to the love with which we sincerely treat them."[171]

Cardinal Bueno y Monreal suggested that to avoid every suspicion of political meddling, the declaration should be entitled simply *De non christianis*, without making any explicit reference to the Jews, and in the text, besides the Jews and the Muslims, the religions of India, China, and Japan should be mentioned.[172] Also the final intervention, on September 30, by Bishop Gahamanyi,[173] bishop of Butan in Ruanda, on behalf of about eighty fathers, concluded with the proposal that the schema "not be on the Jews, but on non-Christians, and that it make some special mention of the Jews and the Muslims."[174]

The suggestions were partially accepted. The declaration on the Jews was modified and entitled *On the Relations between the Church and non-Christian Religions.* The text dealt in the first place with non-Christian religions as a whole, then briefly with Hinduism and Buddhism; then it addressed Islam and finally the Jews, to whom more lines were devoted because of their role in the economy of salvation. On November 20, during the final General Congregation of the third session, the revised text was put to a vote. It garnered 1,651 *placet*, ninety-nine *non placet*, and 242 *placet juxta modum.*[175] Its journey was not yet over.

8. "Let us lift up sacred scripture, not tradition"[176]

Between September 30 and October 6 the council examined the new version, prepared by the Joint Commission, of the schema *Dei Verbum* on divine revelation.[177]

---

[171] Ibid., 586.

[172] AS III/3:11–13.

[173] Jean-Baptiste Gahamanyi (1920–1999), ordained in 1951, consecrated bishop of Butare (Rwanda) in 1962.

[174] AS III/3:141–142.

[175] AS III/8:672.

[176] Thus the *votum* of Bishop Herman Volk: AS III/3:344–345 at 344.

[177] AS III/3:124–366 and 425–511. On *Dei Verbum,* see C. Theobald, "La Révélation: Quarante

In the first session the discussion had been centered on the unity or duality of the fonts of revelation. To break the deadlock, John XXIII had created an *ad hoc* commission including representatives of the two opposing trends, which the Very Reverend Prignon, in his "report" to Cardinal Suenens dated March 2, 1962, described as "on the right" and "on the left."[178] At the meeting held that day, Cardinal Lefebvre had made a frontal attack on the schema presented by Cardinal Ottaviani, creating "the psychological shock needed in order to proceed to a vote," that gave the upper hand to the conciliar "left."[179]

The result of the work of this commission was a new text, distributed to the council fathers in May 1963. As Bishop Schröffer, ordinary of Eichstätt and a progressive member of the Theological Commission, wrote to the participants of the Fulda conference, it was about the "result of a laborious struggle" within the new commission, and therefore nothing more than "a compromise with all the disadvantages that a compromise entails."[180]

The Fulda conference had proposed an official declaration on the schema, based for the most part on Father Rahner's comments, with the recommendation that the schema on revelation not be treated at the beginning of the second session, but only afterward, and not before the schema on the Church. After having personally presented these requests to the Roman authorities, Cardinal Döpfner could reassure his Fulda confrères about the fact that the schema *De Ecclesia* appeared at the head of the daily agenda and that *De fontibus revelatonis* was not listed there.

Three weeks after the close of the second session, the Coordinating Commission told the Theological Commission to proceed with a revision of the schema on divine revelation that had not yet been discussed. Therefore, a theological sub-commission was set up, with the Belgian Bishop Charue

---

ans après 'Dei Verbum,'" in *Revue théologique de Louvain* 36 (2005): 145–165; A. Vanhoye, "La réception dans l'Église de la constitution dogmatique 'Dei Verbum' du concile Vatican II à aujourd'hui," in *Esprit et Vie* 114 (2004): 3–13; *La "Dei Verbum" trent'anni dopo: Miscellanea in onore di Padre Umberto Betti o.f.m.*, ed. N. Ciola, (Rome: Pontificia Università Lateranense, 1995).

[178] Letter from Monsignor Prignon to Cardinal Suenens dated March 2, 1963, in Fonds Prignon, "Card. Suenens: correspondance," in CLG n. 287.

[179] Cf. ibid. Prignon adds: *"Même Mgr Parente se joignit ici à la 'gauche', ce qui amena Franić, je pense, à déclarer: 'etiam Parente corruptum est'"* ["Even Bishop Parente joined the 'left' this time, which led Franić, I think, to declare: 'even Parente has been corrupted'"], (ibid.).

[180] Wiltgen, 175.

presiding, who appointed the Italian Florit co-presider, sharing with him the task of coordinating the revision of the schema.

The "Roman" council fathers insisted that the text confirm that scripture and tradition are two equally important fonts of divine revelation, and that there can be truths contained in tradition that are not found in scripture. The example given was infant baptism, which is based on the Church's tradition, but not on sacred scripture, which limits itself to requiring faith and baptism for salvation (Mk. 16:16). But there was little or no concession to these requests on the part of the progressives, whose *leitmotiv* was still their concern about not harming ecumenism. In this instance, however, ecumenism was invoked because of the dialogue with the protestants, but not with the Oriental Christians, if it is true, as Bishop Franić confided to Fr. Schauf, that there was much discontent among the Orthodox because of the council's new attitude on the subject of the relationship between scripture and tradition.[181]

The new revised version of the text was presented in the hall on September 30, 1964, by Bishop Ermenegildo Florit,[182] who had "converted" to the position of the majority and sought to justify the new document. As always happened, the interventions in the hall in favor and against the text were balanced, but in the voting the majority always confirmed the line taken by the commissions or sub-commissions.

First, Cardinal Ruffini took the floor and pointed out that the schema passed over in silence the constitutive role of tradition. "I am amazed," he declared, "that in this schema on revelation one could forget to say that tradition is not only explicative, but 'constitutive.' I demand that the corresponding passages from the Council of Trent and Vatican I be cited

---

[181] One might also add that Bishop Franić explained that among the Orthodox there was uneasiness about the fact that the Catholic Church could call into question its previous teaching on scripture and tradition, which is also the teaching of Orthodoxy. Spanedda emphasized that he wanted to know what he should teach the people and whether what had been taught before was wrong, as well as all the textbooks, etc. The Spaniards brought honor to their name: Fernandez, the Dominican general superior, and Barbado. Again people are quoting the saying: *Galli quaerunt veritatem* [The Gauls seek the truth] (which is quite flattering to the French), *Germani confundunt veritatem* [the Germans confuse it], *Itali habent* [the Italians have it] *et Hispani defendunt veritatem* [and the Spaniards defend it]." (*Konzilstagebuch von Heribert Schauf*, February 28, 1963, unpublished manuscript version ed. A. von Teuffenbach, 101 [translated from German]).

[182] AS III/3:131–139.

in their entirety."[183] The progressives' position was expounded by Cardinal Döpfner, who on the contrary, speaking in the name of seventy-eight bishops who were German-speaking and from the Nordic countries, sang the praises of the new text, which in his opinion had managed to decide the delicate problem of whether or not all revelation was contained in sacred scripture.[184]

The conservative fathers appeared to be quite unconvinced. The bishop Franić of Split affirmed that the schema, although containing no error, was "notably deficient," because it did not present the integral tradition.[185] Bishop Enrico Compagnone, bishop of Anagni, stressed that there is no need to deviate from the teaching of the Council of Trent and Vatican I, which specified that tradition is more "extensive" than sacred scripture and that revelation is contained not only in scripture, but also in tradition. He requested a repetition at least of the formulation of the Council of Trent and of Vatican I that revelation is contained "*in libris scriptis et sine scripto traditionibus* [in written books and unwritten traditions]."[186] Cardinal Browne objected to the statement that divine revelation could "increase," seeing in it the danger of modernist leanings.[187] Bishop Carli faulted the schema for not stating clearly the historical character of the gospels and for not taking "sufficient account of the errors that are multiplying rapidly, such as *Formgeschichte*. Why was the passage suppressed from the first version which spoke of 'dissipating the errors of our time'?" "It is deplorable that the schema says nothing about the historical veracity of the gospels, concerning Christ's infancy and the post-resurrection. Tradition is as immutable as scripture. This is not stated, and it is a serious defect. Tradition is not sufficiently respected in the whole of chapter 3."[188]

On the opposite front, Dom Christopher Butler, president of the Congregation of English Benedictines, supported freedom of scientific

---

183 Ibid., 142–145.

184 Ibid., 145–147.

185 Ibid., 124–129.

186 Ibid., 203–206 at 205. Enrico Compagnone (1908–1989), Discalced Carmelite, ordained in 1930, bishop of Anagni from 1953 to 1972.

187 AS III/3:187–188.

188 Ibid., 332–335; Fesquet, *Drama*, 389–390.

research so as "to enter into dialogue with non-Catholic exegetes and to prepare the way to an adult and mature Christian faith."[189] The bishop of Mainz, Bishop Hermann Volk, one of the spokesmen of the anti-Roman party, asserted that revelation is expressed first of all in the Church's liturgy: "In the sacred liturgy, sacred scripture is incensed and not tradition, and in this hall we are solemnly expounding sacred scripture and not tradition."[190]

After the debate was closed, on October 6, a new version of the schema was distributed to the council fathers, who were asked to submit their observations before January 31, 1965. In the final intersession they would continue to get requests for changes and additions, but the Doctrinal Commission, especially through the efforts of Florit and his trusted theologian Betti, did not modify the planned approach.[191]

The *Coetus Internationalis Patrum* [International Group of Fathers] sent to their supporters a ten-page critique of the schema, asking them to vote for it only on the condition that the indicated amendments be incorporated. The reservations pertained above all to the relations between scripture and tradition (art. 9), the inerrancy of the scriptures (art. 11), and the historicity of the gospels (art. 19). Despite these requests, the Theological Commission made no revision of the text. The vote on the schema took place at the beginning of the fourth session, between September 20 and 22, 1965.

9. *Gaudium et spes:* The council's "promised land"

a) The Church in the contemporary world

Even before the opening of the council, John XXIII had wanted it to deal with the relations between the Church and the modern world. In a television interview the pope had posed beside a large globe on which were written four words that summed up his speech: *Ecclesia Christi lumen gentium* [The Church of Christ is the light to the nations].

---

[189] Ibid., 353–355.

[190] Quoted in *Third Session Council Speeches of Vatican II*, ed. William K. Leahy and Anthony T. Massimini (Glen Rock, NJ: Paulist Press, 1966), 96.

[191] Cf. R. Burigana, *Dei Verbum: Introduzione, op. cit.*, 57.

When, on December 4, 1962, towards the end of the first session, Cardinal Suenens, citing John XXIII, had proposed to the general assembly that the Church should study its relations as a whole with the world, the pontiff had created the Coordinating Commission and entrusted to the same Suenens the job of developing a new schema that would collect the Church's teachings that were directly related with the problems of the modern world. In its first meeting, in January 1963, the commission decided that the new schema would be entitled *On the actual presence of the Church in the contemporary world* and would have six chapters: on man's vocation; on the human person in society; on matrimony and the family; on human development and cultural growth; on the socio-economic order; and on the community of nations and peace.

In his capacity as promoter of the schema, Cardinal Suenens proposed that the composition of the text be entrusted to a joint *ad hoc* commission, made up of members of the Theological Commission and of the Commission for the Lay Apostolate, with Cardinals Ottaviani and Cento[192] as co-presidents.

The work that began in February was interrupted by the death of John XXIII and was suspended for a time, until a number of experts of the anti-Roman persuasion were added to the commission during the second session.

The composition of the schema was entrusted to a restricted group with a progressive orientation. Among them were Bishop Guano of Livorno, as president, and the Redemptorist Häring as secretary. There were many working meetings, and then on July 3, 1962, Paul VI approved a 29-page draft, to which a 57-page supplement was subsequently added; the document was distributed to the council fathers on the September 30, 1964, during the third session.[193] Never was a conciliar document awaited

---

[192] Fernando Cento (1883–1973), nuncio in Belgium from 1946 to 1953, cardinal in 1958. Member of the Central Preparatory Commission, president of the Commission for the Apostolate of the Laity.

[193] On Schema XIII (later *Gaudium et spes*), besides *Paolo VI e il rapporto Chiesa-mondo*, cf. Enrico Chiavacci, *La costituzione pastorale sulla Chiesa nel mondo contemporaneo: Gaudium et spes* (Rome: Studium, 1967); C. Moeller, *L'élaboration du schéma XIII: L'Église dans le monde de ce temps* (Paris: Casterman, 1968); K. Rahner and Henri De Riedmatten, *L'Église dans le monde de ce temps: constitution Gaudium et spes* (Paris: Mame, 1967); Francisco Gil Hellín, Augusto Sarmiento, Jesús Ferrer, and José María Yanguas, *constitutionis pastoralis Gaudium et spes: synopsis historica* (Pamplona: Eunsa, 1985); Luigi Sartori, *La Chiesa nel mondo contemporaneo: introduzione alla "Gaudium et spes"* (Padua: Ed. Messaggero, 1995).

like schema XIII, which was "supposed to be the first 'proving ground' of the Church's capacity to enter into dialogue with the world."[194]

The "star" schema of the third session, that began with the words "*Gaudium et spes*, "the joys and the hopes, the griefs and the anxieties of the men of this age," was described by Father Congar as "the 'promised land' of the council."[195] The field would be prepared by a series of conferences like that of Father Schillebeeckx on September 16 at the Dutch Documentation Center DO-C. "In the economy of salvation, the world is by definition in a state of implicit Christianity.... The Church must recognize that the soil she is tilling in schema 13 is not a sacred but a holy land."[196]

On Sunday, October 5, eight hundred bishops who were present in Rome for the council proceedings attended the showing of the film The *Gospel According to Matthew* by the Marxist director Pier Paolo Pasolini. The showing had been sponsored by the *Ufficio Cattolico Internazionale del Cinema* (International Catholic Office for Cinema), which a month before that had awarded Pasolini's film the prize for "best religious film of the year."[197]

b) First skirmishes in the hall

Finally, on Tuesday, March 20, 1965, the schema reached the assembly. On the eve of the beginning of the debate, Father Daniélou held a crowded press conference in which he mentioned that the promoter of the schema was Cardinal Suenens, who was convinced that it would be unthinkable to conclude the council without examining the fundamental problems of today's world.

The text was presented by Bishop Emilio Guano on behalf of the commission that had prepared the schema. The document—Guano said—set out "to promote (. . .) dialogue with all men in order to listen to them in their way of seeing their situations and problems" and to make clear "in what way the Church is involved in the progress of our time, what Christians can and must give as their contribution toward

194 Cf. G. Alberigo, *A Brief History*, 78.

195 Fesquet, *Drama*, 292.

196 Ibid., 309.

197 Fesquet, *Diario* [Italian edition], 517.

the solution of the major problems confronting men in this hour of history."[198] The idea underlying the intervention was that humanity was in a period of relentless "progress" and that the Church, having fallen behind, had to find the way and the forms in which "to update itself and to adapt to the times."

Among the first to speak was, as always, Cardinal Ruffini who, although congratulating the authors of the schema, lamented the frequent repetitions that uselessly burdened the text. Among the non-intelligible things, the Cardinal of Palermo cited the sentence of the schema that stated, in typically evolutionist terms, that human nature is the apex of visible creation, towards which, according to God's design, the evolution of the world was following its trajectory through untold ages.

> The dignity of man is spoken of seven times without mentioning the redemption. The word vocation recurs incessantly without any definition of it, and it is used in different senses. The same page talks about the fight against injustice five times. This is a sermon rather than a conciliar constitution! There are things that are said wrongly or at least that I do not understand. For example on the fourth line of page ten it says that human nature appeared as the result of an evolution of countless years. I don't like that, because to say that human nature was prepared by evolution is contrary to the Church's doctrine. On page 15, line 25, it says that the faithful must give proof of intelligence and prudence so as to put their conscience to the test. This is said against a background of "situation ethics." It seems to say in fact that conscience ought be the norm, when, on the contrary, the Church's principles are.[199]

On October 20, Cardinal Lercaro intervened in opposition. "Let us discuss this schema without delay but also without haste. It would be a mistake to take its defects as a pretext for discarding it. This text is situated along the spiritual line of the message of Paul VI. It is enough to serve as a basis for discussion. Experience shows that only discussion makes schemas better."[200]

On November 4 Lercaro intervened a second time on schema XIII to assert that the Church should manifest a more open attitude toward the

---

[198] AS III/5:203–214 at 205.

[199] Ibid., 220–223 at 220.

[200] Ibid., 223–226.

world with regard to poverty, renouncing if necessary some "riches" from its past, such as the scholastic system in the philosophical and theological field and particular academic and educational institutions.[201] Within this vision, he looked forward to future cooperation between the bishop-teacher and the layman-theologian.

Cardinal Ruffini deemed the intervention so serious that he was prompted to write directly to the pope: "What His Eminence Cardinal Lercaro declared in his intervention yesterday seemed to be 'abnormal,' paradoxical, and I would say absurd, because it was contrary to our traditions in the matter of study and education."[202]

c) Teilhard de Chardin's presence at the council

Two lines of the progressive battle array came together over schema XIII in the council, the "optimistic" French line, which was tinged with humanism and Maritainism, and the "pessimistic" German line that was sensitive to the entreaties of protestantism, in particular of the school of Karl Barth. Archbishop Volk, on behalf of seventy fathers, most of them German-speaking,[203] cited the Lutheran theology of the cross, asserting that the schema did not sufficiently take sin into account. The harshest critic was Cardinal John Carmel Heenan,[204] archbishop of Westminster, who had already set up an opposition group called "St. Paul's Conference." He declared that the schema was "unworthy of an ecumenical council of the Church"[205] and proposed to take it away from the commission that had dealt with it thus far. "It would be better to say nothing rather than these banalities and these empty words.... This pitiful schema will make the world laugh.... Even when completed with additions, it would remain insufficient and ambiguous. Without the additions, then, it would

---

[201] AS III/6:249–253.

[202] Letter from Cardinal Ruffini dated November 5, 1964, in F. M. Stabile, *Il Cardinal Ruffini e il Vaticano II, op. cit.*, 138.

[203] AS III/5:586–588.

[204] Ibid., 318–322.

[205] De Lubac, *Quaderni*, 676.

be downright harmful."[206] Either Cardinal Lecaro or Cardinal Döpfner proposed putting off discussion of the schema until the following session so as to be able to examine it more calmly.

The discussion of schema XIII revealed how strong Teilhard de Chardin's influence was on the council.[207] The name of the French paleontologist frequently resounded in the hall. On October 22, Archbishop Hurley[208] of Durban, saluted "the illustrious son of the Church, Teilhard de Chardin," and compared his eschatology with that of St. Paul.[209] On October 26, Bishop Otto Spülbeck,[210] bishop of Meissen, stressed the great influence of Teilhard de Chardin on the modern scientific world, because, "he spoke our scientific language; we believe also that he understood our problems and, therefore, we turn to him to obtain help in the religious questions that arise from our studies."[211] The German bishop ended by asserting that "the difficulties and anxieties of many theologians unfortunately still stand in the way" of the Church's desired progress in this field, "something that goes back to the time of Galileo, four hundred years ago, and for which we are not completely without fault."[212]

On October 23, Father Benedikt Reetz, superior general of the Benedictine Congregation of Beuron, in Germany, and a member of the Conciliar Commission for Religious, openly defended the monks against the criticisms that had aimed at them in the hall by some fathers. He said:

> As a monk and abbot I hardly know the world, but perhaps those forty monks sent to England by Pope Gregory the Great in the early seventh century to "make the Angles angels"—and one of those forty

---

[206] AS III/5:319.

[207] In the *Acta Synodalia* we find Teilhard's name cited in at least eleven different places: cf. Étienne Michelin, *Vatican II et le "surnaturel": Enquête préliminaire 1959–1962* (Venasque: Éditions du Carmel, 1993), 321–326.

[208] Denis E. Hurley (1915–2004), Oblate of Mary Immaculate, South African, ordained in 1939, archbishop of Durban from 1951 to 1992.

[209] AS III/5:341–344.

[210] Otto Spülbeck (1904–1970), German, ordained in 1930, titular bishop of Christopolis in 1955, bishop of Meissen in 1958.

[211] AS III/5:548–549.

[212] Ibid., 549.

was Augustine, who became the first bishop of the Angles—perhaps they too, I say, scarcely knew the world.

I tremble at the idea of addressing the council because obviously those who have been inside a convent since their childhood know nothing of the world. And yet St. Gregory the Great sent to England the monk Augustine to convert it, and he became bishop of Canterbury. And yet St. Benedict, who obviously knew nothing of the world, is about to be proclaimed "patron of Europe" by Paul VI.[213]

Father Reetz then cited numerous passages to show that scripture speaks of the world "in a twofold sense, that is, as a world that has been wounded by sin and as a world that should be consecrated in all its parts."[214] He asked, therefore, that this twofold aspect be made clear in the introduction to the schema.

His final observation was that the philosophical system of Father Teilhard de Chardin, which is marked by "an exaggerated optimism," ought to be kept out of the schema, because it does not take into due consideration "death, sin, the devil, and the resurrection itself."[215] Dom Prou also,[216] the abbot of Solesmes, criticized on October 16 the confusion between nature and grace, the natural and the supernatural order, with an implicit reference to the disciples of Teilhard, *in primis* [especially] de Lubac. "Actually," de Lubac commented in his diary, "he does not blame Teilhard, but rather the theory—a daring one, in my opinion—of the Chenu-Schillebeeckx school, which, on the contrary, claims to speak in the name of St. Thomas."[217]

Meanwhile a brochure by Father Meinvielle, entitled "*Il progressismo cristiano, errori e deviazioni*" ("Christian Progressivism: Errors and Deviations"), was circulating in the council. Among other things, it denounced the responsibilities of heterodox authors like Maritain, Mounier, Teilhard in the drift of contemporary thought.[218]

---

[213] AS III/5:374–377 at 374.

[214] Ibid., 376.

[215] Ibid., 377.

[216] Ibid., 519–520.

[217] De Lubac, *Quaderni*, 689.

[218] J. Meinvielle, *Il progressismo cristiano: Errori e deviazioni* (Rome: Istituto editoriale del

10. A new vision of the Christian family

a) Going beyond *Casti connubii*

The real drama that the West, and especially Europe, would experience in the decades after the council would be the "fall in the birth-rate." Many council fathers, nevertheless, accepted the Malthusian suggestions in the sixties that "prophesied" a catastrophe for mankind if it did not put into effect a rigid "control of births." Through the "pill," science offered the means of accomplishing this, and the Church would have to prove that she was sensitive to the demands of the times.

Article 21 of the fourth chapter of schema XIII was dedicated to "The dignity of matrimony and the family." The text, however, departed from the teaching of the encyclicals *Arcanum*[219] of Leo XIII and *Casti connubii*[220] of Pius XI and from Pius XII's teaching in the talks that he gave to married couples from 1939 to 1943.[221] As a matter of fact, it avoided the traditional distinction between the primary and secondary ends of matrimony and, *de facto*, placed the bond of conjugal love before the procreation of children, leaving open the possibility of "birth-control," as something left up to the conscience of the spouses. In 1963, Doctor John Rock, in a much discussed book, *The Time Has Come*, had maintained the need for a new approach of the churches, and especially of the Catholic Church, to the topic of birth control.[222] In the same year a long article by the Belgian theologian

---

Mediterraneo, 1965).

219 Leo XIII, encylical *Arcanum divinae sapientiae consilium* (February 10, 1880) in AAS 12 (1979): 385–402; EE, 3:94–137.

220 Pius XI, encylical *Casti connubii* (December 30, 1930) on Christian marriage, in AAS 22 (1930): 539–590.

221 For a presentation of the traditional teaching, see the papal teachings edited by the Monks of Solesmes collected in the volumes *Il matrimonio*, Ital. transl. (Roma: Paoline, 1965) and *La famiglia cristiana*, Ital. transl. (Rome: Paoline, 1968). See also Father Noël Barbara, *Catéchisme catholique du mariage* (Tours: Forts dans la foi, 1989).

222 John Rock, *The Time Has Come: A Catholic Doctor's Proposal to End the Battle over Birth Control* (New York: Alfred A. Knopf, 1963). On the myth of population explosion, cf. the critiques in Colin Clark, *Population* (Houston: Lumen Christi Press, 1974); Gérard-François Dumont, *Le festin de Kronos: Réalités et enjeux des évolutions socio-démographiques en Europe* (Paris: Fleurus, 1991); Riccardo Cascioli, *Il*

Louis Janssens appeared, in which he discussed Rock's book and said that perhaps, truly, "the time had come."[223] Besides the Belgians, two Canadian cardinals were moving along these lines: Bishop Roy[224] of Quebec, and Archbishop Léger of Montreal.[225] Roy had as an "expert" [*peritus*] a well-known, dedicated Thomist, Charles de Koninck,[226] a professor at Laval University, who argued for the lawfulness, in some cases, of contraceptive methods.[227]

John XXIII, on Suenens' advice, had created in 1963 a commission to study the problem. Paul VI had reported news about it on June 23, 1964, in a speech to the cardinals[228] and had requested that the council address the subject only in general terms.

The new concept of morality was presented on October 27 by the Patriarch Maximos IV Saigh [Sayegh], who asserted that the Middle Ages, a period of infancy for mankind, were over, and that the world was now entering into an age of maturity.

> Does not this state of mind of today's society perhaps demand a revision of the presentation of the teaching of morality? … The current teaching is excessively marked by the legalism of a bygone era and thoroughly imbued with Roman law. Now, our Christian morality must have a Christocentric character with an expression of

---

complotto demografico (Casale Monferrato: Piemme, 1996); Michel Schooyans, *The Gospel: Confronting World Disorder*, Eng. transl. with preface by Cardinal J. Ratzinger (Catholic Central Verein, 1997).

[223] Louis Janssens, "Morale conjugale et progestogines," in *Ephemerides Theologicae Lovanienses* 39 (1963): 787–826.

[224] Maurice Roy (1905–1985), Canadian, ordained in 1927, bishop of Trois Rivières (1946), then archbishop of Québec (1947–1981), created cardinal in 1965, then president of the Pontifical Councils for the Laity (1967), for Justice and Peace (1967), and for the Family (1973).

[225] G. Routhier, "Famille, mariage, et procréation: Le combat de deux cardinaux canadiens," in *Cristianesimo nella Storia* 23 (2002): 367–428.

[226] Charles de Koninck (1906–1965), Belgian-Canadian philosopher and theologian, founder of the so-called "Laval School" of philosophy. From 1939 to 1956 he was the dean of the Faculty of Philosophy at the University of Laval in Quebec.

[227] Cf. G. Routhier, "Famille, mariage et procréation," *op. cit.*, 379–395. See also C. de Koninck, "Réflexions relatives à la régularisation des naissances," in C.C.C.C. (November 6, 1964).

[228] AAS 56 (1964): 581–589.

> love and of freedom. It must educate each individual to a sense of personal and communal responsibility. Consequently, it is imperative to have a profound revision of our disciplines—which on the other hand are changing in nature.... Many things from the good old days, accepted by our simple, pious grandfathers, are no longer so today. Let us mention for example the treatment given in our catechisms to the Commandments of the Church. According to our catechisms, skipping Sunday Mass once without a reason, or failing to fast once on Friday, is a mortal sin that consequently merits eternal damnation. Is that reasonable? Nowadays, how many adult Catholics believe it?[229]

"Maximos IV was applauded at length" by the progressive sectors of the assembly.[230] The bishop of Cuernavaca Méndez Arceo intervened to say that he was in complete agreement with him.

> One of the principal signs of these times is the growth of the sense of responsibility and of freedom. It is necessary for the Church not to appear only as a defender of religious liberty, but also of freedom in general, wherever it is found. It is necessary to preach the spirit of freedom and love.... Many of our positions are anachronistic. Let us revise them and let us insist on the gospel law, since there is the impression that this is less important than the rest. What a nasty display it is to give the impression of having to brandish mortal sin in order to fill up our churches! Let us center everything on the essentials, that is, on Paschal joy.[231]

When the debate started on October 29, Cardinal Ruffini was the first to speak, in the order of seniority. He expressed his disapproval of the schema which stated "that the final word on the number of children remains with the spouses themselves," and described this teaching as very difficult to accept, "obscure, and full of extremely dangerous ambiguities."

After he cited a pertinent passage from St. Augustine, Cardinal Ruffini added:

---

229 AS III/5:567–569 at 568.

230 Fesquet, *Drama*, 461–462

231 AS III/5: 609–612.

> It is clear, venerable fathers, that Augustine's times were not much different from ours. Licentiousness and lustfulness were rife even then. But the Holy Doctor, a very faithful herald of the Church, did not remain silent with his severe disapproval. We too, as we speak to the men of the modern world, must not refrain from suppressing vices that are contrary to the sanctity of matrimony.[232]

On the next day, Bishop Juan Hervás[233] of Ciudad Real (Spain), a member of the Conciliar Commission on the Sacraments, speaking on behalf of 126 council fathers from all over the world, denounced the naturalistic and materialistic spirit of the schema.

In order to be positive, the bishop said, the document should have begun "by praising the virtues and merits of those spouses who are seeking in marriage their own sanctification or, at least, the faithful fulfillment of the natural law." Special praise should have been given in the schema to those married couples "who deny their own comfort in the imitation of Christ and receive the children whom God gives them with understanding, faith, and joy, as a gift of the creator, while they patiently bear arduous labors and the derision of the world." "Again and again the text says that the number of children should be regulated by the Christian prudence of the spouses, and this is good.... Yet little is said, and indeed rather timidly, about supernatural faith, about confidence in divine providence and about the love and acceptance of the cross—all of which should illuminate Christian prudence. We are not drawing up here a document that is philosophical-hedonistic, or merely technical or scientific, but one that is Christian!"[234]

b) The ends of matrimony

The intervention that created the greatest stir was the discourse of Cardinal Suenens[235] on October 29. In a forceful tone he asserted:

---

232 AS III/6: 52–54 at 53–54.

233 Juan Hervás y Benet (1905–1982), Spaniard, ordained in 1929, bishop of Alinda (1944), then of Majorca (1947), in 1955 titular bishop of Ciudad Real (1955–1976).

234 AAS III/6:217–219 at 217–218; cf. *Third Session Council Speeches of Vatican II*, ed. William K. Leahy and Anthony T. Massimini (Glen Rock, NJ: Paulist Press, 1966), 228–229.

235 Ibid., 57–59.

May I be permitted to express the recommendations that this commission should conduct an extensive investigation among leading moralists, scholars, and university faculty members from different disciplines, laypeople, both men and women, and among Christian spouses.

...The first work of this commission is situated along the line of the faith and should consist of this: to find out whether until now we have brought sufficiently to light the aspects of the Church's teaching on marriage.

...It may be that we have accentuated the verse from scripture: "Increase and multiply," to the point of obscuring the other divine command, "And the two shall be one flesh." (...) It will be up to the commission to tell us whether we have not overemphasized the first end, which is procreation, to the detriment of an equally imperative purpose, which is growth in the marital union.

In the same way, it is up to the commission to respond to the immense problem posed by the current demographic explosion and by overpopulation in many regions of the world. For the first time we must proceed to make such an examination in the light of the faith. The topic is difficult, but the world is waiting, more or less consciously, for the Church to speak her mind in this area and to be "light for the nations."

...The second work of the commission is situated along the line of scientific progress and a more in-depth knowledge of natural ethics. The commission must examine whether the classical doctrine, especially that of the manuals, sufficiently takes into account the new data of today's science. We have made progress since Aristotle and have discovered the complexity of reality in which the biological component interacts with the psychological aspect, the conscious with the unconscious. Now possibilities are constantly being discovered in man, in his power to direct the course of nature. From this results a deeper consciousness of the unity of man, both in his essence as an incarnate spirit and in the dynamism of his whole life, a unity that is like the heart of Thomist anthropology; another result is a more exact appreciation of his reasoning power over the world that is entrusted to him. Who cannot see that in this way we may be led to further research into the problem of what is "secondary or contrary to nature"? Let us follow the progress of science. I entreat you, Brothers. Let us avoid a new "Galileo trial." One is enough for the Church.[236]

[236] Ibid., 58.

After listening to this intervention, Cardinal Ruffini could not refrain from pounding his fist on the table out of indignation, and two days later he unburdened himself to Cardinal Cicognani, the Secretary of State, describing Suenens' remarks as "horrendous" and demanding the removal of the moderator. "It seems that the concept of matrimony, as we have understood it until now, dogmatically and morally," he wrote, "has to change, at least in practice. But is it possible that the Church was mistaken until now, and that adaptation to today's society forces us to declare that what was always held to be immoral is [now] in keeping with morality?"[237]

Bishop Helder Câmara, in contrast, expressed his full enthusiasm for the primate of Belgium: "He has said everything that one could possibly dream of hearing on the subject of birth-control, including the courage to declare—he, a cardinal of the Holy Church, a moderator of the council, right there in St. Peter's Basilica: 'let us not repeat the Galileo trial!'"[238]

Suenens had asked Câmara for a "supportive" intervention, for which the Brazilian Archbishop Fernando Gomes dos Santos[239] had been selected, but then he did not take the floor. The "*claque*" [paid applause] for "Padre Miguel" had also been organized by the same Câmara. "He had notified me," the latter writes, "and we acted in such a way that his pioneering position was warmly applauded in the basilica. Once again he appeared as the leader who opened up the way for us."[240]

The reporter for *Le Monde* commented:

> The least that can be said is that the last two general congregations of Vatican II have inaugurated a new era in the Roman Church. In fact, the interventions by Maximos IV and Cardinals Léger, Suenens, and Alfrink represent such a break with what is called the traditional doctrine on birth control that they mark a radical change of attitude.[241]

---

237 E. Ruffini, letter dated October 30, 1964, to Cardinal Amleto G. Cicognani, Secretary of State, in F. M. Stabile, *op. cit.*, 137; see also L. Declerck and T. Osaer, *op. cit.*, 64–65.

238 Câmara, *Lettres Conciliaires*, 2:696.

239 Fernando Gomes dos Santos (1910–1985), Brazilian, ordained in 1932, bishop of Peedo (1943–1949), then Aracajú (1949–1957), then archbishop of Goiânia (1957–1985).

240 Câmara, *Lettres Conciliaires*, 2:696–697.

241 Fesquet, *Drama*, 482.

Paul VI, who did not share the positions of the progressives on subjects of natural morality, was still upset and in a stormy audience with Suenens reprimanded him for his lack of judgment.[242] About a week later Suenens said that he had to reply "to certain reactions of public opinion," and explained that the decision was in the hands of the "supreme magisterium."[243]

On October 30, Cardinal Ottaviani,[244] with an intervention that was striking because of its personal note—something rare in his interventions, which were always rigorously doctrinal—addressed the council fathers as follows: "The priest who is talking to you is the eleventh of a family of twelve children. His father was a workingman, a laborer, not the boss of a laborer, but a workingman, and despite this he never doubted providence, and never thought about limiting the number of his children, even though there were difficulties. Do we intend, perhaps, to forget Our Lord's words: 'Behold the birds of the air.... consider the lilies of the field' (Mt 6:26, 28)?"[245]

Cardinal Ottaviani's allocution was followed immediately by Cardinal Browne's, which explained in a crystal-clear way the traditional idea of matrimony.[246]

> In the doctrine on matrimony, the teachings originating both from magisterial teaching and from the classical schools of theology are certain:
>
> The primary end, the primary end of the work (*finis primarius operis*), as they say, is the generation and education of children;
> The secondary end is twofold: a) the mutual help, or the mutual services rendered by the spouses to each other in their domestic partnership; b) the remedy to concupiscence.
>
> But, some say, it is necessary to assign a place to marital love also. No doubt, but in order to assign a place to it, one needs to distinguish between the love of friendship, according to which a person wills

---

242 Cf. L. Declerck and T. Osaer, "Les relations entre le cardinal Montini/Paul VI (1897–1978) et le cardinal Suenens (1904–1996) pendant le Concile Vatican II," in *Notiziario* 51 (2006): 49–77.

243 AS III/6:379–381 at 381.

244 Ibid., 85–86.

245 Ibid., 85.

246 Ibid., 86–88.

> and procures the good for a friend as to another self, and the love of concupiscence, according to which a person desires and procures a good for himself.
>
> In the marital partnership, the love that is most anxiously desired so that the spouses' fervor might be steadfast, lasting, and profoundly happy is a love of conjugal friendship of the man and the woman for one another.
>
> In marital life, and especially in the marital act, there is also a sensory delight that the spouse may desire for its own sake insofar as it is united to a decent marital act and that the other party can desire in the same way insofar as it is united to the same act.
>
> The natural course of things in marital life is such that when one of the spouses notices that the other is dominated by the sensory love of concupiscence, his love of friendship for him diminishes to the same extent.
>
> We must therefore be prudent when we defend the rights of conjugal love. It is necessary to make the necessary distinctions so that conjugal love may be fully and virtuously established.
>
> Because this virtuous quality exists in marital life, the spouses must pay attention to the so-called goods of marriage, namely the generation and education of children, fidelity which is preserved by rendering the marital debt, and the sacrament whereby marital life, which is already virtuous on the natural level, is made holy.
>
> Because the marital act is naturally licit, it is enough to intend to preserve the good of fidelity by rendering the marital debt. To render the marital debt as one ought presupposes that the marital act observes the laws of nature but it does not require that it be performed during the period of the spouse's actual fertility. It can be performed legitimately in the so-called infertile periods.
>
> There is no doubt whatsoever that all this belongs to the treasury of the common doctrine of the great theologians and that it is proposed to us in its essential elements in the documents of the magisterium and in particular in the encylicals *Arcananum* of Leo XIII, *Casti connubii* of Pius XI, and in the addresses of Pius XII to obstetricians and physicians.[247]

Unfortunately the family morality formulated in the chapter "The dignity of matrimony and of the family" in *Gaudium et spes* would

[247] Ibid., 87.

incorporate the suggestions of the innovators, rather than those of the defenders of traditional morality. It resulted in an unfortunate synthesis of contrary tendencies.[248]

11. Marxism and communism are again discussed

Marxism and communism were at the center of the debate during the third session, on which Paul VI's encyclical (published two months previously on August 6, 1964) weighed heavily. In it the pontiff deplored the ideological systems that denied God and oppressed the Church in the world, yet he hoped for "the eventual possibility of a dialogue between these men and the Church, and a more fruitful one than is possible in the present, when we can only express our justifiable complaints and repudiations."[249] "For the first time," a contemporary historian observed, "the policy of dialogue with non-believers and socialist regimes entered into an encyclical."[250]

In the general examination of the conciliar schema, which left out all reference to communism, many of the fathers touched on the subject with concern.

On October 22, 1964, either Bishop Stimpfle[251] of Augusta, in Germany, or Bishop Barbieri[252] of Cassano Ionio, in Italy, forcefully requested that the question of communism be addressed. "The main purpose of this council is pastoral," said Bishop Barbieri, "and it may be necessary to avoid condemnations: but it would be a scandal for many believers if the council were to give the impression that it was afraid to condemn the greatest crime of our age, scientific and practical atheism, which is worse in itself and because of its consequences, on the moral and spiritual level, than the atomic bomb itself."[253]

---

[248] Monsignor Philippe Delhaye, one of the four *periti* who worked on his report, described the document as *"une synthèse tenant une moyenne entre plusieurs tendances"* ["a synthesis holding a middle position between two tendencies"] (*Vatican II: L'Église dans le monde de ce temps* [Paris: Cerf, 1967], 2:421).

[249] AAS 56/10 (1964): 651–654 at 654; Eng. transl. par. 105.

[250] A. Riccardi, *Il Vaticano e Mosca, op. cit.*, 269.

[251] AS III/5: 324–327.

[252] Raffaele Barbieri (1898–1968), ordained in 1921, bishop of Cassano Ionio in 1937.

[253] AS III/5:362–364 at 363.

The next day Archbishop Yü Pin, [254] the exiled ordinary of Nanchin in China, in the name of seventy council fathers, attacked the "extended hand" policy and demanded the addition of a new chapter, or at least of a solemn declaration on communism, so as to the satisfy the expectations of the peoples who were groaning under the communist yoke. And this for various reasons:

> (1) *To examine thoroughly a sign of the times:* The Church cannot and must not overlook the question of communism and Marxist materialism—which is a very great and a very clear sign of our times, although the unhappiest one. (2) *To defend the truth*: Communism is militant atheism, crass materialism—in a word, the sum of all heresies. (3) *To vindicate liberty*: There is never absent, wherever communism is in political control, a bloody, or at least legal, persecution or stifling of liberty. (4) *To dispel confusion*: The doctrines of peaceful coexistence, the politics of the outstretched hand, and even a so-called "Catholic" communism have given rise to [dangerous] confusion.... (5) *To satisfy the longing of all people*, especially those groaning under the communist yoke, unjustly undergoing unspeakable anguish.[255]

Many other fathers intervened to request that the schema denounce communism: Archbishop Bolatti[256] of Rosaria in Argentina; Archbishop García di Sierra y Méndez[257] of Burgos in Spain; Bishop Guerra Campos,[258] auxiliary bishop of Madrid; Archbishop Pogačnik[259] of Lubiana in

---

[254] Paul Yü Pin (1901–1978), Chinese, ordained in 1928, archbishop of Nanking (China) from 1946 until his death, created cardinal in 1969.

[255] AS III/5:362–364 at 363. English translation from *Third Session Council Speeches of Vatican II*, ed. William K. Leahy and Anthony T. Massimini (Glen Rock, NJ: Paulist Press, 1966), 158–159.

[256] Ibid., 395–398. Guillermo Bolatti (1912–1982), Chilean, ordained in 1936, auxiliary bishop of Buenos Aires in 1957, titular bishop of Limata in 1957, bishop of Rosario in 1961.

[257] AS III/5:417–419. Segundo Garcia de Sierra y Méndez (1908–1998), Spanish, ordained a priest in 1931, bishop of Barbastro in 1954, coadjutor archbishop of Oviedo in 1959, archbishop of Burgos in 1964.

[258] AS III/5:520–525. José Guerra Campos (1920–1997), Spanish, ordained in 1944, auxiliary bishop of Madrid and titular bishop of Mutia in 1964, bishop of Cuenca in 1973.

[259] AS III/5:525–527. Jože Pogačnik (1902–1980), Slovenian, ordained in 1927, auxiliary bishop of

Yugoslavia; Bishop Wright[260] of Pittsburgh in the United States; and Bishop Bäuerlein[261] of Sirmio in Yugoslavia.

On October 23, 1964, Bishop Carli submitted a written intervention that was as always clear and articulate and deserves to be known in its entirety:

> The silence of the schema concerning a phenomenon that unfortunately exists in the world of our time is astonishing; a phenomenon that proximately affects the natural order and with it the supernatural order; a phenomenon that ought to elicit the grief and anguish of the council—as we read in the preface [to *Gaudium et spes*]—no less than hunger and the population explosion, since it has struck and is striking millions of human beings with suffering and mourning.
>
> The phenomenon, I mean to say, of Marxism, which is intrinsically perverse because it "opposes and exalts [it]self against every so-called god or object of worship, so that [it] takes [its] seat in the temple of God, proclaiming [it]self to be God" (2 Thess 2:4); of Marxism which, covering itself astutely with the mantle of the economy or politics and making use of physical violence, cruelly rages in more than half of the world and lies in wait for the remaining part, sowing so much mourning and sorrow among Catholics, among the separated Christian brethren, and finally among the followers of any religion whatsoever.
>
> Its doctrine and its practice concerning God, man, the world, and eschatology is radically opposed, indeed extremely hostile to Christian doctrine and practice. Dialogue with Marxism seems impossible; but at least let the monologue not be wanting. The Catholic Church, which has this phenomenon before her eyes, and also feels it and endures it in the quick of her flesh, cannot and must not remain silent or speak only euphemistically!

Llubljana and titular bishop of Irenopolis in Isauria in 1963, then archbishop of Ljubljana in 1964.

260 AS III/5:703–705. John Joseph Wright (1909–1979), American, ordained in 1935, auxiliary bishop of Boston and titular bishop of Egee in 1947, bishop of Worcester (Massachusetts) in 1950 and of Pittsburgh in 1959, created cardinal in 1969.

261 AS III/5:730–732. Stjepan Bauerlein (1905–1973), Croatian, ordained in 1929, auxiliary bishop of Sirmio and titular bishop of Heraclea Pontica in 1951, then titular bishop of Sirmio in 1959.

In this third session of the council we have heard many fathers who are concerned about conducting a summary trial about the responsibility of the Jews in the killing of Our Lord Jesus Christ. Such a trial, if not properly to be left solely to the justice and mercy of God, seems to me at least extremely difficult, both because of the excessive interval of time since the crime, and also especially because of the large number of biblical and patristic passages that would have to be subjected to a rigorous exegetical examination, without which the impartiality of the judges could be influenced in some way by the human and Christian pity that is justly owed to a people who, in the last war, was subjected to atrocious and relentless persecution.

Well, now, would it not cause astonishment if our council, so preoccupied with that historical trial, devoted not even one word, pronounced no judgment, and showed no concern at all for the deplorable phenomenon of our time that has the name of communist Marxism? Someone might say: but communism has already been condemned by the papal magisterium! I reply: I do not deny it, but everything else that is found in this schema and in some of the others was proclaimed also by the supreme pontiffs, especially by Pius XII of venerable memory, with even greater clarity, fullness, and precision; even our council thinks it good that these things should be repeated solemnly and in a conciliar manner!

I ask therefore that this supreme heresy of our time also be treated explicitly and competently, so that future generations will not have to believe that Vatican II was celebrated in an era in which the whole Catholic world was living in peace and tranquility.

Let the Church not be content to suffer and groan and flee but, after the example of the Woman of the Apocalypse (Apoc 12:2 ff.), let her fearlessly cry out at the sight of the red dragon; let her testify solemnly and collegially to the truth; let her not refuse an ecumenical service and consolation not only to her own bishops, priests and lay people, but also to the separated Christian brethren, and also to all persons who profess a religion, who as a result of Marxism suffer hunger, prison, exile, persecution, or death; finally let her make a maternal warning to Catholics resound, especially to laborers and intellectuals who, under the pretext of economic progress or pseudo-science, are deceived by this pestilential doctrine and could be confirmed in their error by the council's silence.

> Let the Church publicly set forth how she and her children ought to behave with regard to contemporary Marxism; with what means she intends to call those who have been deceived back to the right path!
>
> Venerable Brothers, I have plainly manifested to you my thinking on this topic. In doing so it seemed to me as if I were the executor of the Last Will of our lamented confrère Archbishop Józef Gawlina, who recently passed away († September 20, 1964), who many times before his sudden death, strengthened by the knowledge and living experience that he had in this regard (he was, in fact, exiled from Poland and was the Ordinary of the Poles in exile), had complained to me about the surprising silence of the conciliar schemas concerning so weighty a doctrinal and pastoral problem.[262]

In the fourth session the topic was white-hot, and it would be explosive.

12. The "updating" of religious life

A further clash occurred over the schema on religious, which was debated in the hall from November 10 to 12, when it was sent back to the commission.[263] In late September 1964, The Roman Union of Superior Generals, represented by about a hundred superior generals, endeavored to define a common course of action. On October 7, 1964, the Executive Committee of the Union met at the Generalate of the Oblates of Mary Immaculate. Present, among others, were the superior generals of the Franciscans, Dominicans, Carmelites, Benedictines, Oblates of Mary Immaculate, Marists, and Eudists. Although dissatisfied with the schema, they decided to emend it with a series of proposals that they would circulate among the council fathers in late October.

Cardinal Spellman, as he opened the debate on November 10, asserted that, with the introduction of some modifications, the text could be accepted. Spellman denounced the risks of the so-called modernization or "updating" of religious life, in an implicit polemic against Cardinal Suenens who in a book devoted to the *Apostolic Development of the Religious*

---

262 AS III/5:439–441. The Latin text was published in its entirety in *Bollettino Diocesano di Segni* (December 1964): 79–81.

263 AS III/7:422–497 and 569–663; see also Wiltgen, 212–222; N. Tanner, "The Church in the World (*Ecclesia ad extra*)," *op. cit.*, 270–387.

Woman (published in English as *The Nun in the World*),[264] had proposed a radical reform of women's religious life and saw in Vatican Council II the opportunity to carry it out. This reform, for the primate of Belgium, would have to redefine the role of women religious, by giving them an adequate "social training"[265] and by making them spiritual directors of lay women.[266] To this end it would be necessary to eliminate mercilessly certain "out-of-date" and "redundant" devotions that tended to "make the life of prayer mechanical and to atrophy it,"[267] and to transform the "spiritual exercises" of women religious so as "to amend and simplify them, to give their piety a more biblical, liturgical, ecclesiastical and apostolic basis."[268]

Cardinal Suenens invited nuns to be more sincere and open in their mutual relations and to engage in "constructive self-criticism" of their religious practices."[269] He added that women religious must avoid giving the impression of "living outside the world they are trying to save,"[270] as though isolated in a ghetto; the religious habit will have to be completely adapted to relations with the world[271] and dispense with forms and rituals that no longer are part of our era.[272] The concept of "obedience" also will have to be revised: the renunciation of one's own will must not be placed before the service of the common good. The common good sometimes requires that subjects assert their point of view before superiors make a decision.[273]

In the General Congregation of November 11, neither Cardinal Suenens nor Cardinal Döpfner[274] expressed satisfaction with the schema and the

---

264 Cf. L.-J. Suenens, *The Nun in the World: New Dimensions in the Modern Apostolate* (Westminster, MD: The Newman Press, 1963).

265 Ibid., 146–149.

266 Ibid., 166–167.

267 Ibid., 118.

268 Ibid., 118.

269 Ibid., 119.

270 Ibid., 18.

271 Ibid., 131.

272 Ibid., 131.

273 Ibid., 139.

274 AS III/7:431–436.

proposed emendations that has been sent in. Döpfner maintained that the schema lacked "*Schwerpunkte*, (the main or crucial points)" the "cardinal points of the desired renewal and updating";[275] Suenens demanded new rules for the convents, in order that the women religious would be treated as "*feminae vere adulate* (truly grown-up women)."[276] He looked forward to new, more democratic and representative structures of government, so as to avoid the concentration of power in the hands of only one superior, and excessively "passive" and "childish" obedience.

On the same day the council fathers heard replies to these two interventions by Father Anastasio of the Most Holy Rosary,[277] superior general of the Discalced Carmelites and president of the Roman Union of Major Superiors, on behalf of 185 fathers; by Franciscan Archbishop Perantoni[278] of Lanciano on behalf of 370 fathers; by Archbishop Sartre,[279] former archbishop of Tananarive, on behalf of 265 council fathers and of 250 superior generals of congregations of women religious; and by Jesuit Bishop Richard Guilly[280] of Georgetown in British Guyana, on behalf of 263 fathers; all were in favor of the schema, albeit with suitable modifications.

Bishop Guilly found it "truly surprising" that the schema on religious contained "so little about the other orders and congregations that are dedicated strictly to contemplative life." It is precisely 'these men and these women who with their prayers and their austerities, their silence and their sacrifices, contribute more than all the others to the advancement of the Church's apostolate."[281]

---

[275] Ibid., 431.

[276] Ibid., 439–442 at 439.

[277] Ibid., 453–455. Anastasio Ballestrero (1913–1998), ordained in 1936, superior general of the Order of Discalced Carmelites from 1955 to 1967, archbishop of Bari in 1973, then of Turin in 1977, created cardinal in 1979. See his book, *Autoritratto di una vita: Padre Anastasio si racconta* (Morena [Rm]: Edizioni OCD, 2002). Various recollections about the council and interesting anecdotes on 98–207.

[278] AS III/7:458–460.

[279] Ibid., 460–462. Victor Sartre (1902–2000), French Jesuit, ordained in 1932. archbishop of Tananarive (Madagascar) from 1955 to 1960.

[280] Richard Lester Guilly (1905–1996), English, ordained in 1938, apostolic vicar of British Guyana in 1954, titular archbishop of Adraa, bishop of Georgetown in Antilles from 1956–1996.

[281] AS III/7:462–464 at 463.

The representatives of the Roman Union, although not enthusiastic about the schema, were aware of the fact that, should it fail, it would run the risk of being even more profoundly modified according to the ideas of Suenens and Döpfner. These two, in contrast, were counting on a rejection of the schema, precisely because they wanted it to be completely rewritten.

The backers of the progressive alliance realized, nonetheless, that they did not have sufficient numbers to reject the schema, and they agreed to seek to modify it by means of *modi*. The watchword was, therefore, to vote *placet iuxta modum*, but to propose modifications contrary to the ones suggested by the Roman Union. During the voting on the different chapters, the *placet iuxta modum* ballots sometimes represented the majority opinion in the assembly hall.[282] The revised text returned to the council hall on October 11, 1965, during the fourth session, and was adopted with a final ballot in a public meeting on October 28, 1965.

The debate on priestly formation[283] also brought to light the profound differences that existed between the traditional stance that Cardinal Ruffini[284] and Archbishop Staffa[285] defended and the progressive position espoused by Cardinals Léger,[286] Döpfner,[287] and Suenens.[288] Staffa who had succeeded Ruffini as Secretary of the Congregation of Seminaries and Universities on November 14, asserted: "St. Thomas is not a milestone but a beacon. Let us at all costs keep the fundamental principles of St. Thomas contained in the encylical *Humani generis*."[289]

On that same day Cardinal Léger had attacked St. Thomas and the "philosophia perennis," by stating: "He is an unfortunate man who has only one book! It is an unfortunate Church that has only one doctor! Rather than to impose St. Thomas, let him be declared the prototype of the searcher and let him be proposed as the master and model, and the

---

282 Cf. the votes in AS III/7 and III/8.

283 AS III/7:703–747 and AS III/8:14–45, 239–259.

284 Ibid., 705–708.

285 Ibid., 718–720.

286 Ibid., 708–710.

287 Ibid., 711–714.

288 Ibid., 715–717.

289 Fesquet, *Drama*, 522–523.

one who knew how to place the science of his day at the service of the Church."[290] Cardinal Döpfner intervened in support: "The holiness of the priests is not enough. It is necessary for the priest to be adapted to his time. The soul of theological formation is sacred scripture. I am in complete agreement with Cardinal Léger in regard to St. Thomas...."[291]

Suenens, the primate of Belgium, after declaring that he seconded what had been said before him by Cardinals Léger and Döpfner, insisted at length on the reform of the seminaries, stating that he had personally undertaken one in his own diocese, especially for the purpose of not isolating the seminarians from the outside world.[292] On November 17 Archbishop Garrone[293] launched a heavy attack on the Congregation of Seminaries and proposed entrusting to the episcopal conferences the task of providing for the formation of seminarians.

The fathers finally approved the schema by an overwhelming majority of 2,117 to forty-one.

In the meantime, between November 4 and 6, while the debate on schema XIII was coming to an end, the text on bishops and diocesan government went back to the assembly. It was still the object of almost a thousand amendments for each of the first two chapters. On November 6 the outline on the missions[294] was introduced, presented by Cardinal Agagianian,[295] prefect of the Congregation *De propaganda fide* and president of the conciliar Commission for the Missions. To overcome the opposition to the schema that been manifested above all among many African bishops, the cardinal managed to get the pope—the one exception during the entire council—to come to begin the debate and to recommend the acceptance of the text.[296] Yet despite Paul VI's intervention in the hall, the criticisms proliferated and the schema was withdrawn after only three days.

---

290 AS III/7:709.

291 Ibid., 712.

292 Ibid., 715–717.

293 AS III/8:171–173.

294 AS III/6:327–336.

295 Ibid., 336–340.

296 Ibid., 324–325.

13. Open conflict concerning collegiality

The vote on the first two chapters of the schema De Ecclesia created no particular problems, but a bitter clash took place over the vote on the third concerning the hierarchy, which was considered by many as "the very heart of the council."[297] It was about the way in which collegiality in the Church was to be understood.

Collegiality was, as a matter of fact, understood in three different ways. According to the traditional way of thinking, the pope's power was the unique supreme power in the Church. According to the progressives, the unique subject that possessed this supreme power was the College of Bishops, presided over by the pope. When the latter exercised his power he did so only as the representative of the Episcopal College. The "Third Proposal," towards which Paul VI inclined,[298] saw in the Church two subjects of supreme power: the pope and the College of Bishops in union with the pope. This position undermined the constitution of the Church, because, if the close collaboration between the pope and the College of Bishops is not subjected to a hierarchical principle that governs it, it inevitably becomes a question of an endless search for balance between the two sources of authority. Relations between the pope and the bishops are doomed, in that case, to shift from the supernatural plane to the human and political plane of the balance of powers.

A defense of the traditional concept of the Roman Primacy appeared in 1964 in a series of articles by Abbé Dulac and by Abbé Berto in La *Pensée Catholique*, and two articles by Archbishop Dino Staffa and by Father Ugo Lattanzi in *Divinitas*, which were circulated also in the form of off-prints.[299] Archbishop Staffa, on July 28, had completed a long essay about the two conciliar schemas on the Church and on the bishops, which he forwarded to the council fathers.[300] He said that he was deeply convinced that the positions emerging from the schemas were "opposed to the more common teaching of the saintly fathers, of the Roman pontiffs,

---

[297] R. Aubert, "Lo svolgimento del Concilio," *op. cit.*, 286.

[298] Wiltgen, 228–229.

[299] D. Staffa, "De collegiali Episcopatus ratione," in *Divinitas* 1 (1964): 3–61; U. Lattanzi, "Quid de Episcoporum 'collegialitate' ex Novo Testamento sentiendum sit," in ibid., 62–96.

[300] D. Staffa, "Osservazioni sugli Schemi 'De Ecclesia' e 'De Pastorali Episcoporum munere in Ecclesia,'" July 25, 1964, mimeographed.

of provincial synods, of the holy Doctors of the Universal Church, of theologians and canonists. They are also contrary to century-old norms of ecclesiastical discipline."[301] Staffa cited the works of an Italian Jesuit, Father Vincenzo Bolgeni,[302] and stated that his positions, which already had been refuted in the XVIII century, were substantially identical to those found in the schema *De Ecclesia*. He found it unbelievable that principles unanimously rejected by theologians and canonists as incompatible with the Church's tradition should be proposed again, one hundred and forty years later, as the foundation of a conciliar schema.[303] On September 15 the Roman archbishop handed over to the cardinal moderators a list of more than seventy names of council fathers who supported him, requesting authorization to be the first speaker before the third chapter concerning collegiality was put to a vote.

Despite the fact that article 57, paragraph 6 of the council rules stipulated the right to intervene in the hall when the request was made in advance on behalf of at least seventy council fathers, Archbishop Staffa did not receive permission to speak.

Since no agreement had been reached among the members of the Theological Commission, Bishop Felici announced in the General Congregation of September 21 that Bishop Franić would speak before the vote,[304] thus presenting in a public meeting the opposition's point of view also. Bishop Franić criticized the doctrinal error of the document, which claimed that episcopal jurisdiction devolved on the bishops *ipso facto* from their episcopal consecration, whereas the Church's tradition has constantly affirmed that the bishops derive this power directly from the Roman pontiff and only indirectly from Christ.[305] "It would be altogether new, unheard-of,

301 Wiltgen, 230.

302 On Father Vincenzo Bolgeni of the Society of Jesus (1733–1811), prefect of the Library of the Roman College, then theologian of the Apostolic Penitentiary, see also M. R. Gagnebet, O.P., *L'origine de la jurisdiction collégiale du corps épiscopal au Concile selon Bolgeni* (Rome: Libreria della Pontificia Università, 1961).

303 Monsignor Staffa wrote in those days a review of the recently published volume by G. Alberigo, *Lo sviluppo della dottrina sui poteri della Chiesa universale* [Development of the doctrine on the powers of the Universal Church] for the *Monitor Ecclesiasticus* 4 (1964): 685–694, showing the scientific flimsiness of his thesis.

304 AS III/2:192.

305 Ibid., 193–201.

and anomalous," he said, "for such a teaching, which before the council was considered less common, less probable, and with little foundation, suddenly to become more acceptable, even more ripe for inclusion in a conciliar dogmatic constitution." The schema, moreover, provided for the possibility of conferring the diaconate on men who were already married. "I am convinced along with many others," said Bishop Franić, "that it would create a serious danger for priestly vocations if the council were to approve this clause."[306]

The reports in favor of the document were given by Cardinal König,[307] to whom was the theme of sacramentality was assigned, by Bishop Henríquez Jiménez,[308] who dealt with the last two paragraphs of the chapter, number 28 on priests, and number 29 on deacons, and by Bishop Pietro Parente, who spoke about collegiality.[309] The intervention in favor of collegiality by Bishop Parente, who made it clear that he was speaking as "bishop" and not in the name of the Holy Office, of which he was an assessor, nevertheless "had made a huge impression"[310] precisely because of the position that he held. Parente, already an opponent of collegiality, meticulously refuted Franić, as he appealed to a just-published work on *Lo sviluppo della dottrina dei poteri nella Chiesa universale [The Development of the Teaching on Powers in the Universal Church]* of Giuseppe Alberigo "*qui est laicus, sed bene scripsit de hac re* [who is a layman but wrote well on this subject]."[311]

In Bishop Parente's opinion, collegiality perfectly fit "in the organic unity of the Church, by virtue of which Christ can never be considered as separated from his Mystical Body, nor Peter from Christ, who is his head, nor Peter from the Episcopal College, nor the bishops from Peter.... The whole ontological structure of the Church rests on Holy Orders and on the universal priesthood of Christ."[312] These considerations of a spiritual nature

---

306 Ibid., 199.

307 AS III/2:201–205.

308 Ibid., 211–218. Luis Eduardo Henríquez Jiménez (1913–1991), Venezuelan, ordained in 1937, auxiliary bishop of Caracas and titular bishop of Lamdia in 1962, bishop of Valencia in Venezuela in 1972 and then archbishop in 1974.

309 AS III/2:205–211.

310 Cf. G. Alberigo, *A Brief History*, 118.

311 AS III/2:211. This was the study that had just been refuted by Monsignor Staffa.

312 Ibid., 210.

left standing the juridical ambiguity that saw two different overlapping legal subjects. Nonetheless, Bishop Franić would write, "Who could object, and in the name of what cause, knowing that this prelate was considered among Catholic theologians to be more strict than Cardinal Ottaviani, prefect of the Holy Office?"[313] The astonishment in the hall, after Bishop Parente's intervention, was profound.[314] Cardinal Siri expressed the opinion that Parente "must have been asked by the pope himself to do this. That would explain everything."[315] Cardinal Larraona criticized Parente's intervention and lamented the fact that Franić's had been read before and not after that of the official reporters, as would have been logical.

Then the ballots began, which resulted in a more successful text than had been foreseen. The sensational reversal of position by the theologian from the Holy Office swayed many who were hesitant. In the votes on the individual articles, there were 322 fathers who opposed the existence of the College of Bishops and 325 who refused to admit that episcopal consecration conferred the threefold sacred office in the Church. There was a very large number of fathers who were opposed, but far from the approximately eight hundred that they were hoping to get. Many of them (839) would uphold the proposal to confer the diaconate on young men without imposing on them the law of celibacy. When it came time to vote on the third chapter as a whole, the progressive alliance rejoiced over their new victory.[316] The results were 1,624 *placet*, 572 *placet iuxta modum*, and forty-three *non placet*. Now the discussion moved on to the *modi*, most of which had been prepared by the International Group, to which Archbishop Staffa belonged.

Over the course of the council Bishop Parente progressively distanced himself from the positions of the International Group of Fathers and was "rewarded" for his "conversion." In 1965 he was named secretary of the new Congregation for the Doctrine of the Faith and in 1967 he was

---

313 *L'Église colonne de la vérité, op. cit.*, 262.

314 "The support given by *Monsignor* Parente to the cause of collegiality not only was important from the numerical perspective, but also took on a particular moral significance. From then on the majority movement could count on the support of a representative from the curial circle, which at the beginning of the council had fought the theses of the renewal" (Grootaers, *I protagonisti*, 212).

315 B. Lai, *Il Papa non eletto, op. cit.*, 385.

316 Cf. Robert Prevost, *Vaticano II: Pietro o il caos*, Preface by His Eminence Cardinal A. Ottaviani (Rome: Coletti editore, 1965), 85–86.

created cardinal, titular bishop of San Lorenzo in Lucina. The purple had been denied to Bishop Antonio Piolanti, with whom Parente had collaborated for a long time. Parente died on December 30, 1986, at the age of ninety-five. He vindicated his choices, which had been severely judged in conservative circles.[317]

The Theological Commission's sub-commission on collegiality considered the objections raised by the minority to be of little importance. On November 7, 1964, Archbishop Staffa wrote a long letter to the pope and shared it among the most influential council fathers. In it Archbishop Staffa made several counter-arguments with reference to the question of collegiality and protested the method of the debate, recalling that he had been unlawfully denied the exercise of his right to take part in it.

Within the anti-Roman coalition the conflicts continued between the Girondist wing, which was already behaving like the "party in power," and the Jacobins; the first consisted of the French-speaking group, the second was made up of a number of German and Dutch theologians together with the "Bolognese group."[318]

One of the "boldest" of them was already explaining, in writing no less, how the ambiguous passages of the schema would be interpreted after the council. These documents ended up in the hands of a group of cardinals and "Roman" religious superiors, who forwarded them to the pontiff. At this point Paul VI was forced to acknowledge reality.[319] His theological adviser, Carlo Colombo, proposed a *Nota explicativa praevia* (Preliminary Explanatory Note) to be published as an appendix to the schema, which would explain the principles followed in the schema *De Ecclesia*."[320] It was Paul VI's intention that this note should play a role analogous to that of the *Relatio* by Bishop Gasser[321] in First Vatican Council, which had given the

---

[317] Cf. *Scritti del card. Pietro Parente dal 1933 al 1976*, ed. Monsignor Michele Di Ruberto (Rome: Città Nuova, 1976).

[318] On the two wings, cf. J. Grootaers, "La collégialité vue au jour le jour en la IIIe session conciliaire," in *Irénikon* 38 (1968): 183–194 at 186–187.

[319] Cf. Wiltgen, 232.

[320] On the *Nota praevia* see J. Grootaers and G. Thils, *Primauté et Collégialité* (Peeters Publisher and Booksellers, 1986), and the articles by C. Toisfontaines, G. Caprile, and V. Carbone in *Paolo VI e i problemi ecclesiologici al Concilio*; the reconstruction by Philips in *Carnets conciliaires*, 136–140, and the many documents published by G. Caprile in "Contributo alla storia della 'Nota explicativa praevia,'" *op. cit.*

[321] Vinzenz Gasser (1809–1879), Austrian, ordained in 1833, consecrated bishop of Brixen in 1857.

official interpretation of the document on papal infallibility. On October 31 Colombo proposed to Monsignor Philips that he compose the text of the note, on which there was already a memorandum by Father Bertrams,[322] who was considered, however, to be too "Roman"[323] in his thinking. Philips immediately set to work and in less that fifteen days the *Nota explicativa was drawn up*.

14. The "black week": but for whom?

a) Bishop Felici's announcements

On the morning of Saturday, November 14, a close-packed group of council fathers knelt in prayer in St. Peter's at the tomb of St. Josaphat, whose feast was celebrated that day. Saint Josaphat, a martyr of the Uniate Church in the seventeenth century, was an indomitable defender of unity and of Catholic truth, and the group of fathers prayed for his assistance against the innovators.[324] They knew that Paul VI, through the Secretary of State, had asked the president of the Theological Commission, Ottaviani, to compose a document that would "interpret" the schema on collegiality so as to specify that the consent of the Roman pontiff constituted a necessary and essential element of the authority of the Episcopal College.[325] After they entered the hall that morning, the fathers received a booklet, to which was joined: "by order of the higher authority"—that is, of Paul VI—a *Nota explicativa praevia*, proposed to the fathers by the Theological Commission before the ballots on the emendations to the third chapter of the schema *De Ecclesia*. Thus began what the progressives described as the "black week" of the council.[326]

---

322 Wilhelm Bertrams (1907–1995), German Jesuit, professor of Canon Law at the Gregorian University, conciliar *peritus*.

323 In a handwritten memorandum dated November 10, 1964, the pope expresses the desire that the *Nota* be prepared however by bishop Colombo together with Monsignor Philips and Monsignor Bertrams (text in G. Caprile, "Contributo alla storia della 'Nota explicativa praevia,'" *op. cit.*, 664–665).

324 R. Prevost, *op. cit.*, 99–100.

325 J. Grootaers, *Primauté et collégialité, op. cit.*, 109–113.

326 Luis Antonio G. Tagle, "The 'Black Week' of Vatican II…," in HVT 4:388–452; Caprile, 3:74; Wiltgen, 234.

That Saturday the secretary general informed the assembly that starting on the following Tuesday, November 21, voting would begin on the chapters of the future constitution on the Church[327] and, in his second intervention, he explained that the meeting on November 21 would be a public session, presided over by the supreme pontiff. The significance of the interpretative document, however, was yet not clear. Not until Monday morning did the bomb go off in the hall, when the secretary general made three important announcements, intended for all the council fathers, including the presidents and moderators. The first two announcements referred to Archbishop Staffa's letter, but without citing it, and the third to the *Nota explicativa*.[328]

On the first point Bishop Felici reported that some fathers had complained to the higher authority because of the non-observance of procedural rules in the discussion on chapter III and because of some dubious points in a doctrinal matter. The question had been studied carefully and they could be sure that there had been no violation of the rules; as to the doubts concerning the doctrine contained in chapter III, they had been submitted to the competent Theological Commission.

The second notification concerned the "theological note," or degree of authority, that must be assigned to the schema on the Church, as it was submitted for the final vote. On this point, Bishop Felici confirmed that the council did not have a doctrinal, but rather a pastoral character, and its teaching should not be considered as a dogma or an infallible definition, but should be accepted as issuing from the supreme magisterium of the Church.

Before the third announcement the secretary general attracted still more attention by declaring slowly in a loud voice: "This is of very great importance," and he continued to intone these words: "By order of the higher authority we are transmitting to the fathers an explanatory note previous to the emendations regarding chapter 3 of the schema *De Ecclesia*: the teaching set forth in this same chapter 3 is to be explained and understood according to the intention and the language of the note."[329] The *explanatory note*, therefore, came directly from the supreme pontiff.

"It is regrettable perhaps, but that is how it is; they are now cornered into voting *Placet*, even if not everything is acceptable," noted Congar,

---

327 AS III/7:667, 702, 711.

328 AS III/8:10–13.

329 Ibid., 10.

summing up the state of mind of someone who sought to rein in the progressive fathers and theologians who would have liked to express their protest publicly.[330]

At this point, in profound silence, the conciliar assembly listened to the four "observations" with which the commission, at the pope's command, had amended the text.[331] 1) When it says that "the bishops constitute a College" one should not think of a juridical College in which all the bishops, including the pope, would be one level of equality; 2) When it says that one becomes a "member of the College in virtue of episcopal consecration and of hierarchical communion with the Head and the members of the College," it means that the nature of the episcopal office requires a juridical determination on the part of the ecclesiastical hierarchy which can consist either in the assignment to an ecclesiastical office or in the designation of the portion of the flock that will be subject to the bishop; 3) It is stated in the text that the College of Bishops, which does not exist without its head, "is equally the subject of a supreme and plenary power over the universal Church. The distinction does not concern two powers (the pope and the Episcopal College), but the two ways in which the Roman pontiff, who always has the fullness of power, can exercise it: by himself or in union with the bishops, who are directed and convoked by him; 4) There is a difference, the note explains again, between the exercise of the supreme pontiff's personal power over the universal Church and the exercise of the collegial power of the bishops with the pope. The supreme pontiff can exercise his power at any moment, as he pleases, but his collegial power is not always operative. The final sentence of the note sums up its meaning: "This hierarchical communion of all bishops with the supreme pontiff is unmistakably hallowed in the tradition of the Church."[332]

That same day Cardinal Ruffini wrote to the pope to express the extent of his joy on account of the proclamations that Bishop Felici had read in the hall, "which dispelled every anxiety and clarified the text of the same chapter without leaving any ambiguity," but also to reveal to Paul VI his concerns about "a movement that would be organizing to mitigate the significance of the aforementioned proclamations."[333]

---

330 Congar, *Journal*, 680.

331 AS III/8:11–13.

332 Ibid., 12.

333 E. Ruffini, letter dated November 16, 1964, in F. M. Stabile, *op. cit.*, 140.

The next day each council father received a printed copy of the *Nota explicativa praevia*. After that, on November 19, the council approved by 2,099 votes to forty-six (*non placet*) the rewriting of chapter 3 by the Theological Commission.[334] The document undoubtedly toned down the importance of the text on collegiality, even though Bishop Parente wrote that the *Nota explicativa* was not necessary and added nothing to the text of the declaration, while in fact denying that it had the character of a conciliar document.[335] Cardinal Siri, on February 10, expressed his bewilderment at the article by Cardinal Parente.[336] Don Dossetti, on the contrary, revealed to Bishop Carlo Colombo, Paul VI's trusted theologian, the extent of his "indescribable sense of anguish."[337] It was a defeat for the Jacobin wing, but, as Philips noted, "The pope has gained his objective, that is, to win over the minority to himself."[338] The Belgian theologian clarifies this point in his book on *Lumen gentium*: "It is never desirable in a council for a majority to triumph over a minority; history shows this.... To attain this unity Paul VI endeavored with all his might, tirelessly, so much so that his inclusive [*comprensivo*] attitude toward the minority at times irritated the majority group."[339]

b) The revolt of the bishops

That day, "Black Thursday," in addition to the *Nota praevia*, other actions aggravated the disappointment of the anti-Roman front: the postponement of the discussion on religious liberty, the corrections to the text on ecumenism, and the proclamation of the Blessed Virgin's Motherhood of the Church.[340]

---

334 AS III/8:177.

335 Cf. P. Parente, "Visione della Chiesa nella dottrina del Concilio ecumenico," in *Città Nuova* 2 (1965): 15–17 at 17. The article was reprinted in *L'Avvenire d'Italia* (January 21, 1965).

336 Letter from Siri to Felici dated February 10, 1965, in ASV, Conc. Vat. II, Busta 345. I, 1 fol.

337 Cf. G. Alberigo, *A Brief History*, 74–76 at 74.

338 Philips, *Carnets conciliaires*, 136.

339 G. Philips, *La Chiesa e il suo mistero: Storia, testo e commento della* Lumen gentium, Ital. transl. (Milan: Jaca Book, 1975), 50.

340 Cf. V. A. Berto, "Remarques sur un 'incident' conciliaire," in *Itinéraires* 91 (1965): 60–70.

The new outline on religious liberty by the Secretariat for Promoting Christian Unity, composed in the month of October especially by Fr. Murray and Bishop Pavan, had been sent to the Theological Commission, which approved it on November 9, and was distributed to the council fathers on the seventeenth of the same month. The *Coetus Internationalis*, after examining the document, realized that, compared with its predecessor, this was a totally new schema: in fact, the text had been expanded from about 250 lines to 500, with only seventy lines from the original document, and, as such, required the time necessary for a careful examination of it, before the vote that was to take place in a public session. About 150 council fathers, invoking article 30.2 of the rules, asked that the vote be put off until the fourth session, so as to have more time for a serious study of the new schema. Cardinal Tisserant, president of the assembly, did not accept the proposal, and announced the vote for the next day. At this point, one of the signers of the petition, Bishop Carli, made an appeal to Cardinal Roberti, the president of the administrative tribunal of the council, to denounce as unlawful the decision by Tisserant and the four moderators to put the schema to a vote.[341] The request got its desired effect. The tribunal of the council approved of the appeal and the judges decided to postpone the discussion until the fourth session.

On the following day, November 19, Cardinal Tisserant, president of the Board of Presidency, informed the assembly that the declaration of religious liberty could not be submitted to the fathers, inasmuch as—after the changes introduced—it was really a new document that would be postponed until the next session.[342] The announcement that the vote was to be postponed set off a furious reaction. In the basilica many left their places and went away from the gallery so as to meet for lively discussion in little groups and furtive gatherings. In the hall, Fesquet writes, bishops were heard crying out: "We've been betrayed!" One of them, an American, let slip the insult: "The bastards!"[343] Bishop Reh,[344]

[341] Wiltgen, 236–237.

[342] AS III/8:415.

[343] Fesquet, *Drama*, 539.

[344] Francis Frederick Reh (1911–1994), from the United States, ordained in 1935, bishop of Charleston in 1962, rector of the Pontifical North American College and bishop of Macriana in Mauretania in 1964, bishop of Saginaw in 1968.

rector of the American College in Rome, and two experts, Monsignor Quinn[345] of Chicago, and Fr. McManus[346] of Washington, after consulting with Cardinal Meyer, produced a booklet, addressed to the supreme pontiff, entitled *Instanter, instantius, instantissime*, that contained only one sentence: "We ask that the declaration on religious liberty be voted on before the end of the present session of the council, for fear that the confidence of Christians and non-Christians could be diminished."[347] The press spoke of a "revolt" by the American bishops.

Monsignor Prignon recalls that Cardinals Frings, Döpfner, König, Léger, Lebfebvre, Meyer, Ritter, Silva Henríquez, Landázuri Ricketts and Alfrink got together and agreed on the text of a letter to Paul VI, in which they asked him personally to revoke the decision to postpone, as announced by Cardinal Tisserant. The letter was delivered on the following day, after having received as well the signatures of Lercaro, Liénart, Rugambwa, and others.[348] The pope, however, refused to intervene, since the tribunal of the council had already pronounced its decision. He said, "We have to respect the conscience of every bishop. If they feel the need for more time to decide some questions, we have to give it to them."[349]

The dissatisfaction of the progressives increased when, shortly after Cardinal Tisserant's intervention, Secretary General Felici, while announcing that the final vote on the schema *De oecumenismo* would take place the next day, added that "At the last moment some modifications had been introduced by the higher authority," and distributed mimeographed pages with nineteen new revisions that the Holy Father made to the schema on ecumenism that had already been voted on in its entirety by the assembly. The secretary announced that "Such corrections were introduced for a greater clarity in the text on the part of the secretary for Promoting Christian Unity, who thus accepts the kind suggestions

---

345 John Quinn Weitzel, M.M. (1928–1986), American, ordained in 1955, bishop of Samoa-Pago Pago in 1986.

346 Frederick Richard McManus (1923–2005), from the United States, ordained in 1947, professor at Catholic University of American from 1967 to 1973, consultor of the Pontifical Preparatory Commission on the Sacred Liturgy of Vatican Council II, conciliar *peritus*, consultor of the Secretariat for Promoting Christian Unity.

347 AS V/3:89–91 at 89.

348 Fonds Prignon, "Rapport sur les travaux conciliaires depuis le 25–9–1964," in CLG, n. 1057.

349 Divine Word Service, September 15, 1964.

authoritatively made to him."[350] This meant that Cardinal Bea had approved of them against his will.

Then Felici gave the floor to Bishop De Smedt, the reporter on the schema on religious liberty.[351] The dissatisfaction of the progressives was only waiting for a pretext to show itself. When, in the course of his intervention, the bishop of Bruges said that "The Church should be free of political powers,"[352] frenetic applause broke out in some sectors of the hall. Two moderators joined in with the acclamation even though—Fesquet recalls—this kind of display was strictly forbidden in the council.[353] The end of the Thursday's Congregation resembled the conclusion of a political meeting.

Whereas the *Nota praevia* had alarmed the German-language fathers and theologians in particular, the modifications to the document on ecumenism disquieted the French progressives above all. "It is undeniable," Congar noted on November 19, "that this morning was CATASTROPHIC from the point of view of the ecumenical climate."[354] On that same day, Arrighi confided to Congar: "Willebrands and I have not slept for three nights. The *De oecumenismo* is being called into question."[355] Congar, when he found out that the *modi* introduced in the text were said to have come from his confrère Luigi Ciappi, noted, "I must say that this does not surprise me. Fr. Ciappi is a poor and petty soul, for whom the papal system, understood in the most literally unyielding and limited manner, is an absolute, which occupies the ENTIRE space."[356] The Benedictine from Chevetogne, Emmanuel Lanne, mentions having taken part in "a very restricted and rather secret commission," made up of Willebrands, Duprey, and Thils that examined the forty *modi*, proposed by Paul VI on *De oecumenismo*, accepting only nineteen revisions and rejecting twenty-one.[357] Actually, in the previous two days, Bishop Willebrands had realized

---

350 AS III/8:422.

351 Ibid., 449–456.

352 Ibid., 450–451.

353 Fesquet, *Drama*, 539.

354 Congar, *Journal*, 690.

355 Ibid., 688.

356 That is, leaves room for nothing else. Ibid., 695.

357 E. Lanne, *Il monastero di Chevetogne, op. cit.*, 542–543.

that the pope would not be able to promulgate the document as it stood, because of the manifest irenicism of the text and, with Cardinal Bea, he had approved some modifications. The schema was approved with 2,129 votes in favor and sixty-four against and eleven blank ballots. Thus the final week of the third session came to an end.

According to Wiltgen the liberal-progressives had four major reasons to be disssatisfied with the attitude of the supreme pontiff in this predicament.[358] In the first place, his decision to add an explanatory note on collegiality, which had been communicated to the assembly on November 16. In the second place, the postponement of the decree on religious liberty, on which a vote had been expected. In the third place, the revisions to the final schema on ecumenism. Finally, the sudden announcement that Paul VI made on November 18, the closing day of the third session, bestowing on the Most Blessed Virgin Mary the title of "Mother of the Church," a title that the Conciliar Commission had refused to include in the text of *Lumen gentium*.[359] Paul VI, after having sought in vain to have Mary proclaimed Mother of the Church by the council fathers, was forced to do it on his own initiative. Nonetheless, the mere announcement of the event made the progressive fathers and theologians indignant, like Otto Semmlroth, who in his diary accused the pope of placing himself with this act "again formally in opposition to the council."[360]

15. The promulgation of *Lumen gentium*

On November 21, 1964, the day of the solemn closing of the third session, the council fathers adopted, after three stormy sessions of discussion, the dogmatic constitution on the Church, *Lumen gentium*, which included the

[358] Wiltgen, 234–235.

[359] *L'Osservatore Romano* (November 20, 1964). Father Roschini compiles the texts in which Paul VI expresses in vain his hope that the council fathers will proclaim Mary Mother of the Church. See the speeches on August 15, 1963, October 11, 1963, November 17, 1963, the closing speech of the second session of the council, the address on May 18, 1964, and finally the announcement to the faithful on November 18, 1964, three days before the official proclamation; but not one of them succeeded in moving the council fathers (G. M. Roschini "Maria SS. solennemente proclamata da Paolo VI 'Madre della Chiesa,'" in *Marianum* 26 [1964]: 326–327).

[360] Cf. Semmelroth, *Diario* (November 19, 1964), cf. L. A. G. Tagle, "The 'Black Week' of Vatican II...," 447.

debated chapter on collegiality, with 2,151 votes against five.[361] The text was divided into eight chapters: the mystery of the Church; the people of God; the hierarchical constitution of the Church; the laity; the universal call to holiness in the Church; consecrated religious; the eschatological character of the pilgrim Church on earth; the Blessed Virgin Mary in the mystery of Christ and of the Church.

The hermeneutic discussion of what was called the *Magna Charta*[362] of the council started immediately. *L'Osservatore Romano*, on March 3, 1965, published in a frame on its first page an unsigned article on the *Nota praevia* that described it as the "authentic source of the interpretation of the great conciliar document," repudiating all attempts to minimize its importance.[363] The debate, however, was far from over. No. 8 of the constitution Lumen gentium asserted that:

> this Church (of Christ) constituted and organized in the world as a society, subsists in (*subsistit in*) the Catholic Church, which is governed by the successor of Peter and by the bishops in union with that successor, although many elements of sanctification and of truth can be found outside of her visible structure. These elements, however, as gifts properly belonging to the Church of Christ, possess an inner dynamism toward Catholic unity.[364]

The expression *subsistit* in was the object of contradictory interpretations. Alexandra von Teuffenback, who devoted an extensive study to it,[365] maintained that the phrase, whose author is said to have been the secretary

---

361 Text in AS III/8:784–836; see also COD, 849–898.

362 Cf. G. Dejaifve, "La 'Magna Charta' de Vatican II: La constitution 'Lumen gentium,'" in *Nouvelle Revue Théologique* 97 (1967): 3–22. For an in-depth commentary on the document, see B. Gherardini, *The Ecumenical Vatican Council II*, 255–281.

363 See also the special issue of *Divinitas* dated December 1965, with articles by C. Balić, Ch. Boyer, J. Brinktrine, M. Browne, L. Ciappi, A. Gutiérrez and U. Lattanzi.

364 Cf. COD, 854.

365 Cf. A. von Teuffenbach, *Die Bedeutung, op. cit.*; a summary restatement can be found in *Idem*, "'Subsistit in': [LG 8] una formula discussa," in Associazione Teologica Italiana, *Annuncio del Vangelo, forma Ecclesiae* (Cinisello Balsamo, San Paolo, 2005), 395–403; this is also the position of J. Ratzinger, "The Ecclesiology of the constitution *Lumen gentium*," in *Pilgrim Fellowship of Faith*, ed. Stephan Otto Horn and Vinzent Pfnür (San Francisco: Ignatius Press, 2005), 123–152 at 147 ff.

of the Doctrinal Commission, Tromp,[366] must be understood, not as an ecumenical overture, but as the reaffirmation of Catholic identity according to the guidelines of Pius XII.[367] Just as widespread, however, is the thesis of those who interpret the expression *subsistit in* to mean also the subsistence of the Church of Christ in the Christian communities that are separated from Rome.[368]

The Civiltà Cattolica, for instance, described as "greatly significant" the assertion that "there is no absolute and total identification between the Church of Christ and the Catholic Church:"

> The Church of Christ is (*est*) not the Catholic Church, but subsists in (*subsistit in*) it, because churches, communities and ecclesial elements exist also outside the visible confines of the Catholic Church. In other words, the reality of the Church of Christ overlaps with the reality of the Catholic Church, so that this Church is a true Church of Christ; but at the same time, it extends beyond her, including ecclesial realities that are not visibly a part of the Catholic Church.[369]

The Congregation for the Doctrine of the Faith declared in *Dominus Jesus*,"[370] with greater authority, that Vatican Council II had used the

---

[366] Pastor Wilhelm Schmidt, a protestant observer at the council, in a letter to Father Mathias Gaudron dated August 3, 2000, declares that he suggested the formula to Father Ratzinger, who then transmitted it to Cardinal Frings (*Le Sel de la Terre* 49 [2004]: 40).

[367] Von Teuffenbach's thesis was adopted by Father Karl J. Becker, S.J., director of Teuffenbach's doctoral thesis at the Gregorian ("'Subsistit in' [Lumen gentium, 8]: un articolo di P. Karl Josef Becker, S.J.," in *L'Osservatore Romano*, December 5–6, 2005); one of his confreres argued against it: see Francis A. Sullivan, S.J. "A Response to Karl Becker on the Meaning of 'subsistit in,'" in *Theological Studies* 67 (2006): 395–409.

[368] Cf. F. A. Sullivan, "The Significance of the Vatican II Declaration That the Church of Christ 'Subsists in' the Roman Catholic Church," in R. Latourelle, ed., *Vatican II: Assessment and Perspectives* (Mahwah, NJ: Paulist Press, 1989), 2:272–287.

[369] "Dalla 'società perfetta' alla Chiesa 'mistero,'" in *Civiltà Cattolica*, 3230 (1985): 105–119 at 118. G. Philips, one of the chief authors of *Lumen gentium*, for his part writes: "The Church of Christ 'is found in' the Catholic Church.... As for us, we would be tempted to translate: there we find the Church of Christ in all its fullness and strength" (G. Philips, *La Chiesa e il suo mistero, op. cit.*, 111).

[370] Declaration *Dominus Iesus* by the Congregation for the Doctrine of the Faith (August 6, 2000), in AAS 92 (2000): 744–764, and in Denz-H, n. 5088.

expression "*subsistit in*" to affirm that "the single Church of Christ… subsists in [*subsistit in*] the Catholic Church, governed by the Successor of Peter and by the bishops in communion with him," even though there are elements of sanctification and truth outside its structure. The Very Rev. Fernando Ocariz, in his presentation of the Declaration *Dominus Jesus*, asserted that the "precise interpretation" is this:

> The unique Church "subsists" (*subsistit*) in the Catholic Church, governed by the Successor of Peter and by the other bishops. With this statement, Vatican II meant that the one Church of Jesus Christ continues to exist despite divisions among Christians; and, more precisely, that only in the Catholic Church does the Church of Christ subsist in all its fullness, whereas outside its visible structure there are "elements of sanctification and truth" belonging to the Church itself (cf. n. 17). At this point, the text of *Dominus Iesus* mentions that some non-Catholic Christian communities preserve, among those "elements of sanctification and truth," the valid Episcopate and the valid Eucharist and, therefore, are particular Churches, that is to say, parts of the one People of God in which the one, holy, catholic, and apostolic Church is present and operative (Vatican Council II, *Christus Dominus*, n. 11), as is the case with the Orthodox Churches. There is therefore only one Church (subsisting in the Catholic Church), and at the same time true non-Catholic particular Churches exist. This is not a paradox: there is only one Church, of which all the particular Churches are parts even though there is no ecclesial fullness in some of them (the non-Catholic ones), inasmuch as their union with the whole is imperfect, due to a lack of full communion with him who, according to the will of the Lord, is the principle and foundation of the unity of the Episcopate and of the entire Church (the bishop of Rome, Successor of Peter: cf. Vatican Council II, *Lumen gentium*, n. 23).[371]

On that same day, November 21, 1964, the council fathers approved the decree *Orientalium Ecclesiarum*, on the Eastern Catholic Churches[372] (with 2,110 votes in favor and thirty-nine against) and the decree *Unitatis Redintegratio* on ecumenism (2,137 votes in favor and eleven against),

---

371 Presentation of the Declaration *Dominus Iesus* of the Congregation for the Doctrine of the Faith on August 6, 2000.

372 Test in AS III/8:837–845. See also COD, 900–907.

which was made up of an introduction and three chapters, with twenty-four paragraphs.[373] According to Father Congar, this "great and fine document… conveys the spirit of John XXIII who… could be considered its founding father."[374] Monsignor Gherardini, on the contrary, comments that the document seems to be decidedly open to syncretism, and its echo of Karl Rahner's "anonymous Christians" or of the "implicit Christians" of Edward Schillebeeckx "is recognizable a million miles away."[375]

In sketching a summary of the third conciliar period Cardinal Bea wrote:

> The central ecumenical event of this session, or one could even say of this year, is without a doubt the definitive vote and promulgation of the conciliar decree on ecumenism. This represents the official theoretical and practical stance taken by the Catholic Church, as such, with regard to the cause of union and the ecumenical movement; and this significance was widely recognized almost everywhere.[376]

In his final allocution,[377] Paul VI briefly recapped the two months of work, stressing especially the reflection on the Church, which was explored in her "mystery" and in her "fundamental constitution."

At the end of his speech the supreme pontiff proclaimed the Virgin Mary "Mother of the Church."[378] The proclamation was greeted with long

---

[373] Text in AS III/8:845–859 and in COD, 908–920. Cf. B. Gherardini, "'Unitatis redintegratio' ha quarant'anni," in *Divinitas* 48/2 (2005): 217–232; M. Velati, "L'ecumenismo al concilio: Paolo VI e l'approvazione di Unitatis redintegratio," in *Cristianesimo nella storia* 26 (2005): 427–476, including as an appendix (465–476) the diary of Bishop Willebrands written shortly after the events (November 14–20, 1964).

[374] Y. Congar, *Introduction à* Unitatis redintegratio, *Documents conciliaries* (Paris: Centurion, 1965), 1:165–166.

[375] B. Gherardini, *The Ecumenical Vatican Council II, op. cit.*, 232. See also the closely-argued critique by Pierre-Marie, O.P., "Bref examen critique de Unitatis Redintegratio," in *L'Unité spirituelle du genre humain*, 163–192.

[376] Schmidt, *Bea*, 532. Alberigo, for his part, writes: "The old outlook according to which unity would be realized through the 'return' of the 'heretics' and 'schismatics' to the Roman Church was finally left behind" (G. Alberigo, *A Brief History*, 86).

[377] AS III/8:909–918.

[378] Ibid., 916.

applause in the assembly,[379] but was the cause of disappointment among the "observers" and the more "ecumenical" fathers.[380] The Abbé de Nantes[381] wrote that Paul VI behaved like a motorist who brakes on a curve so as to stay on the road, in order to bring all his passengers to their destination without shaking them up too much.[382]

16. Paul VI sets aside the tiara

Describing the final Mass of the session, with it twenty-four concelebrants, as "a mixture of liturgical innovations... and of the old rite," Father de Lubac noted, "I look at the statue of St. Peter with his head covered by the tiara: will it be possible to remove it? It would be perceived as a sacrifice."[383]

A week before, on November 13, Paul VI had come down from the pontifical throne that was set up under the bronze baldachin of Saint Peter's, and had placed "upon the altar of the council" the tiara that had been given to him by the people of Milan on the occasion of his

---

[379] Cf. V. Carbone, "Maria Madre della Chiesa: Una pagina di storia del Concilio Vaticano II," in *L'Osservatore Romano*, February 3, 1988.

[380] Cf. R. Laurentin, "La proclamation de Marie 'Mater Ecclesiae' par Paul VI," in *Paolo VI e i problemi ecclesiologici al Concilio*, 376–388. Father Henri Denis (1921–1951) notes: "Father de Lubac is horror-stricken. He said to me, Father Denis, this is the end of the council. There is no more John XXIII, no more *aggiornamento*" (H. Denis, *Église, qu'as-tu fait de ton Concile?* [Paris: Le Centurion, 1985], 138).

[381] Georges de Nantes (1924–2010), French, ordained in 1948, parish priest from 1958 in Villemaur-sur-Vanne in the Aube, where he founded the Brothers of the Sacred Heart of Jesus. In 1963 he settled in Saint-Parres-lès-Vaudes, coming into conflict with the bishop, who suspended him *a divinis*. In 1956 he published *"Lettres à mes amis,"* which then became *La Contre-Réforme catholique au XXe siècle*. In 1970 he called his movement "The League of the Catholic Counter-Reformation" (more commonly "Catholic Counter-Reformation"). See his book *Liber accusationis* [an English translation of the subtitle follows:] *To our Holy Father Pope Paul VI, by the Grace of God and the Law of the Church Sovereign Judge of all Christ's Faithful, We Present a Complaint against our Brother in the Faith, Pope Paul VI, on account of Heresy, Schism, and Scandal* (Saint-Parres-lès-Vaudes, La Contre-Réforme catholique, 1973).

[382] *La Contre-Réforme Catholique* 50 (1971): 4.

[383] De Lubac, *Quaderni*, 771.

coronation as pontiff.[384] Bishop Helder Câmara describes the event in these words, "The basilica, in a moving silence, watched Paul VI who came forward with the tiara in hand, placed it on the altar and went back happy! There was delirium."[385] De Lubac wondered, "What does this gesture mean? To sell a tiara in order to get for it (they say) two million? Or to renounce the tiara with a symbolic gesture of renouncing the rituals of temporal power? The two opinions make the rounds almost everywhere over the course of the day."[386] Congar, who was not present at the ceremony, but who compiled responses to it, comments with a trace of skepticism, "The pope brought his tiara and offered it for the poor. If this is the discarding of the tiara, if there is not another one after it, that is good. Otherwise, it would be a spectacular gesture without consequence. In short, he should have put on the altar, not A tiara, but THE tiara."[387] In those days Father Congar was downcast by the development that the assembly activities seemed to take, but in his *Diary*, although showing that he is discouraged, he does not give up: "I think," he writes, "that the history of ecclesiology should have first priority. It alone will break the deadlock for certain questions, by showing where this or the other position comes from."[388]

On November 14, the Spanish-Argentine Bishop Vincente Zazpe[389] wrote in his *Diary*: "The Church and the council have remained in the hands of central Europe. The only thing that counts is what they say. On the other hand, there is no current of thought or any group to hold them back or provide a balance. Even the pope is not a containing force. Neither America nor Africa nor Italy nor Spain counts."[390]

In those same days the following irreverent image of the conciliar assembly was attributed to Bishop Antonino Romeo: "A sinister comedy of three

---

[384] On the event, which is not recorded in the *Acta Synodalia*, see *L'Osservatore Romano* (November 14, 1961); Caprile, 4:431–432; Norman Tanner, "The Church in the World..." *op. cit.*, 372–376.

[385] Câmara, *Lettres Conciliaires*, 2:751.

[386] De Lubac, *Quaderni*, 734.

[387] Congar, *Journal*, 675.

[388] Ibid. 697.

[389] Vincente Faustino Zazpe Zarategi (1920–1984), Spanish, ordained in 1948, bishop of Rafaela in Argentina (1961), then archbishop of Santa Fe (1969).

[390] Cited in G. Alberigo, "Major Results, Shadows of Uncertainty," in HVT 4:617–640 at 631.

thousand good-for-nothings, with gold crosses on their chests, who don't even believe in the Trinity or the Virgin, at least some of them don't."[391]

The journalist for *Le Monde*, for his part, sketched this summary:

> In three years, four centuries have been bridged. The reform of the curia, the urgency of which becomes more apparent with each passing day, will definitely be undertaken; contact has been restored with non-Catholic Christians; the real problems of the secular world have been considered. Vatican II has clearly sided with the ideals of universal fraternity, equality, and liberty. The Jews have been unequivocally rehabilitated. Pastors have carried the day over jurists, the New Testament over the Old. A theology of evolution and human progress has been begun. Tomorrow the blunders and manipulations will be forgotten. The new impetus given will be remembered.... The strength of the council is indomitable. Its progress may be slowed slightly, but it cannot be stopped. Vatican II is more a departure point than an end point. Like Jerusalem and Bombay.[392]

On January 6, 1965, Paul VI informed Cardinal Cicognani that the final session of the council would begin on September 14, and a little later it was learned that the pope would celebrate some Masses in Italian in various Roman parishes beginning on March 7.

---

[391] Fesquet, *Drama*, 416.

[392] Fesquet, *Drama*, 557.

VI

1965: The Fourth Session

1. From the third to the fourth session

The year 1965 opened in a climate of alarm and worry about the Church's situation. In his Wednesday general audiences Paul VI began to lament the spread of heterodox theological statements, as he censured the spirit of unrest and almost of rebellion that was circulating.[1] Jean Madiran[2] went so far in his *Itinéraires* as to mention the possibility of a schism in the Church by December.[3]

On September 11, on the eve of reopening the council, the pope published the encylical *Mysterium fidei*, which reaffirmed the mystery of the real presence of Christ in the Eucharist and recalled the lasting importance

---

[1] Cf. Giovanni Turbanti, "Toward the Fourth Period," in HVT 5:1–48 at 7.

[2] Jean Madiran, pseudonym for Jean Arfel (1920–), founder and editor of the monthly magazine *Itinéraires* (1956–1996), then of the daily newspaper *Présent*, is one of the most renowned French Catholic writers. Besides the previously cited works by him, see *L'hérésie du XXe siècle* (Paris: Nouvelles Éditions Latines, 1968); *Le Concile en question: correspondance Congar-Madiran sur Vatican II et sur la crise de l'Église* (Bouère: DMM, 1985); *Chroniques sous Benoît XVI* (Versailles: Via Romana, 2010). About him see Daniele Masson, *Jean Madiran* (Maule: Difralivre, 1989).

[3] Cf. J. Madiran, "Un schisme pour décembre," in *Itinéraires* 95 (1965): 2–41.

of the technical terms in the dogmatic formulas of theology. "We can see that some of those who are dealing with this most holy mystery in speech and writing are disseminating opinions on Masses celebrated in private or on the dogma of transubstantiation that are disturbing the minds of the faithful and causing them no small measure of confusion about matters of faith."[4] The encylical was presented as a reaction to the heterodox tendencies that were rife in the Dutch Church, so much so that Cardinal Alfrink, on the very day of the first General Congregation of the session, held a press conference to justify what was going on in his country.[5] Bishop Willebrands was saying that the encylical was saying nothing new of importance, and that in the space of five years it would no longer be spoken of, while Dom Lanne, of the Abbey of Chevetogne, judged it "catastrophic,"[6] also because the pope had published it just two days before the new session, as if to emphasize the independence and superiority of his teaching authority.[7]

The goal-line that Paul VI set for the council, however, did not change, as was made evident by the consistory on February 22, in which he created twenty-seven new cardinals, from twenty nations, mainly Africans. Among the new prelates clad in purple were individuals close to him, like the theologian Charles Journet, the "prophet" of the Christian Working Youth (*Jeunesse Ouvrière Chrétienne*) Joseph Cardijn, and his "master," Father Giulio Bevilacqua, who died three months after receiving the cardinal's hat. Other prelates who were created cardinals included three Eastern patriarchs (among them Maximos IV Saigh [Sayegh]), the archbishop of Prague, Josef Beran, and the archbishop of Zagreb, Franjo Seper,[8] as well as Archbishop Lorenz Jäger, one of the pioneers of ecumenism.

---

[4] Paul VI, encylical letter *Mysterium fidei* (September 1, 1965), in AAS 57 (1965): 753–774 at 755.

[5] The primate of Holland protested "against the unilateral, negative, twisted way in which people have been speaking for months in the international press, almost slanderously, about the Catholic community in the Netherlands," whereas he emphasized its "vitality" (Address by Cardinal Bernard Alfrink to the *Centre Hollandais de Documentation*, in DO-C, September 15, 1965). See also the report about the speech in *L'Avvenire d'Italia*, cited in R. La Valle, *Il Concilio nelle nostre mani, op. cit.*, 36–42.

[6] Congar, *Journal*, 774.

[7] Cf. ibid.

[8] Franjo Seper (1905–1981), Croatian, ordained in 1930, coadjutor archbishop (1958), then archbishop of Zagreb from 1960 to 1968. Created cardinal in 1965, became secretary of the Congregation for the Doctrine of the Faith (1968–1981).

Between December 1964 and the first months of 1965 symbolic "ecumenical" gestures proliferated, with the restitution to the Orthodox Churches of some relics (of St. Andrew to Patras, of St. Saba to Jerusalem, of St. Titus to Crete, and of St. Mark to Alexandria).[9] On October 5 one of the flags captured on October 7, 1571, by the Christian fleet in the battle of Lepanto, was returned to Turkey. Until then it had been preserved in the Basilica of Saint Mary Major in Rome. On April 9, 1965, *L'Osservatore Romano* published news of the creation of the Secretariat for Non-believers.[10] The presidency of the body was entrusted to the Austrian, Cardinal König, who had often served as an intermediary between the Holy See and the communist governments; the secretary was the Salesian Don Vincenzo Miano,[11] who would make a name for himself by his initiatives for dialogue between Christians and Marxists and between the Church and Freemasonry.[12] The same König specified, on the other hand, that the secretariat was not formed to organize the fight against atheism, not even the militant variety, but rather to enter into dialogue with it.[13]

The secretariat completed the "three circles" foreseen by the encylical *Ecclesiam suam*: after the one for relations with the separated brethren of other Christian churches, and the one for relations with other religions, now there was also a secretariat for dialogue with the non-believers.

On April 25, the second encylical of the pontificate was published: *Mense maio*,[14] dedicated to Mary. The pope invited the faithful to pray to Mary for the success of the council and above all for peace, which is mentioned,

---

9 Cf. A. Tornielli, *Paolo VI, op. cit.*, 415.

10 The secretariat was transformed by John Paul II into the Council for Dialogue with Non-Christians and was then absorbed, in 1993, into the Pontifical Council for Culture (cf. Niccolò Del Re, in MV, 385–386).

11 Vincenzo Miano (1910–1980), Salesian, ordained in 1933. Professor of philosophy at the Salesian Athenaeum. Expert at the council during the last session. See his article "Les tâches du Sécretariat pour les non-croyants," in *Concilium* 23 (1967): 111–116.

12 Cf. Rosario Francesco Esposito, S.S.P., *La riconciliazione tra la Chiesa e la Massoneria: Cronaca di alcuni avvenimenti e incontri*, with an introduction by Don Vincenzo Miano, S.D.B., Giordano Gamberini and Giovanni Caprile, S.J. (Ravenna: Longo, 1979).

13 Cf. Ricardo Burigana and Giovanni Turbanti, "The Intersession: Preparing the Conclusion of the Council," in HVT 4:453–616 at 609.

14 Paul VI, encylical *Mense maio* (April 25, 1965), in AAS 57 (1965): 353–358.

as Tornielli observes,[15] no less than fourteen times in the scarcely 120 total lines of the letter, in which Paul VI described the international situation as being "more obscure and uncertain than ever, inasmuch as new, serious threats endanger the supreme good of peace in the world."[16]

2. The conservatives' new initiatives

a) The corrections by the *Coetus Internationalis*

The months that preceded the fourth session saw a final attempt at an attack on the part of the *Coetus Internationalis* that had been strengthened by the relative success achieved with the *Nota praevia explicativa.* On December 18, 1964, the *Coetus* had composed a letter containing fifteen pages of corrections that they suggested making to the text. In the month of January, 1965, a series of observations were publicized on the relation between scripture and tradition; in June of 1965 the *Coetus* sent to the council fathers a new document containing twenty pages of improvements to the fourth version of the schema.[17]

On July 25, Bishop Proença Sigaud, Archbishop Lefebvre, and Bishop Carli addressed a letter to the supreme pontiff, requesting that, in keeping with the provisions of the rules, even the conciliar minority might also officially present their reports in the hall, especially on important issues such as religious liberty, divine revelation, the Church in the modern world, and relations between the Church and non-Christian religions. They asked furthermore that the spokesmen for the minority's position be granted the necessary time to prepare their interventions; that the spokesmen be

---

15 Cf. A. Tornielli, *Paolo VI, op. cit.*, 415.

16 Encylical *Mense maio, op. cit.*; Ital. transl. in Paolo VI, *Tutti i principali documenti* (Vatican City: Libreria Editrice Vaticana, 2002), 212–221 at 215.

17 Cf. Caprile, 5:53–54; Wiltgen, 247. Before the opening of the fourth session, Archbishop Lefebvre sent a copy of the list of emendations to the Abbé de Nantes, who replied that, in his opinion, it was necessary to reject the schema of the Secretariat for Promoting Christian Unity as a basis of discussion and not to try to improve it by means of revisions (François-Marie des Anges, *Pour l'Église*, vol. II, 1963–1969, *Dans l'oeil du cyclone* [Saint-Parres-les-Vaudes/Paris: Éd. de la Contre-Réforme Catholique, 1993], 149–150).

appointed by the minority itself; that their reports might be printed and distributed in time, and that each speaker have the right to reply briefly.[18]

On August 11, Cardinal Cicognani, Secretary of State, replied to Bishop Carli, informing him that the supreme pontiff, after having carefully examined the proposal, refused the request and chided the fathers for being associated in a group of the sort that would divide the assembly.

> But I must tell Your Excellency that it caused come surprise that this request had been presented in the name of a *"Coetus Internationalis Patrum idem in re theologica et pastorali sentientes"* ["International Group of Fathers who think alike in theological and pastoral matters"], in other words, by a particular group within the council. The initiative could serve as a precedent for the official rise of other "alliances," to the detriment of the conciliar assembly: indeed, as Your Excellency understands, this tends to deprive the fathers of that freedom of judgment and of choice that must be guaranteed above any particular interest, and it tends to accentuate tendencies and divisions among the fathers themselves, whereas one must do everything possible to attenuate them for the sake of serenity, concord, and finally the good outcome of the council and the honor of the Church. The undertaking cannot, therefore, be approved in itself, and it is good that the abovementioned *Coetus* does not function as a representative body of the position of the fathers who belong to it."[19]

The hypocrisy of the reply was obvious. First of all, the internal rules of the council, that Paul VI had reviewed and approved, formally encouraged in article 57 the formation of groups of council fathers who shared the same viewpoint in theological and pastoral matters. But, above all, the communiqué pretended not to know that within the council a progressively orientated "alliance" had been formed by one "particular" group there, well before the same thing had happened with the *Coetus Internationalis*. Moreover, the organized progressive minority worked with much greater force and efficacy than did the conservative minority.

The secretary of the *Coetus*, Abbé Berto, wrote to Bishop Carli that all the Church's affairs are "in the hands of a small permanent committee of the

---

18 Text of the letter in Caprile, 5:53. See also Wiltgen, 247–248.

19 Text in Caprile, 5:53–54.

episcopacy, which is, itself, a prisoner of 'secretaries,' 'theologians,' observers, and informants, who are not bishops, but are all 'progressives.' This cabal, I would be willing to say this 'mafia,' rules despotically, tyrannically, and heaven help the bishop who may have a wish independent of it."[20]

The problem for the conservative minority was how to oust the progressive minority from the dominant positions. On August 13, Archbishop de Proença Sigaud and Archbishop Lefebvre met again at Solesmes with Dom Prou, abbot of the monastery and superior general of the French Benedictines, devise a new overall strategy. The last phase of the council appeared to be the most delicate, likely to contain surprises and unexpected occurrences.

b) Cardinal Siri's criticisms

In a letter sent to the pope on the eve of the fourth session,[21] Cardinal Siri, who was acting independently from the *Coetus Internationalis*, set forth his critical evaluations on the three schemas: *De libertate religiosa, De Ecclesia in mundo huius temporis,* and *De revelatione.*[22]

The schema *De libertate religiosa*, he wrote, is "extremely and seriously perplexing"[23] especially for the following reason. It not only asserts but defends "religious liberty" repeatedly for all religious communities. Not "all" religious communities know the truth about God and live in accordance with divine law, nor even with natural theology and natural law; on the contrary, everywhere outside the Catholic Church one

---

[20] Letter from Father Berto to Bishop Carli dated May 2, 1965, in N. Buonasorte, "Per la 'pura, piena, integra fede cattolica,'" *op. cit.*, 139.

[21] Cf. AS V/3:352–354.

[22] "I think that at least with regard to these three schemas it is necessary to act boldly *ante sessionem concili* [before the council session]," Siri wrote to Cardinal Ruffini on August 6, 1965 (A-Siri, Conc. Vat. II, fasc. 1965, draft from Siri to Ruffini dated August 6, 1965), inviting him to intervene personally with the pope also. The cardinal of Palermo wrote back from Chianciano on August 12 that, while he shared Siri's concerns, it seemed to him that one should not confront the pope with new objections, after the ones that he himself had forwarded with Ottaviani and Larraona, which had caused him "so much displeasure as to make him wish for death" (Letter from Ruffini to Siri dated August 12, 1965, ibid., and in F. M. Stabile, *op. cit.*, 142).

[23] AS V/3:352.

finds errors, frequently deficiencies and even immoral and bloodthirsty deviations. With regard to the evil use of freedom, God "tolerates," he does not "legitimize." "It seems, therefore, necessary to conclude that we cannot defend 'religious liberty' in a case where objectively speaking there is evil; we can only 'tolerate' it, and do this only when stricter limits imposed by the demands of the common good do not enter in."[24]

The schema *De Ecclesia in mundo huius temporis*, also is "profoundly perplexing and frightening." "I really fear," the cardinal of Genoa wrote, "that the Christian people may be scandalized when they read a conciliar act that touches on aspects that directly concern the supernatural mission of the Church. I fear likewise that public opinion—at times not to be despised—may accuse this schema of being Maritainian in its inspiration. I do not mean here to refer to one Outstanding Man, but rather to his self-styled disciples, who go under the name of Maritainists."[25]

Finally, the schema *De Revelatione* "leaves to be desired a greater clarity concerning the constitutive tradition" that is part of the Church's habitual usage and of the common method of the theological schools. A more explicit clarity is desirable in placing "before and above all other means of hermeneutics, tradition and the magisterium of the Church."[26]

Cardinal Siri's criticisms, which were added to those of the *Coetus*, left its mark. On September 15, Cardinal Cicognani, at the instructions of Paul VI, forwarded the note to Bishop Felici, asking him to make these considerations known to the respective conciliar commissions.[27]

On September 24, Cardinal Ottaviani received from the pope, by way of Bishop Felici, a letter which said that it was the will of the supreme authority that the sub-commission speak more clearly about the "constitutive nature of tradition, as a source of revelation."[28]

---

24 Ibid., 353.

25 Ibid., 353.

26 Ibid., 354.

27 Cf. ASV, Conc. Vat. II, Busta 343, letter from Cicognani to Felici dated Sept. 15, 1965, 1 fol. See also AS V/3:352.

28 AS V/3:377.

3. The opening of the fourth session

On Wednesday, September 14, the fourth session of the council began, the final session that Raniero La Valle, in *Avvenire*, introduced as the session of "dialogue with the world."[29] In the liturgical ceremony Paul VI used neither the tiara nor the gestatorial chair (*sedes gestatoria*). In the opening speech[30] he intended to capture "the spirit" of the council that was about to conclude, asserting that it would be characterized not by condemnation but rather by love. Then the pope announced two unexpected "innovations": the institution of a Synod of Bishops (*Synodus episcoporum*), chosen for the most part from the episcopal conferences and approved by him, which were to be convoked "according to the needs of the Church, by the Roman pontiff, for his consultation and collaboration, when, for the general welfare of the Church, it will seem opportune to him";[31] and his impending visit to the United Nations Organization, on the occasion of the twentieth anniversary of its foundation, so as to bring to it a message of brotherhood and peace.

The Synod, instituted with the motu proprio *Apostolica sollicitudo*,[32] was an ecclesiastical body, without any real authority, apart from what the pontiff granted it ("*Nostrae potestati directe atque immediate subiectum*" [directly and immediately subject to our authority]), but the institution thereof, the first of the "post-conciliar era," combined with the trip to the United Nations,[33] seemed like a positive sign to the progressive circles, who had been disappointed after the "black week."[34] The discussion turned to the conciliar hall, where debate and voting on eleven schemas that had already been submitted to the assembly were on the agenda.

---

[29] Cf. R. La Valle, *L'Avvenire* (September 12, 1965), in *Il Concilio nelle nostre mani, op. cit.*, 3.

[30] Cf. AS IV/1:125–135; Ital. transl. in Caprile, 5:1–7.

[31] Caprile, 5:6.

[32] Cf. AAS 57 (1965): 771–780.

[33] Ibid., 776. The new Code of Canon Law, although limiting its competencies, places the Synod of Bishops (canons 342–348) before even the College of Cardinals and the Roman curia itself, as an administrative body assisting the supreme pontiff. Cf. N. Del Re, in MV, 986–988.

[34] On the first reactions to the *Synodus Episcoporum*, cf. M. Faggioli, *Il vescovo e il Concilio: Modello episcopale e aggiornamento al Vaticano II* (Bologna: Il Mulino, 2005).

4. The battle over religious liberty

a) Again the conservatives critique the schema

The first General Congregation of the fourth session opened with the debate on religious liberty. The cardinal moderators did not take into account the *Animadversiones criticae* (critical observations) of the document sent to them, on July 23, by the *Coetus Internationalis* and proposed, as a basis for the definitive declaration, the fourth version of the schema, on which the experts Murray and Pavan had worked, in close collaboration with Bishop De Smedt. This was the same De Smedt, who then served as its spokesman, on September 15, 1965, in the first congregation of the fourth session.[35] Seventy speakers took the floor on this subject,[36] on which, 218 new corrections had been sent in between the end of the third session and mid-February 1965.[37]

In the opening session, after Cardinals Spellman[38] and Frings spoke,[39] Cardinal Ruffini's intervention began a series of three increasingly intense critiques. The archbishop of Palermo foresaw the consequences that the declaration on Religious Liberty could have in Italy on the Lateran agreements incorporated in article 7 of the Constitution of the Italian Republic.

> With the pact between the Holy See and Italy, signed on February 11, 1929, it was established at the beginning that the Catholic, apostolic, Roman religion is the state religion and moreover the sole one; furthermore many special rights are reserved to ecclesiastics and to Catholics, for example exemption from military service, except in times of war, for clerics *in sacris* [in Holy Orders] and for religious men who have taken their vows…, full freedom to administer Church properties without any intervention by the civil authorities…, the validity of religious matrimony in the sight of the state also, the

[35] AS IV/1:196–199.

[36] Ibid., 200–431 and IV/2:11–21.

[37] AS IV/1:605–881.

[38] Ibid., 200–201.

[39] Ibid., 201–203.

> reservation of matrimonial cases to the ecclesiastical tribunals, the right to teach the Catholic religion in state schools.... If our declaration were to be approved, as it is shown to us today, then by virtue of this same declaration, all these aspects would be easily contested by our enemies, with an easy hope of victory.[40]

Cardinal Siri, in an intervention with a more doctrinal edge, recalled how man received freedom from God and is able to commit sin freely: an act that was not approved, but simply tolerated by God.

> The schema tries to defend freedom, and in general freedom should be defended in every way. But for us who are the successors of the apostles, it is more important to defend the divine order, it is more important to defend the divine law. Because if in defending freedom we undervalue the law, surely both theoretical and practical evils will result, which will foster indifferentism, both insofar as the fruits of the apostolate are concerned, and also through the illusion that many will believe that they can save their own souls by doing whatever they please and by deferring for a long time or forever their conversion to the true faith. I ask that we pay more attention to what the theological sources say about religious liberty and especially to what Leo XIII, Pius XI, and Pius XII said. If we introduce changes into their teaching by not discussing the true religion, at least on the basis of natural law, then I fear that we will diminish the value of the theological sources and will weaken our own authority.[41]

Cardinal Arriba y Castro, archbishop of Tarragona, spokesman for the Spanish episcopacy, delivered a short but limpid speech confirming the fundamental principle whereby

---

[40] Ibid., 204–207 at 206. In 1969 Paul VI had declared that he was not denying the possibility and the appropriateness "of reconsidering by common agreement several clauses of the concordat, for the purpose of an eventual combination thereof, which would result from a bilateral agreement, without prejudice to the constitutional guarantee assured by the Lateran Pacts within the jurisdiction of the Italian state" (Speech to the new ambassador from Italy on July 5, 1969, in *Insegnamenti* 7 [1969]: 476). So began a process that ended in the new concordat signed in Villa Madama on February 18, 1984, by the Secretary of State, Cardinal Casaroli, on behalf of the Holy See, and by the president of the council Bettino Craxi on behalf of the Italian state (on the nature and the consequences of it, cf. R. de Mattei, *L'Italia cattolica e il Nuovo Concordato* [Rome: Centro Culturale Lepanto, 1985]).

[41] AS IV/1:207–208 at 208.

> only the Catholic Church has the right and the duty to preach the gospel. Therefore proselytism by non-Catholics among Catholics is illicit, and to the extent permitted by the common good it must prevented not only by the Church but also by the state. Let the sacrosanct Second Vatican Council therefore see to it that it does not decree the ruin of the Catholic religion in nations where this religion is practically the only one. Indeed, once one has begun the discussion [about religious freedom], both in speech and in writing, there are many, especially among the most destitute, who, say: "It seems that all religions are equal." And they are very near concluding, "Therefore, none of them is important."[42]

This was the common approach of the Spanish bishops who, for the first time, showed a fighting spirit and solidarity in the council hall.[43] They seemed to foresee what would happen after the council, with the transformation of the concordat between Spain and the Holy See, the fall of the Franco regime, and the invasion of secularism in society.

b) The two groups confront each other

On September 16, five cardinals spoke in favor of religious liberty: Ritter,[44] Silva Henríquez,[45] Meouchi,[46] Slipyj,[47] and Jäger.[48] Speaking against it were

---

[42] Ibid., 209–210.

[43] This was the line taken by Bishop Angel Temiño Sáiz of Orense, in "Sobre la libertad religiosa en España," in *Revista Española de Teologia* XXIII/3 (1963): 277–308 and Father Jesus Muñoz, S.J., dean of the Faculty of Theology of the Pontifical University of Comillas, in his *Libertad religiosa aqui hoy* (Santander: Universidad Pontificia Comillas, 1964).

[44] AS IV/1:225–226.

[45] Ibid., 226–229.

[46] Ibid., 233–236. Pierre-Paul Meouchi (1894–1975), Lebanese, ordained in 1917, Maronite patriarch of Antioch from 1955 until his death, created cardinal in 1965. Member of the Commission for Eastern Churches.

[47] AS IV/1:236–239.

[48] Ibid., 239–241.

Bishops Carli,[49] Morcillo González,[50] Tagle[51] (in the name of forty-five Latin American bishops), and Velasco[52] (bishop in exile of Hsiamen in China). The last-mentioned bishop asserted that the schema encouraged pragmatism, indifferentism, religious naturalism, and subjectivism. Similar critiques were made by Del Campo[53] (naturalistic humanism), Alvim Pereira[54] (indifferentism), Gasbarri[55] (laicism, indifferentism, irenicism) and De Sierra y Mendez[56] (naturalism, indifferentism).

Bishop Carli cited the passage from the famous allocution of Pius XII, according to which "That which does not correspond to the truth and to the moral norm objectively has no right either to make propaganda or to spread."[57] His theses were repeated, on September 17, by Cardinal Florit[58] and Cardinal Ottaviani.[59]

The first asserted that

> The state's indifference in religious matters comes from its indifference towards their very nature. Indeed, the state is a natural society whose end is the common good of the citizens. Thus it belongs to the nature of the state to care for the whole common good (especially temporal

[49] Ibid., 263–266.

[50] Ibid., 245–248. Casimiro Morcillo González (1904–1971), Spanish, ordained in 1926, had been appointed auxiliary bishop of Madrid in 1943, and then became titular bishop of Bilbao (1950–1995) and Saragozza (1955–1964). He returned to Madrid in 1964 as archbishop. During the council he was part of the Secretariat.

[51] AS IV/1:274–277. Emilio Tagle Covarrubias (1907–1991), Chilean, ordained in 1930, archbishop of Valparaíso (Chile) from 1961 to 1983.

[52] AS IV/1:252–254.

[53] Ibid., 314–317.

[54] Ibid., 323–325. Custódio Alvim Pereira (1915–2006), Portuguese, ordained in 1937. Archbishop of Lourenço Marques (Mozambique) from 1962 to 1974.

[55] AS IV/1:325–327.

[56] Ibid., 328–330.

[57] Ibid., 266.

[58] Ibid., 284–292.

[59] Ibid., 299–301.

> good on this earth). But the common good has a much broader scope than the public order. It is made up of various and greater goods, such as truth and virtue, and furthermore the right disposition of the citizens and of society with regard to God, who gave life to society. Therefore attaining religious truth, preserving and defending it pertain to the natural end of the state. It follows from this that the limitations of religious liberty are not only of a public nature, but also and especially a necessity of religious truth.[60]

Cardinal Ottaviani insisted on the need to include in the schema

> a solemn affirmation of the objective, natural, and true right to freedom that the Church should enjoy because of her origin and mission, which are both divine.... It would be better to distinguish between physical constraint and moral constraint, or, even more than moral constraint, moral obligation. God does not constrain and yet he obliges, and therefore the gospel says, "He who believes and is baptized shall be saved; he who does not believe shall be condemned." And therefore, even/also Christ and the Church can impose a moral obligation, and in religious matters, that obliges in conscience.[61]

On the other hand some cardinals from Eastern Europe spoke in favor of religious freedom. They saw in the principle of religious freedom a line defense against communist totalitarianism. Among them, besides Slipyj who had intervened on September 16, were Cardinals Seper[62] (on September 17), Wyszyński,[63] and Beran[64] (on September 20). In particular the intervention of the archbishop of Prague, Beran, who had been freed from a communist prison the previous spring, had repercussions. He referred to the process against the heretic, Jan Hus, that ended at the stake, at Constance, in 1417, and described it a "trauma," that was "an obstacle to religious progress.... So history also warns us, that in this council the

---

[60] Ibid., 286.

[61] Ibid., 299–300.

[62] Ibid., 292–294.

[63] Ibid., 387–390.

[64] Ibid., 393–394.

principle of religious liberty and liberty of conscience must be enunciated in very clear words without any restrictions, which might stem from opportunistic motives."[65] The prelates from Eastern Europe, however, confused a factual situation, in which Catholics had the right to appeal to religious freedom against their persecutors, with a matter of principle that imposed on Catholic states the profession of the true religion, in obedience to the dictate of the First Commandment.

When Cardinal Urbani, patriarch of Venice, on behalf of thirty-two Italian bishops, declared himself in favor of the text by De Smedt, the coalition of the Italian episcopacy, which had been solid up till then, cracked.[66] Paul VI's decision to entrust to Urbani the presidency of the Italian Bishops' Conference seemed to be bearing the expected fruit.[67]

The final words on the schema on religious liberty were the opposing interventions of Cardinal Dante[68] and of the Swiss theologian Charles Journet,[69] both of them cardinals recently created by Paul VI. Journet, accompanied by the Abbé Pierre Mamie,[70] his secretary, and by Father Georges Cottier,[71] rarely attended the discussions, because of his deafness that kept him from following the debates accurately. With a printed intervention that was decidedly Maritainian, he wanted to bring to bear in support of the declaration on religious liberty his authority as a theologian, asserting that it deserved the utmost approval: *"Mihi videtur maxime approbanda."*[72]

---

65 Ibid. English translation in *Council Daybook*, 3:35–36 at 36.

66 Ibid., 211–213.

67 G. Routhier, "Finishing the Work Begun," *op. cit.*, 68.

68 AS IV/1:422–423.

69 Ibid., 424–425. Charles Journet (1891–1975), Swiss, ordained in 1917. Professor at the Major Seminary of Fribourg, was created cardinal in February 1965. About him see, among other studies, *Montini, Journet, Maritain: une famille d'esprit*, Acts of a Study Day in Molsheim, June 4–5, 1999 (Brescia: Pubblicazioni dell'Istituto Paolo VI, 2000); Guillaume de Thieulloy, *La théologie politique du cardinal Journet* (Paris: Téqui, 2009).

70 Pierre Mamie, born in 1920, Swiss, ordained in 1946, auxiliary bishop (1968), then bishop of Lausanne, Geneva, and Fribourg from 1970 to 1995. Secretary of Cardinal Journet during the council.

71 Georges Cottier (1922–), Swiss Dominican. Professor of philosophy in Fribourg, secretary of the review *Nova et Vetera* edited by Charles Journet. Created cardinal in 2003. *Peritus* at the council during the fourth session.

72 AS IV/1:425.

Cardinal Dante emphasized, on the contrary, the fact that the declaration expressed what the supporters of Catholic liberalism wanted in the nineteenth century, from Lamennais to Montalembert, echoing the tenth declaration of the French Revolution on the rights of man, that reads: "No one should be persecuted because of his opinions, including religious ones, as long as their manifestation does not disturb the public order that is established by law."[73]

Concerning the doctrine of "just limits," mentioned in the declaration, such as "peace, civil rights, public morality," Cardinal Dante observed:

> a) If the state that has established these "limits" is Christian, it conforms these same principles (precisely those things, namely peace, etc.) to the natural law, and specifically adapts its laws and its juridical order to it more or less; hence the terms peace, civil law, public morality are assured of having a decent, reasonable meaning.
>
> b) But if the state is pagan, then these "limits," if they do not leave the natural law out of consideration entirely, are generic, and can easily become an instrument of oppression (*tyrranide*), not only against false religions, but also against the one true religion; indeed the interpretation of the meaning of these limits depends on those who manage the state.
>
> c) Finally, if the state is communist, these "limits," *i.e.* peace, civil rights, and public morality, have an entirely different or even contrary meaning, because this type of state has clearly established or usually establishes such "limits" against the law of nature.
>
> Therefore these "limits" are a sure instrument of oppression, and what the declaration on religious liberty wants to obtain, namely freedom of religion, is a thousand miles away from us. On the contrary, the more rigorously a religion seems to a communist state to comply with the natural law, the more violently is it persecuted by the state itself."[74]

---

[73] Ibid., 422.

[74] Ibid., 423.

c) Vatican Council II and Freemasonry

Like Cardinal Dante, Archbishop Lefebvre too, in his intervention, recalled that the origin of religious liberty was to be sought "outside the Church, with the self-styled philosophers of the eighteenth century: Hobbes, Locke, Rousseau, Voltaire,"[75] and in the mid-nineteenth century Lamennais and the Catholic liberals tried in vain to adapt this notion to the teaching of the Church. They were condemned by Pius IX and by Leo XIII. "This year (1965)," the French archbishop added, "the Freemason Yves Marsaudon published a book, *L'oecuménisme vu par un franc-maçon de tradition* (Ecumenism as Seen by a Traditional Freemason).[76] The author of the book expresses in it the Freemasons' desire that our council solemnly proclaim religious freedom.... What more do you want in order to be well informed?"[77]

Baron de Marsaudon's book was dedicated to John XXIII, and was supposed to serve as a "bridge" between the Church and Freemasonry. Among other things, one reads in it:

> In these days, our brother Franklin Roosevelt has claimed for all men the possibility "of adoring God by following their principles and their convictions." This is tolerance and ecumenism as well. We, traditional Freemasons, venture to paraphrase and transpose this advice of a famous statesman by adapting it to the circumstances: Catholics, Orthodox, protestants, Jews, Muslims, Hindus, Buddhists, freethinkers, free believers, are for us only [given] names; Freemason is the family name [of them all].[78]

Then Marsaudon explicitly referred to the "revolution of freedom of conscience desired by John XXIII":

---

75 AS IV/2:409–411 at 409.

76 Cf. Yves Marie Marsaudon, *L'oecuménisme vu par un franc-maçon de tradition*, Preface by Charles Riandey (Paris: Éditions Vitiano, 1964). Yves Marie Marsaudon (1895–1985), French, state official, was a member of the Supreme Council of the Scottish Rite, then of the National Grand Lodge of France. See his other book, *Souvenirs et réflexions: un haut dignitaire de la franc-maçonnerie de tradition révèle des secrets* (Paris: Vitiano, 1976). Marsaudon had met Archbishop Roncalli several times when he was nuncio in Paris.

77 AS IV/2:410.

78 Y. Marsaudon, *L'oecuménisme vu par un franc-maçon de tradition, op. cit.*, 126.

> We do not think that a Freemason worthy of this name, who is himself committed to practice tolerance, would be unable to rejoice unconditionally over the irreversible results of the council, whatever the momentary conclusions may be.[79]

In 1960, Father Giovanni Caprile, and the *Civiltà Cattolica*'s expert on Masonic problems, had published a small volume on Freemasonry, in which he recalled that "the philosophical and pseudo-religious principles professed by that sect are completely antithetical to all of Christianity;[80] the book contained more than two hundred documents issued by the Apostolic See condemning Freemasonry.[81] In the course of the council, Caprile championed a *rapprochement* between the Church and Freemasonry that had its roots, as he wrote, precisely in the assembly hall.[82] Father Caprile explained that "the council did not speak of Freemasonry, but… there was

---

[79] Ibid., 120.

[80] G. Caprile, *La Massoneria* (Colle Don Bosco [Asti]: Universale LDC, 1960), 45.

[81] Cf. G. Cantoni, "La Massoneria nei documenti del Magistero della Chiesa," in Cesnur (Centro Studi sulle Nuove Religioni), *Massoneria e religioni*, ed. M. Introvigne (Leumann: Elle Di Ci, 1994), 133–161.

[82] Cf. José Antonio Ferrer Benimeli, S.J., and Giovanni Caprile, S.J., *Massoneria e Chiesa cattolica ieri, oggi e domani*, 2nd ed. with an updated appendix, edited by Fr. G. Caprile, S.J., (Roma: Edizioni Paoline, 1982), 85–94. Fr. Caprile had authored vehemently polemical works against Freemasonry between 1957 and 1960. After the council he arrived at the conviction that it was to be hoped that there could be "a productive encounter not only on the level of ideas, but also on the level of a possible collaboration between the Church and the authentic Freemasonry that has as the foundation of its statues a firm belief in God and in human fraternity" (ibid., 131). During the council, the activity of "occult forces" was denounced by the French Catholic scholars Léon de Poncins (1897–1976) and Pierre Virion (1898–1988). By the first author see *Christianisme et Franc-maçonnerie* (Chiré-en-Montreuil: Diffusion de la Pensée, 1975); by the second cf. *Bientôt un gouvernement mondial* (Paris: Téqui, 1967), which brings to light the project for a "new Christianity" by the apostate canon Paul Roca (1830–1893). On that historical personage see also Marie-France James, *Esotérisme, occultisme, franc-maçonnerie et christianisme au XIXème et XXème siècle: Explorations bio-bibliographiques*, Preface by Emile Poulat (Paris: Nouvelles Éditions Latines, 1981), 228–230. On the topic of the council and Freemasonry, see also the study by Father Paolo Siano, F.I., "Alcune note su Concilio e postconcilio, tra storia, ermeneutica e massoneria," in *Fides catholica* 2 (2009): 317–382.

talk about it in the council."[83] He began his progressive "transfer" precisely at a time when the Secretariat for Non-believers had been trying, since its inception, to initiate "dialogue" with Freemasonry as well. "Let us dialogue not only with Christians of other confessions in our search for the unity desired by Christ," the secretary of the secretariat, Don Vincenzo Miano wrote, "But also the Jews, the Muslims, the Hindus, and even the secular ideologies, although excluding all impossible syncretism, because we think that even in these religious faiths and ideologies, which are so different or even opposed, we can find positive elements and reasons for deepening our own faith-experience. How could and should this not be done with Freemasonry, especially given its historical Christian ancestry?"[84]

d) Paul VI's decisive intervention

The interventions for and against the declaration on religious liberty were equally numerous and authoritative. But the outcome of the vote, in this case and in others, did not reflect the objective fissure in the council hall. Paul VI wanted to avoid this rupture, but he needed at least an indicative vote on the schema before leaving for his visit to the U.N., fearing the consequences on the international level of a postponement of the voting.

On the evening of September 20, the directive bodies of the council (Moderators, Board of Presidency, and Coordinating Commission) met in a plenary session, and decided after a spirited discussion that in light of the strong and authoritative critiques that the document had been subjected to, it was better to set aside the topic of religious liberty.[85] The reaction, however, was violent, especially on the part of the press organizations with wider circulation. Then, on September 21, something happened that no one was expecting: Paul VI decided to intervene in that turbulent development by giving the peremptory order that the fathers were invited to pass judgment on the text that same morning.[86] They proceeded to a vote, and by some

---

[83] *Massoneria e Chiesa cattolica, op. cit.*, 88–89.

[84] Note by Vincenzo Miano, S.D.B., in R. F. Esposito, *La riconciliazione tra la Chiesa e la massoneria, op. cit.*, 11–16 at 16. Cardinal König, president of the Secretariat, rejected in 1980 the anti-Masonic declaration of the German Bishops' Conference, continuing to work to abolish the excommunication for Freemasonry.

[85] Cf. G. Routhier, "Finishing the Work Begun," *op. cit.*, 97–100.

[86] AS IV/1:564.

mysterious psychological mechanism that melted the opposition, out of 2,220 present, there were 1,997 ballots marked *placet*, against 224 *non placet*, and one abstention. The result of this first ballot already forecast the outcome of the debate in the following General Congregation.[87] During an audience granted to De Smedt, Paul VI showed his satisfaction with the text, adding, "This document is first-rate [*capitale*]. It establishes the Church's attitude for several centuries. The world awaits it."[88]

When the fifth version of the schema was put to a series of votes on October 26 and 27, hundreds of *modi* accompanied the ballots marked *placet iuxta modum*. The document was reviewed once again and the sixth version was distributed to the fathers on Wednesday, November 17. The next day, the *Coetus Internationalis* managed to distribute to eight hundred fathers a letter in which, while admitting that there had been remarkable improvements, it noted that the criterion determining the limits of religious liberty ought to have been not the preservation of law or of order, but rather the common good, of which order and law are only a part. The fundamental thesis of the Secretariat for Promoting Christian Unity was instead that the neutrality of the state should be considered as the normal condition and that there does not have to be cooperation between Church and state except "in particular circumstances." At issue was a position that, quite obviously, modififed the traditional teaching of the Church on this point.

When the whole of the text was put to a vote, on November 19, 1965, 1,954 fathers declared themselves in favor and 249 against.[89] The text had therefore received much more than the required two-thirds majority, but the number of negative votes was among the highest ever for a conciliar document. "Despite all his efforts," Gilles Routhier observes, "Paul VI had not succeeded in putting together the consensus he so badly wanted, even at the price of compromises for which many reproached him."[90]

Those opposed to the decree on Religious Liberty did not surrender. A statement by Cardinal Siri, dated November 27, revealed the reasons for

---

87 P. Pavan, "Testimonianza," *op. cit.*, 188; see also V. Carbone, "Il ruolo di Paolo VI nell'evoluzione e nella redazione della Dichiarazione 'Dignitatis humanae,'" in *Paolo VI e il rapporto Chiesa-mondo.* "It is to a great extent thanks to the pope," Grootaers points out, "that the plan for the declaration succeeded in avoiding countless shoals so as finally to arrive safe and sound" ("Paul VI et la déclaration conciliaire 'Dignitatis humanae,'" *op. cit.*, 87).

88 G. Routhier, "Finishing the Work Begun," *op. cit.*, 113.

89 For the results of the voting, cf. AS IV/7:95–96.

90 G. Routhier, "Finishing the Work Begun," *op. cit.*, 122.

his "*summae perplexitatis* [utmost bewilderment]" in regard to the limits of civil power in religious matters.[91] On December 3, Bishop Giuseppe Di Meglio,[92] a specialist in international law, publicized a letter that said that the results of the vote indicated "that for a notable number of council fathers the teaching and practical applications of the schema are not acceptable in conscience. In fact, the fundamental principle of the schema has remained unchanged despite the amendments that have been introduced: that is, the right of error.... Since the declaration on religious freedom has no dogmatic value, the negative votes of the council fathers will constitute a factor of great importance for the future studies of the declaration itself, and particularly for the interpretation to be placed on it."[93]

Father Murray, one of the "fathers" of the document, replied to this declaration by recalling that the partisans of the "more modern theory of religious liberty" were convinced that the "dignity of the human person" was what required this liberty.[94]

According to *Dignitatis humanae*,[95] the human person has the right, by virtue of his dignity, not to be hindered from the practice of his own religious worship, whatever it may be, in private or in public, unless it disturbs the peace and public morality; the right to human freedom is founded on the self-same dignity of the human person (no. 2). It is not a question of an "affirmative" right to freedom of conscience, but of a "negative" right not to be hindered in exercising it: or else a right to "immunity from coercion in religious matters" in public and private worship (no. 4). With that, the document had cancelled out the fundamental distinction between "the internal forum," that concerns the eternal salvation of individual believers, and the "external forum" that is related to the public good of the community of the faithful.[96] The Church has always taught religious liberty in the internal forum, because no man can to be forced to believe. But this interior freedom which, as such, no external force can coerce,

---

91 AS V/3:633–635.

92 Giuseppe Di Meglio (1907–1994), ordained in 1929, served in the nunciature in Vienna (1937), and the one in Berlin (1938), and after the war in the Congregation of the Holy Office.

93 Wiltgen, p. 251.

94 Cf. D. Gonnet, "L'apport de John Courtney Murray," *op. cit.*, 205–215.

95 Text in AS IV/7:663–673.

96 Cf. D. Staffa, article "Foro" in EC, 5:1531–1534.

does not imply religious liberty in the external forum, that is to say the public practice of any worship whatsoever or the profession of any error. Religious liberty was invoked, after *Dignitatis humanae*, in order to suppress every type of "protection" of the Catholic Church by the states, but the refusal on the part of the civil authority to recognize the mission and role of the Church and the existence of an objective natural law that is to be safeguarded, opened the door, at the same time, to the spread of relativism and to the spread of other religions, starting with Islam. Relativism asserted itself by denying to the state any form of religious and moral censorship as it faced rampant de-Christianization. Islam, in the name of this same religious freedom, demanded the construction of mosques and minarets, which were destined to surpass in number the churches that had been abandoned or transformed into hotels and supermarkets.

5. Schema XIII: criticisms from opposite sides

a) The presentation of the schema

On September 21, in the 132nd General Congregation, while the discussion on religious liberty was coming to an end, the council began the discussion of the draft of the pastoral constitution on the *Church in the Modern World*, the so-called "schema 13," a number that defined it as the last of the council's documents in logical and chronological order.[97] The project, wrote Raniero La Valle in *L'Avvenire d'Italia*, was destined to "show mankind the most advanced stage, as it were the new frontier to which the Church, starting with the great witness of John XXIII, had set out and was advancing in these years."[98]

In early February 1965, in Ariccia, in the vicinity of Rome, the schema had been completely revised in the course of a week's work, in which

[97] Text in AS IV/3:435–552. Cf. G. Turbanti, *Un concilio per il mondo moderno: La redazione della costituzione pastorale "Gaudium et spes" del Vaticano II* (Bologna: Il Mulino, 2000); see also J. A. Komonchak, "Le valutazioni sulla 'Gaudium et spes': Chenu, Dossetti, Ratzinger," in Joseph Doré and A. Melloni, *Volti di fine Concilio: Studi di storia e teologia sulla conclusione del Vaticano II* (Bologna: Il Mulino, 2001), 116–153 at 125–136. Chenu's speech was reprinted in *Peuple de Dieu dans le monde* (Paris: Foi vivante, 1966), 11–34.

[98] R. La Valle, *Il Concilio nelle nostre mani, op. cit.*, 102.

twenty-nine council fathers, thirty-eight experts, and about twenty laymen had participated, not counting the male and female auditors.[99] It was just the beginning of a frenetic series of new revisions of the text (seven for the doctrinal part and as many again for the "attachments"), in which a leading role was played by Monsignor Philips[100] and the major criticisms came from Archbishop Karol Wojtyla, the author of an alternative proposal that was not accepted. After it had been examined by the Central Sub-commission and by the Mixed Commission (the Theological Commission and the Commission of the Apostolate of the Laity), the text was finally approved by the Coordinating Commission on May 11 and by the pope on May 28. But Cardinal Ruffini confided to Cardinal Siri that schema 13 "should be radically redone so as to frame it in terms of the proper mission of the Church; otherwise the council would become a session of the U.N.O."[101]

The German and French theologians, who disagreed among themselves on what judgment to pass on the document, met on September 17 at Regina Mundi for a "'conciliar strategy' meeting."[102] "Schema 13 should not be rejected or demolished, because that would play into the hands of the conservatives, but it should be improved," Congar recommended.[103]

On September 21, because the reporter, Bishop Guano, was sick, the text was presented in the hall by Bishop Garrone, who emphasized that the problem of man was "the soul of the entire schema," which intended to offer, in summary form, the fundamental outlines of a "Christian anthropology."[104] The next day, in a conference held at the Dutch Center of Documentation, Chenu passionately defended schema 13, responding especially to the reservations that the German theologians had put forth.[105] The criticisms of the text that "was constructed as a sociological treatise

[99] Cf. C. Moeller, *L'élaboration du schéma XIII, op. cit.*, 108–114; G. Turbanti, *Un concilio per il mondo moderno, op. cit.*, 502–614.

[100] Cf. C. Moeller, *L'élaboration du schéma XIII, op. cit.*, 116–120.

[101] Letter from Cardinal E. Ruffini to Cardinal G. Siri dated August 12, 1965.

[102] The expression is used by Congar, who gives an account of the meeting: Congar, *Journal*, 779–780.

[103] Ibid., 779.

[104] AS IV/1:553–558.

[105] *L'Avvenire d'Italia* (September 23, 1965) and G. Turbanti, *Un concilio per il mondo moderno, op. cit.*, 643–651.

rather than a conciliar decree," as Alberigo writes,[106] came, as a matter of fact, from the opposite side of the assembly.

At the end of the discussion, Bishop Garrone said that the commission would take into account all the observations and would strive to produce a new, shorter, and clearer text.

b) Critiques of the document's optimism

The German-speaking bishops and theologians, like Rahner[107] and Ratzinger,[108] challenged the overly optimistic tone of the document, which was due, in their opinion, to the influence of the French theologians. Bishop Höffner,[109] bishop of Münster, asserted, in the name of eighty-four German-speaking bishops, that chapter 3, which dealt with man's social and economic life, had to be completely redone because the text gave the impression that sincere cooperation among men was the sole condition for a just social order. Speaking in the name of ninety-one council fathers from German-speaking and Nordic countries, Cardinal Döpfner[110] asserted that the schema had made great progress, but the natural and supernatural orders were not clearly distinguished and the serious consequences of the state of sin were not set forth appropriately. The group from Bologna also made their misgivings plain. Dossetti wrote an intervention for Cardinal Lercaro that called the whole schema into question by pointing out all "its defects and ambiguities."[111] There was a big difference, Lercaro

---

[106] Cf. G. Alberigo, *A Brief History*, 100.

[107] Cf. K. Rahner, "Über den Dialog in der pluralistischen Gesellschaft," in *Stimmen der Zeit* 176 (1965): 321–330.

[108] Cf. J. Ratzinger, "Angesichts der Welt von heute: Überlegungen zur Konfrontation mit der Kirche im Schema XIII," in *Wort und Wahrheit* 20 (1965): 439–504. A revised version appeared in an anthology of Ratzinger's essays, *Dogma und Verkündigung*, and was translated into English as "The Christian in the Modern World," in J. Ratzinger, *Dogma and Preaching* (San Francisco: Ignatius Press, 2011), 162–180.

[109] Joseph Höffner (1906–1987), German, ordained in 1932, bishop of Münster in 1962, titular archbishop of Aquileia and archbishop of Cologne in 1969. Created cardinal that same year.

[110] AS IV/2:28–33.

[111] Text in AS IV/1:761–764. For the original Italian, cf. G. Lercaro, *Per la forza dello Spirito, op. cit.*, 253–261. See also J. A. Komonchak, "Le valutazioni sulla 'Gaudium et spes,'" *op. cit.*, 136–144.

declared, between "thoroughly supernatural Christian optimism" and "the naturalistic optimism that easily and timidly follows and undergoes the phenomenology of human progress and does not know or else avoids the principle whereby everyone and everything 'will be salted with fire' (Mk 9:49), with the fire of the cross and of the Spirit of Christ."[112]

Cardinal Bea[113] criticized the almost unintelligible Latin of the document, calling for a revision of its style, so as to allow an efficacious distribution of it in modern languages. On September 22, Cardinal Ruffini[114] deplored the fact that the Church was presented "almost on her knees," "as though in a guilty attitude before the world."[115] Cardinal Siri[116] and Cardinal König[117] who spoke after him, demanded the insertion into the schema of fundamental elements that it lacked, such as sin, the truth of the cross, the need for repentance and the hope for the resurrection in Christ.

Archbishop Amici[118] of Modena, acting as spokesman for a group of Italian bishops, asserted that the entire text needed to be revised, because neither its form nor its substance was satisfactory. By thus communicating little to those who wanted to know the true Christian conception of life, the schema did not succeed in establishing a point of dialogue with modern man.

To Archbishop Giuseppe D'Avack,[119] titular archbishop of Leontopolis, the document seemed to be imbued with naturalism. At least in its conclusions, he asked, let the schema explain the "secret of Christianity," a "secret" whereby love can be lived out only with the help of the grace that Christ merited for man through the cross.[120]

---

[112] G. Lercaro, *Per la forza dello Spirito, op. cit.*, 255–256.

[113] AS IV/1:576–596.

[114] AS IV/2:21–23.

[115] Ibid., 22.

[116] Ibid., 24–25.

[117] Ibid., 26–27.

[118] Ibid., 34–36. Giuseppe Amici (1901–1977), ordained in 1926, consecrated bishop of Troia in 1951, bishop of Foggia in 1954 and of Cesena in 1955, archbishop of Modena in 1956.

[119] Giuseppe D'Avack (1899–1979), ordained in 1923, archbishop of Camerino from 1946 to 1964, then titular archbishop of Leontopolis in Pamphylia.

[120] AS IV/2:44–45.

On September 23, Bishop Lourdusamy,[121] coadjutor to the archbishop of Bangalore, speaking in the name of sixty-two Indian bishops, gave his support of the text, but he too requested some improvements, so that the argumentation of the schema might be founded more on theology than on natural philosophy.[122]

Cardinal Rugambwa[123] (Bukoba, Tanzania) and Cardinal Shehan[124] (Baltimore) were in favor of it, while Bishop Antonio de Castro Mayer criticized it because it failed to point out the incompatibility between the Christian concept of the world and the one championed by Marxist dialectical materialism.[125] Among the many who then took the floor were: [1] Cardinal Frings, who asked that the text be completely reorganized, because of the dangerous confusion that it introduced between human progress, which results from dialogue, and supernatural salvation, which is the fruit of the Church's mission,[126] and [2] the archbishop of Krakow, Karol Wojtyla, who on September 28 gave what some would consider his most important speech at Vatican Council II,[127] clinching the personalist anthropology that he had already had to occasion to expound in the hall.[128]

The proposals were extremely varied. From a petition to the pope asking him to define dogmatically "the universal brotherhood of man" (Bishop

---

121 Duraisamy Simon Lourdusamy (1924–), Indian, ordained in 1951, auxiliary bishop of Bangalore and titular bishop of Sozusa in 1962, coadjutor archbishop of Bangalore and titular archbishop of Philippi in 1964, created cardinal in 1996.

122 AS IV/2:380–383.

123 Ibid., 366–368. Laurean Rugambwa (1912–1997), Tanzanian, ordained in 1943. Bishop of Bukoba from 1953 to 1968, created cardinal in 1960, archbishop of Darres-Salaam from 1968 to 1992. Member of the Commission for the Missions.

124 AS IV/2:368–370. Lawrence Shehan (1898–1984), from the United States, ordained in 1922, archbishop of Baltimore from 1961 to 1974, created cardinal in 1965. Member of the Commission for the Discipline of the Clergy and of the Christian People.

125 AS IV/2:371–373.

126 Ibid., 405–406 at 406.

127 Cf. George Weigel, *Witness to Hope: The Biography of Pope John Paul II* (New York: Harper-Collins Publishers, 2001), 168–169 (more generally on Archbishop Wojtyła's presence at the council, see 145–180, and *Actes et acteurs*, 105–129). The text of the speech is in AS IV/2:660–663.

128 AS III/5:298–300 and 680–683.

Soares de Rezende[129] of Beira in Mozabique), to the petition of Bishop Ddungu[130] of Masaka in Uganda, who, speaking in the name of ninety-four bishops, deplored the fact that the theme of racial discrimination was handled in a very superficial and confused way: only four lines were dedicated to this problem and its solution.[131] Bishop Fernandes,[132] auxiliary of the archbishop of Delhi, speaking in the name of all the Indian bishops and of more than one hundred other council fathers from Asia, Africa, Europe, Latin America and Canada, asked for the creation of a permanent post-conciliar commission "for the promotion of international justice and of the integrated development of all peoples."[133]

c) Teilhard de Chardin mentioned again in the hall

Bishop Méndez Arceo,[134] who spoke on September 28, wanted instead to point out the schema's "inexplicable silence" on psychoanalysis, a genuine "scientific revolution" that placed Freud's "brilliant discovery" on the same level as those of Copernicus and Darwin. Along the same line the Indian archbishop D'Souza opined, "In the past year, one of the moderators exclaimed that 'one Galileo case is enough.' But meanwhile we have had, among others, the case of Lamennais, the cases of Darwin, Marx, Freud, and, finally, the case of Teilhard de Chardin."[135] Bishop Câmara, who considered Bishop D'Souza "a friend" and "a great council father,"[136] deplored, however, the excessive clarity of the intervention,

---

[129] AS IV/2:643–645. Sebastiào Soares de Rezende (1906–1967), Portuguese, ordained in 1928, bishop of Beira (Mozambique) from 1943 until his death.

[130] Adrian Kivumbi Ddungu (1923–2009), Ugandan, ordained in 1952. Bishop of Masaka (Uganda) from 1961 to 1998.

[131] AS IV/3:110–111.

[132] Angelo Fernandes (1913–2000), Indian, ordained in 1937, coadjutor archbishop of Delhi from 1959 to 1967.

[133] AS IV/2:720–722.

[134] Ibid., 625–628.

[135] Ibid., 477–479 at 478.

[136] Câmara, *Lettres Conciliaires*, 2:843.

which ran the risk of being counterproductive. Cardinal Suenens, who did not think otherwise, was in his opinion more skillful: "When Father Michel (Suenens) needs to use the big guns, he does not do so in the basilica, but in print."[137]

Grand Master Marsaudon, in the book that Archbishop Lefebvre had cited in the hall, had identified Teilhard de Chardin's evolution of the cosmos as the meeting point between Freemasonry and Christianity.

> Knowledge, philosophy, and metaphysics draw near to one another. Between the Masonic formula of the Great Architect of the Universe and the Omega-point of Teilhard de Chardin, it is hard to discern what would keep thinking men from coming to an agreement. Currently Teilhard de Chardin is certainly the author who is read most, both in the Freemason lodges and in the seminaries.[138]

Archbishop de Proença Sigaud[139] also mentioned the French Jesuit's name, but in order to criticize roundly his influence on the council. For the archbishop of Diamantina, schema 13 had had recourse to Teilhard de Chardin's dangerous idea about the "construction of the world," while forgetting that the tower of Babel also tried to be a new creation of the world.

> "This 'Teilhardian' (Teilhard de Chardin) idea about the construction of the world with God is dangerous. The tower of Babel was a 'construction of the world.' The hedonism of the Greeks and Romans was a 'construction of the world.' Nevertheless, these did not lead to God, but to sin and corruption and ultimately to the destruction of the nations."[140]

---

137 Ibid., 844.

138 Y. Marsaudon, *op. cit.*, 60.

139 AS IV/2:47–50.

140 Ibid., 49.

d) Overpopulation and birth-control

In the course of the discussion of schema 13, the problem of Christian matrimony and of "birth control" was dealt with once again on September 29.[141] The text formulated some principles of a general character, asserting that it was up to the spouses to "determine the number of children," but without specifying the means by which that could happen. Cardinal Ruffini[142] judged that the nature of matrimony was very poorly described and that it emerged much more clearly from *Casti connubii*[143] by Pius XI, especially as far as the distinction between primary and secondary ends was concerned. The secondary ends were extolled so much in the schema as to seem indispensable, even if it were to mean "avoiding procreation." The cardinal brought to light the parts of the text that, in his opinion, seemed to sow doubts and confusion along the path of wedded couples with, for instance on page 49, where the document said that spouses, in starting and governing their own family, "should be guided by their conscience, which has been properly formed by God's law, and it is their task to determine the number of children, in accordance what God's gifts permit and what true love dictates."[144] From such expressions, according to the cardinal, doubts and anxieties could arise even among virtuous and religious spouses, not only with regard to the *vexata quaestio* (much-debated question) of "the pill," inanely called the Catholic question, but also concerning the way to arrange married life in general. In particular, one truth of the utmost importance is not affirmed in the schema: that it is always shameful, dishonest, and contrary to nature to deprive the matrimonial act of its natural procreative power.

The schema was defended, however, by Cardinals Léger,[145] Suenens,[146] and Colombo.[147] Léger declared the decision to reaffirm the teaching of

---

141 J. Grootaers and J. Jans, *La régulation des naissances à Vatican II: une semaine de crise* (Louvain: Peeters, 2002).

142 AS IV/3:17–20.

143 Pius XI, encylical *Casti connubii, op. cit.*, 541–573. The encylical declares, "The child holds the first place among the blessings of matrimony" (Denz-H, n. 3704).

144 AS IV/3:18.

145 Ibid., 21–25.

146 Ibid., 30–33.

147 Ibid., 33–37.

Pius XI's *Casti connubii* "very serious." Colombo, while declaring that he was in favor of the "personalist" approach to matrimony, confirmed the reasons for a clear-cut refusal of contraceptive practices.

On October 7, Bishop Mariano G. Gaviola[148] of Cabanatuan City (Philippines), expressed in the hall his surprise at the attitude that the fathers seemed to have taken on the "population explosion." The fact that the schema affirmed the right of parents to decide the number of their children, he said, is surprising, because "it seems to agree with the theory that the overpopulation of the world will be a certain fact, at a time not too distant from our own." Everyone knows, Bishop Gaviola continued, that the proponents of birth control and planned parenthood "derive their chief arguments from the theory of overpopulation" and that frequently "their real motive is economic profit rather than a true concern for the common good."[149] The bishop concluded by making an appeal that "the very great number of true Christian families" that accept the children sent by God, might not be "left in oblivion."[150]

The intervention by Bishop Elias Zoghby,[151] patriarchal vicar of the Melkites of Egypt, on September 29, was a "bomb" that, as the newspapers put it, went off in the hall. In fact, the prelate brought into the debate the indissolubility of marriage, coming to the defense of the "innocent spouse" in a divorced couple and hoping that in this case the council would decide to apply the practice of the Orthodox Churches.[152] The "dossier" to prepare his intervention had been prepared by the Benedictine, Dom Olivier Rousseau, a disciple of Dom Beauduin.[153] The next morning, Cardinal Journet replied forcefully, reiterating that the positive, divine command of the indissolubility of marriage did not allow the Church to make exceptions or derogations.[154] Journet, as Father Wenger mentions,

---

148 Mariano Gaviola y Garcés (1922–1998), Filipino, ordained in 1949, bishop of Cabanatuan (1963–1967), then titular Bishop of Girba (1967) and archbishop of Lipa (1981–1992).

149 AS IV/3:645–647 at 645.

150 Ibid., 647.

151 Elias Zoghby (1912–2008), Egyptian, ordained in 1936, vicar to the Melkite patriarch for Egypt, imprisoned in 1954 by the Nasser regime, and kidnapped in 1982 by pro-Nasser terrorists.

152 Cf. AS IV/3:45–48.

153 Cf. E. Lanne, "Il monastero di Chevetogne," *op. cit.*, 537–538.

154 Cf. AS IV/3:58–59.

had been asked by Paul VI himself to intervene and had worked on his text until one o'clock in the morning.[155]

Other speakers dwelt on the distinction between the primary end and the secondary end of matrimony. Father Schillebeeckx, in a conference held on September 29, claimed to reverse, in the name of St. Thomas, the relation of priority between the ends of matrimony that had been established by the tradition and magisterium of the Church.[156] On October 23, 1965, Cardinal Suenens spent more than an hour with Paul VI, persistently requesting: 1) the radical reform of the curia; 2) the establishment of a post-conciliar commission to implement Vatican II; 3) and above all a clear stance in favor of birth control. Faced with this persistence the pope replied: "Let's do it this way: put yourself in my shoes: imagine that you are the pope and write the declaration that you would like to write in the sight of God and considering humanity. Bring this declaration to me without delay and I promise you to study it on my knees."[157] Suenens did not wait to be asked twice, and after consulting with Bishop Albert Prignon, rector of the Belgian College, Bishop Joseph Reuss, auxiliary of Magonza, and Bishop Victor Heylen, professor of moral theology at Louvain, he brought the pope a text that Câmara describes as "a masterpiece."[158]

Among the interventions that followed, the one by the new archbishop of Turin, Michele Pellegrino,[159] former professor of ancient Christian literature, caused a sensation. It made an appeal for freedom of research and was critical of the excessive punishments that had been meted out during the modernist crisis, adding that they had continued into recent times.[160] "I," said Bishop Pellegrino, "knew a religious in exile, certainly not

---

[155] Cf. A. Wenger, "Discussione," in *Paolo VI e il rapporto Chiesa-mondo*, 39.

[156] Cf. R. La Valle, *Il Concilio nelle nostre mani, op. cit.*, 189–192.

[157] Câmara, *Lettres conciliaires*, 2:952.

[158] Ibid.

[159] Michele Pellegrino (1903–1986), ordained in 1925. Professor at the University of Turin from 1943 to 1965, archbishop of Turin in 1965, created cardinal in 1967. Cf. *Padre Michele Pellegrino, testimonianze e ricordi* (Fossano: Edizioni Diocesi di Fossano, 2003).

[160] Cf. AS IV/3:135–137.

voluntarily, for having expressed ideas that can be read today in the conciliar documents. There are many *'periti'* of the council who are exercising great influence yet in the past have had the same difficulties."[161]

So ended, on October 1, the debate on the chapter from schema 13 that was dedicated to matrimony.

6. Paul VI at the U.N.O.: a symbolic event

a) The speech in the Glass Palace

There are events that by their symbolism characterize more deeply the history of a book or of a doctrinal document. Such an event, certainly, was Paul VI's visit to the United Nations Organization in New York on October 4, 1965, an event that left a decisive imprint on the final session of the council. It was the feast day of St. Francis of Assisi and that year marked the twentieth anniversary of the foundation of the United Nations.[162] The pope was received at the Glass Palace by the secretary general of the institution, the Burmese U-Thant, and by president-on-duty, the Italian Amintore Fanfani. About two thousand delegates were present, representing 115 countries, almost all the nations of the world. At 3:30 p.m. the pope gave his eagerly awaited discourse, from the green, marble podium of the great hall of the Glass Palace.[163] Paul VI, speaking in French, claimed to be an "expert in humanity" and praised the service rendered to humanity by the U.N.O., a body to which the task of "building peace" belonged by right.

> Our message is intended, in the first place, as a solemn moral ratification of this most noble institution. This message comes from Our historical experience; as an 'expert in humanity,' We bring to this

---

[161] Ibid., 136.

[162] Cf. R. Morozzo della Rocca, "L'umile dovere di servire la pace," in *Avvenire* (April 20, 2008); Emma Fattorini, "Il Papa 'esperto di umanità,'" in *Il Sole 24 ore* (April 13, 2008).

[163] Cf. Paul VI, "Address to representatives of the states," in *Insegnamenti* 3 (1965): 507–516 [French original], Italian translation 516–523.

Organization the approbation of Our recent Predecessors, that of the entire Catholic Episcopacy, and Our own, convinced as We are that this Organization represents the necessary path of modern civilization and of world peace."[164]

Paul VI who saw "the most serious threat of a breach of peace" in the "inequalities between one class and another and between one nation and another," then lifted up in a trembling voice his cry against war:

> You await this word from Us, which We cannot pronounce without being aware of its seriousness and solemnity: *never again some against others*, never, never again! Was it not above all to that end that the United Nations Organization was born: against war and for peace? Listen to the lucid words of a great man who has passed away, John Kennedy, who proclaimed four years ago: "Humanity will have to put an end to war, or else war will put an end to humanity." There is no need for long speeches in order to proclaim the highest purpose of your Institution. It is enough to recall the fact that the blood of millions of human beings, that countless unprecedented sufferings, useless massacres, and appalling ruins sanction the pact that unites you, in an oath that must change the future history of the world: never again war, never again war! Peace, peace is what should guide the destinies of the peoples and of all mankind.[165]

The exclamation "*jamais plus la guerre, jamais plus la guerre* [never again war, never again war]" summed up the meaning of the papal trip. The American columnist Walter Lippman saw the essence of the trip in the "moral ratification"—by the pope—of the United Nations and in the message that "the first crusade of mankind is the crusade against war and for peace."[166]

---

[164] Ibid., 508 [translated from French]; cf. 517. In the "fraternal collaboration of peoples" promoted by the United Nations, Paul VI saw the realization of "the ideal of humanity on its pilgrimage in time," and perceived "the heavenly gospel message becoming earthly" (ibid., 521).

[165] Ibid., 510–511 translated from French; cf. 519–520.

[166] R. La Valle, *Il Concilio nelle nostre mani, op. cit.*, 252. The Abbé de Nantes, for his part, saw the inauguration of an era in which "the Church is silently disowning the ancient order of Christendom, its faith, and its crusade" ("Lettres à mes amis," no. 215 dated October 31, 1965, the Feast of Christ

In New York, Paul VI met the Foreign Minister of the Soviet Union, Gromyko, who was received in an official audience "the importance of which was emphasized by the location," according to the press release of the Soviet news agency Tass.[167] In the brief meeting, Gromyko mentions, the pontiff dwelt upon the possibility of some collaboration between different ideologies to promote peace.[168]

On the day that Paul VI was at the U.N.O., Bishop Bettazzi called for the canonization of Pope John, "father and master of all men of good will."[169] The initiative was considered rash and was blocked by Cardinal Suenens, and also by the will of Paul VI himself.[170]

b) The pacifist appeal in the council hall

On October 5, back from New York, the pope summed up the meaning of his mission before the reassembled council. Paul VI arrived at Saint Peter's directly from the airport and, when he entered the basilica, the applause completely drowned out the singing of the hymn *"Tu es Petrus."* Turning to the council fathers he said in Latin, "We give thanks to the Lord, venerable brothers, to have had the fortune to announce a message of peace, in a sense to men of all the world. The gospel message has never before had such a large audience nor, we can say, an audience more ready and disposed to listen to it…." "It is regrettable," the pope added, "that the interpreter at such a luminous hour should have been our most humble person…. It is regrettable, but let this not lessen our joy in the prophetic value assumed by our announcement: In the name of Christ we have preached peace to men."[171]

Paul VI's cry at the U.N.O, "No more war! No more war!" reechoed several times in the council hall. At the request of Cardinal Liénart, the

---

the King), so as to celebrate its "marriage" with the world ("Lettres à mes amis," no. 218 dated December 8, 1965).

[167] Cf. V. Gaiduk, *op. cit.*, 29.

[168] Cf. Andrej Gromyko, *Memoirs* (New York: Doubleday, 1989), 211–212.

[169] AS VI/3:258–261.

[170] Cf. G. Alberigo, *A Brief History*, 101–102.

[171] AS, IV/1:36–38 at 37. English translation in *Council Daybook* 3:97–98 at 97.

papal speech was inserted into the conciliar *Acta*.[172] Liénart himself,[173] on October 6, affirmed that, given modern weapons, the classical distinction between a just and an unjust war had become less clear and men should no longer think of defending their rights with weapons. The pacifist appeal of Paul VI was taken up also by Cardinals Alfrink[174] and Léger[175] and by the Benedictine Dom Butler,[176] who called on the council to condemn the possession and use of nuclear weapons. Concerning the problem of peace, Cardinal Duval,[177] archbishop of Algiers, spokesman for a group African bishops, observed that a new way of thinking and a change of heart (*metanoia*) should be determined. Therefore it was necessary to emphasize more comprehensively how the problems of hunger, ignorance, and injustice were the evil that leads to war.[178] Warm applause greeted, on October 7, Cardinal Ottaviani's unexpected peroration on behalf of peace, the conditions necessary to promote it, the pursuit of an historical and not utopian objective, and a unique global society that would include all the nations of the world.[179]

Bishop Boillon[180] of Verdun referred in the hall to the "fast" for peace by twenty Christian women,[181] the first in a series of "non-violent" actions that would characterize the conciliar era. "Non-violence," the daily *Le Monde* wrote on October 10–11, "had made its entrance into Rome on tiptoe."

In the years in which the Vietnam War and the pacifist and third-world movements pointed out a "third way" between capitalism and communism, Paul VI's appeal took on an undeniable political significance far beyond his

---

172 Ibid., 28–36.

173 AS IV/3:397–400.

174 Ibid., 509–510.

175 Ibid., 510–512.

176 Ibid., 613–617.

177 Léon-Étienne Duval (1903–1996), French, ordained in 1926, Bishop of Constantine (Hippo) in Algeria in 1946, archbishop of Algiers in 1954, created cardinal in 1965.

178 AS IV/3:601–606.

179 Ibid., 642–644.

180 Pierre Boillon (1911–1996), French, ordained in 1935, Bishop of Verdun from 1963 to 1986.

181 AS IV/3:732–735.

intentions. The historian Victor Zaslavsky has documented the fact that the founder of the pacifist movement was, in the fifties, Stalin, for whom the "struggle for peace" was a product for export, as he naturally contrasted the "just wars" (those of U.S.S.R. and its allies) and the "unjust wars" started by the Western camp.[182] In this sense, as Riccardo Burigana writes, "Paul VI's speech at the Glass Palace on arms reduction and the campaign against world hunger brought into prominence topics that were dear to communist propaganda, in clear contrast with the models of the West."[183]

The United Nations, founded in 1945, gathered up the "moral" heritage of the League of Nations and the utopian dream of the American President Woodrow Wilson of establishing a new world order under the banner of peace, progress, and justice. Pius XII had contrasted the U.N.O., as a model of international organization, and the Catholic Church, the source of authentic justice and true values. Under his pontificate, the Jesuit journal *Civiltà Cattolica* had denounced the institutional mistake of the U.N.O, which admitted the U.S.S.R. into its Security Council with the right to veto, but excluded the Spain of General Franco while condemning it in its second assembly.[184] The United Nations had shown in particular its failure on the occasion of the Soviet invasion of Hungary in 1956, and, on the level of international law, it showed itself incapable, like the League of Nations before it, of guaranteeing peace and security in the world.

On the level of ideology, starting in the seventies, socialist-communist and feminist thought became the guideline for the international activity of the U.N.O., which began a systematic campaign to promote and implement an anti-birth policy and became one of the main "ideological laboratories" of anti-Christian secularism.[185] In 1998 the Pontifical Council

---

182 Cf. Victor Zaslavsky, *Lo stalinismo e la sinistra italiana: Dal mito del Urss alla fine del communismo, 1945–1991* (Milan: Mondadori, 2004).

183 R. Burigana, "Il Partito comunista e la Chiesa," *op. cit.*, 223.

184 See the lucid articles by Fr. A. Messineo, S.J., "I paradossi della politica internazionale," in *Civiltà Cattolica* 2299 (1946): 3–11; *idem*, "La seconda assemblea generale delle Nazioni Unite," *ibid.*, 2318 (1947): 97–105; *idem*, "Il declino delle Nazioni Unite," *ibid.*, 2458 (1952): 373–385. See also A. Riccardi, *Le politiche della Chiesa* (Cinisello Balsamo: San Paolo, 1997), 84–100.

185 Cf. Agostino Carloni, "Il fallimento dell'ONU," in *Cristianità* 330–331 (2005): 19–24; Eugenia Roccella e Lucetta Scaraffia, *Contro il Cristianesimo: L'ONU e l'Unione Europea come nuova ideologia*, with an appendix edited by Assuntiana Morresi (Casale Monferrato [AL]: Piemme, 2005); M. Schooyans, *The Hidden Face of the United Nations* (St. Louis: Central Bureau, 2001); R. de

for the Family declared that "for thirty years, the conferences sponsored by this organization [the U.N.O.] have provoked and nurtured unfounded fears about demography, especially in the southern countries,"[186] and John Paul II, in his encylical *Evangelium vitae* spoke of an "objective conspiracy against life," that implicitly involves even "international institutions, engaged in encouraging and carrying out actual campaigns to make contraception, sterilization, and abortion more widely available."[187]

7. Non-Christian religions and *Nostra aetate*

On October 11 the assembly in the hall addressed the problem of "non-Christian" religions, with whom Cardinal König once again suggested the need for "dialogue."[188] He recommended that the Christians should get used to considering non-Christian religions in terms of their genuine significance, namely, that they are interiorly (*ad intra*) paths on the search for God. The Church constitutes the necessary means for the salvation of all men, even those who do not believe in her, but only subjectively and implicitly respond to the promptings of grace. Hence, the necessity for a dialogue that may dispose the spirit to accept the values that are found in non-Christian religions (Islam, Hinduism, Buddhism), which are as though orientated to Christ and the Church. On that same day, a document by the *Coetus Internationalis* was distributed which invited the council fathers to express themselves with a *non placet* either in the balloting on most of the articles of the decree, or in the vote on the whole text.

On the last working day of the previous period, November 20, 1964, an extensively rewritten text that began with the words *Nostra aetate* had been passed by a large majority.[189] The worries of the *Coetus* concerned the part dedicated to the other religions more than the part related to the Jews.

Mattei, *La dittatura del relativismo* (Chieti: Solfanelli, 2008), 47–66.

[186] Pontifical Council for the Family, "Declaration on the Decrease of Fertility in the World" (February 27, 1998), no. 2.

[187] John Paul II, encylical *Evangelium vitae* (March 25, 1995), no. 17.

[188] Cf. AS IV/4:137–138.

[189] The various versions of the text are presented, together with the definitive version approved by a vote on October 28, 1965, in the book by Marie-Thérèse Hoch and Bernard Dupuy, *Les Églises devant le judaïsme: Documents officiels 1918–1978* (Paris: Cerf, 1980), 321–334.

With regard to the Jews, the *punctum dolens* (sore spot) was the cancellation of the charge of deicide against the Jewish people: but with some slight emendation the group would accept the document. But the first part of the text (nos. 1-3) was what stirred up the clearest opposition.[190] The declaration, according to the fathers of the *Coetus*, came to reduce the difference between Christianity and the other religions and, in so doing, both "delays the conversion of [the] peoples" of the world, and "quenches or weakens zeal for missionary vocations."[191]

Other criticisms were made of the text by the Arabian bishops and finally by some progressive sectors. In the opinion of Father Laurentin, for example, it lacked an explicit condemnation of the traditional teaching of deicide,[192] which according to the French theologian was the origin of anti-Semitism. In the new version of the text, after the word *"deplorat,"* the rewrite had in fact deleted the words "*et damnat*" that clearly condemned the accusation of deicide. The same complaint was expressed by Jacques Maritain, who opined, "If the council accepts this omission, it is taking a big step backward by comparison with the condemnations of racism and anti-Semitism issued by Pius XI."[193] On the other hand, Paul VI, while celebrating the rites of Passion Sunday that same year, in a sermon given at a Roman parish, had referred to Christ's death while attributing the responsibility for it to the Jewish people.[194] The theologian Ratzinger reported to Congar that "The pope was thought to be convinced of the collective responsibility of the Jewish people in the death of Christ."[195]

The Arab States continued to be convinced that the text might be concealing a political, pro-Zionist plan and was pressuring the Holy See to abandon it. Meanwhile, in the first months of 1965, Bishop Carli had published a strong theological criticism of the schema in two articles that were widely circulated among the council fathers.[196] The Bishop of Segna

---

190 Cf. Mauro Velati, "Completing the Conciliar Agenda," in HVT 5:185–274 at 213.

191 Ibid., 214.

192 Cf. ibid., 216–220.

193 Letter from Journet to Paul VI dated October 13, 1965, cited in M. Velati, "Completing the Conciliar Agenda," *op. cit.*, 220.

194 Paul VI, *Insegnamenti*, 3:209.

195 Congar, *Journal*, 749 (3 April 1965).

196 Cf. L. Carli, "La questione giudaica davanti al Concilio Vaticano II," in *Palestra del Clero* 44

produced the scriptural proofs for the collective responsibility of the Jews for the death of Jesus.

Cardinals Bea and Lercaro kept pressing for the emancipation of the Jews from all guilt in the passion and death of Christ, which should be attributed to the sins of all men. Cardinal Luigi Ciappi, master of the Sacred Palace, referring to St. Thomas,[197] replied that the Jews had truly been guilty of deicide and that the Church had to do her utmost for their conversion.[198] The observations of Cardinal Browne were similar: according to him the text should not give the impression that the Church was saying that "the… perseverance (of the Jews) in Judaism is without fault."[199] Paul VI agreed to the proposals of Ciappi and Browne and the text was changed according to their recommendations. Moreover, some suggestions by Maximos IV were approved, and after these changes, Willebrands, De Smedt, and Duprey[200] traveled to the Middle East and paid a visit to all the patriarchs. The secretary prepared an Arabic translation of the text, with a positive section on the Muslims that came before the section on Judaism. On October 13, Cardinal Bea informed the fathers that the text had been revised once again, and he explained why the word "deicide" had been alternately included and omitted in successive versions.[201]

In a conference given several days earlier for the Brazilian episcopacy on the theme "The problem of our attitude toward the Jewish people," Bea affirmed that based on a detailed examination of the New Testament passages one could not speak about the culpability of the Jewish people for the crime of deicide. According to the cardinal, one could not accuse the leaders of the Jewish people either of such a specific crime, inasmuch as it is doubtful that they had adequately understood the human-divine nature of Jesus.[202]

(1965): 185–203, and "È possibile discutere serenamente della questione giudaica?" *ibid.*, 465–476. See also Léon de Poncins, "Le problème juif face au Concile," (brochure, 1965).

197 Cf. *Summa Theologiae* III, q. 47 a. 5 ad 3.

198 Cf. AS V/2:643–644 at 644.

199 Ibid., 645.

200 Pierre François Marie Joseph Duprey (1922–2007), French, ordained in 1950, secretary of the Pontifical Council for Promoting Christian Unity in 1983, consecrated Bishop of Tibari in 1990.

201 AS IV/4:722–725.

202 Cf. R. La Valle, *Il Concilio nelle nostre mani, op. cit.*, 343. Cardinal Bea himself wrote a preface for

The ballots on the revisions that had been made to the schema on non-Christian religions ended on October 15. With 2,023 voting, 1,763 of the council fathers expressed their satisfaction with the corrections made to the text, while 250 voted against them, with one *placet iuxta modum* and one abstention.[203] The text was then sent to Paul VI, who decided to put it to the vote on October 28 in a public session.

Paragraph 2 of the Declaration *Nostra aetate* reads that the non-Christian religions "often reflect a ray of that truth which enlightens all men." Bishop Pietro Rossano comments on the document as follows: "Let us suppose, for example, that a Christian, a Jew, a Muslim, a Buddhist, a Hindu, and a humanist without any particular religious faith met in order to seek together the ways and the means of helping their neighbor to achieve, peace, liberation, truth, communion, and hope, which are the supreme objectives of human life on earth. I ask myself: on which of them is the Holy Spirit present? Perhaps only on the Christian?" Rossano concludes that his faith "does not authorize him to suppose that he is the sole bearer of the Spirit of God."[204] It should be observed that a group of Catholic scholars, including Father Georges Anawati[205] from Cairo, became part of the Arab and Arab-Christian opposition to the conciliar document. Along the lines of the Orientalist Louis Massignon,[206] they had been championing for some time

---

the booklet by Fr. G. Caprile, *La responsabilità degli ebrei nella crocifissione di Gesù* (Florence: Edizioni Spiritualità, 1964), which stressed that the Jewish people must be acquitted of the charge of deicide.

203 AS IV/4:824.

204 Pietro Rossano, "Lo Spirito Santo nelle religioni e nelle culture non cristiane," in Comunità di Sant'Egidio, *Il dialogo non finisce: Pietro Rossano e le religioni non cristiane*, ed. Mario Marazziti (Brescia: Morcelliana, 1994), 94–95. Pietro Rossano (1923–1992), ordained in 1946, was auxiliary Bishop of Rome until his death.

205 Georges C. Anawati (1905–1994), Egyptian Dominican, ordained in 1939, known for his studies of Islamology, founded and headed the *Institut des Études Orientales* in Cairo. See his works, *L'Islam à la croisée des chemins* (Fribourg: Éditions Universitaires Fribourg, 1986); *L'ultimo dialogo: La mia vita incontro all'Islam*, Ital. transl. (Venice: Marcianum Press, 2010). About him see Jean-Jacques Pérennès, *Georges Anawati: Un chrétien égyptien devant le mystère de l'islam* (Paris: Cerf, 2008).

206 On the French Orientalist Louis Massignon (1883–1962), see G. Basetti Sani, *Louis Massignon (1883–1962)* (Florence: Alinea, 1985); Louis Massignon et le dialogue islamo-chrétien," in *Louis Massignon et le dialogue des cultures*, ed. Daniel Massignon (Paris: Cerf, 1990), 247–264; M. Introvigne, "Louis Massignon: 'Il mistico spione,'" in *Il Foglio* (November 12, 2005).

a new Islamic-Christian relation.[207] The disciples of Massignon, Riccardi observes, had the ability to transform the opposition to the decree *De Iudeis* into the request for a conciliar pronouncement on Islam: "that way the Islamic faith also entered into the conciliar document."[208]

The Declaration *Nostra aetate* affirms in paragraph 3 that "The Church has also a high regard for the Muslims. They worship God, who is one, living and subsistent, merciful and almighty, the creator of heaven and earth, who has also spoken to men."[209] Paragraph 16 of *Lumen gentium* completes paragraph 3 of *Nostra aetate* by affirming the special relation (*ordinatio*) of the Muslims to the people of God, because, "these profess to hold the faith of Abraham, and together with us they adore the one, merciful God, mankind's judge on the last day."[210] The principal beneficiary of the conciliar declaration *Nostra aetate* was, even more than the Judaism, Islam, which for the first time became an object of a consideration that related it with Christianity.[211] Many of the progressives, who fought so much to remove any element of doctrinal incompatibility between Christianity and Judaism, were among those who in the Arab-Israeli crisis of the following years systematically defended the Arab countries and Islam against the State of Israel, which in their view was guilty of acting as the symbolic resistance, in the Middle East, of that Western civilization whose extinction they were looking forward to.

The Roman curia then provided for itself in 1974 a Commission for Religious Relations with Muslims, within the Vatican Secretariat for Relations with Non-Christians.[212]

---

207 Cf. A. Riccardi, *Le politiche della Chiesa, op. cit.*, 108–109.

208 Ibid., 108. On this topic see François Jourdan, *Dio dei cristiani, dio dei musulmani: Che cosa ci unisce, che cosa ci divide?* with a preface by Rémi Brague, Ital. transl. (Turin: Lindau, 2008).

209 COD, 969.

210 Ibid., 861.

211 Cf. Alexandre del Valle, *Le totalitarisme islamiste à l'assaut des démocraties* (Syrtes, 2002); Ital. transl. *Il totalitarismo islamista all'assalto delle democrazie* (Castellazzo Bormida [AL]: Solinum, 2007), 449.

212 On the relations between the Catholic Church and the Islamic world after the Second Vatican Council, see for example Comunità di Sant'Egidio, *Cristianesimo e Islam: L'amicizia possibile* (Brescia: Morcelliana, 1989); Mahmut Aydin, *Modern Western Christian Theological Understandings of Muslims since the Second Vatican Council* (Washington, DC: Council for Research in Values and

8. Compromise on the constitution *Dei Verbum*

The schema *De fontibus revelationis* (On the Sources of Revelation) had been withdrawn in the first session, at the intervention of John XXIII, and entrusted to a special mixed commission, presided over by Cardinals Ottaviani and Bea, which had overhauled it and produced the new schema *De divina revelatione* (On Divine Revelation), that was sent to the fathers on April 29, 1963. Paul VI let the council discuss it in the third session, from September 30 until October 6, 1964, but the vote was put off until the final session. The text, corrected and revised by the Doctrinal Commission, was re-examined by the same commission under the direct control of Paul VI.

The two principal problems concerned the relations between scripture and tradition and the historicity of the gospels. The sub-commission, in response to the pope's appeal, proposed adding the word "directly" to the statement that "the whole of Catholic doctrine cannot be proved from sacred scripture." Both the *Biblicum* and Father Rahner resolutely opposed this change and on October 4, in the fourth meeting, the commission decided to stick to the original formulation without the word "directly."[213] De Lubac[214] describes the heated debate within the commission between the "two sources of revelation party," led by Parente, Ottaviani, and Boyer, and the party of the opposition, Butler, Schöffer, Henríquez, and McGrath. The "Third Party" (Colombo, Philips, Florit) prevailed; to it we owe the compromise text that reached the hall on October 29, 1965.[215] After long discussions and negotiations a formula was found that both the majority of the commission and the pope were disposed to accept. "It is not from sacred scripture alone that the Church draws her certainty about everything which has been revealed."

As far as the historicity of the gospels was concerned, chapter V had had as many as 313 votes *placet iuxta modum*, after paragraph 19 in the same

Philosophy, 2002): Michael Louis Fitzgerald, "From Heresy to Religion: Vatican II and Islam," in *Europe and Islam: Evaluations and Perspectives at the Dawn of the Third Millennium*, ed. Mahmoud Salem El Sheikh (Florence: Florence University Press, 2002).

213 See the reconstruction in John W. O'Malley, *What Happened at Vatican II*, *op. cit.*, 277–278.

214 Cf. de Lubac, *Quaderni*, 847–848.

215 Christophe Theobald, "The Church under the Word of God," in HVT 5:275–362 at 335.

chapter had received sixty-one *non placet*.[216] The text stated that "the sacred authors wrote the four gospels… but always in such fashion that they told us the honest truth about Jesus."

Paul VI requested that the truthfulness of the gospels be defended with the formula "things that are truthful and worthy of historical faith" in place of "honest truth." The debate, during the session of the Doctrinal Commission, led to the correction of paragraph 19, that had already been voted on, in these terms: "Holy Mother Church has firmly and with absolute constancy held, and continues to hold, that the four gospels just named, whose historical character the Church unhesitatingly asserts, faithfully hand on what Jesus Christ… did and taught."[217]

Dei Verbum declares that "there exists a close connection and communication between sacred tradition and sacred scripture" (no. 9), and they "form one sacred deposit of the word of God, committed to the Church" (no. 10). Cardinal Vanhoye[218] described as "surprising" the expression chosen by the council to describe scripture: "as a matter of fact, taken literally, it declares that the written text is an act of speaking, *locutio,*"[219] a "living act," as Roger Schutz and Max Thurian described it;[220] sacred tradition, for its part, has the dynamic function of "transmitting" this same word. It "takes the word of God entrusted by Christ the Lord and the Holy Spirit to the apostles, and hands it on to their successors" (no. 9). The final impression is of a text that is at least hazy.

---

216 Cf. AS IV/2:54–55.

217 Cf. COD, 978.

218 Albert Vanhoye (1923–2006), French, ordained in 1954 in the Society of Jesus, created cardinal in 2006.

219 Albert Vanhoye, "La parola di Dio nella vita della Chiesa: La recezione della 'Dei Verbum,'" in R. Fisichella, ed., *Il Concilio Vaticano II, op. cit.* 29–45 at 30.

220 Cf. R. Schutz and M. Thurian, *La parole vivante au Concile* (Taizé: Presses de Taizé, 1996), 120.

9. The council and communism: the story of a missing condemnation

a) Schema XIII and communism

In December of 1964, Bishop Pierre Haubtmann,[221] who was responsible for coordinating the new reworking of schema 13, had requested the collaboration of the Salesian Giulio Girardi[222] with regard to the chapter on atheism. In February of 1965, at Ariccia, the text by Girardi, which suggested a more positive approach to Marxist humanism, was preferred to the text by Archbishop Wojtyla, which demanded a more clear-cut affirmation of the Church's rights in society.[223] Girardi would later leave the priesthood to become a theoretician and prominent protagonist of liberation theology.

When Bishop Haubtmann, in an audience granted to him on February 16, presented to the pope the "open" and "dialogical" outline of the schema that would have to avoid any condemnation of communism, Paul VI encouraged him to pursue this line: "*Oui* [Yes]," he said, "*C'est à la fois délicat e indispensable* [It is both sensitive and strictly necessary]."[224] The new text, subjected to discussion in the council hall between September and October of 1965, made no explicit reference to communism. A condemnation, indeed, according to those who composed the document, would go against the pastoral character of Vatican II and would constitute an obstacle to "dialogue" with the communist regimes. In the discussion, however, the request for a clear condemnation of communism was repeated by numerous fathers who were dissatisfied with the schema.[225]

---

221 Pierre Haubtmann (1912–1971), French priest, national chaplain of *Action Catholique Ouvrière* from 1945 to 1962, conciliar *peritus*. Cf. Philippe Bordey-Ne, "La collaboration de Pierre Haubtmann avec les experts Belges," in *The Belgian Contribution*, 585–610.

222 Giulio Girardi (1926–2012) Salesian, ordained in 1955, professor at various universities, consultor of the Secretariat for Non-believers. Expelled from the Salesian Congregation and suspended *a divinis* in 1977. See his books *Marxism and Christianity*, translated by Kevin Traynor (New York: Macmillan, 1968); *Credenti e non credenti per un mondo nuovo* (Assisi: Cittadella, 1969).

223 Cf. G. Turbanti, "Il problema del comunismo al Concilio," *op. cit.*, 169–173; *idem, Un Concilio per il mondo moderno, op. cit.*, 505–521.

224 Ibid., 172.

225 On this discussion cf. V. Carbone, "Schemi e discussioni," *op. cit.*, 38–45.

On September 11, the Lebanese patriarch, Maximos IV Saigh,[226] maintained that to save humanity from atheism it was necessary, instead of condemning Marxism, to denounce the causes that provoke atheistic communism, by proposing "a dynamic mysticism and a vigorous social morality, and by showing that the source of the workers' striving for their true liberation is found in Christ."[227] "We all know," he added, "that many of those who call themselves atheists are not really against the Church; there are some of them who are very close. They are seeking in truth, as Paul VI said, a more lively presentation of God, a religion in accord with the historical evolution of humanity, and above all a Church that sustains not only the poor, but the effort of solidarity with the poor." "Let us show," said the patriarch at the rhetorical climax, "that the true socialism is Christianity, lived out completely in the just distribution of goods and in the fundamental equality of all."[228]

The Yugoslav Cardinal Seper[229] proved to be against a condemnation of communistic atheism, asserting that part of the responsibility for modern atheism must be assigned to those Christians who stubbornly continued to defend the established order and the immutability of social structures. "Therefore, we clearly proclaim that this rigid conservatism and this immobility that some do not cease to ascribe to the Catholic Church, are foreign to the true evangelical spirit."[230] Still more explicit was Cardinal König,[231] who invited Catholics in countries subject to communism to give witness to the living God by collaborating sincerely with the economic and social progress of the regime, so as to show that greater energies can spring from religion than from atheism.[232]

Clemente Riva,[233] in the September 28 issue of *L'Avvenire d'Italia*, and René Laurentin in the September 2 issue of *Le Figaro*, stressed particularly

---

[226] AS IV/5:451–454.

[227] Ibid., 451.

[228] Ibid., 452.

[229] Ibid., 435–437.

[230] Ibid., 436.

[231] Ibid., 454–456.

[232] Ibid., 455.

[233] Clemente Riva (1922–1999), Rosminian, ordained in 1951, titular Bishop of Atella in 1975, auxiliary Bishop of Rome from 1975 to 1998.

the reasons given by Cardinal König: the roots of atheism must be sought within Christianity because it is the fault of those Christians who do not have a right notion of God and a precise image of man and shirk the duty to dialogue with the world.

Father Pedro Arrupe,[234] the new superior general of the Society of Jesus, began speaking in the council by affirming that the Church, after two thousand years, had not yet found efficacious ways to defend her message: it was necessary to revise her pastoral methods, by contrasting atheism to the witness of a Christian community that is not isolated or, as it were, enclosed in a ghetto, but immersed in the world.[235]

There were many contrary opinions, however, such as that of Bishop de Castro Mayer[236] and of other prelates like the Italian Cardinal Ermenegildo Florit[237] and the Czechoslovakian Jesuit, Bishop Pavel Hnilica,[238] titular bishop of Rusado, in Czechoslovakia, who had been ordained clandestinely and had recently arrived in the West.

Bishop Hnilica began his speech by asserting that what the schema said about atheism was so little "that to say only that is the same as saying nothing." He added that a large part of the Church is suffering "under the oppression of militant atheism, but this cannot be deduced from the schema, which nevertheless claims to speak about the Church in today's world!" "History will justly accuse us of cowardice or blindness on account of this silence," the speaker continued, while recalling that he was not speaking in the abstract, because he had been in a concentration and labor camp along with seven hunded priests and religious. "I speak from my direct experience and from that of priests and religious whom

---

234 Pedro Arrupe (1907–1991), Spanish Jesuit, ordained in 1936, elected May 22, 1965, superior general of the Society of Jesus, a post which he kept until 1983. Cf. Bartolomeo Sorge, "Arrupe," in DHCJ, 1697–1705.

235 AS IV/2:481–484. See also Caprile, 5:106–109.

236 Ibid., 371–373. P. Corrêa de Oliveira, "Lucida e relevante intervenção do bispo-diocesano no Concilio," in *Catolicismo* 179 (1965): 8.

237 AS IV/2:456–460.

238 Pavel Hnilica (1921–2006), Slovak Jesuit, clandestinely ordained a priest (1950) and a bishop (1951) by Bishop Robert Pobozny (1890–1972) of Roznava. In December 1951 he was forced to leave Czechoslovakia and to flee to the West. On May 13, 1964, Paul VI made public his episcopal rank and Bishop Hnilica was able to participate together with the fathers in the remaining sessions of the council.

I have known in prison and with whom I have borne the burdens and dangers of the Church."[239]

Archbishop Florit suggested that the council should assert unambiguously (*verbis univocis*) that the atheistic character of dialectical materialism is not accidental. Since there are Catholics who absurdly maintain that it is possible to adhere to the economic teaching of the Marxist system, without thereby accepting its atheism, it is necessary for the council to affirm the impossibility of this distinction.

In the opinion of Bishop Elko,[240] too, the bishop of Pittsburgh for the Ruthenians in the United States, it was necessary to speak "about dialectical materialism as the plague of modern society and to condemn it fittingly, so that the future ages might not have to hold us responsible for our fear and cowardice, if we shall have dealt with it only indirectly."[241]

Bishop Rusnak,[242] auxiliary bishop of Toronto for the Ukrainians in Canada, expressed himself in similar words: "It would be a scandal and an act of cowardice if a council of the twentieth century neglected to denounce before public opinion the errors and lies of communism."[243]

In the 138th General Congregation on September 29, 1965, the voice of Cardinal Josef Slipyj, the major archbishop of Ukraine in the U.S.S.R., was raised: "In the hall," he said, "there has been talk of atheism, according to the Western concept, but many speakers seem unaware of the existence in the East of countries where it has set up as a system and all sorts of methods are adopted to eradicate the Catholic Church and every other religion. And this is no secret to anyone."[244]

In his turn Cardinal Antonio Bacci affirmed, "Every time an ecumenical council has been assembled, it always resolved the major problems that were causing trouble at that time and condemned the errors of the moment. To

---

239 AS IV/2:629–631.

240 Nicholas Thomas Elko (1909–1991), from the United States, ordained in 1934. bishop of Pittsburgh for the Ruthenians from 1955 to 1967.

241 AS IV/2:480–481 at 480.

242 Michael Rusnak, C.Ss.R. (1921–2003), Ukrainian Redemptorist, ordained in 1949, auxiliary bishop of Toronto and titular bishop of Zternicus in 1964, eparch of the Slovakian Eparchy of Sts. Cyril and Methodius of Toronto in 1980.

243 AS IV/2:639–642.

244 AS IV/3:106–110 at 107.

remain silent on this point would be, I think an unpardonable lapse, as well as a collective sin.... This is the great theoretical and practical heresy of our times; and if the council does not deal with it, it may seem to be failed council!"[245]

b) The mysterious pigeonholing of the anti-communist appeal

On October 7, 1965, the discussion on the draft of the constitution *Gaudium et spes* was concluded. On Friday, October 8, Bishop Felici made it known that the fathers could present in writing observations on the schema until the following day. The *Coetus Internationalis Patrum* prepared a petition asking that, "... after paragraph no. 19 of the schema, *The Church in the Modern World*, which deals with the problem of atheism, there be added a new and suitable paragraph that expressly deals with the problem of communism."[246] If Vatican II has an eminently pastoral character, the petition affirmed, "is there any other problem that is more pastoral than the problem of preventing the faithful from becoming atheists through communism?" If the council were to be silent on a problem of such importance, this silence, in the minds of the faithful, would be equivalent "to a tacit repeal of all that the recent supreme pontiffs have said and written against communism." The existence of pronouncements by so many popes is not a reason to ignore the problem, because "the solemn consensus of the whole council gives greater force and efficacy to the argument"; nor "is it possible for the Christians of the Church of Silence to have greater suffering in the future than what they have now."[247]

Here, now, in translation an English translation, is the entire proposed amendment:

---

245 AS IV/2:669–670.

246 The text of the petition in AS IV/2:898–900. See the reconstruction of the whole incident in "Il comunismo e il Concilio Vaticano II," by Bishop L. M. Carli, in the volume edited by Don Giovanni Scantamburlo, *Perchè il Concilio non ha condannato il comunismo? Storia di un discusso atteggiamento* (Rome: L'Appennino, 1967), 177–240; cf. also Caprile, 5:119–121, 402–411; A. Wenger, *Vatican II, op. cit., Quatrième session*, 147–173; Wiltgen, 272–278; V. Carbone, "Schemi e discussioni," *op. cit.*, 45–68; G. Turbanti, "Il problema del comunismo al Concilio," *op. cit.*, 173–186; P. Levillain, *La mécanique politique, op. cit.*, 343–360.

247 G. F. Svidercoschi, *op. cit.*, 604–605.

A specimen of the proposed addition.

After paragraph 19 of the Schema "On the Church in the Modern World," which deals with the problem of atheism, to be revised according to the suggestions submitted by the fathers, let the following new paragraph be added: No. 19.b. (The problem of communism):

Any form of atheism whatsoever must be rejected because it is contrary to the doctrine of the Church. But the form that since the past century down to our day has exerted the greatest influence to the detriment of the Christian faithful, and of the followers of any religion, and therefore worries the pastors of the Church, is the one that spreads widely under the name of Marxist socialism or communism, and under the pretense of economic and social progress wretchedly deceives an enormous number of persons.

In fact, given its denial of the existence of God and of any religious order, above all a supernatural order, communism by logical necessity, as history has proved, is led to undermine in many ways even the fundamental principles of the natural order. And indeed, to restrict ourselves only to the most important ones, it denies the spirituality and immortality of the human soul; it rejects true freedom, especially in religious matters; it violates in many respects the genuine dignity of the human person, of the family, and of the marital union; it does not recognize any permanent, unchanging norm of the moral and civil law; the only just and moral thing in its view is anything that is useful for the dictatorship of its own party (cf. the intervention of Cardinal Wyszyński on September 20, 1965); it does not admit the right to private property; it considers struggle between the social classes as a necessary means for the attainment of terrestrial goods; it has such a totalitarian concept of the state that almost no worthy place is acknowledged for individuals or intermediate social groups.

For all these reasons communism is to be rejected not only because it is infected with the plague of atheism, but also because on account of its aforementioned extremely serious errors it has been declared intrinsically perverse by the magisterium of the Church (cf. encylical *Divini redemptoris*).

For an even more serious reason the doctrine of communism is to be deemed pernicious, because especially in our times, in many places, it is put into practice by civil and political authorities using every means possible, and thus it is propagating itself and is being imposed either by violence or by cunning. The result is that, while the rights of God and human rights are still downtrodden by communism, the

> Catholic Church herself, which cannot accept that doctrine and that praxis, is unjustly impeded in carrying out her divine mission, and in her members is subjected to the most abject persecution.
>
> For these reasons the Catholic Church, urged by such a great disaster for souls, has never ceased to lead the Christian faithful away from the doctrines and practice of communism, with repeated condemnations and warnings also. Even today she feels obligated by her very serious pastoral duty to pronounce the same judgment by means of the ecumenical council.
>
> Whereas the Church as a whole shares in the sufferings of her members who suffer in various ways from the persecution by communism, she solemnly confirms both the revealed and the natural truths impugned by communism. She ardently exhorts her children, indeed all men of good will, not to let themselves be deceived by the false hope of being able licitly to harmonize their religious faith with the dictates of communism, not even in the economic or social field. The Church proclaims that the life of true progress is not found in the teachings and the practice of communism, as is already evident from the lamentable experience of a good many nations, but in the sound political principles that conform to the divine law, both natural and positive.
>
> Finally, she urges all those in authority to work, by means of justice and charity, to eliminate those unjust conditions of civil society that unfortunately make smooth the path to communism."[248]

The reasons listed on an attached page to persuade the council fathers to support the request for a new paragraph on the problem of communism were classified as positive and negative. Among the "positive reasons" it was repeated that if "Vatican Council II has an eminently pastoral character," then "is there any other problem that is more pastoral than the problem of preventing the faithful from becoming atheists through communism? As a matter of fact, very many think because they are not atheists they can support communism."[249] Among the negative reasons, from an opposite point of view, the following called for the requested addition:

---

248 Italian text in L. M. Carli, "Il comunismo e il Concilio Vaticano II," *op. cit.*, 217–218. The complete Latin text of the *modus* was published in the *Bollettino Diocesano di Segni* (December 1965): 97–98.

249 L. M. Carli, "Il comunismo e il Concilio Vaticano II," *op. cit.*, 222–223.

1) If the council were to remain silent on communism, this silence, in the minds of the faithful, would be equivalent, by an unfair yet inevitable logic, to a tacit repeal of all that the recent supreme pontiffs have said and written against communism, and also of the condemnations imposed on several occasions by the Holy Office. The psychological harm that would result, not to mention the contempt for the teaching authority of the Church, would be enormously consequential. Furthermore the Church could easily be accused of opportunism, of human respect, of caring more about the Jews than about the Christians who are subject to persecution.

2) Communism ardently longs for and expects the council's silence: and this certainly has a very serious significance. There is no doubt that communism, through an enormous effort of propaganda, would exploit the council's silence to its own advantage, with a lamentable confusion of ideas among the faithful.

3) Just as Pius XII of venerable memory is accused today by some, quite unjustly of course, of silence with regard to the victims of Nazism, so too, after the council, the Episcopal College would quite rightly be accused of silence with regard to the victims of communism."[250]

c) The petition vanishes

At first 334 fathers replied to the invitation of the *Coetus Internationalis Patrum*. Their petitions, on as many separate pages and duly signed, were delivered personally by Bishop de Proença Sigaud and Archbishop Lefebvre to the secretary general of the council, on the via Serristori 10, at midday of October 9, 1965, the last day when emendations could be submitted.[251] To these 334 were added another seventy-one new petitions in support that arrived late and were presented to the secretary general about ten days later; there were also thirty more that the *Coetus* received in early November, but they were not submitted because they were too late.[252] These last two groups of supporters should be counted also,

[250] Ibid., 223–224. Latin text in AS IV/2:900.

[251] Cf. V. Carbone, "Schemi e discussioni," *op. cit.*, 46.

[252] The exact numbers can be found, among other places, in a copy belonging to Archbishop de

because October 9 was the deadline for accepting new *emendations*, but it did not exclude the acceptance of new *supporters* of emendations that had been submitted in time.

The petition, therefore, was received from 435 council fathers in all: a remarkable number considering that: a) the invitation was not extended to each and every council father, because of the difficulty of delivery to their residences, since they were dispersed in a hundred different places; b) the fathers had so much work in those days, the final closing period of the council, and received so much printed matter from every side, that one may suppose that many did not have the opportunity to pay attention to the petition.

On Monday, October 11, the petition came into the hands of Monsignor Achille Glorieux,[253] secretary of the Mixed Commission responsible for the preparation and revision of the schema on The Church in the Modern World, as well as Rome correspondent for the French Catholic daily, *La Croix*. He, however, did not pass it on to the commission that was working on the schema, under the pretext of not wanting to hinder their work. The petition had been signed by a good 454 prelates from eighty-six countries, who were dumbstruck when on Saturday, November 13, they received the new text in the hall, without any mention of their requests. "The fact that one man had been able to keep such a significant document from reaching the conciliar commission to which it was officially addressed is one of the great tragedies of the Second Vatican council and may go down in history as the greatest scandal that has damaged the serious deliberations of this sacred assembly," commented Father Wiltgen in his Divine Word News Service.[254]

The very serious guilt of Monsignor Glorieux is obvious. One cannot assume his good faith, but it is, in fact, permissible to presume malice. How else can one imagine that he would decide to pigeonhole the petition without consulting anyone? And whom would he consult? As we shall see a little later, it seems to rule out the possibility that Bishop Felici, the secretary of the council, was involved. It is more logical to suppose that Cardinal Tisserant was involved.

Proença Sigaud preserved in the Archives in Ecône (E 02–11–002).

[253] Achille Glorieux (1910–1999), French, ordained in 1934. Conciliar *peritus*, secretary of the Pontifical Council for the Laity (1966), then titular archbishop of Beverley (1969), pro-nuncio in Egypt (1973–1984).

[254] Cf. Divine Word Service, November 23, 1964.

That same day, October 11, Bishop Carli sent a letter of protest to the council presidency, denouncing the arbitrary action of the commission that had ignored a document of such great importance.[255] Monsignor Glorieux stated, falsely, that the document from the *Coetus* had arrived at the commission past the deadline for submission, but he was proved wrong by the secretary of the council himself, Bishop Felici.[256] Despite the protests, in the General Congregation of November 15, Bishop Garrone, reporter of the Commission for the Schema of the Conciliar Constitution, declared that the commission's "manner of proceeding" was in keeping with the "pastoral purpose" of the council, with the "expressed will" of John XXIII and Paul VI, and with the tenor of the discussions that had taken place in the hall on this subject.[257] Bishop Carli then submitted a formal appeal, which he made known in print. The rules, in fact, provided that all emendations, even those not included in the text of the schema, were nevertheless to be printed and made known to the assembly. The petition of the 454 bishops, on the contrary, mysteriously vanished.

On that same day, Bishop Felici sent to the pope a memo about Bishop Carli's appeal.[258] In the afternoon the pope had the following note delivered to Bishop Felici:

> 11/15/65
>
> To keep or to withdraw the appeal?
>
> 1) Was the conduct of Mixed Commission illegal?
>
> 2) After the intervention *"iuxta modum"* the thesis of the petitioners would be brought to the knowledge of the fathers with the pertinent observations.
>
> A) Is it prudent?
>
> If rejected: the council seems to have rejected the condemnation of communism, which has already been condemned
>
> If approved: what is the fate of the Catholics in communist countries?

[255] Cf. V. Carbone, "Schemi e discussioni," *op. cit.*, 53–54.

[256] Cf. G. Turbanti, "Il problema del comunismo," *op. cit.*, 180.

[257] Cf. G. F. Svidercoschi, *op. cit.*, 607.

[258] Cf. ASV, Conc. Vat. II, Busta 343, secretary general Sept.-Nov. 1965, memorandum from Bishop Felici dated November 15, p. 2 ff.

B) Is it consistent with the promises of the council?
- not to enter into "political" topics
- not to pronounce anathemas
- not to speak about communism (1962).[259]

The last point should be emphasized, because it looks like the confirmation of the "promise" made by the Vatican to the Soviet government not to condemn communism in any form. This was the condition that the Kremlin demanded in order to permit the participation of observers from the patriarchate of Moscow at Vatican II. The fact that this compromise was "informal" and not "official," in no way diminishes its reality.

On the morning of November 16, Bishop Felici, in accordance with the instructions that he had received, had a new meeting with Bishop Carli who insisted that the council should in some way reiterate the condemnation of communism. Bishop Felici, in reporting the meeting to the pope, confirmed that the emendation had been submitted according to the rules and that the commission should have considered it.[260] In a further note dated November 20, Bishop Felici repeated to the pope that Bishop Carli's appeal seemed to be well founded and that the procedural irregularity could not be justified by alleging the late submission of the petition.[261]

On November 23, Father Wiltgen's news agency circulated a lengthy bulletin on the incident. By that time the scandal exploded in the press. Paul VI, at this point, had a closed meeting called by the substitute of the Secretary of State, Archbishop Dell'Acqua, to deal with the problem. On November 26, in the papal office on the third floor of the Apostolic Palace, Cardinals Tisserant and Cicognani met with Bishops Garrone, the reporter for the schema on the Church, Felici, the council secretary, and Dell'Acqua. Before starting the meeting, Cardinal Tisserant had given the pope a letter in which he stated among other things:

> Anathemas have never converted anyone, and although they were useful at the time of the Council of Trent, when the princes could force their subjects to convert to protestantism, they no longer work

---

259 Ibid., memorandum from Paul VI, p. 1 f.

260 Cf. ibid., note from Bishop Felici about the petition presented by Bishop Carli, in which he reconstructs the entire incident (p. 3 ff.).

261 Cf. ASV, Conc. Vat. II, Busta 343, memorandum from [Cardinal] Felici dated November 20, 1965, p. 3 ff.; see also AS IV/6:445.

> today when everyone has the sense of his own independence. As I already told Your Holiness, a conciliar condemnation of communism would be considered by most people as a political move, something that would cause enormous damage to the authority of the council and of the Church herself."[262]

The pope presided over the meeting, and after he read Cardinal Tisserant's letter he briefly explained the *status quaestionis*. There were two questions: one of method, the other of merit. Under the heading of method, several irregularities emerged, not only of Monsignor Glorieux, who had not forwarded the petition to the Council of the Presidency, but also of the council itself, presided over by Cardinal Tisserant, who had not taken Bishop Carli's appeal into consideration. Cardinal Tisserant made the incredible excuse of not convoking the Council of the Presidency to examine the appeal, because Cardinal Wyszyński, a member of the same council, was very strong in his mind-set against communism.[263] Under the heading of merit, on the other hand, all those present agreed with the position of Tisserant and of Paul VI himself, that it was not opportune for the council to renew expressly the condemnation of communism. Turning again to Monsignor Glorieux, who was presented to public opinion as the one only responsible for the incident, and who in a memorandum sought to lighten his responsibility, Cardinal Tisserant wrote to him on December 4, "Your responsibility will not be exaggerated beyond measure by historians of the council. May those who are well informed pardon your oversight."[264]

The text was again revised according to the *modi* submitted by the fathers and was examined by the competent Mixed Commission of the council. The section concerning atheism (nos. 19-21) remained substantially unchanged. Among the few approved emendations the most significant is found in no. 21, which reads:

> The Church has already repudiated and cannot cease repudiating, sorrowfully but as firmly as possible, those poisonous doctrines and

[262] ASV, Conc. Vat. II, Busta 34, Tisserant to Paul VI, Rome, November 26, 1965, p. 1. See also V. Carbone, "Schemi e discussioni," *op. cit.*, 58.

[263] Cf. V. Carbone, "Schemi e discussioni," *op. cit.*, 59.

[264] Cited in V. Carbone, "Schemi e discussioni," *op. cit.*, 61–62.

> actions which contradict reason and the common experience of humanity, and dethrone man from his native excellence.[265]

The commission, therefore, followed the line indicated by the governing bodies of the council, in the closed meeting on November 26, over which the pope presided. The procedural irregularity was acknowledged, but the bad faith of Monsignor Glorieux was not admitted. As for the substance, the emendations and the corresponding *modi* for the mention and condemnation of communism were not accepted. It was clear that this was no fortuitous incident, but a definite purpose to avoid a condemnation of communism, so as to respect the agreements reached in 1962 with the Soviet government. Bishop Carbone maintained that there is no trace an agreement of this kind in the archives of the council,[266] but in the above-cited memo dated November 15, which Carbone himself reports,[267] Paul VI had explicitly mentioned among "the promises of the council" the one "not to speak about communism," and wrote in parentheses the date "1962" with an obvious reference not to the pastoral approach of the council, but to the negotiations conducted that year between Cardinal Tisserant and Metropolitan Nikodim.[268]

d) The council fathers protest against the pacifism of schema 13

Connected with the theme of communism was the topic of peace, about which there were disagreements among the council fathers. On November 17, the outcome of the vote on this question was forty-five *non placet* and 523 *placet iuxta modum*.

---

[265] AS IV/7:247.

[266] Cf. V. Carbone, "Schemi e discussioni," *op. cit.*, 67–68.

[267] Cf. ibid., 55.

[268] Antonio Socci has correctly pointed out the importance of the memorandum dated November 15 in "Le prove del patto scellerato tra il Vaticano e il Cremlino," in *Libero* (January 21, 2007), and "Le riunioni e i messaggi che provano il patto Vaticano-Urss ai tempi di Paolo VI," in *Libero* (January 23, 2007).

The archbishop of New Orleans, Philip Hannan,[269] became the promoter of a *modum*, which was widely circulated among the fathers, asking for the revision of paragraphs 84 and 85 (80 and 81 of the definitive version), which said that every use of nuclear weapons was absolutely illicit. In a statement released by the Divine Word News Service, Archbishop Hannan, while referring to the Soviet menace, asserted that "paragraph 85 ignores the fact that the possession of nuclear weapons by some nations has protected vast areas of the world from possible aggression. The protection of these areas would be very uncertain if there were no nuclear arms."[270]

When it became clear that the new text contained nothing substantially different from the preceding one, ten council fathers distributed a circular letter, translated into various languages, which stressed that "the defense of a large portion of humanity from aggression is not a crime to be condemned but on the contrary a great service rendered to mankind."

> The cause of war and conflicts is injustice and not the possession of scientific weapons (for example, the cause of the Second World War was not the possession of arms on the part of some nations, but injustice). The true remedy for war and conflicts is the eradication of injustice and the securing of peace, founded on liberty and justice. To state that scientific weapons cause war is as illogical as to say that the law and the police in a city are the causes of the crimes and disturbances in the city itself. The inclusion of these assertions and ideas in the schema will certainly be harmful to the cause of liberty in the world.[271]

The first of the ten signers was the cardinal of New York, Francis Spellman. Their position was that of Pius XII, who when speaking about the use of nuclear, chemical, and bacteriological weapons, admitted the use of them as an extreme means of legitimate defense when faced with an unjust aggression with the same means.[272] On December 3, the *Coetus*

---

269 Philip Matthew Hannan (1913–1988), ordained in 1939, auxiliary bishop of Washington and titular bishop of Hierapolis in 1956, archbishop of New Orleans from 1965 until his death.

270 Caprile, 5:494.

271 Ibid., 496.

272 Cf. Pius XII, address on October 19, 1953, in DRM, 15:417–428; speech on September 30,

Internationalis Patrum directed a final appeal to the council fathers to vote against the entire schema because it made no mention of communism, and because of the document's ambiguous position on the ends of matrimony, on conscientious objection, and on total war.[273]

10. The final public sessions

As of October 6, after the introductory report of Bishop Romolo Compagnone, bishop of Anagni, discussion had begun on the renewal of religious life. On October 8, the schema was approved with 2,126 affirmative votes and thirteen negative votes out of 2,142 voters, after all the partial votes of the previous days had been positive. The document on priestly formation and the declaration on Christian education were approved in the General Congregations from October 11 to 15. Within the assembly there was no lack of fathers who opposed obligatory celibacy. On October 12, the pope, by means of a letter sent to Cardinal Tisserant, asked the council not to discuss ecclesiastical celibacy, affirming that this "ancient, sacred, and providential" law should be not only preserved but reinforced.[274]

On October 17, a few days after the final vote on the document on priestly formation, Cardinal Ruffini wrote to Paul VI to complain about the meager references to the traditional magisterium and to the teaching of St. Thomas in the formation of the clergy. "I feel, Most Holy Father, a deep bitterness upon learning that the teachings of this magisterium, which were imparted particularly in papal encylicals, are disregarded. If the popes of the past are not listened to, one fears that the same will continue to be done in the future."[275]

1954, in DRM, 16:167–169. The position of Pius XII was confirmed by moral theologians such as Father Eberhard Welty, O.P. (*A Handbook of Christian Social Ethics*, 2 vols. [New York: Herder and Herder, 1960, 1963], 2:406–408; Johannes Messner (*Ética social, política y económica a la luz del derecho natural* [Madrid: Rialp, 1967], 777–880). For an up-to-date treatment of the topic, cf. R. de Mattei, *Holy War, Just War: Islam and Christendom at War* (Madera: Chronicles Press, 2007).

[273] Text in Caprile, 5:497.

[274] AS IV/2:40.

[275] AS V/3:447–448.

At the end of the debate on the schema concerning priestly life and ministry, on October 26, Bishops Foley[276] (Lancaster), Fares[277] (Catanzaro), Pechuan[278] (Cruz del Eje), and Compagnone[279] (Anagni) took the floor. In Foley's opinion, a reference in the schema to clerical garb would be necessary: the clothing may certainly be different in different places, but all the clothing should be distinctive of a particular state; Fares dwelt on a lacuna in the text, namely on the silence that it kept about the sacrament of penance; Pechuan would have liked a clearer reference to the relations that bind priests to Mary, the Mother of priests; Compagnone, in the name of eighty-five fathers, would have expected a clearer exhortation to priestly holiness in the schema.

The last speech was the one Archbishop Pellegrino.[280] On that day Father Congar noted in his *Diary*: "Little by little we are escaping from [the era of] Pius IX and Pius XII (I mention them here only from the point of view of their refusal of the world as it is). Everything is cohering: the work of the council, even though it was so little thought through in advance, and has been conducted [from a human point of view] in the way that it has been, is extraordinarily consistent. The page is being turned over on Augustinianism and on the Middle Ages."[281] In the corridors of the council some cardinals began to walk around in "clerical garb," like simple priests: among the first were Cardinals Suenens and Léger.[282]

On October 28, 1965, the seventh anniversary of the election of John XXIII, five conciliar documents were promulgated by Paul VI in a public session: the decrees, *Christus Dominus*,[283] on the pastoral office of bishops

---

[276] AS IV/5:188–191. Brian Charles Foley (1910–1999), English, ordained in 1937, bishop of Lancaster in 1962.

[277] Ibid., 191–194. Armando Fares (1904–1980), ordained in 1927, archbishop coadjutor of Catanzaro and archbishop of Squillace in 1950, archbishop of Catanzaro in 1956.

[278] AS IV/5:194–196. Enrique Pechuán Marín (1913–1983), Argentine, ordained in 1938, bishop of Cruz del Eje in 1963.

[279] Ibid., 197–199.

[280] AS IV/5:200–203.

[281] Congar, *Journal*, 825–826.

[282] Cf. Câmara, *Lettres conciliaires*, 2:967.

[283] Text in AS IV/5:564–583; see also COD, 921–939.

(2,139 votes in favor, two against, one invalid); *Perfectae caritatis*,[284] on the renewal of religious life (2,325 votes in favor, four against); *Optatam totius*,[285] on priestly formation in keeping with the spirit of the council (2,318 votes in favor, three against); the two declarations, *Gravissimum educationis*[286] (2,290 votes in favor, thirty-five against), on the new principles of Christian education, and *Nostra aetate*,[287] on the Church's relations with the non-Christian religions (2,221 votes in favor, eighty-eight against, one invalid). None of the sixteen documents that were approved, except the decree *Inter mirifica*, had such a high number of *non placet* votes.

After October 29, the General Congregations were suspended for ten days, to give more time to the commissions that had to process the *modi*. On November 10 the decree *Apostolicam actuositatem* on the apostolate of the laity was also approved with 2,210 voting *placet*, two *non placet*, and two *placet iuxta modum*.[288]

The eighth public session, which Cardinal Lercaro deemed "the most beautiful and most enthusiastic session of the entire council," took place on November 18.[289] Father de Lubac led the procession of concelebrants with the Holy Father, and Bishop Câmara seemed to see Teilhard de Chardin himself in the person of the French Jesuit. In his periodical circular letter Câmara wrote: "I assure you that if Teilhard were still on earth—in China or in the U.S.A. or in any other place of exile—Pope John would have made him come as an expert and he would have concelebrated yesterday with Paul VI."[290] On October 16, in the Great Hall of the Domus Mariae,

---

284 Ibid., 584–593; see also COD, 939–947.

285 Ibid., 593–605; see also COD, 947–959. The monograph by Alois Greiler examines the various phases of the origin of the Vatican II decree on seminaries and the role of the individual members of that "second-string" commission, and especially of the Benedictine Paul Augustin Mayer (described by the author as "manager, driving force and author of *Optatam totius*"). Cf. Alois Greiler, *Das Konzil und die Seminare: Die Ausbildung der Priester in der Dynamik des Zweiten Vatikanums*, Foreword by P. A. Cardinal Mayer, O.S.B., Annua Nuntia Lovanensia 48 (Louvain, Paris, Dudley, MA, 2003), 363.

286 Text in AS IV/5:606–616; see also COD, 959–968.

287 Ibid., 616–619; see also COD, 968–971.

288 Cf. AS IV/6:298.

289 Letter dated November 21 in Lercaro, *Lettere*, 409.

290 Câmara, *Lettres conciliaires*, 2:1054.

which was full of council fathers, young priests, and religious, de Lubac had spoken about "Teilhard of Chardin, a disciple of St. Paul," and declared that the reading from St. Paul about the Word of God who "descended and ascended that he might fill all things" [*cf.* Eph 4:10] is found again in his French confrère's idea of the cosmic Christ.[291]

In his homily Paul VI restated his desire to complete the reform of the Roman curia and announced the opening of the canonical processes for the beatification of Pius XII and of John XIII.[292]

After the Mass, in the midst of applause, two documents were promulgated: the constitution *Dei Verbum*[293] on Divine Revelation, on which the debate between conservatives and reformers had started at the beginning of the council,[294] and the decree, *Apostolicam actuositatem*[295] on the apostolate of the laity. Of the 2,350 votes cast, the first document got 2,344 "yes" votes and only six "no." The second document, with 2,342 voting, got 2,340 "yes" and two "no": practically unanimous.[296]

The text of *Dei Verbum*, the conciliar document with the longest gestation period, which had started the doctrinal battle of the council, now seemed to satisfy everyone. The solid support for the text can be explained by the fact that in *Dei Verbum*, as in *Lumen gentium*, there is no dogmatic definition, and, unlike the other documents, such as *Dignitatis humanae*, no traditional concept is denied or called into question. What is new, rather, is the way of addressing the issues, that "pastoral" spirit that aroused the utmost satisfaction on the part of Father de Lubac.[297]

In his final intervention Cardinal Suenens wanted to thank, on behalf of the assembly, the Secretary Felici, and to pay homage, he recalls, "to a man who for four years implacably obstructed all the ideas that we defended. He opposed the inclinations of the council twenty-four hours a day; he truly

---

[291] Vittorio Citterich, "L'ispirazione paolina di Teilhard de Chardin," in *Avvenire d'Italia* (October 17, 1965).

[292] Text of the homily in AS IV/6:689–695.

[293] Text in AS IV/6:597–609; see also COD, 971–981.

[294] According to B. Dupuy, "The theological debate on revelation would remain for historians the fundamental debate of Vatican II" (*Vatican II: La Révélation divine* [Paris: Cerf, 1968], 1:62).

[295] AS IV/6:609–632; see also COD, 981–1001.

[296] Concerning the votes on the two documents, see AS IV/6:687–688.

[297] Cf. H. de Lubac, *La Révélation divine* (Paris: Cert, 1983), 154.

fought, with consummate skill, playing all the procedural cards against us, never giving in, not even when faced with an overwhelming majority, always seeking to make his own point of view triumph."[298]

11. The historic day, December 7

a) The promulgation of the final documents

The fourth session was characterized by an almost frenetic activity, with 256 votes taken between September 20 and December 6, 1965, (47% of all of the votes during the entire council) and the solemn approval of two constitutions, six decrees, and three declarations, that is, eleven of the sixteen documents in all that were issued by Vatican II.[299]

On December 4 the 167th General Congregation took place. In the afternoon, the pope presided over an ecumenical prayer service for the more than one hundred observers and guests in the Basilica of Saint Paul Outside the Walls. A great number of bishops and Catholic observers prayed with them. Congar knelt at the tomb of St. Paul and invoked Luther, "who had wanted to reaffirm 'the gospel' for which Paul had struggled."[300]

In this same place John XXIII had celebrated, on January 25, 1959, the conclusion of the Week of Prayer for Christian Unity, and, immediately after, in a remote little room of the adjacent Benedictine Abbey, had announced to a limited group of cardinals his decision to convoke the council.

On Sunday, December 5, an inter-denominational prayer meeting took place, in the presence of Paul VI—the first one in which a pope participated. In the course of it the representatives of all the religious confessions on hand recited passages from sacred scripture.[301] That day the pope had de Lubac, Jean Guitton, and the Lutheran theologian Oscar Cullman over for dinner.[302] The next day the final General Congregation celebrated its

---

298 Suenens, *Diario*, 60.

299 G. Alberigo, "The Conclusion of the Council and the Initial Reception," in HVT 5:541–572 at 541.

300 Congar, *Journal*, 865.

301 Cf. Caprile, 5:455–456.

302 Cf. de Lubac, *Quaderni*, 898–901.

last deliberation with the vote on schema 13. There were as many as 483 votes against the fifth chapter concerning peace and the promotion of the community of nations, but in the concluding vote on the entire text, the number of votes against the text decreased, but it still reached the level of 251. This vote was far from unanimous, but the pope nevertheless decided to promulgate it the following day.

On December 7 the final public session of the council took place. This was an historic day not only because of the promulgation of the remaining four schemas, but because of the symbolic character that it came to take on. Before the final Mass, a public embrace between Paul VI and the metropolitan of Heliopolis, Melito, who had arrived from Constantinople representing the patriarch Athenagoras, confirmed the annulment of the excommunication that representatives of the pope had imposed on the "Orthodox" Church on July 16, 1054.

At the beginning of the session, in the presence of the pope, the secretary general of the council Felici presented for the approval of the fathers the four last documents: the Declaration *Dignitatis humanae*[303] on religious liberty (2,308 in favor, seventy against); the decrees *Ad gentes*[304] on the missionary activity of the Church (2,394 in favor, five against), and *Presbyterorum ordinis*[305] on priestly ministry (2,390 in favor, four against); and finally

303 Text in AS IV/7: 663–673; see also COD, 1001–1011. Theologians faithful to the traditional teaching of the Church have given different interpretations of *Dignitatis humanae*: some assert that the document is in continuity with the traditional magisterium of the Church (cf. Victorino Rodríguez, O.P., "Estudio historico-doctrinal de la declaración sobre la libertad religiosa del Concilio Vaticano II," in *La Ciencia Tomista* 93 [1966]: 193–339; Brian W. Harrison, *Le développement de la doctrine catholique sur la liberté religieuse* [Paris: Dominique Martin Morin, 1988]; Basile (Valuet), O.S.B., *Liberté religieuse et tradition catholique* [Le Barroux: Abbaye Sainte-Madeleine, 1998]). The rupture with tradition was pointed out by M. Lefebvre, *Ils l'ont découronné, op. cit.*, Engl. transl. *They Have Uncrowned Him, op. cit.*; Bernard Lucien, *Grégoire XVI, Pie IX et Vatican II: Études sur la liberté religieuse dans la doctrine catholique* (Tours: Forts dans la Foir, 1990) (the author later modified his opinion); M. Davies, *The Second Vatican Council and Religious Liberty, op. cit.*; Michel Martin, "Le Concile Vatican II et la liberté religieuse," in *De Rome et d'ailleurs*, special issue (January 1986): 1–106. Some of the better studies are *Lettre à quelques évêques sur la situation de la Sainte Église* and the *Mémoire sur certaines erreurs actuelles, suivies d'une annexe sur la liberté religieuse* (Paris: Société Saint Thomas d'Aquin, 1983), composed by an international group of theologians and university professors.

304 Text in AS IV/7:673–704; see also COD, 1011–1042.

305 Text in ibid., 704–732; see also COD, 1042–1069.

the pastoral constitution *Gaudium et spes*[306] on the relations of the Church with the world (2,309 in favor, seventy-five against). Contrary to custom, prolonged applause, difficult to interpret, underscored the announcement of the seventy *non placet* votes[307] for *Dignitatis humanae*. "The day of the promulgation of *Dignitatis humanae* was certainly a happy one for me," the Jesuit Giacomo Martina wrote, summing up the feelings of a vast array of progressives. "The distinction between thesis and hypothesis had been abandoned, and religious liberty now had its true foundation."[308]

The *Coetus Internationalis* had valiantly opposed this document, which in the balloting on November 19 had received as many as 249 *non placet* votes. Nonetheless as the biography of Archbishop Lefebvre recalls, "On December 7, in a public session attended by the pope, the final vote showed that the *Coetus's* numbers had fallen to seventy *non placets*,"[309] more or less the same number of votes (seventy-five) cast against *Gaudium et spes.*

b) The unsuccessful condemnation of communism

The constitution *Gaudium et spes* was the sixteenth and last document officially promulgated by the Second Vatican Council. It intended to be a completely new definition of the relations between the Church and the world. The Church described herself as "a sacrament for the world" (cf. nos. 42, 45) claiming that it is her task to understand "the signs of the times" and to interpret them in the light of the gospel (nos. 4, 11), in "dialogue with the world" (no. 43). The formula for this was to live the truth of Christianity within the world's way of thinking so as to make the former more understandable and acceptable to modern man. Joseph Ratzinger, at that time a theologian, described this formula as the true and proper "testament" of the council:

---

306 Text in ibid., 733–739; see also COD, 1069–1135.

307 "How should it be interpreted? Noble rejoicing over the undaunted resistance of a minority; gratification at seeing the negative votes noticeably decreased in comparison to the preceding vote; a kindly admonition to the opponents to tell them that, despite everything, the schema had passed? We will not venture to say for certain" (Caprile, 5:500).

308 G. Martina, "The Historical Context...," *op. cit.*, 51.

309 B. Tissier de Mallerais, *op. cit.*, 311.

> If it is desirable to offer a diagnosis of the text as a whole, we might say that (in conjunction with the texts on religious liberty and world religions) it is a revision of the *Syllabus* of Pius IX, a kind of countersyllabus.... [A]s such it represents, on the part of the Church, an attempt at an official reconciliation with the new era inaugurated in 1789."[310]

For Cardinal König too, the document "marks a turning point in the Church's thinking about history that closes the era of the *Syllabus* and of *Pascendi*."[311] An illustrious theologian like Monsignor Brunero Gherardini, however, formulates a severe judgment:

> This capsized the thought of St. Thomas Aquinas, who taught that God cannot create for ends which are foreign to his own reality. Vatican II, on the other hand, made man "the only creature on earth which God willed for itself" (GS 24).... So the extreme limits of idolatrous anthropocentrism had already been reached. It was not longer a question of whether man believed or not, it was sufficient that he be the "center and crown" (GS 12) of all creation: creatures being willed and created by God to serve man, "subordinated to the integral perfection of the human person" (GS 59).[312]

In *Gaudium et spes* any form of condemnation of communism is missing. The fact was so remarkable "as to lend credence to the rumor of an explicit agreement between the patriarch of Moscow and the Holy See."[313] The council's silence on communism in fact constituted a striking omission by the historical gathering. Referring to this silence, Bishop Helder Câmara wrote in November 1965: "The Second Vatican Ecumenical Council said

---

[310] J. Ratzinger, *Principles of Catholic Theology*, 381, 382.

[311] F. König, *Chiesa dove vai?, op. cit.*, 108.

[312] B. Gherardini, *The Ecumenical Vatican Council II*, 220. This constitution," Monsignor Hubert Jedin comments in turn, "was greeted enthusiastically, but its subsequent history has already showed that at that time its significance and importance had been widely overestimated and that it had not been understood how profoundly the 'world' that they wanted to win for Christ had penetrated into the Church" (*Il Concilio Vaticano II, op. cit.*, 151).

[313] A. Riccardi, *Il Vaticano e Mosca, op. cit.*, 281.

very many things, by its words and by its silences."[314] Plinio Corrêa de Oliveira, who had fought on the opposite side, recalls in his turn:

> Presided over by John XXIII and later by Paul VI, the ecumenical council of Vatican II was the largest in the history of the Church. It was agreed that all the major topics of the day related to the Catholic cause would be discussed. That the attitude of the Church toward her greatest adversary at that time be among these topics was essential, absolutely essential! In her almost two-thousand-year history, the Church had never encountered such a powerful, brutal, and cunning adversary, so completely opposed to her doctrine. A discussion of contemporary religious problems facing religion that fails to deal with communism would be as flawed as a worldwide medical convened to study today's major diseases that omits any reference to AIDS.[315]

Gaudium et spes sought dialogue with the modern world, in the conviction that the journey that it made from humanism and protestantism, up to the French Revolution and Marxism, was an irreversible process. Modernity was really on the eve of a profound crisis that would manifest its first symptoms, a few years later, in the Revolution of '68. The council fathers ought to have made a prophetic gesture by challenging modernity instead of embracing its decomposing body, as it unfortunately happened.

The conciliar court would have been a place *par excellence* in which to the start a trial of communism analogous to what the Nuremburg trial was for National Socialism: not a trial of a penal character, and not even an *ex-post-facto* trial of the conquered by the conquerors, as Nuremburg was, but rather a cultural and moral trial, before the event, of the victims confronting their persecutors, as the so-called dissidents had begun to do.[316]

---

314 Câmara, *Lettres conciliaires*, 1:438.

315 P. Corrêa de Oliveira, "Communism and Anticommunism on the Threshold of the Millennium's Last Decade," in *The Wall Street Journal* (February 27, 1990) [available at http://www.tfp.org/tfp-http://www.tfp.org/tfp-home/statements/communism-and-anticommunism-on-the-threshold-of-the-milleniums-last-decade.html.).

316 Since the 1920s and 1930s extensive literature had drawn the attention of public opinion worldwide to the crimes of communism. Only in 1997 did the *Black Book of Communism* appear (Engl. transl. Harvard University Press, 1997), edited by the French historian Stéphane Courtois, which offered documentary proof of it.

c) The reasons for the conservatives' defeat

The next four votes, one for each conciliar schema, were followed by comprehensive vote on the four documents related to their final approval and proclamation, according to the procedure established by article 2 of the rules.[317]

After the approval of the four decrees there appearred "an obvious spirit of joyous gratitude on the part of the bishops as they met for the last time in Saint Peter's Basilica. There was an almost effusive atmosphere of joy when at the end they all embraced and gave one another the kiss of peace before departing."[318]

One can ask at this point how it was possible that, after the harsh debates in the hall, which had brought to light the existence of opposing alignments that were balanced in the number and the authority of their respective interventions, when it came time to vote they always managed to approve the schemas by an overwhelming majority, and at the moment when the documents were promulgated it would even happen that someone who had voted against a document would sign it, as Bishop de Castro Mayer and Archbishop Lefebvre did in the case of *Dignitatis humanae* on religious liberty.[319] There were different kinds of reasons. First of all, one must keep in mind the "democratic" process of the conciliar assembly, which appeared to be a sort of ecclesiastical parliament, governed by rules and, above all, by the "philosophy" of modern democracy. One has to recall in this regard the existence of different concepts of the parliamentary system. The liberal tradition, which is substantially individualistic, protects the rights of the minority, before and after the vote (in Great Britain the "Shadow Governments" and "Her Majesty's Opposition" come to mind). In the democratic concept that originated with Rousseau, the will of the majority, at the time of its expression, is no longer the numerical sum of

---

317 Cf. AAS IV/7:804–850.

318 J. Ratzinger, *Theological Highlights of Vatican II* (New York, etc.: Paulist Press, 1966), 181.

319 Cf. AS, IV/7:809 and 823. "Archbishop Marcel Lefebvre's and Bishop Antonio de Castro Mayer's support was officially registered in the council's *Acta*. If later Archbishop Lefebvre stated several times that he did not put his signature on the declaration [on] religious liberty—as with *Gaudium et spes*—it was a claim in line with his opposition before and after the promulgation, and the result of an error or a memory slip.... In our opinion, the archbishop's signing *Dignitatis humanae* takes nothing away from the value of his fight against religious liberty" (B. Tissier de Mallerais, *op. cit.*, 312–313 and, in more detail, 311–313).

individual wills but rather becomes "a general will," a collective will, to which particular groups and individuals must bend.[320] The Second Vatican Council seemed to want to replace the "absolutist" model of Trent and of Vatican I with a new "democratic" model, which replaced the supreme will of the Roman pontiff with that of the assembly, although still united with the same pontiff. The truth of tradition was replaced by a "social will", which was worked out collectively and acknowledged socially. The will of the conciliar assembly was equivalent to the "general will" of Rousseau: a sacred and absolute will to which the fathers, observing the laws that they had made for themselves, felt obliged in conscience to subordinate their own ideas and opinions.[321]

The fact that the assembly was ecclesiastical and not political "sacralized," so to speak, the expression of the "general will," giving it a transcendent value. Moreover, once a schema was promulgated by the pope, it was no longer a schema, but a magisterial act, thus changing its theological nature.

One could object at this point that the council fathers knew very well that the council's magisterium had no guarantee of infallibility, especially after Popes John XXIII and Paul VI themselves had specified its pastoral character. It should be mentioned, however, that in the century following Vatican Council I the possibility of "resisting" incorrect decisions of a pontiff had never been taken into consideration by the theologians, who on the contrary had stressed the papal prerogatives even in the exercise of the ordinary magisterium. Father Frederick William Faber,[322] one of the greatest spiritual writers of the nineteenth century, had explained

---

[320] Cf. Jacob L. Talmon, *The Rise of Totalitarian Democracy* (Boston: Beacon, 1952); B. Baczko, "Le contrat social des Français: Sieyès et Rousseau," in *The French Revolution and the creation of modern political culture*, ed. Keith Michael Baker (Oxford: Pergamon Press, 1987); Augustin Cochin, *Les Sociétés de Pensée et la Révolution en Bretagne* (Paris, 1921).

[321] The political concept of Georg Friedrich Hegel (1770–1831) is also descended from the Rousseauian theory of the "general will." Like Rousseau, Hegel describes the passage from the particular will of individuals to the ethical universality of the "general will," distinguishing between civil society, which expresses the multiplicity of the individual particular interests, and the state, which brings about—at a higher level of "universality"—the common good. Cf. R. de Mattei, *La sovranità necessaria* (Rome: Il Minotauro, 2001), 107–110.

[322] The Oratorian Father Frederick William Faber (1808–1892), a convert to Catholicism in 1845, was one of the most popular religious writers at the turn of the twentieth century. About him see Ronald Chapman, *Father Faber* (London: Burns and Oates, 1961).

that devotion to the pope is an essential part of Christian piety,[323] and generations of priests had been trained to obey the Roman pontiff without qualification. Toward the papacy, as with regard to Our Lady, the "Roman" bishops practiced "maximalism," while not considering the problem of the moral limits of obedience.

"Our Creed is the pope, our morality is the pope, our life is the pope," St. Luigi Orione, for example, wrote to his priests. "Our love, our heart, our reason for living is the pope; for us the pope is Jesus Christ; to love the pope and to love Jesus are the same thing; to listen to and follow the pope is to listen to and follow Jesus Christ; to serve the pope is to serve Jesus Christ; to give one's life for the pope is to give one's life for Jesus Christ."[324] The possibility of a pope who could err on the doctrinal level or fall into ambiguity, or even into heresy, although admitted in theory by all theologians, was considered unrealistic and consequently had never been taken into consideration.[325]

For many fathers, undermining the supreme pontiff's authority or impairing the unity of the episcopal assembly meant jeopardizing their own authority as pastors. "To govern," wrote Cardinal Siri, "is to guide with authority a community towards a goal. If there is no authority, or ability to create an obligation of conscience, there is no true government."[326] Therefore, although he did not share many of the choices made by John XXIII and Paul VI, the archbishop of Genoa felt toward papal authority the same "obligation of conscience" that he demanded from his subjects.[327] Many conservative council fathers conducted themselves in the same way.

---

[323] Cf. F. W. Faber, "Devotion and fidelity to the Pope," a conference given on January 1, 1869, in the Oratory in London; Italian translation in *Il Papa nel pensiero degli scrittori religiosi e politici*, 2 vols. (Rovigo-Rome: Istituto Veneto Arti Grafiche – *La Civiltà Cattolica*, 1927), 2:230–237 at 233.

[324] Don Luigi Orione, *Lettere* (Rome: Postulazione della Piccola Opera della Divina Provvidenza, 1929), 2:44.

[325] The best study of these points remains the *Hypothèse théologique d'un Papa hérétique*, Part II of the study by Arnaldo Xavier da Silveira, *La nouvelle Messe de Paul VI: Qu'en penser?* (Chiré-en-Montreuil, Diffusion de la Pensée française, 1975), 213–334.

[326] G. Siri, "Memorie," in *Idem, Un vescovo ai vescovi* (Pisa: Giardini, 1991), 13.

[327] "The most interesting property of the law," he had written, "is that it generates an obligation in conscience. The juridical order is essentially based on this interior world, on this profound bond" (G. Siri, *La ricostruzione sociale* [Rome: AVE, 1943], 104).

A witness, Father Ralph Wiltgen, comments as follows on the final vote on religious liberty:

> Nearly all of the seventy negative votes had been cast by the hard core of the International Group of Fathers. And yet, after the voting was done, they were as ready as the next man to accept the promulgated decree. Basically, this was the attitude of all council fathers, whether they belonged to the liberal or the conservative camp; each was convinced that his position on a given topic was the correct one, the one which would bring greater blessing upon the Church and mankind. But these men, trained in Church law, also realized that both sides could not be right. And ultimately they went along with the majority view, when this finally became clear and was promulgated by the pope as the common doctrine taught by the Second Vatican Council.[328]

To insist unyieldingly on one's opposition to conciliar decisions would require perhaps, besides an excellent theological knowledge of the nature of magisterial acts, a "prophetic" attitude, like the one evoked by the Abbé de Nantes when he stated, on the eve of the fourth session, that one bishop alone would be able to make the *aggiornamento* of Vatican II fail: he wrote, "It would be enough," he wrote, "for only one of the fathers—and I reminded some of them about this—to rise up and proclaim before all that the faith prevents him from accepting a certain proposition; all he would need to do would be to challenge their enormous lethargy, to threaten to leave the council… if this or that proposal is voted on, accepted, promulgated…. If such a man were in the council tomorrow, his appeal to the truth revealed by God would be enough to stop all the machinery of subversion!"[329]

The French priest's words may seem "quixotic," but only an attitude of strong psychological impact could have changed the course of events at that moment. The occasion for a sign of public protest could have been, for example, the scandal of the pigeonholing of the anticommunist petition. The roots of the defeat of the fathers of the *Coetus Internationalis* are to be sought in a weakness that was more psychological than doctrinal.

---

[328] Wiltgen, 252.

[329] Georges de Nantes, "Lettre à mes amis," no. 211 (September 1, 1965): 13.

Archbishop Lefebvre stressed, however, the psychological weight of papal approval, admitting that he had signed many documents of the council "under moral pressure from the Holy Father," since, he said, "I cannot separate myself from the Holy Father; if the Holy Father signs, morally I am obliged to sign."[330]

Although in the first phase of the council main problem of the conservative fathers was their lack of organization, in the last two final they lacked instead the will to resist to the end. On the other hand, there was no lack of will and determination either among the progressive minority or in Pope Montini himself, who never wanted to make his will prevail thanks to numerical strength alone. He sought to have the will of the majority become a *consensus unanimis* and was disposed to make concessions and strategic retreats just to get the assent of the minority. The attitude of Paul VI in the council has been variously appraised, but the portrait that Monsignor Prignon gives in one of his confidential reports to Ambassador Poswick is one of the most accurate:

> It is difficult to believe in the congenital hesitancy of someone who, on more than one occasion, displayed an iron will and unfailing perseverance in the line of conduct that he mapped out.... On the other hand his concern with convincing the minority did not lead Paul VI to give in to them on the essentials, nor did it prevent him from running the risk of a hardening of the majority or keep him from employing rather "sensational" forms of opposition. The modifications that he made at the last minute, after the final vote, to the document on ecumenism testify also to an uncommonly decisive character.... As for me, I think that Paul VI, fully aware of his role as supreme arbiter, wanted to stand above the "partisan" fray, and above all succeeded in doing so, and that he ceaselessly aimed at getting unanimity. He was right also at the moment when he agreed to what, according to ill-informed minds, could appear to be a limitation of the primacy and a correction to the Vatican I dogma reaffirming in theory and in practice the indefeasible rights of the successor of Peter and the perfect consistency between the two councils.[331]

---

[330] B. Tissier de Mallerais, *op. cit.*, 312.

[331] Fonds Prignon, "Rapport sur la 3e session du Concile: 25 octobre-21 novembre," in CLG, no. 1058.

d) The final homily of Paul VI

During the public session on December 7, immediately before the concelebration of Mass, the secretary for Promoting Christian Unity, Jan Willebrands climbed into the pulpit and read in French the text of a joint declaration in which the Catholic Church and the "Orthodox" Church of Constantinople decided to "deplore" the reciprocal sentences of excommunication and the subsequent events that had led to the severance of ecclesial communion.[332] At that very moment the same text was read in the patriarchal Basilica of Constantinople, in the presence of the patriarch and seven legates of the pope, headed by Cardinal Shehan, the archbishop of Baltimore. The act annulling the excommunication was formally completed with the reading of the pontifical brief, *Ambulate in dilectione* by Bishop Willebrands.[333] The pope, in this papal brief, declared that he and the Orthodox primate "remove both from memory and from the midst of the Church the sentences of excommunication which followed these events… and they commit these excommunications to oblivion."[334]

In the homily at the Mass that followed,[335] Paul VI mentioned that the council had brought about a meeting between "the religion of God who became man" and "The religion (for such it is) of man who makes himself God,"[336] without the two religions entering into conflict, which did not fail to arouse "astonishment and scandal."[337] "Secular humanism," was presented to the council's consideration, but the contact had not caused "a clash, a battle, a condemnation," as might have happened.

---

332 Cf. AS IV/7:651–654; Caprile, 5:508–509; P. Chenaux, "L'influence des écoles théologiques dans la rédaction de la constitution pastorale *Gaudium et spes* (1962–1965)," in *Annuarium Historiae Conciliorum* 35 (2003): 150–166.

333 Text in Caprile, 5:509–510.

334 Ibid., 509. English translation in "Catholic-Orthodox Delegation," in *Council Daybook: Vatican II, Session 4* (Washington, D.C.: National Catholic Welfare Conference, 1966), 286.

335 Text of the homily in AS IV/7:654–662; Ital. transl. in Caprile, 5:501–505.

336 AS IV/7:658.

337 A. Wenger, *Les trois Rome, op. cit.*, 190.

> The Catholic religion and human life reaffirm their alliance with one another, the fact that they converge on one single human reality: the Catholic religion is for mankind. In a certain sense it is the life of mankind.... Secular humanism, revealing itself in its horrible anti-clerical reality has, in a certain sense, defied the council. The religion of the God who became man has met the religion (for such it is) of man who makes himself God. And what happened? Was there a clash, a battle, a condemnation? There could have been, but there was none. The old story of the Samaritan has been the model of the spirituality of the council. A feeling of boundless sympathy has permeated the whole of it.[338]

The homily by Paul VI on December 7, centered completely on the relation between the Church and the world, can be considered the conclusive message of the council and the interpretive key that the pope proposed for it. It was linked thematically with the opening discourse of John XXIII on October 11, 1963. Romano Amerio draws a comparison between the diagnosis of his own age made by Paul VI in this document and the one made by Pius X in the encylical, *E supremi apostolatus*.[339] Like Paul VI, Pope Sarto had recognized that the spirit of modern man is a spirit of independence that dedicates all creation to itself. Yet although the diagnosis of the two popes is identical, the value judgment that they pass on modernity is different, if not contradictory.

> Just as St. Pius X, citing St. Paul (2 Thess 2:4), saw modern man making himself a god and claiming adoration, so Paul VI explicitly says that "the religion of the God who made himself man, has met the religion (for such it is) of man who makes himself God." Pope Paul however, ignoring the fact that the confrontation involves rival principles, thinks that thanks to the council the confrontation has not produced a clash, or a struggle, or an anathema, but an immense sympathy and a new attention to the needs of man on the part of the Church.[340]

---

338 AS IV/7:661; English translation in *Council Daybook* 3:359–362 at 360.

339 St. Pius X, encylical *E supremi apostolatus* (October 4, 1903), in ASS 36 (1903–1904): 129–139; English text, "On the Restoration of All Things in Christ," at the EWTN website: www.ewtn.com/library/ENCYC/P10SUPRE.HTM

340 R. Amerio, *Iota Unum, op. cit.*, 95.

Father Congar did not hide his satisfaction: "The pope's speech: very much in the tone of *'Ecclesiam suam'*; a veritable declaration of the complete acceptance of the modern human being and of the primacy of anthropology."[341]

The French theologian added contentedly:

> Looking at things objectively, I did a great deal to prepare for the council, elaborating and diffusing the ideas that the council consecrated. At the council itself, I did a great deal of work. I could almost say *"Plus omnibus laboravi"* [I worked harder than any of them (cf. 1 Cor 15:10)], but that would, no doubt, not be true: think of Philips, for example.[342]

Congar claimed paternity in the partial or total drafting of many documents: *Lumen gentium, De revelatione, De ecumenismo, Declaration on non-Christian religions, schema 13, De missionibus, De Libertate religiosa, De presbyteris.*[343] But to attribute to theologians only, such as Congar, Rahner, or Philips, the doctrinal fatherhood of the council would be to do an injustice to some council fathers, like Cardinal Suenens, who not only played a governing role in the council but also exercised a profound theological influence on it. Câmara, recalling Suenens role, described it, not incorrectly, "a perfect image of Vatican II."[344]

Father Kobler, for his part, has pointed out how Paul VI was the true "theoretician" of Vatican II while the theologians were only the "engineers"[345] called to help carry out his program for the renewal of the Church, "which can be summed up in three words: *totus homo phaenomenicus*, that is, the whole man as a phenomenological reality."[346]

All told, the conciliar assembly held 168 General Congregations, approving, in five different sessions, sixteen documents: four constitutions,

---

[341] Congar, *Journal*, 870 (December 7).

[342] Ibid., 870–871.

[343] Cf. ibid., 871. Cf. A. Melloni, "Yves Congar al Vaticano II: Ipotesi e linee di ricerca," in *Rivista di Storia della Chiesa in Italia*, 50/2 (1996): 516–520; R. Burigana and G. Turbanti, "The Intersession: Preparing the Conclusion of the Council," in HVT 4:453–616 at 509–510.

[344] Câmara, *Lettres conciliaires*, 2:895.

[345] Cf. J. F. Kobler, "Were theologians the engineers of Vatican II?" *op. cit.*, 242–243.

[346] *Idem, Vatican II: Theophany and the Phenomenon of Man* (London - New York: Peter Lang, 1991), 83–189 at 83.

nine decrees, and three declarations, with 3,058 council fathers taking part in the work. In all the conciliar deliberations, the utmost concessions had been made to win the goodwill of those who happened to be separated from the Church.[347] Now everyone was looking forward to its fruits.

12. The curtain falls on the Second Vatican Council

On the morning of December 8, 1965, on the spacious steps of Saint Peter's Basilica, on a windy day and under an intermittently overcast sky, the solemn final ceremony of the Second Vatican Council took place. Starting at nine o'clock in the morning, a crowd estimated to be around 300,000 gathered between the square and the Via della Constituzione. A little after ten, while all the bells in the city of Rome tolled, the long procession began, with the council fathers preceding Paul VI, who was being transported in the *sedia gestatoria*. As Hubert Jedin, the historian of the councils, recalls in his memoirs with certain bitterness, the ceremony "did not correspond to the idea that I had of the solemnity proper to an ecumenical council. It was a demonstration and, as such, a concession to the age of the masses and to the mass-media."[348]

Seated beside Paul VI during the ceremony were the four cardinal moderators, the winners of the council, and Cardinal Ottaviani, the big loser. According to Wiltgen, none of them had had as much influence as Cardinal Frings. His theological expert was the young Father Ratzinger, but Frings had depended above all on Father Rahner. Little by little, as the council drew to a close, Ratzinger, a disciple of Rahner, had proved to be in disagreement with him on many points, concerning which he would openly take his distance after the council.[349]

The final appeal of the council was addressed to the world. The pope

---

[347] Cf. P. Corrêa de Oliveira, "Chiuso il Concilio: Momento di straordinaria importanza nella storia dell'umanità," in *Idem, Rivoluzione e Contro-Rivoluzione, op. cit.*, 313–316.

[348] H. Jedin, *Lebensbericht* (Mainz: Kommission für Zeitgeschichte, 1984). Citation at p. 321 of the Italian translation, *Storia della mia vita* (Brescia: Morcelliana, 1987).

[349] Cf. Wiltgen, 285. A similar itinerary was followed by Father Arturo Medina Estévez, theologian of Cardinal Silva Henríquez, with whom he had differences of opinion after the end of the council. Cardinal Silva Henríquez would level the way for the social communist Allende in Chile, while Monsignor Medina, later a cardinal, would become the rallying point for the conservatives, especially in liturgical matters.

announced in French the messages that would be read by as many cardinals and then personally delivered by him to the representatives of the different groups to which they were directed: rulers, scientists, artists, women, workers, the poor, the sick, and the suffering, youth. The message to intellectuals,[350] read by Cardinal Léger, was delivered to Jacques Maritain, assisted by Jean Guitton and by the Polish philosopher Stefan Swieżawski,[351] auditors at the council. As he delivered the message to them, Paul VI whispered "The Church is grateful for your life-long work."[352] Seven years earlier, in 1958, Cardinal Pizzardo, prefect of the Congregation for Universities, had forbidden the Catholic University of the Sacred Heart in Milano to confer a degree *honoris causa* on the French philosopher, the theoretician of that integral humanism that the *Civiltà Cattolica* had vehemently criticized. Father Congar noted in his *Diary*, "The council is going to shine forth in the world. Today it is achieving its Pentecostal moment, of which John XXIII had spoken."[353] Hans Küng, unanimously elected for the second time on December 10 as dean of the theological faculty at Tübingen, saw some of the proposals coming true that he had advanced five years earlier in his book, *Council, Reform and Reunion.* Vatican II, he wrote, "may not have been allowed to do much of what it could have done. But it has achieved far more than most people expected."[354]

After the messages to the world, there was a reading by Archbishop Felici of the apostolic letter, *In Spiritu Sancto*, with which the pope declared the Second Vatican council closed. Then Paul VI gave the final blessing, amidst applause from the crowd, and proclaimed in a loud voice: "Go in peace, the council is ended." It was 1:21 p.m. on Wednesday, December 8, 1965, when the bells of Saint Peter's announced the conclusion of the twenty-first ecumenical council of the Church.

That evening, the Italian Prime Minister, Aldo Moro, gave a dinner in honor of the foreign delegations that had come to Rome for the council.

---

350 Italian text in Caprile, 5:520.

351 Stefan Swieżawski (1907–2004), Polish, professor of philosophy at the University of Lublin. Cf. Jerzy Kalinowski and Stefan Swieżawski, *La philosophie à l'heure du Concile* (Paris: Société d'Éditions Internationales, 1965).

352 Maritain, *Carnet de notes* (Paris: Desclée de Brouwer, 1965) at December 8, 1965.

353 Congar, *Journal*, 874.

354 Küng, *My Struggle*, 444.

At the end of the meal, he mentioned that the assembly had intended to address, among its principal topics, "those concerning the Church's position with regard to the cultural, social, and moral achievements of the modern world and the relations with the Christian Churches, with every confession, with every religion, and finally with all men."[355]

On September 24, Paul VI had met in the Vatican the journalist from *Corriere della Sera*, Alberto Cavallari, to explain the meaning of the conciliar message. "It is necessary to be simple and shrewd," said the pope, "in grasping the meaning of the years that we are experiencing. The Church wishes to become many-sided so as better to reflect the modern world. To become this she has decided to sink the plow into unproductive grounds, even into the hardest grounds, in order to shift, to enliven, to bring to light what remains buried. This plowing causes shocks, stresses, and problems. My predecessor had the job of sinking the plow. Now the job of guiding it has fallen into our poor hands." The pope confirmed "the need for the Church to be open" to the world, regarding this as the essence of "dialogue," and he denied the existence of a crisis in the Church. "The council itself goes to show that alongside a crisis of faith in the world, there is fortunately not a crisis in the Church"[356]

[355] Caprile, 5:527.

[356] Alberto Cavallari, "Colloquio con Papa Paolo VI," in *Corriere della Sera* (October 3, 1963), reprinted in *Idem, Il Vaticano che cambia* (Milan: Mondadori, 1966), 44–45.

VII

The Conciliar Era (1965–1978)

1. The era of the "Conciliar Revolution"

The expression "post-conciliar era," designating the years following the conclusion of the Second Vatican Council, is historically improper because it assumes a nonexistent break between the historical phase opened by the council and the one immediately following. It would be more correct to speak about the "era of the council," to designate in the strict sense the twenty years (1958-1978) that elapsed between the beginning of the pontificate of John XXIII and the end of the pontificate of Paul VI, the two pontiffs who respectively opened and closed Vatican II and, historically, were the personification thereof. The conciliar era as a whole, as Plinio Corrêa de Oliveira described it,[1] was a "cultural revolution" in the Church, that brought about profound transformations in the mentality and customs of the hierarchy and of the faithful. This era naturally does not conclude with the death of Paul VI: the very fact that his two successors decided to take the names John Paul attests to the intended continuity between the two popes of the council and those who followed them. It is undeniable, however, that on the historical level the death of Paul VI marks a *caesura*, a moment of interruption between two eras that is not theological but certainly historical.

---

[1] Cf. A-IPCO, March 30, 1988.

From 1962 on people started talking about the "spirit of the council," meaning by this term a psychological attitude of rupture and of optimistic trust in the future of the Church, committed above all to its *"aggiornamento"* and its "dialogue" with the world.[2] In this sense the conciliar document that most closely summarizes the conciliar spirit is the pastoral constitution *Gaudium et spes*, promulgated on December 7, 1965. To it should be added three other texts of significant relevance: the decree *Unitatis redintegratio* on ecumenism, dated November 21, 1964, the declaration *Nostra aetate* on the Church's relations with non-Christian religions, dated October 28, 1965, and the declaration *Dignitatis humanae*, also dated December 7, 1965.[3] The common perspective of these texts is ecumenism and the decisive contribution to their composition came from Cardinal Bea's Secretariat for Promoting Christian Unity.[4] The ecumenical sphere was the one that had allowed the greatest development of a tendency toward the future, presented as "fidelity to the future united Church, the Church of the final goal of the ecumenical journey."[5]

Apart from the doctrinal evaluation of the conciliar documents, there is no doubt that the Second Vatican Council appeared and was experienced by many, even those in important positions, as an "momentous turning point," a veritable "revolution" in the Church. Father Battista Mondin writes that "1965, the year in which Vatican II ended, can be taken as an epochal date for the history of theology,"[6] because from that time on, theology lost its speculative character and gained an eminently practical bent, following the slant of the "pastoral," non-dogmatic council: "The orientation towards praxis and 'inculturation' is the chief characteristic

---

2 For a well-grounded critique of this "spirit," see B. Gherardini, *The Ecumenical Vatican Council II*, 48–54.

3 On the unity and coherence of the three documents, cf. Florian Kolfhaus, *Pastorale Lehrverkündigung: Grundmotiv des Zweiten Vatikanischen Konzils: Untersuchungen zu "Unitatis redintegratio", "Dignitatis humanae", und "Nostra aetate"* (Berlin: LIT, 2010).

4 Cf. Barthe, *op. cit.*, 132–133.

5 L Sartori, *Teologia ecumenica oggi* (Padua: Libreria Gregoriana, 1987), 32–33; *Idem, Spirito Santo e storia* (Rome: Ave, 1977), which is the basis for the article "Segni dei tempi" ["signs of the times"] by Gianni Gennari in *Nuovo Dizionario di spiritualità*, ed. Stefano De Fiores and Tullo Goffi (Cinisello Balsamo: San Paolo, 1999), 1400–1422.

6 G. B. Mondin, *Storia della teologia* (Bologna: ESD, 1997), 4:664.

of the theology of the years 1965-1995. 'Praxology' and 'inculturation' are two facets of this major anthropological turn that took place in the theology of that period."[7] Theologians tried to introduce a distinction between doctrine, which in itself is unchangeable, and its formulation, which is bound up with the changeable linguistic structures of history. But the abandonment of clear, rigorous Thomistic language was not without its consequences on the theological level.[8] Pastoral language and practice modified the old system of values, without managing to create a new one. The Belgian philosopher Marcel De Corte observed this lucidly:

> Indeed, one does not change one's language like a garment.... By refusing to use the language of scholasticism, in which the natural effort of the human mind setting out in search of the truth has arrived at an unequalled degree of perfection, the council threw overboard at the same time that realism of which the Church had always had custody until the council. Into the emptied wineskin was poured not a new wine, but rather the wind of all the storms of human subjectivity, and with stupefied horror we see the ravages of this in the Church and in Christian civilization. In repudiating the language, the sign of concepts, they repudiated the things, and in repudiating the things, they embarked all at once, to the great astonishment of the fathers themselves, or of most of them, upon permanent subversion and revolution.[9]

The documents approved by the council were "framework laws" devoid of dogmatic content, but also of legal force, which allowed ample room for experimentation. Their implementation was left not only to the competent Roman congregations, but also and above all to the episcopal conferences. "The conciliar decisions," Jean Madiran wrote in the pages

---

[7] Ibid., 665.

[8] See Associazione Teologica Italiana, *Il linguaggio teologico oggi*, ed. Alfredo Marranzini (Milan: Ancora, 1970), in particular Carlo Molari, "La problematica del linguaggio teologico," 39–95. "For theology one could say that the overall meaning of theological formulas cannot be determined solely by their ideational contents or by existing relations within the system of faith, but must be identified within the broadest framework of the culture and historical experiences from which it draws its expressive categories" (ibid., 53).

[9] Marcel De Corte, *L'intelligence en péril de mort* (Paris: Collecction du Club de la culture française, 1969), 17. [Translated from French.]

of *Itinéraires*, "are the 'point of departure' for a whole implementation: an implementation of the decisions that had been promulgated, in keeping with the promulgated decisions."[10]

"It is not up to the council to say everything," Bishop Helder Câmara declared in the final days of Vatican II. "There are some implicit statements that it is our task to make explicit."[11] "What happened in Rome" at the council, the theologian Joseph Ratzinger observed for his part, "was only the formulation of a mandate whose execution must now be undertaken."[12] The conciliar documents were sufficiently ambiguous to allow different and sometimes conflicting interpretations. The same fathers who had fought most vigorously against the approval of some conciliar documents, proposed interpreting and applying them "in the light of tradition," in opposition to those who claimed to be applying them in terms of a discontinuity with the past.

2. The reform of the curia by Paul VI

The "reform" of the curia, the chief objective of the progressive minority, was also the first achievement of the conciliar era.[13] The curial edifice built over the centuries by the preceding pontiffs was systematically demolished. This required, at the start, a symbolic event, and this was the transformation of the Congregation of the Holy Office, which was renewed in fact and in name, precisely on the eve of the conclusion of the council, with the motu proprio *Integrae servandae*.[14] On the afternoon

---

[10] J. Madiran, "Un schisme pour décembre," *op. cit.*, 3. [Translated from French.]

[11] Câmara, *Lettres conciliaires*, 2:1026. A Belgian industrialist, Jacques Lannoye, on behalf of a group of friends, offered Cardinal Suenens and Bishop Helder Câmara financial support to fuel the "sacred flame" of the council after its conclusion (ibid., 887, 884–885).

[12] J. Ratzinger, *Theological Highlights of Vatican II*, 183.

[13] Cf. N. Del Re, *La curia Romana: Lineamenti storico-giuridici* (Rome: Edizioni di Storia e Letteratura, 1970); J. Sánchez y Sánchez, "La curia Romana hasta Pablo VI: las grandes líneas de su evolución histórica," in *Revista española de derecho canónico* 32 (1976): 439–458; *Idem,* "Ante una nueva reforma de la curia Romana: Entre el respeto y la esperanza," in *Estudios canónicos en homenaje al Profesor D. Lamberto de Echeverría* (Salamanca: Universidad Pontificia de Salamanca, 1988), 245–264.

[14] Cf. AAS 57 (1965): 952–955, Ital. transl. in Caprile, 5:466–467. The motu proprio was followed

of December 6, 1965, *L'Osservatore Romano* published the decree that abolished the Index of Forbidden Books and transformed the Holy Office into the Congregation for the Doctrine of the Faith, asserting that "it now seems better that the defense of the faith should come about through diligence in promoting doctrine."

The Index of Forbidden Books (*Index librorum prohibitorum*) had been created in 1558, through the work of the Congregation of the Roman Inquisition, which later (1908) became the Holy Office. The Index published in 1948, which remained in force until 1966, was the final edition of the catalogue of forbidden books that the congregation had started publishing in 1559.[15] The reform of the Holy Office carried the signature of Cardinal Ottaviani himself, who in the council hall had strenuously defended the role of the institution, which until then had been called *"Suprema."* On June 14, 1966, a notification from the pro-prefect of the Congregation for the Doctrine of the Faith declared that the Index would no longer have the legal force of ecclesiastical law. Many theologians felt authorized by this development to present themselves as the new and best accredited interpreters of the faith and of the word of God. On July 17, 1967 the anti-modernist oath imposed by St. Pius X was suppressed and replaced with a simple profession of the Creed.[16]

Equally eloquent in their significance were the appointments that followed. The ruling class of ecclesiastics who had guided the Church in the years immediately following the death of Pius XII was completely replaced. On February 4, 1966, Archbishop Gabriel-Marie Garrone, ordinary of Toulouse and vice-president of the French Episcopal Conference, was appointed pro-prefect of the Congregation of Seminaries and Universities, the dicastery that the progressives were denouncing as the one most

by the notification *Post litteras apostolicas* dated June 4, 1965. The Holy Office had been established, with the name of the Sacred Congregation of the Roman and Universal Inquisition, by Paul III, with the constitution *Licet ab initio* (July 21, 1542). See the critiques of Paul VI's reforms by R. Amerio, in *Iota unum, op. cit.*, 159–162, and by P. Pasqualucci, in *Giovanni XXIII, op. cit.*, 277–287.

[15] *L'Index librorum prohibitorum 1600–1966*, ed. J. M. De Bujanda (Geneva: Centre d'Études de la Renaissance, Université de Sherbrook, 2002), compiles all the authors and the writings placed on the index from 1600 until 1966, for a total of around 3,000 authors and 5,000 writings. See also Bruno Neveu, *L'erreur et son juge: Remarques sur les censures doctrinales à l'époque moderne* (Naples: Bibliopolis, 1993); Hubert Wolf, *Inquisition, Index, Zensur* (Paderborn: Ferdinand Schöningh, 2001).

[16] Cf. AAS 59 (1967): 1058.

dominated by conservative influence. "I recall," Congar noted, "that Msgr. Garrone had specifically asked for the reform of the congregation in a speech at the council. That means the formal notice for him to put his idea into action."[17] The post that was assigned to him, Monsignor Francesco Spadafora observed, "was authorization to demolish those glorious institutes, of which only the memory remains today."[18] Carlo Falconi, too, emphasized in *L'Espresso* that the appointment of Archbishop Garrone represented "a very heavy blow to what, under the guidance of Cardinal Pizzardo, had been for many years, along with the Holy Office, the most battle-seasoned stronghold of Pacellian reaction within the curia."[19] On January 13, 1968, Garrone definitively replaced Cardinal Pizzardo at the head of the Congregation of Seminaries and Universities.

Equally emblematic was the choice of Canon Charles Moeller, a fervent disciple of Dom Beauduin, to the post of undersecretary of the Congregation for the Doctrine of the Faith.[20] "Both nominations are significant," Congar wrote, "and even rather sensational, especially the second.... With Moeller, what we have is 100% ecumenism, what we have is openness to humankind, interest in human searchings, in culture, what we have is dialogue."[21]

On June 29, 1967, Paul VI appointed a new substitute of the Secretariat of State: Archbishop Giovanni Benelli,[22] who twenty years

[17] Congar, *Journal*, 876.

[18] F. Spadafora, *Il postconcilio: Crisi, diagnosi e terapia* (Rome: Edizioni Settimo Sigillo, 1991), 87.

[19] C. Falconi, "Salgono gli amici di Papa Giovanni," in *L'Espresso*, February 13, 1966. See also R. Laurentin, "Ce qui signifie l'entrée de Mgr Garrone à la Curie Romaine," in *Le Figaro*, February 4, 1966.

[20] "After my parents—Canon Moeller would say one day—Dom Beauduin is the one who taught me everything" (Bernard Chaberon, "Le chanoine Charles Moeller sous-secrétaire au Saint-Office," in *Le Phare-Dimanche*, February 27, 1966). "Dom Lambert Beauduin had foretold the election of Cardinal Roncalli. But had he dreamed of the most distinguished appointment of his disciples to the Holy Office, six years after his death?" ("Paul VI a nommé le chanoine Moeller sous-secrétaire du Saint-Office," in *La Cité*, January 14, 1966).

[21] Congar, *Journal*, 878.

[22] Giovanni Benelli (1921–1982), ordained in 1943, titular archbishop of Tusuros and apostolic pro-nuncio in Senegal in 1966, substitute of the Secretariat of State from 1967 to 1977, then appointed archbishop of Florence and Cardinal in 1977.

before had been his private secretary. Archbishop Agostino Casaroli, with whom Benelli often differed in his views, was called to direct the Council of Public Affairs, the Church's "Ministry of Foreign Affairs." On December 30, 1967, Cardinal Ottaviani went into early "retirement" by submitting a letter of resignation from his office of pro-prefect of the Sacred Congregation for the Doctrine of the Faith. On January 6, 1968, Paul VI accepted his resignation and appointed to that position the Yugoslav Cardinal Franjo Seper. Several days later, at Frascati's lodgings, the journalist Gianna Preda met Cardinal Ottaviani who, despite the "delicate health" attributed to him by the press, seemed to her to be in the best of health, "erect, steady, sure, smiling, without fears of any kind, benign and severe."[23] "What we need in these times," said he who described himself as "the policeman of the Church," "is a man like Savonarola. Or a saint with all the influences of holiness, in such an indifferent world," where "no one fears sin. They have lost the fear and the concept of sin. Everything is permitted."[24]

After Ottaviani and Pizzardo, two other curial officials were dismissed: Cardinal Benedetto Aloisi Masella, prefect of the Congregation of the Discipline of the Sacraments, and Cardinal Arcadio Maria Larraona, prefect of the Congregation of Rites. In February 1968, a resignation was sent in also, at the request of Paul VI, by Cardinal Giacomo Lercaro from his post as archbishop of Bologna. Among the reasons for the dismissal was a homily that had displeased Paul VI, in which Lercaro had gone well beyond the Holy See's official line, condemning the American bombardments in Vietnam as contrary to the gospel and calling for their immediate cessation.[25] On February 4, 1966, the appointment of Cardinal Urbani as director of the Italian Episcopal Conference had definitively closed the "era" of Cardinal Siri.

In early 1968, the pope replaced the head of the Diocese of Rome, Cardinal Luigi Traglia, with Cardinal Dell'Acqua who, after receiving the purple hat, had initially been destined for the new prefecture of Economic Affairs of the Holy See. Dell'Acqua was mentioned also as a possible Secretary of State, but in 1969 Cardinal Jean Villot succeeded Cardinal Amleto Cicognani in that capacity.

---

23 "'Finalmente sono libero' dice il cardinale Ottaviani," interview with Gianna Preda, in *Il Borghese*, February 15, 1968, 291–293.

24 Ibid., 292.

25 Cf. A. Tornielli, *Paolo VI, op. cit.*, 481–483.

On November 21, 1970, Paul VI published the motu proprio *Ingravescentem aetatem*, which defined "the age of the cardinals in relation to their office."[26] The constitution introduced, among other things, an age limit for appointments: seventy for curial functionaries, seventy-five for heads of dicasteries of "prefects."

The reform was completed by the apostolic constitution *Romano pontifici eligendo* dated October 1, 1975, which excluded cardinals over the age of eighty from the active electorate in a conclave and from any curial position. The College of Cardinals was radically transformed as a result, with the creation of one hundred forty-four new cardinals, the great majority of them non-Italians, over the course of six consistories held during 1965 and 1977. The weight of the curia was further limited both by the institution of the new Synod of Bishops and by the development of the episcopal conferences announced by Paul VI as an expression of collegiality in the governance of the Church.[27]

We should also mention the institution, in 1967, of the Council for the Laity and of the Peace and Justice Commission, both entrusted to another representative of the progressives, Cardinal Roy, and the development of three secretariats, for Promoting Christian Unity, for Non-Christians and for Non-believers, which assumed the role of true dicasteries. For the new Cardinal Parente, a collaborate of Cardinal Ottaviani who had "converted" to more advanced ideas, the institution of the three secretariats was the result of "the council's attitude of dialogue, convinced that even error can be a basis for a deeper, more conscious conquest of truth."[28] The new physiognomy of the curia was expressed by the constitution *Regimini ecclesiae universae*[29] dated August 15, 1967, which put into effect the general reform of the organs of the Holy See. The constitution hallowed an absolutely new principle: cardinal prefects, members of dicasteries, whether cardinals or bishops, the secretaries, and the consultors "cannot remain in office more than five years." The pope was still free to confirm them after that five-year term. At the death of the pontiff, in any case, all

---

26 AAS 62 (1970): 810–813.

27 G. Zizola, *Il Sinodo dei vescovi: Cronaca, bilancio, documentazione* (Turin: Borla, 1968); R. Laurentin, *Le Premier Synode: Histoire et bilan* (Paris: Éd. du Seuil, 1968).

28 P. Parente, "Discorso alla Pontificia Università Urbaniana dell' 11 novembre 1967," cited in G. Zizola, *Il Sinodo dei vescovi, op. cit.*, 228.

29 AAS 59 (1967): 885–928.

had to vacate their offices, leaving the newly-elected pope with the option of employing a completely different ruling group. The principle whereby the curia served as the factor of continuity between one pontificate and the next was definitively set aside.

The disbanding of the corps of the Noble Guard on September 15, 1970, as part of the implementation of the motu proprio *Pontificalis domus* dated March 28, 1968,[30] was not an irrelevant event. Instituted by Pius VII in 1801, with the name "Broken Lances," the corps of the Pontifical Noble Guard had distinguished itself, in the 170 years of its existence, by its fidelity and unbounded devotion to the pontiff.[31] In his addresses to the Patricians and the Roman Nobility, Pius XII had emphasized all the spiritual riches which in the Christian past had characterized the nobility, entrusting to them the mission of affirming them and spreading them throughout the modern world.[32] "You, the Guard of Our person," he had said to the Noble Guard on December 26, 1942, "are our shield, great with the nobility which is the privilege of blood, and which already before your admission to the corps was resplendent in you as the pledge of your devotion, because, as the ancient proverb says, *bon sang ne peut mentir* [good blood cannot lie]."[33]

From the perspective of the distribution of power, the post-conciliar period only partially transferred responsibilities from the center to the periphery. In reality the Roman curia did not lose its strength, but a new ruling class replaced the old one. The real novelty was the transfer of power from the Holy Office to the Secretariat of State, which ended up directing the nine congregations, the three secretariats, and the various commissions. Among other things, an organization was instituted that almost resembled a "Council of Ministers" in civil governments, made up of the periodic meeting of all the cardinals who headed dicasteries under the presidency of the cardinal Secretary of State, whose duties thus came to acquire a new and very different importance.[34]

---

[30] AAS 60 (1968): 305–315.

[31] Cf. Giulio Patrizi Di Ripacandida, *Quell'ultimo glorioso stendardo: Le guardie nobili pontificie dell'11 maggio 1801 al 15 settembre 1970*(Vatican City, 1994).

[32] Ćf. P. Corrêa de Oliveira, *Nobiltà ed élites tradizionali analoghe nelle allocuzioni di Pio XII al Patriziato e alla Nobiltà romana*, Ital. transl. (Milan: Marzorati, 1993).

[33] Cited in ibid., 36.

[34] N. Del Re, article "curia Romana," in MV, 433–439 at 436.

At the distance of a little more than twenty years from the reform by Paul VI, John Paul II carried out a new reorganization of the Roman curia with the constitution *Pastor bonus* dated March 1, 1989,[35] which essentially preserved the preceding framework. This changed the physiognomy of the Church, under its organizational aspect as well, reducing its role as "custodian" of the truth and augmenting its role as a political "force" on the international scene.

3. The explosion of the crisis: the new Dutch catechism

The new centralization of power did not manage to contain the centrifugal forces that were running through the body of the Church. The first symptoms of a crisis appeared before the conclusion of the council. In early February 1965, the book by Michel de Saint-Pierre,[36] *Les nouveaux prêtres* [The New Priests], had a tremendous success, selling more than 200,000 copies. The protagonist of the novel, who describes the religious crisis that was beginning in Europe, is a priest from a "red" parish on the periphery of Paris who is at odds with his progressive confrères.[37] Congar, in his *Journal*, relates that Paul VI, receiving Bishop Ancel, asked him what he thought about the picture drawn by Saint-Pierre in his book. "The Holy Father also thought it an over-simplification, a false image, made up with some accurate fragments. He had not granted the author, Michel de Saint-Pierre, the audience he had requested. But (Del Gallo[38] told us) the Holy Father is rather uneasy about the Dutch situation."[39]

---

[35] AAS 80 (1988): 841–912. See *La curia Romana nella costituzione apostolica "Pastor Bonus,"* ed. Piero Antonio Bonnet and Carlo Gullo (Vatican City: Libreria Editrice Vaticana, 1990).

[36] Michel de Grosourdy, Marquis of Saint-Pierre (1916–1987), was a successful writer and journalist. Some of his works, like *Les aristocrates* (Paris: La Table Ronde, 1954) and *Les nouveaux aristocrates* (Paris: Calmann-Levy, 1961), were adapted for film. Cf. Jean Paulhan, *Michel de Saint-Pierre* (Paris: La Table Ronde, 1972).

[37] Ten years later Michel de Saint-Pierre signed *Les fumées de Satan* [The Smoke of Satan], an impressive denunciation of the most blatant cases of doctrinal and liturgical deviation by the Church in France. The volume compiled more than three thousand scandalous episodes, ranging from praise of group sex to a refusal to administer baptism to newborns (André Higuot and Michel de Saint-Pierre, *Les fumées de Satan* [Paris: La Table Ronde, 1976]).

[38] Luigi del Gallo di Roccagiovine (1922–), ordained in 1950, consecrated bishop of Campli in 1983.

[39] Congar, *Journal*, 721.

In July of 1965 the English Jesuit magazine *The Month* published a worrisome analysis of the situation of the Church in Holland,[40] describing it as "its heaviest crisis since the Reformation"[41] and identifying the greatest dangers as "a certain dogmatic relativism, together with a sham ecumenism, and the disappearance of a personal life of prayer among a large number of our Catholic people."[42]

The Dutch crisis exploded in October 1966 with the publication, sponsored by the bishops of the Netherlands, of the new *Dutch Catechism* containing profoundly ambiguous statements about sin, redemption, the Eucharist, Our Lady's virginity, the role of the Church and of the pope: in other words, on almost all the essential points of the Catholic faith.[43] An *ad hoc* commission of cardinals chosen by Paul VI, in dialogue with the cardinals and bishops of that nation, proposed a series of modifications and supplements to the new *Dutch Catechism*, conversationally and without any ultimatum.[44] The observations were openly contested by a large part of the Dutch Catholic establishment, headed by the cardinal primate, Bernard Jan Alfrink, the principal defender of the new *Dutch Catechism*.

In early January 1969, in Noordwijkerhout, on the North Sea, there was a meeting of the Dutch Pastoral Council, an organization created in 1967, which included more than one hundred representatives of the bishops, the priests, and the lay faithful. The nine bishops who were members of the council—including Cardinal Alfrink—voted in favor of the so-called "Declaration of Independence," in which Dutch Catholics were invited to reject the teaching of the encylical *Humanae vitae*. On that same occasion the Dutch Pastoral Council—with the bishops abstaining—aligned itself in favor of the new *Dutch Catechism*, rejecting the corrections suggested by Rome and asking that the Church remain open to "radical new approaches" to moral topics, which were not mentioned in the final motion yet emerged from the proceedings of the council, such as pre-marital relations, homosexual unions, abortion, and euthanasia.[45]

---

[40] E. Schoenmaeckers, S.J., "Catholicism in the Netherlands," in *The Month* 6 (1965): 335–346.

[41] Ibid., 346.

[42] Ibid., 343. See also "Gli ardui tentativi del riformismo olandese," in *Il Regno* 10 (1965): 307–308.

[43] Cf. the critique made by Monsignor Pier Carlo Landucci in *Miti e realtà* (Rome: La Roccia, 1968), 291–323.

[44] Cf. AAS 60 (1968): 685–691.

[45] Cf. M. Schmaus, L. Scheffczyk, and Joachim Giers, *"Exempel Holland: theologische Analyse und*

The results of Holland's "Declaration of Independence" from Rome were disastrous. In 1966, the year of the publication of the new *Dutch Catechism*, 35% of the inhabitants of Holland declared some affiliation with the Catholic Church. In 2006 there were fewer than half that many, down to 16%. Today Holland is the [Western] country in which the Christian identity is the most diluted and the Muslim presence the most aggressive and invasive.[46]

Bishop Joannes Gijsen,[47] who was consecrated bishop of Roermond by Paul VI in 1972, wrote: "It is not surprising that all this would change the very life of the Church like a revolution: church attendance fell off rapidly; confession was considered superfluous and was replaced by communal 'penance services'; piety lost its depth and flickered out; the value of the rich Catholic heritage was barely acknowledged. Slowly the idea spread that the Catholic Church should associate with other Christian churches and form with them a generic church; various initiatives along these lines were made in keeping with the slogan of promoting ecumenism."[48]

4. The dissent against *Humanae vitae*

A new dispute burst onto the scene on July 25, 1968, when Paul VI published the encylical *Humanae vitae*.[49] After the conclusion of the council, the commission to study the new questions regarding married life, which had been instituted by John XXIII and then expanded by Paul VI to include seventy-five members, had continued its work, and toward the

---

Kritik des Niederländischen Pastoralkonzils (Berlin: Morusverlag, 1972).

[46] See Giulio Meotti, "Nella casbah di Rotterdam," in *Il Foglio*, May 14, 2009; Sandro Magister, "L'Eurabia ha una capitale: Rotterdam," www.chiesa.espressonline.it, May 19, 2009; *Idem*, "In Olanda non c'è più posto per il Bambino Gesù: O invece sì," ibid., December 30, 2009, which cites the reportage of Marina Corradi, "Ad Amsterdam che cosa resta del Natale," in *Avvenire*, December 23, 2009.

[47] Joannes Baptist Matthijs Gijsen (1932–2007), Dutch, ordained in 1957, bishop of Roermond from 1972 to 1996, then bishop and bishop emeritus of Reykjavik, in Iceland (1996–2007).

[48] J. B. M. Gijsen, "Esbozo de la historia del catolicismo en Holanda, especialmente durante la época de 1700 a 1970," in M. Schmaus, L. Scheffczyk, and J. Giers, *op. cit.*, 7–43 at 40. See also L. Laevendecker, "Du cardinal Alfrink au cardinal Simonis: Vingt ans de catholicisme hollandais," in *Le retour de certitudes: Événements et orthodoxie depuis Vatican II* (Paris: Le Centurion, 1967), 122–141.

[49] Paul VI, encylical *Humanae vitae*, dated July 25, 1968, in AAS 60 (1968): 481–503.

end of June 1966 it submitted its own reports to a group of cardinals who were commissioned to give their opinion and to forward the whole dossier to the pope. Public opinion was increasingly convinced that Paul VI would change the traditional teaching of the Church about birth control, also because family planning was regarded almost everywhere as a necessity in the modern world and the contraceptive pill was presented as an instrument of women's "liberation."[50] Between 1966 and 1968, Paul VI seemed to waver before making a painful and tormented decision.[51] Finally, with the encylical *Humanae vitae*, contrary to the opinion of the majority of the experts he had consulted,[52] the pope reaffirmed the Church's traditional position on artificial contraception.[53] This was, according to Romano Amerio, the most important act of his pontificate.[54]

---

[50] L. Scaraffia, "Rivoluzione sessuale e secolarizzazione," in *L'Osservatore Romano*, July 25, 2008, recalls the impetus given to the sexual revolution by research in the United States by Alfred Kinsey (1896–1956), who dates of birth and death coincide with those of the Marxist-Freudian ideologue Wilhelm Reich (1897–1957).

[51] The journalist Alberto Cavallari, in his interview with Paul VI on September 24, 1963, records that the pope told him that "being open to the world" meant "responding to the questions of contemporary man, today's Christian," some of which were "particularly difficult." "Take birth control, for example. The world is asking what we think about it and we have to give a response. But what response? We cannot remain silent. Speaking is a big problem. For centuries the Church has never had to confront things like this. And this matter is, let us say, foreign to the men of the Church, and also humanly embarrassing. And so the commissions meet, and the mountains of reports and studies grow. Oh, they are studying so much, you know. But then it is up to us to decide. And in deciding we are alone. Deciding is not something easy like studying. But we must say something. What? … Actually it is necessary for God to enlighten us" (A. Cavallari, *Il Vaticano che cambia, op. cit.*, 51.)

[52] Cf. J. De Broucker, *Le dossier Suenens: Diagnostic d'une crise* (Paris: Éd. Universitaires, 1970); Robert McClory, *Turning Point: The Inside Story of the Papal Birth Control Commission…* (New York: Crossroad Publishing Company, 1997).

[53] On the encylical, from a traditional perspective, see, among other works, Ermenegildo Lio, O.F.M., *Humanae vitae e infallibilità: Paolo VI, Il Concilio e Giovanni Paolo II* (Vatican City: LEV, 1986); *"Humanae vitae": 20 anni dopo,* Acts of the 2nd International Congress of Moral Theology in Rome, November 9–12, 1988 (Milan: Edizioni Ares, 1989); Ralph M. McInerny, *What Went Wrong with Vatican II* (Manchester, NH: Sophia Institute Press, 1998); Stéphane Seminckx, *La réception de l'encyclique "Humanae vitae" en Belgique: Étude de théologie morale* (Rome: Pontificia Universitas Sanctae Crucis, 2006); M. Schooyans, *La profezia di Paolo VI: L'enciclica Humanae vitae* (Siena: Cantagalli, 2008).

[54] Cf. R. Amerio, *Iota unum, op. cit.*, 135–141 at 136.

A few days later, on July 30, 1968, under the headline "Against Pope Paul's encylical," *The New York Times* published a statement signed by more than two hundred theologians, calling on Catholics to disobey the encylical of Paul VI.[55] This declaration, known also as the "Curran Statement," after one of its promoters, Father Charles Curran,[56] a theologian at the Catholic University of America, is, according to Ralph McInerny, a fundamental document for anyone who wants to understand "what went wrong with Vatican II."[57] This was something the likes of which had never been seen in the long and tormented history of the Church. But the exceptional fact, as Leo Declerck emphasizes, was that the objections came not only from theologians and priests, but also from some episcopates, among them, *in primis*, the Belgian episcopate, headed by Cardinal Primate Leo Suenens.[58] The *Déclaration de l'Épiscopat belge sur l'encylique* Humanae Vitae [Declaration of the Belgian episcopate on the encylical *HV*], dated August 30, 1968, was, along with the statement of the German episcopate, one of the first drawn up by an Episcopal Conference, and it served as a model of dissent for other episcopates.[59] The main author of the document was Monsignor Philips, the chief contributor to *Lumen gentium*, who during the council had distinguished himself as a representative of the "Third Party."

A group of leading figures from the council who were against the encylical of Paul VI, among them Cardinals Suenens, Alfrink, Heenan, Döpfner, and König, met in Essen to coordinate their opposition to the document,[60] and on September 9, 1968, during the *Katholikentag* in Essen, in the presence of the papal legate, Cardinal Gustavo Testa, an overwhelming majority voted

---

[55] "Against Pope Paul's encylical," in *The New York Times*, July 31, 1968.

[56] Charles Curran (1934–), ordained in 1958, was a *peritus* at the council, then a professor at Catholic University of America, which fired him (1986) because of his attitude of open dissent against the Catholic magisterium in matters of morality. See his book, *Loyal Dissent: Memoirs of a Catholic Theologian* (Washington: Georgetown University Press, 2006).

[57] Cf. R. McInerny, *What Went Wrong with Vatican II, op. cit.*, 60 ff., and the article by Cardinal Francis J. Stafford, "1968, l'anno della prova," in *L'Osservatore Romano*, July 25, 2008.

[58] Cf. the study, based on documents from the Suenens, Moeller, Philips, and Prignon archives, by L. Declerck, "La réaction du cardinal Suenens et de l'épiscopat belge à l'encyclique Humanae vitae: Chronique d'une Déclaration (juillet-décembre 1968)," in *Ephemerides Theologicae Lovanienses* 84/1 (2008): 1–68.

[59] Cf. L. Declerck, "La réaction du cardinal Suenens," *op. cit.*, 1–2.

[60] Ibid., 75.

for a resolution to revise the encylical. From Suenens' correspondence with Bishop Huyghe,[61] bishop of Arras, we know about many other reactions, such as that of Cardinal Pellegrino, archbishop of Turin, who described the encylical as "one of the tragedies of papal history,"[62] expressing in those words a judgment no different from the one pronounced during that same period by Brother Roger Schutz of Taizé.[63]

At the symposium of European bishops held in Coir in July 1969, Cardinal Suenens, during his concluding conference, read a dramatic appeal by Hans Küng to abolish obligatory celibacy for priests.[64] Three years later a group of theologians signed the so-called "Manifesto of the Thirty-three," calling for freedom from celibacy.[65] This request was consistent with the role that progressive theology attributed to sexuality: an instinct that a human being should not repress through asceticism, but rather "liberate," thus finding in sex a form of personal human "fulfillment."[66]

The theologian (later cardinal) Leo Scheffczyk,[67] speaking in 1988 in Rome at a congress observing the twentieth anniversary of *Humanae vitae*, explained clearly the mechanism used by the dissident theologians to set up their "magisterium" against papal teaching authority. One "places alongside the infallible magisterium a so-called fallible magisterium, as though fallibility belonged to that magisterium almost like a permanent

[61] Gérard-Maurice-Eugène Huyghe (1909–2001), French, ordained in 1933, consecrated bishop of Arras in 1962.

[62] L. Declerck, "La réaction du cardinal Suenens," *op. cit.*, 49.

[63] Ibid.

[64] Cf. L. Declerck and T. Osaer, *op. cit.*, 75.

[65] Cf. *Regno-Documentazione* 17 (1972): 244–246.

[66] In 1976 Father Innocenzo Colosio (1910–1997), an eminent Dominican scholar of spirituality, pointed out the downfall of asceticism and mysticism within the Catholic Church, as a consequence of a false spirituality that asserted itself after the council (I. Colosio, "Agonia della mistica nell'attuale congiuntura ecclesiale?" in *Rivista di Ascetica e Mistica* 3 [1976]: 105–116), while the Stigmatine Father Cornelio Fabro (1911–1995) denounced the devastation of Catholic morality as the work of the "porno-theologians" (*L'avventura della teologia progressista* [Milan: Rusconi, 1974]).

[67] Leo Scheffczyk (1920–2005), German theologian, ordained in 1947, professor at the Universities of Tübingen and Munich, created cardinal in 2001.

attribute."[68] Given that the magisterium very rarely invokes its infallibility, and normally requires the assent of the faithful with regard to its statements in an "authentic" form, the dissidents "devise the equation: infallibility is the inability to err, whereas authenticity is the ability to err, and therefore also uncertainty, which is inherently more liable to rejection."[69] The chief reason for the crisis of the magisterium goes back in reality to the abandonment of the role of tradition in the life of the Church.

The seriousness of the *Humanae vitae* case is confirmed by a fact that concerns Pope Paul VI personally: in the ten years following that document, the pontiff, as though traumatized by dissent that came from some prominent figures of the council who were closest to him, did not publish another encylical, after having published seven between 1964 and 1968.

5. 1968: the revolution in society

At this point there is no way to ignore the historical correlation between the two major events of the twentieth century: Vatican Council II and the 1968 Revolution.[70]

The 1968 Revolution was a non-"spontaneous" movement that had a precise plan to transform society. The "scientific socialism" of Marx and Lenin had obviously failed in its Promethean dream of building the new edifice of modern civilization, paying a dreadful human price: wars, revolutions, hundreds of millions of victims throughout the world.[71]

---

[68] L. Scheffczyk, "Responsabilità e autorità del teologo nel campo della teologia morale: il dissenso sull'enciclica 'Humanae vitae,'" published jointly in the acts of the congress by the John Paul II Pontifical Institute of the Lateran University and the Centro Accademico Romano della Santa Croce (Rome, 1989), 283.

[69] Ibid.

[70] For general studies on 1968, see Peppino Ortoleva, *Saggio sui movimenti del 1968 in Europa e in America,* with an anthology of materials and documents (Rome: Editori Riuniti, 1988); Arthur Marwick, *The Sixties Cultural Revolution in Britain, France, Italy and the United States c. 1958–1974* (Oxford: Oxford University Press, 1998); Roger Kimball, *The Long March: How the Cultural Revolution of the 1960s Changed America* (San Francisco: Encounter Books, 2000); *Enciclopedia del '68* (Rome: Manifestolibri, 2008); Enzo Peserico, *Gli "anni del desiderio e del piombo"* (Milan: Sugarco, 2008).

[71] See a general overview in: R. de Mattei, *1900–2000: Due sogni si succedono: La costruzione, la*

Never had there been so much talk about human progress and liberation and never had so much blood been spilled in history, to the point of offering a veritable holocaust to the fetish of modernity. Nineteen sixty-eight ratified the failure of that utopia, while also presenting itself as a new revolutionary "dream." Under this aspect, instead of being enclosed within the limits proposed by the historian Eric Hobsbawm,[72] between 1914 and 1991, the twentieth century could be restricted to the fifty years running from 1918, the end of the First World War, to 1968, the year of the student protests.

The Revolution of 1968 certainly had a strong impact in the Church, as well as in society, but the "conciliar about-face" in turn fostered the outbreak of the student revolt. The slogan of Sixty-eight, "it is forbidden to forbid," had its origins in the conciliar aversion to any form of condemnation and doctrinal prohibition. "The demands of the movement of May '68," wrote Fr. Laurentin, "coincided to a great extent with the major ideas of the council, in particular of the conciliar constitution on the Church and the world."[73] Parishes, Catholic and protestant groups held meetings and assemblies, like the debate organized by CRAC (*Comité révolutionnaire d'agitation culturelle*) [Revolutionary Committee for Cultural Agitation] on June 8, 1968, in the Richelieu Amphitheater in Paris, on the topic "From Che Guevara to Jesus Christ."[74] Moreover, Laurentin writes, "Vatican II was already to some extent the dissent of a group of bishops who banded together against the curia that was trying to stage an institutionally prefabricated council."[75]

On May 21, 1968, the magazine *Témoignage chrétien* published an appeal "to introduce the revolution into the Church."[76] Conjuring up that atmosphere again, with particular reference to the French Dominicans,

---

distruzione (Rome: Edizioni Fiducia, 1989); French transl. *De l'utopie du progrès au règne du chaos* (Losanna: L'Âge d'Homme, 1993).

[72] Eric Hobsbawm, *The Age of Extremes: The Short Twentieth Century, 1914–1991* (New York: Vintage Books, 1994).

[73] R. Laurentin, *Crisi della Chiesa e secondo Sinodo episcopale* (Brescia: Morcelliana, 1969), 14.

[74] Ibid., 15.

[75] Ibid., 16.

[76] Cited in Gerard Cholvy and Yves-Marie Hilaire, *Histoire religieuse de la France contemporaine* (Toulouse: Privat, 1988) 3:307.

Cardinal Schönborn[77] recalls: "It was like during the French Revolution: the only thing missing was the guillottine."[78]

In Italy, too, at the dawn of the Sixty-eight uprising there were, as Roberto Beretta recalls, "the ferment of Vatican Council II, the impatience with its implementation, the expectations—justified or not—as to some of its developments, the interpretations of so many fashionable theologians of the time, discussions of young 'committed' believers, who were often 'the best,' the most avant-garde and educated *crème* of the laity, the executive boards of the ecclesial labor union movement."[79] As one leafs through the documents of Sixty-eight, one discovers in fact how the student leaders and the promoters of Catholic dissent cited the conciliar documents and some documents by the popes extensively: the favorites were the encylical *Pacem in terris* by John XXIII, the constitutions *Lumen gentium* and *Gaudium et spes* of Vatican II, and the encylical *Populorum progressio* by Paul VI.[80]

The religious-ecclesial dispute began in Italy with the "*contro-quaresimale*" ["counter-Lenten sermon," followed by a university sit-in] in Trent, followed in September by the occupation of the Cathedral of Parma. On the 22nd of that month the Florentine community of Isolotto sent a letter of solidarity to the demonstrators in Parma, underscoring the necessity for a discerning choice "between those who are on the side of the gospel of the poor and those who serve two masters, God and money."[81] Don Enzo Mazzi, the leader of the Isolotto community, was dismissed by Cardinal Florit from his position as pastor and became the center of the first Italian "base community," followed by many others.

Some of the chief representatives of the movement like Mario Capanna[82] and Marco Boato[83] came from Catholic environments; Capanna, a writer

---

[77] Christoph Schönborn (1945–), Austrian, Dominican Friar, ordained in 1970, titular bishop of Sutri and auxiliary bishop of the Archdiocese of Vienna (1991), of which he became archbishop in 1995. Created cardinal in 1998.

[78] Cited in E. Habsburg-Lothringen, *Das Ende des Neuthomismus, op. cit.*, 118.

[79] Roberto Beretta, *Cantavamo Dio è morto: Il 68 dei cattolici* (Casale Monferrato: Piemme, 2008), 16.

[80] Ibid., 61.

[81] G. Martina, *La Chiesa in Italia, op. cit.*, 162.

[82] Cf. Mario Capanna, *Formidabili quegli anni* (Milan: Rizzoli, 1988).

[83] Cf. Marco Boato, *Contro la Chiesa di classe: Documenti della contestazione ecclesiale in Italia* (Padua: Marsilio, 1969).

for the *Cattolica* of Milan, recalls: "We spent whole nights studying and discussing the theologians who were then considered borderline: Rahner, Schillebeeckx, Bultmann… together with the documents of the council."[84]

Another exponent of the "*Lotta Continua*" ["Ongoing Struggle"] of those years, Paolo Sorbi, the protagonist of the "counter-Lenten sermon" on the square in front of the Cathedral of Trent, writes, "We were interpreters of the thought of Don Milani, Don Mazzolari, Father Balducci, and Don Camillo Torres—persons who handed on to us the dream of a utopia that we sought to achieve on earth. Now, words are like stones. We took those words seriously and radicalized them."[85]

The Catholic '68' developed in two directions: a "charismatic" line and a "political" line, one destined to lead to Catholic Pentecostalism,[86] the other to revolutionary terrorism or liberation theology.[87]

In the first case, the theologians who at the council had tried to separate the charismatic dimension of the Church (the "soul") from its hierarchical structure (the "body"), now championed a vision in which the traditional institutions, from dioceses to parishes, were dissolved in the name of new "charisms." Father Laurentin, in early 1974, saluted "the prodigious expansion of the 'movement of Pentecost' in Catholicism,"[88] and Cardinal Suenens devoted a pastoral letter to the "rediscovery of the Holy Spirit," expressing his admiration for the charismatic movement.[89]

---

[84] Interview by *Avvenire* (March 20, 1998). On the influence of Catholicism on the Sixty-eight movement, cf. Mario Cuminetti, *Il dissenso cattolico in Italia 1965–1980* (Milan: Rizzoli, 1983); Michele Brambilla, *Dieci anni di illusioni: Storia del Sessantotto* (Milan: Rizzoli, 1994); R. Beretta, *Il lungo autunno: Controstoria del Sessantotto cattolico* (Milan: Rizzoli, 1998); Rocco Cerrato, "Il Sessantotto e il mondo cattolico in Italia," in *1968: fra utopia e Vangelo: Contestazione e mondo cattolico*, ed. A. Giovagnoli (Rome: Ave, 2000).

[85] Paolo Sorbi, "Mea culpa sul '68," in *Avvenire*, March 26, 1998. Sorbi, who proclaimed "There can be no revelation without revolution," would go from the *Lotta Continua* to the Italian Communist Party, only to end up with managerial responsibilities in the Italian pro-life movement and a program on Radio Maria.

[86] Cf. L. G. Suenens, *A New Pentecost?* Eng. transl. (New York: Seabury, 1975).

[87] Cf. E. Peserico, *Gli "anni del desiderio e del piombo," op. cit.*

[88] R. Laurentin, "La prodigieuse expansion du 'mouvement de Pentecôte,'" in *Le Figaro*, January 21, 1974; *Idem, Pentecôtisme chez les catholiques: risques et avenir* (Paris: Beauchesne, 1974).

[89] Cf. "Le cardinal Suenens évoque le climat de foi, de jeunesse et de spontanéité du renouveau

In the second case, the Christian presence was transformed into a political utopia, dissolving the transcendent dimension of the Church of Christ. "The destruction of theology...," Cardinal Ratzinger recalls, "was now occurring through its politicization as conceived by Marxist messianism."[90] For his part, Gianni Baget Bozzo wrote: "Vatican II had made current the idea that the God-bearing people changes history and changes it in terms of universal criteria; in other words, it had introduced utopia into Catholic language."[91]

The consequences were catastrophic. "In 1968," Cardinal Stafford recalls,[92] "something terrible happened in the Church. Within the ministerial priesthood, among friends, divisions occurred everywhere that would never again be healed; those wounds continue to afflict the entire Church."[93] Another illustrious prelate, Cardinal Caffarra,[94] observes that Sixty-eight was not the cause but the outcome of an historical process that started in the distant past.

"The dissent against *Humanae vitae*, the controversy over the new *Dutch Catechism* and the birth of Marxist-style 'liberation theology' are the outcome—which not accidentally appeared precisely in 1968—of more-than-centuries-old processes, of dynamics that already existed before the council, against which not even preconciliar theology had set up an

charismatique," in *Le Monde*, July 19, 1973. In a later book, devoted to *Ecumenism and Charismatic Renewal: theological and pastoral orientations* (Ann Arbor, MI: Servant Books, 1978), Suenens hoped for a merger of the ecumenical movement with Catholic Pentecostalism, asserting that "the Charismatic Renewal can serve as a dynamic leverage to raise the Christian people in ecumenical hope" (p. 107). On the origins of "Catholic Pentecostalism," cf. Kevin and Dorothy Ranaghan, *Catholic Pentecostals* (Paramus, NJ: Paulist Press, 1969); Joseph Crehan, S.J., "Charismatics and Pentecostals," in *Christian Order* 11 (1972): 678–689. See also the critical but precise overview by Enrico Zoffoli, *Carismi e carismatici nella Chiesa* (Rome: Edizioni Dehoniane, 1991).

90 J. Ratzinger, *Milestones*, 137.

91 G. Baget Bozzo, *L'intreccio: Cattolici e comunisti 1945–2004* (Milan: Mondadori, 2004), 130.

92 James Francis Stafford (1932–), from the United States, ordained in 1957, titular bishop of Respecta (1976), bishop of Memphis (U.S.A.) in 1982, then archbishop of Denver (1986–1996), president of the Pontifical Council for the Laity (1996), created cardinal in 1998.

93 F. Stafford, "1968: L'anno della prova," *op. cit.*

94 Carlo Caffarra (1938–), ordained in 1961, consecrated bishop of Ferrara-Comacchio in 1995, archbishop of Bologna in 2004, created cardinal in 2006.

adequate barrier, so that the reaction itself to the dissidents on the part of conservative ethical and theological thought in the immediate wake of 1968 displays a serious 'inadequacy.'"[95]

6. Liberation theology

a) The birth of CELAM

The most radical expression of the politicization of the Catholic world was the birth and the development of "liberation theology."[96] The phenomenon was connected to two historical events that are typical of the post-conciliar period: the encylical by Paul VI, *Populorum progressio*, and the Medellín Conference.

The first somewhat prominent meeting of Latin American theologians had taken place in Petrópolis, Brazil, in February 1964, when the council was still in progress. On that occasion a group of theologians gathered for the purpose of applying in Latin America the conciliar innovations and organizing a course for professors on Latin American theology faculties, with input from European theologians.[97] During the council, moreover, the Episcopal Conference of Latin American Bishops (CELAM) met three times in Rome between 1963 and 1965. These assemblies were described by their president, Bishop Larraín, as "the first case, in all of Church history, of the realization of the concept of episcopal collegiality," which in the future was

---

[95] C. Caffarra, "Il sesso è libero, cioè relativo," in *Il Foglio*, October 7, 2008.

[96] Cf. *La nuova frontiera della teologia nell'America Latina*, ed. R. Gibellini (Brescia: Queriniana, 1975); B. Mondin, *I teologi della liberazione* (Rome: Borla, 1977); Philip Berryman, *Liberation Theology: The Essential Facts about the Revolutionary Movement in Latin American and Beyond* (New York: Pantheon Books, 1987); Lucia Ceci, *La teologia della liberazione in America Latina: L'opera di Gustavo Gutiérrez* (Milan: Franco Angeli, 1999); I. Ellacuría and J. Sobrino, *Mysterium Liberationis, op. cit.*; S. Scatena, *In populo pauperum: La Chiesa latinoamericana dal Concilio a Medellín* (1962–1968) (Bologna: Il Mulino, 2007); *Idem, La teologia della liberazione in America Latina* (Rome: Carocci, 2008). The remote ideological roots of the movement are clearly identified by Julio Loredo in *Revolution in the Church: tracing the roots of liberation theology* (Pro-Manuscripto, 1992).

[97] Cf. L. Ceci, *La teologia della liberazione, op. cit.* 60–61.

certain to be a "vehicle for the spirit of the council."[98] As one of the Latin American council fathers, Bishop Marcos McGrath, recalls, "During the months when the bishops were staying in Rome for the council, CELAM promoted for its members regular meetings with speakers on various topics of the council, besides personal and group meetings…; and weekly study sessions on the current topics of the council, since the main groups had gathered around the Brazilian and the Chilean episcopates. These various groups that met all over Rome… developed proposals for the documents that many bishops would support."[99]

One initial, significant attempt to implement Vatican II in the Latin American political, social, and cultural context was the extraordinary assembly of CELAM that was held from October 11 to 16, 1966, in Mar del Plata (Argentina), on the subject of "*Presencia activa de la Iglesia en el desarrollo y en la integración de América Latina*" ["The Church's active presence in the development and integration of Latin America"].[100] The frame of reference was Latin American reality in light of *Gaudium et spes*. Since the conference in Bandung in 1955, the theme of "development" had started to express the aspirations of the third world countries and, as far as Latin America was concerned, had been supported by some pan-continental organizations like the *Comisión Económica Para América Latina* (CEPAL), founded in 1949 and dependent on the United Nations, the Interamerican Bank for Development and even the *Alianza para el Progreso*, the program of American aid for Latin American that was carried out between 1961 and 1970.[101]

---

[98] Quoted in *Criterio* 1475 (1965): 355. During the discussion of the schema *De episcopis ac de diocesium regimine*, a proposed amendment suggested inserting into the conciliar document an explicit reference to CELAM as an example of a supranational Episcopal Conference.

[99] Cf. L. Ceci, *La teologia della liberazione, op. cit.*, 57–58. Cf. M. G. McGrath, "Unas notas sobre Paolo VI y la colegialidad episcopal en América Latina," in *Paolo VI e la collegialità episcopale*, Colloquio internazionale di studio, Brescia (25–26–27 settembre 1992) (Brescia-Rome: Studium, 1995), 236–240.

[100] Cf. Vicente Oscar Vetrano, "Crónica de la X Asemblea del CELAM en Mar del Plata," in *Criterio* 1526 (1967): 432–437.

[101] Cf. Albert Otto Hirschman, *Problemi dell'America Latina* (Bologna: Il Mulino, 1961), particularly pages 22–42 in regard to CEPAL.

b) The encylical *Populorum progressio*

The theme of development had also made its way into the documents of the magisterium, particularly in the Johannine encylicals *Mater et magistra* and *Pacem in terris*, as well as in the pastoral constitution *Gaudium et spes*, and it had something of a reception at the level of theological reflection in some European authors.[102]

In 1967 the encylical *Populorum progressio* appeared.[103] The original text had been composed in French, which was unusual for an encyclical yet revealed the pope's intellectual sources, particularly the contribution to the document made by Father Lebret,[104] who had died a few months earlier in 1966. In the document Paul VI admitted the existence of "situations" the injustice of which "cries out for God's attention" and of violations of human dignity in which armed revolt could be legitimate.

> Lacking the bare necessities of life, whole nations are under the thumb of others; they cannot act on their own initiative; they cannot exercise personal responsibility; they cannot work toward a higher degree of cultural refinement or a greater participation in social and public life. They are sorely tempted to redress these insults to their human nature by violent means. Everyone knows, however, that revolutionary uprisings—*except where there is manifest, longstanding tyranny which would do great damage to fundamental personal rights and dangerous harm to the common good of the country*—engender new injustices, introduce new inequities, and bring new disasters. The evil situation that exists, and it surely is evil, may not be dealt with in such a way that an even worse situation results.[105]

---

[102] L. Ceci, *La teologia della liberazione, op. cit.*, 77–78. On the theology of development see Angelo De Gennaro, "Teologia dello sviluppo," in *Correnti teologiche postconciliari*, ed. Alfredo Marranzini (Rome: Città Nuova, 1974), 149–169.

[103] Paul VI, encylical *Populorum progressio* (March 26, 1967), in Paolo VI, *Insegnamenti, Encicliche*, 79–119.

[104] Louis-Joseph Lebret (1897–1966), French Dominican, ordained in 1928. Was appointed an expert at the council in early 1964 and was then commissioned to prepare the encylical *Populorum progressio* (1967).

[105] Paul VI, encylical *Populorum progressio, op. cit.*, nos. 30–31.

The papal passage dedicated to the case of "manifest, longstanding tyranny" was easily exploited by some theologians who developed the thesis of the legitimacy of revolution, once peaceful attempts had been made. "The encylical of Paul VI *Populorum progressio,*" according to Gustavo Gutiérrez,[106] "resounds like a trumpet in Latin America."[107]

Gustavo Gutiérrez Merino, a thirty-five-year-old Peruvian priest, after studying in Europe, had participated in the council together with the Brazilian priest Hugo Assman[108] and with the support of CELAM proposed developing in South America the more radical demands of the council.

"In Rome," Gutiérrez recalls, "I met my spiritual director from Louvain, Gustave Thils (he was one of the experts), a dear friend from those years at Louvain, Charles Moeller, who was very much involved in the work of the commissions, but also other professors of mine like de Lubac, whom I knew well, Congar, Chenu, whom I also knew, Martelet[109] and Roger Aubert.[110] They were all experts at the council, and since I had a relation of friendship with them, that gave me the opportunity to have a very direct confrontation. Finally the theology that I had studied—in those days it was called 'progressive'—found a hearing in the Church."[111]

---

[106] Gustavo Gutiérrez Merino (1928–), Peruvian, ordained in 1959. After studying in Belgium, he taught in Latin America and in the United States. His main work is *A Theology of Liberation: history, politics and salvation*, Eng. transl. (Maryknoll, NY: Orbis Books, 1973). In 1983 he was condemned by the Congregation for the Doctrine of the Faith.

[107] G. Gutiérrez, "La Chiesa e i poveri visti dall'America Latina," in *Il Vaticano II e la Chiesa*, ed. G. Alberigo and J. P. Jossua (Brescia: Paideia, 1985), 231–260 at 248.

[108] Hugo Assman (1933–2008), Brazilian, ordained in 1961 in Italy, student of Father Josef Fuchs, S.J. (1912–2005) at the Gregorianum, left the priesthood ten years later to marry a Brazilian woman with whom he had two children, and took a job as an instructor at the Methodist University of San Paolo. His basic text is *Theology for a Nomad Church*, Eng. transl. (Maryknoll, NY: Orbis Books, 1975).

[109] Gustave Martelet (1916–) French Jesuit, disciple of Teilhard de Chardin, professor at the *Centre Sèvres* in Paris and at the Gregorian University in Rome. Theologian of the French-speaking bishops from Africa at the council. See his book, *Teilhard de Chardin prophète d'un Christ toujours plus grand* (Brussels, Éditions Lessius, 2005).

[110] Roger Aubert (1914–2009), Belgian, ordained in 1938, historian and theologian, professor at the University of Malines from 1952 to 1983.

[111] L. Ceci, *La teologia della liberazione, op. cit.*, 50. See also Rosino Gibellini, *Il dibattito sulla*

Another European theologian whose lesson Gutiérrez further developed was Edward Schillebeeckx, who had underscored the importance for modern man of historical praxis, whereby one began to build the kingdom of God.[112] No less relevant in Gutiérrez' theological formation was Karl Rahner, with his theory of the "anonymous Christian" or "implicit Christian."[113] According to him even outside of Christianity, among atheists, there are human beings justified by grace, in whom the Holy Spirit is present. Gutiérrez had looked to Rahner since the years of his studies in Lyons, attracted above all by the idea of the "supernatural existential" as something constitutive of human nature. This concept, as Gutiérrez went on to emphasize, allowed Rahner to affirm that man as a whole and every human being is existentially touched by grace.[114] Starting from this Rahnerian perspective, which is not far from de Lubac's concept of the supernatural, Gutiérrez would elaborate a philosophy that rejected the distinction between secular history and salvation history, affirming that "there is only one history" and that Christian salvation includes an "integral liberation" of man which is to be realized in history and through history.[115]

c) The Medellín Conference

The general conference of the Latin American episcopate held in Medellín, in Colombia, from August 26 to September 6, 1968, was the point of arrival for the ideological process that the council had begun and the point of departure for the spread of liberation theology on an international scale.

---

teologia della liberazione (Brescia: Queriniana, 19902); *Idem,* "Chiesa e liberazione in America Latina (1968–1972)," in *L'America Latina fra Pio XII e Paolo VI*, ed. A. Melloni and S. Scatena (Bologna: Il Mulino, 2006).

112 Cf. E. Schillebeeckx, *The Church and Mankind* (Glen Rock, NJ: Paulist Press, 1965).

113 See Karl Rahner, "Anonymous Christians," in *Theological Investigations*, vol. VI (Baltimore: Helicon Press, 1969), 390–398; *Idem,* "Anonymous Christianity and the missionary task of the Church," in *Theological Investigations*, 12:161–178 *Idem,* "Observations on the problem of the 'anonymous Christian,'" in *Theological Investigations*, 14:280–294; Anita Röper, *The Anonymous Christian* (New York: Sheed and Ward, 1966), which takes the ideas of Rahner and Schillebeeckx as its inspiration.

114 Cited in G. Gutiérrez, *La verità vi farà liberi: Confronti*, Ital. transl. (Brescia: Queriniana, 1990), 37.

115 Ibid., 38.

For Schillebeeckx, liberation theology represented essentially "the spirit of Medellín fallen into [reduced to] a theology."[116]

The official topic of the conference, which had been convoked by Paul VI, was "The Church in the transformations of Latin America in light of the council." The historical and social transformations of the Latin-American continent were to be seen in the light of the transformation of the Church promoted by the Second Vatican Council. Oscar Beozzo pointed out that Medellín had its roots in Paul Gauthier's group, "Church of the Poor," which had been organized at the time of the first session of the council,[117] after John XXIII had alluded to this topic in his address on September 11, 1962.[118] The group "Church of the Poor" had proposed the so-called "pact of the catacombs," signed on November 16, 1965, in the Catacombs of Domitilla by forty bishops, most of them from the third world. The signatories pledged to lead a life of struggle for the poor and of solidarity with their needs, in keeping with the new principles of Vatican II.[119]

The council event had been a moment of encounter for the bishops of the former colonial nations of Asia, Africa, and Latin America, who were also responsible for the document known as the "Message of the Seventeen Third World Bishops."[120] The first signatory was Bishop Helder Câmara and, besides him, eight Brazilian bishops and one Colombian signed their names. In this message the bishops declared that the peoples of the third world were "the proletariat of humanity today" and recalled that the Church's social teaching, reaffirmed by the Second Vatican Council, condemned all collusion of the Church with "the imperialism of money." Describing feudalism, capitalism, and imperialism as "inhumane systems,"

---

[116] E. Schillebeeckx, "Befreiungstheologie Zwischen Medellin und Puebla," in *Orientierung* 43/1 (1979): 6–10 at 7, cited in Scatena/L. Ceci, *La teologia della liberazione, op. cit.*, 27; O. J. Beozzo, "Medellin: Inspirations e racines," in *Volti di fine Concilio, op. cit.*, 361–393.

[117] Cf. O. J. Beozzo, "Medellin: Inspirations et racines," *op. cit.*, 362–363.

[118] John XXIII, DMC, 4:519–528.

[119] Cf. L. Ceci, *La teologia della liberazione, op. cit.*, 52. On the group "Church of the Poor" and concerning the "pact of the catacombs," cf. Caprile, 5:354–356. The "pact" is reprinted in Bonaventura Kloppenburg, "O pacto da Igreja Serva e Pobre," in *Concilio Vaticano II* (Petrópolis: Vozes, 1966), 4:526–528.

[120] The document, published for the first time in Paris on August 31, 1967, by *Témoignage Chrétien*, can be found also in *Il Regno/documentazione*, XIII, n. 151/2 (1968): 19–22 and, for Latin America, in *Criterio*, XL, nn. 1537–1538 (1967): 936–941.

the signatories declared unacceptable the exploitation of the peoples of the third world by the rich nations and the very "economic system currently in force" that allowed the rich countries to become more and more wealthy, while the poor countries, in comparison, became impoverished. While exhorting governments to endeavor to "put an end to class struggle," they concluded by saying that this struggle was often started by the rich and not by the poor. This was a theme repeated many times in the post-conciliar period, especially in Latin America.[121]

Liberation theology had its vigorous expression in Ecclesial Base Communities (EBC). They appeared in Brazil in the second half of the 1950s and spread especially in the immediate post-conciliar period, when they were included in the pastoral plans of several episcopal conferences.[122] In the name of the centrality given to the Word of God, of which they considered themselves spokesmen, replacing the Church, the Base Communities championed class struggle of the Marxist variety for the purpose of bringing about the "Kingdom of God" on earth.[123]

Twenty years after the council, the "Instruction on Certain Aspects of the 'Theology of Liberation'" by the Congregation for the Doctrine of the Faith[124] formulated an explicit condemnation of liberation theology, without however successfully eradicating its profound influence in Latin America.

---

121 Cf. L. Ceci, *La teologia della liberazione, op. cit.*, 59.

122 Cf. ibid., 68; José Marins, "Communità ecclesiali di base in America Latina," in *Concilium* 20/6 (1984): 571–582; Faustino Luiz Couto Texeira, *A gênese das CEBs no Brasil: Elementos explicativos* (San Paolo: Paulinas, 1988).

123 Cf. *Comunidades eclesiais de base: utopia ou realidade*, ed. Afonso Gregory (Petrópolis: Vozes, 1973), 53 ff. See also L. Gonzaga Fernandes, "Gênese, Dinâmica e Perspectivas das CEBs do Brasil," in *Revista Eclesiástica brasileira* 42/167 (1982): 456–464. On Base Communities in Brazil, see the compelling critique of P. Corrêa de Oliveira, Gustavo Antonio Solimeo, and Luíz Sergio Solimeo, *As CEBs ... das quais muito se fala, pouco se conhece: A TFP as descreve come são* (San Paolo: Editora Vera Cruz, 1982).

124 Congregation for the Doctrine of the Faith, Instruction *Libertatis nuntius* (August 6, 1984) in Denz-H, nn. 47304741 (AAS 76 [1984]: 890–899); *Idem*, "Instruction on Christian Freedom and Liberation," *Libertatis conscientia* (March 22, 1986); in Denz-H, nn. 4750–4776 (AAS 79 [1987]: 554–591). Various aspects of the doctrine of liberation theology had already been condemned by John Paul II in his speech to CELAM in Puebla in 1979 (cf. Giovanni Paolo II, *Insegnamenti*, 2:188–211 and 212–230).

In an article published in 2007 in the *Revista Eclesiástica Brasileira*,[125] Father Clodovis Boff[126]—brother of the more famous Leonardo[127] and with him one of the chief representatives of the revolutionary movement—conducted a lucid self-critique of his thought, admitting that the basic error of liberation theology lay in having made the "option for the poor" its epistemological axis or center, in effect displacing the transcendent primacy of God. In this inversion of the epistemological primacy, "the first operative principle of theology is no longer God, but the poor person."[128] The root of this error, according to Boff, goes back to the "anthropological revolution" in modern thought that posits man as the new *axis mundi*.[129] At the origins of the anthropological trend of modernity, in his opinion, are protestantism (especially in Schleiermacher's liberal formulation), modernism, and the transcendental theology of Rahner.[130] Boff says nothing about the council, which in this development was the immediate antecedent of liberation theology, but the ideological and existential choices of the Brazilian Franciscan and of his travelling companions, during and after the council, were the eloquent confirmation of this continuity.

7. "The smoke of Satan" in the temple of God

The council had been over for three years then, and the situation appeared to be white-hot. Although Michel de Saint-Pierre could be considered a "traditionalist," the same could not be said of Jacques Maritain, the old

[125] Clodovis M. Boff, O.S.M., "Teologia da Libertação e volta ao fondamento," *Revista Eclesiástica Brasileira*, 268 (2007): 1001–1022.

[126] Clodovis M. Boff (1944–) Brazilian, Servant of Mary, professor at the Franciscan Theological Institute of Petropolis and at ISER (Institute of Religious Studies) in Rio de Janeiro.

[127] Leonardo Boff (1938–) Brazilian, Capuchin Friar, ordained in 1964, student of Rahner in Germany, then professor in Petropolis, was one of the originators of liberation theology. Condemned in 1984 by the Congregation for the Doctrine of the Faith, he left the priesthood in 1992 and married, taking a position at the University of Rio de Janeiro. See his book *Jesus Christ Liberator: a critical Christology for our times* (Maryknoll, NY: Orbis Books, 1978).

[128] Clodovis M. Boff, O.S.M., "Teologia da Libertação e volta ao fondamento," *op. cit.*, 1004.

[129] "axis around which the world revolves"; *ibid.*

[130] Ibid., 1009.

friend of Giovan Battista Montini, who, in a book published in 1966, *Le Paysan de Garrone*, wrote that the modernism of the time of Pius X seemed like "only a modest hay fever" compared with contemporary neo-modernism.[131]

On January 18, 1967, Cardinal Journet delivered to Paul VI Maritain's suggestions for a new "Profession of Faith" that would re-establish the basic truth of Christianity.[132] On that occasion Paul VI asked Journet for a judgment on the situation in the Church. "Tragic" was the lapidary response of the Swiss cardinal.[133]

On May 13, 1967, at the invitation of the Portuguese episcopate, Paul VI made an unexpected lightning trip to Fatima, where he was the first pope to preside at a liturgical celebration at the place of the apparitions, at the Cova da Iria. On that same day, the pope published the apostolic exhortation *Signum magnum*, in which he recalled the consecration of the world to Mary's heart made by Pius X and invited "all the sons of the Church to renew personally their own consecration to the Immaculate Heart of Mary, Mother of the Church."[134] In Fatima, Paul VI spoke about the urgency of peace "within the Church and in those countries where religious liberty is suppressed" and also about peace in the world, "which is neither happy nor calm," but refused Sister Lucia's request to have a conversation with him. The presence of Paul VI in Fatima might have offered an historic opportunity to reveal the third secret and to set in motion the fulfillment of Our Lady's requests, but it was not so. In reality, starting precisely with that journey, the message of Fatima lost its hold on the mass media and on the faithful.[135]

---

131 Cf. J. Maritain, *The Peasant of the Garrone*, Eng. transl. (New York: Holt, Rinehart and Winston, 1968), 5. The Belgian philosopher Marcel De Corte (1905–1994) described Christian progressivism in those years as "the modernist heresy in the convulsive stage and triumphant in the Church" (*La grande eresia,* Ital. transl. [Rome: Volpe, 1970], 100).

132 On the "Credo" of Paul VI see, among other commentaries, C. Pozo, *El credo del Pueblo de Dios: Comentario teológico* (Madrid: Biblioteca de Autores Cristianos, 1968).

133 Cf. Interview with Cardinal George Cottier by Gianni Valente in *30 Giorni* (2008/4): 46–61.

134 Paul VI, Homily during the Mass celebrated in Fatima, May 13, 1967, in *Insegnamenti* 5 (1967): 229–239.

135 Cf. A. Tornielli, *Paolo VI, op. cit.*, 461. As the journey drew near, Pope Montini reopened the dossier on Fatima and asked the Holy Office to examine it. The secret became known not only to a few persons, but to a "plenary meeting" of the Supreme Congregation that was held in the Vatican

What was happening in those dramatic years did not escape Paul VI. In December 1968, in an epoch-making speech, he uttered the impressive words: "The Church today is going through a moment of anxiety. Some are practicing self-criticism, one might say to the point of self-destruction. It is like an acute, complex internal upheaval that no one would have expected after the council.... The Church is being struck by those who are part of it."[136]

Three years later, in his homily on the Feast of Saints Peter and Paul on June 29, 1972, referring to the situation of the Church, Paul VI stated with equal clarity that he had

> the sense that the smoke of Satan had entered the temple of God through some crack. There is doubt, uncertainty, equivocation, anxiety, dissatisfaction, conflict. There is no confidence in the Church.... Doubt has entered our awareness and it has entered through the windows that ought to have been opened to the light.... In the Church too this state of uncertainty prevails; it was thought that after the council would come a day of sunlight for the history of the Church. What came instead was a day of clouds, storm, darkness, searching, uncertainty....[137]

Paul VI, in reality, was presenting the situation in a way that was more problematic than dramatic. Turning to the cardinals on December 15, 1969, in a speech dedicated to the difficult interpretation of the "signs of the times," he declared:

> How is the Church today? The recent council produced a state of concern [*attenzione*] and, in certain respects, of spiritual tension.... Inside and outside of it, the Church has shown not the calm fervor that the council made us hope for, but in some restricted but significant sectors, a certain uneasiness [that] presents contrasting negative and positive phenomena.... But this does not do away with the fact that this symbolic ship, the Church, is again experiencing the force of the

---

on March 1, 1967.

136 Paul VI, Discourse at the Lombard Seminary in Rome (December 7, 1968), in *Insegnamenti* 6 (1968): 1188–1189.

137 Paul VI, Homily for the ninth anniversary of his enthronement (June 29, 1972), in *Insegnamenti* 10 (1972): 707–709.

> great storm characteristic of our time, which sometimes brings to our lips the imploring cry of the frightened disciples: "Save us, Lord, we are perishing" (Matt 8:25).... It is necessary to be attentive observers, to be wise critics. Today everything is being transformed; everything becomes a problem; and everywhere there is danger of illusion, even for those who are good.[138]

He considered his time as "a period of transformation," a "rapidly developing age" in which the Church would have to "be updated" in order to produce a simultaneous reform of spiritual society and secular society.

> Our era is young; look at the renewal. It is not a time turned in on itself; not a period of decadence, in which skeptical people predominate, those who almost make a profession of being negligent, to whom nothing about anything is important. They are the false prophets; they cannot guide us; they do not give us the enthusiasm and the truth of things; they do not imbue us with the energies and the ability to enjoy the immense gift of life. Consequently our time is surely an era of renewal. After that remark, what do we see? That the Church is precisely in the vanguard. She is extensively renewing herself, for the purpose of perfecting all that is hers: her catechism, her rites, her liturgy, her associations, her doctrinal heritage. Let us make sure to leave behind what is transitory, and let us work instead to preserve intact the substance, all the fruitful seed.[139]

The existence of a serious crisis however was confirmed by—of all people—some theologians from the ranks of the progressives. We will recall only a few significant pronouncements.

The historian Hubert Jedin, who at the council had collaborated as *peritus* with Cardinal Frings, at first tried to oppose the idea of a "crisis of the Church" but was forced to take note of its existence. In a famous conference that he gave to the German Bishops' Conference, entitled "Church History

---

[138] Paul VI, Address on December 15, 1969, to the Sacred College of Cardinals, in Paolo VI, *Insegnamenti*, 7:796–798.

[139] Paul VI, Homily on September 3, 1967, at www.vatican.va (the text is missing from the volume Paolo VI, *Insegnamenti*).

and Crisis of the Church," published in Italian by *L'Osservatore Romano*[140] itself on September 17, 1968, Monsignor Jedin elucidated five phenomena related to the actual crisis of the Church:

> 1. an ever-spreading uncertainty about the faith, caused by the free diffusion of theological errors from pulpits, in books and articles;
> 2. the attempt to transfer into the Church the forms of parliamentary democracy through the introduction of the right to participate on all three levels of ecclesiastical life, in the universal Church, in the diocese, and in the parish;
> 3. the desacralization of the priesthood;
> 4. the free "structuring" of the liturgical celebration instead of carrying out the *Opus Dei*;
> 5. ecumenism as a protestantizing process.[141]

Father Henri de Lubac himself, one of the "fathers" of the council, in a conference held on May 19, 1969, at the University of Saint Louis in Missouri (United States) on "Church in Crisis," denounced the use and abuse of the main conciliar documents. The constitution *Dei Verbum*, he said, becomes the pretext for "a narrow biblicism which disregards any and all tradition and in the process manages to swallow itself up," developing "the notion of a 'faith-in-the-future' in which it is hard to see what, if anything is left of the gospel of Jesus Christ." The constitution *Lumen gentium* is interpreted "so as to transform the Church into a vast democracy" and to criticize what is called "the institutional Church" in the name of an ideal of Christianity" that strikes at "the divine constitution of the Church." Openness to the world in *Gaudium et spes* becomes "a forgetfulness of salvation [through the cross] and of the gospel, a tending toward secularism, a loosening of faith and morals … [and] finally … a loss of identity, in a word, the betrayal of our obligation toward the world."

> We know, too, how the decree on religious liberty is falsified, when, contrary to its most explicit teaching, some conclude that there is no longer any need to preach the gospel… How many more analogous observations might be made concerning the constitution on the

---

[140] Cf. H. Jedin, "Kirchengeschichte und Kirchenkrise," in *Aachener Kirchenzeitung*, December 29, 1968 and January 5, 1969; Ital. transl. in *L'Osservatore Romano*, January 15, 1969.

[141] *Idem, Storia della mia vita, op. cit.*, 326–327.

> liturgy, which some have turned into a mockery, as well as the decrees on ecumenism, the religious life, and others? The word "renewal" can cover a multitude of abuses![142]

While aware of the process of self-destruction of the body of the Church, Paul VI had not modified his basic optimism. On the night of July 20–21, 1969, man set foot on the moon for the first time. The pope watched the event on television in his summer residence at Castel Gandolfo, and a few minutes after the space ship touched down on lunar soil, he addressed the astronauts via satellite connection: "Honor, greetings, and blessings to you, conquerors of the moon, pale lamp of our nights and of our dreams. Bring to her, with your living presence, the voice of the spirit, the hymn to God, our creator and our Father."[143] In this undertaking, the pope had said in his Angelus message on July 13, man "appears to us as a giant. He appears divine, not in himself, but in his principle and in his destiny. Honor to man, honor to his dignity, to his spirit, to his life."[144]

8. The defeat of the conservatives after the council

The group of conservative cardinals that had gravitated around the *Coetus Internationalis Patrum*, folded in the years immediately afterward, putting up only weak resistance to the beginning of the conciliar reforms.

Cardinals Ottaviani and Ruffini were now bent over with age and the weight of the defeats that they had suffered. The younger Cardinal Siri

---

[142] H. de Lubac. "Church in Crisis," conference given at the University of Saint Louis (Missouri), May 29, 1969; reprinted in *Theology Digest* 17 (1969): 312–325 at 318–319. A revised French version of the conference was also published in *Nouvelle Revue Théologique* 91 (1969): 550–569, from which the Italian citation cites the following additional text: "What a mockery there is, alas, all too frequently, in the ostentatious pretense of boldly applying the principles enunciated by the council for the 'suitable renewal' of religious life, while contradicting them! This perhaps is where the devastation wreaked by the crisis appears to be simultaneously most serious and most significant.... What wretched realities, what desertions of all kinds, what sorts of degradations take place, in certain cases to the point of perversion, which are then hidden under the banner of 'prophetic witness' or 'the demands of truth,' under the mendacious word 'renewal'!"

[143] Paul VI, Message (July 21, 1969), in *Insegnamenti* 7 (1969): 499–500.

[144] Ibid., 493–494.

tried to become the promoter of a resistance movement, creating a review[145] that could oppose the progressive theology that was invading the Church, especially after the birth of *Concilium*, the mouthpiece of international progressivism.[146] "I am busy organizing the Catholic revival after the council," Siri writes in his *Diary* on October 20, 1964, "seeking to create a front that will be very clear against the defects that appeared in the council or as a result of the council. God has allowed us to get all the wrinkles out: praise be to him!"[147] The new review, *Renovatio*, debuted in 1966; according to the editor chosen by Siri, Gianni Baget Bozzo,[148] "was at one time an attempt to accept the council and to present in a different way the themes that had been put forward by progressive theologies."[149]

---

[145] A-Siri, fald. "Renovatio." Cardinal Ruffini was received by Paul VI on January 4, 1966, and spoke to him about the plan: "I confided to His Holiness what I wrote to Your Eminence about the appropriateness of a periodical that would publish sound doctrine in the critical times that we are going through, and would make headway, when necessary, against the review *Concilium* (which seems to me to cause His Holiness himself concern)" (ibid.). Siri, in turn, spoke about it with Cardinal Ottaviani, who strongly encouraged him.

[146] The founders of *Concilium*, many of whom had played a decisive role as conciliar *periti*, were Antoine van den Boogaand, Paul Brand, Yves Congar, Hans Küng, Johannes Baptist Metz, Karl Rahner, and Edward Schillebeeckx. Cf. Hadewych Snijdewind, "Genèse et organisation de la Revue internationale de théologie 'Concilium,'" in *Cristianesimo nella storia* 21 (2000): 645–673.

[147] Siri, *Diario*, 391.

[148] Gianni Baget Bozzo (1925–2009), after a youthful experience in the Dossettian left, founded the reviews *L'Ordine Civile* and *Lo Stato* to resist the formation of the center-left. Invited in 1966 by Cardinal Siri to edit *Renovatio*, he was ordained by Cardinal Siri himself in 1967. After resigning in 1978 from the editorial board of *Renovatio*, in the spring of 1984 he was elected deputy to the European Parliament as a candidate of the Italian Socialist Party (PSI). This candidacy resulted in a canonical process that led to his being suspended *a divinis* on August 4, 1985. He ran for office again in 1989 and remained in Strasbourg until 1994. The penalty was then revoked by Siri's successor, Cardinal Giovanni Canestri. After leaving the PSI in 1994, he participated in the founding of *Forza Italia* and edited its publication, *Carta dei Valori*.

[149] G. Baget Bozzo, *I tempi e l'eterno: Intervista su un'esperienza teologica*, ed. Claudio Leonardi and Giovanni Tassani (Genoa: Marietti, 1988), 37. "When I went to see Cardinal Siri to propose to him the founding of *Renovatio*," Baget Bozzo recalls, "the cardinal was a defeated, anguished man. In a few years, from being the pope's candidate for the papacy, he had gone to the status of a rejected minority, considered at the level of public opinion to be semi-heretical. I asked him whether he was willing to help me found a review that accepted the council and accepted it as a doctrinal event,

For twenty years (1966-1986) the review began with an editorial by the archbishop of Genoa, not signed, but clearly penned by him,[150] along the lines of what would then become "the hermeneutic of continuity." In 1975, the cardinal of Genoa rode onto the battlefield with his "Reflections on the Contemporary Theological Movement,"[151] which then became what has remained his theological testament: *Gethsemane*. In the "contemporary theological movement" he denounced the errors of Pelagianism, Arianism, and modernism. These are "combined more or less consciously, with more or less subtlety, and sometimes also guile, in a speculative amalgam, without precise outlines and without basic references, which serves as a basis for a rush towards integral humanization of all religion."[152] Siri dwelt in particular on the errors of three contemporary authors: Henri de Lubac, Karl Rahner, and Jacques Maritain, concluding that as a result of the errors present in the theological movement, "the gospel message and the teaching of the Church about the new creation, about the renewal of man, and of everything, has been fundamentally altered."[153]

Like Siri, Bishop Luigi Carli, too, while denouncing the existence of a crisis of the Church—or, as he put it more accurately, "in the Church"—which had as it basis "a crisis of faith,"[154] proposed interpreting the council in the light of tradition, denouncing the misrepresentation and exploitation of its documents.

The line of accepting the council was chosen, at first, by three other bishops too, who with Bishop Carli had guided the *Coetus Internationalis:* Archbishop Marcel Lefebvre, Bishop Antonio de Castro Mayer, and Archbishop Geraldo de Proença Sigaud.

---

and defended within these parameters what we considered to be binding in tradition" (ibid., 38).

150 The editorials of *Renovatio* and the notes to the clergy that had appeared earlier in the Genoese *Rivista Diocesana* are collected in G. Siri, *Il dovere dell'ortodossia: Editoriali di "Renovatio" e note al clero* (Pisa: Giardini, 1987).

151 G. Siri, *Riflessioni sul movimento teologico contemporaneo* (Rome: Fraternità della Santissima Vergine Maria, 1975); the text was then included in an expanded 1980 edition, which was translated into English as *Gethsemane: Reflections on the Contemporary Theological Movement* (Chicago: Franciscan Herald Press, 1981).

152 Ibid., 51.

153 Italian edition, 73. [The citation cannot be found in the English translation.]

154 L. M. Carli, *Nova et vetera: Tradizione e progresso nella Chiesa dopo il Vaticano II* (Rome: Istituto Editoriale del Mediterraneo, 1969), 17.

Around 1968, however, the positions of Archbishop de Proença Sigaud and of Bishop de Castro Mayer began to diverge. Archbishop Sigaud made a "political" choice and moved closer to the military regime that in 1964 had deposed the "progressive" president João Goulart. Bishop de Castro Mayer aligned himself with Archbishop Lefebvre, gradually breaking off relations with the Roman ecclesiastical authorities.[155] In 1968 Archbishop Lefebvre asked the bishop of Campos from Rome:

> Has the moment perhaps not arrived to say what we think about the council, to conduct a study on each schema so as to show their ambiguities, their disastrous tendencies, to ask that a commission be appointed to interpret and revise them? Personally I do not hesitate to say so in all my conversations. I am getting ready to write an article on the following topic: the post-conciliar spirit has nothing to do with the council.
>
> For my part I am convinced that what we are presently witnessing is a direct result of the council. One does not dismantle all the truths of tradition without ruining the edifice of the Church.
>
> You mention then a very serious problem that we can no longer remain silent about, at least in our private conversations, namely: the Holy Father's attitude in some documents, but especially in his acts. How to describe it? How to judge it when the whole tradition of the Church condemns it?[156]

---

[155] On October 5, 1969, in a letter to Archbishop Lefebvre, in which he announced the painful defection of Archbishop Sigaud, Bishop de Castro Mayer wrote: "And so, I dare once again to have recourse to your charity, to your advice. The situation of the Church could not be more terrible! The new *Ordo Missae* does not agree well with dogma. It is the beginning of a capitulation to protestantism. It is the disavowal of Trent and of Pius V. Can we pastors of souls follow a *'via media,'* without saying anything and allowing each priest to follow his own conscience or lack thereof, with the resulting dangers for many souls? And if we say openly what we think, what will be the consequences? Dismissal, which causes confusion for many believers and scandal for the weakest! Can we in conscience run the risk of such consequences? These are very painful cases of conscience. I do not know what support the good cause has in Rome. Such support will be able to ward off the thunderbolts that threaten the faith and the piety of many Catholics. I apologize if I am troubling you with all this, but I ask you for a word that might enlighten and comfort me" (Letter from Bishop Castro Mayer to Archbishop Lefebvre dated October 5, 1968, in A-Ecône 05–01).

[156] Letter from Archbishop Lefebvre to Bishop de Castro Mayer dated May 28, 1968, in A-Ecône 05–01.

In Latin America, Plinio Corrêa de Oliveira upheld his strongly critical attitudes toward progressivism in the temporal order, according to his own vocation as a layman committed to the "*consecratio mundi*" ["consecration of the world"].[157] In two months, in July and August 1968, the militant activists of Tradition Family and Property (TFP) collected more than 1,500,000 signatures against the communist infiltration in the Church on the streets of 158 cities in Brazil. The petition was presented officially at the Vatican on November 7, 1969; no response ever arrived from the Holy See, but progressivism suffered a major setback in Brazil.[158]

9. The Vatican *Ostpolitik*

The international policy of "*détente*" toward communism begun by John F. Kennedy was continued in the 1970s by U.S. President Nixon and by his Secretary of State Kissinger. The objective was identical to the policy that Willy Brandt, German Socialist Chancellor, developed on a European scale: the idea of a "convergence" between the Western bloc and the communist bloc.

In the ecclesiastical field, Archbishop Casaroli, the "Foreign Minister" of Paul VI, pursued a policy of understanding with communism similar to that of Brandt and Kissinger. In the wake of negotiations about the participation of Orthodox observers in the council,[159] Archbishop Casaroli began to make journeys to Budapest and Prague (1963-1973), to Belgrade (1966-1970), to Warsaw (1967-1974), to Moscow (1971), and to Cuba (1974).

The Soviet foreign minister Andrej Gromyko was received at the Vatican in 1966, 1970, 1974, and 1975. In 1970 audiences were granted to three heads of the communist guerilla forces in Angola, Guinea, and Mozambique. In 1971 Paul VI received the Yugoslav dictator Josef Tito and in 1973 the Rumanian dictator Nicolae Ceausescu.

During the meeting with Tito on March 29, 1971, Pope Montini welcomed his guest, declaring that the Yugoslav constitution contained principles such as the "humanization of the social sphere," the "strengthening

157 R. de Mattei, *The Crusader of the Twentieth Century, op. cit.*, 180–183.

158 Ibid., 153–154.

159 Cf. G. Barberini, *L'Ostpolitik della Santa Sede, op. cit.*, 250 ff.

of solidarity and collaboration among men," "respect for human dignity," and "the general development of man as a free person."[160] The conviction was that Marxism and Christianity shared some common values that they could leverage so as to reach the objective of international peace.

The new strategy of the Holy See was revealed by Casaroli himself, one year after his trip to Moscow, in a speech on "The Holy See and Europe" that he gave in Milan on January 20, 1972,[161] in which the archbishop stressed that the service of humanity and of peace was a primary duty of the Holy See, in order to avoid a nuclear catastrophe as well.

One of the most famous victims of the Vatican *Ostpolitik* was Cardinal József Mindszenty, primate of Hungary and hero of the anti-communist resistance. Mindszenty, who had been a prisoner from 1948 to 1956, took refuge after the Hungarian revolt in the American embassy in Budapest and always remained resolutely opposed to any idea about dialogue or negotiations with communist governments, convinced that that could only strengthen them. He steadfastly disputed the Vatican *Ostpolitik*, telling the Secretary of State, Cardinal Villot: "Why do you appoint bishops in the countries of the Eastern bloc? It would be better if there were none, rather than those whom the governments allow you to appoint."[162] On November 1, 1973, when Paul VI asked him to renounce his title of archbishop of Esztergom and primate of Hungary, the cardinal replied with a respectful but clear refusal. Paul VI took it upon himself to declare the primatial archdiocese vacant, informing Cardinal Mindszenty on November 18, 1973, of his dismissal as archbishop.[163]

---

[160] A. Casaroli, *op. cit.*, 269.

[161] Cf. *Relazioni Internazionali* (February 12, 1973): 161–165.

[162] A. Wenger, *Le cardinal Villot, op. cit.*, 260.

[163] The announcement of the removal of Cardinal Mindszenty was made in *L'Osservatore Romano*. According to the *Giornale d'Italia* dated February 6–7, 1974, the Vatican had "offered his head on a silver platter to his Herod, the communist government of Budapest." The February 13 issue of the Zürich newspaper *Die Weltwoche* wrote that now Rome itself was the one to martyr Mindszenty, since it was worried about getting rid of its anachronistic image for the sake of the Vatican's new *Ostpolitik*. On February 5, 1974, when the news of his dismissal had become common knowledge, Cardinal Mindszenty issued a communiqué in which he declared that he had never resigned from his post as archbishop nor from his rank as primate of Hungary, underscoring that "the decision was made solely by the Holy See" (*Memorie, op. cit.*, 372).

Supporters of the *Ostpolitik* maintained that communism would last a long time and that the negotiations would allow communism to separate itself from atheism and to evolve automatically into a political system "with a human face." The communist leaders, for their part, were aware of the imminent collapse of the system and, in order to survive, had undertaken the policy of "dialogue" and of the "outstretched hand." They conceded little or nothing, giving assurances that would never be honored.[164] In fact, the *Ostpolitik* "propped up" communism instead of depriving it of all support, thus delaying its fall for years.

The policy of Vatican *détente* had many critics throughout the world, starting with those who were supposed to have been its beneficiaries. In 1976, Father Alessio Ulisse Floridi,[165] who for fifteen years had been a regular contributor to the *Civiltà Cattolica* as its "Sovietologist," published a book in which he analyzed the Holy See's new strategy toward the communist countries from an unusual angle: that of Soviet "dissent," showing that the Christians in Eastern Europe who were supposed to be the beneficiaries of the policy of *détente*, were in reality its victims.[166] "The absolute necessity of avoiding the outbreak of a nuclear war is something, no doubt, that nobody can deny. Yet," Father Floridi asked, "is this requirement really so absolute as to take precedence over the rights of God or to be used also as a deterrent in order to be able to proceed to the enslavement of entire nations?"[167]

After the fall of communism, Bishop (later cardinal) Ján Korec judged the *Ostpolitik* as follows:

---

[164] Cf. Casaroli, *op. cit.*, 72–73.

[165] Alessio Ulisse Floridi (1920–1986), Jesuit, ordained in 1949 in the Slavonic Byzantine Rite, "Sovietologist" of the *Civiltà Cattolica* until 1965, when he was reassigned first to Brazil, then to the United States, where he conducted his missionary apostolate among the Eastern-rite Catholics.

[166] Cf. A. U. Floridi, *Mosca e il Vaticano, op. cit.* Later, recalling the participation at the Second Vatican Council of "observers" from the Patriarchate of Moscow, which was notorious for its direct dependence on the Kremlin, he declared, "It is certain that on the Kremlin's part there was an intense interest in preventing any possible attempt by the council to condemn communism officially.... The Russian Orthodox Church dismissed its reservations about the council only after it became clear that the council would not condemn communism" ("In tema di 'dissenso' e di 'ostpolitik,'" Interview with Father Alessio U. Floridi by R. de Mattei in *Cristianità* 32 [1977]). Among the main critiques of the *Ostpolitik* are those by the German writer Reinhard Raffalt, *Wohin steuert der Vatikan? Papst zwischen Religion und Politik* (Munich: Piper, 1973).

[167] A. U. Floridi, *Mosca e il Vaticano, op. cit.*, 61.

> In our country the most dangerous thing was that they called on the carpet the most precious thing that we had, namely the so-called clandestine Church. I myself received the order to stop ordaining priests secretly. For us it was truly a catastrophe, as though they had abandoned us, thrown us away.... This was the greatest sorrow of my life. The communists thus held in their hands the public pastoral ministry of the Church. If some priest in his parish devoted himself to the altar servers, he was deprived of the state approval without which no priest could minister. The Church was condemned to shut herself up in her places of worship and then to die out.... Our hope was the clandestine Church, which silently collaborated with the priests in the parishes and formed young men who were prepared to make sacrifices: professors, engineers, physicians who were ready to become priests. I ordained about 120 of them. These persons labored in silence among the youth and the families, and secretly published magazines and books. In reality the *Ostpolitik* sold out this activity of ours in exchange for the vague and uncertain promises of the communists.[168]

On April 10, 1974, after Archbishop Casaroli's trip to Cuba, the *Folha de San Paulo* published as an advertising supplement a declaration entitled "The Vatican policy of *détente* toward the communist governments. Non-intervention or resistance for the TFP?"[169] In it Plinio Corrêa de Oliveira wrote in the name of the Brazilian TFP, in respectful but firm language, words that expressed the state of mind of a multitude of Catholics throughout the world.

---

[168] Ján Korec, Interview in *Il Giornale*, July 18, 2000. Ján Chryzostom Korec, S.J. (1924–) Slovak, ordained in 1950, consecrated bishop in 1951, bishop of Nitra from 1990 to 2005, created cardinal in 1991.

[169] The manifesto appeared in the days following a visit to Cuba by Archbishop Agostino Casaroli. In the course of the journey, which took place from March 27 to April 5, 1974, at the invitation of the Cuban episcopate, Archbishop Casaroli had conversations with government representatives and with Fidel Castro. The following year he was in the German Democratic Republic and from July 30 to August 1, 1975, took part, as the special delegate of Paul VI, in the Helsinki Conference on "security," signing its final document in the name of the Holy See. On the trip to Cuba see also Riccardo Cannelli, "Il viaggio a Cuba di Monsignore Casaroli," in *L'America Latina fra Pio XII e Paolo VI: Il cardinale Casaroli e le politiche vaticane in una Chiesa che cambia*, ed. A. Melloni and S. Scatena (Bologna: Il Mulino, 2006), 195–235.

The Vatican policy of *détente* toward the communist governments creates a situation which affects anti-communist Catholics deeply, but much less, however, as anti-communists than as Catholics. For at any moment a supremely embarrassing objection may be put to them: Does not their anti-communist action lead to a result that is precisely opposed to the one intended by the vicar of Christ? And how can one consider a Catholic to be consistent if he moves in an opposite direction from the Pastor of Pastors? This question leads all anti-communist Catholics to a consideration of these alternatives: To cease the struggle?—Or to explain their position?

To cease the fight, we cannot. And we cannot cease it because of a demand of our conscience as Catholics. For if it is a duty of every Catholic to promote good and fight evil, our conscience imposes on us the responsibility of propagating the traditional doctrine of the Church, and of fighting communist doctrine....

The Church is not, the Church never was, the Church never will be such a prison for consciences. The bond of obedience to the successor of Peter, which we will never break, which we love in the depth of our soul, to which we give the best of our love, this bond we kiss at the very moment in which, [crushed] by sorrow, we affirm our position. And kneeling, gazing with veneration at the figure of His Holiness Paul VI, we express to him our fidelity.

In this filial act we say to the Pastor of Pastors: Our soul is yours, our life is yours. Order us to do whatever you wish. Only do not order us to stay idle in face of the assailing red wolf. To this, our conscience is opposed.[170]

---

170 P. Corrêa de Oliveira, "The Vatican Policy of Détente Toward the Communist Governments" (http://www.tfp.org/tfp-home/statements/the-vatican-policy-of-detente-towards-the-communist-governments.html). The document was originally published in its entirety in *Catolicismo* 280 (1974), in thirty-six Brazilian newspapers, and later reprinted in seventy-three newspapers and magazines in eleven countries, eliciting no objection whatsoever regarding its orthodoxy and canonical correctness.

10. The post-conciliar period and the liturgy

a) The *Novus Ordo Missae*

Don Giuseppe Dossetti saw in the constitution on the liturgy the interpretive key of the conciliar *corpus* of writings and the hermeneutic criterion for interpreting its documents,[171] and Cardinal Danneels[172] considered the liturgical reform begun by the council and carried out by Paul VI as perhaps the most profound change in the life of the Catholic Church.[173]

Article 54 of the constitution *Sacrosanctum concilium*, combined with article 40 concerning the role of the episcopal conferences, had given the latter the option of introducing the vernacular in the celebration of Mass. Based on this, on Sunday, March 7, 1965, during the council, a form of the Mass began to be celebrated in Italy that called for many parts in the vernacular and the altar turned toward the people. Paul VI celebrated in Italian that day in a Roman parish and exhorted the parishioners to collaborate in implementing the reform. On March 4, 1967, the recitation of the Canon of the Mass aloud and in the vernacular was authorized. In that same month the book *The Torn Tunic* by Tito Casini[174] appeared, which contained a harsh critique of the ongoing liturgical reform. The fact that Cardinal Bacci had written the preface to it made a great impression.

Paul VI had entrusted to the *Consilium ad Exsequendam Constitutionem de Sacra Liturgia* [Consilium for the Implementation of the Constitution on the Sacred Liturgy], established in 1964, the task of revising the liturgical books (missal, breviary, ritual, pontifical) and of carrying out the reforms concerning more active participation by the faithful, such as the use of

---

171 G. Dossetti, *Per una "Chiesa eucaristica": Rilettura della portata dottrinale del Vaticano II: Lezioni del 1965*, ed. G. Alberigo and G. Ruggieri (Bologna: Il Mulino, 2002).

172 Godfried Danneels (1933–), ordained in 1957, bishop of Anversa in 1977, then of Malines-Brussels from 1979 to 2009, created cardinal in 1983.

173 Cf. G. Danneels, "Le réforme liturgique de Paul VI et ses enjeux pour la vie de l'Église," in *Le rôle de G. B. Montini, op. cit.*, 4.

174 Cf. Tito Casini, *The Torn Tunic: Letter of a Catholic on the "liturgical reform,"* with a preface by Cardinal Antonio Bacci, Eng. transl. (Britons, 1971); *idem, Nel fumo di Satana: Verso l'ultimo scontro* (Florence: Il carro di San Giovanni, 1976).

national languages and concelebration.[175] The climax of the *Consilium*'s work, directed by Monsignor Bugnini, was the development of the new *Ordo Missae*, which was promulgated by Paul VI in the Consistory of April 28, 1969.[176] The *Consilium* had accomplished its mission and was replaced, in 1970, with the newly created Congregation for Divine Worship. In May 1970 the new *Missal* was ready. This was, as the Jesuit historian Giacomo Martina observed, "a genuine liturgical revolution, much more important than the one started by the Council of Trent."[177]

There were those who tried to place all the responsibility for the *Novus Ordo* on the shoulders of Monsignor Bugnini, interpreting his removal from office as Pope Montini's response to the treason of which he was supposedly the victim. The testimonies to the contrary are utterly conclusive and not surprising. Paul VI, one of his biographers Yves Chiron wrote, will no doubt go down in history as the pope who brought the Second Vatican Council to its conclusion, but also as the one who gave the Church a new Mass.[178] From the 1930s on, in fact, the young Montini, under the influence of Father Bevilacqua, had been a follower of the "liturgical movement," in which he saw the ecclesial expression of Maritain's humanism.[179]

Once the new rite was in force, some eminent members of the hierarchy, as well as many theologians and laypeople, criticized it severely.[180] In late

---

175 On September 26, 1964, the *Consilium* authorized the optional use of the vernacular in all the rites except the Preface and the Canon of the Mass.

176 On April 3, 1969, the apostolic constitution *Missale Romanum* was promulgated, which consisted of two documents: the *Institutio generalis missalis Romani* and the new *Ordo Missae* strictly speaking, in other words, the text of the Mass and the rubrics that accompany it (cf. AAS 61 [1969]: 217–226). The breviary acquired its new form on February 2, 1971 with the *Institutio generalis de liturgia horarum* (cf. AAS 63/2 [1971]: 527–535).

177 G. Martina, *Storia della Chiesa* (Brescia: Morcelliana, 1995), 3:359.

178 Cf. Y. Chiron, *Paul VI, op. cit.*, 289.

179 Cf. Virginia Pontiggia, "L'interesse per la liturgia in G. B. Montini: gli anni giovanili alla FUCI," in *Liturgia: temi e autori, op. cit.*, 38–52.

180 Among the many critical studies on the "new Mass" and the Liturgical Reform, most of them composed by lay scholars, we mention: A. X. Vidigal da Silveira, *La nouvelle Messe de Paul VI qu'en penser?, op. cit.*; J. Vaquié, *La Révolution liturgique* (Chiré-en-Montreuil: Diffusion de la Pensée Française, 1971); L. Salleron, *La Nouvelle Messe* (Paris: Nouvelles Éditions Latines, 1971, 1976); Wolfgang Waldstein, *Hirtensorge und Liturgiereform* (Schaan [Fl]: Lumen gentium, 1977); Klaus

October 1969, Cardinals Ottaviani and Bacci presented to Paul VI a "Brief Critical Examination of the *Novus Ordo Missae*" composed by a select group of theologians of various nationalities. In their cover letter to the pope they said that "the *Novus Ordo Missae*... represents, as a whole and in its details, a striking departure from the Catholic theology of the Holy Mass, as it was formulated in the 22nd session of the Council of Trent, which, in fixing definitively the 'canons' of the rite, erected an insurmountable barrier against any heresy that might attack the integrity of the mystery."[181]

Monsignor Ferdinando Antonelli himself, secretary of the new Congregation for Divine Worship, who had followed the whole iter [journey] of the liturgical reforms, from Pius XII to Paul VI, had expressed on July 23, 1968, to Archbishop Benelli, substitute to the Secretary of State, his "concerns about the liturgical reform which is becoming increasingly chaotic and aberrant."[182] Even the progressives admitted that the *Novus Ordo Missae* expressed a new theology of the "people of God" on its journey through history: an immanentist ecclesiological vision that presupposed the common priesthood of the faithful and was quite different, according to Alberigo, from the vision of the encylicals *Mediator Dei* and *Mystici Corporis* by Pius XII.[183]

Gamber, *Die Reform der Römischen Liturgie* (Regensburg: F. Pustet, 1979) (the French edition of this work contains prefaces by Cardinals Silvio Oddi, Joseph Ratzinger, and Alfons M. Stickler; English edition: *Reform of the Roman Liturgy: Its Problems and Background* [San Juan Capistrano: Una Voce Press, 1993]) ; Michael Davies, *Pope Paul's New Mass* (Dickinson, TX: The Angelus Press, 1980); *Die heilige Liturgie*, ed. Franz Breid (Steyr: Ennsthaler, 1997); *Autour de la Question Liturgique avec le cardinal Ratzinger* (Fontgombault: Association Petrus a Stella, 2001); English edition: Looking Again at the Question of the Liturgy with Cardinal Ratzinger (Farnborough, Hampshire: St. Michael's Abbey Press, 2001); R. de Mattei, *La liturgia della Chiesa nell'epoca della secolarizzazione* (Chieti: Solfanelli, 2009); Martin Mosebach, *The Heresy of Formlessness: The Roman Liturgy and its Enemy*, Engl. transl. (San Francisco: Ignatius Press, 2006).

181 This study, sponsored by Una Voce of Italy, has been reprinted by the same association together with a "New Critical Examination of the *Novus Ordo Missae* ("Il Novus Ordo Missae: due esami critici," in *Una Voce*, supplement to issue 48–49 [1979] of the journal).

182 F. Antonelli, "Note sulla riforme liturgica," *op. cit.*, in N. Giampetro, *Il card. Ferdinando Antonelli, op. cit.*, 257.

183 Cf. G. Alberigo, "Il popolo di Dio nell'esperienza di fede," in *Concilium* 20 (1984): 940–958; *Idem,* "La riforma conciliare nel cammino storico del movimento liturgico e nella vita della Chiesa," in *Transizione epocale, op. cit.*, 505–525.

Based on these facts, there were more and more calls from Catholics of every nationality asking for the restoration of, or at least "equal status" for, the traditional Mass.[184] We must mention among others a 1971 "memorandum" with which more than one hundred outstanding personages from all over the world asked the Holy See "to be willing to consider with the utmost seriousness what a tremendous responsibility it would incur in the sight of the history of the human spirit if it did not agree to allow the traditional Mass to live perpetually."[185]

b) The secularization of the liturgy

The problem of the new rite was soon accompanied by the problem of the new liturgical practice. In August 1976, the journalist Dino Pieraccioni wrote:

> When you attend Mass celebrated on a sort of makeshift table in front of the altar… when you see at some Masses a sort of "combined" offertory in which the bread and wine are offered with one formula; when you hear prayers of the faithful improvised here and there throughout the Church by the individual participants…; when at the sign of peace you see the celebrant leave the altar and stroll among the nearby concelebrants or even among the congregation, walking around the pews; when at communion the faithful take the consecrated hosts by themselves…; when instead of the traditional hymns (in Italian or in Latin, it makes no difference) that everyone knew and sang from memory, you hear some tunes and ditties that have no musical (much less religious) value whatsoever, is this really implementing the liturgical reform and following the will of the council?[186]

---

[184] Catholics made three international pilgrimages to Rome to confirm their fidelity to the traditional Mass and the catechism of St. Pius X (cf. Guglielmo Rospigliosi, "La manifestazione dei cattolici tradizionalisti riconfermano la fedeltà al messale e al catechismo," in *Il Tempo*, June 19, 1970). A collection of the appeals until 1980 can be found in *…Et pulsanti aperietur (Lc 11, 10)* (Clarens: Una Voce, 1980).

[185] Among the signers were: Romano Amerio, Jorge Luis Borges, Marcel Brion, Agatha Christie, Henri de Montherlant, Augusto Del Noce, Robert Graves, Grahame Green, Julien Green, Yehudi Menuhin, Malcolm Muggeridge, Marius Schneider, and Bernard Wall. See the text and the list of signatories in *Una Voce* 7 (1971): 1–10.

[186] Dino Pieraccioni, "Il Concilio, la tradizione, le fughe in avanti," in *Il Resto del Carlino*, August 18, 1976.

In theory, the *Novus Ordo* of Paul VI established a set of norms and prayers that regulated the celebration of the Holy Sacrifice of the Mass as a replacement of the old Roman Rite; in fact, the liturgical practice revealed in the existence of a new shape-shifting rite. In the course of the reform, in fact, a whole series of innovations and variants were gradually introduced, many of them not foreseen either by the council or even by the constitution *Missale Romanum* by Paul VI.[187]

Quid novum? What's new is not just the replacement of the language of the Latin rite with the vernacular languages, but also the altar understood as a "table," so as to underscore the banquet aspect instead of the sacrifice; the *celebratio versus populum* instead of *versus Deum*, with the resulting abandonment of celebration facing east, in other words, toward Christ, symbolized by the rising sun; the lack of silence and recollection during the ceremony and the theatricality of the celebration, often accompanied by irreverent songs, with the priest often reduced to the status of "presider at the assembly"; the hypertrophy of the Liturgy of the Word in comparison with the Liturgy of the Eucharist; the "sign" of peace replacing the genuflections by the priest and the faithful as a symbol of the transition from the vertical dimension to the horizontal dimension of the liturgical action; communion received by the faithful standing and in the hand; the access of women to the altar; concelebration as a tendency toward the "collectivization" of the rite; above all the change and replacement of the prayers of the Offertory and the Canon. In particular the elimination of the words *Mysterium Fidei* from the Eucharistic formula can be considered, as Cardinal Alfons Maria Stickler[188] observed, as the symbol of the demystification and thus of the humanization of the central nucleus of the Holy Mass.[189]

The guiding thread of these innovations can be expressed in the thesis that if we want to make the faith of Christ accessible to contemporary

---

[187] R. de Mattei, *La liturgia della Chiesa nell'epoca della secolarizzazione, op. cit.*, 30–31.

[188] Alfons Maria Stickler (1910–2007), Austrian, ordained in 1937, professor of Canon Law at the Pontifical Salesian University, where he served as rector from 1958 to 1966. prefect of the Vatican Apostolic Library (1981), pro-librarian of the Holy Roman Church, and titular archbishop of Bolsena in 1983, created cardinal in 1985.

[189] Cf. A. M. Stickler, "Erinnerungen und Erfahrungen eines Konzilperitus der Liturgiekomission," in *Die heilige Liturgie, op. cit.*, 176. Cardinal Stickler mentions that the *Sacramentarium Gelasianum*, the most ancient missal of the Roman Church, clearly contains in the original text (in Codice Vaticano, Reg. lat. 316, foglio 181v), the formula *"mysterium fidei"* (*op. cit.*, 174).

man, we must live out and present that faith within the thought and mentality of today. The traditional liturgy, because of its inability to adapt to the contemporary mindset, would distance man from God, thus incurring guilt for the loss of God in our society. The liturgical reform set out to adapt the rite, without impairing the essence of the sacrament, so as to make it possible for the Christian community to "participate in the sacred" in a way that could not be achieved through the patterns of the traditional liturgy.

The dominant idea of the liturgical reform was the idea of the "active participation" of the faithful, which, as Gilles Routhier emphasizes, "entered Vatican II through the constitution on the liturgy, before invading, so to speak, the conciliar documents in their entirety."[190] Through this principle of *participatio actuosa*, the whole community becomes the subject and the producer of the liturgical action, from the perspective of a radical secularization of the liturgy.[191] "The seemingly so modest expression: conscious, full, and active participation, is a spy for unforeseen difficulties,"[192] notes Father Angelus Häussling, emphasizing the relation between the *actuosa participatio* of the liturgical reform and the sort of active participation which, in Rahner's school, was called the "anthropological revolution" (*anthropologische Wende*) of theology.

The one who acts is not so much the priest *in persona Christi*, that is, God himself, but the community of believers, *in persona hominis* [in the person of man], so as to represent the demands of this modern world which a disciple of Rahner describes as "holy and sanctified in its profanity, that is, holy in the form of anonymity."[193] The result of the liturgical reform "as it was carried out concretely… was not revival but devastation,"[194] wrote Cardinal Ratzinger, who maintains that "the crisis

---

[190] G. Routhier, *Il Concilio Vaticano II, op. cit.*, 101.

[191] Cf. Michael Kunzler, "La liturgia all'inizio del terzo millennio," in *Il Concilio Vaticano II: Recezione e attualità alla luce del Giubileo*, ed. R. Fisichella (Cinisello Balsamo: San Paolo, 2000), 217–231.

[192] Angelus A. Häussling, O.S.B., "Liturgiereform: Materialien zu einem neuen Thema der Liturgiewissenschaft," in *Archiv für Liturgiewissenschaft* 31 (1989): 1–32 at 29.

[193] Luis Maldonado, *Secularización de la liturgia* (Ediciones Marova, 1970). Citation at p. 473 of the Italian edition, *Secolarizzazione della liturgia* (Rome: Edizioni Paoline, 1972).

[194] J. Ratzinger, "In memory of Klaus Gamber," in *Joseph Ratzinger: Collected Works*, vol. 11, chapter 29 originally published as the preface to K. Gamber, *La réforme liturgique, op. cit.* See also *idem*,

in the Church that we are experiencing today is to a large extent due to the disintegration of the liturgy."[195]

In the apostolic letter *Ecclesia Dei*[196] dated July 2, 1988, John Paul II asked the bishops and all those who exercise pastoral ministry in the Church "to guarantee respect for [the] rightful aspirations" of all those Catholic faithful "who feel attached to some previous liturgical and disciplinary forms of the Latin tradition." In 2007 Cardinal Ratzinger, who had since become Pope Benedict XVI, issued the motu proprio *Summorum pontificum*,[197] in order to satisfy "the just aspirations" of the faithful of the old traditional Rite and to come "to an interior reconciliation in the heart of the Church."[198] With the motu proprio the pope restored the full right of citizenship to the ancient Roman Rite, which juridically had never been abrogated, although in fact it had been "forbidden" for forty years.[199]

11. The Jubilee Year in 1975

In 1974, Paul VI announced, with the Bull *Apostolorum limina*,[200] the twenty-fifth Jubilee Year of the Church, according to the traditional way of reckoning them established by Paul II. Attending the ritual of the opening of the Holy Door, on Christmas Eve of 1974, were also several Buddhists invited by the Secretariat for Non-Christians. On December 14, 1975,

---

Introduction to the Liturgy (San Francisco: Ignatius Press, 2000).

195 J. Ratzinger, *Milestones*, 146–149.

196 Cf. John Paul II, apostolic letter *Ecclesia Dei* (July 2, 1988), in AAS 80 (1988): 1498. Citation at paragraph 5.c.

197 Cf. Benedict XVI, apostolic letter *Motu proprio data* on the use of the Roman liturgy prior to the reform carried out in 1970, *Summorum Pontificum* (July 7, 2007), in AAS 99 (2007): 777–781, accompanied by a letter, *"Ad omnes catholicae Ecclesiae episcopus ritus romanis"* ["To all the Roman-rite bishops of the Catholic Church"], ibid., 795–799.

198 Ibid.

199 Jean Madiran tells the story of this prohibition in France, from November 1969, when Cardinal Marty (1904–1994), president of the Episcopal Conference, declared that, starting on January 1, 1970, the new *Ordo Missae* would be obligatory and used only in French (cf. J. Madiran, *Histoire de la messe interdite*, 2 vols. [Versailles: Via Romana, 2007 and 2009]).

200 Paul VI, Bull *Apostolorum limina* (May 23, 1974), in AAS 66 (1974): 289–307.

in Saint Peter's Basilica, on the tenth anniversary of the rescinding of the excommunications between the Church of Rome and the Church of Constantinople, the pope, unexpectedly, bent over and kissed the foot of Metropolitan Meliton of Calcedonia, head of the "Orthodox" delegation.

Twenty-five years had passed since the triumphal Holy Year of Pius XII and the Church appeared to be torn apart by a profound crisis.[201] The collapse of dogmatic certainties; the relativism of the new permissive morality; the anarchy in the area of discipline; the defections from the priesthood and the millions of faithful who stopped practicing their faith; the removal from the churches and the disposal of altars, altar rails, crucifixes, statues of saints, and sacred vestments: all this presented the picture of a veritable devastation.[202]

The "springtime of faith" that was supposed to follow the Second Vatican Council appeared rather to be a severe winter, as evidenced especially by the collapse of vocations and the abandonment of religious life.[203]

From 1939 to 1963 the dicastery of the Holy Office had granted a total of 563 dispensations from the celibate priesthood. In the years following the council the number of dispensations grew until it reached 3,335 for the years between 1963 and 1970.[204] "For the first time in history," Father Giacomo Martina wrote in 1977, "we have witnessed the abandonment of

---

201 The bibliography on this topic is enormous. Besides the book-length interview of V. Messori with Cardinal J. Ratzinger, *The Ratzinger Report, op. cit.*, and the volume by R. Amerio, *Iota Unum, op. cit.*, see also Dietrich von Hildebrand, *The Trojan Horse in the City of God* (Chicago: Franciscan Herald Press, 1967); *idem, Devastated Vineyard* (Harrison, NY: Roman Catholic Books, 1985); C. Fabro, C.P.S., *L'avventura della teologia progressista, op. cit.*; Bernard Monsegú, C.P., *Posconcilio*, 3 vols. (Madrid, Studium, 1975–1977); Wiegand Siebel, *Katholisch oder konziliar: Die Krise der Kirche heute* (Munich-Vienna: A. Langen – G. Müller, 1978); G. Siri, *Gethsemane, op. cit.*; Georg May, *Der Glauben in der nachkonziliaren Kirche* (Vienna: Mediatrix Verlag, 1983); A. Sinke Guimarães, *In the Murky Waters of Vatican II, op. cit.*

202 The United States is the country that offers the most certain statistics on this devastation. Cf. the unsparing picture drawn by Roger Finke and Rodney Stark in *The Churching of America, 1776–1990: Winners and Losers in Our Religious Economy* (New Brunswick, NJ: Rutgers University Press, 1992).

203 Cf. Francesco José Fernández de la Cigoña, "El invierno postconciliar," in *Verbo* 393–394 (2001): 329–358, who reports impressive data about the collapse of the then-flourishing religious life in Spain.

204 Cf. G. Martina, *Storia della Chiesa, op. cit.*, 376–377.

the priesthood, albeit with all the necessary dispensations, by thousands of priests within the space of a few years."[205]

The overall assessment on the fortieth anniversary of the council (1965-2005), with regard to the total and proportional losses of the major religious institutes, would be more dramatic. Whereas there were 329,799 male religious in the principal men's institutes in 1965, in 2005 only 214,913 remained; their number had diminished by one-third in the forty years after the council.[206]

In 1973, the 1600th anniversary of the death of the indomitable bishop of Alexandria, St. Athanasius, Bishop Rudolf Graber[207] of Regensburg, who had been a council father, recalled the Arian crisis of the fourth century.

> Why is so little done to strengthen the pillars of the Church, so as to avoid their collapse? If there is still anybody convinced that the events taking place in the Church are incidental, or that these are passing difficulties, it means that he is beyond recovery.... But the responsibility of the leaders of the Church is even greater, if they do not deal with these problems or if they think that they can remedy the evil with a bit of patchwork. No: this is about the whole thing; this is about the Church; this is about a kind of Copernican revolution that has broken out within the Church itself, a gigantic revolution in the Church.[208]

The American Bishop Robert Dwyer,[209] on July 30, 1975, wrote a letter to Paul VI in which he outlined a striking description of the Catholic decadence in the United States, especially with regard to the

---

[205] G. Martina, *La Chiesa in Italia negli ultimi trent'anni*, Preface by Clemente Riva (Rome: Studium, 1977), 142.

[206] Cf. the study by the Claretian Angelo Pardilla, *I religiosi ieri, oggi e domani* (Rome: Editrice Rogate, 2007). A similar picture of nuns is drawn by the same author: *Idem, Le religiose ieri, oggi e domani* (Vatican City: Libreria Editrice Vaticana, 2008).

[207] Rudolf Graber (1903–1992), German, ordained in 1926, bishop of Regensburg from 1962 to 1981.

[208] R. Graber, *Athanasius und die Kirche unserer Zeit* (J. Kral, 1973). Citations from the Italian edition, *Sant'Atanasio e la Chiesa del nostro tempo* (Brescia: Civiltà, 1974), 28, 79.

[209] Robert Joseph Dwyer (1908–1976), from the United States, ordained in 1932, bishop of Reno (Nevada) in 1952 and then archbishop of Portland (Oregon) from 1966 to 1974.

devastation in the liturgical sphere.[210] "No enemy," the prelate concluded, "had wreaked this devastation, but rather the children of the family themselves."[211] Two years later Archbishop Arrigo Pintonello,[212] in an open letter to the Italian bishops, presented a similar picture of the anarchy in the Church: "a true scourge of God much more vast and destructive than the one by Attila, with consequences that ought to deprive of sleep those who are responsible for the life and governance of the Church, who inexplicably remain silent."[213]

Meanwhile, in France, the Abbé Louis Coache[214] spoke about "apostasy," whereas on May 7, 1973 the Abbé Georges de Nantes arrived in Rome to present to the pope a brochure concerning the dramatic situation of the Church and the responsibilities of the ecclesiastical leaders. The gesture was evaluated in various ways, but it caused a tremendous stir.[215]

In Italy, too, starting in January 1975, an "anti-modernist" publication, *Sì sì, no no*, edited by a priest, Francesco Putti, began to document

---

210 Text of the letter, with the title, "Una cattedrale devastata," in *Sì sì, no no*, 3 (1978): 2.

211 R. J. Dwyer, "Una cattedrale devastata," *op. cit.*, 3.

212 Arrigo Pintonello (1908–2001), ordained in 1932, bishop of Theodosiopolis in Arcadia in 1953, military ordinary of Italy from 1953 to 1966, archbishop of Terracina-Latina, Priverno and Sezze from 1967 to 1971. Archbishop Pintonello founded in 1975 the review *Seminari e teologia*, which set out to "record the echo of sorrow—we should say—of true anguish of so many priests and laypeople, concerned about the fate to which seminarians and religious students seem to be condemned" (*Seminari*, 1 [1975]: 1). One of his most active collaborators was Don Ennio Innocenti (1932–) priest of the Roman clergy from 1957 on, a writer and journalist; about him see *Don Ennio Innocenti: La figura, l'opera, la milizia* (Rome: Biblioteca Edizioni, 2004).

213 A. Pintonello, "Lettera agli Ecc.mi vescovi," in *Seminari e Teologia* 3 (1977): 1–4 at 4.

214 Louis Coache (1920–1994), French, ordained in 1943, parish priest in Montjavoult (Oise), founded in 1968 the newsletter *Le combat de la foi* to defend the faith against the new heresies. In 1985 he handed over the center in Flavigny, which he organized in 1971, to Archbishop Lefebvre's Society of Saint Pius X. Cf. Louis Coache, *Vers l'apostasie générale* (Paris: La Table Ronde, 1969); *Idem, Les batailles du combat de la foi* (Chiré-en-Montreuil: Éditions de Chiré, 1993).

215 G. de Nantes, *Liber Accusationis*, available in English translation at www.scribd.com/doc/76591221/Liber-Accusationis . Cf. Domenico Celada, "De Nantes e il Vaticano," in *Il Tempo*, May 7, 1973.

unsparingly the responsibility of ecclesiastics for the conciliar trend.[216] The resistance to progressivism began to spread throughout Europe.

12. The "Lefebvre case"

Ten years after the conclusion of the council the "Lefebvre case" exploded, so called after the French archbishop who from 1974 on embarked on an open conflict with the Holy See on the subject of the new Mass and the conciliar reforms.[217]

On June 6, 1969, Bishop Charrière[218] of Fribourg had authorized Archbishop Lefebvre to open in his episcopal see an international boarding school named after St. Pius X. Given the increase in applications for admission, the French bishop acquired in Ecône, in the Valais, a second house that became the center of formation for the international Priestly Society of Saint Pius X, which was erected canonically on November 1, 1970, in the Diocese of Lausanne-Geneva-Fribourg. In November 1972, seven years after the conclusion of Vatican II, Archbishop Lefebvre gave a speech in Rennes in which for the first time he expressed a strongly negative judgment on the Second Vatican Council.[219] The Holy See forbade Archbishop Lefebvre to ordain his seminarians. Yet on June 29, 1976, in the presence of a crowd of Catholics who had gathered from all over the world, the French archbishop conferred the subdiaconate on thirteen of his seminarians and the priesthood on another thirteen, thus incurring

---

[216] About Don Francesco Maria Putti (1909–1984), cf. F. Spadafora, *Araldo della fede cattolica*, pro-manuscripto (Rome: Arti Grafiche G.A.D.I., 1993). We should also mention the work of the priest Don Luigi Villa, founder of the review *Chiesa viva* in which he documented especially the alarming adherence of some ecclesiastics to Freemasonry.

[217] Besides the previously cited works by C. Siccardi and B. Tissier de Mallerais, see Luc Perrin, *L'affaire Lefebvre*.

[218] François Charrière (1892–1976), Swiss, ordained in 1917, bishop of Lausanne, Geneva, and Fribourg from 1945 to 1970, then bishop emeritus.

[219] See M. Lefebvre, *A Bishop Speaks: Writings and Addresses 1963–1976* (Dickinson, TX: Angelus Press, 1977), 117–141; second unabridged edition (Kansas City: Angelus Press, 2007), 119–142. Later Archbishop Lefebvre expresses his critiques in the works, *I Accuse the Council* (Dickinson, TX: Angelus Press, 1982); *Open Letter to Confused Catholics*, transl. Rev. Michael Crowdy (Dickinson, TX: Angelus Press, 1986); and *They Have Uncrowned Him* (Dickinson, TX: Angelus Press, 1988).

"suspension *a divinis*." A meeting with Paul VI at Castel Gandolfo on September 11, 1976 did not lead to a solution to the problem.

In 1977, Princess Elvina Pallavicini[220] invited Archbishop Lefebvre to her historic palace in Rome to explain his own reasons. The conference unexpectedly revived curiosity about and attention to the existence of a Roman patrician class and nobility; they were still alive and feisty, and Princess Pallavicini was a vocal representative thereof.[221] The pressures put on the Roman noblewoman to cancel the conference[222] were to no effect, due to her strong personality and independence. In addition to the four hundred invited guests who attended the event in the Throne Room of the palace on the Quirinal Hill, an equal number crowded the antechamber.

In his speech Archbishop Lefebvre calmly posed questions instead of formulating answers:

> It is impossible to conceive of the Catholic Church as anything but continuity, as tradition, as the heir of her past. It is impossible to understand a Catholic Church that breaks with her past, with her tradition, and precisely because of the impossibility of imagining such a thing, I find myself in a rather strange situation: that of a bishop who has been suspended for having founded a seminary in Switzerland, a seminary that was legally, canonically erected, a seminary that welcomes many vocations; and eight years after its foundation we have many houses in the United States, one in Canada, in England, in France, in Switzerland, in Germany, and even in Italy here in Albano. How can it be that while continuing to do what I myself have done during fifty years of my life, with the congratulations and the encouragement of the popes, and in particular of Pope Pius XII who honored me with his friendship, I should find

[220] Princess Elvina Pallavicini (1914–2004), winner of the military bronze medal of honor for her efforts on behalf of the monarchist partisans during the German occupation of Rome, had made her Roman palace on the Quirinal Hill an important meeting place for the ecclesiastical and political circles and the nobility of the capital.

[221] Cf. Benny Lai, "Il Vaticano e il patriziato," in *La Nazione* (June 7, 1977) and the investigation by Emilia Granzotto, "Tutti i nobili di Roma," in *Panorama* (June 14, 1977).

[222] During the turbulent days that preceded the meeting, among those who intervened to dissuade Princess Pallavicini were Duke Carlo Colonna on behalf of King Umberto II, Archbishop Andrea Cordero of Montezemolo, the Grandmaster of the Order of Malta Angelo de Mojana, and the Cardinal vicar of Rome Ugo Poletti.

> myself today being considered as an enemy of the Church? How is this possible, how is it conceivable? I had the opportunity to say this to the pope in the last audience that I had on September 11. I told him: I cannot understand the reason why, unexpectedly, after having formed seminarians for my whole life the way I am forming them today, whereas before the council I had all sorts of honors, excluding only the cardinalate, now, after the council, while doing the same thing, I find myself suspended *a divinis*, practically considered a schismatic, practically excommunicated as an enemy of the Church. I do not think that such a thing is possible or conceivable. Therefore something in the Church has changed, something that was changed by the men of the Church, in the history of the Church.[223]

Archbishop Lefebvre was presented as the "head" of the traditionalists. In reality he was only the most visible expression, amplified by the mass media, of a phenomenon that went far beyond him personally and had its roots and its first cause in the problems raised by the council and by its implementation. The resistance to the actualization of the conciliar reforms began in sectors of the lower clergy and of the laity, as had happened during the French Revolution, when pastors and farmers had been the ones to promote the revolt of the Vendée and the anti-revolutionary insurgencies in Europe. The French archbishop was the most famous but not the only representative of a vast, ramified resistance movement, which unfortunately sometimes led to schism or to a loss of faith.

13. The "Italian way" to communism

In Italy the post-conciliar period found its expression in political action more than in theological reflection. This resulted from the role that the Church had always had in the peninsula and from the specific political sensibility that Paul VI had had since his youth. In the post-conciliar years something was presented as a "religious choice" that was in reality a "political choice" by the ecclesiastical authorities and was centered above all on the party of the Catholics in power.

---

[223] M. Lefebvre, *La Chiesa dopo il Concilio* (Rome: Society of St. Pius X, 1977), 4. In that same year Archbishop Lefebvre expressed himself more radically in *Le coup de maître de Satan: Ecône face à la persécution* (Martigny: Éditions Saint-Gabriel, 1977).

The modernist movements of the early twentieth century had had one of its most significant exponents in Romolo Murri,[224] founder of that Christian Democratic Party that had been eyed attentively by the communist leader Antonio Gramsci, who identified its revolutionary potential.[225] The modernist journal itself, *Nova et Vetera*, had maintained that the task of Christianity should be to supply Marxism with a religious soul.[226] Giulio Girardi, one of the authors of *Gaudium et spes*, who wrote *Marxism and Christianity*[227] in 1966 and then founded Christians for Socialism, proposed in the aftermath of the council a synthesis between the two philosophies.

More cautiously, but with the same conviction that Marxism was the future, *La Civiltà Cattolica* invited its readers in 1966 to face "clear-sightedly and prudently" "the risk involved in any dialogue between Catholics and communists, in the hope, if not the certainty, that the seed sown in their minds and hearts might one day bear its fruits."[228]

As of September 1972, Paul VI had a trusted ally at the head of the Italian Episcopal Conference in the person of the secretary, Archbishop Enrico Bartoletti. Bartoletti made "a substantial contribution to the transition by the Italian church in the post-conciliar period,"[229] writes one of his close collaborators at the time, Father Bartolomeo Sorge, noting many times that when he went to visit him "I met some of the

---

224 Romolo Murri (1870–1944), founder of the Christian Democratic Party, was excommunicated by St. Pius X in 1909. Like many modernists, he joined fascism, only to return shortly before his death to the bosom of the Church. About him see the article by M. Guasco in DSMCI 2:414–442, with a bibliography; *Idem, Romolo Murri e il modernismo* (Rome: Cinque Lune, 1968).

225 "Democratic Catholicism does what communism could not do: it blends, orders, enlivens, and commits suicide.... The popular politicians are to the socialists as Kerensky was to Lenin" (A. Gramsci, "I popolari," in *L'Ordine Nuovo* 24 [November 1, 1919], reprinted in *Ordine Nuovo 1919–1920* [Turin: Einaudi, 1954], 286).

226 Cf. Daniela Sarasella, *Modernismo* (Milan: Editrice Bibliografica, 1995), 80.

227 G. Girardi, *Marxismo e Cristianesimo* (Assisi: Cittadella, 1966).

228 Giuseppe De Rosa, S.J. "Cattolici e comunisti oggi in Italia," in *Civiltà Cattolica* 2782 (1966): 305–314 at 312. See the fuller treatment in *Idem, Chiesa e comunismo in Italia* (Rome: Coines, 1970).

229 B. Sorge, S.J., *La traversata: La Chiesa dal Concilio Vaticano II ad oggi* (Milan: Mondadori, 2010), 126 and, more generally, 126–133.

most famous Catholic challengers who resulted from him!"[230] During Bartoletti's term as secretary, Catholics lost the referendum on divorce (in which the secretary of the CEI did not want to get involved), witnessed the growth and strengthening of the Italian Communist Party, and saw the disbanding of the traditional Catholic associations. Italian Catholic Action went from 3,600,000 registered members in 1963 to 1,600,000 in 1969. From 1969 on, under the new general president of the association, Vittorio Bachelet,[231] what happened was, according to Father Martina, "a genuine demobilization of the complex central apparatus set up by Gedda."[232] Ten years later there were eight hundred registered members,[233] while Catholic dissent was increasing.[234]

The relativist mentality, denounced in 1960 by the "Letter of the Italian Episcopate on Secularism,"[235] had gradually made its way into Italian society after the council. On December 1, 1970, divorce was introduced, later confirmed by the popular referendum of May 12, 1974. Divorce was followed by the new family law, which legally codified the demands of libertarian and egalitarian feminism. Commenting on the results of the May 12 referendum with his students at the Gregorianum, Father Giacomo Martina responded without hesitation that this was "one of the final acts (but not the final one!)" of an "irreversible process" of secularization that

---

230 Ibid., 130.

231 Vittorio Bachelet (1926–1980), professor of Economic Public Law at the University of Rome, president of Catholic Action from 1964 to 1973. On February 12, 1980, while conversing with his assistant Rosy Bindi, he was assassinated by a commando of the Red Brigades in the entrance hall of the faculty of Political Science.

232 G. Martina, *La Chiesa in Italia, op. cit.*, 149.

233 Cf. A. Tornielli, *Paolo VI, op. cit.*, 529.

234 In the book by D. Saresella, *Dal Concilio alla contestazione: Riviste cattoliche negli anni del cambiamento (1958–1968)* (Brescia: Morcelliana, 2005), there is a detailed reconstruction of the debate generated, in the years during and immediately after the council, by the Italian publications that can be classified as part of the Catholic "dissent."

235 *Il laicismo: Lettera dell'episcopato italiano al clero* (March 25, 1960), no. 3, in *Enchiridion della Conferenza episcopale italiana: Decreti, dichiarazioni, documenti pastorali per la Chiesa italiana*, vol. I: *1954–1972* (Bologna: EDB, 1985), 76–95. The decision to compose the letter had been made during the sixth meeting of the CEI in October 1959.

had been going on since the French Revolution.[236] The Jesuit historian, like so many other representatives of the Catholic world, was convinced that history was following its unstoppable course which had to be fostered because "it signaled the passage from a predominantly sociological faith to a more personal faith." This was the "adult Catholicism" that claimed to reinterpret, in the light of the council, the immanentistic demands that had been characteristic of modernism.

It was in this climate of relativism and secularism that the secretary of the Italian Communist Party (PCI), Enrico Berlinguer, launched his proposal for an "historic compromise" between Catholics and communists. The following years, between 1974 and 1976, saw the greatest electoral successes of the PCI.[237] After the political elections of 1976 began the series of so-called "national solidarity" governments led by Giulio Andreotti with the decisive support of Enrico Berlinguer's PCI.[238] The ultimate objective was the entrance of the communists into the Christian Democratic government. In that way, after the failure of the Chilean experiment, Catholic Italy would be the first country in the world in which communism would have won power democratically. The man chosen to lead this delicate operation to a successful issue was the president of the Christian Democrats (DC), Aldo Moro, who in his final political speech on February 28, 1978, sought to convince the Christian Democratic senators and deputies of the necessity of an agreement with the communists.[239]

On March 16, 1978, the day scheduled for a vote of confidence in a government headed by Giulio Andreotti, with the external support of the PCI, the Red Brigades abducted Aldo Moro on the *Via Fani* in Rome, massacring the five men in his escort in the ambush.[240] Paul VI

---

236 Cf. G. Martina, *La Chiesa in Italia, op. cit.*, 183.

237 Many Catholic candidates came forward on the Communist slates. "If it is a cause of scandal to vote for someone who ran on the Communist Party slate," declared Prof. Pietro Scoppola in an article in *Il Populo* on May 21, 1976, "it would be a much more serious cause of scandal to condemn them" (cited in S. Magister, *La politica vaticana e l'Italia, op. cit.*, 481).

238 Cf. Arturo, Gismondi, *Alle soglie del potere: Storia e cronaca della solidarietà nazionale, 1976–1979* (Rome: Sugarco: 1987).

239 Cf. Francesco Damato, "L'ultimo discorso sui rapporti col Pci," in *Il Giornale*, May 10, 1978.

240 The group of Brigadiers on the *Via Fani* also included Alessio Casimirri, the son of two Vatican citizens (his father had been assistant director of the Vatican Press Office), whose marriage had been blessed by the then substitute of the Secretary of State Archbishop Montini. Alessio Casimirri,

was distressed over it. The following day, through a communiqué of the Secretariat of State, he informed the public that he would give all his moral and material support to save the life of the president of the Christian Democrats, his friend from his youth.[241] The Holy See collected an enormous sum of money and tried in vain to intervene in a practical way to save the life of the hostage. On April 22, the pope wrote an open letter "to the men of the Red Brigades," as he described the terrorists on the *Via Fani*, begging them, on his knees, to free Aldo Moro, unconditionally, "not so much because of my humble and affectionate intercession, but by virtue of his dignity as our brother in the human race."[242] The distraught appeal remained unanswered. On May 9 the lifeless body of the president of the Christian Democrats was found in the trunk of a Renault, on the *Via Caetani*, a few meters away from the headquarters of the PCI and the DC. The secretary of Paul VI, Monsignor Macchi, recalls that this was "a deadly blow that left its mark on him personally, since he was already weakened by illness and advanced age."[243]

On May 13, in the Basilica of Saint John Lateran, the pope attended the funeral celebrated by Cardinal Vicar Ugo Poletti[244] and gave a speech that sounded almost as though it were reproaching God for not having granted the request to spare Aldo Moro.[245] The tragic incident had been a tremendous blow to Paul VI, hastening the decline of his strength.

---

with his wife Daniela Algranati, managed to throw the police off his trail and to settle abroad as an expatriate (cf. A. Tornielli, *Paolo VI, op. cit.*, 610–613).

241 See: A. Tornielli, *Paolo VI, op. cit.*, 596–613; Giuliano Ferrara, "L'Affaire Moro e il gioco delle coincidenze simboliche incrociate: L'addio alla Repubblica di Montini e alla pietà laica e cattolica," in *Il Foglio*, May 10, 2008.

242 Paul VI, April 22 Letter to the Red Brigades, in *Insegnamenti* 16 (1978): 298–299. Moro's wife, Eleonora, did not approve of the petition by Paul VI, which she described as "a peculiar initiative," and refused to attend the funeral rites in the Basilica of Saint John Lateran.

243 *Paolo VI e la tragedia di Aldo Moro: 55 giorni di ansia, tentativi, speranze e assurda crudeltà*, ed. Pasquale Macchi, Preface by Cardinal Agostino Casaroli (Milan: Rusconi, 1998), 44.

244 Ugo Poletti (1914–1997), ordained in 1938, auxiliary bishop of Novara in 1958, archbishop of Spoleto in 1967, auxiliary archbishop of Rome in 1969, vicar general of Rome and cardinal in 1973.

245 The pope's prayer for Aldo Moro, in *Insegnamenti* 16 (1978): 362–373.

14. The proximate and remote causes of the "world split apart"

While Soviet imperialism was extending its shadow over the world, in June of that year Aleksandr Solzhenitsyn gave a memorable speech at Harvard entitled "A World Split Apart,"[246] in which he denounced the West for yielding in the face of real-world socialism. The Russian dissident identified the basic error as "the prevailing Western view of the world which was born in the Renaissance and found political expression since the Age of Enlightenment. It became the basis for political and social doctrine and could be called rationalistic humanism or humanistic autonomy: the proclaimed and practiced autonomy of man from any higher force above him. It could also be called anthropocentricity, with man seen as the center of all."[247] This concept, according to Solzhenitsyn:

> started modern Western civilization on the dangerous trend of worshiping man and his material needs. Everything beyond physical well-being and the accumulation of material goods, all other human requirements and characteristics of a subtler and higher nature, were left outside the area of attention of state and social systems, as if human life did not have any higher meaning. Thus gaps were left for evil, and its drafts blow freely today.[248]

Communism was, according to Solzhenitsyn, the most radical and consistent form of modern humanism, "so that Karl Marx was able to say, in 1844, that 'communism is naturalized humanism.'"[249] He added that:

> The communist regime in the East could endure and grow due to the enthusiastic support from an enormous number of Western intellectuals who (feeling the kinship!) refused to see communism's crimes, and when they no longer could do so, they tried to justify these crimes. The problem persists: In our Eastern countries, communism has suffered a complete ideological defeat; it is zero and less than zero.

---

246 Aleksandr Solzhenitsyn, *A World Split Apart* (New York: Harper & Row, 1978).

247 Ibid., 47, 49.

248 Ibid., 49.

249 Ibid., 53. A penetrating analysis of the communist system, along the same lines, was penned during those same years by Igor Safarevic in *Il socialismo come fenomeno storico mondiale* (Milan: La casa di Matriona, 1980), with an introduction by A. Solzhenitsyn.

> And yet Western intellectuals still look at it with considerable interest and empathy, and this is precisely what makes it so immensely difficult for the West to withstand the East.[250]

The path followed from renaissance humanism on is, according to the Russian author, the cause for modern man's loss of a spiritual life.

> It is trampled by the party mob in the East, by the commercial one in the West. This is the essence of the crisis: the split in the world is less terrifying than the similarity of the disease afflicting its main sections. If, as claimed by humanism, man were born only to be happy, he would not be born to die. Since his body is doomed to death, his task on earth evidently must be more spiritual: not a total engrossment in everyday life, not the search for the best ways to obtain material goods and then their carefree consumption. It has to be the fulfillment of a permanent, earnest duty so that one's life journey may become above all an experience of moral growth: to leave life a better human being than one started it. It is imperative to reappraise the scale of the usual human values; its present incorrectness is astounding.[251]

Solzhenitsyn's speech was the subject of commentary throughout the world. What struck the most attentive observers, such as Eugenio Corti,[252] was the fact that Christians, even Catholics, had not immediately noticed in that speech the similarity to the concept of history that had been typical of them when Catholic culture had not entered into its current state of confusion: the historical vision that identifies the beginning of de-Christianization in the passage from medieval theocentrism to modern anthropocentrism and immanentism.

---

[250] A. Solzhenitsyn, *op. cit.*, 55.

[251] Ibid., 57, 59.

[252] Cf. Eugenio Corti, *Il fumo nel Tempio* (Milan: Ares, 1997), 130. Among the works of Eugenio Corti (1923–), the most widely known is *Il cavallo rosso* (Milan: Ares, 1972–1983); English translation, *The Red Horse* (San Francisco: Ignatius Press, 2002). Besides *Il fumo nel Tempio*, on the crisis of the Catholic world in the post-conciliar period, he also wrote *Le responsabilità della cultura occidentale nelle grandi stragi del nostro secolo* [The responsibilities of Western culture in the great massacres of our century] (Milan: Mimep-Docete, 1998).

In 1959, Plinio Corrêa de Oliveira had outlined the big picture of this process of de-Christianization of society in *Revolution and Counter-Revolution*. The work of this Brazilian thinker, unlike that of the Russian dissident, was inspired by the supernatural hope of someone who trusts in the indestructible strength of the Catholic Church. The book concluded with an homage of filial devotion to the newly elected Pope, John XXIII, and with an expression of absolute confidence in the triumph of the Immaculate Heart announced by Our Lady at Fatima. In the appendix to the new edition of the work published in Italy in 1977, the Brazilian thinker, who thirty-five years before had denounced the infiltration of liturgical errors into Catholic Action, saw in the historical events of his own time the development and the fruits of those errors that go back to the modernist crisis of the early twentieth century. The dialogue with the world had been a surrender to the enemy, which now constituted a terrible threat.

Plinio Corrêa de Oliveira's point of view was not that of the theologian, but of a layman, philosopher, historian, and man of action. Based not on the theological merit of the conciliar documents but on the reality of the facts and on their historical consequences, he denounced the "enigmatic, disconcerting, dreadful, and apocalyptically tragic silence that the Second Vatican Council kept with regard to communism."[253]

> This council intended to be pastoral and not dogmatic. In fact it had no dogmatic import. Moreover, its omission with respect to communism may make it go down in history as the a-pastoral council par excellence. With its up-to-date tactics—about which, nevertheless, the least that can be said is that they are debatable on the theoretical-practical plane[254]—the Second Vatican Council attempted to drive away, so to speak, bees, wasps, and birds of prey. Its silence on communism let the wolves run free. The work conducted by this council cannot be written down as really pastoral: neither in history nor in the Book of Life.
>
> It is harsh to say it. Yet the factual evidence points, in this sense, to Vatican Council II as one of the greatest calamities, if not the greatest, in the history of the Church. As a result of it the "smoke of Satan" has

253 This judgment is expressed in the 1977 appendix of P. Corrêa de Oliveira, *Rivoluzione e Contro-Rivoluzione, op. cit.*, 168.

254 Later Plinio Corrêa de Oliveira expressed more explicitly his evaluation on the theoretical level, stating that in some conciliar documents he noted a dissonance with traditional teaching (cf. A-IPCO, Incontro del 22 giugno 1984) and even a certain systematic ambiguity that is incompatible with full orthodoxy (cf. A-IPCO, Riunione del 20 agosto 1980).

penetrated into the Church to an unthinkable extent, and it is still spreading day by day, with the terrible force of expanding gases. To the scandal of countless souls, the Mystical Body of Christ has entered into a sinister process that could be called self-destruction.[255]

15. Twenty years of Church history

In 1978 in Italy the Catholic party in power sought at all costs to avoid a conflict over abortion, renouncing all forms of obstructionism in Parliament and seeking to prevent a new referendum in the country. The *Official Gazette* dated May 22 published Law 194, which introduced abortion, signed by members of Parliament who were all Christian Democrats,[256] starting with the president of the Republic Giovanni Leone and the Prime Minister Giulio Andreotti.[257] According to one of the signers of the law, the Minister Tina Anselmi, Paul VI had exhorted the Christian Democratic ministers not to resign and to remain in office even though they would have to sign the law.[258]

On June 29, 1978, the day of the Feast of Saints Peter and Paul, in his final public liturgy, a Mass celebrated in the Vatican Basilica, the pope, visibly suffering, presented a veritable assessment of the fifteenth anniversary of his pontificate.

Paul VI reviewed in his homily the whole time "during which the Lord entrusted his Church to Us," while "the natural course of our life

---

[255] P. Corrêa de Oliveira, *Rivoluzione e Contro-Rivoluzione, op. cit.*, 168–169. Plinio Corrêa de Oliveira stressed this judgment in a 1976 article "Autoritratto filosofico," reprinted in *Rivoluzione e Contro-Rivoluzione, op. cit.*, 365–426 at 388. At a meeting on May 17, 1989, he declared: "When in the last part of *Revolution and Counter-Revolution* I wrote that the Second Vatican Council was the greatest calamity in all of Church history, I maintained something that I would maintain today much more vehemently than before" (A-IPCO, May 17, 1989).

[256] See Giambattista Sciré, *L'aborto in Italia: Storia di una legge* (Milan: Bruno Mondadori, 2008); Giulia Galeotti, *Storia dell'aborto* (Bologna: Il Mulino, 2004).

[257] Cf. *Gazzetta ufficiale della Repubblica Italiana*, anno 119, n. 140, May 22, 1978, p. 3646. "I considered the problem involved in countersigning that law (as Leone did in signing it), but if I refused I would not only start a crisis after having scarcely begun to plug up the leaks, but besides enduring the law on abortion the DC would also lose the presidency and that would truly be more serious" (G. Andreotti, *Diari 1976–1979: gli anni della solidarietà* [Milan: Rizzoli, 1981], 73).

[258] *La Gazzetta del Mezzogiorno*, August 30, 1994, cited in Alfredo Mantovano, *La Democrazia cristiana e l'aborto: perché fu "vero tradimento,"* in *Cristianità*, 232–233 (1994): 13–15 at 13.

is drawing to its sunset." In this retrospect the aged pontiff recalled as an "important act" of his pontifical teaching authority the profession of faith which ten years earlier, on June 30, 1968, he had solemnly pronounced as "the Credo of the People of God," in a moment when "facile doctrinal experimentation seemed to be shaking the certitude of so many priests and faithful" and addressed a "worried but firm appeal to those who were involved in drawing others after them, by word, by their writings, by their conduct, on the paths of their personal opinions and then on those of heresy and schism, disorienting the consciences of individuals and the entire community…." "We warn them paternally," he concluded: "let them take care not to disturb the Church further; the moment of truth has come, and it is necessary for each one to know his own responsibilities with regard to decisions that ought to safeguard the faith, the common treasure that Christ, who is the Rock [*Pietra*], entrusted to Peter [*Pietro*], *Vicarius Petrae*, "Vicar of the Rock", as St. Bonaventure calls him."[259]

In these words a truth cropped up which current events had not impaired: the rock of Peter, thanks to his universal primacy and the infallibility of his magisterium, provides the foundation on which Jesus Christ instituted his Church and on which she will remain steadfast, by virtue of a divine promise, until the end of time. "Thou art Peter and upon this rock I will build my Church… and I will give to thee the keys of the kingdom of heaven" (Mt 16:18-19). These words of the gospel, which are so rich in supernatural hope, sparkled in the gilded mosaic of the cupola of Saint Peter's Basilica over the council fathers throughout the Second Vatican Council. They expressed an insurmountable truth: the popes, as private individuals, pass on, but the institution of the papacy survives every disaster, summing up and concentrating within it the Church, which is the Mystical Body of Christ.

In mid-July Paul VI left Rome to move to his summer residence in Castel Gandolfo. His end arrived unexpectedly. The pope of the council died at 9:40 p.m. on August 6, 1978, in the same papal villa where Pius XII had breathed his last on October 9, 1958.[260] Twenty years of Church history had elapsed since then.

---

[259] Paul VI, *Insegnamenti* 16 (1978): 519–525.

[260] There were countless messages of condolence for the death of Paul VI. The most striking of all were the words of the former Grandmaster of the Grand Orient of Italy, Giordano Gamberini: "This is the first time in the history of modern Freemasonry that the head of the largest western religion has died while not in a state of hostility toward the Masons. And for the first time in history the Masons can pay their homage at the tomb of a pope, without ambiguity or contradictions" (*Rivista Massonica* 5–6 [1978]: 290).

Conclusion

From the death of Paul VI to today another thirty years have passed, the minimal interval required to allow an historian to evaluate objectively the events of his time. What has happened since then is not history, but a chronicle of the dramatic era in which we are living. Despite the positive seeds of rebirth that can be glimpsed in recent years, the crisis of the Church unfortunately has not come to an end in the last three decades, nor will it be possible for it to come to an end until its profound causes have been eliminated.

At the conclusion of this volume allow me to turn with veneration to His Holiness Benedict XVI, in whom I recognize that successor of Peter to whom I feel indissolubly bound, expressing my deep gratitude to him for having opened up the doors to a serious debate on the Second Vatican Council. I emphasize that I intended to offer to this debate the contribution not of a theologian but of an historian, joining however in the requests of those theologians who respectfully and filially ask the vicar of Christ on earth to promote a more in-depth examination of Vatican Council II, in all its complexity and to its full extent, so as to verify its continuity with the twenty preceding councils and to dispel the shadows and doubts that for a half century have caused the Church to suffer, yet certain that the gates of hell will never prevail against her (Mt 16:18).

Glossary of Technical Terms and Abbreviations

(Foreign language terms are in Latin unless otherwise indicated.)

Ad extra: externally, in its external relations.
Ad interim: for the meantime.
Ad intra: internally, in its internal relations.
Aggiornamento [Italian]: updating.
Ancien Régime [French]: the old monarchical government in France before the Revolution of 1789.
Aspersorium: aspergillum, used for sprinkling holy water.
Camerlengo [Italian]: chamberlain, administrator.
***Celebratio versus populum*:** celebration of Mass with the priest facing toward the people instead of *versus Deum* "towards God" (*i.e.* facing the altar together with the people).
Chanson de geste [French]: a medieval epic poem, usually celebrating legendary events and figures. Plural *chansons de geste*.
Claque [French]**:** members of an audience paid to applaud.
Conciliarism: the theory that the highest authority in the Catholic Church is that of an ecumenical or general council.
Coetus Internationalis Patrum: "International Group of Fathers," a group of conservative council fathers organized to oppose the innovative agenda of a large number of council fathers from Western Europe.
De Ecclesia: the conciliar schema "On the Church."
De fontibus revelationis: the conciliar schema "On the Sources of Revelation."
De unitate ecclesiae: the conciliar schema "On the unity of the Church."

Desideratum, plural ***desiderata***: something desired as essential.

Détente [FRENCH]: relaxation of tensions between hostile nations or blocs.

Diarchy: rule by two supreme authorities (*cf.* monarchy, rule by one authority).

Dicastery: general term for an administrative body in the Roman curia (*e.g.* a Congregation, a Pontifical Council or Commission).

Dubio: "a doubt," a formal question that is submitted to a Roman dicastery.

Episcopal conference: the assembly of the Catholic bishops of a country or a geographical region.

Ex-novo: anew, as something new.

Febronianism: the 18th-century theory that final ecclesiastical authority belongs to the whole Church and not just to the papacy.

Girondist: a member of the moderate republican party in the French legislative assembly in 1791.

Horatii and Curatii: two sets of male triplets, the former Romans, the latter from Alba Longa, who, according to Livy's account, fought to settle a war between their two fatherlands in the seventh century B.C.

Ibid.: "At the same place," in the work just cited.

Idem: "the same one," the same author just cited.

In luce et in Cruce: an aspiration, a prayer that a departed person died "in light and in the cross," *i.e.* a Christian death.

In persona Christi: "in the person of Christ," the manner in which an ordained priest or bishop acts in celebrating the sacraments.

In primis: among the first.

Inter alia: among other [secondary sources].

Intersession: the interval between two sessions of the ecumenical council.

Iure divino: by divine law.

Jacobin: a member of the radically egalitarian political group that engaged in terrorist activity during the French Revolution.

Katholikentag [GERMAN]: Catholic conference.

Kerygma [GREEK]: proclamation, preaching.

Latae sententiae: "the sentence already having been passed"; refers to a canonical penalty incurred by an act itself, with no need of a formal ecclesiastical judgment.

Latreutic: having to do with *latria* [GREEK], divine worship.

Lex orandi lex credenda: "the law of prayer is the law of belief," the conviction that liturgy defines faith.

Magisterium: the formal teaching authority of the Church.

Modus, plural ***modi:*** a recommended revision or modification.

Motu proprio: a document issued by the pope "on his own initiative."

Mysterium iniquitatis: the mystery of evil.

Non placet: "it does not please," conventional formula for a vote against a proposal.

Non possumus: we cannot.

Nota praevia: Preliminary note (especially to the Vatican II dogmatic constitution on the Church, *Lumen gentium*, sometimes referred to as the "Explanatory Note").

Nouvelle théologie: new theology (French movement between the two World Wars)

Novator, plural ***novatores:*** innovator.

Novus Ordo Missae: The new Missal promulgated by Paul VI as part of the post-conciliar liturgical reform; sometimes referred to as "the *Novus Ordo*."

Op. cit.: in the work previously cited.

Opus Dei: the work of God (often referring to the liturgy)

Ordo Missae: "Order of the Mass," a Missal with its rubrics.

Ostpolitik [German]: Foreign policy with regard to the East bloc.

Papabile [Italian]: likely to be a candidate for the papacy.

Passim: here and there (in a work cited).

Peritus, plural ***periti:*** an "expert" in theology, canon law, etc., officially appointed to assist with the work of the conciliar commissions or, in a broader sense, invited to Rome by a council father as an advisor.

Petrine: having to do with the prerogatives of St. Peter the Apostle.

Placet: "it pleases," conventional formula for a vote in favor of a proposal.

Placet iuxta modum: "it pleases subject to modification," conventional formula for a qualified vote in favor of a proposal.

Positio: an official report at a certain stage of a process of beatification.

Possibilist: someone who advocates a policy of accomplishing what is possible instead of standing on principle.

primus inter pares: first among equals.

Procura: General House or administrative center of a religious order or congregation.

Professio Fidei: Profession of Faith.

Ratio modi: the reason for or rationale of a *modus* (a recommended revision or modification).

Relatio Generalis: General Report.

Romanità [Italian]: the Roman way of doing things; the "Roman-ness" of someone who has learned those lessons well.

Schema, plural **schemas** [in Greek, *schema*, plural *schemata*]: an outline or preliminary text destined to become a conciliar document.

Suprema: the "highest-ranking" dicastery, the Holy Office.
Suspensio a divinis: a canonical penalty prohibiting a cleric from performing the sacramental acts of the power of Holy Orders.
Versus populum: see *Celebratio versus populum.*
Votum, plural ***vota***: recommendation.

The Translators

Patrick T. Brannan, S.J., worked in Rome as a translator for the 34th General Congregation of the Society of Jesus and for two Synods of Bishops. He translated *The Papacy, the Episcopacy, and Collegiality* by Wilhelm Bertrams and, more recently, the Conciliar Deliberations on *Nostra aetate* from Latin for The Institute for Jewish-Catholic Relations at St. Joseph University in Philadelphia.

Michael J. Miller has translated numerous volumes by and about Joseph Ratzinger / Benedict XVI, including a new edition of *Church, Ecumenism and Politics* and *Joseph Ratzinger: Life in the Church and Living Theology: Fundamentals of Ecclesiology with Reference to Lumen gentium,* by Maximilian Heinrich Heim.

Kenneth D. Whitehead is the author of *One, Holy, Catholic, and Apostolic: The Early Church Was the Catholic Church* and *A Short Guide to Ancient Heresies;* he translated *The Second Vatican Ecumenical Council: A Counterpoint for the History of the Council* by Archbishop Agostino Marchetto.

Index

C

D

E

F

H

K

L

M

N

Q

R

T

U

V

X

Y

Z

Other titles available from Loreto Publications

www.loretopubs.org • 603 239 6671

The Twenty Ecumenical Councils, Fr. Clement Raab, OFM.

This brief and positive sketch of the twenty great events in Catholic history, so vibrant with life and so far-reaching in their consequences, will afford the reader a very definite and appreciable knowledge of the nature and history of Holy Mother Church. Originally published in 1937, this re-issue of Fr. Raab's classic work on the history of the Ecumenical Councils did not include anything about Vatican II, because its convocation still lay in the future. We have not added to his work since so much has already been written of the newest council elsewhere. Softcover - 136 Pages - $11.95

The Great Commentary on The Gospels

Cornelius aLapide, S.J.

Cornelius aLapide, S.J. (1568-1637) is a giant figure in the history of Catholic biblical interpretation. To read aLapide 400 years later is to enter a nearly forgotten world of biblical interpretation. It is hard to decide which is more more striking, the breadth and density of aLapide's interpretative matrix or his audacity in summoning all these resources to the interpretation of the sacred text. ALapide himself takes a breathtakingly high view of Scripture's purpose. . . aLapide also prefaces his commentary with thirty-eight "canons of interpretation," which reflect a wise and prayerful method." It is clear that the Fathers hold pride of place for aLapide in his interpretative work. - From Scott Hahn's Review

- 6"x 9" Book format
- 2,900+ Pages in four volumes
- First complete English translation
- Sewn Binding & Headbands
- Bonded Leather Covers & Satin Ribbons
- Discussion of Greek and Hebrew words
- $199. Per four volume set

Other titles available from Loreto Publications

www.loretopubs.org • 603 239 6671

After the Boston Heresy Case, Gary Potter

To go after something is to inquire into it, to be in search of it, to seek the truth about it. In this book, veteran Catholic journalist Gary Potter goes after the truth concerning one of last century's principal religious controversies, the so-called Boston Heresy Case, and its chief figure, Fr. Leonard Feeney, S.J. Originally published in 1993 by Catholic Treasures this re-issue has been newly typeset and slightly revised by the author. Softcover, 272 pages, $14.95

They Fought the Good Fight, Br. Thomas Mary Sennot

Orestes Brownson & Father Feeney "The documents and facts presented in They Fought the Good Fight: Orestes Brownson and Father Feeney, speak for themselves, not only illuminating the similarity of "liberal Catholicism," "Americanism," and post-conciliar "neo-Modernism," viz. a willingness to compromise on doctrine for the sake of friendship, which in every instance postulates a repudiation in principle or practice of the axiom extra ecclesiam nulla salus, and a minimization of devotion to Our Lady as Mediatrix of All Graces. Not all the problems of the Church in the U.S.A began after the Council." —Father Peter Fehlner, O. F. M., Conv.
Softcover, 440 pages, $17.95

The Loyolas and the Cabots, Sister Catherine, M.I.C.M.

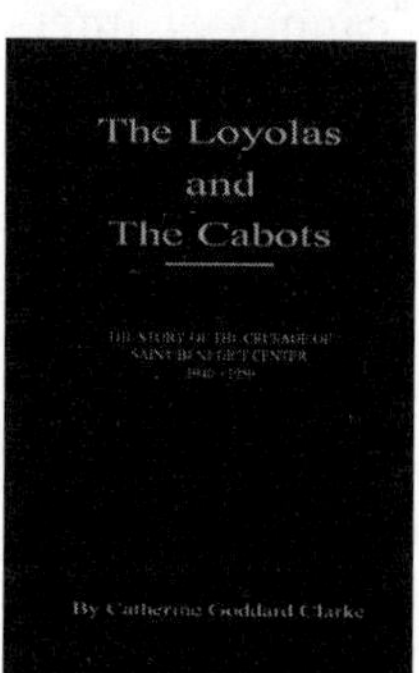

Did you ever hear of Father Feeney? Despite what the liberals say, he was a devout Catholic priest who defended the teachings of the Church. This book tells how the authorities in the Boston Archdiocese and the Society of Jesus ("Loyolas") teamed up with the Boston Yankee Masons ("Cabots") to silence a priest whose "embarrassing" insistence on Catholic doctrine disturbed their liberal agenda. An inspiring story, well told. Softcover, 302 pages, $9.95

Other titles available from Loreto Publications

www.loretopubs.org • 603 239 6671

The Sources of Catholic Dogma, Heinrich Denzinger

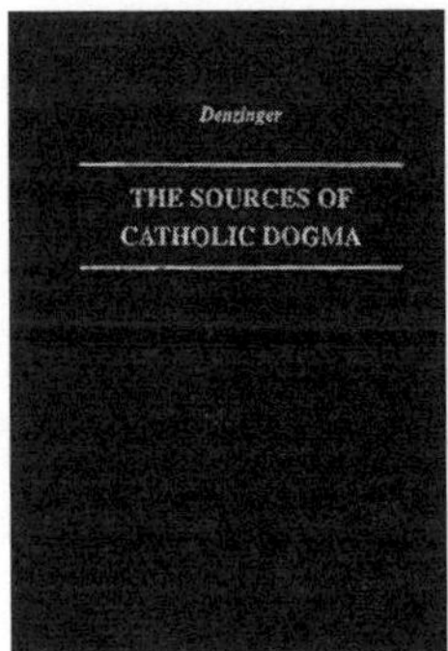

In this age of doctrinal latitude and speculative innovation there is a pressing need for a comprehensive source book on authentic Catholic dogma that is magisterially anchored while at the same time both practical and non-voluminous. You have such a book in this English translation of Father Heinrich Denzinger's Enchiridion Symbolorum et Definitionum. Since it was first published a century and a half ago, this collection of articles of faith and morals has enjoyed universal appeal and approbation since the pontificate of Blessed Pope Pius IX. The edition being offered here by Loreto is that issued in 1957. Hardcover, 634 Pages, $34.95

Gate of Heaven, Sr. Catherine, M.I.C.M

The author exudes both her own joy in living the sacramental life within the Catholic Church, and her holy indignation over the fact that liberal Catholic clergymen in the United States were teaching that one's personal sincerity of conscience was an acceptable substitute for the one and only means of salvation given by Christ. Sister Catherine demolishes all the ambiguous subterfuges that in her day were undermining the doctrinal clarity that in centuries past left no doubt as to the whereabouts of the only way of salvation. Softcover, 150 pages, $8.95

Our Glorious Popes, Sr. Catherine, M.I.C.M

The author takes us on a journey through four hundred years of *tempus ecclesiae*, from the entrance of St. Peter into the fearsome capital of Satan's doomed empire, to the triumph of the Council of Chalcedon, held under St. Leo I. Vividly brought to life is the maturation of the Church Militant from its infancy in Jerusalem. The remaining bulk of information dovetails into the major periods of religious crises and tells of those heroic popes who steered the Church through these gravest trials. This book restores hope and confidence in the might of the papacy. Sewn Softcover, 266 pages, $12.95

The Second Vatican Council, the twenty-first in the history of the Church, was opened by John XXIII on October 11, 1962, and closed by Paul VI on December 8, 1965. Despite the expectations and hopes of so many people, the period that followed it was not a "springtime" or a "pentecost" for the Church but rather, as Paul VI himself and his successors acknowledged, a time of crises and difficulties. This is one of the reasons why a lively hermeneutical discussion has begun, in which the authoritative voice of Pope Benedict XVI has intervened, inviting Catholics to read the documents of the Council in continuity with the Tradition of the Church.

To the ongoing debate Roberto de Mattei offers the contribution not of a theologian but of an historian, through a rigorous reconstruction of the event, of its roots and consequences, based chiefly on archival documents, diaries, correspondence and testimonies of those who were its protagonists. From the well-documented, fascinating picture drawn by the author emerges "an unwritten story" of Vatican II which helps us to understand not only the events of yesterday but also the religious problems of the Church of today.

"The history of the Council is to be rewritten, or at least to be completed. In this spirit I propose a history of the Council, 'an unwritten story,' not so much on account of the novelty of the testimonies and the episodes that emerge from it, as on account of the new reconstruction and interpretation of the facts that is offered. Neither the researcher who 'unearths' new documents nor the 'chronicler' who piles up the ones that are already known is the real historian, but rather the one who, based on the published or unpublished documentation at his disposal, is able to order it, understand it, and narrate it, framing the events within a philosophy of history that, for the Catholic historian, is first of all a theology of history."

Roberto de Mattei, Introduction

"A work that is as erudite as it is relevant. I am certain that thanks to its rigorous historical-critical method it will convince a vast readership."

Cardinal Walter Brandmüller, President Emeritus of the Pontifical Committee for Historical Sciences

"I am very grateful to Professor de Mattei for his extraordinary work on the history of Vatican II."

Bishop Luigi Negri, Bishop of San Marino-Montefeltro

"A complete, non-ideological picture, which no doubt was missing until now."

Francesco Agnoli, Il Foglio

"The Roman historian—vice-president of the CNR, the most refined intellectual of Italian traditionalism—is rarely elusive in dealing with crucial problems.

Alberto Melloni, Corriere della Sera

Roberto de Mattei teaches Church History at the European University of Rome, where he is the head of the Faculty of Historical Sciences. He is Vice President of the National Research Council [*Consiglio Nazionale delle Ricerche,* CNR], and a member of the Boards of Directors of the Historical Institute for the Modern and Contemporary Era and of the Italian Geographical Society. He is President of the Lepanto Foundation and edits the scholarly journals *Radici Cristiane* [Christian Roots] and *Nova Historica*. Moreover he collaborates with the Pontifical Committee for Historical Sciences, and the Holy See awarded him the insignia of the Order of Saint Gregory the Great in recognition of his service to the Church. Among his more recent published works: *Blessed Pius IX* (Gracewing, 2004); *Holy War, Just War: Islam and Christendom at War* (The Rockford Institute: Chronicles Press, 2007); *La dittatura del relativismo [The dictatorship of relativism]* (Chieti: Solfanelli, 2007); *Turkey in Europe: Benefit or Catastrophe?* (Gracewing, 2009).